Tasmania

Charles Rawlings-Way, Meg Worby
Gabi Mocatta

TASMAN SEA

VICTORIA

Cape Liptrap (140km)

Wilsons Promontory

Tidal River

Cape Liptrap

BASS STRAIT

To Melbourne (140km)

Spirit of Tasmania Ferries
(Overnight trip to Melbourne, approx. 10 hours or 430km)

FURNEAUX GROUP

KENT GROUP

Hogan Island

Curtis Island

Erith Island
Dover Island
Deal Island

Inner Sister Island
Outer Sister Island
Stanley Point
Palana
B85

Cape Frankland

Flinders Island
Emita
Prime Seal Island
Whitemark
Badger Island
Strzelecki National Park

Babel Island
Sellars Point
Cameron Inlet
Lady Barron
Vansittart Island
Franklin Sound

Cape Barren Island
Cape Barren
Swan Island
Clarke Island

Banks Strait

Cape Portland

Waterhouse Island
Anderson Bay
Noland Bay

Ringarooma Bay

Eddystone Point
Bay of Fires

St Helens Point
Georges Bay
St Helens
Scamander

BAY OF FIRES (p194)
Wander white-blond beaches of hourglass-fine sand and sapphire-blue seas

Gladstone
Mt William (216m)
Mt William National Park

Derby
B82

Mt Horror (676m)
Bridport
B84
Scottsdale
Lilydale
B82

A3
Mathinna
Ben Lomond National Park
Legges Tor (1573m)
Mt Barrow (1413m)

Launceston

LAUNCESTON (p202)
Savour the best *millefeuille* this side of the Equator at one of the city's Parisian patisseries

George Town
Low Head
Beaconsfield
Narawntapu National Park
Port Sorell
Latrobe
Deloraine

Devonport
Ulverstone
Penguin
Burnie

Mole Creek
Mt Roland (1231m)
B12
Lake Barrington

St Valentine Peak (1106m)
Black Bluff (1339m)
B18

Wynyard
Rocky Cape
Rocky Cape National Park
A2

Stanley
Table Cape
Smithton
Edith Creek
Three Hummock Island

Waratah

Savage River
Savage River National Park
Arthur River

Perkins Bay
Walker Island
Robbins Island
Perkins Island
Montagu

Hunter Island

Hope Channel
Studland Bay

Woolnorth Point
Hunter Passage

Cape Rochon

Marrawah

Bluff Hill Point
Arthur Pieman Protected Area
Mt Norfolk (759m)
C249

Kenneth Bay
Sandy Cape

TARKINE WILDERNESS (p268)
Absorb yourself in the Tarkine rainforest, a mysterious – and vulnerable – domain of gnarled myrtles, glow worms, manferns and giant blue freshwater crayfish

King Island

Cape Wickham
Disappointment Bay
Egg Lagoon
Cowper Point
Yambacoona
Naracoopa
Sea Elephant Bay
Loorana
Currie
Grassy
B25
Mt Stanley (213m)
Stokes Point
Stokes Seal Bay

KING ISLAND DAIRY (p307)
Sample some Bass Strait Blue, Seal Bay Triple Cream and Stokes Point Smoked Cheddar from the excellent King Island Dairy – a genuinely local gourmet experience

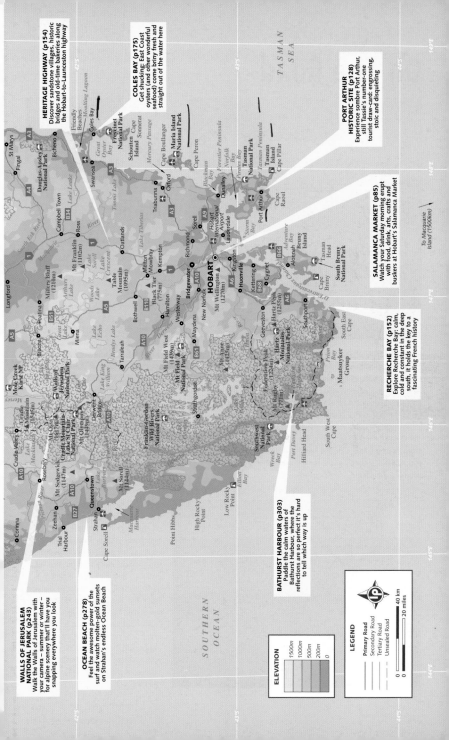

WALLS OF JERUSALEM NATIONAL PARK (p243)
Walk the Walls of Jerusalem with your camera – summer or winter – for alpine scenery that'll have you snapping everywhere you look

OCEAN BEACH (p278)
Feel the awesome power of the surf and watch molten-gold sunsets on Strahan's endless Ocean Beach

BATHURST HARBOUR (p303)
Paddle the calm waters of Bathurst Harbour, where the reflections are so perfect it's hard to tell which way is up

RECHERCHE BAY (p152)
Explore Recherche Bay: calm, cold and constant in the deep south, it holds the key to a fascinating French history

HERITAGE HIGHWAY (p154)
Discover sandstone villages, historic bridges and old-time bakeries along the Hobart-to-Launceston highway

COLES BAY (p175)
Get shucking: East Coast oysters (and other wonderful seafood) come briny fresh and straight out of the water here

PORT ARTHUR HISTORIC SITE (p128)
Experience sombre Port Arthur, still Tassie's number-one tourist draw-card: engrossing, stoic and disquieting

SALAMANCA MARKET (p85)
Watch your Saturday morning erupt with food, drink, arts, crafts and buskers at Hobart's Salamanca Market

ELEVATION

1500m
1000m
500m
200m
0

LEGEND

Primary Road
Secondary Road
Tertiary Road
Unsealed Road

0 ___ 40 km
0 ___ 20 miles

To Macquarie Island (1500km)

SOUTHERN OCEAN

TASMAN SEA

On The Road

COORDINATING AUTHOR Meg Worby
We had hiked the challenging Overland Track (p290) for six days, in constant sunshine – lucky, since it bucketed down the minute we got back to the city. Ominous Mt Wellington (p88) sulked behind clouds as we arrived at a waterfront hotel for the ultimate bath. The staff didn't blink at our muddy gaiters, packs and beanies. Their excellent umbrella later turned inside out (just after this photo was taken) as we walked across the docks to sample the local seafood… but in my book, packet pasta and cask wine at Pelion Hut after hiking 17km on day four were just as good!

COORDINATING AUTHOR Charles Rawlings-Way
There's something calming, welcoming, benign – dare I say English! – about the green, safe-haven folds of the Huon Valley (p144). After weeks spent haring around the state and two arduous days on Bruny Island (p136) – lashed by howling rain in the south, parched by the sun in the north – I rounded a lazy Channel Hwy bend south of Franklin (p145) and the broad Huon River unfurled before me in a shimmering band. I pulled over to admire the serene scene: this is a place that's good for the soul! Next stop, beyond the hills, Tasmania's Deep South…

GABI MOCATTA After a long day's East Coast (p165) research, I'd checked in after dark at a beachside B&B in Swansea (p171). I wanted to be up early for sunrise, so I took an early wander and was joyful to find a perfect little cove all to myself. There was the whole Freycinet Peninsula (p175) before me across the calm waters of Great Oyster Bay, and the sun a great silver orb, painting the whole scene impossibly bright. That day started with a salute to the sun and a long, salty-cool dip in the clear waters of the bay.

For full author biographies see p351

Tasmania Highlights

Here at Lonely Planet, we think we know Tasmania. Our head office is in Melbourne, after all – it's only a ferry ride away. When we have holidays, loads of our favourite destinations are right here in this book – sometimes it seems as though half the office is hiking the Overland Track! Here our staff and authors share a few of their top spots. But we like your own suggestions as much as you like ours. So we asked our travellers – you – about your favourites. Did we miss your own secret highlight? Share it with our community of travellers at lonelyplanet.com/australia.

GRANT DIXON

1 WINEGLASS BAY

Wineglass Bay and the walk to and from Coles Bay are so beautiful they're in danger of being loved to the point of overpopulation (p177). So pack a bit of extra water and sun protection and be prepared to walk just a bit further down the beach to avoid the crowds.

'Chris_t' (online name), traveller

CRADLE MOUNTAIN WILDLIFE

I love the way possums, wallabies and wombats roam free here (p289).

Margaret Thomas, Perth, Western Australia

3

ANDREW BAIN

SARA-JANE CLELAND

2

DOVE LAKE

My daughter and I had a great few hours here, circling the lake in the shadow of Cradle Mountain (p289). See super hikers head off overland, see everyone from toddlers to oldies visit and paddle, or walk in the peace of a warm windless day (if you are lucky like us). Simply find a warm rock and observe. This is soul food.

'Chris_t' (online name), traveller

GRANT DIXON

4

TASMAN PENINSULA

Three-hundred-metre cliffs stand against the forces of nature, protecting the land from ferocious seas. The Tasman Peninsula (p121) offers much more than convict ruins, including great walks, superb natural rock formations and fantastic diving.

'Boonedog' (online name), traveller

PORT ARTHUR

Tasmania is haunted. It's no secret, ask any of the locals and they'll be happy to share their favorite ghost story. Take a ghost tour of historic Battery Point in Hobart (p85) for a spine-tingling experiance, or test your courage with a ghost tour at Port Arthur (p127). Beware the parsonage…

Kate Slomkowski, Hamden, Connecticut, USA

5

CHRIS MELLOR

BLACK BLUFF

On Boxing Day we hiked up Black Bluff mountain (p252). It was an amazing climb, tough in part (for me anyway) and completely wild at the summit. I was really surprised to find a deep blue lake near the top – we felt like the only humans on earth. The next day my other half hauled his mountain bike up it and threw himself back down again for some adrenalin-fuelled fun.

Louise Vicente, Lonely Planet staff, London, UK

6

GRANT DIXON

PAINTED CLIFFS, MARIA ISLAND

Camping on Maria Island one moonlit night, I crept out of the tent for night-time ablutions and quite literally bumped into a grazing (or was he dozing?) wombat. I was as surprised as he was, and we eyed each other in sleepy shock for up for a long moment before he trundled off into the poa grass. You can get that close to wildlife here (p168).

Gabi Mocatta, Lonely Planet author, Hobart, Tasmania

7

HOLGER LEUE

FRANKLIN RIVER

Whether you raft it or just look at it in awe, check out this mighty river, subject of some of Australia's most passionate and influential environmental campaigning (p287).

'Djebru' (online name), traveller

9

GRANT DIXON

TREVOR CREIGHTON

8 ### CYCLING

World Heritage wilderness and quaint towns are all accessible by bike (p59), with myriad options and scenic backroad routes to choose from. The hardy trek up to Cradle Valley is a particularly rewarding example.

Quentin Frayne, Lonely Planet staff, Melbourne, Victoria

RUSSELL FALLS

Russell Falls may not be one of the world's largest waterfalls but in my book it's definetly worth the hike (p116). The tree ferns and streams lend a feeling of serenity and isolation where the modern world just melts away. It's a cool, lush environment that needs no improvement and you feel lucky just to be there.

**Selena Symons,
Western Australia**

10 STRAHAN

Enjoy the slap and murmur of waves against the hull as your bed gently rocks. This is one way to sleep like a baby. We got to Strahan (p277) and there was barely a bed to be found. It was March and silly me thought tourist numbers would be down! Hadn't planned it but found a bed on an unusual hostel on a yacht at the pier.

'Chris_t' (online name), traveller

12 SOUTH COAST TRACK

The 83km South Coast Track is a true wilderness experience, snaking along Tassie's rugged southern coastline (p152). The mud can be something to behold.

'Djebru' (online name), traveller

QUEENSTOWN

Queenstown's copper-mining industry cleared the surrounding hills of every single tree (p283). Consequently, Queenstown looks like a small town on the surface of Mars, and it's great for mountain-biking.

Peter Smiley, Melbourne, Victoria

13

LINDSAY BROWN

TAHUNE FOREST AIRWALK

Don't forget to do the short little walk that starts just to the right of the bridge (p148). The walk goes through rainforest and old-growth trees, and you might see a platypus like I did!

'Regazza' (online name), traveller

14

SIMON FOALE

RICHARD CUMMIN

15 **HISTORIC HOBART**

Hobart is an amazing place built top to bottom from stone (p77). Some of the B&Bs we stayed in were over 100 years old. Cool!

'Aphra' (online name), traveller

ROB BLAKERS

16 STYX VALLEY

If you want to get into some classic, tall, old-growth forests that are contentious in terms of logging, the Styx Valley (p302) is about an hour's drive from Hobart. You can see some amazing Eucalyptus regnans out there, or Mountain Ash – the tallest flowering trees in the world – surrounded by huge tree ferns.

Ed Parker, Lonely Planet contributing author, Hobart, Tasmania

BRUNY ISLAND

Cloudy Bay on South Bruny Island is heaven on earth (p136). Watch thousands of birds take to the air as you drive 3km along the hard sand of Cloudy Bay beach to reach a brilliant camping ground behind the dunes and a million miles from anywhere. Enjoy spectacular views and kookaburra songs while you sip your morning camp coffee and watch for the whales that visit.

Jane Hart, Lonely Planet staff, Melbourne, Victoria

HOLGER LEU

17

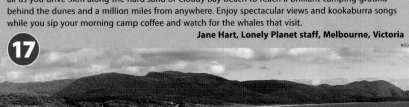

SALAMANCA MARKET

A Hobart tradition, the Salamanca Market takes place every Saturday, rain or shine (p85). You can find hand-made wool sweaters, Huon pine wood products, wines, cheeses, organic fruit and vegetables, pre-loved clothing, arts and crafts. Mingle with the locals and grab a beer at Knopwood's Retreat (p105) to end the day.

Kate Slomkowski, traveller, Hamden, Connecticut

RICHARD I'ANSON

18

JOHN SONE

19 MT WELLINGTON

One overcast morning, I drove to the summit to check out the mountain rock-scapes in the mist (p88). I entered the cloudy veil above Fern Tree, winding down the window to breathe in the damp forest perfume. Not far from the summit, the clouds began to feather, fray, then dissipate altogether – I shot out of the gloom onto the sunlit summit, surrounded on all sides by a rolling ocean of cloudtops.

Charles Rawlings-Way, Lonely Planet author

Contents

Regional Map Contents

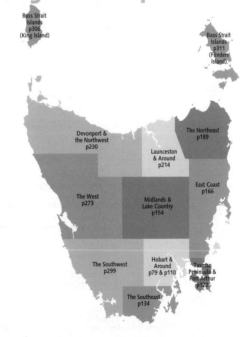

Bass Strait Islands p306 (King Island)

Bass Strait Islands p311 (Flinders Island)

Devonport & the Northwest p230

The Northeast p189

Launceston & Around p214

East Coast p166

The West p273

Midlands & Lake Country p154

The Southwest p299

Hobart & Around p79 & p110

Tasman Peninsula & Port Arthur p122

The Southeast p134

Destination Tasmania

There's an expression from the 1980s: 'Wake up Australia, Tasmania is floating away!' These days, however, mainland Australia is wide awake to the loveliness of its Apple Isle and holds it close to its heart.

Like any new love affair, there's a lot you can do in the space of a week. Top of your to-do list should be a close encounter with the state's wild places: the curves of Wineglass Bay, the far-flung Tarkine forests, the crags of Cradle Mountain. Almost a quarter of Tassie (as it's affectionately known) is classed as a World Heritage Area or national park – an inspirational backdrop of jagged mountain peaks and near-impenetrable rainforest, soaring sea cliffs and fragile alpine moorlands. Experience it first hand with world-class bushwalking, sea-kayaking, white-water rafting and cycling, or just bum around on a deserted beach. And while you're outside, grab a deep breath of Australia's purest air in the abundant sunshine – in the height of summer, Hobart (Tassie's capital city) enjoys more than 15 hours of sunlight every day (more than Darwin or Sydney).

When you wander in from the wilderness, you'll discover the table is laid. A highlight of any Tasmanian trip is sampling the local gourmet fare, especially fresh seafood, luscious fruits, outstanding dairy products and cellar-worthy cool-climate wines.

There's also no shortage of urban virtue here, delivered with less attitude and more charm than in Australia's mainland states. Hobart and Launceston, Tasmania's duelling cities, compete over more than just the quality of their local beer (Cascade and James Boag's respectively). Hobart, Australia's southernmost city, has views to rival Sydney's, and continues to evolve into a cosmopolitan hub with new-found urban cool. Following in its wake, Launceston has been busy transforming itself from colonial backwater into boutique harbour. A rigorous arts scene infuses both centres, while beyond the city limits small-town Tassie has almost as much to offer: colonial accommodation, cafés, festivals, reputable restaurants, traditional rural warmth and sandstone villages that look like film sets.

Of course, there was a time when Tassie wasn't so wonderful, when young islanders left in droves seeking careers, new haircuts and pub bands that played more than just *American Pie* and Billy Idol covers. Forever the butt of mainland jokes, Tasmanians had little to feel proud about. The stigma of isolation and a brutal colonial history have been difficult to reconcile and remain embedded in the landscape: don't be surprised if somewhere along the road you find yourself crossed with a mournful spirit or an inexplicable sense of sadness. This bloody past is captured in much of the island's literature and is a conflict that continues to be played out in today's academic 'history wars'.

But as this new century has matured, the exodus to the mainland has stalled. Tasmania gained more people than it lost in 2007, as 1200 Australians moved south across the perilous span of Bass Strait permanently. The allure varies: a lifestyle change for stressed-out Sydneysiders, climate relief for overheated Queenslanders, a room with a view for Melburnians, and a chance to come home for ex-Tasmanians now that things are looking up. A steady flow of Australians (especially Victorians) choose to holiday here each year, encouraged by increased flights with lower fares into Hobart and Launceston.

It seems the wee southern isle has never evoked more fondness in the hearts of mainlanders, who don't mind admitting what they find precious about

FAST FACTS

Population: 493,000

Area: 68,332 sq km

Number of national parks: 19

Number of surviving Tasmanian Tigers: 0 (but we can't be sure)

Reward for a fox sighting: $1000

Unemployment rate: 4.8% (the lowest in three decades)

Number of tourists: over 800,000 in 2007 (42% from overseas)

Number of Tasmanian-born princesses: 1 (Mary Donaldson, Crown Princess of Denmark)

Tassie-born Australian cricket captains: 1 (Ricky Ponting)

Number of cattle on King Island: more than 89,000

Tasmania. Intense debate over environmental affairs rages, as Tasmanian conservation once again became a federal election issue in 2007. Construction of the controversial Tamar Valley pulp mill, vehemently opposed by some mainland powerbrokers, remains the subject of heated legal wrangling. More than ever, there's conflict over what the big island thinks the little island should be protecting. Should they fight for a close-knit community, jobs for locals and a sequestered way of life? Or should it be for the wilderness, justly famous beyond these island shores? Should it be for both?

For the answers to these questions and more, start your own love affair with Tasmania. The island is flush with renaissance spirit – now is the perfect time to bite into the Apple Isle's goodness.

Getting Started

Tasmania is an excellent family-holiday destination and is ideally suited to a self-drive trip – but don't try to cover too much ground in a short period of time. Distances might appear to be short on a map, but often take longer to drive than you expect due to narrow, winding roads. You might want to concentrate your touring in a specific region rather than darting from one coast to the other, otherwise you could find yourself spending most of your holiday in the car, when you're really here for the fresh air.

WHEN TO GO

December, January and February are the busiest times for tourism: with average temperatures around 21°C, it's almost warm enough to swim and you don't need a beanie (unless you're hiking, which calls for a beanie at all times!). You can expect to see a variety of fantastic festivals and events, including the sails coming into Hobart at the end of the Sydney to Hobart Yacht Race and the wonderful food festival 'The Taste' (p94). However, accommodation is heavily booked (and often more expensive, as is petrol), and roads and restaurants are more crowded. You may want to avoid Tasmania's prime destinations during school holidays when Tasmanians themselves love to camp in national parks. Exact dates vary, but the main period is from mid-December to late January, and again at Easter; see p324 for more information. (For a useful list of school holidays in all Australian states, check out www.dest.gov.au).

See Climate Chart (p320) for more information.

The great advantage of visiting in winter is that tourist numbers and prices are low (look for specials), and it can seem as if you have parts of the island to yourself, including all kinds of cosy accommodation.

In terms of Tasmania's highly variable weather, the winter months are generally cold, wet and cloudy (average 12°C), but days are often clear, crisp and sunny – ideal for sightseeing and short bushwalks. Autumn brings beautiful colours and mild temperatures, but towards the end of the season the days (even sunny ones) are usually quite cold and windy. Spring tends to be windy, too. Temperatures in early September can be chilly, and snowfalls can still occur in the mountains, but by spring's end the weather is improving.

COSTS

Tasmania is a tourism-conscious state that provides options for visitors on all budgets. These days, overseas travellers and Australians may find it more expensive than they expect. The biggest whack to the wallet is transport, both for getting there – your options are restricted to planes and ferries – and getting around. You can really blow out on top-quality food, too (and we suggest you do!), but there's wonderful fresh produce available if you'd rather self-cater.

How much you should budget for depends on how you travel and how you'll be occupying yourself. If sightseeing and having a good ol' time are integral (staying at midrange hotels, motels or B&Bs, and sampling the many great restaurants here), then $150 to $200 per day (per person travelling as a couple) should do it. You can easily spend more by regularly taking tours and staying in top-end guesthouses.

At the budget end, if you camp or stay in hostels, cook your own meals, look at the view for entertainment and travel around by bus (or in your own vehicle), you could probably eke out an existence on $60 to $70 per day; for a budget that realistically enables you to have a good time, raise the stakes to $80 or $90 per day. Staying in places for longer periods and/or travelling in a group will help lower your costs. See the Directory for a few ideas on how to sleep cheaply (p316) and earn a few dollars along the way (p330).

HOW MUCH?

Dorm bed in a hostel $22–28

Copy of *Mercury* newspaper $1.20

10oz glass of beer $3.50

Souvenir T-shirt $30

Street treat (curried scallop pie) $4

See also Lonely Planet Index on the Quick Reference page

TRAVELLING RESPONSIBLY

For information on 4WD touring, read *Cruisin' Without Bruisin'*, a free brochure available at most visitors centres around the state or online from the Parks & Wildlife Service (www.parks.tas.gov.au/recreation/4wd /4wd.html). Whether you're travelling on bush tracks or in a conventional vehicle on a highway, watch out for rampant Tasmanian wildlife on the road and try to avoid driving at dusk, when many animals become more active and harder to see. Sadly, you're likely to see more dead animals on the road than live ones in the bush.

Travellers must discard all plants, fruit and vegetables before their arrival. The state's 'disease-free' status is one of the things that makes its produce attractive to buyers, and the state government has stringent rules to ensure the island maintains this agricultural advantage. To this end, plants, fruit and vegetables cannot be brought into the state without certification.

Live fish that can breed in Tasmanian waters cannot be brought into the state. Anglers must not bring live bait into Tasmania and, in order to prevent the introduction of disease into native and recreational fisheries and aquaculture industries, they should also wash, disinfect and dry their gear before packing it for their trip.

Phytophthora is a root rot that's spread in soil and is devastating flora in parts of the state. Always clean dirt off your shoes and equipment before and after you spend time in the bush. For more information about responsible bushwalking, see p56.

Finally, be sure never to disturb or remove items from sites significant to Tasmanian Aborigines.

PREDEPARTURE READING

Readers who love the travel, history or biography genres should seek out Nicholas Shakespeare's masterfully researched book *In Tasmania*. The English writer discovered family connections when he moved here. His investigation into the past and the people who labelled the island 'a Hades or a Heaven' is also an exposé of the devilish Anthony Fenn Kemp, the 'Father of Tasmania' (not a dad you'd really want to have).

If you're a foodie, three recommended publications are Graeme Phillips' *Eat Drink Tasmania*, updated annually ($15 from visitor information centres, newsagents and bookshops) and *Tasmania's Cellar Door & Farm Gate Guide*, plus *Cool Wine & Food, Cool Wilderness* – a series of free Tourism

---

DON'T LEAVE HOME WITHOUT...

- Waterproof gear and warm clothing (even in midsummer); layers are a good idea (thermal leggings and tops are almost a uniform in Hobart)

- A wetsuit, if you're planning on entering the ocean for more than 30 seconds

- Sunscreen and sunglasses – UV radiation down here is still high, despite the reputation for bleak weather

- Comfy, sturdy walking shoes so you can explore national parks and walking tracks; but also pack shoes to wear out at night – pub bouncers often enforce dress codes

- A hearty appetite for sampling the local food and wine – and the energy to walk it all off

TOP 10

SOUTHERN OCEAN

Canberra

Tasman Sea

TASMANIA Hobart

TOP READS

Tasmania's people, places and creatures, its unique wilderness and complex history are explored in these critically acclaimed books. For reviews see p37.

1 *For the Term of His Natural Life* Marcus Clarke

2 *Death of a River Guide* Richard Flanagan

3 *The Sound of One Hand Clapping* Richard Flanagan

4 *Cape Grimm* Carmel Bird

5 *The Boys in the Island* Christopher Koch

6 *The Alphabet of Light and Dark* Danielle Wood

7 *English Passengers* Matthew Kneale

8 *A Child's Book of True Crime* Chloe Hooper

9 *Fate of a Free People* Henry Reynolds

10 *Thylacine* David Owen

TOP FESTIVALS & EVENTS

Tasmanians don't need much of an excuse for a celebration (see p323 for more information):

1 **Hobart Summer Festival** (www.hobartsummer festival.com.au) Late December to early January; includes The Taste food festival (p94)

2 **Falls Festival** (www.fallsfestival.com) Marion Bay rock fest, late December to early January (p94)

3 **Ten Days on the Island** (www.tendaysonthe island.org) Statewide biennial island culture and festivities, March (p323)

4 **Sydney to Hobart Yacht Race** (www.rolexsyd neyhobart.com) The finish of one of the world's greatest open-ocean yacht races; late December to early January (p61 and p94)

5 **Cygnet Folk Festival** (www.cygnetfolkfestival.org) Banjos and balladry, January (p142)

6 **Antarctic Midwinter Festival** (www.antarctic -tasmania.info) Brrrr… June (p94)

7 **Festivale** (www.festivale.com.au) Food and good-times festival, February (p207)

8 **Australian Three Peaks Race** (www.three peaks.org.au) Easter (p207)

9 **Australian Wooden Boat Festival** (www .australianwoodenboatfestival.com.au) Biennial gathering of yachts, dinghies and tall(ish) ships, February (p94)

10 **Tasmanian Craft Fair** (www.tascraftfair.com .au) Arts and crafts, October (p240)

TOP OUTDOOR ACTIVITIES

Tassie boasts a renowned coastline, numerous national parks and pristine wilderness…(see p56):

1 Hiking the famed Overland Track through Cradle Mountain–Lake St Clair National Park (p290)

2 Walking to (and swimming in) Wineglass Bay on the utterly photogenic Freycinet Peninsula (p179)

3 Pelting down the slopes of Mt Wellington into Hobart on a mountain bike (p88)

4 Arguing over stalactites vs stalagmites (they 'might' go up but 'tights' come down) as you spelunk into a cave at Hastings (p151) or Mole Creek (p242)

5 Kicking back on a Gordon River cruise out of Strahan (p279)

6 Exploring abandoned beaches and rocky headlands around the Bay of Fires (p194)

7 Paddling around the gorgeous D'Entrecasteaux Channel by sea-kayak (p136)

8 White-water rafting down the awesome Franklin River (p287)

9 Casting a trout fly across the serene waters of the Lake Country (p161)

10 Carving up the cold surf at far-flung Marrawah beach (p265)

Tasmania brochures available at visitor information centres and online (www.discovertasmania.com; click on 'Activities & Attractions', then 'Food and Wine'). These publications might help you to plan your gastronomic tour as they detail the best restaurants, cafés, wineries and farm stores around the state, classified by region, along with info on annual foodie/ boozy events. (The *Cellar Door* brochure also has a helpful chart detailing when particular foods are in season.)

The Photographer, The Cook & The Fisherman is put together by well-known Tasmanians Richard Bennett, a photographer with a love of the sea, and fisherman/chef duo George and Jill Mure.

The World of Olegas Truchanas is a classic 'retro read' about the photographer who was mentor to Peter Dombrovskis, whose images you will see everywhere: Dombrovskis' magnificently mysterious photo of the Franklin River became symbolic of a major campaign to save it (see p38). Along these wild lines, discover what all the fuss is about in *For the Forests*, edited by Helen Gee, about the history of Tasmanian forest campaigns in the 20th century. Also check out a beautiful book called *The Forests* by photographer Matt Newton and academic/poet Pete Hay. Newton's *Shack Life* is a pleasing record of that great Tasmanian institution, the shack (a rambling cottage in the hills or by the water).

INTERNET RESOURCES

Discover Tasmania (www.discovertasmania.com) Comprehensive details of key destinations, festivals, tours and accommodation.

Lonely Planet (www.lonelyplanet.com) Unbiased accommodation reviews on Hotels & Hostels; travellers trading information on the Thorn Tree bulletin board.

Parks & Wildlife (www.parks.tas.gov.au) Extensive information on Tasmania's national parks, World Heritage areas, flora and fauna.

Pure Tasmania (www.puretasmania.com.au) Corporate site with a regional holiday planner (alpine, coast, Hobart and Launceston).

Tasmania Online (www.tas.gov.au) Government site with links to other Tasmanian websites.

The Gobbler (www.the-gobbler.blogspot.com) Foodie blog with links to other Tasmanian and national sites.

This Tasmania (www.thistasmania.com) Online magazine with great articles and excellent photography.

Itineraries
CLASSIC ROUTES

NORTHWEST AT ITS BEST
Two Weeks / Launceston to Cradle Mountain to Strahan to Stanley

Pick up a car in **Launceston** (p202), then take a stroll through Lonnie's **Cataract Gorge** (p202). Trundle through the eclectic attractions (seahorses, gold mines, lighthouses and wineries) around the **Tamar Valley** (p213) and the **Pipers River Region** (p221). Loop through the historic towns of **Evandale** (p225) and **Westbury** (p222) before drifting west to **Deloraine** (p239) and the caves at **Mole Creek** (p242). A roundabout route (via Moina) takes you to iconic **Cradle Mountain–Lake St Clair National Park** (p289), arguably Australia's top national park. From here, drive southwest to the lunar landscapes of **Queenstown** (p283) and ride the West Coast Wilderness Railway to **Strahan** (p277). If you have time, take a boat trip on the mirror-surfaced Gordon River. From Strahan, track north through the vast, tree-crowded **Arthur Pieman Conservation Area** (p268), catch a wave in **Marrawah** (p265), then clamber up the Nut in **Stanley** (p260). An ocean dip at idyllic **Boat Harbour Beach** (p258) is the perfect journey's end before wandering back to Devonport or Launceston.

From Tassie's second city into its legendary western wilderness, this 800km drive is a feast for the eyes. Breathe some of the world's cleanest air, tweak your tastebuds in the Tamar Valley and pump your legs up Cradle Mountain and the Nut.

EAST COAST CRUISER Two Weeks / Hobart to Port Arthur to Maria Island to Freycinet Peninsula to St Helens to Launceston

Craving some heavy history and serious sunshine? Spend a few days kicking back in Australia's smallest, southernmost capital **Hobart** (p77), beneath megalithic **Mt Wellington** (p88). Hobart these days is a surprisingly cosmopolitan town – good coffee, brilliant eateries and a vigorous arts scene. Next, head for the dramatic crags of the **Tasman Peninsula** (p121) for a couple of days, and pay your respects at eerie **Port Arthur** (p127). History lesson over, wind your way back north, stopping to growl at the Tasmanian devils in **Taranna** (p126) and for a surf at **Eaglehawk Neck** (p124). Near Copping, look out for the shortcut to the east coast via the wiggly **Wielangta Forest Drive** (p168). Hit the beach for a swim at **Orford** (p166), then take a boat out to **Maria Island National Park** (p168) for a couple of days and nights of camping, bushwalking and sipping wine on some rare west-facing east-coast beaches. Go gourmet in **Swansea** (p171) – the foodie hub of the east coast – then get your cameras ready for the **Freycinet National Park** (p175) and **Wineglass Bay** (p177), a surefire starter on every Tasmanian wilderness calendar. North of here are the chilled-out fishing towns **Bicheno** (p181) and **St Helens** (p190) – both worth a day or two of beach time and fish-and-chip dinners. Finish off your trashy holiday novel on the beach at **Binalong Bay** (p194) near the **Bay of Fires** (p194). From St Helens you can continue north to check out the Forester kangaroos in **Mt William National Park** (p196), or head west through historic tin-mining **Derby** (p196), **Bridestowe Estate Lavender Farm** (p198) near Scottsdale and the wine-soaked **Pipers River Region** (p221) to Launceston.

Adhere to the 'When in Rome' adage and hit the east coast – where Taswegians come to swim, surf and sun themselves. From sombre Port Arthur to the underrated northeast, this 700km tour rattles the skeletons in Tasmania's closet and reveals the island's true holiday colours.

UP THE GUTS: HOBART TO LAUNCESTON

10 days / Hobart to Bruny Island to Huon Valley to The Midlands to Launceston

Pick up a set of wheels in **Hobart** (p78). Don't miss a walk around **Battery Point** (p91) and the waterfront, and if you're flying in for the weekend, Saturday's sensational Salamanca Market (p85). You'll never forget a few days spent meandering through the hills, valleys and waterways south of Hobart. Load up the car and set off on a loop taking in the unspoiled beaches and forests of **Bruny Island** (p136) across the D'Entrecasteaux Channel from sea-salty **Kettering** (p136), artsy-craftsy **Cygnet** (p142), and far-flung **Dover** (p149). Detour to sway through the treetops at **Tahune Forest AirWalk** (p148), take a short walk in the **Hartz Mountains National Park** (p148) and go underground at **Hastings Caves & Thermal Springs** (p151). If you're here in late summer, make sure you pick up a bag of fresh, crunchy apples by the roadside in the Huon Valley – this isn't called 'the Apple Isle' for nothing!

Truck back through Hobart and hit the **Heritage Highway** (p154), the original route between Hobart and Launceston that opened up the Midlands for settlement from the 1820s. It's only 200km between Tassie's two major cities, but a string of gorgeous sandstone-built towns complete with country pubs, tea rooms and colonial accommodations will tempt you to linger for two or three days. **Oatlands** (p155) has more Georgian sandstone buildings than any other town in Australia; **Ross** (p156) is a cutesy heritage town with a great bakery, an historic bridge, a friendly pub and plenty of places to stay; and **Campbell Town** (p158) makes a handy pit stop en route to laid-back **Launceston** (p202). Reward yourself with a tour and a taste at the hallowed **Boag's Brewery** (p205).

From Hobart in the deep south to the northern lights of Launceston, this 500km trail takes in the verdant wonders of the Huon Valley and D'Entrecasteaux Channel south of Hobart, and the historic sandstone towns strung out along the Heritage Highway.

History

Tasmania's short written history is bleak and powerful. But like the rest of Australia, it has a much longer story, that of its *palawa*, or 'first man': the term some Tasmanian Aborigines use to describe themselves. Depicted as a people all but wiped out in an attempted genocide, their culture survives today, despite the fact that their home became Britain's prison island in the first years of the 19th century. In 1804 74 convicts were shipped out to Van Diemen's Land (as Tasmania was then known), with 71 soldiers, plus their 21 wives and 14 children. Early Tasmania was dominated by the mentality, 'If it grows, chop it down; if it runs, shoot it'. Penal settlements were built in the island's most inhospitable places. Macquarie Harbour, on the harsh west coast, became Tasmania's first penal site in 1822, and by 1833 roughly 2000 convicts a year were sent to this end of the earth as punishment for often trivial crimes.

Sites along the west coast harbour stone engravings, thought to be important symbols of Tasmanian Aboriginal beliefs; they also had knowledge of astronomy.

The community quickly developed a very particular character: lawlessness and debauchery were rife. Yet it was also defined by great pioneering innovation and courage. Tasmanian culture has undergone a transition from shame and an increasing number of Tasmanians now identify with their convict past – or their indigenous heritage.

TASMANIAN ABORIGINES
The Land Bridge & the Ice Age

Tasmania was part of the supercontinent Gondwana until it broke away and drifted south 160 million years ago. Aboriginal people probably migrated across a land bridge that joined Tasmania to the rest of Australia at least 35,000 years ago. The sea level was much lower then and the Tasmanian climate much drier and colder. Aborigines settled the extensive grasslands on the western side of Tasmania, where they hunted wallabies. When the last ice age ended between 18,000 and 12,000 years ago, the glaciers retreated, sea levels rose and tall forests became established in the western half of the island, while in the east, rainfall increased and new grasslands developed. Most people abandoned their caves and shelters and followed the animals they hunted to the more open, eastern tracts of land. Tasmania 'floated away' from mainland Australia and a distinctive existence began for the people, animals and plants of the island.

For more information, see the excellent *Deep Time: Continuing Tasmanian Aboriginal Culture* brochure available at the Hobart Visitor Information Centre.

Life on the Smaller Island

The culture of the Tasmanian Aborigines diverged from the way people were living on the mainland, as they developed a sustainable, seasonal culture of hunting, fishing and gathering. They produced more sophisticated boats

TIMELINE

60,000–35,000 BC	12,000–8000 BC	1642
Aborigines settled in Australia sometime during this period	Tasmania's Aborigines are separated from the mainland when sea levels rise	Abel Tasman discovers Tasmania and names it Van Diemen's Land after a Dutch governor

and used them to hunt seals and mutton birds on and around the offshore islands. While mainland groups developed more specialised tools for hunting, such as boomerangs, *woomeras* and pronged spears, the Tasmanian people continued to use simpler tools, such as ordinary spears, wooden *waddies* (war clubs) and stones.

Those who remained in the west lived mainly on the coast. Aboriginal women collected shellfish (mussels, abalone and oysters), the remains of which make up the enormous middens around Tasmania's coastline. Both men and women wore necklaces of shell. They sheltered in bark lean-tos and protected themselves from the island's cold weather by rubbing a mixture of ochre, charcoal and fat on their skin.

Sails, Guns & Fences

The first European to spy Tasmania was Dutch navigator Abel Tasman, who bumped into it in 1642. He named this new place Van Diemen's Land after the Dutch East Indies' governor. It's estimated there were between 5000 and 10,000 Aborigines in Tasmania when Europeans arrived, living in 'bands' of around 50 people, each claiming rights over a specific area of land and being part of one of the nine main language groups. These included the Nuenonne people in the southern area and the Tommeginne in the North.

European sealers began to work Bass Strait in 1798 and they raided tribes along the coast, kidnapping Aboriginal women as workers and sex slaves. The sealers were uninterested in Aboriginal land and eventually formed a reciprocal trade relationship with the Aborigines. Some accounts suggest the sealers traded dogs and other items for accompaniment back to their islands by Aboriginal women and occasionally men.

Risdon Cove, on the Derwent River, became the site of Australia's second British colony in 1803. One year later the settlement moved to the present site of Hobart, where fresh water ran plentifully off Mt Wellington.

During this period, despite some initial friendly exchanges and trade, an unknown number of peaceable Aboriginal people were killed as European fences and farming encroached on their hunting grounds and significant places. In return, Aboriginal people began to carry out their own raids. In 1816 Governor Thomas Davey produced his 'Proclamation to the Aborigines', which represented settlers and Aborigines living together amicably – in direct contrast to the realities of a brutal conflict.

By the 1820s these territorial disputes had developed into the so-called Black Wars, as Aboriginal people increasingly refused to surrender their lands, women and children without a fight. In 1828 martial law was declared by Lieutenant-Governor Arthur. Aboriginal groups were systematically murdered, arrested or forced at gunpoint from districts settled by whites; arsenic on bread and steel traps designed to catch humans were used. Many more succumbed to exotic diseases.

The level of frontier violence across Australia is disputed in the acrimonious and highly political 'history wars', as detailed in Stuart McIntyre's *The History Wars* (2003).

1700s	1788	1798
Captain Bligh cleverly plants the isle's first apple tree	The First Fleet arrives at Sydney with its cargo of convicts	'Straitsmen', a rough bunch of sealers, make their home and their living in Bass Strait

Meanwhile, a disapproving Tasmanian establishment contemptuously termed the descendants of sealers and Aboriginal women 'half-castes', and even though Cape Barren was designated an Aboriginal reserve in the 1880s, there was continual pressure on the islanders to adopt European farming ways and assimilate with mainlanders.

THE BLACK LINE

European contact with Tasmania increased after the British arrived at Sydney Cove in 1788 – Van Diemen's Land was a convenient pit-stop en route to New South Wales.

By now, the British were concerned at how it might look to the world if their actions led to the extinction of an entire people: this would appear an 'indelible stain upon the government's character'. In 1830, in an attempt to flush out all Aborigines and corner them on the Tasman Peninsula, a human chain of about 2200 men known as the 'Black Line' was formed by settlers and soldiers, moving through the settled areas of the state from Moulting Lagoon, through Campbell Town, to Quamby's Bluff. Three weeks later, the farcical manoeuvre had succeeded in capturing only an old man and a boy, and confirmed settlers' fears that they couldn't defeat the Aborigines by force of arms. The *Hobart Courier* mocked the exercise: it had cost half the annual budget. In turn, it must have given the Aboriginal people an awful sense that their time was running out.

A PARALLEL PRISON

As a result, Lieutenant-Governor Arthur consented to George Augustus Robinson's plan to 'conciliate' the Aboriginal people. In effect Robinson enticed and cajoled virtually all of the Aborigines in mainland Tasmania to lay down their arms, leave their traditional lands and accompany him to new settlements. In doing so, he became the first European to walk across much of the state, adding the title of 'explorer' to that of missionary. There is strong historical evidence that the people of Oyster Bay, including their prominent chief Tongerlongetter, whom Robinson regarded as 'a man of great tact and judgement', followed him to a succession of settlements in the Furneaux Islands based on the promise of sanctuary and land. Instead, they were subjected to attempts to 'civilise' and Christianise them, and made to work for the government.

After enduring a number of moves, including to Sarah Island on the west coast, they were finally settled at Wybalenna (Black Man's Houses) on Flinders Island. One by one, the people began to die from a potent mixture of despair, homesickness, poor food and respiratory disease. In 1847 those who had managed to survive petitioned Queen Victoria, complaining of their treatment and referring to the 'agreement' they thought Robinson had made with Lieutenant-Governor Arthur on their behalf. Wybalenna was eventually abandoned and the survivors transferred to mainland Tasmania. Of the 135 who had been sent to Flinders Island, only 47 lived to make the journey to Oyster Cove, south of Hobart. The new accommodation here

1803	1804	1822–53
Risdon Cove, Australia's second British penal settlement, is established	Tasmania's first permanent colonial settlements are established, at Sullivan's Cove (Hobart) and George Town	Convicts are imprisoned at various penal settlements around the state, including at Sarah Island and Port Arthur

proved to be substandard and the Aborigines once again experienced the criminal neglect of the authorities, and growing demoralisation. Within a decade, half of them were dead.

TRUGANINI'S STORY

Truganini's life was lived out during the white invasion and her death became a symbol for the attempted genocide of Tasmania's Aboriginal people. By all accounts a lovely looking and intelligent woman, she was born on Bruny Island in either 1803 or 1812, the daughter of Mangana, the chief of the Nuenonne people. Along with her husband, Woureddy, she left her island home to travel with George Robinson; accounts also suggest she lived with sealers as a young woman, an experience which left her unable to bear children. When she was older, Truganini lived with fellow Tasmanian Aborigines in the derelict environment of Wybalenna on Flinders Island and afterwards at the disastrous Oyster Cove settlement.

It is remarkable given the times that Truganini lived into her seventies. When she died in Hobart in 1876, the Tasmanian Government declared that she was the last of the island's Aborigines and that her race was extinct (in fact, she was outlived by Suke and Fanny Cochrane, two women of tribal parentage). The announcement of her death, and the resulting funeral procession through Hobart, aimed to 'end the native problem'; this demise was taken as fact – and still is in some encyclopaedias and school history lessons.

Against her wishes to be buried in the mountains behind Oyster Cove or dropped deep into the D'Entrecasteaux Channel, Truganini's 4ft skeleton was instead displayed for many years as a public curio in the Tasmanian Museum. Much to the chagrin of the Royal Society in Tasmania, other parts of her contested remains were shipped to Britain by the Royal College of Surgeons in London and were only repatriated in 2002. It took more than a lifetime for Truganini's wishes to be granted and her ashes finally scattered in the channel beside her beloved Bruny Island. Travellers can visit a memorial to Truganini at The Neck on Bruny Island (p137) and there is a memorial on Mt Nelson, at the top of the Truganini Track.

MAPPING VAN DIEMEN'S LAND

Nearly 130 years after Abel Tasman's able efforts, Tasmania was sighted and visited by a series of other European sailors including captains Tobias Furneaux, James Cook and William Bligh. Between 1770 and 1790 they all visited Adventure Bay on Bruny Island and believed it to be part of the Australian mainland, rather than an island off an island (off an island). In 1792 Admiral Bruni D'Entrecasteaux explored the southeastern coastline more thoroughly, mapping and naming many of its features. Most major Tasmanian landmarks still bear the French names he gave them.

Truganini's people knew Bruny Island as Lunawanna-Alonnah, names adopted by two present-day settlements there.

The reference to 'Truganini in chains' in the Midnight Oil song *Truganini* is not correct: it's more likely to be a metaphor for the appalling treatment of Tasmania's Aboriginal people.

1830	**1853**	**1856**
The Black Line, a human chain of 2200 men, tries and fails to flush out Tasmania's Aborigines	The Anti-Transportation League lobbyists are successful, bringing an end to convict transportation	The state changes its name from Van Diemen's Land to Tasmania to remove stigma

In 1798 Lieutenant Matthew Flinders circumnavigated Van Diemen's Land and proved that it was an island. He named the rough stretch of sea between the island and the mainland Bass Strait, after George Bass, the ship's surgeon.

Australia's Second Settlement

The European discovery of Bass Strait shortened the journey to Sydney from India or Africa's Cape of Good Hope by a week.

In the late 1790s Governor King of NSW decided to establish a second settlement in Australia, south of Sydney Cove. Port Phillip Bay in Victoria was initially considered, but the site was rejected due to a lack of water on the Mornington Peninsula and, in 1803, Tasmania's Risdon Cove was chosen. A year later, the settlement was moved 10km away to the present site of Hobart. The threat of French interest in the island suggested the need for a settlement up north, on a site proclaimed 'George Town' on the Tamar River.

Exploring Coast to Coast

The establishment of George Town in 1804 attracted new settlers, resulting in a demand for more land. Settlers initially spread along the southern coast towards Port Arthur, along the east coast and around the Launceston area.

Tasmania's coast has claimed over a thousand ships. One of the most treacherous spots was King Island in Bass Strait – take the virtual tour at www.kingisland .net.au/~maritime.

By 1807 an overland route from Hobart to Launceston had been forged. The earliest buildings were rough timber huts, but, as towns developed, settlers with stone masonry skills arrived. Stone was readily available for construction work and many early stone buildings have survived; some of the best examples of these buildings can be found in Richmond (p109) and the small towns along the Midland (Heritage) Highway (p154).

To the settlers, Tasmania's big unknown was its rugged hinterland, where difficult, mountainous country barred the way. The first Europeans to cross the island were escapees from Macquarie Harbour; many escaped, but only a few survived the journey across to Hobart Town.

Then, in 1828, George Frankland was appointed Tasmania's surveyor-general. Determined to map the entire state, he sent many surveyors on long, arduous journeys during the 1830s, often accompanying them. By 1845, when Frankland died, most of the state was roughly mapped and catalogued.

LET'S DO THE TIME WARP AGAIN

As you explore Tasmania you'll often come across gracious old heritage homes and properties managed by the **National Trust** (☎ 6344 6233; www.nationaltrusttas.org.au; 413 Hobart Rd, Launceston). Many are staffed by volunteers and have rather specific opening hours, but if you do fancy a spot of time travel, be sure to talk with the attendants as they are often passionately knowledgeable about stories in the area. Step onto the well-worn flagstones of the Georgian Regency mansion, Clarendon near Evandale (p225), convict-built Franklin House in Launceston (p206) and the colony's first lawyer's digs, Runnymede in Hobart (p87) – all are well worth a visit.

1870s	1932	1932
Gold and tin are discovered in the state's north, signalling the beginning of mining interests in Tasmania	Tasmanian Joseph Lyons becomes Australia's first (and only) Tasmanian prime minister	The Lyell Hwy is opened, linking Tasmania's west coast with Hobart

Building roads across the mountainous west was difficult and many were surveyed across all sorts of landscapes before being abandoned. But in 1932 the Lyell Hwy from Hobart to Queenstown was finally opened for business, linking the west coast to Hobart.

CONVICT LIFE
Sarah, Maria & Arthur: the Worst of the Worst

The actual site of the first penal settlement in Tasmania was on small Sarah Island, in Macquarie Harbour on the west coast. The prisoners sent there were those who had committed further crimes after arriving in Australia. Their severe punishment was the manual labour of cutting down Huon pine in the rainforest. It's believed conditions were so dreadful here that some prisoners committed murder in order to be sent for trial and execution in Hobart. Today, visitors can tour Sarah Island and hear more about convict life here on cruises out of Strahan (p279).

The number of prisoners sent to Van Diemen's Land increased in 1825; in the same year the island was recognised as a colony independent of NSW and another penal settlement was established, this one on the east coast of Maria Island, where prisoners were treated more humanely.

In 1830 a third penal settlement was established at Port Arthur on the Tasman Peninsula. Shortly after its construction, the other two penal settlements closed – Maria Island in 1832 and Sarah Island in 1833.

Punishments meted out to convicts at Port Arthur, which, like its predecessors, was considered escape-proof, included weeks of solitary confinement, sometimes in total darkness and silence. The worst prisoners were sent to work in the coal mines of nearby Saltwater River Arthur (p131), where they were housed in miserably damp underground cells. A visit to Port Arthur (p127) evokes the terrible conditions suffered by prisoners during this era.

A Name Change & a New Image

In 1840 convict transportation to NSW ceased, resulting in an increase in the number of convicts being sent to Van Diemen's Land; there was a peak of 5329 new arrivals in 1842. In 1844 control of the Norfolk Island penal settlement (in the Pacific Ocean, 1610km northeast of Sydney) was transferred from NSW to Van Diemen's Land and by 1848 'VDL' was the only place in the British Empire to which convicts were still being transported.

Vociferous opposition to the continued transportation of convicts came from free settlers, who in 1850 formed the Anti-Transportation League to successfully lobby for change. The last convicts transported to the colony arrived in 1853.

Van Diemen's Land had been the most feared destination for British prisoners for more than three decades. During those years a total of 74,000

London-born Marcus Clarke visited Tasmania in the 1870s and wrote *For the Term of His Natural Life* (1874), an epic novel about convict life. Today it's still considered a ripping yarn.

Robert Hughes' compelling bestseller, *The Fatal Shore* (1987), offers a colourful and exhaustive historical account of convict transportation from Britain to Australia.

The website www .portarthur.org.au is an introduction to one of the most powerful historic sites in Australia; in a twist of fate, a tragic massacre occurred here in 1996.

1934	1935	1945
Construction of the 7km Pinnacle Rd up Mt Wellington begins, creating employment for thousands of men during the Depression	Tasmanian Errol Flynn stars in *Captain Blood*, in which his character is sold as a slave to Olivia de Havilland, escapes, and becomes a pirate...(art mirrors life?)	Arguably the world's toughest open-ocean yacht race, the Sydney-to-Hobart Yacht Race is run for the first time

convicts had been transported to the island. The majority of these people had served out their sentences and settled in the colony, yet so terrible was its reputation that in 1856 – the year it achieved responsible self-government – it changed its name to Tasmania in an attempt to free its image once and for all from the shackles of its past.

GOLD, BUT NO GREAT RUSH

Tony Wright's *Bad Ground: Inside the Beaconsfield Mine Rescue* is the definitive account of the tragedy.

In the 1870s gold was discovered near the Tamar River as was tin in the northeast. These discoveries prompted a deluge of international prospectors. In the northeast a number of Chinese miners arrived, bringing their culture with them. Tourism authorities are constructing a themed 'Trail of the Tin Dragon' through the northeast to highlight this aspect of the state's history (see p190).

Mining was a tough way of life and most people didn't make their fortunes. Individual prospectors grabbed the rich, easily found surface deposits, but once these were gone the miners had to form larger groups and companies to mine deeper deposits, until eventually these either ran out or became unprofitable to work. Remains of the mine workings at Derby (p196) and the still-operating (and now-notorious) mine at Beaconsfield can be visited today. For a brief summation of the Beaconsfield gold mine disaster of April 2006, see p218.

Once it was realised that there was mineral wealth to be found. prospectors randomly explored most of the state. On the west coast, discoveries of large deposits of silver and lead resulted in a boom in the 1880s and an associated rush at Zeehan. In fact, so rich in minerals was the area that it ultimately supported mines significant enough to create the towns of Rosebery, Tullah and Queenstown. Geological exploitation went unchecked, however, and by the 1920s, copper mining at Queenstown had gashed holes in the surrounding hills, while logging, pollution, fires and heavy rain stripped the terrain of its vegetation and topsoil. The environment has only begun repairing itself over the past few decades.

The Parks & Wildlife Service's website (www .parks.tas.gov.au) has a section dedicated to exploring the past, with information on historic sites, plus whaling, sealing and shipwrecks off the state's coast.

The rich belt of land from Queenstown to the northern coast is still being mined in several places, but this is now being done with a little more environmental consideration and fewer visible effects than in the past. New finds will undoubtedly occur in this mineral-rich belt and may well see industry pitted against conservation interests yet again.

TASMANIA LAST CENTURY

Although it was ignored in the initial Federal ministry, Tasmania officially became a state when Australia's Federation took place in 1901. For Tasmanians, as for mainlanders in the new Commonwealth of Australia, the first half of the 20th century was dominated by war, beginning with the dispatch of a contingent of 80 Tasmanian soldiers to South Africa and the

1972	1975	1982–83
Lake Pedder is flooded as part of hydro-electric industrialisation	Hobart's Tasman Bridge collapses, killing twelve, when the ore carrier Lake Illawarra crashes into it	The Franklin River Blockade is staged to oppose construction of a dam in the area, and is ultimately successful

Boer War, through the Great War and WWII, with the Depression of the late 1920s thrown in for bad measure.

The state's post-WWII economy was reassuringly buoyant, with industrial success embodied by Bell Bay's aluminium refinery and the ongoing developments of the powerful Hydro-Electric Commission. However, by the 1980s it had suffered a worrisome decline. Subsequent years saw economic unease reflected in climbing 'emigration' levels to the mainland (especially among the under-30s) and falling birth rates.

Saving the Wilderness

In 1910 an Austrian, Gustav Weindorfer, reached the summit of Cradle Mountain. Throwing his arms out, he declared that the magnificence of the place, 'where there is no time and nothing matters', was something the people of the world should share – it later became a national park. In the 20th century, the extinction of the thylacine (see p54) and the flooding of Lake Pedder in the late 1960s and early '70s led to the birth of the green movement in 1972, when concerned groups got together to form the United Tasmania Group. Ten years later, thousands of people acted to stop the damming of the Franklin River in 1984–85. Leaders in these movements became a force in Australian federal politics, the Greens Party, under the leadership of Bob Brown, who has been a senator since 1996 (see p50); the Greens became national in 2003 when WA joined the party.

The long-running debate between pro-logging groups, pro–pulp mill corporations and conservationists keen to protect Tasmania's old growth forests and wild heritage continues (with some new 'bad guys', in the form of property developers, being added to the mix). Environmental issues are never far from the headlines – see p46 for more information.

TASSIE TODAY

At the start of the 21st century, the exodus of young, educated Tasmanians has begun a slow reversal, with a revival of Tasmania's economy heralding a new era of optimism. An improved unemployment rate, record levels of investment, increased exports, a statewide real estate boom, a small but significant growth in the population and a surge in tourist numbers have seen Tasmania finally shrugging off mainlanders' insults.

Backed by strong tourism campaigns, vocal supporters in mainstream media, a respected arts scene and the emergence of several excellent local brands that wind up in shopping trolleys across the country, Tasmania's image change is well underway as it fosters its reputation as a 'pure' holiday isle and lifestyle haven.

Tasmanian Aborigines continue to claim rights to land and compensation for past injustices. Acknowledgement of the treatment meted out to Aborigines by Europeans has resulted in the recognition of native titles

In 1997 the Tasmanian parliament became the first in Australia to formally apologise to the Aboriginal community for past actions connected with the 'Stolen Generation'.

1996	2004	2006-2007
The Port Arthur massacre stuns the nation, and eventually results in stricter gun-control laws in Australia	Launceston-born Ricky Ponting makes Tasmanians proud when he becomes captain of Australia's test cricket team	Tasmania breaks through to win the Pura Cup (formerly the Sheffield Shield) interstate cricket competition for the first time

Trying to find a convict in your family tree? To help with genealogy searches, check the website of the Tasmanian Family History Society (www.tasfhs.org).

to land. In 1995 the state government returned 12 sites to the Tasmanian Aboriginal community, including Oyster Cove, Kutikina Cave and Steep Island. Wybalenna was added to this list in 1999, and areas of Cape Barren and Clarke Islands in 2005.

It's interesting to note that the subject of Tasmania's early treatment of Aborigines is still a very contentious one. Sydneysider and journalist Keith Windschuttle released a controversial book in 2002 entitled *The Fabrication of Aboriginal History, Volume One: Van Diemen's Land 1803–1847*, which argues that the violence committed against the Tasmanian Aborigines has been vastly overstated; a second volume is due to be published. *Whitewash: On Keith Windschuttle's Fabrication of Aboriginal History* (edited by academic and historian Robert Manne) was released in reply and is a collection of arguments from noted historians refuting Windschuttle's claims.

Good places to learn about Aboriginal art and culture are Tiagarra (p230), the Aboriginal cultural centre and museum in Devonport, and the new Living History Museum of Aboriginal Cultural Heritage, outside Cygnet in the southeast (p142).

2007	2008	2008
The issue of the pulp mill in the tourism- and winery-rich Tamar Valley becomes a political hot potato during the federal election	Prime Minister Kevin Rudd apologises to Australia's Aboriginal 'Stolen Generation'; Tasmanian Aboriginal activist Michael Mansell questions whether financial compenstion will follow	Labor Premier Paul Lennon resigns; the furore over the pulp mill continues

The Culture

REGIONAL IDENTITY

Tasmania has often been dismissed as Australia's cultural backwater, a blip on the travel radar compared with the siren call of the east coast. How many times has this little heart-shaped island state been left off maps of Australia? In Aussie vernacular, the 'map o' Tassie' is more likely to be used to describe 'hair down there'. Given all this, it would be no great surprise to find Tasmanians harbouring yacht-sized inferiority complexes and well-cooked chips on their shoulders.

Yet these days they don't appear to have much of either, now they're truly on the national map and the traveller's hit list. Tasmanians (old-timers and newcomers) are some of the friendliest, most laid-back people you'll encounter. Despite a dark history that is just coming to light, the extreme beauty of the wilderness and the now-established arts and foodie scenes are the staples of a burgeoning identity.

If Australia's national identity is rooted in its past, this is particularly true in Tasmania's case. The seminal colony was characterised by extreme hardship, resentment at being sent so far with so little, and an incalculable sense of loss of loved ones and homes left behind. This struggle against nature and tyranny created a culture based on the principles of a 'fair go' and back-slaps for challenges to authority. You can add to this the convict experience of Van Diemen's Land and a heightened sense of isolation from the rest of the country.

Tasmanian culture is now arguably richer for embracing indigenous culture, but it hasn't always been this way. By accepting that Tasmanian settlers wiped out the island's Aboriginal population, the rest of Australia could potentially say: 'at least we weren't as bad as *that*…' However, contemporary Tasmania now chooses to recognise its 40,000-year-old indigenous heritage as an ongoing culture, with a future as well as a past. You'll see it in the landscape – carvings and paintings in once-inhabited caves, coastal middens of shells that yielded meals, quarries where stone tools were fashioned. Importantly, new generations of Tasmanian Aboriginal people are acknowledging their identity and some of the island's best cultural centres are devoted to their unique traditions. It's also true that Tasmanian indigenous identity is complex, and remains as debated as it is celebrated. For more, see p31.

The greater Tasmanian identity is mirrored in the island's remarkable landscape: dark foliage and craggy peaks whipped by notorious winds, with short winter days and the stark clarity of the light down here. The environment fosters a keen sense of adventure and a certain toughness. Rather than hiding indoors behind solid stone, Tasmanians embrace their wilderness beneath a thin layer of Gore-Tex. Once an adversary, the landscape is now adored. Getting into it, over it or on top of it is something the Tassie work–life balance allows.

In the countryside the hedgerows, old stone dwellings and neat gardens seem to endure in the face of an austere landscape. These things give the British an instant affinity with the place to this day (try tallying up UK expat B&B owners on your travels). Colonial doilies and a stolid 'meat and two veg' mentality are still ingrained, but Tasmania's tastes are shifting. The first genuine croissants and espresso were served in Hobart in the 1980s. Since then the food scene has leapt out of the deep-fryer and into the wood-fired pizza oven, as the new Tasmania tries on a gourmet crown for size, and dishes up an increasingly multicultural menu.

Eminent Tasmanian historian Henry Reynolds' *Fate of a Free People* reexamines the history of the Aboriginal relationship with Tasmania's colonial invaders, asking questions such as did Aborigines tamely surrender their lands and just what happened to their petition to Queen Victoria.

LIFESTYLE

The moody settings and often gloomy subject matter of many books by Tassie authors have led to the coining of the term 'Tasmanian Gothic'.

Australians have been sold to the world as outdoorsy, sporty, big-drinking country folk, but despite the stereotypes, many Australians can barely swim a lap and loads wouldn't be seen dead in an Akubra hat. But you *are* more likely to see an array of outdoor wear in Tasmania (of the boot-and-beanie variety) and there's more country composure than urban verve. Everything moves at a slower pace, which can leave you content or frustrated, depending on your state of mind.

The drinking thing: Hobart's original reputation for drunken lawlessness has settled down into a historical hangover, but boozing outdoors is still a familiar thing to most Tasmanians. Wine and beer duke it out for the title of number-one beverage. Wines from the Tamar Valley are readily available, even in smaller towns, while the two main local beers (Cascade and James Boags) are available in more variety and are more likely to be on tap here than on the mainland. You can also whet your whistle with a wide range of local ciders and ginger beers.

The 'Australian Dream' has long been to own a rambling house on a quarter-acre block – sprawling suburbia is endemic in Australian towns and cities. Tasmanian homes often enjoy astoundingly beautiful views of water or mountains; a room *without* a view and swathes of natural light is considered a rip-off down here! Open the door of an average Tasmanian suburban home and you'll probably find a married heterosexual couple with two kids, though it's increasingly likely they'll be de facto or onto their second marriage. These days, attitudes towards gay and lesbian couples in Tasmania are much more tolerant than they were just over a decade ago, before the Tasmanian parliament repealed the state's antigay laws. This brought Tasmania into compliance with the 1994 UN ruling on this issue, and eliminated Australia's only remaining state law banning same-sex relations.

Billing itself as 'Tasmania's Journal of Discovery', www.thistasmania.com covers everything from adventure travel to local recipes, with fabulous photography.

Our typical Tassie family (with a water view) will have an average of 1.4 children, probably called Jack and Isabella, Australia's names of the moment. The average gross wage of either parent is probably around $1010 per week (compared with $1128 in New South Wales).

Like most Australians, our typical Tassie family probably loves the sun (and the sun does shine down here, despite the wintry rep). Australians have the highest rate of skin cancer in the world, accounting for over 80% of all new cancers diagnosed each year. Wearing sunscreen and hats, our family is proud of Tasmania's wilderness and its unique vegetation – they probably know a number of secret camping spots, and may well take the tent into a national park every holiday. Younger Tasmanians often camp on their weekends with tight-knit posses of mates, or they might try a spot of beach cricket, kayaking or fishing, after which there'll be plentiful bounty: abalone, oysters from the rocks, squid or flathead. On other weekends they probably watch sport, check out the local footy, go to the movies or head to the shops, which will no doubt involve a stop for a latte at some point.

ECONOMY

Run by one guy from Howrah in Hobart, www.tasmaniantimes.com is a 'forum of discussion and dissent' and a way to check the pulse of local issues like the proposed Tamar Valley pulp mill or political goings-on.

In 2008 Tasmania was breaking previous economic records, largely driven by a population boom (see opposite) and the range and affordability of urban and rural real estate. Although prices have spiked in many areas, it's still possible to bag yourself a bargain – often with water views, plenty of land and access to nearby wilderness. Gross State Product is growing at 3.1% (higher than the national rate) and exports rose by over 17% to around $3.71 billion in the year up to September 2007. Strong jobs growth is also reflected in Tasmania's steadily rising participation rate. A 6.1% unemployment rate in December 2007 isn't the lowest it's ever been, but it's not far off the mark (though it's still above the national average of 4.6%). Deregulating shop trading hours has led to growth in the retail sector.

Apart from being a seaport and a base for Antarctic activities, Hobart's economic success is based on tourism, fishing and forestry; other industries include a zinc smelter and a high-speed catamaran manufacturing facility. Launceston derives its wealth from wool, wine, agriculture, niche manufacturing and resource processing at the nearby Bell Bay industrial site. In the fertile northwest, Burnie has a thriving dairy industry and specialised manufacturers in addition to the traditional port, pulp and paper industries. Nearby Devonport is the tourism gateway to the state, welcoming the ferries from the mainland.

POPULATION

Demographers believe Tasmania's population will soon pass the half-million mark. Most people live on the northern and southeastern coasts, where fertile, undulating countryside and accessible harbours invited European settlement. The population density is around seven people per square kilometre (although no-one's within shouting distance in the southwest). The majority live in and around Hobart and Launceston: greater Hobart has a population of around 203,600, while about 137,900 people live in the greater Launceston area.

Australia's population topped 21 million in 2007 due to a strong birth rate and overseas migration, and Tasmania has followed suit. Its recent economic fortune has seen significant population growth (about 1200 people a year) to reach a new population record of 494,500 in late 2007.

Around 16,000 people of Aboriginal descent live in Tasmania. The state has the lowest percentage of overseas-born residents (around 11% of the population, compared with 24% for Australia overall, and 29% in Western Australia). Of the overseas-born residents, about half are from the UK, and most Tasmanians have a British ancestry.

For articles of current social relevance, local (and mainland) poetry and short stories, see the elegant *Island* magazine online: www .islandmag.com.

SPORT

If you're an armchair sports fan, Tasmania has much to offer. The Australian Rules football season has passions running high from about March to September, and when it ends, it's simply time for the cricket season to begin.

Tasmanians avidly follow the national **Australian Football League** (AFL; www.afl .com.au), and Aurora Stadium in Launceston hosts a handful of well-attended AFL matches each year – both St Kilda and Hawthorn (Melbourne-based teams) have been playing regular-season games here in recent years, and Hawthorn at least look set to continue the habit (wearing specially badged 'Tasmania Hawks' guernseys). The **AFL Tasmania** (www.footballtas.com.au) website lists scheduled games and ticketing information. **Redline Coaches** (www.redline coaches.com.au) runs a Hobart-to-Launceston bus service on game days.

Tasmania has two football leagues of its own: the **Northern Tasmanian Football League** (NTFL; www.ntfl.com.au) and the **Southern Football League** (SFL; www .southernfootball.com.au). Squads from either end of the state occasionally play an intrastate match.

Cricket is played during the other, nonfootball half of the year (November to March), and the state has produced two outstanding Australian batsmen in recent decades: the legendary, moustached David Boon, and current Australian captain Ricky Ponting, widely regarded as the best batsman in the world. Tasmania hosts one day international (ODI) and international test matches at Bellerive Oval, east of the Derwent River in Hobart – usually one test and one or two ODIs every summer.

The Tasmania Tigers compete in the interstate Pura Cup competition (formerly the Sheffield Shield), which they won for the first time in 2007. There are lower-key district cricket matches across the state right through summer. Contact the **Tasmanian Cricket Association** (☎ 6282 0400; www.tascricket.com .au) for tickets and match fixtures.

Hobart's harbour comes alive with spectators and party-goers for the finish of the famous **Sydney to Hobart Yacht Race** (www.rolexsydneyhobart.com), and the lesser-known Melbourne to Hobart race, at New Year. See p61 for details.

ARTS

For information on Hobart's vibrant arts scene, see the Salamanca Arts Centre website (www .salarts.org.au).

Cinema

Most people need little introduction to Australia's vibrant movie industry, one of the earliest established in the world and a playground for screen greats Errol Flynn (a Hobart lad, see below), the beloved and missed Heath Ledger, 'our' Nicole (Kidman) and Russell Crowe (born in New Zealand, but wishes it was South Sydney). Very few Australian movies are set or shot in Tasmania, however. Worth checking out are Roger Scholes' *The Tale of Ruby Rose* (1988), a psychological drama about a couple living in the Tasmanian highlands in the 1920s, and *The Sound of One Hand Clapping* (1998), based on Richard Flanagan's harrowing book (and scripted and directed by Flanagan). Set in a remote Tasmanian hydroelectric construction camp, Flanagan's tale traces the impact of war, displacement and abandonment on successive generations of a single family of European migrants. *Young Einstein*, a cult film in 1988, was the madcap account of Tasmanian apple farmer Albert Einstein, who discovers the Theory of Relativity in 1905 when he is sitting under an apple tree, and an apple…well, you can probably guess. In 1906 he invents rock and roll. The movie starred comedian Yahoo Serious (and his hairstyle). It also featured a soundtrack by big Australian music names Paul Kelly, Icehouse, The Saints, The Models and Mental as Anything, and introduced the rest of Australia to the extraordinary beauty of the Tasmanian landscape in cinemas across the country.

Craft & Design

A strong crafts movement has existed in Tasmania since the turn of the century. The Design Centre of Tasmania (p206) in Launceston displays and sells work by Tasmanian artisans. The galleries, shops and market at

---

IN LIKE FLYNN

The song *Errol* by Aussie band Australian Crawl goes *'Ohh, Er-rol. I would give anything, just to be like him…'*, referring to the legendary Tasmanian actor Errol Flynn, who somehow made his way from the Apple Isle to the Big Apple and beyond, to Hollywood. Born in Hobart in 1909, Errol attended numerous schools in Hobart, Sydney and in England. After many jobs (as sailor, gold-hunter, slave-trader and journalist, if you believe all the publicity), Errol drifted into acting with his first role as Fletcher Christian in *In the Wake of the Bounty*, filmed in Sydney in 1933. By 1935 he had moved to Hollywood and became a celebrated star when he featured in *Captain Blood*. He starred in over 60 films and gained screen-idol status playing such swashbucklers as Robin Hood and Don Juan. The expression 'in like Flynn' means a dead certainty or sure thing – usually in the sexual sense. Old Errol certainly established a reputation for bedding women with the greatest of ease.

Flynn died of a heart attack in 1959; from his three marriages he fathered a son and three daughters (but who knows how many outside the vows!). Despite a somewhat tarnished movie-star image created by a private life of divorces, alcohol abuse and sex scandals (recounted in his autobiography *My Wicked, Wicked Ways*), he is affectionately remembered as the devilishly handsome leading man and quintessential Hollywood hero.

Hobart's Salamanca Place also exhibit and sell crafts, with an emphasis on wood-turning, pottery, weaving and photography, while regional crafts-people advertise their creative efforts throughout the state.

Pottery and furniture-making have been particularly important, with cedar pieces from colonial times highly prized today. Contemporary furniture designers such as Patrick Hall, John Smith and Peter Costello (not the politician!) are nationally recognised for their highly refined and often sculptural use of Tasmania's superb native timbers, such as Huon pine and sassafras. Photography also has a strong tradition here, due to the diversity of landscape and the clarity of the light. For more see p38.

Literature

Tasmania's unique culture and landscape and its historical treatment of Tasmanian Aborigines and convicts have inspired and burdened writers of both fiction and nonfiction. The island has become the adopted home of a number of seasoned writers, including novelist Robert Dessaix and British writer Nicholas Shakespeare (see p18 for information on Shakespeare's excellent book *In Tasmania*).

Marcus Clarke, a prolific writer who was born in London but spent most of his life in Australia, visited Tasmania in the 1870s and wrote the novel *For the Term of His Natural Life,* an epic about convict life.

Queensland-born poet Gwen Harwood lived in Tasmania from 1945 until her death in 1996, and much of her work, such as *The Lion's Bride* (1981) and *Bone Scan* (1988), explores the island's natural beauty and the history of its Aboriginal population.

Hobart author Richard Flanagan is one of Australia's best-known (and biggest-selling) contemporary literary stars. His award-winning novel *Death of a River Guide* (1995) weaves together Tasmanian history and myths in a story set on the Franklin River – it makes an excellent introduction to Tasmanian history and life. His next novel, *The Sound of One Hand Clapping* (1997), won a national literary award, while the film of the same name was also well received (see). More recently Flanagan wrote an enigmatic (and very violent) fictional account of convicts on Sarah Island in *Gould's Book of Fish* (2002), followed by *The Unknown Terrorist* (2006).

Christopher Koch is a Hobart-born author. His novels include *The Boys in the Island* (1958), an account of growing up in Tasmania; *The Year of Living Dangerously* (1978), which was made into a high-profile film; and *Out of Ireland* (1999), worked around the journal of a revolutionary Irishman who finds himself exiled in Van Diemen's Land.

Carmel Bird, born in Launceston but now living in Melbourne, is known for the quirky black humour of her stories and novels, including *Red Shoes* (1998), short-listed for the prestigious Miles Franklin award. Her latest offering, *Cape Grimm* (2004), is set in northwest Tassie.

Matthew Kneale was short-listed for the Booker Prize for the historical fiction novel *English Passengers* (1999), a witty stew of multiple narratives telling the interwoven stories of a mid-19th-century expedition to Van Diemen's Land and the trials of the Tasmanian Aborigines.

Danielle Wood, one-time journalist with Hobart's *Mercury* newspaper, won the 2003 *The Australian*/Vogel Literary Award (the country's richest and most prestigious award for an unpublished manuscript) with her debut novel, *The Alphabet of Light and Dark*. Exploring family history, it's set in Bruny Island's lighthouse and inspired by the adventures and stories of Wood's great-great-grandfather.

Keen readers should get hold of the latest copy of Tasmania's quarterly literary journal, *Island* (www.islandmag.com), which publishes local writers'

For a quarterly list of all the latest local books, check out this bookshop's website: www.fullers bookshop.com.au /tasmaniana.html.

TRUCHANAS & DOMBROVSKIS

What would be the odds of two men from Baltic states, each of them finishing up in Tasmania, being top wilderness photographers, each dying out there, each devoted one to the other?

Max Angus

On calendars, postcards and greeting cards, in books and on posters throughout Tasmania you will no doubt see breathtaking images of the state's incredible wilderness. Many of the best photographs will bear the name of Peter Dombrovskis; his story, and that of his mentor, Olegas Truchanas, is an extraordinary one.

Olegas Truchanas (1923–72) was born in Lithuania and came to Tasmania as a refugee in 1945; Peter Dombrovskis (1945–96) was born to Latvian parents in a refugee camp in Germany near the end of WWII, and arrived in Tasmania with his mother in 1950. Both men came to Australia from war-ravaged countries, an experience that possibly left their senses open to the pristine, peaceful beauty of their new country. Both took reverential photographs of remote wilderness areas, and these beautiful images came to inspire the establishment of conservation movements in Tasmania and on the mainland.

Truchanas photographed Lake Pedder and campaigned passionately to save it from being flooded as part of a hydroelectricity scheme (p301); he also acted as a father-figure and mentor to Dombrovskis. In turn, Dombrovskis' stunning photographic images of the remote and wild Franklin River were central to the ultimately successful 1980s campaign (p287) to save the river from meeting the same fate as had befallen Lake Pedder. Dombrovskis' image of the Franklin's Rock Island Bend, in particular, became a national icon. The philosophy of both men was simple and effective: if people could see the beauty of these wild places, then they might be moved to protect them.

Sadly, both men died alone in the wilderness of the southwest, in the pursuit of their art. When Truchanas drowned while photographing the Gordon River in 1972, the year Lake Pedder was flooded, it was Dombrovskis who found his body. Dombrovskis died of a heart attack while on a photographic expedition in the Western Arthur Range in 1996.

Both photographers have left an amazing legacy of images. These days it is a little difficult to find examples of Truchanas' work, although an extensive collection of his wilderness photographs was compiled by Max Angus in *The World of Olegas Truchanas*. Dombrovskis' images are more readily available.

If you like Dombrovskis' work, check out *On the Mountain,* a selection of images of Mt Wellington, which was Dombrovskis' home for the greater part of 50 years. This book also contains a personal reflection on the mountain and its significance by Richard Flanagan and an account of its natural history by academic Jamie Kirkpatrick. *Wild Rivers* by Bob Brown contains photographs of the Franklin River taken by Dombrovskis and is accompanied by the author's account of his own experiences on that river. The newest book featuring Dombrovskis' photography is *Simply,* the first collection of his work in five years.

short stories, poetry, reviews, extracts from forthcoming novels and a variety of articles and essays.

Painting & Sculpture

Tasmania's art scene flourished from colonial times, particularly in the early 19th century under the governorship of Sir John Franklin and the patronage of his wife, Lady Jane Franklin. One of the first artists to successfully capture the Australian landscape's distinctive forms and colours was John Glover, an English artist who migrated to Tasmania in 1830. The English sculptor Benjamin Law also arrived in Tasmania in the 1830s and sculpted busts of two of the better-known Tasmanian Aborigines, the married couple Truganini and Woureddy (for more on their lives, see p27). Hobart-born William Piguenit has been called 'the first Australian-born professional painter'. He painted romantic Tasmanian landscapes, including Lake St Clair and Lake

Writers and keen readers should have a look at the website of the Tasmanian Writers' Centre (www .tasmanianwriters.org).

Pedder, in the 1870s, and his works were among the first exhibited by the Art Society of Tasmania, founded in 1884.

In 1938 the Tasmanian Group of Painters was founded to foster the work of local artists. Founding members included Joseph Connor, a Hobart-born landscape watercolourist who was one of the early Australian modernists. Since the 1940s a strong landscape watercolour school has developed in Tasmania, with artists such as Max Angus and Patricia Giles among the best known.

Tasmanian sculptor Stephen Walker has produced many bronze works that adorn Hobart's public spaces – he was also responsible for a sculptural tribute to the Midlands at the Steppes (p161), near Great Lake. Other notable contemporary artists include Bea Maddock, whose serialised images incorporate painting and photography, and Bob and Lorraine Jenyns, both sculptors and ceramists. Since the early 1980s Tasmania's art culture has been revitalised and the new wave includes printmaker Ray Arnold, painter David Keeling, photographer David Stephenson and video maker Leigh Hobbs.

The Tasmanian Museum & Art Gallery (p87) in Hobart has a good collection of Tasmanian colonial art and exhibits relating to Tasmanian Aboriginal culture. Galleries and studios in Hobart's Salamanca precinct (p84) are full of locally produced treasures. Also worth visiting are the Inveresk site of the Queen Victoria Museum & Art Gallery (p205) in Launceston, Burnie's Regional Art Gallery (p253) and the Devonport Regional Centre (p231). On your travels around the island, you'll also find plenty of smaller contemporary galleries to enjoy.

Performing Arts

The **Tasmanian Symphony Orchestra** (www.tso.com.au) is highly regarded and tours nationally and internationally. It gives regular performances at Hobart's Federation Concert Hall (p106), its home venue, and in Launceston's Princess Theatre (p212).

Tasmania's professional contemporary dance company is **TasDance** (www.tasdance.com.au), which is based in Launceston and tours statewide and interstate. It performs dance and dance-theatre, and often collaborates with artists in other fields. Another innovative company is **IHOS Opera** (www.ihosopera.com) in Hobart, an experimental music and theatre troupe.

Terrapin Theatre (www.terrapin.org.au) is a leading Australian contemporary performing arts company that has created puppetry productions for audiences of all ages both locally and internationally. Its works combine a variety of puppetry styles, including object theatre, black theatre, shadow puppetry and mobile interactive performances.

If you fancy a night of theatre, dance or music, venture to Hobart's Theatre Royal (built by convicts in 1837): www.theatreroyal.com.au.

Food & Drink

Tasmania has a blossoming food and wine culture, grown from a superb range of seafood, juicy berries and stone fruits, award-winning dairy products and cheeses, beers of international reputation and, of course, excellent cool-climate wines. Locals (and travellers!) are reaping the rewards.

Innumerable farms, orchards, vineyards and small enterprises are busy supplying fresh local produce, and buyers (restaurants, markets, food stores and individuals) are snapping it up. Dishes on menus throughout Australia feature Tasmanian oysters, scallops and salmon, and King Island cream appears on dessert menus from Sydney to Perth. Hobart and Launceston eateries offer even more still in the way of local goods.

Despite the relatively newfound fascination with tucker and Tasmania's reputation as a gourmet's paradise, at heart Tasmanians are still mostly simple eaters. Foodies may find themselves despairing in some country towns, especially where the local pub is the only eatery. Occasionally you'll find mutton(bird) dressed up as lamb. This is changing, however, as the influx of mainlanders and immigrants has led to a rise in dining standards, better availability of produce and a frenetic buzz about food in general.

Before We Eat: A Delicious Slice of Tasmania's Culinary Life, by Bernard Lloyd and Paul County, is a great, glossy book tracing the history of Tassie food and drink.

STAPLES & SPECIALITIES

Tasmania's best food comes from the sea, garnered from some of the purest waters you'll find anywhere. Genuine specialties for you to try include oysters at Coles Bay near Freycinet Peninsula National Park and Barilla Bay near Hobart; or ocean trout from the waters of Macquarie Harbour.

Fish like trevalla (blue eye) and striped trumpeter are delicious, as is the local Atlantic salmon, largely farmed in the Huon estuary. Rock lobster (usually called crayfish – fantastic tasting, and usually fantastically expensive), abalone, scallops, mussels and oysters are among the crustaceans and shellfish available.

Tasmania is known for its high-quality beef, based on a natural, grass-fed (as opposed to grain-fed) production system and free from growth hormones, antibiotics and chemical contaminants. Beef from King Island and Flinders Island is where it's at; and if you see it on a menu and the wallet allows, tuck into premium Wagyu beef from Robbins Island in Bass Strait. Flinders Island also farms prime lamb. These meats are available Tasmania-wide and in upmarket restaurants throughout Australia, and command a ransom on overseas markets (Wagyu shifts for up to $300 per kg in Tokyo).

When We Eat: A Seasonal Celebration of Fine Tasmanian Food and Drink, by Liz McLeod, Bernard Lloyd and Paul County, is the companion guide to *Before We Eat*. This title covers the availability of seasonal foods in the state, accompanied by great recipes and photographs.

You may also spy game meats on some restaurant menus – quail, wallaby and farmed venison are often available (and occasionally mutton bird). Wallaby meat is tender, lean and has a mild flavour. It's commonly found in the pies of Tasmania's countryside bakeries.

There's a brilliant cheese industry here, somewhat hampered by the fact that all the milk must be pasteurised, unlike in Italy and France, the homes of the world's best cheeses. Despite that, the results can be great: to confirm, slap some local leatherwood honey over a slice of blue cheese.

Visit Pyengana Cheese Factory (p193), not far from St Helens, for sensational cheddar; Grandvewe Cheeses (p141), just south of Woodbridge, which produces organic cheese from sheep and cows milk; Ashgrove Farm Cheese (p239), near Deloraine, for traditional cheeses like Rubicon red, smoked cheddar and creamy Lancashire; and the big daddy of them all, King Island Dairy (p307), for superb brie and rich, thick cream, among other dairy delights. Alternatively, head for the cheese section of the supermarket, which will no doubt stock many of the state's finest cheeses.

Tasmania's cold climate means its berries and stone fruit are sublime, and picking your own (in season) is a great way to sample and enjoy them. Sorell Fruit Farm (p123) is a favourite – it gives visitors the opportunity to pick all sorts, including raspberries, cherries, apples and pears. Roadside stalls in the Huon and Tamar Valleys offer the chance to buy freshly picked fruits. Other places worth a visit for their fantastic homemade fruity produce include Christmas Hills Raspberry Farm Café (p241) near Deloraine, Kate's Berry Farm (p174) outside Swansea, and Eureka Farm (p187) in Scamander.

Needless to say, the jams, sauces, fruit wines, ciders and juices made from Tasmanian fruits are excellent, and make great souvenirs of your stay. Lots of varieties are available at gourmet food stores and from stalls at Hobart's Salamanca Market (p85); otherwise, head to the Gourmet Sauce Co (p225) west of Evandale, or Fleurtys (p141) near Woodbridge in the southeast.

Without having to look very hard, you'll also find fantastic honey, chocolate and fudge, mushrooms, asparagus, olive oil, walnuts, and mustards and relishes. Locals are getting creative and showing off their agricultural skill, growing or harvesting some wonderfully diverse products, including buckwheat, *wasabi, wakame* (edible seaweed) and saffron. Black truffles are even being harvested in the north of Tasmania, with an idea to capture the French market in the other half of the year.

> Check out *Tasmania Wine & Food – Cellar Door & Farm Gate Guide*, a free brochure published by Tourism Tasmania and available at most visitors centres. See Predeparture Reading (p18) for more.

DRINKS

You can wash down all this delicious local fare with great beverages, including refreshing soft drinks (plenty of local stuff under the Cascade brand) and fruit juices – be sure to try the sparking apple juice.

Expect the best coffee in Hobart and Launceston, decent stuff in most other large towns, and a sniff of a chance of good coffee in many rural areas (but if you're lucky, some better accommodation might supply plunger coffee, tea leaves and teapots in guest rooms, instead of cheap instant coffee and teabags).

Tasmania excels in the beer and wine department, and is now recognised for its whiskies, some of which are doing well as exports.

Beer

Tasmanian beer will be fairly familiar to North Americans and to lager enthusiasts from the UK. It may taste like lemonade to the European real-ale addict, but full-strength beer can still pack a punch. Standard beer generally contains around 5% alcohol, while low-alcohol (light) beer contains between 2% and 3.5%. It's invariably chilled before drinking, even in wintry Tasmania.

In terms of breweries, there's Cascade Brewery in the state's south, based in Hobart, and James Boag's Brewery in the north (Launceston). Cascade produces the very drinkable Cascade Premium Lager and Pale Ale. Visitors tend to ask for 'Cascade' expecting to get the bottle with the distinctive label bearing a Tasmanian Tiger, but you're unlikely to get Premium unless you ask specifically for it – you'll probably get Cascade Draught. Boag's produces similar-style beers to the Cascade brews such as James Boag's Premium Lager and Boag's Draught. See p88 for details of tours of the Cascade Brewery, and p205 for information on touring Boag's Brewery.

> Travellers who want to eat their way around the Apple Isle should go to www.discovertasmania .com.au, click on 'Activities', then 'Food & Wine', and start salivating.

Wine

Since the mid-1950s Tasmania has gained international recognition for producing quality wines, characterised by their full, fruity flavour, along with the high acidity expected of cool, temperate wine regions. Today more than 140

THE INVISIBLE BEER LINE

The definitive example of Tasmanian parochialism is the local loyalty to regionally brewed beer: in the south it's Cascade; in the north, James Boag's. Up until quite recently you could draw a line from Strahan through Ross to Bicheno, north of which no sane publican would serve Cascade; south of which any mention of Boag's would provoke confusion and ridicule. These days things are much less exclusive, but we challenge you to uphold the traditional drinking rules!

---

vineyards across the state are producing award-winning pinot noirs, rieslings and chardonnays, and Tassie wineries are growing a large percentage of the grapes for many of the top Australian sparkling brands.

Grapes are grown all over the state, but it's simple enough to split Tassie into three wine growing regions: the north around Launceston, the south around Hobart and the east coast around Bicheno. Throughout these areas there are a growing number of larger operators with sophisticated cellar doors; well-known names include Tamar Ridge, Clover Hill, Pipers Brook, Freycinet, Domaine A and Moorilla Estate. There are also dozens of smaller, family-owned vineyards quietly going about the business of fine-wine-making, some open to the public by appointment only, others with restricted opening hours.

Start with some wine tastings right at the cellar door, where you can also pick up bottles of your preferred drops more cheaply than in retail outlets. Many wineries have such tastings; some of them are free but most charge a small fee (usually a few dollars), which is refundable if you purchase any wine. Bear in mind that the key word here is 'tasting', not 'guzzling' – you won't get endless glasses of the vineyard's finest, just enough in the bottom of a glass to whet your appetite.

The Tamar Valley and Pipers River area is home to a number of well-established wineries, including Rosevears Estate (p215), Tamar Ridge Wines (p217) and Pipers Brook (p221). Wineries are dotted down the east coast from Bicheno to Dunalley, including the well-respected Freycinet Vineyard (p173). Further south, in the Huon Valley area, you'll find Hartzview Vineyard (p141), Panorama Vineyard (p144) and Home Hill (p145), among others. A major producer in the Derwent River Valley is Moorilla Estate (p88), established in 1958, making it the oldest vineyard in southern Tasmania. The Coal River Valley, easily accessed from Richmond and Hobart, is home to an increasing number of wineries, among them Meadowbank Estate, Coal Valley Vineyard and Puddleduck Vineyard (p109).

If your visit to Tasmania is short but you'd still like to learn more about the state's wine industry (not to mention taste some drops, and purchase lots of bottles!), visit the Tasmanian Wine Centre (p107) in Hobart. They can arrange worldwide shipping of wine purchases.

There are a number of excellent vineyard restaurants (usually serving lunch only); see the boxed text, opposite, for our pick of vineyard eateries.

CELEBRATIONS

Celebrating in Tasmania often involves equal amounts of food and alcohol. A birthday could well be a barbecue (barbie) of steak (or seafood), washed down with a beverage or two. Weddings are usually a big slap-up dinner, though the food is sometimes less than memorable.

If you get the chance, don't miss one of Tasmania's major food festivals: the week-long festival 'The Taste' (aka the Taste of Tasmania) is staged around the waterfront as part of the Hobart Summer Festival (p94), while Launceston celebrates the three-day Festivale (p207) in City Park in February.

To get an idea of the number of grape-wreathed properties around the island, and how to find them, see www.tasmanianwine route.com.au.

Tasmania's wines are expensive compared with similar mainland wines – you'll fork out more than $20 for an acceptable bottle of wine – but the best of them are superb. See www .winediva.com.au /regions/tasmania.asp.

Cradle Mountain also gets in on the act, warming up winter visitors with the three-day Tastings at the Top in mid-June. Many other regions also celebrate their produce.

For many events, especially in the warmer months, Tasmanians fill the car with an esky, tables, chairs, a cricket set or a footy, and head off for a barbie by the lake/river/beach/mountains.

At Christmas the more traditional baked dinner is often replaced by a barbecue, in response to the warm weather. In recent times, seafood has become more popular still: perhaps a whole baked trout or salmon, or prawns, served with a cold salad rather than hot baked veggies.

WHERE TO EAT & DRINK

The Tasmanian taste for the unusual usually kicks in at dinner only. Most people still eat cereal for breakfast, or perhaps eggs and bacon on weekends. They devour sandwiches for lunch, with most sandwich fillings in cafés now coming on grilled, fancy-pants Italian bread such as focaccia, on bagels, or on Turkish bread (also known as *pide*). They may also enjoy other café fare such as quiche, salad or pasta dishes – and then eat anything and everything in the evening.

A competitively priced place to eat is in a pub. Most serve two types of meals: bistro meals, which are usually in the $13 to $24 range and are served in the dining room or lounge bar; and bar (or counter) meals, which are filling, no-frills meals eaten in the public bar and costing around $7 to $15.

The quality of pub food varies enormously. Upmarket city pubs will change their menus as much as midrange restaurants do, while standard country pubs will stick to the tried and true meals like schnitzels, roasts and basic seafood. The usual meal times are from noon to 2pm and 6pm to 8pm.

Solo diners find that cafés and noodle bars are welcoming, and good fine-dining restaurants often treat you like a star, but sadly, some midrange places may still make you feel a little ill at ease.

One of the most interesting features of the dining scene is the Bring Your Own (BYO), a restaurant that allows you to bring your own alcohol. If the restaurant also sells alcohol, the BYO bit is usually limited to bottled wine only (no beer, no casks of wine) and a corkage charge is added to your bill. The cost is either per person or per bottle, and ranges from a few dollars per person to $15 per bottle in fancy places. Be warned, however, that BYO is a custom that is slowly dying out, and many if not most licensed restaurants don't like you bringing your own wine, so ask when you book.

Most restaurants open at noon for lunch and from 6pm or 7pm for dinner. Australians usually eat lunch shortly after noon, and dinner bookings are usually made for 7.30pm or 8pm.

The nickname 'Apple Isle' stemmed from the state's huge apple production, based largely in the Huon Valley. At its peak during the 1960s there were over 2000 orchards exporting eight million boxes of apples, mainly to the UK.

Some species of Tasmanian fish are more sustainable than others. Check out the Australian Marine Conservation Society's Sustainable Fish Finder (www.amcs.org .au), which categorises about 60 species of locally harvested seafood into three sections: Say No, Think Twice, and Better Choice.

TOP FIVE VINEYARD RESTAURANTS

Here are a few places worth heading to for a long, leisurely lunch with some beaut Tassie wines (definitely book ahead):

- **Meadowbank Estate** (p110) Cambridge near Hobart
- **Home Hill Winery Restaurant** (p145) Ranelagh in the Southeast
- **Moorilla Estate** (p88) Hobart
- **Strathlynn** (p215) Rosevears in the Tamar Valley near Launceston
- **Bay of Fires Wines** (p221) Pipers River near Launceston

Quick Eats

There's not a huge culture of street vending in Tasmania. Most quick eats traditionally come from a corner shop or milk bar (a small shop selling basic provisions), which serves old-fashioned hamburgers (with bacon, egg, pineapple and beetroot if you want) and other takeaway foods. Every town has at least one busy fish and chip shop, particularly in the beachside areas.

American-style fast food is common, though many Aussies still love a meat pie, often from a milk bar but also from bakeries, kiosks and some cafés. Traditional pies are of the steak-and-gravy variety, but many bakeries offer more gourmet fare in their pastry casings. Be on the lookout for a Tasmanian speciality, the scallop pie.

Pizza has become one of the most popular fast foods; most are of the American style (thick and with lots of toppings) rather than Italian style. That said, more and more wood-fired, thin, Neapolitan-style pizzas can be found in pizzerias and restaurants around the state.

VEGETARIANS & VEGANS

Vegetarian eateries and vegetarian menu selections, including choices for vegans and coeliac-sufferers, are becoming common in large towns and are forging a stronger presence in areas visited by tourists. Small-town Tasmania mostly continues its stolid dedication to meat (especially where the local pub is the only eatery). Cafés seem to always have vegetarian options, but take care with risotto and soups, as meat stock is often used. Vegans will find the going much tougher, but there are usually dishes that are vegan-adaptable at restaurants.

Vegetarians and vegans feeling neglected as they travel around the state should make a beeline for Sirens (p101) restaurant and Nourish (p101) as soon as they reach Hobart. For coeliac-sufferers, a growing number of eateries are offering gluten-free options, and larger supermarkets usually stock gluten-free bread and pasta.

EATING WITH KIDS

Dining with children in Tasmania is relatively easy. If you avoid the flashiest places, children are generally welcomed, particularly at Chinese, Greek or Italian restaurants. It's usually fine to take kids to cafés and you'll see families dining early in bistros and pub dining rooms. For more, see Children (p320).

Many places that do welcome children don't have separate kids' menus: it's better to find something on the regular menu (say a pasta or salad) and ask to have the kitchen adapt it slightly to your children's needs. Places catering to kids usually offer everything straight from the deep fryer: crumbed chicken, chips and that kind of thing. It's probably fine to bring toddler food in with you and just ask for a highchair.

Good news for travelling families, weather permitting, is that there are plenty of picnic spots, and sometimes free or coin-operated barbecues in parks.

BILLS & TIPPING

The total at the bottom of a restaurant bill is all you really need to pay. It should include GST (as should menu prices) and there is no 'optional' service charge added. Waiters are paid a reasonable salary, so they don't rely on tips to survive. Often, though, especially in urban Australia, people tip a few coins in a café, while the tip for excellent service can go as high as 15% in whiz-bang establishments. The incidence of add-ons (bread, water, surcharges on weekends etc) is rising.

MORE FABULOUS FOODIE EXPERIENCES

Here are some of our island-wide favourites. Also check out the smorgasbord of gourmet delights in the Loosen Your Belts itinerary (p74).

- Pick your own fresh berries at Sorell Fruit Farm (p123)
- Slurp oysters fresh from the Freycinet Marine Farm on the Freycinet Peninsula (p179) or Barilla Bay (p118) near Hobart
- Attend the Festivale in Launceston (p207)
- Pan-fry the trout you just caught yourself in a highland lake – fish never tasted so good (p161)
- Worship the gastronomic gods at one the new breed of Tassie food temples: Peppermint Bay (p142), Marque IV (p102), Stillwater (p211) or Angasi (p195)
- Scoff down fresh fish and chips from the floating fish punts at Hobart's Constitution Dock (p101)
- Coffee in Tasmania is something that no longer comes from a jar. Get espressoed at our fave coffee shops: Retro (p101) in Hobart, and Tant pour Tant (p211) in Launceston

---

HABITS & CUSTOMS

Tasmanian table manners are fairly standard. Avoid talking with your mouth full, wait until everyone has been served before you eat, and don't use your fingers to pick up food unless it can't be tackled another way.

If you're invited over for dinner at someone's house, always take a gift. You may offer to bring something for the meal, but even if the host downright refuses – insisting you just bring your scintillating conversation – still take a bottle of wine. Flowers or a box of chocolates are also acceptable.

'Shouting' is a revered custom where people in a bar or pub take turns to buy drinks for their group. Just don't leave before it's your turn to buy! At a toast, everyone should touch glasses.

EAT YOUR WORDS

Australians love to shorten everything, including people's names, so expect many other words to be abbreviated. Here are some words you might hear in Tassie:

barbie – a barbecue, where (traditionally) smoke and overcooked meat are matched with lashings of coleslaw, potato salad and beer

esky – an insulated ice chest to hold your tinnies (see below), before you hold them in your tinny holder

pav – pavlova, the meringue dessert topped with cream, passion fruit, kiwi fruit or other fresh fruit

pot – a medium glass of beer (in Victoria and Tasmania)

sanger – a sandwich

surf 'n' turf – a classic 1970s pub meal of steak topped with prawns, usually in a creamy sauce; also known as reef 'n' beef

snags – sausages

Tim Tam – a commercially produced chocolate biscuit that lies close to the heart of most Australians. Try a 'Tim Slam': nibble off two opposing corners, dip one into your cup of tea/coffee, suck it through like a straw then slam down the whole delicious mess!

tinny – usually refers to a can of beer, but could also be the small boat you go fishing in (and you'd take a few tinnies in your tinny, in that case)

tinny holder – insulating material that protects your hand from your icy beer, and nothing to do with a boat

Vegemite – salty, dark-brown breakfast spread, popular on toast: adored by Aussie masses, maligned by visitors

Smoking is illegal in Tasmania's indoor cafés, restaurants and pubs and bars, but many places have built new outside areas for the purpose.

Environment

THE LAND

Adrift some 240km south of Victoria across tumultuous Bass Strait, Tasmania is the smallest Australian state, and the only one that's an island. To its east is the Tasman Sea, which separates Australia and New Zealand; to its west and south is the cold, steely Southern Ocean, maintaining a buffer between Australia and Antarctica. Tasmania is 296km from north to south and 315km from east to west. Including its lesser islands, it has an area of 68,332 sq km.

Although Tasmania's highest mountain, Mt Ossa, stands at only 1617m, much of the island's interior is extremely rugged. One indication of the dearth of flat land is the proximity of the centres of its two largest cities, Hobart and Launceston, to extremely steep hills.

The state's coastline is beautiful in every sense of the word, with a multitude of coves and beaches, shallow bays and broad estuaries, the result of river valleys being flooded by rising sea levels after the last ice age. By contrast, the Central Plateau, which was covered by a single ice sheet during that ice age, is a bleak, harsh environment, completely unsuitable for farming; Australia's deepest natural freshwater lake, Lake St Clair (167m deep), is up here.

Showing the scars of recent glaciation, most of the island's western half is a twisted nest of mountainous ranges and ridges. The climate here is inhospitable, with annual rainfall of a discouraging 3m or more, and for much of the year, uncompromising seas pummel the coast into submission. Yet the cliffs, lakes, rainforests and wild rivers of this magnificent region are among Tasmania's greatest attractions – sweet temptation for walkers, adventurers and photographers. Conversely, the rain-shadowed east coast is usually dry, sunny and beachy-keen.

Find out more about Antarctica on the Australian Government website, www.aad.gov.au, where you can watch videos of life aboard expeditions on the icebreaker *Aurora*, which sails from Hobart.

ENVIRONMENTAL HISTORY

Despite a long history of bad, often atrocious, environmental management, Tasmania is famous for its pristine wilderness areas. Both the air and water in parts of the state are claimed to be the purest on the planet, while the Tasmanian Wilderness World Heritage Area, which blankets approximately 20% of the island, is an international smash hit. Yet, ironically, the preservation of much of the environment that Tasmania is proud of has been achieved only by protracted campaigns on rivers and in forests, in the media, and in parliaments and courts.

Gold was discovered in Tasmania in the 1870s and prospectors started exploring most of the state in search of mineral wealth, finding tin, silver, copper and lead. The subsequent prolonged exploitation of natural resources inevitably clashed with environmental preservation. In the late 1960s and early '70s, the unsuccessful efforts of bushwalkers and conservationists to stop Lake Pedder in the southwest from being flooded for hydroelectric purposes (see p301) resulted in the formation of what's believed to be the world's first Green political party. The lessons learnt during the fight for Pedder were crucial in enabling a new generation of activists to execute a vastly more sophisticated campaign a decade later, one that saved the Franklin River – one of the finest wild rivers on the planet – from being flooded for similar purposes (see p287). The Franklin River campaign saw the conservation movement mature as a political force and gain acceptance as an influential player in the corridors of policy-making power.

A successful campaign in the late 1980s to prevent construction of a pulp mill in the northwest saw a Green independents' party form, led by Bob

Brown (see the boxed text, p50). Subsequently, five of its members were elected to state parliament, and the Greens held the balance of power in the Tasmanian parliament from 1989 to 1998. Changes to the number of state parliamentarians, however, resulted in three of the four sitting Tasmanian Greens members losing their seats in the 1998 state election and a significant muting of the Greens' parliamentary voice. In the 2002 election, the Greens increased their state parliament representation to four seats. This held steady in 2006.

Despite Tasmania's relatively new-found appreciation for its wild areas, the balance between conservation interests and industry (especially old-growth logging, pulp milling and mining) remains uneasy at best.

TODAY'S ENVIRONMENTAL ISSUES

On a collision course since the 1960s, Tasmania's environmental conservationists and prodevelopment interests continue to bang heads today.

During the 2004 Australian federal election, logging and the preservation of Tasmanian's old-growth forests became a central campaign issue. 'Old-growth' is a term generally used to describe forest which has had little human disturbance and is ecologically mature. Such forests provide the best habitat for the widest range of species and therefore, according to the Wilderness Society and many other groups, are the most important ecosystem for conserving biodiversity. In a statistic provided by the Wilderness Society, less than 20% of Tasmania's original, presettlement old-growth forests remain today. More than half of what remains (including large parts of the Styx, the Tarkine and northeastern Tasmania) is unprotected and targeted for logging and wood-chipping. In 2004, the left-wing federal Labor Party took a proconservation stance, and lost several parliamentary seats in Tasmania as a result.

In the 2007 federal election, the focus shifted to the proposed Tamar Valley pulp mill and fears of pollution and further old-growth logging. The logging issue was less of a turning point in the election result this time around, but Labor regained the seats it lost in 2004 by appearing to adopt a 'maybe we will, maybe we won't' approach to the pulp mill.

All this is just the latest in a *looong* saga of political glad-handing, lawsuits, resignations, pay-outs and allegations of mismanagement surrounding both the Tasmanian Government and Gunns Ltd, the Tasmanian timber and woodchip conglomerate looking to develop the mill. At the time of writing, the situation was still muddy, unresolved and bound up in spite – a real political hot potato, and a real mess. Every Tasmanian has an opinion on whether or not the mill should proceed – pull up a stool in a pub and see what the locals think! For more on the pulp mill, see the boxed text, p220.

Meanwhile, climate change continues to both enthral and terrify Tasmanians. Some think a few degrees of extra warmth will do wonders for Tassie's tourist industry; some look at their gorgeous but low-lying coastal estates and quiver in their waterproof boots.

WILDLIFE
Animals

The distinctive mammals of mainland Australia – the weird and wonderful marsupials and monotremes isolated here for at least 45 million years – are also found in Tasmania. Marsupials, including wallabies and pademelons, give birth to partially developed young that they then protect and suckle in a pouch. Monotremes (platypuses and echidnas) lay eggs but also suckle their young. Most are nocturnal and the best time to see them in the wild is around dusk. The smaller mammals can be difficult to find in the bush, but there are plenty of wildlife parks around the state where they can be seen.

AUSTRALIAN ENVIRONMENTAL CHALLENGES   Tim Flannery

The European colonisation of Australia, commencing in 1788, heralded a period of catastrophic environmental upheaval, with the result that Australians today are struggling with some of the most severe environmental problems to be found anywhere. It may seem strange that a population of just 21 million, living in a continent the size of the USA minus Alaska, could inflict such damage on its environment, but Australia's long isolation, its fragile soils and difficult climate have made it particularly vulnerable to human-induced change.

Damage to Australia's environment has been inflicted in several ways, the most important being the introduction of pest species, destruction of forests, overstocking rangelands, inappropriate agriculture and interference with water flows. Beginning with the escape of domestic cats into the Australian bush shortly after 1788, a plethora of vermin – from foxes to wild camels and cane toads – have run wild in Australia, causing extinctions in the native fauna. One out of every 10 native mammals living in Australia prior to European colonisation is now extinct, and many more are highly endangered. Extinctions have also affected native plants, birds and amphibians.

The destruction of forests has also had a profound effect on the environment. Most of Australia's rainforests have suffered clearing, while conservationists fight with loggers over the fate of the last unprotected stands of old-growth trees. Many Australian rangelands have been chronically overstocked for more than a century, the result being the extreme vulnerability of both soils and rural economies to Australia's drought and flood cycle, as well as the extinction of many native species. The development of agriculture has involved land clearance and the provision of irrigation, and here again the effect has been profound. Clearing of the diverse and spectacular plant communities of the Western Australian wheat belt began just a century ago, yet today up to one-third of that country is degraded by salination of the soils. Between 70kg and 120kg of salt lies below every square metre of the region, and clearing of native vegetation has allowed water to penetrate deep into the soil, dissolving the salt crystals and carrying brine towards the surface.

In terms of financial value, just 1.5% of Australia's land surface provides over 95% of agricultural yield, and much of this land lies in the irrigated regions of the Murray-Darling Basin. This is Australia's agricultural heartland, yet it too is under severe threat from salting of soils and rivers. Irrigation water penetrates into the sediments laid down in an ancient sea, carrying salt into the catchments and fields. If nothing is done, the lower Murray River will become too salty to drink in a decade or two, threatening the water supply of Adelaide, a city of over a million people.

Despite the scale of the biological crisis engulfing Australia, governments and the community have been slow to respond. In the 1980s, coordinated action began to take place, but not until the 1990s were major steps taken. The establishment of **Landcare** (www.landcareaustralia .com.au), an organisation enabling people to effectively address local environmental issues, and the expenditure of $2.5billion through the National Heritage Trust Fund have been important national initiatives. Yet so difficult are some of the issues the nation faces that, as yet, little has been achieved in terms of halting the destructive processes. Individuals are also banding together to help. Groups like the **Australian Bush Heritage Fund** (www.bushheritage.asn .au) and the **Australian Wildlife Conservancy** (AWC; www.australianwildlife.org) allow people to donate funds and time to the conservation of native species. Some such groups have been spectacularly successful; the AWC, for example, already manages many endangered species over its 5260-sq-km holdings.

So severe are Australia's problems that it will take a revolution before they can be overcome; sustainable practices need to be implemented in every arena of life, from farms to suburbs and city centres. Renewable energy, sustainable agriculture and water use lie at the heart of these changes, and Australians are only now developing the road map to sustainability that they so desperately need if they are to have a long-term future on the continent.

Tim Flannery is a naturalist, explorer, writer and climate change activist. He was named Australian of the Year in 2007, and is currently an adjunct professor at Macquarie University in NSW. Flannery's books include The Future Eaters *(1994) and* The Weather Makers *(2006).*

Tasmania's fauna is not as varied as that of the rest of Australia and it has relatively few large mammals. Its best-known marsupial, the Tasmanian tiger, which resembled a large dog or wolf and had dark stripes and a stiff tail, was officially declared extinct in 1986, but hadn't been sighted with any certainty since 1936 (see the boxed text, p54).

BIRDS

Some extremely rare birds are found in Tasmania; one of the best known is the orange-bellied parrot, of which only a small number survive, on the buttongrass plains of the southwest. They winter on the mainland and make the treacherous crossing of Bass Strait to reach their breeding grounds in southwest Tasmania. More common, but also threatened with extinction, is the ground parrot. To see it you'll need to visit Melaleuca in the southwest (see p304) and wait in the specially constructed bird-hide.

Many twitchers stalk the dry sclerophyll forest on the eastern side of Tasmania to try to catch a glimpse of the uber-rare forty-spotted pardalote, found mainly on Bruny Island (p136) and in Mt William National Park (p196).

There's a wide variety of seabirds, parrots, cockatoos, honeyeaters and wrens here too. Birds of prey (hawks, owls, falcons and eagles) are also on the prowl.

Black Currawongs

The black currawong *(Stepera fuliginosa)*, found only in Tasmania, lives primarily on plant matter and insects, but will sometimes kill small mammals or infant birds. You'll often see this large, black, fearless bird goose-stepping around picnic areas. You get the feeling they'd just as soon have your eye out as steal your sandwich!

Mutton Birds

The mutton bird (a name derived from a Norfolk Island marine officer who nicknamed a closely related bird the 'flying sheep') is more correctly called the short-tailed shearwater *(Puffinus tenuirostris)*. It lives in burrows in sand dunes and migrates annually to the northern hemisphere. These small birds fly in spectacular flocks on their way back to their burrows (the same ones every year) at dusk. They are still hunted by some Tasmanians, notably around Flinders Island, and you'll occasionally see cooked mutton bird advertised for sale.

The Australian Museum's online resource, www .amonline.net.au, links you to hundreds of fact sheets on Australia's environment: geology, water, biodiversity and marine life to name a handful.

Penguins

The fairy penguin *(Eudyptula minor)* is the smallest penguin in the world, and lives in burrows in Tasmania's sand dunes. There are plenty of penguin rookeries around Tasmania where you can see them waddle from the ocean to their nests just after sunset, including at Bruny Island (p137), Burnie (p253), Penguin (of course!; p251), Low Head (p221) and King Island (p307).

KANGAROOS & WALLABIES

The kangaroo and wallaby species found in Tasmania are related to those found on the mainland, but are usually smaller. The largest marsupial is the forester kangaroo *(Macropus giganteus)*, which at one stage looked like becoming extinct because it favoured crop-rich farmland for its lunch. The Narawntapu National Park (p219) and Mt William National Park (p196) have been set aside to preserve this impressive bouncer.

The Bennetts wallaby *(Macropus rufogriseus)* thrives in colder climes – this is the beast that you are most likely to see begging for food at the Cradle Mountain–Lake St Clair National Park (p289) or Freycinet National

Park (p175). Don't feed them, though, because the animals are meant to be wild and should be feeding themselves – also, giving them processed foods such as bread causes a fatal disease called 'lumpy jaw'. Bennetts wallabies stand just over 1m in height and can seem very friendly, but be careful, as these and other native animals can sometimes be aggressive.

If you spy any shorter, rounder wallabies hiding in the forest, then you'll have seen a pademelon *(Thylogale billardierii,* also known as a rufous wallaby). This smaller species is shyer than its larger relatives.

PLATYPUSES & ECHIDNAS

The platypus *(Ornithorhynchus anatinus)* and echidna *(Tachyglossus aculeatus)* are the only living monotremes – mammals which lay eggs.

Monotremes are often regarded as living fossils, and although they display some intriguing features of their reptile ancestors (egg-laying, and that their reproductive, defecatory and urinary systems utilise a single outlet), they suckle their young on milk secreted from mammary glands.

The platypus lives in water and has a ducklike bill, webbed feet and a beaver-like body. You're most likely to see one in a stream or lake, searching out food in the form of crustaceans, worms and tadpoles with its electrosensitive bill.

Echidnas are totally different and look similar to porcupines, covered in impressively sharp spikes. They primarily eat ants, and have powerful claws for unearthing their food and digging into the dirt to protect themselves when threatened. They're common in Tasmania but if you approach one,

---

SIMPLE STEPS FOR SAVING THE FORESTS   Senator Bob Brown

Tasmania's wild and scenic beauty, along with a human history dating back 30,000 years, is a priceless heritage available to all of us. The waterfalls, wild rivers, lovely beaches, snow-capped mountains, turquoise seas, and wildlife are abundant and accessible for locals and visitors alike.

Because we are all creations of nature – the curl of our ears is fashioned to pick up the faintest sounds of the forest floor – we are all bonded to the wilds. No wonder that in this anxiety-ridden world there is such a thirst for remote, pristine, natural places. Yet around the world, wilderness is a fast-disappearing resource and Tasmania is no exception.

This year 150,000 truckloads of the island's native forests, including giant eucalypt species producing the tallest flowering plants on earth, will arrive at the woodchip mills, en route to Japan. After logging, the forests are firebombed and every wisp of fur, feather and flower is destroyed. These great forests, built of carbon, are one of the world's best hedges against global warming. They are carbon banks. Yet they are being looted, taken from our fellow creatures and all who come after us. The log trucks on Tasmania's highways are enriching banks of a different kind.

Over two decades ago, people power saved Tasmania's wild Franklin and Lower Gordon Rivers (p287), which nowadays attract hundreds of thousands of visitors to the west coast. Those visitors, in turn, bring jobs, investment and local prosperity. Saving the environment has been a boon for the economy and employment.

The rescue of Tasmania's forests relies on each of us, and there are plenty of ways we can help. We can help with letters or phone calls to newspapers, radio stations or politicians; with every cent donated to the forest campaigners; and in every well-directed vote. The tourist dollar speaks loudly in Tasmania, so even overseas travellers, who cannot vote, should take the opportunity to write letters to our newspapers and politicians. With each step we take, we move toward ending this destruction of Tasmania's wild and scenic heritage.

Senator Bob Brown was elected to the Tasmanian parliament in 1983 and first elected to the Senate in 1996. His books include The Valley of the Giants (The Wilderness Society, with Vica Bayley, 2005). Read more about Bob Brown at www.bobbrown.org.au.

PULP FICTION

It's an age-old argument in Tasmania: should the state preserve old-growth forests and steer away from unsustainable forestry industries, or should they boost employment and stimulate the economy at all costs? In a state with a historically more robust bank balance, the issue might not be so contentious, and perhaps a proposal such as the Tamar Valley pulp mill might never have been floated. But this is Tasmania, a place where such battle lines often become volatile schisms, tearing through the very identity of the island.

As with any new development, the pulp mill has pros and cons. On the 'pros' side of the fence, the mill will be a boon for both local and state-wide economies, bringing in much-needed investment and export dollars. Its construction and operation will provide ongoing employment for countless northerners. More abstractly, the mill also represents progress and global validation: two things Tasmania's fragile, bottom-of-the-world psyche has always craved. On the 'cons' side, there is the fear of the loss of Tassie's unique forests and with it native habitat. The prospect of a hazy pall of pulp-smoke across the wineries of the Tamar Valley, one of Tassie's main tourist draws, and yet more log-trucks jamming island roads is also far from appealing. Effluent disposal and local marine ecology are other sensitive issues. And where does all that pulp go? It seems absurd to sell a base substance overseas for others to convert into more profitable, value-added products – the pulp created here would be exported to Japan and turned into paper. Opponents of the mill say it doesn't make economic sense for Tasmania to sell a base substance overseas so other countries can add value to it.

Either way, you're sure to draw an opinion from whomever you ask – keeping an open mind will help you see both the forest and the trees.

all you're likely to see up close is a brown, spiky ball. However, if you keep quiet and don't move, you might be lucky: they have poor eyesight and will sometimes walk right past your feet.

POSSUMS

There are several varieties of possum in the state, one of which is the sugar glider *(Petaurus breviceps)*, which has developed webs between its legs, enabling it to glide from tree to tree. The most common and boldest is the brushtail possum *(Trichosurus vulpecula)*, which lives and sleeps in trees but descends to the ground in search of food. Possums show little fear of humans, and regularly conduct late-night food heists at camping grounds. A shyer relation is the smaller ringtail possum *(Pseudocheirus peregrinus)*.

SNAKES & SPIDERS

There are only three types of snake found in Tasmania, but they're all poisonous. The largest and most dangerous is the tiger snake *(Notechis scutatus)*, which will sometimes attack, particularly in late summer. The other snakes are the copperhead *(Austrelaps superbus)* and the smaller white-lipped whip snake *(Drysdalia coronoides)*. Bites are very rare, as most snakes are generally shy and try to avoid humans. If you do get bitten, don't try to catch the snake, as there's a common antivenin for all three – instead, get to hospital for treatment.

The eight-legged critter with the longest reach (up to 18cm) on the island is the Tasmanian cave spider *(Hickmania troglodytes)*, which spins horizontal mesh-webs on the ceiling of a cave to catch insects such as cave crickets. Other local species include the Tasmanian funnel-web, huntsman and white-tailed spiders.

See p346 for more on things that go bite in the night.

TASMANIAN DEVILS

The obnoxious Tasmanian devil *(Sarcophilus harrisii)* mostly eats insects, small birds and mammals, and carrion, and can often be seen at night feasting

Young adult kookaburras hang out with their parents, helping to feed their siblings – behaviour common to many Australian bird species, due to harsh conditions.

TOP FIVE WILDLIFE PARKS

Tasmania's wildlife is fabulously accessible for most visitors – you may encounter a pademelon or wallaby on a bush walk at dusk, or get lucky and spot a platypus in a quiet stream (sadly, you'll no doubt also see a lot of road-kill on your travels). If you're after more meaningful interaction with the local wildlife (including devils), stop by the following wildlife parks:

- **Bonorong Wildlife Centre** (p110) Educative park near Richmond. Protection and rehabilitation of native wildlife.
- **East Coast Natureworld** (p183) Just north of Bicheno. Aviary, seething snake pits and free-roaming native animals.
- **Something Wild** (p114) Near Mt Field National Park. Devils, wombats, quolls and maybe a platypus or two.
- **Tasmanian Devil Conservation Park** (p126) In Taranna on the Tasman Peninsula. A quarantined breeding centre for devils to help protect against Devil Facial Tumour Disease.
- **Trowunna Wildlife Park** (p242) Two kilometres west of Chudleigh. Specialises in devils and wombats.

---

on road-kill (a habit that unfortunately often leads to it becoming road-kill itself). It's about 75cm long and has a short, stocky body covered in black fur with a white stripe across its chest.

Devil Facial Tumour Disease (DFTD, a fatal, communicable cancer) infects up to 75% of the wild population. Quarantined populations have been established, but efforts to find a cure have been depressingly fruitless. The actual beast is nothing like the Warner Bros cartoon, but financial contributions from this company to help save the devil are rumoured. Check out www.tassiedevil.com.au and the website of the **Department of Primary Industries, Water & Environment** (DPIWE; www.dpiwe.tas.gov.au – click on 'Weeds, Pests & Diseases', then 'Animal Diseases') for more DFTD info. To make a tax-free donation to the devils' cause, log on to www.devilsindanger.com.au.

The Mammals of Australia, edited by Ron Strahan, is a complete survey of Australia's somewhat offbeat mammals. Every species is illustrated and almost everything known about them is covered in individual species accounts, written by the nation's experts.

WHALES

Southern right whales *(Eubalaena australis)* migrate annually from Antarctica to southern Australia to give birth to their calves in shallow waters. So named because they were the 'right' whales to kill, they were hunted to the point of extinction while sustaining a lucrative industry around Tasmania. They are still seen off the Tasmanian coast (sometimes in Hobart's Derwent River estuary; see the boxed text, p86) and occasionally beach themselves.

Long-finned pilot whales *(Globicephala melas)* are more commonly involved in beach strandings in Tasmania. In late 2004 there were two mass strandings of pilot whales within one day of each other (one on King Island, the other on Maria Island), reigniting the debate about what causes such tragic incidents (for now, the answer remains a mystery).

WOMBATS

Wombats have large brains and live in complex burrows where they can remain for a week, surviving on just a third of the food a sheep would need.

Wombats *(Vombatus ursinus)* are very solid, powerfully built marsupials with broad heads and short, stumpy legs (the weightlifters of the animal kingdom), weighing up to 35kg. They live in underground burrows that they excavate, and are usually very casual, slow-moving animals, partly because they don't have any natural predators to worry about.

ENDANGERED SPECIES

Since Europeans arrived, Tasmania has lost more than 30 species of plants and animals – most famously, the thylacine, or Tasmanian tiger. Currently, over 600 types of flora and fauna are listed under the state's Threatened Species Protection Act.

Among Tasmania's threatened birds are the forty-spotted pardalote, orange-bellied parrot and wedge-tailed eagle. Tasmania is also home to the largest invertebrate in the world, the giant freshwater crayfish, whose numbers have been so depleted by recreational fishing and habitat destruction that it's now illegal to take any specimens from their natural habitat.

INTRODUCED SPECIES

In mid-2001, Tasmania received some of the worst environmental news imaginable for native animals: a fox had been spotted near Longford in the state's north. Fox predation puts nearly 80 of the island's indigenous land species at enormous risk because of their vulnerability to attack from an animal against which they have no defence. Just as horrifying as the original sighting and subsequent reports of the European red fox in other parts of the state is the revelation that the foxes were deliberately introduced to Tasmania, probably for the purposes of hunting. A full-time fox taskforce has been set up by the state government, though it may be too late to eradicate the threat to Tasmania's biodiversity that the animal poses. If you see a fox or evidence of one, phone the **Fox Hotline** (☎ 1300 369 688).

The second-biggest entrenched threat to native wildlife in Tasmania is the feral cat (unless the speed-obsessed car drivers who kill incalculable numbers of native animals count as introduced pests). The cat has established itself throughout the state, including in the southwest and central highlands.

Feral dogs, goats and pigs can also be found in Tasmania, but they're not nearly so widespread as on the mainland. Even rabbits, which are a problem in rural areas, have had trouble penetrating the state's natural forests; this is just as well, because it appears that one of science's most touted weapons against the animal – calicivirus – is not particularly effective in cool, wet areas.

The ABC TV nature documentary *The Terrors of Tasmania* looks at the lifestyle of the maligned and iconic Tasmanian devil, now struggling with the real-life nightmare of Devil Facial Tumour Disease.

Plants

Tasmania's myriad flora ranges from the dry forests of the east, through the alpine moorlands of the centre to the rainforests of the west. Many of the state's plants are unlike those found in the rest of Australia and have ties with species that grew millions of years ago, when the southern continents were joined at the hip as Gondwanaland. Similar plants are found in South America and fossilised in Antarctica.

Many of Tasmania's trees are unique to the state – the island's native pines are particularly distinctive. The best known is the Huon pine (see p55), which can live for thousands of years, but there are other slow-growing island pines, including the king billy pine, celery-top pine and pencil pine, all of which are commonly at higher altitudes and live for around 500 years. Some pencil pines on the Central Plateau have managed to hang in there for 1000 years,

WATCHING WILDLIFE *Tim Flannery*

Tasmania is jam-packed with wallabies, wombats and possums, principally because foxes, which have decimated marsupial populations on the mainland, were slow to reach the island state (the first fox was found in Tasmania only as recently as 2001). It is also home to the Tasmanian devil – the Australian hyena, but less than one-third the size of its African ecological counterpart. They're common on the island. In some national parks you can watch them tear apart road-killed wombats. Their squabbling is fearsome; their shrieks ear-splitting. It's the nearest thing Australia can offer to experiencing a lion kill on the Masai Mara.

David Owen's little hardback *Thylacine* investigates the great fascination with the Tasmanian tiger, hunted to extinction and now a treasured symbol of Tasmania and of the conservation movement worldwide.

but they're especially vulnerable to fire – one-third of the plateau's pencil pines have been charred to a crisp over the past 200 years.

The dominant tree of the wetter forests is myrtle beech – similar to European beeches. Tasmania's many flowering trees include the leatherwood, which is nondescript most of the year but erupts into bright flowers during summer, when it's covered with white and pale-pink flowers that yield a unique and fragrant honey.

Many of Tasmania's eucalyptus trees also grow on the mainland, but down on the island they often grow ludicrously tall. The swamp gum *(Eucalyptus regnans,* known as mountain ash on the mainland) can grow to 100m in height and is the tallest flowering plant in the world. Look for it in the forests of the southeast, where you'll also find the state's floral emblem, the Tasmanian blue gum *(Eucalyptus globulus).*

In autumn you might catch an eye-full of the deciduous beech, the only truly deciduous native plant in Australia. It usually grows as a fairly straggly bush with bright green leaves. In autumn, however, the leaves become golden and sometimes red, adding a splash of colour to the forests. The easiest places to see the display are the Cradle Mountain and Mt Field National Parks.

A notable component of the understorey in Tasmanian forests is the infamous horizontal scrub (see opposite), a plant that can make life hell for bushwalkers attempting to avoid established tracks. More familiar to bushwalkers, and considerably more benign, is buttongrass. Growing in thick clumps up to 2m high, this unique Tasmanian grass prefers broad, swampy areas like the many flat-bottomed valleys pressed out by ice ages. Buttongrass plains are usually so muddy and unpleasant to walk over that in many places, the Parks & Wildlife Service has incorporated sections of elevated boardwalk into tracks crossing such areas, for both walker comfort and the protection of the environment.

Another interesting specimen is the cushion plant, which is found in alpine areas and at first sight resembles a green rock. In fact, it's an extremely tough, short plant that grows into thick mats ideally suited to helping it cope with

---

TIGER, TIGER, BURNING BRIGHT

The story of the Tasmanian tiger (*Thylacinus cynocephalus,* or thylacine), a striped, nocturnal, dog-like predator once widespread in Tasmania, has two different endings. Version one says thylacines were hunted to extinction in the 19th and early 20th centuries, the last captive tiger dying in Hobart Zoo in 1936. No specimen, living or dead, has been conclusively discovered since then, despite hundreds of alleged sightings.

Version two maintains that thylacines continue a furtive existence deep in the Tasmanian wilderness. Scientists ridicule such suggestions, but the tantalising possibility of remnant tigers makes them prime corporate fodder – Tasmanian companies plaster tiger imagery on everything from beer bottles to licence plates.

In recent years, scientists at Sydney's Australia Museum began scripting another possible ending to the tiger saga. Kicking off version three, biologists managed to extract DNA from a thylacine pup preserved in alcohol since 1866. Their aim was to successfully replicate the DNA, with the long-term goal of cloning the species. Needless to say, there were many obstacles, and the project drew criticism from those who would rather have seen the money spent on helping current endangered species. In early 2005 the project was shelved due to the quality of the extracted DNA being too poor to work with, but science may well add a new twist to the tiger's tale sometime in the future.

For information on the Tassie Tiger and the cloning project, visit www.austmus.gov.au/thylacine. Another good source of information is at www.parks.tas.gov.au/wildlife/mammals/thylacin.html. You can also see black-and-white footage of a tiger in captivity at the Tasmanian Museum & Art Gallery in Hobart (p87).

TASMANIAN CONSERVATION ORGANISATIONS

The **Tasmanian Conservation Trust** (TCT; ☎ 6234 3552; www.tct.org.au; 102 Bathurst St, Hobart; ⊙ 9am-5pm Mon-Fri) is the state's primary nongovernmental conservation organisation. In addition to managing its own campaigns, the TCT hosts the Tasmanian offices of two other Australian environmental organisations: the National Threatened Species Network, which undertakes public education programs aimed at students, landholders and the wider community, and the Marine and Coastal Community Network, which has particular interests in the establishment of no-take marine reserves and the promotion of safe marine waste-management practices.

The **Wilderness Society** (Map p82; ☎ 6224 1550; www.wilderness.org.au; 130 Davey St, Hobart; ⊙ 9.30am-5pm Mon-Fri) works hard to ensure the preservation of several important areas, including the Styx Valley (see the boxed text, p302), which contains the tallest hardwood eucalypt forests on earth, and the Tarkine Wilderness (p268), which occupies 3500 sq km between the Arthur and Pieman Rivers. Both areas are under threat from logging.

---

its severe living conditions. It's not so tough, however, that it can tolerate footprints – stepping on one can destroy thousands of tiny leaves, which take decades to regenerate.

HORIZONTAL SCRUB

The skinny horizontal scrub *(Anodopetalum biglandulosum)* is a feature of the undergrowth in many parts of Tasmania's southwest. It grows by sending up thin, vigorous stems whenever an opening appears in the forest canopy. The old branches soon become heavy and fall, then put up shoots of their own. This continuous process of growth and collapse creates dense, tangled thickets – bushwalkers have been rumoured to completely disappear into it when venturing off the beaten track. You can see twisted examples of horizontal on nature walks in the southwest and in the Hartz Mountains (p148).

HUON PINE

Prized by shipbuilders and furniture makers for its rich golden hue, rot-resisted oils and fine grain, Tasmania's Huon pine *(Lagarostrobos franklinii)* is one of the slowest-growing and longest-living trees on the planet. Individual trees can take 2000 years to reach 30m in height and live to 3000 years, a situation overlooked by 19th-century loggers and ship builders who plundered the southwest forests in search of this 'yellow gold'. Fortunately it's now a protected species – most of the Huon pine furniture and timberwork you'll see around the state is recycled, or comes from dead trees salvaged from riverbeds and hydroelectric dams. Some older trees remain – one 2500-year-old beauty can be viewed during a cruise on the Gordon River (see p279).

KING'S LOMATIA

This endemic Tasmanian plant, a member of the *Proteaceae family,* has flowers similar to those of the grevillea, and grows in the wild in only one small part of the Tasmanian Wilderness World Heritage Area. Studies of the plant's chromosomes have revealed that it's incapable of reproducing sexually, which is why it must rely on sending up shoots to create new plants. Further research has shown that there's absolutely no genetic diversity within the population, which means that every king's lomatia in existence is a clone. It's the oldest known clone in the world, thought to have been around for at least 43,600 years.

NATIONAL PARKS

About one quarter of Tasmania is given over to national parks and reserves. For full details, see p63.

The Parks & Wildlife Service website, www.parks.tas.gov.au, has comprehensive information on Tasmania's amazing flora and fauna: click on 'The Nature of Tasmania'.

Tasmania Outdoors

If Tasmania was a person, it would be very much the 'outdoors type'. The state-wide dress code – beanie, walking boots and woollen shirt – is a source of *haute couture* embarrassment for many, but allows locals the freedom to lurch into the wilderness at any moment. The bushwalks you can do here are among the best (and the most taxing and treacherous) in Australia: if you really want to test your mettle, try propelling yourself up Federation Peak or the Western Arthurs. If you're more of a water-baby, white-water rafting on the Franklin River is charged with environmental grandeur and excitement, or you can join the hardened core of Tassie surfers who carve up the southern swell. Abseiling and rock climbing on the Tasman and Freycinet Peninsulas is a thrill a minute, while cycling around the state is a great way to see the countryside – roads are untrafficked and generally well surfaced. Horse riding also happens around the state in various locales, including the Tasman Peninsula, near Cradle Mountain and Huonville – keep an eye out as you tour the island.

For those who want less physically demanding activities, there's boating on the Arthur and Pieman Rivers in the Northwest, sea-kayaking in the Southeast, and walks through the Hastings Caves in the south. If you have a yacht (or can afford to charter one) you can spend lazy days exploring the bays and inlets of the D'Entrecasteaux Channel. If you're a trout fisher with a hankering for seclusion, you'll find plenty of fish (and no humans) around the Central Plateau lakes.

Some useful online info sources:

Networking Tasmanian Adventures (www.tasmanianadventures.com.au) Lists operators and activities, categorised as either 'wild' (scuba diving, white-water rafting, abseiling etc) or 'mild' (fishing, scenic flights, river cruises etc).

Parks & Wildlife Service (www.parks.tas.gov.au) Click on 'Outdoor Recreation'.

Tourism Tasmania (www.discovertasmania.com) Click on 'Activities & Attractions' then 'Outdoor Activities'.

A fossil of the giant conifer *Fitzroya tasmanensis*, which grows only in Chile, was recently discovered near Cradle Mountain: more evidence of Tasmania's links to the Gondwana supercontinent.

BUSHWALKING

The best-known of Tasmania's many superb bushwalks is the six-day, 65km Overland Track through Cradle Mountain–Lake St Clair National Park (p290). In fact, most of the state's great walks are in national parks – see the National Parks & Nature Reserves chapter (p63) and relevant chapters throughout this book. Bear in mind that entry fees apply to all Tasmanian national parks (see p64).

Books, Maps & Equipment

Shelves of books have been written specifically for walkers in Tasmania. Lonely Planet's *Walking in Australia* has info on some of Tasmania's best (longer) walks. Even if you're not growing a beard and going bush for weeks on end, you can still experience Tassie's famed wilderness on foot – the Parks & Wildlife Service's *60 Great Short Walks* brochure (free from visitors centres) lists the state's best quick ambles, with durations from 10 minutes to all day. Check the **Parks & Wildlife Service** (www.parks.tas.gov.au/recreation/bushwalking .html) website for more info.

The *Tasmania's Great Short Walks* brochure (freely available at visitors centres) lists 60 of the state's best short walks, with durations from 10 minutes to all day.

Other compilations of walks throughout the state include *A Visitor's Guide to Tasmania's National Parks* by Greg Buckman, *120 Walks in Tasmania* by Tyrone Thomas, which covers a wide variety of short and multiday walks, or *Day Walks Tasmania* by John Chapman and Monica Chapman. There are

THE TASMANIAN TRAIL

The Tasmanian Trail is a 480km route from Devonport to Dover, geared towards walkers, horse riders and mountain bikers. Most of the trail is on forestry roads, fire trails or country roads; it passes towns, pastoral land and forests, and there are camping spots about every 30km. All the information you need to follow the trail is in the *Tasmanian Trail Guide Book,* which costs $25 and is available in many bookshops, outdoor-equipment shops and visitors centres. See www .tasmaniantrail.com.au or the website of the **Parks & Wildlife Service** (www.parks.tas.gov.au/recrea tion/tastrail.html) for more information.

also detailed guides to specific walks or areas, including *South West Tasmania* by John Chapman and *Cradle Mountain-Lake St Clair & Walls of Jerusalem National Parks* by John Chapman and John Siseman. Jan Hardy and Bert Elson's short-walk books are also worth hunting down (covering Hobart, Mt Wellington, Launceston, the Northeast and the Northwest).

Tasmap produces excellent maps available from visitors centres. In Hobart you'll also find them at Service Tasmania (p84) and the Tasmanian Map Centre (p81), as well as state-wide outdoors stores.

Shops specialising in bushwalking gear and outdoors equipment proliferate around the state: see p107 for options in Hobart, p212 for Launceston, and p230 for Devonport. A number of shops, hostels and activity operators can also organise rental of outdoors gear.

Code of Ethics & Safety Precautions

The **Parks & Wildlife Service** (PWS; ☎ 6233 6191; www.parks.tas.gov.au) publishes a booklet called *Tasmania's Wilderness World Heritage Area: Essential Bushwalking Guide & Trip Planner,* which has sections on the basics of planning, minimal impact bushwalking, first aid and what gear you need to bring to cope with Tasmania's changeable weather (the booklet is available online at www.parks .tas.gov.au/recreation/mib.html). You can pick up PWS literature at Service Tasmania (p84), at any national park visitors centre or ranger station, or download it from the PWS website.

Tasmanian national parks are 'fuel stove only' areas. A brochure outlining regulations relating to these and other areas under this classification is available from the PWS.

In Tasmania (particularly in the west and southwest), a fine day can quickly become cold and stormy at any time of year – always carry warm clothing, waterproof gear and a compass. In addition, you should always carry a tent, rather than relying on finding a bed in a hut, particularly on popular walks such as the Overland Track.

On all extended walks, you must carry extra food in case you have to sit out a few days of particularly inclement weather. This is a very important point, as the PWS routinely hears of walkers running out of food in such instances and having to rely on the goodwill of better-prepared people they meet along the way to supplement their supplies. In the worst of circumstances, such lack of preparation puts lives at risk: if the bad weather continues for long enough, everyone suffers.

Tasmanian walks are famous for their mud, so be prepared: waterproof your boots, wear gaiters and watch where you're putting your feet. Even on the Overland Track, long sections of which are covered by boardwalk, you can sometimes find yourself up to your hips in mud if you're not careful. A few basic pointers for the uninitiated:

▪ Bushwalkers should stick to established trails, avoid cutting corners and taking short cuts, and stay on hard ground where possible.

Lonely Planet's *Walking in Australia* describes Tasmanian walks of varying length and difficulty, including short jaunts through Mt Field National Park and around Maria Island, as well as the Overland Track and a seven-day excursion along the South Coast Track.

■ Before tackling a long or remote walk, tell someone about your plans and arrange to contact them when you return. Make sure you sign a PWS register at the start and finish of your walk.

■ Keep bushwalking parties small.

■ Where possible, visit popular areas at low-season times.

■ When camping, always use designated camping grounds. When bush camping, try to find a natural clearing to set up your tent.

■ When driving, stay on existing tracks or roads.

■ Don't harm native birds or animals; these are protected by law.

■ Don't feed native animals.

■ Carry all your rubbish out with you; don't burn or bury it.

■ Avoid polluting lakes and streams: don't wash yourself or your dishes in them, and keep soap and detergent at least 50m away.

■ Use toilets provided; otherwise bury human waste at least 100m from waterways.

■ Boil all water for 10 minutes before drinking it, or use water-purifying tablets.

■ Don't take pets into national parks.

■ Don't light fires in any bush environment; use only fuel stoves for cooking.

■ On days of total fire ban, don't light any fire whatsoever, including fuel stoves.

Guided Walks

The *Guide to Free Camping in Tasmania* by S and S Collis ($15) lists over 60 sites (and will pay for itself on the first night!).

A veritable plethora of companies offer guided walks ranging from one-day excursions to multiday epics involving accommodation in everything from tents to upmarket lodges, plus trips that blend foot power with time on a bike, bus or canoe.

Some well-established companies offering trips along the Overland Track to Walls of Jerusalem and other popular destinations include **Craclair Tours** (☎ 6339 4488; www.craclair.com.au) and **Tasmanian Expeditions** (☎ 1300 666 856, 6339 3999; www.tas-ex.com) – see p329 for the low-down on these and other companies. Also hitting trails in the Cradle Mountain area is **Tasman Bush Tours** (☎ 6423 2335; www.tasmanbushtours.com).

If you like your walks with a touch more luxury than an inflatable camp mat, a leaky tent and reconstituted faux-potato, you can have your wishes fulfilled. Many companies offer guided multiday walks, with gourmet dinners, wine, hot showers and a real bed en route (for a premium, of course!):

Bay of Fires (☎ 6391 9339; www.bayoffires.com.au) A four-day walk along this photogenic, rock-strewn stretch of coast in the Northeast; see p195.

Cradle Mountain Huts (☎ 6391 9339; www.cradlehuts.com.au) Six-day walk along the Overland Track, staying in private huts; see p294.

Freycinet Experience (☎ 1800 506 003; www.freycinet.com.au) A fully catered, lodge-based, four-day stroll down the famous peninsula; see p178.

Maria Island Walk (☎ 6227 8800; www.mariaislandwalk.com.au) Another four-day option, this time on Maria Island (a national park off the east coast); see p171.

CANOEING, RAFTING & SEA-KAYAKING

Planning on walking the Overland Track? Look no further than the excellent Parks & Wildlife website www.overlandtrack.com.au, where you can make a booking, access maps and learn about minimal-impact hiking.

Tasmania is famed for white-knuckle, white-water rafting on the Franklin River (p288). See the 'Franklin River Rafting Notes' at www.parks.tas.gov.au/recreation/boating for a raft of priceless advice. Other rivers offering rapid thrills include the Derwent (upstream from Hobart), the Picton (southwest of Hobart) and the Mersey in the north.

For a more sedate paddle, try the Arthur (p267) and Pieman (p269) Rivers in the northwest, and the Ansons River (p194) in the northeast. You can rent canoes at Arthur River. The Huon, Weld, Leven and North Esk Rivers also attract their fair share of canoes and rafts.

Sea-kayaking centres include Kettering, southeast of Hobart (p136), from where you can explore the D'Entrecasteaux Channel, Bruny Island and the south coast; and Coles Bay, the launching place for Freycinet Peninsula explorations (p177). You can also have a paddle around the Hobart docks (p91). See the 'Leave No Wake' notes at www.parks.tas.gov.au/recreation /misk for how to tackle sea-kayaking in a sustainable way.

CAVING

Tasmania's limestone karst caves are among the most impressive in Australia. The caves at Mole Creek (p242), Gunns Plains (p252) and Hastings (p151) are open to the public daily. Both Mole Creek and Hastings offer the chance to get troglodytic on cave tours – see regional chapters for details.

CYCLING & MOUNTAIN BIKING

Cycling is a terrific way to tour Tasmania and engage with the island landscapes, especially on the dry east coast. To cycle between Hobart and Launceston via either coast, allow between 10 and 14 days. For a 'lap of the map' by bike, allow between 18 and 28 days. If you're planning a cycling trip, **Bicycle Tasmania** (www.biketas.org.au) is a solid source of information. Click on 'Routes to Ride by Region' for details of two- and three-week circuits. See p337 for further cycle touring tips.

Short- and long-term bike rental is available in Hobart (p91) and in Launceston (p213). If you prefer a guided cycling tour, contact **Island Cycle Tours** (☎ 1300 880 334, 6228 4255; www.islandcycletours.com) or **Tasmanian Expeditions** (☎ 1300 666 856; 6339 3999; www.tas-ex.com); see p329 for more information. Island Cycle Tours also offers a two-wheeled descent of Mt Wellington (p89) behind Hobart. **Green Island Tours** (☎ 6376 3080; www.cycling-tasmania.com) offer group guided and self-guided tours of the northeast, east and west coasts. Prices start at $490/675/1050 for six-/eight-/12-day self-guided tours including accommodation; guided group tour prices start at $1350/1690 for nine/11 days.

There are no dedicated mountain biking trails within parks in Tasmania, but there are plenty of fire trails and off-the-beaten-track tracks around to explore – ask at bike shops. On the competition front, check out January's four-day, 200km **Wildside Mountain Bike Race** (www.wildsidemtb.com), which wheels through the west coast wilderness from Cradle Mountain to Strahan. There's also the multisport **Freycinet Lodge Challenge** (www.tasultra.org), held in Freycinet National Park every October.

For information on low-impact mountain biking, see www.parks.tas.gov.au /recreation/bikes.

There's a refreshing summary of all the things you can do outdoors in Tasmania at www.leather woodonline.com (click on 'Travel & Leisure').

FISHING

Brown trout were introduced into Tasmania's Plenty River in 1866, followed by Lake Sorell in 1867. Innumerable lakes and rivers have subsequently been stocked, including artificial lakes built by Hydro Tasmania for hydroelectricity production. Trout have thrived, and today anglers make the most of the state's inland fisheries. The Tamar River is another great fishing area, with a series of 10 fishing pontoons (accessible by disabled fishers) between Launceston and George Town. The George Town (p219) area is particularly good for both freshwater and saltwater fishing.

A licence is required to fish Tasmania's inland waters; there are bag, season and size limits on most fish. Licence costs vary from $18 for one day to $73.50 for the full season, and are available from sports stores, Service Tasmania outlets, post offices, visitors centres and some country shops and

---

THE GREAT TASMANIAN BIKE RIDE

Over nine days in February, the super-popular Great Tasmanian Bike Ride wheels across Tasmania in random years, exploring different cycling routes in the state each time. Rain or shine, the ride covers around 500km to 600km each ride, with a rest day, and draws a couple of thousand riders (supported by a crack team of volunteers), with most cyclists camping along the way.

This well-organised event costs about $850 to participate in, including camp sites and meals (BYO tent and bike), and is organised by **Bicycle Victoria** (☎ 1800 639 634, 8636 8888; www.bv.com .au); contact them for details. They rotate their 'Great Rides' between NSW, Victoria and Tasmania, but should be able to tell you if a Tassie one is scheduled!

---

petrol stations. In general, inland waters open for fishing on the Saturday closest to 1 August and close on the Sunday nearest 30 April; the best fishing is between October and April. Different dates apply to some places and these (plus other essential bits of information) are all detailed in the *Fishing Code* brochure you'll be given when you buy your licence. See the **Inland Fisheries Service** (www.dpiw.tas.gov.au) website for details.

The sparsely populated Lake Country (p159) on Tasmania's Central Plateau is a region of glacial lakes and streams, and is home to the state's best-known spots for brown and rainbow trout: Arthurs Lake, Great Lake, Little Pine Lagoon (fly-fishing only), Western Lakes (including Lake St Clair), Lake Sorell and the Lake Pedder impoundment. On some parts of Great Lake you're only allowed to use artificial lures, and you're not allowed to fish any of the streams flowing into Great Lake.

If you want to bone up on Tassie trout before you unpack your rod, get a copy of *Tasmanian Trout Waters* by Greg French. Also worth a look is the bimonthly *Tasmanian Fishing & Boating News* ($4), available online at www.tasfish.com. In Hobart, the spot for spot-on lures and fishing info is **Spot On Fishing Tackle** (Map p82; ☎ 6234 4880; 89 Harrington St; ☺ 9am-5.30pm Mon-Fri, 9am-3.45pm Sat).

Tasmanian trout (brown and rainbow) can be difficult to catch as they're fickle about what they eat; the right lures are needed for the right river, lake, season or weather. If you find you just can't hook them yourself, there are dozens of operators offering guides, lessons and fishing trips – **Trout Guides & Lodges Tasmania** (www.troutguidestasmania.com.au) is a great starting point.

Rod fishing in saltwater is allowed year-round without a permit, but size restrictions and bag limits apply. If you're diving for abalone, rock lobsters or scallops, or fishing with a net, recreational sea fishing licences are required. These are available from post offices, Service Tasmania or online from the **Department of Primary Industries & Water** (www.dpiw.tas.gov.au). There are on-the-spot fines for breaches of fishing regulations.

Meanwhile, on the east coast, ocean charter fishing is big business. See www.fishnet.com.au for a directory of operators.

The wild brown trout are teeming in Tasmania's 3000 lakes and rivers, but it may help to have your own accredited trout guide to find the buggers: www.troutguidestasmania .com.au/fisheryfly.htm.

ROCK CLIMBING & ABSEILING

Although clear skies are desirable for rock climbing and Tasmania's weather is often wet, the sport nonetheless thrives around the state, as does abseiling. There are some excellent cliffs for climbing, particularly along the east coast where the weather is usually best. The Organ Pipes on Mt Wellington above Hobart (p88), the Hazards at Coles Bay (p178), the cliffs on Mt Killiecrankie on Flinders Island (p312) and Launceston's Cataract Gorge (p202) offer brilliant climbing on solid rock. Climbing fiends often see images of the magnificent rock formations on the Tasman Peninsula (p121) and head straight for that region, but the coastal cliffs there are impossible to climb if the ocean swell is too big.

If you want to climb or abseil with an experienced instructor, try one of these outfits:

Aardvark Adventures (☎ 6273 7722; www.aardvarkadventures.com.au)
Freycinet Adventures (☎ 6257 0500; www.freycinetadventures.com.au)
Tasmanian Expeditions (☎ 1300 666 856; 6339 3999; www.tas-ex.com)

SAILING

The D'Entrecasteaux Channel and Huon River south of Hobart are wide, deep and tantalizing places to set sail, with more inlets and harbours than you could swing a boom at (although conditions can be difficult south of Gordon). Fleets of white sails often dot Hobart's Derwent River in summer – many Hobartians own yachts and consider the city's nautical opportunities among its greatest assets.

For casual berths in Hobart (overnight or weekly), contact the **Royal Yacht Club of Tasmania** (☎ 03-6223 4599; www.ryct.org.au) in Sandy Bay, or the **Hobart Ports Corporation** (☎ 03-6235 1000; www.hpc.com.au), which manages berths right in the city. North of the bridge, you can anchor in Cornelian Bay or New Town Bay. There's a great marina at Kettering, in the channel south of Hobart, but it's usually crowded so finding a mooring isn't always easy.

If you're an experienced sailor, hire a yacht from **Yachting Holidays** (☎ 03-6224 3195; www.yachtingholidays.com.au), based in Hobart. Charter of a six-berth vessel is $700 per day, with reduced rates for long rentals or in the off-peak (April to November) period. Skippered charter is also available.

For cruising and trailer boat owners, a useful publication is *Cruising Southern Tasmania* ($27.50), available from Service Tasmania (p84) in Hobart.

During the peak summer holiday period, Discovery Rangers provide a range of free activities for all visitors to Tasmania's national parks and reserves. Check park noticeboards.

SCUBA DIVING & SNORKELLING

National Geographic magazine says that Tasmania offers the 'most accessible underwater wilderness in the world'. Visibility ranges from 12m in summer to 40m in winter, with temperate waters offering unique biodiversity. There are excellent scuba-diving opportunities around Rocky Cape on the north coast, on the east coast, and around the shipwrecks of King and Flinders Islands. At Tinderbox near Hobart and off Maria Island there are marked underwater snorkelling trails. There's also a new artificial dive site created by the scuttling of the *Troy D* off the west coast of Maria Island; see www.troyd.com.au for info.

If you want to learn to dive, diving courses in Tasmania are considerably cheaper than on the mainland. **Dive Tasmania** (www.divetasmania.com.au) can give you information on affiliated diving businesses and equipment hire around the state. Otherwise, contact dive operators in Eaglehawk Neck (p125), Bicheno (p183), St Helens (p191), Wynyard (p257) and King Island (p307).

SKIING

There are two petite ski resorts in Tasmania: Ben Lomond (p226), 55km southeast of Launceston, and Mt Mawson (p117) in Mt Field National Park,

---

SYDNEY TO HOBART YACHT RACE

Arguably the world's greatest and most treacherous open-ocean yacht race, the **Sydney to Hobart Yacht Race** (www.rolexsydneyhobart.com) winds up at Hobart's Constitution Dock every New Year's Eve. As the storm-battered maxis limp across the finish line, champagne corks pop and weary sailors turn the town upside down. On New Year's Day, find a sunny spot by the harbour, munch some lunch from the Taste of Tasmania food festival (p94) and count the spinnakers on the river. New Year's resolutions? What New Year's resolutions?

TOP 10 BEACHES

Pack your swimsuit, brace yourself for a cold water collision, and jump right in! In a state of gorgeous (and often empty) coastline, these are our favourite beaches:

- **Wineglass Bay** (p177) Consistently voted one of the top beaches in the world – once you've seen it, you'll understand why. Well worth the sweaty trek in.

- **Binalong Bay** (p194) Binalong time since you had a dip? Head for this long crescent of sand just north of St Helens.

- **Friendly Beaches** (p177) Often overshadowed by its near neighbour (Wineglass Bay), but offering just as lovely, and more-accessible, white sand and impossibly clear water.

- **Seven Mile Beach** (p118) A seven-mile stretch, just 15km from Hobart. When the swell is working the point break here is awesome!

- **Boat Harbour Beach** (p258) The drive down the steep access road offers postcard-perfect views of this divine little bay.

- **Marrawah** (p265) Hardcore ocean surf for harder-core surfers.

- **Adventure Bay** (p136) A few European explorers also considered this a good place to spend some down time.

- **Fortescue Bay** (p127) A little slice of heaven, complete with low-key camping ground.

- **Trousers Point** (p312) A kooky name indeed, but this magnificent beach makes the waters of Bass Strait look unfeasibly alluring.

- **Stanley** (p260) A long arc of Bass Strait sand with The Nut looming as a backdrop.

80km northwest of Hobart. Both offer cheaper, though much less-developed, ski facilities than at mainland resorts in Victoria and New South Wales (rope tows are still used on some runs!). Despite the state's southerly latitude, snowfalls tend to be patchy and unreliable.

The website www .magicseaweed.com provides updates on surf conditions (swell, wind and temperature) at Bicheno, Clifton Beach, Cloudy Bay, Scamander and the legendary Shipstern Bluff.

SURFING

Tasmania has dozens of wicked surf beaches, but the water is (pardon our French) bloody cold – steamer wetsuits are mandatory! Close to Hobart, the most reliable spots are Clifton Beach and Goats Beach (unsigned) en route to South Arm. The southern beaches on Bruny Island (p137), particularly Cloudy Bay, offer consistent swells. The east coast from Bicheno north to St Helens has solid beach breaks when conditions are working. Eaglehawk Neck (p124) on the Tasman Peninsula is also worth checking out. The east coast from Ironhouse Point south to Spring and Shelly Beaches near Orford (p166) has consistent surf; King Island (p306) also gets its share. At Marrawah (p265) on the west coast the waves are often towering – hardcore corduroy all the way to South America! Australia's heaviest wave, Shipstern Bluff off the south coast, isn't recommended for anyone other than serious pros. Gnarly...

Websites with surf reports and conditions updates include www.surftas mania.com and www.tassiesurf.com.

SWIMMING

The north and east coasts have plenty of sheltered, white-sand beaches offering excellent swimming, although the water is (to understate it) rather cold. There are also sheltered beaches near Hobart, including Bellerive and Sandy Bay, but these tend to receive some urban pollution – things will be less soupy further south at Kingston and Blackmans Bay, or east at Seven Mile Beach. On the west coast, the surf can be ferocious and the beaches aren't patrolled – play it safe.

National Parks Reserves

You'll probably see the slogan 'Tasmania – Australia's Natural S██████ in literature, and it's not a bad summary – a greater percentage of la███ over to national parks or reserves in Tasmania than in any other Aus███ state. In total, the Tasmania Parks & Wildlife Service (PWS) manages ██ reserves (including 19 national parks) covering 25,083 sq km – over a third of Tassie's total area. Add more than 2000km of walking tracks (including some of Australia's finest), unique flora and abundant fauna to the mix and you've baked yourself a mecca for naturalists, bushwalkers, wildlife-watchers, campers, photographers and anyone else with a yearning for going bush. But you don't have to rough it to experience the wilderness down here – guided walks, scenic flights and river cruises open this world up to the soft-option seeker. More hirsute outdoorsy types trek through inspiring natural beauty in the challenging southwest for as long as their supplies last, or escape civilisation for long days on the free-flowing Franklin River.

Tasmania's National Parks, Forests & Waterways – Visitors' Guide, freely available at visitors centres, is a glossy little brochure chock-full of useful information on key sites and activities.

NATIONAL PARKS

Forget Cascade and Boags for a minute – Tasmania's finest feature is its 19 national parks. Walk on their trails, trek to their peaks, lie on their beaches or just take in the awesome diversity of their environments – highland lakes, ocean-swept beaches, complex caves, wild rivers, craggy coastline, wildlife-rich islands, jagged mountain ranges and lush temperate rainforest. Most of the parks are easily accessed by vehicle, but two (Savage River, in the heart of the Tarkine wilderness, and the Kent Group, a group of Bass Strait islets) are virtually inaccessible. Walls of Jerusalem National Park has no road access direct to the park itself, but there is a car park about a half-hour walk from the park boundary.

Public access to the national parks is encouraged as long as the safety and conservation regulations are observed. In all parks you're asked to do nothing to damage or alter the natural environment – and please don't feed the wild animals. See p57 for information about responsible bushwalking within national parks.

Most people visit the national parks during the summer months (December to February), when the days are long and the weather is usually warm – although Tasmania has received snow in December! There are advantages to visiting outside these months, though – the main one being the smaller crowds. Autumn can be lovely as the foliage changes colour, winter sees snow on the peaks, and spring brings out a surge of wildflowers. See p17 for more climatic considerations.

Contacts

Tassie's national parks are managed by the **Parks & Wildlife Service** (PWS; Map p82; ☎ 1300 135 513; www.parks.tas.gov.au; 134 Macquarie St, Hobart). Major local offices and visitors centres include the following:

Cradle Mountain–Lake St Clair National Park Cradle Valley (☎ 6492 1110); Lake St Clair (☎ 6289 1172)

Franklin-Gordon Wild Rivers National Park Queenstown (☎ 6471 2511); Strahan (☎ 6472 6020)

Freycinet National Park (☎ 6256 7000)

Mt Field National Park (☎ 6288 1149)

Southwest National Park Mt Field (☎ 6288 1149); Huonville (☎ 6264 8460)

Park Fees

Visitors fees apply to all national parks, even when there's no ranger's office. Funds from the park entry fees remain with the PWS and go towards maintaining and making improvements to walking tracks, camping grounds, toilets, lookouts and picnic facilities, as well as towards a trainee program and the popular summer 'Discovery Ranger' activities (opposite).

There are two types of passes: per vehicle and per person. A vehicle pass includes up to eight passengers, and costs $22/56/90 for 24 hours/ eight weeks/one year. The one-year pass costs $66 if you buy it during the low season (May to October). An individual pass costs $11/28 for 24 hours/eight weeks.

The longer-term passes represent better value if you're staying in Tasmania for a while or visiting more than a few parks. For most visitors, the eight-week holiday pass is the best bet. Passes are available at most park entrances, at many visitors centres, aboard the *Spirit of Tasmania* ferries, at Service Tasmania (p84) and online at www.parks.tas.gov.au/natparks /current_fees.html.

The website of the Parks & Wildlife Service (www .parks.tas.gov.au) is an absolute gold mine of information. Download fact sheets on all parks, walks, plants and wildlife, campgrounds within parks and loads more.

Facilities

Staffed information centres are at both ends of the Cradle Mountain–Lake St Clair National Park, as well as Freycinet, Mt Field and Narawntapu National Parks. These are open daily and have helpful staff, useful walking information and educational displays on the history and ecology of their parks.

The 16 most accessible parks (ie not the Savage River, Kent Group and Walls of Jerusalem National Parks) all have short walking tracks, toilets, shelters and picnic areas for day-visitors to enjoy. Many also have barbecues. The entire World Heritage area and most national park areas have been declared 'fuel-stove-only' to protect the area's natural environment – this means no campfires. Dogs are definitely not allowed in any national parks.

Camp sites are available in all accessible parks except for the Hartz Mountains, Mole Creek Karst and Rocky Cape National Parks. Some sites are free, while others have a small charge per person ($2.50 to $12) in addition to park entry fees. Ben Lomond, Cradle Mountain–Lake St Clair, Freycinet, Maria Island and Mt Field National Parks also have accommodation options inside their boundaries, ranging from basic huts to five-star resorts. See the regional chapters for more information.

You'll find short walks suitable for wheelchair users and some prams at the Cradle Mountain–Lake St Clair, Freycinet, Mt Field, Tasman and Franklin-Gordon Wild Rivers National Parks (though wheelchair users may require assistance on these walks).

> If you plan on camping in Freycinet National Park from mid-December to Easter (early April), you'll need to fill out a ballot online at www.parks.tas .gov.au/natparks/freyci net/ballot.pdf.

WORLD HERITAGE AREAS

Covering 20% of Tasmania, the huge and internationally significant Tasmanian Wilderness World Heritage Area contains the state's four largest national parks – Southwest, Franklin-Gordon Wild Rivers, Cradle Mountain–Lake St Clair and Walls of Jerusalem – plus the Hartz Mountains National Park, the Central Plateau Conservation Area, the Adamsfield Conservation Area, a section of Mole Creek Karst National Park, the Devils Gullet State Reserve and part of the Liffey Falls State Reserve.

The region was first accepted for listing as a World Heritage area in 1982, acknowledging that these parks make up one of the last great, temperate wilderness areas left in the world. An area nominated for World Heritage status must satisfy at least one of 10 criteria; the Tasmanian Wilderness World Heritage Area satisfied a record seven categories. In 1989 the World Heritage area was enlarged to 13,800 sq km.

The area is managed by the PWS, the same government agency that runs the national parks. Most of the area is managed as a publicly accessible wilderness, but, being so large, most of it is accessible only to bushwalkers who can carry at least one week's food. There are, however, a few slightly less demanding ways to visit. For information on guided walks, kayaking tours and scenic flights (including landings and walking time), see the boxed

> *The Overland Track: one walk, many journeys* booklet ($12) covers the cultural heritage, unique native animals, vegetation and landscapes that make the walk one of the most scenic in Australia. Purchase it online at www.parks.tas.gov.au.

FREE-RANGING ACTIVITIES

A fantastic program of free, family-friendly 'Discovery Ranger' activities, including guided walks, spotlight tours, slide shows, quiz nights and games, is held at the most popular national parks during the peak season (usually from the week before Christmas until the start of school in early February).

National parks that stage these activities include Cradle Mountain–Lake St Clair, Freycinet, Maria Island, Tasman, Mt Field, Narawntapu and South Bruny. There are also nature-based events scheduled in Hobart and Launceston. Ask at visitors centres, or go online for the full rundown: www.parks.tas.gov.au/education/discovery_ranger.

TASMANIA'S NATIONAL PARKS

Park	Features	Activities	Best time to visit	Page
Ben Lomond National Park	alpine flora, the state's main ski field	walking, skiing, rock climbing	year-round	p226
*Cradle Mountain–Lake St Clair National Park	moorlands & mountain peaks, the famed Overland Track, Australia's deepest freshwater lake	walking, scenic flights, wildlife-spotting	year-round	p289
Douglas-Apsley National Park	dry eucalypt forest, river gorges, waterfalls, wildlife, waterhole-swimming	walking, swimming	summer	p185
*Franklin-Gordon Wild Rivers National Park	two grand wilderness watercourses, deep river gorges, rainforest, Frenchmans Cap, Aboriginal sites	rafting, cruises (from Strahan)	summer	p287
Freycinet National Park	picturesque coastal scenery, Wineglass Bay, granite peaks, great beaches, walks	walking, abseiling, sea-kayaking, scenic flights, fishing	summer	p175
*Hartz Mountains National Park	alpine heath, rainforest, glacial lakes, views of the southwest wilderness	walking	spring, summer	p148
Kent Group National Park	Bass Strait islets (mostly inaccessible), fur seals, sea birds, historical significance	wildlife-watching	year-round	p315
Maria Island National Park	traffic-free offshore island with convict history, peaceful bays, fossil-filled cliffs	walking, cycling, swimming	summer	p168
Mole Creek Karst National Park	more than 200 limestone caves & sinkholes, some open to the public	walking, caving	year-round	p242
Mt Field National Park	abundant flora & fauna, alpine scenery, high-country walks, Russell Falls, Mt Mawson ski field	walking, skiing, wildlife-watching	year-round	p116

text on p303. There are also scenic flights over the area out of Hobart (p93), Strahan (p281) and Cradle Valley near Cradle Mountain (p294).

In December 1997 the Macquarie Island World Heritage Area was proclaimed for its outstanding geological and faunal significance, but as a subAntarctic island located 1500km southeast of mainland Tasmania, Macquarie Island is difficult to get to! See p336 for details of one company offering cruises to this remote isle.

Several of Tasmania's national parks comprise the Tasmanian Wilderness World Heritage Area. There are only 166 such natural World Heritage areas in the world; to find out what gives these places 'outstanding universal value', see http://whc.unesco .org/en/list.

OTHER PROTECTED AREAS

Apart from the national parks, the PWS manages a further 423 reserves of land. These reserves are usually established around one significant, protected feature – often wildlife – but have fewer regulations than national parks and allow degrees of activities such as mining, farming, forestry and tourism development. Many of these places are very small and include caves, waterfalls, historic sites and some coastal regions. Usually there are no entry fees to these areas, except where the government has actively restored or developed the area and needs to recoup some costs.

Categories of reserves managed by the PWS include state reserves such as the Hastings Caves (p151) in the southeast and the Nut (p260) in Stanley; conservation areas including the Arthur Pieman Conservation

Mt William National Park	long sandy beaches, protected grey Forester kangaroos	walking, fishing, swimming	spring-summer	p196
Narawntapu National Park	north-coast lagoons, wetlands, tea-tree mazes, native wildlife	swimming, walking, wildlife-spotting	summer	p219
Rocky Cape National Park	bushland, rocky headlands, caves used by Aborigines, exceptional marine environment	swimming, fishing, walking	summer	p259
Savage River National Park	cool temperate rainforest inside the Tarkine wilderness; utterly secluded, no road access	walking	summer	p269
South Bruny National Park	wild southern cliffs, surf & swimming beaches, heathlands, wildlife	walking, swimming, surfing, wildlife-spotting, bird-watching, ecocruises	spring-summer	p137
*Southwest National Park	vast multi-peaked wilderness; one of the world's most pristine natural wonders	walking, swimming, scenic flights, mountaineering, kayaking	summer	p302
Strzelecki National Park	mountainous slice of islandscape, rare flora & fauna	walking, rock-climbing, wildlife-watching, swimming	summer	p312
Tasman National Park	spectacular sea cliffs and rock formations, offshore islands, forests, bays & beaches	walking, diving, surfing, ecocruises, fishing, sea-kayaking,	spring-summer	p127
*Walls of Jerusalem National Park	spectacular, remote alpine & mountain wilderness, no road access	walking	summer	p243

* Part of the Tasmanian Wilderness World Heritage Area

Area (p268) in the state's northwest and the Bay of Fires (p194) in the northeast; nature reserves, which cover the marine reserves listed below; and historic sites including high-profile spots like Port Arthur (p127) and the Richmond Gaol (p109).

FOREST RESERVES

These are small areas that have been given some protection inside larger state forests. They are on crown land and their primary purpose is for timber production. Many of the waterfalls and picnic areas on the state's scenic forest drives are in this type of reserve, which doesn't have real protection

The Tasmanian National Parks Association (TNPA; www.tnpa.asn.au) is a nonprofit, nongovernment organisation committed to the protection of Tasmania's national parks and reserves, and to giving park users a voice.

VOLUNTEERING WITH THE PARKS & WILDLIFE SERVICE

The Tasmanian government's **Parks & Wildlife Service** (www.parks.tas.gov.au/volunteer) runs extensive volunteer and community partnership programs throughout the state, generally involving maintenance work in Tassie's national parks. Tasks range from building repair and renovation to wildlife management, weed control, replanting and track maintenance. Interested? Check out the Volunteer Activity Calendar on the website or contact the regional volunteer facilitator (north, south or northwest).

TOP 10 WALKS

Walking is absolutely the best way to see Tasmania's wilderness in its full glory (and it's not a bad way to walk off all that great local food and wine, either). Pack comfy walking shoes, thick socks and hit the tracks. Following are our favourite walks, ranging in length from 20 minutes to six days:

- **Overland Track** (p290) Six stunning days through Cradle Mountain–Lake St Clair National Park
- **Wineglass Bay** (p177) Climb up over the saddle (about 45 minutes each way) to Freycinet Peninsula's famous beach
- **Cataract Gorge Walk** (p202) Explore Launceston's gorgeous gorge on the outskirts of town
- **Tasman Coastal Trail** (p124) Awesome three- to five-day trail along the Tasman Peninsula clifftops
- **Truganini Track** (p118) A hilly, two-hour return climb through sclerophyll bushland between the southern suburbs of Taroona and Mt Nelson
- **Russell Falls Walk** (p116) A short jaunt from the car park at Mt Field National Park
- **Dove Lake Circuit** (p294) A three-hour lake lap at Cradle Mountain–Lake St Clair National Park
- **South Coast Track** (p303) An 85km epic along the south coast in the Southwest National Park
- **The Nut** (p260) Sweat it out on the seep slopes of the Nut in Stanley
- **Tahune AirWalk** (p148) Take a knee-trembling treetop walk about 1½ hours south of Hobart

---

from future alterations. During weekdays some forestry roads are closed to private vehicles; if the roads are open, drive slowly and give way to logging trucks (they ain't gonna stop). There are no entry fees to forest reserves.

MARINE RESERVES

Tasmania is becoming increasingly aware of the significance and vulnerability of its marine environment. Marine reserves aim to protect fragile ecosystems, so fishing or collecting living or dead material within their boundaries is illegal. There are marine reserves at Tinderbox (p120) near Hobart, at Ninepin Point near Verona Sands south of Hobart, in the waters around the northern part of Maria Island (p168), around Governor Island off the coast at Bicheno, at Port Davey and Bathurst Harbour in the southwest, on Macquarie Island and around the Kent Group of islands in eastern Bass Strait (these islands are already a national park; see p315). Reserves contain 'no take areas', known as Sanctuary Zones, from which you can't remove anything, fishy or otherwise; and 'restricted take areas', known as Habitat Protection Zones, in which limited fishing is permitted.

In 1999 the federal government established a 370-sq-km marine reserve 170km south of Hobart. The Tasmanian Seamounts Marine Reserve is a deep-sea reserve in which any activities that could threaten its population of rare animals and plants have been outlawed, including mining and trawling (though fishing can still occur down to 500m).

Legges Tor summit, in Ben Lomond National Park, is the second-highest point in Tasmania (1572m). The highest is Mt Ossa in Cradle Mountain–Lake St Clair National Park (1617m). Hobart's Mt Wellington peaks at a relatively lowly 1270m.

---

19 NATIONAL PARKS IS BARELY ENOUGH

If Tasmanian conservation groups had their wicked way, there would be at least two more national parks in Tassie, namely the Tarkine (see p268) and the Styx Valley of the Giants (p302), where the swamp gum (*Eucalyptus regnans,* known as 'mountain ash' on the mainland) grows to 100m in height – the tallest flowering plant in the world. The Great Western Tiers near Deloraine (p239) would also get a guernsey. Read more about the campaigns to protect these threatened areas on the Tasmania webpage of the **Wilderness Society** (www.wilderness.org.au/regions/tas).

JOURNEYS

Any visit to Tasmania, whether it's a long-weekend dash or a month-long 'lap-of-the-map', will offer up a bounty of fine food and drink, as well as the chance to propel yourself into the island's famed wilderness and cross paths with its abundant wildlife. More subtly, Tasmania serves as a portal into Australia's colonial past: what you'll discover is often disquieting and may leave you feeling decidedly spooked!

Tasmanian Gothic

There's an unspoken sadness to Tasmania that's undeniable, lacing the landscape and infusing the manmade environment with melancholy. Bound to a savage industrial, convict and indigenous past, here are just some of the places that will make you ponder, reflect, or send a shiver up your spine.

① Northwest Aboriginal Sites

Tasmania's Northwest is endowed with a rich archaeological record (p265). Aboriginal shell middens, petroglyphs, hut depressions, seal hides and stone artefacts litter the coast, telling the deeply saddening story of the people who once lived here.

② Richmond Bridge

Richmond Bridge (p109) is haunted by George Grover, the 'Flagellator of Richmond', who died here in 1832. The nearby Richmond Gaol (1825; p109) predates Port Arthur by five years. Its history is engrossing but the atmosphere is unrelentingly grim.

③ Port Arthur Remembrance

It wasn't enough for 12,500 convicts to serve their sentences at Port Arthur in dehumanizing conditions from 1830 to 1877: in 1996, a gunman killed 35 tourists here. The Port Arthur Historic Site (p128) is weighted with menace and memory.

④ Cannibals & Escapees

Woebegone Sarah Island (p283) was the cruellest, most isolated Tasmanian penitentiary. Still, several convicts escaped: some turned to cannibalism to survive; others hijacked a ship and sailed to South America!

Take a Walk on the Wild Side

Whether you're a broke-ass backpacker or wallowing in lucre, some bushwalking is probably near the top of your Tassie 'Things To Do' list. Take a luxury, fully catered guided walk, or strike out solo. Lethargic? You can still get a feel for Tassie's forests, beaches and wildlife just off the road.

Author Tip
You're old and wise enough to know that the number one *worst* item to bring on any bushwalk – in Tasmania or anywhere else – is thin socks. Wear 'em thick, and wear 'em proud!

① Tarkine Encounter
An ancient swathe of rainforest, buttongrass plains and wickedly wild beaches, the Tarkine Wilderness (p268) is relatively undiscovered (and alarmingly unprotected). Traverse its fringes on a driving adventure, or take a guided tour into its forested heart.

② South Coast Epic
Take a week-long walk along the legendary South Coast Track (p303), traversing the Southwest National Park from Melaleuca to Cockle Creek. A once-in-a-lifetime experience you'll tell your grandchildren about.

③ Bay of Fires Walk
Our favourite Tasmanian guided walk is the four-day, three night Bay of Fires Walk (see the boxed text, p195) on the northeast coast. Pristine coastline, ecolodge accommodation, fine food and wine: this is bushwalking in style!

④ The Overland Track
Many come to Tassie just to walk the five-day Overland Track (p290) in Cradle Mountain–Lake St Clair National Park. Deft management maintains its purity: craggy peaks, tarn shelves, eucalypt forests and icy-cold lakes.

⑤ Devil of a Time
Devil Facial Tumour Disease (DFTD) threatens to decimate the Tasmanian Devil population. Before they go the way of the Tasmanian Tiger, support the Devils' cause at the Tasmanian Devil Conservation Park (p126).

⑥ Hartz Mountains National Park
Hartz Mountains National Park (p148) offers brilliant, bite-sized day-walks (from 20 minutes to five hours) across elevated alpine moorlands, with views from mountain passes across the untamed Tasmanian Wilderness World Heritage Area.

Tasting Tasmania

There are sumptuous culinary experiences to be had all over Tasmania. Sure, it's all the fresh air and water, but local enthusiasm for the good life has something to do with it too. Enjoy a great feed from north to south, by the roadside, the bayside, or a romantic fireside.

① How do you like *them* Apples?

Tasmania's southeast accounts for 85% of the state's apple crop. Munch on crisp apples bought from a Huon Valley (p146) roadside stall near Cradoc, Cygnet and Franklin.

② Cheese Please

The unpretentious King Island Dairy (p307) is a cheese-lover's decadent dream. Pick up a scorecard and taste-test every award-winning cheese, from bries to blues, then purchase a round or three to take home.

③ Seafood on the Road

Rip into fresh crayfish, oysters, scallops or flounder straight off the boat in a fishing town such as St Helens (p190), or snack on fish and chips along the Hobart waterfront (pictured; p85).

④ The Taste Festival

Fine food and wine producers share a table with locals and travellers at premier festival The Taste (p94) in Hobart. There's free admission to over 70 stalls at Princes Wharf.

⑤ Freycinet Marine Farm

For just-out-of-the-water oysters, go to Freycinet Marine Farm (p179). Enjoy them on the deck of the farm's tasting rooms with a fine Freycinet riesling. Ahhhh…

⑥ Pyengana

Pyengana's (p193) impossibly green fields are home to happy milking cows and happy dairy farmers. Drop in at Pyengana Dairy Company to sample alluring homemade ice-creams and mouth watering cheddars.

⑦ Binalong Bay Bounty

Satisfy your stomach with a meal at Binalong Bay's wonderful restaurant, Angasi (p195). It's a tough choice: look at the astounding view or concentrate on your plate! Legendary salt-and-pepper squid and lobster tortellini.

Drinking Down South

Tasmania is as about as chilly and southern as Australia gets, but this hasn't stopped the locals from working up a powerful thirst. The island is justly famous for its beers, but more recently a terrific wine industry has emerged. Peppy cool-climate drops fill the glasses of the state's restaurants.

① Good for what Ales You

Hobart's gothic-looking Cascade brewery has been bubbling out the beers since 1824: fine stouts, ales and lagers that are acclaimed around Australia and the world. Roll up to South Hobart and take a working tour of the brewery (p88).

② Top Drops in Northern Tassie

Go vineyard-hopping for cool-climate wines in the Tamar Valley (p213) and the nearby Pipers River Region (p221). Book lunch at one of the excellent vineyard restaurants (p43) then fill the boot with pinot noirs, rieslings, chardonnays and bottles of bubbly.

③ Northern Brews

Launceston's much-lauded Boag's Brewery (p205) wages an age-old battle with Cascade (in Hobart) for the palates and stomachs of Tasmania's beer drinkers. Both brands come in more plentiful varieties down here, and both make juices and ciders too.

Hobart & Around

Australia's second-oldest city and southernmost capital, Hobart dapples the foothills of Mt Wellington, angling down to the slate-grey Derwent River. The town's rich colonial heritage and natural charms are accented by a spirited, rootsy attitude: hip festivals and top-notch food and drink abound. Laid-back to near-horizontal, Hobartians hang out in cafés joking about the daily 'rush minute', dressed ready to plunge into the wilderness at any moment. On summer afternoons the sea breeze blows and yachts tack across the river; on winter mornings the pea-soup 'Bridgewater Jerry' fog lifts to reveal the snowcapped summit of the mountain.

It's a gorgeous place, but until quite recently Hobart was far from cosmopolitan or self-assured. This was a town of instant coffee and tragic cover bands, where the stigma of history and a downtrodden economy furrowed every brow. It's taken a while for Hobartians to feel comfortable in their own skins, but with a happy island economy, there's money in pockets – and you can get a good latte! In fact, locals have become protective of their town, shouting 'Hypocrites!' at Sydney and Melbourne escapees who've invested in Hobart's Georgian and Federation houses. The mainland attitude to Hobart has shifted from derision to delight, investors recognising that Tassie's abundant water, stress-free pace and cool climate are precious commodities. Hobart's essential attractions – the waterfront, the architecture, the market, mountain and river – have always been here, but these days Hobart is boutique, not backward. Also, not far from town are some great beaches, mountains and historic villages.

HIGHLIGHTS

- Elbowing through the crowds at Hobart's Saturday **Salamanca Market** (p85)
- Boning up on architectural history as you stroll through historic **Battery Point** (p85)
- Gawping at the view from the summit of **Mt Wellington** (p88)
- Anticipating the tasting session at the end of a **Cascade Brewery** (p88) tour
- Sipping a Friday night beer at Hobart's best pub, **Knopwood's Retreat** (p105)
- Window shopping for menus along the **North Hobart restaurant strip** (p102)
- Swimming on one of seven empty miles at **Seven Mile Beach** (p118)
- Feeling the cold-water spray of Russell Falls on your face on a day trip to **Mt Field National Park** (p116)

★ Mt Field National Park

★ Seven Mile Beach

Cascade Brewery
Mt Wellington ★ ★ ★ Salamanca Market;
Battery Point;
Knopwood's Retreat;
North Hobart
Restaurant Strip

HOBART & AROUND

HOBART

☎ 03 / pop 203,600

No doubt about it, Hobart's future is looking rosy. Tourism is booming, and the old town is treading gingerly onto the world stage. Plan on staying a while – you'll need at least a week to savour the full range of Cascade beers flowing from the city's pubs.

HISTORY

Hobart's original inhabitants were the semi-nomadic Mouheneenner band of the Southeast tribe, who called the area Nibberloonne. In 1803 Van Diemen Land's first European settlers pitched their tents at Risdon Cove on the Derwent's eastern shore, which became the site of the first massacre of the Mouheneenner (Risdon Cove was returned to the Aboriginal community by the state government in 1995). The colony relocated a year later to the site of present-day Hobart, where water running off Mt Wellington was plentiful.

When Britain's gaols overflowed with sinners in the 1820s, Hobart's isolation loomed as a major selling point. Tens of thousands of convicts were chained into rotting hulks and shipped down to Hobart Town to serve their sentences in vile conditions. In the 1840s, Hobart's sailors, soldiers, whalers and rapscallions boozed and brawled shamelessly in countless harbourside pubs.

With the abolition of convict transportation to Tasmania in 1853, Hobart started to toe a slightly more moral line, and the town came to rely on the apple and wool industries for its fiscal fortitude.

In the 20th century Hobart stuttered through the Great Depression and World Wars, relying more heavily on industry (paper, zinc and chocolate production, most notably) and the deep-water Derwent River harbour to sustain it. Hobart has always been a key Australian port. Unlike inland cities, ports look outwards to the world, and bring the world to them via trade and travellers. Harbourside pubs sustain this traffic with the same free-floating spirit – the day Hobart's waterfront is no longer the place to go for a beer is the day Hobart loses its sea-born soul.

Indeed, the city has only ever partially sobered up, but today's convicts are more likely to be white-collared than bad company at the bar. Skeletons rattle in Hobart's closet – indigenous Tasmanians and thousands of

---

HOBART IN...

Two Days

Get your head into history mode with a stroll around **Battery Point** (p85) – coffee and cake at **Jackman & McRoss** (p103) will sustain your afternoon explorations of nearby **Salamanca Place** (p84). Bone up on maritime history at the **Maritime Museum of Tasmania** (p87) before a promenade along the Sullivans Cove waterfront and fish and chips for dinner from **Flippers Fish Punt** (p101) on Constitutions Dock. Wash it down with a few Cascades at **Knopwood's Retreat** (p105), the quintessential Hobart pub.

On day two recuperate over a big breakfast at **Retro Café** (p101) then blow out the cobwebs with a ramble around the rocks on **Mt Wellington** (p88) – on a clear day the views are jaw-dropping. Come down to earth with dinner, drinks and some live music at **Republic Bar & Café** (p106), North Hobart's happening hub.

Four Days

If you've got a bit more time on your hands, take a **river cruise** (p93) north to the **Cadbury Chocolate Factory** (p88), followed by a wine-splashed lunch at **Moorilla Estate** (p88). If beer is more your vice, take a tour of the legendary **Cascade Brewery** (p88) in South Hobart. Snooze the afternoon away on the sunny lawns of the **Botanical Gardens** (p89) before a classy dinner at **Marque IV** (p102).

Feeling energetic? On day four take the **Pedal 'N' Paddle** challenge (p91) – plummeting down the flanks of Mt Wellington on a bike, followed by sea-kayaking around the Hobart docks. If you're just not Iron Man material, take a photo-worthy day trip to nearby **Richmond** (p109) or the waterfalls and peaks of **Mt Field National Park** (p116).

HOBART & SUBURBS

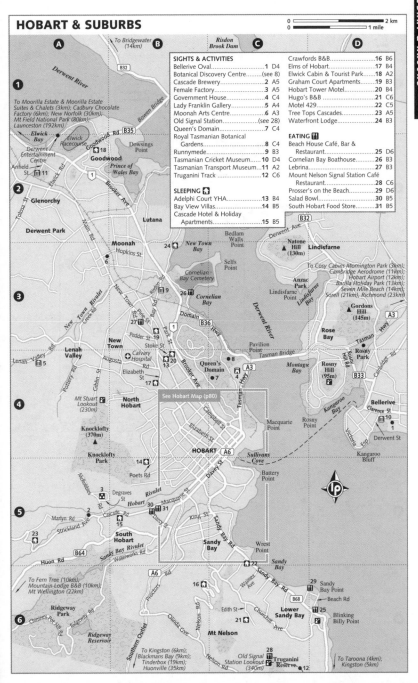

SIGHTS & ACTIVITIES	
Bellerive Oval	1 D4
Botanical Discovery Centre	(see 8)
Cascade Brewery	2 A5
Female Factory	3 A5
Government House	4 C4
Lady Franklin Gallery	5 A4
Moonah Arts Centre	6 A3
Old Signal Station	(see 28)
Queen's Domain	7 C4
Royal Tasmanian Botanical Gardens	8 C4
Runnymede	9 B3
Tasmanian Cricket Museum	10 D4
Tasmanian Transport Museum	11 A2
Truganini Track	12 C6

SLEEPING	
Adelphi Court YHA	13 B4
Bay View Villas	14 B5
Cascade Hotel & Holiday Apartments	15 B5

Crawfords B&B	16 B6
Elms of Hobart	17 B4
Elwick Cabin & Tourist Park	18 A2
Graham Court Apartments	19 B3
Hobart Tower Motel	20 B4
Hugo's B&B	21 C6
Motel 429	22 C5
Tree Tops Cascades	23 A5
Waterfront Lodge	24 B3

EATING	
Beach House Café, Bar & Restaurant	25 D6
Cornelian Bay Boathouse	26 B3
Lebrina	27 B3
Mount Nelson Signal Station Café Restaurant	28 C6
Prosser's on the Beach	29 D6
Salad Bowl	30 B5
South Hobart Food Store	31 B5

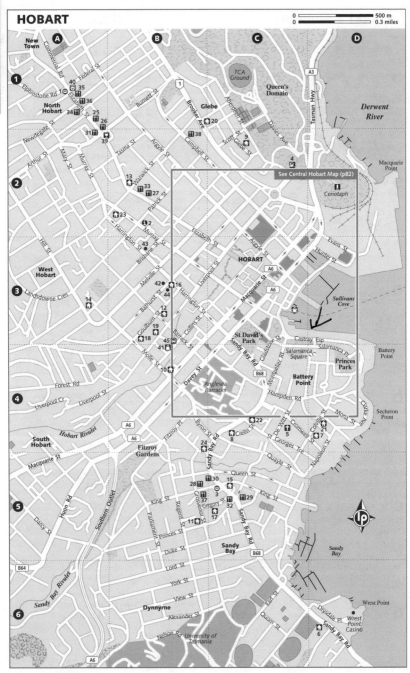

HOBART & AROUND

HOBART

See Central Hobart Map (p82)

convicts suffered here – but the old town's shimmering beauty and relaxed vibe scare away the ghosts of the past.

ORIENTATION

Hobart is sandwiched between Mt Wellington and the wide Derwent River estuary. With scant flat land, the city has spread along the riverbanks – it's now about 20km long, and very narrow. The steep western suburbs streets will give your thighs a workout!

The city centre is compact and navigable, with a grid of one-way streets encircling the Elizabeth St Mall. The visitors centre, banks, bus stops and post office are on Elizabeth St; the main shopping area extends west from the Mall.

Salamanca Pl, a grandiose row of Georgian sandstone warehouses, lines the southern fringe of Sullivans Cove, the city's harbour and social epicentre. Just south of Salamanca Pl (usually just called 'Salamanca') is Battery Point, Hobart's increasingly gentrified early colonial district. South of Battery Point is cashed-up Sandy Bay, home to the University of Tasmania and the landmark/eyesore Wrest Point Casino.

The northern side of the city is bounded by the Queen's Domain (usually just called 'The Domain'), a bushy hillock that harbours the Botanical Gardens. From here the Tasman Bridge arcs across the river to the eastern shore and the airport (16km from the CBD). North Hobart is the city's bohemian enclave – the Elizabeth St strip sustains cafés and restaurants by the dozen. The snoozy eastern shore suburbs probably won't wake up as you pass

through (unless you're at Bellerive Oval for the cricket).

Maps

The visitors centre supplies basic city maps. For more comprehensive coverage try the *Hobart & Surrounds Street Directory* ($18) or the UBD *Tasmania Country Road Atlas* ($31), available at larger newsagents and bookshops. Travellers with disabilities should check out the useful *Hobart CBD Mobility Map* from the visitors centre.

Hobart map sources:

Hobart visitors centre (Map p82; ☎ 6230 8233; www.hobarttravelcentre.com.au; cnr Davey & Elizabeth Sts; ☺ 8.30am-5.30pm Mon-Fri, 9am-5pm Sat, Sun & public holidays; ▣)

Royal Automobile Club of Tasmania (RACT; Map p80; ☎ 6232 6300, 13 27 22; www.ract.com.au; cnr Murray & Patrick Sts; ☺ 8.45am-5pm Mon-Fri)

Service Tasmania (Map p82; ☎ 1300 135 513; www.service.tas.gov.au; 134 Macquarie St; ☺ 8.15am-5pm Mon-Fri)

Tasmanian Map Centre (Map p82; ☎ 6231 9043; www.map-centre.com.au; 100 Elizabeth St; ☺ 9.30am-5.30pm Mon-Fri, 10am-4pm Sat) Bushwalking maps and Lonely Planet guides.

INFORMATION
Bookshops

Fullers Bookshop (Map p82; ☎ 6224 2488; www.fullersbookshop.com.au; 140 Collins St; ☺ 9am-6pm Mon-Fri, to 5pm Sat, 10am-4pm Sun) Super range of literature and travel guides, plus a café upstairs.

Hobart Book Shop (Map p82; ☎ 6223 1803; www.hobartbookshop.com.au; 22 Salamanca Sq; ☺ 9am-6pm

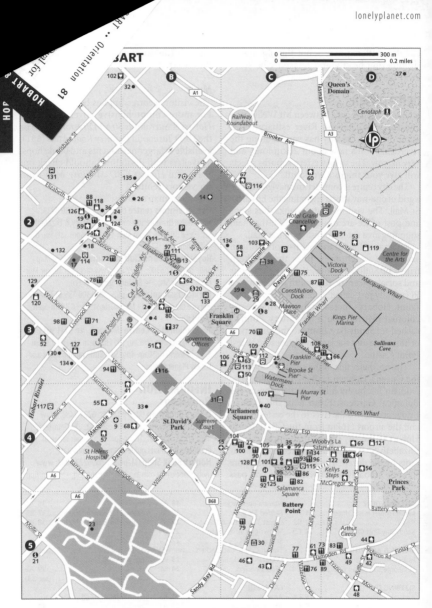

Mon-Fri, to 5pm Sat, 10am-5pm Sun) Tasmania-centric titles, Tassie writers and second-hand selections.

Wilderness Society Shop (Map p82; ☎ 6234 9370; www.wilderness.org.au; Shop 8, The Galleria, 33 Salamanca Pl; ⏰ 9am-6pm Mon-Fri, to 5pm Sat & Sun) Environmental publications, wildlife posters, DVDs, maps and calendars.

Emergency

Police, Fire & Ambulance (☎ 000)
Hobart Police Station (Map p82; ☎ 6230 2111; www.police.tas.gov.au; 43 Liverpool St; ⏰ 24hr)

Internet Access

Expect to pay $5 to $6 per hour at internet cafés:

Drifters Internet Café (Map p82; ☎ 6224 6286; www.errolflynn.com.au; Shop 9/33 Salamanca Pl; ⏳ 9am-6.30pm) Printing, scanning and faxing available.

Mouse on Mars (Map p82; ☎ 6231 5421; www.mouse onmars.com.au; 1st fl, 112 Liverpool St; ⏳ 10am-10pm) Statewide wi-fi hotspots (see website for details), plus cheap long-distance calls, tour-booking desk and backpacker info.

HOBART & AROUND

Outzone (Map p82; ☎ 6224 0775; 1st fl, 3/66 Murray St; ☽ 10am-7pm Sat-Thu, to 10pm Fri)
Pelican Loft (Map p82; ☎ 6234 2225; 1st fl, 35a Elizabeth St; ☽ 8.30am-7pm Mon-Fri, noon-4pm Sat & Sun)
Service Tasmania (Map p82; ☎ 1300 135 513; www.service.tas.gov.au; 134 Macquarie St; ☽ 8.15am-5pm Mon-Fri)
State Library (Map p82; ☎ 6233 7529; www.statelibrary.tas.gov.au; 91 Murray St; ☽ 9.30am-6pm Mon-Thu, to 9pm Fri, to 12.30pm Sat) Thirty minutes free for Australians; $5.50 for international visitors.

Internet Resources
Hobart City (www.hobartcity.com.au) City council website.
LIVE Tasmania (www.livetasmania.com) Theatre, puppetry, dance and music listings.
The Dwarf (www.thedwarf.com.au) Online gig guide.
Totally South (www.totallysouth.com.au) Southern Tasmania tourist guide.
Welcome to Hobart (www.welcometohobart.com.au) Official visitors guide.

Media
The visitors centre stocks free Tassie tourist publications highlighting Hobart's attractions. Hobart's long-running newspaper the *Mercury* (aka 'the Mockery') is thin on quality global reportage but handy for discovering what's on where; the Thursday edition lists entertainment options. The free monthly *Sauce* entertainment rag provides detailed arts listings.

Medical Services
Australian Dental Association Emergency Service (☎ 6248 1546) Advice for dental emergencies.
Chemist on Collins (Map p82; ☎ 6235 0257; www.chemistoncollins.com.au; 93 Collins St; ☽ 9am-5.30pm Mon-Thu, to 6pm Fri, 9.30am-4pm Sat)
City Doctors & Travel Clinic (Map p82; ☎ 6231 3003; www.citydoctors.com.au; 93 Collins St; ☽ 9am-5pm Mon-Fri) Standard consultation is $60.
Macquarie Pharmacy (Map p82; ☎ 6223 2339; 180 Macquarie St; ☽ 8am-10pm)
Royal Hobart Hospital (Map p82; ☎ 6222 8423; www.dhhs.tas.gov.au; 48 Liverpool St; ☽ 24hr) Argyle St emergency entry.
Salamanca Medical Centre (Map p82; ☎ 6223 8181; 5a Gladstone St; ☽ 8.30am-6pm Mon-Fri, 10am-3pm Sat, noon-3pm Sun) Bulk-billing doctors; free for Australian Medicare Card holders.

Money
The major banks have branches around Elizabeth St Mall, open 9am to 5pm Monday to Friday:

ANZ Bank (Map p82; ☎ 13 13 14; www.anz.com.au; 40 Elizabeth St)
Commonwealth Bank (Map p82; 13 22 21; www.commbank.com.au; 81 Elizabeth St)
National Bank (Map p82; ☎ 13 22 65; www.nab.com.au; cnr Elizabeth & Liverpool Sts)
Westpac Bank (Map p82; ☎ 13 13 31; www.westpac.com.au; 28 Elizabeth St)

Post
The following **Australia Post** (☎ 13 13 18; www.auspost.com.au) branches are open 9am to 5pm Monday to Friday:
General Post Office (GPO; Map p82; cnr Elizabeth & Macquarie Sts)
North Hobart (Map p80; 412 Elizabeth St)
Sandy Bay (Map p80; cnr Sandy Bay Rd & King St)

Tourist Information
Hobart visitors centre (Map p82; ☎ 6230 8233; www.hobarttravelcentre.com.au; cnr Davey & Elizabeth Sts; ☽ 8.30am-5.30pm Mon-Fri, 9am-5pm Sat, Sun & public holidays; ☐) Brochures, maps, information and statewide tour and accommodation bookings. Collect a copy of the useful *Welcome to Hobart* booklet.

Useful Organisations
Parks & Wildlife Service (Map p82; ☎ 1300 135 513; www.parks.tas.gov.au; 134 Macquarie St; ☽ 9am-5pm Mon-Fri) Information and fact sheets for bushwalking and all national parks; inside the Service Tasmania office.
Sustainable Living Tasmania (Map p82; ☎ 6234 5566; www.sustainablelivingtasmania.org.au; 1st fl, 102 Bathurst St; ☽ 9am-5pm Mon-Fri) Community resource centre stocking environmental publications.
Wilderness Society Office (Map p80; ☎ 6224 1550; www.wilderness.org.au; 130 Davey St; ☽ 9.30am-5pm Mon-Fri) Head office on the outskirts of the city.
YHA Office (Map p82; ☎ 6234 9617; www.yha.com.au; 9 Argyle St; ☽ 9am-5pm Mon-Fri) YHA's Tasmanian HQ is at Montgomery's Private Hotel & YHA (p96).

SIGHTS
Most of Hobart's big-ticket sights are in or near the city centre and waterfront area, within easy walking distance of each other. On the city outskirts are historic houses, wineries and the famous Cascade Brewery, plus the stoic bulk of Mt Wellington.

Salamanca Place
This picturesque row of four-storey sandstone warehouses on Sullivans Cove (Map p82) is a classic example of Australian colonial architecture. Dating back to the whaling days of the

---

SALAMANCA MARKET

Every Saturday morning since 1972, the open-air **Salamanca Market** (Map p82; ☎ 6238 2843; www.hobartcity.com.au; ✆ 8.30am-3pm Sat) has lured hippies and craft merchants from the foothills to fill the tree-lined expanses of Salamanca Pl with their stalls. Fresh organic produce, secondhand clothes and books, tacky tourist souvenirs, ceramics and woodwork, CDs, cheap sunglasses, antiques, exuberant buskers, quality food and drink – it's all here, but people-watching is the real name of the game. Rain or shine – don't miss it!

1830s, Salamanca Pl was the hub of Hobart Town's trade and commerce, but by the mid-20th century many of the buildings had fallen into ruin. The 1970s saw the dawning of Tasmania's sense of 'heritage', from which flowed a push to revive the warehouses to house restaurants, cafés, bars and shops – an evolution that continues today. The development of the quarry behind the warehouses into **Salamanca Square** has bolstered the atmosphere. The eastern end of Salamanca Pl has been the subject of major developments in recent years, including the conversion of four old wheat silos into luxury apartment towers.

Operating behind the scenes here is a vibrant and creative arts community. The nonprofit **Salamanca Arts Centre** (Map p82; ☎ 6234 8414; www.salarts.org.au; 77 Salamanca Pl; ✆ shops & galleries 9am-6pm) occupies seven Salamanca warehouses, home to 75-plus arts organisations and individuals, including shops, galleries, studios, performing arts venues (including the Peacock Theatre, p107) and versatile public spaces. Check the website for the latest happenings.

To reach Salamanca Pl from Battery Point, descend the well-weathered **Kellys Steps**, wedged between warehouses halfway along the main block of buildings.

Battery Point

An empty rum bottle's throw from the once-notorious Sullivans Cove waterfront, the old maritime village of **Battery Point** (Map p82; www.batterypoint.net) is a nest of tiny lanes and 19th-century cottages, packed together like shanghaied landlubbers in a ship's belly. Its name derives from the 1818 gun battery that

stood on the promontory, protecting Hobart Town from nautical threats both real and imagined. Built in 1818, the guardhouse is now Battery Point's oldest building. The guns were never used in battle and the only damage they inflicted was on nearby windowpanes when fired during practice.

During colonial times Battery Point was a salty maritime enclave, home to master mariners, shipwrights, sailors, whalers, coopers and merchants. Architectural styles here reflect the original occupants' varying jobs (and salaries), ranging from one- and two-room fishermen's cottages (like those around Arthur Circus), to lace-festooned mansions. Most houses are still occupied by Hobartians; many are now guesthouses where you can stay (usually for a pretty penny) and absorb the village atmosphere.

While away an afternoon exploring on your own, or follow our walking tour (p91). Stumble up **Kellys Steps** (Map p82) from Salamanca Pl and dogleg into **South St** (Map p82) where the red lights once burned night and day and many a lonesome sailor sheltered from the storm. Spin around the picturesque **Arthur Circus** (Map p82), then explore **Hampden Rd** (Map p82) where slick cafés and restaurants cater to a more dignified clientele than the ale houses of the past. Check out **St George's Anglican Church** (Map p80) on Cromwell St or shamble down **Napoleon St** (Map p80) to the waterfront where yachts strain against their moorings in the tide. For a fortifying stout, duck into the salty Shipwrights Arms Hotel (p98).

The **Anglesea Barracks** (Map p82) were built adjacent to Battery Point in 1811. Still used by the army, this is the oldest military establishment in Australia. Inside is the volunteer-staffed **Military Museum of Tasmania** (Map p82; ☎ 6237 7160; fax 6223 1111; cnr Davey & Byron Sts; admission free; ✆ 10am-noon Tue, other times by appointment). Free 45-minute guided tours of the buildings and grounds depart the front gates at 11am every Tuesday.

See also Narryna Heritage Museum (p87).

The Waterfront

Hobartians flock to the city's waterfront like seagulls to chips. Centred around **Victoria Dock** (Map p82; a working fishing harbour) and **Constitution Dock** (Map p82; chock-full of floating takeaway-seafood punts; see p101) –

it's a brilliant place to explore. The obligatory Hobart experience is to sit in the sun, munch some fresh fish and chips and watch the harbour hubbub. If you'd prefer something with a knife and fork, there are some superb restaurants around here too; head for Elizabeth St Pier (p101).

Celebrations surrounding the finish of the annual Sydney to Hobart Yacht Race (p61) also revolve around Constitution Dock at New Year. The fabulous food festival The Taste (p94) is also in full swing around this time – there are so many people around the waterfront, Hobart feels like it could be Monaco! The waterfront on New Year's Eve is both an exhilarating and nauseating place (depending on how late you stay out).

Hunter St (Map p82) has a row of fine Georgian warehouses, most of which comprised the old Henry Jones IXL jam factory. It's occupied these days by the Art School division of the University of Tasmania and Hobart's glam-est hotel, the uber-swish Henry Jones Art Hotel (p97) and its affiliated restaurants and galleries. These developments have remained true to the area's heritage and retain the original façades, but not all of the hotel's neighbours can make the same claim. It's no secret that the design of the large, modern hotel and apartment complex at the corner of Davey and Hunter Sts has few admirers; many Hobartians consider it totally inappropriate for the historic area (and you'd be forgiven for feeling the same way about the naff hotel and concert hall opposite too).

Most of the Hobart waterfront area is built on reclaimed land. When the town was first settled, Davey St marked the shoreline and the Hunter St area was an island used to store food and imported goods. Subsequent projects filled in the shallow waters and created the land upon which the Hunter St and Salamanca Pl warehouses were constructed. On Hunter St itself, there are markers indicating the position of the original causeway, which was built in 1820 to link Hunter Island with the long-since-demolished suburb of Wapping.

Historic Buildings

Hobart's cache of amazingly well-preserved old buildings makes it exceptional among Australian cities. There are more than 90 buildings classified by the National Trust here – 60 of these are on Macquarie and Davey Sts. The intersection of Macquarie and Murray

---

WHALES IN THE DERWENT

In the 1830s Hobartians joked about walking across the Derwent River on the backs of whales and complained about being kept awake at night the ocean giants cavorting offshore. In typical Tasmanian style, the ensuing whaling boom was catastrophic, driving local populations of southern right and humpback whales to near extinction. Though still endangered, the occasional forgiving whale returns to the Derwent during June–July northbound and October–November southbound migration. If you spy one, call the Parks & Wildlife Service Whale Hotline on ☎ 0427 WHALES (☎ 0427-942 537).

Sts features a gorgeous sandstone edifice on each corner. For detailed information contact the **National Trust** (Map p82; ☎ 6223 5200; www .nationaltrust.org.au; cnr Brisbane & Campbell Sts; ☼ 9am-1pm Mon-Fri), or pick up the *Hobart's Historic Places* brochure from the visitors centre.

Ruminating over the court rooms, cells and gallows of the **Penitentiary Chapel Historic Site** (Map p82; ☎ 6231 0911; www.penitentiarychapel .com; cnr Brisbane & Campbell Sts; tours adult/concession & child/family $8/7/16; ☼ tours 10am, 11.30am, 1pm, 2.30pm), writer TG Ford mused, 'As the Devil was going through Hobart Gaol, he saw a solitary cell; and the Devil was pleased for it gave him a hint, for improving the prisons in hell.' Take the excellent National Trust-run tour, or the one-hour **Penitentiary Chapel Ghost Tour** (☎ 0417-361 392; www.hobartghosts.com; adult/child/concession $10/6/8; ☼ 8.30pm) held most nights (bookings essential).

Presiding over an oak-studded park adjacent to Salamanca Pl is the low-lying, sandstone **Parliament House** (Map p82; ☎ 6233 2200; www.parlia ment.tas.gov.au; Salamanca Pl; 45min tours free; ☼ tours 10am & 2pm Mon-Fri except when parliament sits), completed in 1840 and originally used as a customs house. No-one knows what it was used for, but there's a tunnel under Murray St from the building to the Customs House Hotel opposite (a few MPs looking unsteady on their feet?).

Take a backstage tour of Hobart's prestigious **Theatre Royal** (Map p82; www.theatreroyal.com .au; 29 Campbell St; 1hr tours adult/concession & child $8/6; ☼ tours 10.30am & noon Mon, Wed & Fri), built in 1837 and Australia's oldest continuously operating theatre. See p106 for performance details.

Hobart's **Real Tennis Club** (Royal Tennis Club; Map p82; ☎ 6231 1781; www.hobarttennis.com.au; 45 Davey St; ☼ 9am-6pm Mon-Fri) dates from 1875 and is one of only five such courts in the southern hemisphere (the others are in Melbourne, Ballarat, Sydney and Romsey in country Victoria). Real (or 'Royal') tennis is an archaic form of the highly strung game, played in a jaunty four-walled indoor court. Visitors can watch, take a lesson ($45) or hire the court ($15 per hour).

Runnymede (Map p79; ☎ 6278 1269; 61 Bay Rd, New Town; adult/child/family $8/6/16; ☼ 10am-4.30pm Mon-Fri, noon-4.30pm Sat & Sun) is a gracious 1840 sandstone-and-slate residence 5km north of the city centre. It was built for Robert Pitcairn, the first lawyer to qualify in Tasmania, and named by a later owner, Captain Charles Bayley, after his favourite ship. It's now managed by the National Trust – delightfully doddery volunteers staff the house and conduct free tours if you're interested. To get here, take bus 15 or 20.

Finally being recognised as an important historic site (one in four convicts transported to Van Diemen's Land was a woman!), the **Female Factory** (Map p79; ☎ 6223 1559; www.female factory.com.au; 16 Degraves St, South Hobart; tours adult/child/ concession/family $10/5/8/25; ☼ 9am-4pm, 1hr tour 9.30am, extra 2pm tour Dec-Apr) was where Hobart's female convicts were incarcerated. Major archaeological work is ongoing and tour bookings are essential. It's not far from the Cascade Brewery (p88) – combining the two makes for a fascinating afternoon. To get here by public transport, take bus 43, 44, 46 or 49 and jump off at stop 16.

Other notable edifices include the 1864 **Town Hall** (Map p82; 50 Macquarie St), which takes its architectural prompts from the Palazzo Farnese in Rome, and the austere **St David's Cathedral** (Map p82; cnr Murray & Macquarie Sts).

Museums & Galleries

The enduring **Tasmanian Museum & Art Gallery** (Map p82; ☎ 6211 4177; www.tmag.tas.gov.au; 40 Macquarie St; admission free; ☼ 10am-5pm) incorporates Hobart's oldest building, the Commissariat Store (1808). The museum features Aboriginal displays and colonial relics; the gallery curates a collection of Tasmanian colonial art. There are free guided tours at 2.30pm from Wednesday to Sunday (hordes of school kids might be a little less interested in proceedings than you are). There's a cool café here too.

Celebrating Hobart's unbreakable bond with the sea, the excellent **Maritime Museum of Tasmania** (Map p82; ☎ 6234 1427; www.maritimetas .org; 16 Argyle St; adult/child/concession/family $7/3/5/16; ☼ 9am-5pm) has a fascinating, salt-encrusted collection of photos, paintings, models and relics (try to resist ringing the huge brass bell from the *Rhexenor*). Upstairs is the council-run **Carnegie Gallery** (admission free; ☼ 9am-5pm), exhibiting contemporary Tasmanian art, craft, design and photography.

Cricket fans should slap a straight six towards Bellerive Oval on Hobart's eastern shore, where the **Tasmanian Cricket Museum** (Map p79; ☎ 6211 4000; www.tascricket.com.au; cnr Church & Derwent Sts, Bellerive; admission adult/child $2/1, tours adult/child $7/2; ☼ 1-3pm match days, plus 10am-3pm Tue-Thu, 10am-noon Fri) resides in willow-and-leather splendour. Oval and museum tours run at 10am on Tuesdays (except on match days). Don't miss the impressive portraits of a latter-day Boonie and a mean-looking Ricky Ponting. Buses 285 and 287 service Bellerive Oval.

The **Allport Library & Museum of Fine Arts** (Map p82; ☎ 6233 7484; www.statelibrary.tas.gov.au; 91 Murray St; admission free; ☼ 9.30am-5pm Mon-Fri, to 2.30pm last Sat of the month) is at the State Library. Inside is a collection of rare books on the Australia-Pacific region, plus colonial paintings, antiques, and a special collection of artworks it dusts off for display several times a year.

Narryna Heritage Museum (Map p82; ☎ 6234 2791; www.nationaltrust.org.au; 103 Hampden Rd; adult/concession/child/family $6/5/3/12; ☼ 10.30am-5pm Tue-Fri, 2-5pm Sat & Sun, closed Jul) is a stately Georgian sandstone-fronted mansion (pronounced 'Narrina') built in 1836, set in established grounds and containing a treasure-trove of domestic colonial artefacts.

The **Moonah Arts Centre** (Map p79; ☎ 6214 7633; www.mac.gcc.tas.gov.au; 65 Hopkins St, Moonah; admission free; ☼ 12.30-5pm Mon-Fri, 10am-2pm Sat) is a community arts centre staging everything from indigenous arts exhibitions and concerts to workshops and special events. Buses departing stop E on Elizabeth St go to groovy Moonah.

Lady Franklin Gallery (Map p79; ☎ 6228 0076; www.artstas.com; Ancanthe Park, 268 Lenah Valley Rd; admission free; ☼ 1.30-5pm Sat & Sun), in a colonnaded 1842 sandstone building called Ancanthe (Greek for 'Vale of Flowers'), displays work by Tasmanian artists. To travel here take bus 6, 7, 8, 9 or 10 to the Lenah Valley terminus from stop G on Elizabeth St.

Train rides are available on the first and third Sundays of each month at the **Tasmanian Transport Museum** (Map p79; ☎ 6272 7721; www.railtasmania.com/ttms; Anfield St, Glenorchy; adult/child $6/3; ☺ 1-5pm Sat & Sun). When the trains run, admission increases to $8/4 per adult/child. At other times, mourn the loss of Tasmania's passenger train network, which called it a day in the mid-1970s. Take bus X1 from stop F on Elizabeth St: the museum is a short walk from Glenorchy bus station.

Tastes of Hobart
CASCADE BREWERY
Around a bend in South Hobart, standing in startling, Gothic isolation, is the **Cascade Brewery** (Map p79; ☎ 6224 1117; www.cascadebrewery.com.au; 140 Cascade Rd, South Hobart; 90min tours adult/child/concession/family $18/7/14/42; ☺ tours 9.30am, 10am, 1pm & 1.30pm Mon-Fri except public holidays, additional summer tours). Australia's oldest brewery, it was established in 1832 next to the clean-running Hobart Rivulet, and is still pumping out superb beer and soft drinks today. Tours involve plenty of stair climbing, with tastings at the end (including Cascade Premium, the global sales smash). Wear flat, enclosed shoes and long trousers (no shorts or skirts); bookings essential. You can take a tour on weekends, but none of the machinery will be operating (brewers have weekends too). See also the boxed text, p42.

To get here, take bus 43, 44, 46 or 49 from Elizabeth St at Franklin Sq and jump ship at stop 18.

MOORILLA ESTATE
Twelve kilometres north of Hobart's centre, **Moorilla Estate** (off Map p79; ☎ 6277 9900; www.moorilla.com.au; 655 Main Rd, Berriedale; tastings free; ☺ 10am-5pm) occupies a saucepan-shaped peninsula jutting into the Derwent River. Founded in the 1950s, Moorilla plays a prominent and gregarious role in Hobart society. Stop by for wine and 'Moo Brew' beer tastings (*ooooh*, the pinot noir…), have lunch or dinner at the outstanding restaurant the **Source** (mains $25-33; ☺ noon-2.30pm daily & 6.30-9pm Fri & Sat), catch a summer concert on the lawns (Alex Lloyd, Cat Empire, The Pretenders et al), or splash some cash for a night in the uber-swish accommodation (p98). Hold your breath for **MONA** (www.mona.net.au), Moorilla's Museum of Old and New Art, which is being dug into the Moorilla peninsula as we speak. It's slated to open in 2010.

To get here take bus X1 from Stop F, or a cruise from the waterfront (see p93).

CADBURY CHOCOLATE FACTORY
A must-see for sweet-tooths and Willie Wonka wannabes is the **Cadbury Chocolate Factory** (off Map p79; ☎ 6249 0333, 1800 627 367; Cadbury Rd, Claremont; adult/child $5/free; ☺ 9am-4pm Mon-Fri except public holidays), 15km north of the city centre. You can enjoy samples, invest in low-priced choc products and watch a chocolate-making video.

Some companies offer day trips and river cruises incorporating the Cadbury tour (see p93), or book directly with Cadbury and make your own way here on bus 37, 38 or 39 to Claremont from stop E on Elizabeth St.

LARK DISTILLERY
Continuing the boozy theme is the **Lark Distillery** (Map p82; ☎ 6231 9088; www.larkdistillery.com.au; 14 Davey St; admission free, tours per person $11; ☺ 10am-6pm Sun-Wed, to late Thu-Sat), near the visitors centre, which produces fruit liqueurs (free tastings) and single malt whisky ($2.50 per tasting). Distillery tours happen at 11am and 2pm, Monday to Saturday. You can also get a bite to eat here, and it morphs into a lounge bar with live music on Thursday, Friday and Saturday nights.

Mt Wellington
Cloaked in winter snow, **Mt Wellington** (Map p89; www.wellingtonpark.tas.gov.au) peaks at 1270m, towering over Hobart like a benevolent overlord. The citizens find reassurance in its constant, solid presence, while outdoorsy types find the space to hike and bike on its leafy flanks. And the view from the top is unbelievable! Don't be deterred if the sky is overcast – often the peak rises above cloud level and looks out over a magic carpet of cotton-topped clouds.

Hacked out of the mountainside during the Great Depression, the 22km road to the top winds up from the city through thick temperate forest, opening out to lunar rockscapes at the summit. If you don't have wheels, local buses 48 and 49 stop at Fern Tree halfway up the hill, from where it's a five- to six-hour return walk to the top via Fern Glade Track, Radfords Track, Pinnacle Track, then the steep Zig Zag Track. The Organ Pipes walk from the Chalet (en route to the summit) is a flat track below these amazing cliffs. Pick up the *Mt Wellington Walks* map ($4.10 from the visitors centre) as a guide. Alternatively, Mt

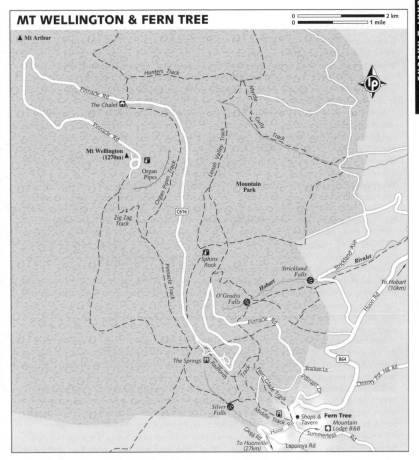

MT WELLINGTON & FERN TREE

▲ Mt Arthur

Hunters Track

Pinnacle Rd

The Chalet

Pinnacle Rd

Mt Wellington
(1270m) ▲

Organ Pipes

Organ Pipes Track

Myrtle Gully Track

Lenah Valley Track

Mountain
Park

C616

Zig Zag
Track

Pinnacle Track

Sphinx
Rock

Strickland Ave

Rivulet

Strickland
Falls

To Hobart
(10km)

Hobart

O'Gradys
Falls

Huon Rd

Pinnacle Rd

The Springs

Radfords

Track

Fern Glade Track

Bracken La

Pillinger Dr

864

Chimney Pot Hill Rd

Silver
Falls

Middle Track Rd

Shops &
Tavern

Fern Tree
Mountain
Lodge B&B

Glegg Rd

Huon

Summerleas Rd

To Huonville
(27km)

Lapoinya Rd

Wellington Walks (p94) runs organized hikes on the mountain from easy to adventurous.

Some bus-tour companies include Mt Wellington in their itineraries (see p93); another option is the **Mt Wellington Shuttle Bus Service** (☎ 0408-341 804; per person return $25), departing the visitors centre at 10.15am and 1.30pm daily. City pick-ups by arrangement; call to book and confirm times.

Feeling more intrepid? Bomb down the slopes on a mountain bike with **Island Cycle Tours** (☎ 1300 880 334, 0418-234 181; www.islandcycle tours.com; tours incl hotel pick-up adult/child $75/70), which provides a van ride to the summit, followed by more than 21km of downhill cruising (mostly on sealed roads, but with off-road options). Tours depart at 9.30am and 1.30pm daily,

with a two-person minimum. There's also the option of combining the 9.30am bike descent with sea-kayaking around the Hobart waterfront; see p91.

Queen's Domain

When Hobart was settled, the leafy hill on the city's northern side was the Governor's private playground, which prevented housing being built. Today the hillock is called the Queen's Domain (Map p79) and is public parkland, strewn with cricket grounds, an athletics stadium, native grasslands and hilltop lookouts. Pedestrian overpasses on the western side provide easy access to North Hobart.

On the hill's eastern side is the small but beguiling **Royal Tasmanian Botanical Gardens**

DAVID BUTTON

David Button is a Hobart architect and all-round Tassie enthusiast, with a penchant for national parks, bushwalking and the good life.

Where can travellers see some well-preserved colonial architecture around Tassie? Tasmania has some of Australia's best early-colonial architecture. The standouts, of course, are Port Arthur (p127) and intact villages like Richmond (p109) in the south, Evandale (p225) in the north, and Ross (p156) in the Midlands.

In Hobart there's Battery Point (p85) and the Tasmanian Museum & Art Gallery (p87), which includes building fabric dating back to 1810 – one of the oldest surviving buildings in Tasmania. The Penitentiary Chapel Historic Site (p86) is a bit grim, but it's an intact remnant of early Hobart Town. Salamanca Pl (p84) is all 1840s and '50s sandstone warehouses that have taken on a new life now – full of restaurants, cafés, boutiques and bars. It's certainly not the hard-drinking place it was in the 1830s when Hobart was an international whaling port.

Your favourite Tasmanian national parks? I like the beaches on the east coast, especially around Freycinet Peninsula National Park (p175). It's accessible – an hour's walk up over the saddle to Wineglass Bay (p179). You don't have to stray very from your car and you're in another world. You can camp at the far end of Wineglass Bay too – about 20 minutes along the beach.

Maria Island National Park (p168) is great for camping, and there are a couple of mountains to climb, lovely beaches and some tranquil, isolated spots. Take a bike too, because there are plenty of gravel tracks and only two rangers' vehicles on the island. I've had some brilliant sunsets there, riding through large groups of kangaroos and wallabies grazing.

How about some short walks? It depends on your mode of transport. If you don't have a car, there are good places close to Hobart. You can walk from the city around Sullivan's Cove, through the docks, around Battery Point and down to Sandy Bay Beach. Otherwise, get a bus up to Fern Tree and explore Mt Wellington (p88). Make sure you've got warm clothing, water and food, and allow a day to make a good job of it.

You can catch a bus up to Mt Nelson and walk down Truganini Track through a valley of dry eucalypt forest. It feels like the Tasmanian bushland as it's always been: almost no signs of human habitation. The undergrowth is thick but the track is fairly clear. It brings you out onto the Channel Hwy at Taroona, from where you can catch a bus back to the city.

The Hartz Mountains National Park (p148) is a pleasant alpine walk in summer – you'll need transport to get there. As with everywhere in Tasmania above 1000m, take some warm and waterproof clothes with you. I went for a walk there last January (the hottest part of summer) and stepped into a blizzard and heavy snow cover. It happens often enough to always be prepared.

In the southeast there's a walk from Cockle Creek to South Cape Bay (p152). It's a two-and-a-bit hours' drive to Cockle Creek from Hobart, then a two-hour walk from there. It's a pretty easy walk – some of it along boardwalks – to one of the wildest ocean beaches in the world, with the huge Southern Ocean swell crashing in. If people want to get away from everything, all alone with just the huge surf on the edge of a primeval forest, it's a magic spot!

As related to author Charles Rawlings-Way

(Map p79; ☎ 6236 3076, tours 6236 3075; www.rtbg.gov .tas.au; Queens Domain; admission free, 1hr tours per person $5; ☙ 8am-6.30pm Oct-Mar, to 5.30pm Apr & Sep, to 5pm May-Aug, tours 11am Mon, Tue & Thu). Established in 1818, it features more than 6000 exotic and native plant species over 14 hectares. Explore the flora in detail at the **Botanical Discovery Centre** (admission free; ☙ 9am-5pm), which also houses a gift shop, kiosk and restaurant. Don't miss TV icon Peter Cundall's veggie patch!

Next door to the Botanical Gardens is palatial **Government House**, the state governor's digs. It's not open to the public and not visible from the road, but you can get a good view of the turrets and towers from high on Queen's Domain.

Bus 17 runs daily to the Botanical Gardens.

Mt Nelson

If Mt Wellington is cloud shrouded, the **Old Signal Station** atop Mt Nelson (Map p79), which is much lower, provides immaculate views over the city and Derwent estuary. When Port

Arthur was operating as a penal site, a series of semaphore stations were positioned atop hills to transmit messages across the colony. The one on Mt Nelson – established in 1811 – was the major link between Hobart and the rest of the colony.

There's a pretty good restaurant beside the signal station (see p104), and there are barbecues and picnic tables here too. To get here, drive up Davey St then take the Southern Outlet towards Kingston and turn left at the top of the hill. Local buses 57, 58 and 156–8 also come here. Alternatively, you can also walk to the top via the 90-minute return Truganini Track (opposite) which starts at Cartwright Reserve beside the Channel Hwy in Taroona.

ACTIVITIES

See also p56 for information on bushwalking, canoeing and rafting, caving, fishing, sailing, skiing, scuba diving and snorkelling around Hobart.

Cycling

A useful navigational tool is the *Hobart Bike Map* ($4 from the visitors centre and most bike shops), detailing cycle paths and road routes. Pick up a pair of wheels from any of the following.

Bike Hire Tasmania (Appleby Cycles; Map p82; ☎ 6234 4166, 0400-256 588; www.bikehiretasmania.com.au; 109 Elizabeth St; ☷ 8.30am-6pm Mon-Fri, 9am-4pm Sat) Quality mountain/road bikes from $35/45 per day.

Derwent Bike Hire (Map p82; ☎ 6260 4426, 0428-899 169, www.derwentbikehire.com; Regatta Grounds Cycleway; ☷ 10am-4pm Sat & Sun Sep-Nov, Apr & May, daily Dec-Mar) Mountain and touring bikes from $20/125 per day/week.

Island Cycle Tours (☎ 1300 880 334, 0418-234 181; www.islandcycletours.com) Organises a range of guided bike trips around the state, including the popular three-hour Mt Wellington Descent (see p89), seven days exploring the east coast or west coast ($2325 all inclusive), and a 13-day lap of the island ($4315). More affordable are its east coast Beachcomber tours: $495/650 per three/four days. You can also combine the Mt Wellington descent with a sea-kayaking experience around the Hobart docks (see right), or hire mountain or touring bikes from $30/160 per day/week.

Indoor Climbing

Climbing Edge (Map p82; ☎ 6234 3575; www.theclimbing edge.com.au; 54 Bathurst St; admission adult/child $14/10, shoe & harness hire $4; ☷ 10am-9.30pm Mon-Fri, to 5pm Sat & Sun) offers world-class climbing walls inside a converted warehouse. Don your nifty rubber shoes, chalk up your paws and up you go.

Sea-Kayaking

Kayaking around the docks in Hobart, particularly at twilight, is a lovely way to get a feel for the city. There are a couple of operators:

Blackaby's Sea-Kayaks & Tours (☎ 0418-124 072, 0438-671 508; www.blackabyseakayaks.com.au) Morning, afternoon and sunset paddles around the Hobart waterfront, running on demand; $50 per person. Ask about paddling adventures further afield (Port Arthur, Fortescue Bay, Gordon River).

Island Cycle Tours (☎ 1300 880 334, 0418-234 181; www.islandcycletours.com) Combines its Mt Wellington Descent (see p89) with a two-hour paddle around the docks after the cycle. The five-hour 'Pedal 'N' Paddle' outing costs $129/119 per adult/child, including a light meal. Departs 9.30am daily; not available July or August.

Swimming & Surfing

Hobart's city beaches look inviting, especially at Bellerive and Sandy Bay, but the water here tends to get a bit soupy. For a safe, clean swim, you'll be better off heading further south to Kingston, Blackmans Bay (p119) or Tinderbox (p120), or east to Seven Mile Beach (p118). The most reliable local surfing spots are Clifton Beach and Goats Beach en route to South Arm.

The **Hobart Aquatic Centre** (Map p80; ☎ 6222 6999; www.hobartcity.com.au; 1 Davies Ave; admission adult/child & concession $5.30/4; ☷ 6am-10pm Mon-Fri, 8am-6pm Sat & Sun) offers recreational moisture when it's raining outside. Inside are leisure pools and 'formal pools' (dressed in a tux?) for lap swimming etc. There's also a spa, sauna, steam room, aqua-aerobics and aerobics for land-lubbers.

WALKING TOUR

Old school versus New World – ready for a Hobart history lesson? Launch your expedition at **Franklin Square (1)**, where skaters collide with canoodling school kids beneath the bird-poo-stained statue of Governor Sir John Franklin. Track northeast down Macquarie St past the 1906 sandstone clock tower of the **General Post Office** (**2**; p84), the 1864 **Town Hall** (**3**; p87) and into the **Tasmanian Museum & Art Gallery** (**4**; p87). Soak up some culture for a while, or duck through the café, out into the courtyard and across the car park. Navigate across Campbell and Davey Sts and shuffle around **Victoria Dock (5)**, where the fishing boats bump and sway.

WALKING TOUR

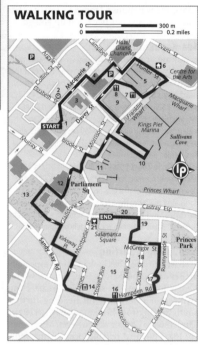

WALK FACTS

Start Franklin Sq
Finish Knopwood's Retreat
Distance 3km
Duration Three hours

Have a quick stickybeak at the renovated **Henry Jones Art Hotel** (6; p97). Formerly the IXL jam factory headed by the entrepreneurial Henry Jones (who did indeed excel), it was once Tasmania's largest private employer. Cross the swing bridge and fishtail towards **Mures** (7; p101) or **Flippers Fish Punt** (8; p101) for a sea-sourced lunch by **Constitution Dock** (9). This place is party central for yachties celebrating the finish of the famous Sydney to Hobart Yacht Race (p61) on New Year's Eve.

Next stop is the slickly reworked **Elizabeth St Pier** (10), jutting into Sullivans Cove – classy accommodation upstairs, restaurants and bars downstairs. If the tide is out, take the low-road steps around **Watermans Dock** (11). Cross Morrison St then wander through the acorn-infested Parliament Sq in front of **Parliament**

House (12; p86). Resist the photogenic façades of Salamanca Pl for now, turning right instead to detour through **St David's Park** (13), with its picturesque pergola, undulating lawns and walls of colonial gravestones. Hobart Town's original cemetery, it became an overgrown eyesore and was converted into a park in 1926. Cut through Salamanca Mews, jag right onto Gladstone St, left onto Kirksway Pl then right onto Montpellier Retreat, arcing uphill towards the colonial delights of **Narryna Heritage Museum** (14; p87), built in 1836.

Hampden Rd leads you into the heart of **Battery Point** (15; p85), Hobart's oldest 'hood. Reconstitute with a coffee and croissant at **Jackman & McRoss** (16; p103), then turn left into Runnymede St to check out **Arthur Circus (17)**, an improbably quaint roundabout lined with eave-free Georgian cottages. After a play on the swings, continue down Runnymede St and turn left into McGregor St, casting an eye up well-preserved **South St (18)** – take away the BMWs and power lines and this could easily be 1856! Turn right onto Kelly St and bumble down **Kellys Steps (19)**, an 1839 sandstone link between Battery Point and the redeveloped warehouses of **Salamanca Place (20**; p84). Not far along is Hobart's best pub, **Knopwood's Retreat (21**; p105). Settle into a couple of quite Cascades and regale the locals with tall tales of your adventures.

HOBART FOR CHILDREN

Parents won't break the bank keeping the troops entertained in Hobart. The free Friday-night music in the courtyard at the Salamanca Arts Centre (p106) is a family-friendly affair, while the street performers, buskers and visual smorgasbord of Saturday's Salamanca Market (p85) captivate kids of all ages. There's always something interesting going on around the waterfront – fishing boats chugging in and out of Victoria Dock, yachts tacking and jibing in Sullivans Cove – and you can feed the whole family on a budget at the floating fish punts (p101) on Constitution Dock.

Rainy-day attractions to satisfy your child (or inner child) include the Tasmanian Museum & Art Gallery (p87), the Maritime Museum of Tasmania (p87), the Cadbury Chocolate Factory (p88) and the Discovery Centre at the Royal Tasmanian Botanical Gardens (p89).

Hobart is a naturally active kinda town: take a boat cruise up or down the river; assail the heights of Mt Wellington or Mt Nelson; rent a bike and explore the cycling paths; pack the teens into the Kombi and go surfing at Clifton Beach. The minute you head out of town the child-friendly options increase, with an abundance of animal parks, beaches, caves, nature walks and mazes to explore; see the Around Hobart section (p100).

TOURS

Most cruises and bus and walking tours run daily during summer (December to February), but schedules and prices vary with the season and demand; call in advance to confirm.

Bus Tours

Bottom Bits Bus (☎ 1800 777 103, 6229 3540; www.bottombitsbus.com.au) Small-group, backpacker-oriented full-day trips from Hobart: Cradle Mountain, Wineglass Bay or Mt Field National Park. All trips $105.

Gray Line (☎ 6234 3336, 1300 858 687; www.grayline .com.au) City coach tours (from adult/child $39/20), plus longer tours to destinations including Mt Wellington ($42/21), Mt Field National Park ($99/50), Bruny Island ($155/110) and the Huon Valley ($163/109). Free hotel pick-ups.

Red Decker (☎ 6236 9116; www.reddecker.com.au) Commentated sightseeing on an old London double-decker bus. Buy a 20-stop, hop-on-hop-off pass (adult/child/concession $25/15/23), or do the tour as a 90-minute loop. Pay a bit more and add a Cascade Brewery tour ($44/25/42) or river cruise ($48/37/46) to the deal.

Tasman Island Cruises (☎ 6250 2200; www.tasman cruises.com.au; full-day tour adult/child $220/150) Take a bus to Port Arthur for a three-hour ecocruise around Tasman Island, then explore the Port Arthur Historic Site and bus it back to town. Includes morning tea, lunch and Port Arthur admission. Departs Hobart visitors centre at 8am; bookings required.

Tassielink (☎ 6230 8900, 1300 300 520; www .tassielink.com.au) Full-day trips to Lake St Clair (adult/child $75/38) and Freycinet National Park ($85/51), or a half-day trip to Huonville and Franklin ($16/8). Tours depart the terminal at 64 Brisbane St. See p338 for info on multiday Explorer Passes.

Cruises

Several boat-cruise companies operate from the Brooke St Pier and Watermans Dock area (Map p82), cruising around the harbour and up and down the river.

Captain Fell's Historic Ferries (☎ 6223 5893; www .captainfellshistoricferries.com.au) Good-value lunch (from $28 per adult) and dinner ($49) cruises on cute old ferries. It also runs coach or double-decker bus sightseeing trips

around town and to Mt Wellington, the Cadbury Chocolate Factory and Richmond.

Hobart Harbour Jet Boat (☎ 0404-078 687; www .hobartharbourjet.com.au) Water-taxi rides to Hobart locales (Moorilla, Bellerive, West Point Casino) from $10 per person, plus splashy hold-onto-your-lunch jet-boat river tours from adult/child $35/20.

Navigators (☎ 6223 1914; www.navigators.net.au) Slick ships sailing north to Moorilla Estate (adult/child $25/12), and south to Port Arthur ($149/110 including site entry and return coach trip), Tasman Island ($65/45) and the Iron Pot lighthouse ($35/18).

Peppermint Bay Cruise (☎ 1300 137 919; www .peppermintbay.com.au/cruises) A five-hour float down the D'Entrecasteaux Channel to the sassy Peppermint Bay development at Woodbridge (see p142). Prices start at adult/child $78/48 including lunch on board; cruise only from $48/28.

Wild Thing (☎ 6224 2021; www.wildthingadventures .com.au) A speedy red boat churning up the froth on tours around the Derwent (adult/child $24/15), Bruny Island (from $125/99), Cape Raoul ($125/99) and the Iron Pot lighthouse ($55/35).

Scenic Flights

Par Avion (☎ 6248 5390; www.paravion.com.au) Scenic flights into the southwest from Cambridge Aerodrome near Hobart Airport. A four-hour Southwest World Heritage Tour including a boat ride on Bathurst Harbour costs adult/child $180/144; an eight-hour Day In The Wilderness tour costs $290/236 including lunch and a visit to Port Davey.

Rotor-Lift Helicopters (☎ 6248 4117; www.rotorlift .com.au) Twenty-minute helicopter flights over Hobart and Mt Wellington for $150, or one-hour sightseeing over Hobart and the Tasman Peninsula for $395. Departing Hobart Airport.

Tasair (☎ 6248 5088; www.tasair.com.au) Thirty-minute flights over Hobart for $94 per person, plus longer flights to the Tasman Peninsula ($125), the east coast ($243) and the Southwest ($243). Departing Hobart Airport.

Walking Tours

Ghost Tours of Hobart & Battery Point (☎ 0439-335 696; www.ghosttoursofhobart.com.au) Walking tours oozing ectoplasmic tall tales departing The Bakehouse in Salamanca Sq at dusk. Bookings essential; $30 per person.

Hobart Historic Tours (☎ 6278 3338, 0429-843 150; www.hobarthistorictours.com.au) Highly informative walking tours of Hobart (10am) and historic Battery Point (3.30pm). Also available is an Old Hobart Pub Tour (5pm) taking in three waterfront watering holes, and a Polar Pathways Walk (10.30am Sat) exploring Hobart's Antarctic heritage. All tours cost adult/child/concession $28/12/25; winter hours vary. Bookings essential.

HOBART & AROUND

Louisa's Walk (☎ 6230 8233; www.livehistory.com
.au; 1½hr tour adult/family $25/60) Engaging tours of
Hobart's female convict heritage at the Female Factory
(p87), interpreted through 'strolling theatre'. Tours depart
Cascade Brewery at 10.30am and 2pm. Great feedback
from readers on this one.

Mt Wellington Walks (☎ 0439-551 197; www.mt
wellingtonwalks.com.au; half-/full-day walk adult
$120/69, child $99/59) Runs organised hikes on Hobart's
high hill, from easy to adventurous.

Penitentiary Chapel Ghost Tour (p86) Historic haunt-
ings at Hobart's old gaol.

Waterways Tours (☎ 6230 8233; www.welcome
tohobart.com.au; adult/concession/family $19/13/40;
⏱ 4.45pm Tue & Thu Jan-Feb, 4.45pm Thu Mar-Dec)
A subterranean tour of the Hobart Rivulet which sluices
along beneath the CBD. Tours depart the council offices
at 16 Elizabeth St, opposite the visitors centre. Bookings
essential.

FESTIVALS & EVENTS

Hobart hosts a cavalcade of festivals and
events throughout the year.

December–January
Falls Festival (www.fallsfestival.com) The Tasmanian
version of the Victorian New Year's Eve rock festival is a
winner! Three days of live Oz and international tunes (Paul
Kelly, John Butler Trio, Kings of Leon etc) at Marion Bay, an
hour south of Hobart.

Hobart Summer Festival (www.hobartsummerfestival
.com.au) Hobart's premier festival, focussed around the
waterfront: two weeks of theatre, kids' activities, concerts,
buskers, New Year's Eve shenanigans and The Taste (see
below).

Sydney to Hobart Yacht Race (p61; www.rolex
sydneyhobart.com) Yachts competing in this annual race
start arriving in Hobart around 29 December – just in time
for New Year's Eve! (Yachties sure can party…)

The Taste On either side of New Year's Eve, this
week-long harbourside event is a celebration of Tassie's
gastronomic prowess. The seafood, wines and cheeses are
predictably fabulous, or branch out into mushrooms, truffles and raspberries! Stalls are a who's who of the Hobart
restaurant scene.

February
Australian Wooden Boat Festival (www.australian
woodenboatfestival.com.au) Biennial event (odd-
numbered years) to coincide with the Royal Hobart
Regatta. The festival showcases Tasmania's boat-building
heritage and maritime traditions.

Royal Hobart Regatta (www.royalhobartregatta.com)
Three days of aquatic yacht-watching and mayhem on the
Derwent River.

March–April
Ten Days on the Island (www.tendaysontheisland.com)
Tasmania's premier cultural festival – a biennial event
(odd-numbered years, usually late March to early April),
celebrating island culture at statewide venues. Concerts,
exhibitions, dance, film, theatre and workshops.

Southern Roots (www.southernroots.com.au) A rootsy
music, food and wine festival in Hobart's Royal Tasmanian
Botanical Gardens, held annually over Easter. Artists like
Keith Urban, John Fogarty and Angus and Julia Stone have
graced the stage.

June
Antarctic Midwinter Festival (www.antarctic-tasmania
.info) Celebrate the winter solstice at this 10-day Hobart
festival, designed to highlight and celebrate Tasmania's
connection with the Antarctic.

October
Royal Hobart Show (www.hobartshowground.com.au)
Enduring rural-meets-urban festival showcasing the state's
primary industries. Showbags, hold-onto-your-lunch rides
and the fecund aromas of nature.

SLEEPING
The pumping-est areas to stay in Hobart are
the Sullivans Cove waterfront and Salamanca
Pl (and to a lesser extent Battery Point),
though prices here are usually sky-high and
vacancy rates low. The CBD has less atmosphere, but most of the backpacker hostels,
pubs with accommodation and midrange hotels are here. To the north of the city centre
are suburban North Hobart and New Town,
where apartments and B&Bs are within walking distance of the North Hobart restaurants.
Accommodation in waterside Sandy Bay is
surprisingly well priced, but it's a fair hike
from town (check that you won't be in for
a long walk). Most of Hobart's motels are
out of town along Brooker Ave heading into
the city from the north (those listed here are
closer in).

Despite Tassie's obvious suitability for
camping, there are no camp grounds within
walking distance of Hobart's city centre (now
there's a business opportunity!). Aside from
the options following under Around Hobart
(p100), there's also a campground at Seven
Mile Beach (p118).

Top-end Hobart accommodation can be
quite reasonable. If your budget stretches to
$200 you can afford something quite special:
designer hotels, historic guesthouses and
modern waterside apartments.

HOBART'S ANTARCTIC LINKS

Tasmania was the last chunk of Gondwanaland to break free from Antarctica, which is now about 2500km south of Hobart across the Southern Ocean. Hobart is arguably the world's leading Antarctic gateway city, and has become a centre for Antarctic and Southern Ocean science: the Australian Antarctic Division has its headquarters at suburban Kingston (p119); the Commonwealth Scientific and Industrial Research Organisation (CSIRO) Division of Marine Research is in Battery Point; and the Institute of Antarctic & Southern Ocean Studies and the Antarctic Climate & Ecosystems Cooperative Research Centre reside on the University of Tasmania campus. Down on the waterfront, the Antarctic Division's garish orange research vessel *Aurora Australis* and the CSIRO's boats *Southern Surveyor* and *MV Franklin* often dock at Hobart's wharves, alongside international research ships.

Pick up a copy of the free *Polar Pathways* brochure from the Hobart visitors centre, which details the key Antarctic sites around town on walking and driving tours. If you're in Hobart in June, check out the 10-day **Antarctic Midwinter Festival** (www.antarctic-tasmania.info), which warms up winter visitors with celebrations highlighting Tasmania's Antarctic connections. Highlights include live music, ice carving and photographic displays, the huskie dog picnic, and cult screenings on the 21 June solstice in the **Longest Night Film Festival** (www.longestnightfilmfestival.com).

For a sense of Antarctic life, check out the climate-controlled Subantarctic Plant House at Hobart's Royal Tasmanian Botanical Gardens (p89), which re-creates the flora (and soundtrack!) of Tasmania's Macquarie Island, en route to Antarctica.

Like the rest of Tasmania, midrange accommodation here isn't exactly a bargain. If you're visiting in January, book as far in advance as humanly possible. Outside peak season and holidays, many plush hotels offer weekend accommodation/dinner deals and walk-in rates, while luxury B&Bs also slash prices.

City Centre

BUDGET

Transit Centre Backpackers (Map p80; ☎ 6231 2400; www.salamanca.com.au/backpackers; 199 Collins St; dm $21-23, tw/d $52/60; 🖳) The cheapest beds in town are at this functional hostel above the Redline Transit Centre. Rooms lead off a huge communal area, which is strewn with grungy couches, bookshelves and a kitchen. The vibe is inclusive and relaxed, with helpful owners and bathrooms cleaner than the dorms.

Hobart Hostel (Map p80; ☎ 6234 6122; www.hobart hostel.com; cnr Goulburn & Barrack Sts; dm $21-26, tw & d with/without bathroom $90/70; 🖳) In a former pub (the ever-rockin' Doghouse), Hobart Hostel offers clean, cheap but cram-'em-in dorms, with better value twins and doubles upstairs. Take up smoking on the tiny deck overlooking Hobart's city rooftops.

Welcome Stranger Hotel (Map p82; ☎ 6223 6655; www.welcomestrangerhotel.com.au; cnr Harrington & Davey Sts; dm/s/d $22/85/99) Only a discerning eye will appreciate the aesthetic qualities of this modern redbrick pub, but upstairs the decent pub rooms (all with en suite) and small backpackers section will appeal to your wallet. It's on a noisy intersection, but windows are double glazed. Downstairs is Hobart's best pool hall. Limited parking.

Narrara Backpackers (Map p80; ☎ 6231 3191; www.narrarabackpackers.com; 88 Goulburn St; dm/s/d/tw $23/60/69/81; 🖳) In a three-level townhouse on the city fringe, casual Narrara has some of the cheapest beds in town, but attracts mixed reports from readers. Travellers slump on couches in front of the TV, working through the pain of last night's efforts.

Pickled Frog (Map p80; ☎ 6234 7977; www.thepickled frog.com; 281 Liverpool St; dm $23-25, s/d & tw $60/65; 🖳) Not for the moderate or meek, this huge, ramshackle hostel fills an old pub on the CBD fringe with party vibes. Cheap beer, big-screen TVs, pool table, shaggy backpackers – you get the picture.

Central City Backpackers (Map p82; ☎ 6224 2404, 1800 811 507; www.centralcityhobart.com; 138 Collins St; dm $23-27, s/d $55/69; 🖳) Smack-bang in the middle of the city, this mazelike hostel has loads of communal space, a great kitchen, OK rooms, friendly staff and extras such as baggage storage and tour desk. Bathrooms a tad shabby; linen extra.

New Sydney Hotel (Map p82; ☎ 6234 4516; www.newsydneyhotel.com; 87 Bathurst St; dm $25) Casual, ebullient downtown pub with small, basic dorms upstairs. Good pub grub, and live music most nights (see p106) – don't expect a monastic retreat. Twelve beds, 12 beers on tap – coincidence?

Montgomery's Private Hotel & YHA (Map p82; ☎ 6231 2660; www.montgomerys.com.au; 9 Argyle St; dm $26-29, s & d with/without bathroom $113/90; 🖳) Attached to Montgomery's pub, this YHA offers clean, bright, secure accommodation right in the middle of town. Spread over three levels are dorms of all sizes, and nifty en suite singles and doubles. A solid, conservative option; family-sized rooms also available.

Waratah Hotel (Map p80; ☎ 6234 3685; www .thewaratah.com; 272 Murray St; s/d $70/90, extra person $40) Known as 'W Block' to truant students from the nearby college, the red-brick Waratah pub is short on charisma (nowhere near as pretty as its namesake native flower), but offers good-value beds a short walk from town. Pub meals downstairs, and a pool table or two.

Astor Private Hotel (Map p82; ☎ 6234 6611; www.astor privatehotel.com.au; 157 Macquarie St; s with/without bathroom $115/75, d $150/89, all incl breakfast) A rambling, downtown, 1920s charmer, the Astor retains much of its character: stained-glass windows, old furniture, ceiling roses and the irrepressible Tildy at the helm. Older-style rooms have shared facilities; newer en suite rooms top the price range. Strict 'No Bogans' policy!

MIDRANGE

Edinburgh Gallery (Map p80; ☎ 6224 9229; www .artaccom.com.au; 211 Macquarie St; s $85, d $125-205; 🖳) This funky, art-filled boutique hotel puts an eclectic stamp on an old Federation home, just to the west of the CBD. Some rooms share immaculate bathrooms, all have quirky, artsy décor (try for a veranda suite). Excellent winter reductions and help-yourself breakfast bar. Gay-friendly too.

Theatre Royal Hotel (Map p82; ☎ 6234 6925; 31 Campbell St; d with/without bathroom $120/100) Exit stage right for theatre-goers (it's right next door to the Theatre Royal), this gracious hotel has spotless rooms (all with TVs) leading off baby-blue corridors. Downstairs are two bars and a restaurant, attracting a yuppie slice of the Hobart social melee.

Harrington's 102 (Map p82; ☎ 6234 9277; www .harringtons102.com.au; 102 Harrington St; d incl breakfast $115-160, extra person $25) After the shock of the naff postmodern office façade subsides, you'll find the rooms here well equipped but a tad small. Still, the price is good given that continental breakfast is included and you're

within walking distance of everywhere. Good winter rates.

Hobart Midcity Hotel (Map p82; ☎ 6234 6333, 1800 030 966; www.hobartmidcity.com.au; cnr Elizabeth & Bathurst Sts; r $135-215) The Midcity strikes a chunky '70s pose, rising nondescriptly into the Hobart skyline. But forget aesthetics: the staff are great, the location is primo, there's 24-hour reception and an on-site restaurant and bar. A perfectly good all-rounder.

Mercure (Map p80; ☎ 6232 6225; www.mercure.com.au; 156 Bathurst St; d $144-244; 🖳) A fave with blow-in yachties, touring rock bands and business bods, the demure Mercure looks a bit 'prison block' but delivers 140 stylishly updated rooms right in the middle of town, each with a little semicircular balcony overlooking the rooftops.

Leisure Inn Hobart Macquarie (Map p82; ☎ 6234 4422; www.leisureinnhotels.com; 167 Macquarie St; d $155-210; 🖳) The architecture here is funky (c 1968), but the ongoing makeover shifts the interior design forward 40 years: coffee-and-cream colours, dark timber floors, flat-screen TVs and natty bathrooms. A great location too, close to the city and waterfront (views to either from most rooms). Internet deals sometimes include breakfast.

Grand Mercure Hadleys Hotel (Map p82; ☎ 6223 4355, 1800 131 689; www.accorhotels.com.au; 34 Murray St; d from $175; 🖳) This sumptuous place has clocked up more than 150 years of hospitality (and almost as many owners) in the heart of the CBD – ideal for meeting-plagued businesspeople. It's acquired plenty of modern embellishments since its colonial beginnings, including a restaurant and lobby bar.

TOP END

Quest Savoy (Map p82; ☎ 6220 2300; www.questapart ments.com.au; 38 Elizabeth St; r $165-250; 🖳 🖳) The Savoy offers super-duper modern studios – all with kitchenette and living/dining area – smack bang in the middle of downtown Hobart. If you're travel-weary, there's a therapeutic spa on site. Quest Waterfront (3 Brooke St) and Quest Trinity House (149 Brooker Ave, Glebe) offer similar rates.

Macquarie Manor (Map p82; ☎ 6224 4999, 1800 243 044; www.macmanor.com.au; 172 Macquarie St; r $200-300) Plush, high-ceilinged heritage rooms and cooked breakfast buffets are the order of the day at this central, well-groomed, Regency-style guesthouse. Enough chesterfields and mahogany writing desks to fill three gentlemen's clubs.

Waterfront & Salamanca Place

MIDRANGE

Customs House Hotel (Map p82; ☎ 6234 6645; www
.customshousehotel.com.au; 1 Murray St; d $125-160)
Renovated, stylish pub rooms (all with en
suite, some with harbour view) are upstairs at
this ever-popular harbourside watering hole,
dating from 1846. The location is magic, but
light sleepers should look elsewhere, especially later in the week when the live music
downstairs cranks up the decibels. Tasty pub
food too.

TOP END

Old Woolstore (Map p82; ☎ 6235 5355, 1800 814 676;
www.oldwoolstore.com.au; 1 Macquarie St; d from $190, apt
d from $215, extra person $35; 🖥) Oodles of parking and superfriendly staff are the first things
you'll notice at this large, lavish hotel/apart-
ment complex. You won't notice much wool
lying around – it hasn't been a wool store for
100 years. Spend up on a roomy apartment
(up to three bedrooms), with kitchen, laundry,
stereo and video.

   Somerset on the Pier (Map p82; ☎ 6220 6600, 1800
766 377; www.staysomerset.com.au; Elizabeth St Pier; apt
from $250; 🖥) In a definitively Hobart location
on the upper level of the Elizabeth Pier, this
stylin' complex offers luxurious apartments
with beaut harbour views and breezy, contemporary design. You'll pay more for a balcony,
but with these views, you won't need to do any
other sightseeing! Winter rates as low as $170.
The same management also runs Somerset on
Salamanca (8 Salamanca Pl).

   Henry Jones Art Hotel (Map p82; ☎ 6210 7700;
www.thehenryjones.com; 25 Hunter St; d $290-390, ste
$390-850; 🖥) Since opening in 2004, superswish
HJs has become a beacon of sophistication.
Absolute waterfront in a restored jam factory,
it oozes class but is far from intimidating (this
is Hobart after all, not Sydney). Modern art
enlivens the walls, while facilities and downstairs distractions (bar, restaurant, café) are
world class. The hotel also makes smart use
of recycled materials.

North & West Hobart

BUDGET

Adelphi Court YHA (Map p79; ☎ 6228 4829; www.yha
.com.au; 17 Stoke St, New Town; dm $24-27, d & tw with/
without bathroom from $75/60) Rooms here occupy
a spruced-up 1950s-style apartment block
built around a courtyard behind a Federation
manor. It's out of the way – 2.5km from the

city – but reasonably close to the North
Hobart strip. Limited reception hours; call
ahead. Take bus 15 or 16 from stop H in
Elizabeth St to stop 8, or any bus leaving stop
E to stop 13, which is close to Stoke St.

   Hobart Tower Motel (Map p79; ☎ 6228 0166; www.ho
barttower.com.au; 300 Park St, New Town; s/d/f from $68/78/96)
The Tower is close to busy Brooker Hwy and
more than a walk from town (the buses that
service Adelphi Court YHA stop nearby), but
the quieter rooms out the back are as good as
any Hobart motel. And what old-fashioned
prices! Management seems to enjoy lagging
behind the pace – they only recently took down
the sign out the front advertising 'Colour TV'.

   Waterfront Lodge (Map p79; ☎ 6228 4748; www
.waterfrontnewtownbay.com; 153 Risdon Rd, New Town; d $75-
115, extra person $15; 🖥) Overlooking the quasi-
industrial New Town Bay and the Cornelian
Bay Cemetery 5km north of the centre, this
funky renovated motel has spotless, modern
units, all with kitchenette. There's also a guest
kitchen. Great value if you don't mind the
outlook or the drive.

   Marquis of Hastings Hotel (Map p80; ☎ 6234 3541;
www.marquishotel.com.au; 209 Brisbane St, West Hobart; s/d
from $85/99, extra person $15) Ask for a water-view
room at the Marquis, another of Hobart's red-
brick '70s pubs with a conjoined motel wing
off to one side. It's a killer hike up vertiginous
Brisbane St, but you can recover with a schnit-
zel and a beer or three at the bar.

MIDRANGE

Grosvenor Court (Map p80; ☎ 6223 3422; www.grosve
norcourt.com.au; 42 Grosvenor St, Sandy Bay; d $130-145, q
$149-290; 🖥) Grosvenor Court is a strange mix
of good and evil: quiet street, obnoxious tiling;
lovely linen, ugly brickwork; exciting leather
lounge suites, weary kitchens. As is often the
case in Hobart (and indeed Tasmania), friendly
owners lessen any disappointment and make
things feel homy. Wireless internet access.

   Lodge on Elizabeth (Map p80; ☎ 6231 3830; www
.thelodge.com.au; 249 Elizabeth St, North Hobart; s/d incl breakfast from $140/160, self-contained cottage from $190; 🖥)
Built in 1829, this old-timer has been a school
house, a boarding house and a halfway house,
but now opens its doors as a value-for-money
guesthouse. Rooms are dotted with antiques
(not for the modernists); all have en suites. The
self-contained cottage overlooks the courtyard
out the back (two-night minimum).

   Graham Court Apartments (Map p79; ☎ 6278
1333, 1800 811 915; www.grahamcourt.com.au; 15 Pirie St,

New Town; d $145-170, extra person $25) Probably Hobart's best-value self-contained option, this block of 23 well-maintained apartments sits amid established gardens in the subdued northern suburbs. Units range from one to three bedrooms (décor from '70s to '90s), with a playground and cots, high chairs and babysitters on call. Wheelchair-accessible units available.

Elms of Hobart (Map p79; ☎ 6231 3277; www .theelmsofhobart.com; 452 Elizabeth St, North Hobart; d incl breakfast $160-230; 🖳) Built in 1917 for the Palfreymans, a haughty Hobart merchant family, this self-assured mansion features beaut gardens (perfect for sunny afternoon G&Ts), six luxurious rooms and cooked breakfasts. Pro: close to the North Hobart action. Con: no kids under 14.

Bay View Villas (Map p79; ☎ 6234 7611, 1800 061 505; www.bayviewvillas.com; 34 Poets Rd, West Hobart; d $169-265, extra adult/child $25/20; 🖳 🐾) Two kilometres up the steep West Hobart slopes from the city, this family-focussed option offers a games room, playground, indoor pool and spa. It looks a bit '80s externally, but the two- and three-bedroom units here are surprisingly hip. East-facing rooms have water views and are pricier (it's not really a bay, but 'Estuary View Villas' doesn't have quite the same ring to it).

TOP END

Corinda's Cottages (Map p80; ☎ 6234 1590; www .corindascottages.com.au; 17 Glebe St, Glebe; d incl breakfast $220-250) Gorgeous Corinda, a renovated Victorian mansion with meticulously maintained parterre gardens, sits high on the Glebe hillside a short (steep!) walk from town. Three self-contained cottages (garden, coach house or servants' quarters) provide contemporary comforts with none of the twee, olde-worlde guff so may Tasmanian accommodations wallow in. Breakfast is DIY gourmet (eggs, muffins, fresh coffee etc). Cheaper rates for longer stays. Outstanding.

Moorilla Estate Suites & Chalets (off Map p79; ☎ 6277 9900; www.moorilla.com.au; 655 Main Rd, Berriedale; d $350-395, extra person $40; 🖳) For a slice of luxury, rent a secluded chalet at Moorilla Estate (p88), 12km north of the city. These modern self-contained pavilions (one- and two-bedroom) are superbly equipped, featuring private balconies, wine cellars, river views and oh-so-discreet service. Over-14s only; wireless broadband.

Battery Point, Sandy Bay & South Hobart
BUDGET
Cascade Hotel & Holiday Apartments (Map p79; ☎ 6223 6385; www.view.com.au/cascadehotel; 22 Cascade Rd, South Hobart; s/d $70/85, extra person $15) Famed for its steaks, the Cascade pub is en route to Cascade Brewery (how handy), on a residential strip 2km from town (Cascade Rd is the continuation of Macquarie St). Behind the pub are four unassuming, self-contained brick units, with free guest laundry and bargain rates.

Shipwrights Arms Hotel (Map p80; ☎ 6223 5551; www.batterypoint.net/shippies; 29 Trumpeter St, Battery Point; d with bathroom $150, s/d without bathroom $75/80) Nested in the Battery Point backstreets, 'Shippies' is one of the best old pubs in town. Soak yourself in maritime heritage at the bar (you can almost taste the brine sheeting down from the sails), then retire to your clean, above-board berth upstairs. Great pub meals in the beer garden.

St Ives Motel (Map p80; ☎ 6224 1044; www.stives motel.com.au; 67 St Georges Tce, Battery Point; d $97-155) Within walking distance of Battery Point and the city is this reasonable option – a curvilicious '80s building with dozens of rooms, all with kitchens. The whole place was getting a makeover when we visited: expect prices to spike when the paint has dried.

MIDRANGE
Hugo's B&B (Map p79; ☎ 6225 1902; www.hugosbb.com .au; 22 Edith Ave, Sandy Bay; s/d incl breakfast from $90/110, extra adult/child $30/20) Down south in Sandy Bay is Hugo's, a modern, unobtrusive B&B with a one-bedroom and a two-bedroom unit, both with sensational Derwent River views. To get here take Regent St (which becomes Churchill Ave) off Davey St, then turn right onto Edith Ave after 2.5km.

Crawfords B&B (Map p79; ☎ 6225 3751; www .crawfordsbb.com; 178 Nelson Rd, Mt Nelson; s/d incl breakfast $100/130) Located on an elbow of Nelson Rd, winding up from Sandy Bay to Mt Nelson, Crawfords' is a homy self-contained unit under the owners' house. Great views and private garden, but beware: chintzy prints and wallpaper. Bus 58 stops nearby.

Battery Point Heritage B&B (Map p82; ☎ 6223 3124; www.batterypointbedandbreakfast.com; 74 Hampden Rd, Battery Point; d incl breakfast $100-165) 'Heritage' is indeed the most apt description for this one (much curlicue, floral print and twee twiddle-dee-dee), but the three rooms here come with hefty cooked breakfasts and rates as good as they get in this neck of the woods.

Blue Hills Motel (Map p80; ☎ 6223 1777, 1800 030 776; www.bluehills.bestwestern.com.au; 96a Sandy Bay Rd, Battery Point; d from $115) Before they painted this modern gem cream and blue, it was a stark and stunning white. There's just no accounting for taste. The same applies inside where it's all a bit 1994, but still, it's in a stellar location on the fringe of Battery Point, and B&B internet deals are solid value.

Prince of Wales Hotel (Map p82; ☎ 6223 6355; www .princeofwaleshotel.net.au; 55 Hampden Rd, Battery Point; r incl breakfast $120-140) A severe '60s glitch in Battery Point's urban planning (would Prince Chas approve?), the POW is nonetheless exquisitely located and offers cheery, spotlessly clean pub-style rooms, all with en suite. Off-street parking.

Mayfair Plaza Motel (Map p80; ☎ 6220 9900; www .mayfairplaza.com.au; 236 Sandy Bay Rd, Sandy Bay; r $120-150) The redevelopment of the Mayfair in the '90s sent Sandy Bay into an architectural tailspin, but if that doesn't bother you, these cavernous modern rooms are well located and pretty good value. There are lots of eating options in the 'hood, and plenty of parking.

Motel 429 (Map p79; ☎ 6225 2511; www.motel429 .com.au; 429 Sandy Bay Rd, Sandy Bay; d $120-160; 🖳) Not far from the casino, this motel's recent face-lift has tarted things up externally but fails to deliver inside, where the rooms remain shamelessly middle-aged. That said, the staff are friendly and everything's clean and shipshape. Deluxe rooms lift the bar a little.

Merre Be's (Map p80; ☎ 6224 2900; www.merrebes .com.au; 17 Gregory St, Sandy Bay; d incl breakfast from $120) On a quiet street close to the Sandy Bay shopping strip, this 1901 colonial house has been transformed into an upmarket B&B with large rooms (some with spa), and almost-as-large bathrooms. Colonial interiors are on the tasteful side of excessive; breakfast is a full buffet affair.

Mountain Lodge B&B (Map p89; ☎ 6239 1005; jfaircloth@bigpond.com; 9 Lapoinya Rd, Fern Tree; s/d incl breakfast $120/125) With one hectare of lovingly maintained mountain gardens and views to Bruny Island, this B&B is superclose to Mt Wellington's walking trails. To get here, head for Mt Wellington but go past the turn-off to the summit then turn left after the Fern Tree Tavern. A bottomless bottle of port eases the chill of altitude.

Battery Point Manor (Map p80; ☎ 6224 0888; www .batterypointmanor.com.au; 13-15 Cromwell St, Battery Point; s $135, d $155-195, incl breakfast) Absorb the magical river views from the outdoor terrace at this homely manor, built c 1834. There's a range of large rooms here, all with en suites, some with king-size beds, as well as a separate two-bedroom cottage.

Woolmers Inn (Map p80; ☎ 6223 7355, 1800 030 780; www.woolmersinn.com; 123-127 Sandy Bay Rd, Sandy Bay; d from $138) A solid choice not too far from the action, despite lashings of brown-brick colonial coach-house style. Spacious studio and two-bedroom units, all with kitchenette, cable TV and video. Some disable-access units too.

Avon Court Holiday Apartments (Map p82; ☎ 6223 4837, 1800 807 257; www.avoncourt.com.au; 4 Colville St, Battery Point; d $140-200, extra adult/child $40/20) Overlook the ugly nouveaux-sandstone exteriors and bland, motel-style interiors and you'll find yourself brilliantly poised in a spacious apartment, right in the heart of Battery Point. Larger apartments sleep up to six. Off-street parking a bonus.

Coopers Cottage (Map p82; ☎ 6224 0355; www .cooperscottage.com.au; 44a Hampden Rd, Battery Point; r $150, extra person $15) Nooked in behind an old-time Hampden Rd shopfront is this self-contained option, perfect for two or three, with extras such as video, CD player and washing machine. The Gods of Décor do not ordain the carpet... Reception is next door at the Village Store.

our pick Tree Tops Cascades (Map p79; ☎ 6223 2839; treetops@treetopscascades.com.au; 165 Strickland Ave, South Hobart; d $150-160, extra person $35) Book ahead for this superb three-bedroom house in an idyllic bush setting, 6km from town near Cascade Brewery. Built on 6 acres, there's a zoo-full of wildlife about: possums, bandicoots and tame kookaburras (which you can feed on the BBQ deck). Three bedrooms means lots of room for families and groups. Buses 46, 47 and 49 run here from bus stop M on Elizabeth St next to Franklin Sq.

Battery Point Boutique Accommodation (Map p82; ☎ 6224 2244; www.batterypointaccommodation.com.au; 27-29 Hampden Rd, Battery Point; d $165, extra person $35) Yet more colonial midrangery, this time in a block of four salmon-coloured serviced apartments (sleeping three, with full kitchens) in Battery Point's heart (somewhere near the left ventricle). Off-street parking a bonus. Direct inquiries to Unit 1.

TOP END

Battery Point Guest House (Map p82; ☎ 6224 2111; www.batterypointguesthouse.com.au; 7 McGregor St, Battery

Point; s/d incl breakfast from $155/190) Originally the coach house and stables for the nearby Lenna of Hobart (below), this stress-free guesthouse is a stone's throw from Salamanca Pl, but is hemmed in by a child-care centre and an apartment tower (no views). Fussless rooms come with cooked breakfast, with discounts on stays of three nights or more. Self-contained cottages also available.

Barton Cottage (Map p82; ☎ 6224 1606; www.barton cottage.com.au; 72 Hampden Rd, Battery Point; s/d incl breakfast from $155/190) In the midst of well-heeled Battery Point is the symmetrical, double-storey Barton Cottage, a National Trust–listed building dating from 1837. Beyond a new red roof and wrought-iron veranda trimmings are six well-appointed rooms, run by the same folks as Battery Point Guest House (p99).

Colville Cottage (Map p82; ☎ 6223 6968; www.colville cottage.com.au; 32 Mona St, Battery Point; s/d incl breakfast from $165/210) An enduring, endearing B&B in Battery Point, where you can peruse the cultured cottage gardens from a shady veranda. There's a welcoming, elegant interior, full of colonial heritage but without the clutter.

Amberley House (Map p80; ☎ 6225 1005; www.amber leyhouse.com.au; 391 Sandy Bay Rd, Sandy Bay; d $180-240) An elegant, high-ceilinged 1890s mansion, Amberley is a top-quality guesthouse with young owners. The rooms have benefited from a face-lift, which has seen the introduction of soothing neutral colours and choice pieces of furniture. Too far from town to walk, but off-street parking is available.

Lenna of Hobart (Map p82; ☎ 6232 3900, 1800 030 633; www.lenna.com.au; 20 Runnymede St, Battery Point; r & ste $205-295) Knocked into shape in 1874, this grand Italianate mansion squats on a bluff above Salamanca Pl amid manicured gardens. The newer concrete wing houses the accommodation – rooms are large and the facilities first class, but the décor is looking dated. More up-to-speed are the apartments at Salamanca Terraces (93 Salamanca Pl), managed through Lenna.

Around Hobart
BUDGET

Elwick Cabin & Tourist Park (Map p79; ☎ 6272 7115; www.islandcabins.com.au; 19 Goodwood Rd, Glenorchy; unpowered/powered sites $20/30, cabins $90-115, 3-bedroom house per d $130) The nearest camping area to town (about 8km north of the centre), with a range of cabins but limited powered sites (book ahead). The three-bedroom houses

sleep eight (extra adult/child $25/20). Tight security and roaming bull mastiff.

Barilla Holiday Park (off Map p79; ☎ 6248 5453; 1800 465 453; www.barilla.com.au; 75 Richmond Rd, Cambridge; unpowered/powered sites $26/28, cabins $85-160; 🖵 🐕) A decent option for those with wheels, Barilla is midway between Hobart (12km) and Richmond (14km), close to the airport and some great wineries. The river-plains grounds are dotted with well-kept cabins, plus minigolf and an on-site restaurant serving wood-fired pizzas.

Cosy Cabins Mornington Park (off Map p79; ☎ 6211 4811; www.cosycabins.com.au; 346 Cambridge Rd, Mornington; cabins from $99; 🐕) Family-friendly cabin park out in the 'burbs (the first suburb you reach approaching the city from the airport). No camping sites, but a passable mishmash of cabins, barbecues, playground and trampoline.

EATING

Downtown Hobart proffers some classy brunch and lunch venues, but when the sun sinks behind the mountain, the city streets are overrun with 'bogans' (Hobart's version of standard, low-IQ, pugilistic hoons), stuck on an endless petrol-wasting loop of the city block – head for the harbour or North Hobart without delay!

The waterfront streets, docks and piers are the collective epicentre of the city's culinary scene – quality seafood is everywhere you look. Salamanca Pl is an almost unbroken string of excellent cafés and restaurants, especially thronging during Saturday morning market festivities. Battery Point's Hampden Rd restaurants are always worth a look, while Elizabeth St in North Hobart has evolved into a diverse collection of cosmopolitan cafés, multicultural eateries and improving pubs. Pub meals citywide are dependable (if somewhat predictable), and are usually big enough to keep you walking for a week.

City Centre

La Cuisine (Map p82; ☎ 6231 1274; 85 Bathurst St; meals $5-8; ⏰ breakfast & lunch Mon-Fri) When La Cuisine opened its doors in the mid-'80s, no-one in Hobart had seen a croissant before. With Basque house cakes, stuffed sourdough rolls, juicy quiches and sensational salads, La Cuisine dragged the city out of the white-bread culinary quicksand. Also at 108 Collins St.

Undertone (Map p82; ☎ 6234 1033; 37a Elizabeth St; meals $5-10; ⏰ breakfast & lunch Mon-Sat) Dig it! Underground Undertone is a hip new record bar-café attracting wired-for-sound city workers and students looking for something different. The hip young staff make a mean coffee, and serve a small but tasty section of salads, frittatas, toasted sandwiches, rolls and gluten-free cakes.

Vanny's (Map p82; ☎ 6234 1457; 181 Liverpool St; meals $6-10; ⏱ lunch Mon-Fri, dinner Mon-Sat) Supermodest café-takeaway plating up cheap Cambodian-style curries and satays, including vegetarian options.

Criterion Street Café (Map p82; ☎ 6234 5858; 10 Criterion St; mains $8-15; ⏱ breakfast & lunch Mon-Sat) It's a short menu on a short street, but Criterion Street Café manages to keep vegetarians happy (try the pan-fried polenta with mushrooms and spinach) and caffeine fiends buzzing. Be seen on the sidewalk tables.

Nourish (Map p82; ☎ 6234 5674; 129 Elizabeth St; meals $8-15; ⏱ breakfast & lunch Mon-Sat, dinner Thu & Fri) Don't eat wheat? Dairy scary? Nourish is a god-sent café for the allergic and intolerant, serving curries, salads, stir-fries, risottos and burgers – all gluten-free, and mostly dairy-free too. Vegetarians and vegans also catered for.

Kafe Kara (Map p82; ☎ 6231 2332; 119 Liverpool St; mains $10-18; ⏱ lunch & dinner Mon-Sat) A pioneering Hobart café with a loyal following, offering early breakfasts and all-day eating in its stylish *looong* room. There'd be a riot if it ever took the chicken salad off the menu. If it does, order a *panini*, pasta or risotto.

Sirens (Map p82; ☎ 6234 2634; 6 Victoria St; mains $18-20; ⏱ dinner Mon-Sat) Sirens serves up creative vegetarian and vegan food in a warm, welcoming space, offset by excellent service and impeccable ethics. But it's not all earnest long-hairs stirring lentils – there's some sophisticated cooking going on in the kitchen! Try the three-cheese beetroot ravioli in champagne, dill and pink peppercorn cream.

The most central self-catering option is **City Supermarket** (Map p82; ☎ 6234 4003; 148 Liverpool St; ⏱ 8am-7pm Mon-Fri, 9am-5pm Sat, noon-5pm Sun).

See also New Sydney Hotel (p95).

Waterfront & Salamanca Place

Salamanca Bakehouse (p82; ☎ 6224 6300; 5 Salamanca Sq; items $3-8; ⏱ 24hr) Gone are the days of nothing-open-past-10pm in Hobart – the Salamanca Bakehouse is open 24/7! Pies, pastries and rolls to soak up the beer and build a better tomorrow for nocturnal drinkers.

Sticky Fingers (p82; ☎ 6223 1077; Murray St Pier; snacks $5-10; ⏱ 11am-10pm) Upbeat, kid-friendly place

for a pit stop, full of sweet treats like sundaes, smoothies, cakes, crepes and vats of ice cream and *gelati*.

Flippers Fish Punt (Map p82; ☎ 6234 3101; Constitution Dock; meals $5-12; ⏱ lunch & dinner) With its voluptuous fish-shaped profile and alluring sea-blue paint job, floating Flippers is a Hobart institution. Not to mention the awesome fish and chips! Fillets of flathead and curls of calamari – straight from the deep blue sea and into the deep fryer.

Retro Café (Map p82; ☎ 6223 3073; 31 Salamanca Pl; mains $6-18; ⏱ breakfast & lunch) So popular it hurts, funky Retro is ground zero for Saturday brunch among the market stalls. Masterful breakfasts, bagels, salads and burgers interweave with laughing staff, chilled-out jazz and the whir and bang of the coffee machine. A classic Hobart café.

Mures (Map p82; ☎ 6231 2121; www.mures.com.au; Victoria Dock; ⏱ lunch & dinner) Mures and Hobart seafood are synonymous. On the ground level you will find a fishmonger (selling the Mures fleet's daily catch), a sushi bar, ice-cream parlour and the hectic, family-focussed bistro Lower Deck (mains $7 to $13), serving meals for the masses (fish and chips, salmon burgers, crumbed scallops). The Upper Deck (mains $20 to $28) is a sassier affair, where patrons can take in silvery dockside views and à la carte seafood dishes.

Zum Salamanca (p82; ☎ 6223 2323; 29 Salamanca Pl; meals $7-15; ⏱ breakfast & lunch daily, dinner Wed-Sat) A long, lantern-lit space receding to a courtyard where metrosexual young staff serve heart-starting breakfasts (muffins, ricotta hotcakes, egg-and-bacon *panini*), moving on to risottos, pastas and pastries to plug stomach holes later in the day.

Vietnamese Kitchen (Map p82; ☎ 6223 2188; 61 Salamanca Pl; mains $8-14; ⏱ lunch & dinner) With slick waterfront eateries closing in on all sides, it's refreshing to discover this cheap, kitsch kitchen, with its glowing drinks fridge and plastic-coated photos of steaming soups and stir-fries. Eat in or takeaway.

Tricycle Café Bar (p82; ☎ 6223 7228; 71 Salamanca Pl; mains $8-16; ⏱ breakfast & lunch Mon-Sat) This newish, red-painted nook just near the Salamanca Arts Centre serves up a range of café classics (BLTs, toasties, free-range scrambled eggs, salads and Fair Trade coffee). Arty types sip wines by the glass from the mirror-backed bar and discuss budgets for upcoming productions.

Jam Packed (Map p82; ☎ 6231 3454; 27 Hunter St; mains $9-20; ✿ breakfast & lunch) Inside the redeveloped IXL Jam Factory atrium next to the Henry Jones Art Hotel, this café is jam-packed at breakfast time. If you're sporting a hangover of some description, the BLT is the perfect reintroduction to life, while the prawn *puttanesca* spaghetti, simmered in olive, tomato and caper sauce, makes a filling lunch.

Sugo (Map p82; ☎ 6224 5690; 9 Salamanca Sq; mains $10-16; ✿ breakfast & lunch) Tomato-red walls, serious coffee and a menu heavy with Italian influences (pasta, pizza, risotto, *panini*) make this a *perfetto* café choice. Kudos to the semi-dried tomato and mozzarella scrambled eggs on cornbread ($12). Oz wines by the glass or bottle.

Machine Laundry Café (Map p82; ☎ 6224 9922; 12 Salamanca Sq; mains $10-17; ✿ breakfast & lunch) Hypnotise yourself watching the tumble dryers spin at this bright, retro-style café, where you can wash your dirty clothes while discreetly adding fresh juice, soup or coffee stains to your clean ones. Five dollars per load.

Fish Frenzy (Map p82; ☎ 6231 2134; Elizabeth St Pier; meals $10-25; ✿ lunch & dinner) A casual, waterside fish nook, perennially overflowing with fish fiends and brimming with deliciously prepared fish and chips, fishy salads (spicy calamari, smoked salmon and brie) and fish burgers. The eponymous 'Fish Frenzy' ($15) delivers a little bit of everything. No bookings.

Saffron (p82; ☎ 6231 4150; 15 Hunter St; mains $13-21; ✿ lunch & dinner) Festooned with subcontinental paraphernalia, Saffron slides back the windows on summer nights so curry-munchers can enjoy the warm airs and Victoria Dock views. The prawn vindaloo will knock your little cottons socks off.

Sals on the Square (Map p82; ☎ 6224 3667; 55 Salamanca Pl; mains $15-28; ✿ breakfast & lunch & dinner) Is it a bar? Is it a café? Is it a food court with occasional live music? Sals somehow manages to be all of the above. Walk past the Salamanca Pl takeaway counter into the wider café-bar fronting Salamanca Sq, where pastas, risottos, steaks, burgers and salads rule the roost.

Mezethes (p82; ☎ 6224 4601; Salamanca Sq; mains $17-28; ✿ breakfast, lunch & dinner) Tried and true Greek dishes and Adonis-like staff come together perfectly at Mezethes. All the classics (moussaka, souvlaki, lamb, fish, *saganaki*, baklava) plus, in true Hellenic style, a dazzling array of starters. The entrée platter ($23 for two) is hard to beat.

Ball & Chain Grill (p82; ☎ 6223 2655; 87 Salamanca Pl; mains $22-42; ✿ lunch Mon-Fri, dinner nightly) This carnivorous cave has been here so long, it's almost convict-era. Predictable, yes, but when you're onto a good thing, stick with it: steaks, grilled game, chicken and seafood with perfectly paired wines.

Catch (p82; ☎ 6234 3490; 11 Morrison St; mains $23-30; ✿ lunch & dinner) Inside the flamboyantly renovated City Mill (cast-iron columns, white-painted timber, black-and-white stripy chairs) is this sharp but relaxed eatery, serving up (you guessed it) seafood, straight from the deep blue sea to you and me. Top service, interstate chefs.

Henry's Harbourside (p82; ☎ 6210 7700; 25 Hunter St; lunch $16-19, dinner $23-35; ✿ breakfast, lunch & dinner) Inside the schmick Henry Jones Art Hotel is this better-than-most lobby eatery. Breakfast is pricey (up to $22); lunch is better value (salads, oysters, fish, vegetarian lasagne); dinner sees prices escalate again, but the food is high-quality stuff. Aim for an atrium table.

Maldini (p82; ☎ 6223 4460; 47 Salamanca Pl; mains $24-34; ✿ breakfast, lunch & dinner) Midrange Italian joint trying to climb the culinary rungs, with essential pasta and risotto dishes plus mains like Sicilian fish stew, osso bucco and baked calamari. Tiramisu and grappa to polish the palate and close out the night.

Marque IV (Map p82; ☎ 6224 4428; Elizabeth St Pier; mains $35-40; ✿ lunch Mon-Fri, dinner Mon-Sat) High-class dining hits waterfront Hobart at Marque IV, a discrete food room halfway along Elizabeth St Pier. You could start with an 'amuse' but, at these prices, it doesn't pay to dally. Begin with a *carpaccio* of cured Marrawah beef on a warm *nicoise* salad, followed by caramelised pork belly with Granny Smith dumplings, walnuts and sage gnocchi. Desserts? Sensational. Wine list? Superb. Service and décor lag very slightly behind.

Gourmet self-caterers should head to Wursthaus (p107) for deli produce or the **Salamanca Fresh Fruit Market** (Map p82; ☎ 6223 2700; 41 Salamanca Pl; ✿ 7am-7pm) for fruit and groceries.

See also T-42° (p105).

North & West Hobart

Kaos Café (Map p80; ☎ 6231 5699; 237 Elizabeth St, North Hobart; mains $5-19; ✿ breakfast, lunch & dinner) A few blocks south of the main action, this laid-back, gay-friendly café busies itself with a tasty assortment of dishes (burgers, salads and risottos), serving until late (usually around 11.30pm). Soak@Kaos (p105) bar is next door.

Amulet (Map p80; ☎ 6234 8113; 333 Elizabeth St, North Hobart; lunch $10-16, dinner mains $22-26; ☺ lunch & dinner daily, brunch Sat & Sun) The stylishly understated Amulet serves innovative, well-priced food infused with a mindset of 'sustainability, seasonality and community'. For lunch, how about asparagus ravioli with lemon crème fraîche, or roast-capsicum soup with pickled eggplant? Dinner choices are just as appealing, and desserts are worth leaving room for.

Rain Check Lounge (Map p80; ☎ 6234 5975; 392 Elizabeth St, North Hobart; mains $12-27; ☺ breakfast & lunch Mon-Sun, dinner Wed-Sat) A slice of mainland urban cool (straight out of Fitzroy or Darlinghurst), Rain Check's cool Moroccan-styled room and sidewalk tables see punters sipping coffee, re-constituting over big breakfasts and convers-ing over impressive Mod Oz dinners.

our pick **Annapurna** (Map p80; ☎ 6236 9500; 305 Elizabeth St, North Hobart; mains $14-17; ☺ lunch & dinner) It seems like half of Hobart lists Annapurna as their favourite eatery (bookings advised). Northern and southern Indian options are served with absolute proficiency – the best Indian meal you'll have on the island, guar-anteed! The *masala dosa* (south Indian crepe filled with curried potato) is a crowd fa-vourite. BYO; takeaway available. Also at 93 Salamanca Pl.

Vanidol's (Map p80; ☎ 6234 9307; 353 Elizabeth St, North Hobart; mains $16-25; ☺ dinner Tue-Sun) A pio-neering North Hobart restaurant (both in location and cuisine), Vanidol's simple pur-ple walls belie a complex menu – a creative confluence of Asian-fusion dishes like beef and vegetables stir-fried in Thai green curry paste with Indian spices ($16). Oodles of veg-etarian options; BYO.

Casablanca (Map p80; ☎ 6234 9900; 213 Elizabeth St, North Hobart; mains $18-34; ☺ dinner Mon-Sat) Loads of Italian choices at this upmarket BYO with down-home quality. If you're after pizza, pasta, risotto, *scallopine* or *cotoletta*, you've come to the right place. Takeaway available. No sign of Humphrey Bogart.

Restaurant 373 (Map p80; ☎ 6231 9186; 373 Elizabeth St, North Hobart; mains $28-33; ☺ dinner Tue-Sat) Artsy, high-end eatery on the Elizabeth St strip in a lovely old shopfront with wide floorboards and splashes of dark red paint and white linen. The young owners give local produce a Mod Oz twist – try the Flinders Island wallaby fillet

with beetroot couscous and native pepper-berry sauce. Excellent service; brilliant wine list and desserts. One of Hobart's best.

Lebrina (Map p79; ☎ 6228 7775; 155 New Town Rd, New Town; mains $35-45; ☺ dinner Tue-Sat) Foodies effuse about Lebrina. Isolated in Hobart's north-ern reaches, it looks small and unremarkable from the outside, but inside it's sheer dining pleasure, from the décor to the service to the wine list – and of course the creative modern food. Bookings essential.

Self-caterers should find what they need at **Fresco Market** (Map p80; ☎ 6234 2710; 346 Elizabeth St, North Hobart; ☺ 8.30am-8pm) or **Woolworths Super-market** (Map p80; ☎ 6211 6911; 189 Campbell St, North Hobart; ☺ 8am-10pm).

See also Republic Bar & Café (p106) and Moorilla Estate (p88).

Battery Point, Sandy Bay & South Hobart

Jackman & McRoss (Map p82; ☎ 6223 3186; 57-59 Hampden Rd, Battery Point; meals $7-11; ☺ breakfast & lunch) Be sure to swing by this conversational, neigh-bourhood bakery-café, even if it's just to gawk at the display cabinet full of delectable pies, tarts, baguettes and pastries. Early-morning cake and coffee may evolve into quiche or soup for lunch. Staff stay cheery despite being run off their feet.

South Hobart Food Store (Map p79; ☎ 6224 6862; 356 Macquarie St, South Hobart; meals $7-14; ☺ breakfast & lunch) OK, so it's a little way out of the city cen-tre, but any trip to the Food Store will reward the intrepid traveller. It's an old shopfront café full of booths, bookish students, brunching friends and kids under the tables. A mod-rock soundtrack competes with the coffee machine, which runs at fever pitch.

Gilt (p80; ☎ 6224 0551; 231 Sandy Bay Rd, Sandy Bay; meals $8-16; ☺ breakfast & lunch daily, dinner Thu-Sat; ☐) Check your guilt at the door and rip into a big Gilt breakfast (a pancake stack or some 'eggus benedictus', perhaps), or graze over dips, tapas or more substantial salads, soups and wraps right through the day. Flamboyantly decorated, with a piano that gets a bashing on weekends. Free internet.

Fish Bar (p80; ☎ 6234 5691; 50 King St, Sandy Bay; meals $8-20; ☺ breakfast, lunch & dinner) A chipper fish-and-chipper, popular with locals for fresh (uncooked) seafood, plus a swathe of cooked fishy combos and subaquatic treats (Thai fish cakes, seafood curry, Cajun-style trevally). Oily-smelling air; worn timber booths.

Francisco's on Hampden (p82; ☎ 6224 7124; 60 Hampden Rd, Battery Point; tapas $9-11, mains $24-27; ☼ lunch Fri, dinner Tue-Sun) Upbeat, noisy tapas bar of the fertile Spanish persuasion, adorned with posters of toreadors and dusky dancing maidens. Try some snacky tapas slooshed down with rioja, or a larger meal (paella, seafood or meat platters) if you want a plate all to yourself.

Chon-Na-Kau Thai Restaurant (p80; ☎ 6223 3600; 50c King St, Sandy Bay; mains $12-17; ☼ lunch &, dinner) No-frills suburban Thai food room where you get what you pay for – Thai beef salad, green chicken curry etc. The food, surpassing; the décor, middling.

Magic Curries (p82; ☎ 6223 4500; 41 Hampden Rd, Battery Point; mains $13-22; ☼ dinner) The Indian cricket team eat here when they're in town, so the food gets the stamp of approval. Settle into a Kingfisher beer and contemplate an Indian fave (from mild to face-meltingly hot, depending on your mood). Ace vegetarian options; takeaway available.

Metz (p80; ☎ 6224 4444; 217 Sandy Bay Rd, Sandy Bay; mains $15-25; ☼ breakfast, lunch & diner) If you haven't been in Hobart for 10 years, you'll be forgiven for looking twice at superslick Metz, once a grungy student bar with rotten floorboards. Today it's an all-day café with a huge outdoor deck, transforming nightly into a bar (DJs Wednesday nights and Sunday afternoons). Less surprising is the menu: salads, pastas, wood-fired pizza, plus upmarket dinner mains.

Da Angelo (Map p82; ☎ 6223 7011; 47 Hampden Rd, Battery Point; mains $17-27; ☼ dinner) An enduring (and endearing) Italian *ristorante*, Da Angelo presents an impressively long menu of homemade pastas, veal and chicken dishes, calzone and pizza with 20 different toppings. Colosseum and Carlton Football Club team photos add authenticity. Takeaway and BYO.

Kelley's Seafood Restaurant (p82; ☎ 6224 7225; cnr James & Knopwood Sts, Battery Point; mains $26-43; ☼ lunch Thu-Fri, dinner Tue-Sat) A Hobart institution, Kelly's is hidden in a geranium-dappled, 1849 sailmaker's cottage in the Battery Point back streets. Creatures from the sea define the menu: try the chowder or the trademark Accidental Occy (tenderised and grilled octopus). Bookings advised.

Piccadilly (Map p82; ☎ 6224 9900; cnr Hampden Rd & Francis St, Battery Point; 4 courses with/without wine $125/80; ☼ dinner) Piccadilly is the latest incarnation of this corner cook-house – with a bit of luck

the French 'assiette' menu (meaning 'selection') will ensure longevity. Expect modern creations like handmade linguini with spanner crab, and caramelised tomato tart with crushed olives and fetta. Ramp it up to five courses if you're hungry.

Sandy Bay self-caterers should head to **Coles Supermarket** (Map p80; ☎ 6234 3291; 246 Sandy Bay Rd, Sandy Bay; ☼ 7am-midnight) or nearby **Woolworths Supermarket** (Map p80; ☎ 6211 6611; 57 King St, Sandy Bay; ☼ 7am-midnight). In South Hobart, the **Salad Bowl** (Map p79; ☎ 6223 7728; 362 Macquarie St, South Hobart; ☼ 7am-late) stocks picnic fodder, wine, cakes, fresh groceries and deli delights.

See also Shipwrights Arms Hotel (p98).

Around Hobart

Mount Nelson Signal Station Café Restaurant (Map p79; ☎ 6223 3407; 700 Nelson Rd, Mt Nelson; lunch $11-19, dinner $20-29; ☼ breakfast & lunch daily, dinner Fri & Sat) Try for a window table at this elegant restaurant with awesome D'Entrecasteaux views, inside Mt Nelson's historic signalman's house. On offer are morning and afternoon teas, lunches, and dinner later in the week (dinner bookings essential in winter). Try the Thai chicken curry or the signalman's beef and burgundy pie.

Beach House Café, Bar & Restaurant (Map p79; ☎ 6225 4644; 646 Sandy Bay Rd, Lower Sandy Bay; mains $12-28; ☼ breakfast & lunch daily, dinner Wed-Sat) A rockin' pub in the '70s, the Beach House is now a stylin' mod café, and the pride (rather than shame) of the snooty Lower Sandy Bay set. Wander along the beach before retiring for creative seafood and pasta, Tasmanian wines and good vegetarian options.

Cornelian Bay Boathouse (Map p79; ☎ 6228 9289; Queen's Walk, Cornelian Bay; lunch $13-26, dinner $25-30; ☼ lunch daily, dinner Mon-Sat) Hip, stylish restaurant-bar in a converted beach pavilion on shallow Cornelian Bay, 3km north of town. On the menu is contemporary cuisine starring quality local produce, with great service. Try the Boat House chowder followed by some crispy Szechwan pepper–spiced chicken.

Prosser's on the Beach (Map p79; ☎ 6225 2276; Beach Rd, Lower Sandy Bay; mains $27-30; ☼ lunch Fri, dinner Mon-Sat) A glass-fronted pavilion by the water on Sandy Bay Point, classy Prosser's is BIG on seafood: try a fresh cray and avocado cocktail with warm citrus dressing, or scallops with Huon Valley mushrooms, chives and lemon sauce. It's a taxi ride from town, but worth the trip. Bookings recommended.

DRINKING

Hobart's pretty young drinkers are 10,000 leagues removed from the rum-addled whalers of the past, but the general intentions remain true: drink a bit, relax a lot and maybe take someone home. Salamanca Pl and the waterfront host a slew of pubs and bars – outdoor imbibing on summer evenings; open fires in winter. North Hobart is another solid (or rather, liquid) option.

Knopwood's Retreat (Map p82; ☎ 6223 5808; 39 Salamanca Pl; ☽ 11am-late) Adhere to the 'when in Rome…' dictum and head for Knoppies, Hobart's best pub, which has been serving ales to seagoing types since the convict era. For most of the week it's a cosy watering hole with an open fire; on Friday nights the city workers swarm and the crowd spills across the street.

T-42° (Map p82; ☎ 6224 7742; Elizabeth St Pier; ☽ 9am-late) Waterfront T-42° makes a big splash with its food, but also draws late-week bar-flies with its minimalist interior, spinnaker-shaped bar, ambient tunes and Charlie, the quintessential Hobart barman. If you stay out late enough, it does breakfast too.

Quarry (Map p82; ☎ 6223 6552; 27 Salamanca Pl; ☽ 11am-late) Yet another slick Salamanca renovation yielding profits, this place lures swarms of sassy Hobart young 'uns, encircled by predatory, aging musos and bombastic businessmen itching their wedding rings. Great Mod Oz menu too (pan-fried haloumi salad; mussel linguini with tomato, fresh basil and chives).

Observatory (Map p82; ☎ 6223 1273; L1, Murray St Pier; ☽ 3pm-late Wed-Sun) The newest bar in town has them queuing at the gates (bouncers are picky – don't dress down). Sip a 'Big O' cocktail as you swan between loungy nooks and the raised VIP platform in a viewless corner of the room (you can pretend you're the Big Cheese, but this ain't the Big Apple…). DJs Friday and Saturday.

Bar Celona (Map p82; ☎ 6224 7557; 23 Salamanca Sq; ☽ 10am-late) The impressive renovation is almost irrelevant here, the main focus drifting between divorcees eyeing each other across the crowd and the effervescent staff, bubbly as champagne in tight yellow T-shirts. The tapas menu deserves scrutiny. DJs on Saturday nights.

IXL Long Bar (Map p82; ☎ 6210 7700; 25 Hunter St; ☽ 5pm-late) Prop yourself at the glowing bar at the Henry Jones Art Hotel (p97) and check out Hobart's fashionistas over cock-tails. If there are no spare stools at the not-so-long bar, flop onto the leather couches in the lobby.

Hope & Anchor Tavern (Map p82; ☎ 6236 9982; 65 Macquarie St; ☽ 11am-late) It wasn't *that* long ago that you wouldn't be caught dead in here (for fear of ending up that way), but these days it's an atmospheric place, cashing in on its 1807 origins. The downstairs bar has pool tables, lounges and regular acoustic acts; upstairs is an amazing, museumlike bar and dining room.

Lower House (Map p82; ☎ 6224 0067; basement, 9-11 Murray St; ☽ noon-late Mon-Sat) Across the road from Parliament House is this hip basement bar, keeping escapee MPs lubricated with top-shelf whiskies, cocktails and a massive wine list. Mature crowd; DJs once a month.

Lizbon (Map p80; ☎ 6234 9133; 217 Elizabeth St, North Hobart; ☽ 4pm-late Tue-Sat) A cool wine bar, Lizbon lures a late-20s crowd with excellent wines by the glass, antipasto platters, smooth tunes, a pool table and intimate nooks and crannies. Occasional live jazz.

Soak@Kaos (Map p80; ☎ 6231 5699; 237 Elizabeth St, North Hobart; ☽ 10am-2pm) Perfect for an intoxicating urban afternoon or evening, gay-friendly Soak is a cloistered little lounge bar attached to Kaos Café (p102). Consume burgers and cakes from the café alongside handsome cocktails, while listening to the resident DJ on Friday and Saturday nights.

See also the Shipwrights Arms Hotel (p98), New Sydney Hotel (p106) and Republic Bar & Café (p106).

ENTERTAINMENT
Nightclubs

It's gotta be said – no-one comes to Hobart for the clubs. Still, the action is here if you know where to look. Anyone wanting to tap into the gay and lesbian scene should head to Kaos Café (p102) or consult the Gay & Lesbian Travellers section in the Directory (p324).

Syrup (Map p82; ☎ 6224 8249; www.syrupclub.com; 39 Salamanca Pl; admission free-$12; ☽ 9pm-late Thu-Sat) Spreading syruplike over two floors above Knopwood's Retreat (left), this is an ace place for late-night drinks and DJs playing to the techno/house crowd.

Mobius (Map p82; ☎ 6224 4411; 7 Despard St; admission free-$10; ☽ 9pm-late Thu-Sat) A pumping, clubby dungeon behind the main waterfront area, Mobius (hey wasn't he the guy in *The Matrix*?) is a going concern. Breakbeats, hip-hop, drum and bass – the crowd gyrates in unison.

HOBART & AROUND

Halo (Map p82; ☎ 6234 6669; 37a Elizabeth St; admission $5-10; ☯ 10pm-late Wed-Sun) Hobart's best-credentialed club is Halo, which sees touring and local DJs spinning acid, hard trance, electro and hip-hop. Access is off Purdy's Mart.

Isobar (Map p82; ☎ 6231 6600; www.isobar.com.au; 11a Franklin Wharf; admission free Wed, $5/8 Fri/Sat; ☯ 10pm-5am Wed, Fri & Sat) Downstairs here is a slick bar (open 5pm Fridays, 7pm Saturdays), while Isobar itself – the club upstairs – plays commercial dance and blows hot and cold with the locals (most of whom seem to be there to pick up).

Live Music

Republic Bar & Café (Map p80; ☎ 6234 6954; www.republicbar.com; 299 Elizabeth St, North Hobart; ☯ 11am-late) The Republic is a raucous Art Deco pub hosting live music every night (often free entry). It's the number-one live-music pub in town, with an always-interesting line-up (Holly Throsby, Sarah Blasko) and an understandably loyal following. Some say the pub food is the best in Tasmania.

New Sydney Hotel (Map p82; ☎ 6234 4516; www.newsydneyhotel.com; 87 Bathurst St; ☯ noon-10pm Mon, to midnight Tue-Sat, 4-9pm Sun) Low-key folk, jazz, blues and comedy playing Tuesday to Sunday nights (usually free), with the occasional pub-rock outfit and end-of-week crowds adding a few decibels. Great pub food, plus budget accommodation upstairs (see p95).

Brisbane Hotel (Map p82; ☎ 6234 4920; 3 Brisbane St; ☯ noon-late) The bad old Brisbane has dragged itself up from the pit of old-man, sticky-carpet alcoholism to reinvent itself as a progressive live-music venue. This is where anyone doing anything original, offbeat or uncommercial gets stage time: punk, metal, hip-hop and singer-songwriters.

Irish Murphy's (Map p82; ☎ 6223 1119; www.irishmurphys.com.au; 21 Salamanca Pl; ☯ 11am-late) Pretty much what you'd expect from any out-of-the-box Irish pub: crowded, lively, affable and dripping with Guinness. Free live music of varying repute from Wednesday to Sunday nights; original acts Thursdays.

Other rowdy waterfront pub-rock options (both free) include the Art Deco **Telegraph Hotel** (Map p82; ☎ 6234 6254; 19 Morrison St; ☯ 11am-late) and the nearby Customs House Hotel (p97), where live music raises the rafters from Wednesday to Sunday nights. See also the Lark Distillery (p88).

FRIDAY NIGHT FANDANGO

Some of Hobart's best live music airs every Friday year-round from 5.30pm to 7.30pm at the Salamanca Arts Centre courtyard, just off Wooby's Lane. It's a free community event that started about eight years ago, with the adopted name 'Rektango', borrowed from a band that sometimes plays here. Acts vary from month to month – expect anything from African beats to rockabilly, folk or gypsy-Latino. Drinks essential (sangria in summer, mulled wine in winter); dancing optional.

CLASSICAL MUSIC

Federation Concert Hall (Map p82; ☎ 6235 3633, 1800 001 190; www.tso.com.au; 1 Davey St; ☯ box office 9am-5pm Mon-Fri) Welded to the Hotel Grand Chancellor, this concert hall resembles a huge aluminium can leaking insulation from gaps in the panelling. Inside, the Tasmanian Symphony Orchestra do what they do best (tickets from $51).

Cinema

State Cinema (Map p80; ☎ 6234 6318; www.statecinema.com.au; 375 Elizabeth St, North Hobart; tickets adult/concession $15/13; ☯ box office noon-10pm) Saved from the wrecking ball in the '90s, the State shows independent and art-house flicks from local and international film makers. There's a great café and bar on site (you can take your wine into the cinema).

Village Cinemas (Map p82; ☎ 6234 7288; www.villagecinemas.com.au; 181 Collins St; tickets adult/child/concession $15/11/12; ☯ box office 10am-10pm) An inner-city multiplex screening mainstream releases. Cheap-arse Tuesday tickets $9.

Theatre

Theatre Royal (Map p82; ☎ 6233 2299, 1800 650 277; www.theatreroyal.com.au; 29 Campbell St; shows $20-60; ☯ box office 10am-5pm) This venerable old stager is Australia's oldest continuously operating theatre, actors first cracking the boards back in 1837. Expect a range of music, ballet, theatre, opera and university revues. See p86 for backstage tour information.

Other thespian outlets:

Playhouse Theatre (Map p82; ☎ 6234 1536; www.playhouse.org.au; 106 Bathurst St; tickets from $20; ☯ box office 7-8.30pm performance nights) Home of the Hobart Repertory Theatre Society (musicals, Shakespeare, kids' plays).

Peacock Theatre (Map p82; ☎ 6234 8414; www
.salarts.org.au; 77 Salamanca Pl; ☽ box office 9am-6pm)
This intimate theatre is inside the Salamanca Arts Centre,
along with a handful of other small performance spaces.

SHOPPING

Shopping in Hobart tends to be a utilitarian and practical experience rather than frivolous or indulgent (particularly when it comes to fashion – it seems most people here dress in preparation for impromptu wilderness experiences), but speciality shops selling Tasmanian crafts and produce are definitely worthwhile. Head to Salamanca Pl for shops and galleries stocking Huon pine knick-knacks, hand-knitted beanies, local cheeses, sauces, jams, fudge and other assorted edibles. The hyperactive Salamanca Market (p85), held here every Saturday, overflows with gourmet Tasmanian produce and sassafras cheeseboards.

The CBD shopping area is the place for less specialised needs, extending west from Elizabeth St Mall through the inner-city arcades. On Elizabeth St between Melville and Bathurst Sts is a swathe of stores catering to the aforementioned outdoors types.

Antiques

Antique stores proliferate across the state, some selling little more than browse-worthy bric-a-brac, others specialising in well-aged articles of jewellery, artworks, furniture and colonial artefacts. This antique bounty echoes back to the settlers who migrated here from Europe in the 19th century, lugging their furniture with them.

There are a few good antique stores in the city centre and around the junction of Hampden Rd and Sandy Bay Rd in Battery Point. Pick up the free *Antique Shops of Hobart* and *Antiquarian & Secondhand Booksellers & Printsellers in Hobart* brochures from the visitors centre, detailing a few options. Our favourites:

Antiques Market (Map p82; ☎ 6234 4425; www
.theantiquesmarket.com.au; 125 Elizabeth St; ☽ 10am-
5.30pm Mon-Fri, to 4pm Sat, noon-3pm Sun)

Bathurst St Antique Centre (Map p82; ☎ 6236 9422;
www.antique-art.com.au; 128 Bathurst St; ☽ 10am-5pm
Mon-Fri, to 1pm Sat)

Food & Wine

Fine Tasmanian produce is available everywhere – barnstorm into the nearest supermarket for great cheeses, sauces and other assorted digestibles. Then hit Saturday morning's Salamanca Market (p85) and walk away with more oil, jams and fudge than you might have planned…

Other essential stops:

Tasmanian Wine Centre (Map p80; ☎ 6234 9995;
www.tasmanian-wine.com.au; 201 Collins St; ☽ 8am-
6pm Mon-Fri, 9.30am-5pm Sat) Stocks a hefty range of
Tassie wines; also organises shipping, winery tours and
educational tastings for groups.

Salmon Shop (Map p82; ☎ 6224 9025; www.tassal
.com.au; 2 Salamanca Sq; ☽ 10am-7pm Mon-Fri, 9am-
5pm Sat, 10am-4pm Sun) Tasmanian salmon in all shapes
and sizes – whole fish, steaks, smoked fillets, burgers,
kebabs – plus marinades and sauces.

Wursthaus (Map p82; ☎ 6224 0644; www.wursthaus
.com.au; 1 Montpelier Retreat, Battery Point; ☽ 8am-
6pm Mon-Fri, to 5pm Sat, 9.30am-4pm Sun) Fine-food
showcase off Salamanca Pl selling speciality smallgoods,
cheeses, breads, wines and pre-prepared meals.

Galleries

Pick up a copy of the *Gallery Guide* brochure from the visitors centre to guide you around Hobart's arty hot spots. Some of the best:

Art Mob (Map p82; ☎ 6236 9200; www.artmob.com
.au; 29 Hunter St; ☽ 10am-late) Gorgeous Aboriginal
fine arts.

Despard Gallery (Map p82; ☎ 6223 8266; www
.despard-gallery.com.au; 15 Castray Esplanade, Battery
Point; ☽ 11am-6pm Mon-Fri, noon-5pm Sat) Top-notch
contemporary Tasmanian arts.

Handmark Gallery (Map p82; ☎ 6223 7895; www
.handmarkgallery.com; 77 Salamanca Pl; ☽ 10am-6pm)
Exquisite local ceramics, glass, wood, jewellery and
textiles, plus paintings and sculpture.

Outdoor Clothing & Equipment

There's a plethora of stores on Elizabeth St catering to outdoorsy types in a state overflowing with national parks and wilderness. See p81 for info on where to buy topographic maps.

Kathmandu (Map p82; ☎ 6224 3027; www
.kathmandu.com.au; 16 Salamanca Sq; ☽ 9.30am-6pm
Mon-Fri, to 5pm Sat & Sun)

Mountain Designs (Map p82; ☎ 6234 3900; www
.mountaindesigns.com; 111 Elizabeth St; ☽ 9am-5.45pm
Mon-Sat, 10am-4pm Sat)

Snowgum (Map p82; ☎ 6231 0777; www.snowgum
.com.au; 119 Elizabeth St; ☽ 9am-5.30pm Mon-Fri,
10am-4.30pm Sat)

Spot On Fishing Tackle (Map p82; ☎ 6234 4880;
www.spotonfishing.com.au; 89-91 Harrington St,
☽ 9am-5.30pm Mon-Fri, to 3.45am Sat) Fishing supplies.

GETTING THERE & AWAY

Air

For information on domestic flights to/from Hobart, see p335.

Bus

There are two main intrastate bus companies operating to/from Hobart:

Redline Coaches (Map p80; ☎ 1300 360 000, 6336 1446; 199 Collins St; www.redlinecoaches.com.au) Operates from the Transit Centre.

Tassielink (Map p82; ☎ 1300 300 520, 6230 8900; 64 Brisbane St; www.tassielink.com.au) Operates from the Hobart Bus Terminal.

Additionally, **Hobart Coaches** (☎ 132 201; www.hobartcoaches.com.au) has regular services to/from Richmond, New Norfolk and Kingston, south along the D'Entrecasteaux Channel and to Cygnet. See those towns for specific timetable/fare info, check online or visit Metro Tasmania's Metro Shop (right) inside the General Post Office on the corner of Elizabeth and Macquarie Sts.

GETTING AROUND

To/From the Airport

Hobart Airport (☎ 6216 1600; www.hiapl.com.au) is at Cambridge, 16km east of town. The **Airporter Shuttle Bus** (☎ 0419-382 240; www.redlinecoaches.com.au/airporter/; 199 Collins St; one-way adult/concession & child $13/6) scoots between the Transit Centre and the airport (via various city pick-up points), connecting with all flights. Bookings essential.

A taxi between the airport and the city centre will cost around $33 between 6am and 8pm weekdays, $38 at other times.

Bicycle

See p91 for details of bike-rental places in Hobart.

Boat

There are plenty of Hobart river cruises (p93), but little by way of commuter ferries. Harking back to 1975 when the Tasman Bridge collapsed and everyone used ferries (the Derwent became a mini Sydney Harbour), Captain Fell's Historic Ferries (p93) runs a weekday service between Hobart and Bellerive, transporting eastern shore residents to/from work. The ferry departs Hobart's Franklin Wharf at 7.50am and 5.25pm; return boats are at 8.15am and 5.40pm. A one-way/return ticket is $4/8.

Bus

Metro Tasmania (☎ 13 22 01; www.metrotas.com.au) operates the local bus network, which is reliable but infrequent outside of business hours. The **Metro Shop** (Map p82; ☒ 8.30am-5.30pm Mon-Fri), inside the General Post Office on the corner of Elizabeth and Macquarie Sts, handles ticketing and enquiries. Most buses depart this section of Elizabeth St, or from nearby Franklin Sq.

One-way fares vary with distances ('sections') travelled (from $2 to $4.50). For $5 you can buy an unlimited-travel Day Rover ticket, valid after 9am Monday to Friday, and all day Saturday, Sunday and public holidays. Buy one-way tickets from the driver (exact change required) or ticket agents (newsagents and most post offices); day passes are only available from ticket agents. Alternatively, buy a book of 10 discounted tickets for use any time of day ($16 to $36, depending on sections).

Car

Timed, metered parking predominates in the CBD and tourist areas like Salamanca and the waterfront. For longer-term parking, large CBD garages (clearly signposted) offer inexpensive rates, often with the first hour for free.

The big-boy rental firms have airport desks and city offices as follows:

AutoRent-Hertz (Map p80; ☎ 6237 1111; www.autorent.com.au; cnr Bathurst & Harrington Sts)

Avis (Map p82; ☎ 6234 4222; www.avis.com.au; 125 Bathurst St)

Budget (Map p82; ☎ 6234 5222, 13 27 27; www.budget.com.au; 96 Harrington St)

Europcar (Map p80; ☎ 6231 1077, 1800 030 118; www.europcar.com.au; 112 Harrington St)

Thrifty (Map p82; ☎ 6234 1341, 1300 367 227; www.thrifty.com.au; 11-17 Argyle St)

Cheaper local firms offering daily rental rates from as low as $25 include the following.

Bargain Car Rentals (Map p80; ☎ 6234 6959, 1300 729 230; www.bargaincarrentals.com.au; 173 Harrington St)

Lo-Cost Auto Rent (Map p82; ☎ 6231 0550, 1800 647 060; www.locostautorent.com; 105 Murray St)

Rent-a-Bug (Map p82; ☎ 6231 0300, 1800 647 060; www.rentabug.com.au; 105 Murray St)

Rent For Less (Map p82; ☎ 6231 6844; www.rentforless.com.au; 92 Harrington St)

Selective Car Rentals (Map p82; ☎ 6234 3311, 1800 300 102; www.selectivecarrentals.com.au; 47 Bathurst St)

Taxi

You'll have no trouble hailing a cab in the busy, touristed areas. Fares are metered.

City Cabs (☎ 13 10 08)

Maxi-Taxi Services (☎ 6234 8061) Wheelchair-accessible vehicles.

Taxi Combined Services (☎ 13 22 27)

AROUND HOBART

You won't have to travel too far from Hobart to swap cityscapes for natural panoramas, sandy beaches and historic sites. Reminders of Tasmania's convict history await at Richmond, and the waterfalls, wildlife and fantastic short walks at Mt Field National Park make an easy day trip. New Norfolk is a curious place to visit, while Seven Mile Beach and the Channel Hwy towns are great for an estuarine escape.

See p93 for info on companies offering day trips out of Hobart.

RICHMOND & AROUND
☎ 03 / pop 750

Straddling the Coal River 27km northeast of Hobart, historic Richmond was once a strategic military post and convict station on the road to Port Arthur. Riddled with 19th-century buildings, it's arguably Tasmania's premier historic town, but like the Rocks in Sydney and Hahndorf in Adelaide, it's become a parody of itself with no actual 'life', just a parasitic tourist trade picking over the bones of the colonial past.

That said, Richmond is undeniably picturesque, and kids love chasing the ducks around the riverbanks. It's also quite close to the airport – a happy overnight option if you're on an early flight. There are no banks in town, but both main street supermarkets have ATMs.

See www.richmondvillage.com.au for more information.

Sights & Activities

The chunky but not inelegant **Richmond Bridge** (Wellington St) still funnels traffic across the Coal River, and is the town's proud centrepiece. Built by convicts in 1823 (making it the oldest road bridge in Australia), it's purportedly haunted by the 'Flagellator of Richmond', George Grover, who died here in 1832.

The northern wing of the remarkably well-preserved **Richmond Gaol** (☎ /fax 6260 2127; 37 Bathurst St; adult/child/family $7/3/18; ☺ 9am-5pm) was built in 1825, five years before the penitentiary at Port Arthur. Like Port Arthur, fascinating historic insights abound, but the mood is pretty grim.

Other interesting historic places include the 1836 **St John's Church** (Wellington St), the first Roman Catholic church in Australia; the 1834 **St Luke's Church of England** (Edward St); the 1825 **Courthouse** (Forth St); the 1826 **Old Post Office** (Bridge St); the 1888 **Richmond Arms Hotel** (Bridge St); and the 1830 **Prospect House** (Richmond Rd), a historic B&B just south of town.

Also here is the curious **Old Hobart Town Historic Model Village** (☎ 6260 2502; www.oldhobart town.com; 21a Bridge St; adult/family $10/25; ☺ 9am-5pm), a re-creation of Hobart Town in the 1820s built from the city's original plans.

Herd the kids into the wooden-walled **Richmond Maze** (☎ 6260 2451; 13 Bridge St; www.towns oftasmania.com/richmond/maze; adult/child/family $7/5/20; ☺ 9am-5pm). They'll be safe, as the resident Minotaur has taken long-service leave. There are also tea rooms here, serving breakfast, light lunches and the obligatory Devonshire tea.

Oak Lodge (☎ 6260 2761; www.nationaltrust.org.au; 18 Bridge St; admission by gold-coin donation; ☺ 11am-3.30pm), opposite the maze, is worth a sticky-beak. It's one of Richmond's oldest homes (c 1831), now owned by the National Trust and operated by the Coal River Historic Society. Inside is a museum and gallery offering an insight into colonial life.

Tours of Richmond (☎ 0409-935 139; www.toursof richmond.com) runs good-value 45-minute daytime walking tours (adult/child $10/5) and nocturnal ghost tours ($25/12.50). Minimum numbers apply; bookings essential.

COAL RIVER VALLEY VINEYARDS

Richmond is also the centre of Tasmania's fastest-growing wine region, the **Coal River Valley** (Map p110; www.coalrivervalley.com.au), with wineries popping up all over the place. Some are sophisticated affairs with gourmet restaurants; some are small vineyards, quietly making wine with cellar doors open by appointment. Some of our favourites:

Coal Valley Vineyard (☎ 6248 5367; www.coalvalley .com; 257 Richmond Rd, Cambridge; mains $16-28; ☺ 9am-4pm Thu-Sun) Sunny terracotta-tiled tasting room and excellent restaurant (open breakfast and lunch Thursday to Sunday). Pinot, riesling and tempranillo.

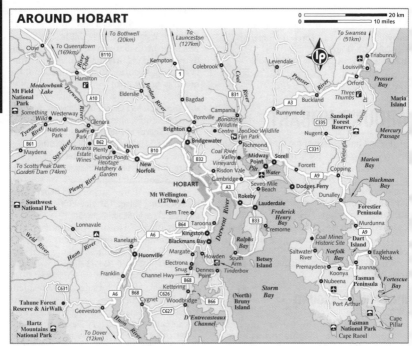

AROUND HOBART

Craigow Vineyard (☎ 6248 4210; www.craigow
.com.au; 528 Richmond Rd, Cambridge; ☺ 11am-5pm
Jan-Mar) Opposite Meadowbank, offering tastings in a
colonial cottage. Great whites: riesling, chardonnay and
sauvignon blanc.

Meadowbank Estate (☎ 6248 4484; www.meadow
bankwines.com.au; 699 Richmond Rd, Cambridge; mains
$15-25; ☺ 10am-5pm) Overlooking the Mt Pleasant
Observatory 9km southwest of Richmond. Acclaimed
restaurant serving lunch daily, plus art gallery and kids play
area. Don't miss *Flawed History*, an in-floor jigsaw by local
artist Tom Samek. Winning pinot gris, sauvignon blanc and
pinot noir.

Puddleduck Vineyard (☎ 6260 2301; www.puddle
duckvineyard.com.au; 992 Richmond Rd, Richmond;
☺ 10am-5pm) Small family-run vineyard producing just
1000 cases per year. Rosé, cabernet, chardonnay and 'Bub-
bleduck' sparkling white.

WILDLIFE PARKS

ZooDoo Wildlife Fun Park (Map p110; ☎ 6260 2444;
www.zoodoo.com.au; 620 Middle Tea Tree Rd; adult/child
$16/10; ☺ 9am-5pm), 6km west of Richmond on
the road to Brighton, has 'safari bus' rides,
playgrounds, picnic areas and enough captive
wildlife – from miniature horses to Tasmanian

devils, wallabies and a nursery farm – to keep
the kids engrossed.

Bonorong Wildlife Centre (Map p110; ☎ 6268
1184; www.bonorong.com.au; 593 Briggs Rd, Brighton;
adult/child $16/9; ☺ 9am-5pm) is about 17km west
of Richmond (or alternatively, signposted off
Hwy 1 at Brighton). 'Bonorong' derives from
an Aboriginal word meaning 'native companion' – there are plenty of those here (devils,
koalas, wombats, echidnas and quolls), fed
daily at 11.30am and 2pm. The emphasis here
is on conservation, education and the rehabilitation of injured animals.

Sleeping
BUDGET

Richmond Cabin & Tourist Park (☎ 6260 2192, 1800
116 699; www.richmondcabins.com; 48 Middle Tea Tree Rd;
unpowered/powered sites $18/24, cabins $60-110; ☎) Over
the back fence of Prospect House, this park
is 1km south of town but provides affordable accommodation in neat, no-frills cabins.
Kids will be happy with the indoor pool and
games room.

Richmond Arms Hotel (☎ 6260 2109; www.richmond
armshotel.com.au; 42 Bridge St; d from $99) Sneaking

into the budget category by $1, the grand old Richmond pub has four good-quality motel-style units in the adjacent former stables. Plans for developing more accommodation are afoot.

MIDRANGE

Richmond Cottages (☎ 6260 2561; www.richmond cottages.com; 12 Bridge St; d $125-165, extra adult/child $30/15) Just can't get enough colonial accommodation? On offer here are two self-contained abodes: Ivy Cottage, a family-friendly, three-bedroom home (complete with claw-foot bath), and behind it The Stables, a rustic one-bedroom cottage with spa. Breakfast provisions provided.

Laurel Cottage (☎ 6260 2397; www.view.com .au/laurel; 9 Wellington St; d $130, extra adult/child $25/18) Ramshackle, two-bedroom convict-brick cottage beside the bridge, with a wood fire. Self-catering kitchen; breakfast provisions supplied. Kids welcome.

Geraldine Cottage (☎ 6260 2397; www.view.com .au/geraldine; 12 Parramore St; d $130-150, extra adult/child $30/25) Run by the same folks as Laurel Cottage (and with similar rates), Geraldine – a former

schoolhouse – is a bit bigger, a bit more refined and a bit newer (yeah, like 1839 is new). More flowers in the garden than a bee could ever service.

Mrs Currie's House (☎ 6260 2766; www.mrscurries house.com.au; 4 Franklin St; d incl breakfast $140, extra person $35) The oldest part of this accommodation was once the Prince of Wales Inn, a rammed-earth structure dating from the 1820s. On offer are four tastefully furnished rooms, plus cooked breakfasts, open fires and snooker-table-flat lawns. Mrs Currie lived here for 80 years last century.

Daisy Bank Cottages (☎ 6260 2390; www.daisybank cottages.com; Daisy Bank, off Middle Tea Tree Rd; d incl breakfast $140-150) This place is a rural delight: two spotless, self-contained units (one with spa) in a converted 1840s sandstone barn. There are loft bedrooms, views of the Richmond rooftops and plenty of farmy distractions for the kids.

Richmond Colonial Accommodation (☎ 6260 2570; www.richmondcolonial.com; 4 Percy St; d $140-160, extra adult/child $30/15) Manages three (Willow, Bridge and Poplar) well-equipped, family-friendly historic cottages around town.

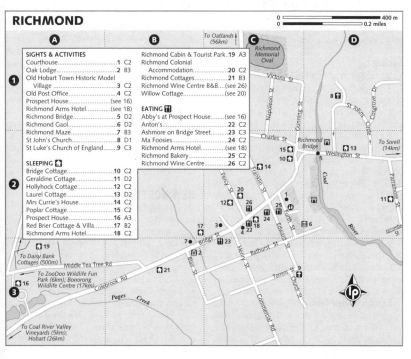

RICHMOND

0 —— 400 m
0 —— 0.2 miles

SIGHTS & ACTIVITIES
Courthouse...................................1 C2
Oak Lodge.....................................2 B3
Old Hobart Town Historic Model
  Village......................................3 C2
Old Post Office.............................4 C2
Prospect House.....................(see 16)
Richmond Arms Hotel............(see 18)
Richmond Bridge.........................5 D2
Richmond Gaol.............................6 D2
Richmond Maze............................7 B3
St John's Church...........................8 D1
St Luke's Church of England........9 C3

SLEEPING
Bridge Cottage...........................10 C2
Geraldine Cottage.......................11 D2
Hollyhock Cottage......................12 C2
Laurel Cottage............................13 D2
Mrs Currie's House.....................14 C2
Poplar Cottage............................15 C2
Prospect House...........................16 A3
Red Brier Cottage & Villa..........17 B2
Richmond Arms Hotel................18 C2

Richmond Cabin & Tourist Park..19 A3
Richmond Colonial
  Accommodation.......................20 C2
Richmond Cottages....................21 B3
Richmond Wine Centre B&B...(see 26)
Willow Cottage....................(see 20)

EATING
Abby's at Prospect House........(see 16)
Anton's.......................................22 C2
Ashmore on Bridge Street..........23 C3
Ma Foosies.................................24 C2
Richmond Arms Hotel.............(see 18)
Richmond Bakery.......................25 C2
Richmond Wine Centre.............26 C2

To Oatlands
(56km)

Richmond
Memorial
Oval

Victoria St
Napoleon St
Cumming St
St Johns Circle
Cosgrove St

Charles St
Richmond
Bridge
To Sorell
(14km)
Wellington St

Percy St
Franklin St
Edward St
Coal St
River
Parramore St
Jacombe St

Bridge St
Henry St
Bathurst St
Blair St

Middle Tea Tree Rd
To Daisy Bank
Cottages (500m)

To ZooDoo Wildlife Fun
Park (6km); Bonorong
Wildlife Centre (17km)
Colebrook Rd

Pages Creek

Torrens St
Church St
Commercial Rd

To Coal River Valley
Vineyards (5km);
Hobart (26km)

All are self-contained with a roll-call of colonial touches.

Hollyhock Cottage (☎ 6260 1079; www.hollyhock cottage.com.au; 3 Percy St; d $160) Hollyhock is a cutesy National Trust–listed brick-and-timber cottage off the main street, renovated using original materials, with a few modern indulgences like a double spa. Breakfast provisions supplied. Mind your head on the convict-height doors.

Prospect House (☎ 6260 2207; www.prospect-house .com.au; 1384 Richmond Rd; d $160-180; 🖳) About 1km west of Richmond is this haughty Georgian mansion, built in 1830, offering heritage-style guest rooms in converted outbuildings. The grounds evoke an old-money rural splendour, and there's an upmarket restaurant here too (see right). Dinner, bed and breakfast costs $249 for two.

TOP END

Red Brier Cottage & Villa (☎ 6260 2349; www.redbrier cottage.com.au; 15 Bridge St; d cottage/villa $140/200, extra person $50) There are two mod accommodation styles on offer here: an intimate, fully equipped cedar cottage lashed with heritage décor, and a plush modern villa with king-size beds, two en suites, spa, flat-screen TVs, sound system and fantastic private garden with barbecue. Both sleep four.

Eating

Richmond Bakery (☎ 6260 2628; off Edward St; items $3-8; 🕐 breakfast & lunch) Pies, pastries, sandwiches, croissants, muffins and cakes – take away or munch in the courtyard. If the main street is empty, chances are everyone is in here.

Ma Foosies (☎ 6260 2412; 46 Bridge St; dishes $6-12; 🕐 breakfast & lunch) Cosy tearoom serving breakfast till 11.30am (pancakes, stuffed croissants, bacon and eggs) and an array of light meals, including ploughman's lunch, grilled *panini*, quiche and lasagne. Gluten-free menu available.

Anton's (☎ 6260 1017; 42a Bridge St; mains $8-13; 🕐 lunch Tue-Sun, dinner Fri-Sun) Next to the pub, this small shop churns out first-class pizzas (try the Indian curry and lamb), plus pasta, antipasto, salads, desserts and *gelati*. Grab some picnic bits and head for the river, or there are a couple of tables inside and out.

Richmond Wine Centre (☎ 6260 2619; 27 Bridge St; mains $12-25; 🕐 breakfast & lunch daily, dinner Wed-Sat) Don't be duped by the name – this place dedicates itself to fine food as well as wine.

Slink up to an outdoor table then peruse the menu. Tassie produce reigns supreme. There's also a B&B here.

Ashmore on Bridge Street (☎ 6260 2238; 34 Bridge St; mains $13-18; 🕐 breakfast & lunch daily, dinner Tue) Cheery corner food room with the sun streaming in through small-paned windows. Order up a big breakfast (scrambled eggs, cinnamon French toast with berry compote), and zingy lunches (beef lasagne, garlic prawns, Caesar salad). The best coffee in town too.

Richmond Arms Hotel (☎ 6260 2109; 42 Bridge St; mains $13-22; 🕐 lunch & dinner) This laid-back sandstone pub, popular with day-tripping, moustachioed bikers, has an uncreative but reliable pub-grub menu (plus a kids' menu). The streetside tables are where you want to be. Coal River Valley wines available.

Abby's at Prospect House (☎ 6260 2207; 1384 Richmond Rd; mains $27-30; 🕐 dinner) Classy restaurant in an 1830 mansion just west of town. The menu includes established staples like duck breast (we hope they don't take them from the pond), saddle of venison and beef eye fillet; the wine list highlights local drops. Good reports from readers.

Getting There & Away

If you have your own wheels, Richmond is a 20-minute drive from Hobart. If not, you can get to Richmond on a scheduled bus service with **Tassielink** (☎ 1300 653 633; www.tassielink.com.au) from the Hobart Bus Terminal (64 Brisbane St), Monday to Friday at 9.15am, 1.30pm, 4.30pm and 5.30pm (one way $6.40).

The **Richmond Tourist Bus** (☎ 0408-341 804; per person return $25; 🕐 9.15am & 12.20pm) runs a twice-daily service from Hobart, with three hours to explore Richmond before returning. Call for bookings and pick-up locations.

NEW NORFOLK & AROUND
☎ 03 / pop 9000

Cropping up unexpectedly amid the lush, rolling countryside (and heavy industry) of the Derwent Valley is New Norfolk, disarmingly referred to by locals as 'Norfick'. Here, 38km north of Hobart, the Derwent River narrows to just a few hundred metres across, and black swans rubberneck across the water – an Irish ex-con was so impressed, he knocked up the first house here in 1808. By the 1860s the valley had become a hop-growing hub, which explains all the old oast houses dotted around

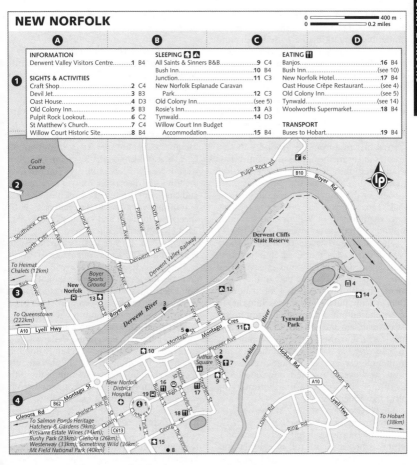

NEW NORFOLK

0 ___ 400 m
0 ___ 0.2 miles

INFORMATION		
Derwent Valley Visitors Centre.........1	B4	

SIGHTS & ACTIVITIES		
Craft Shop..................................2	C4	
Devil Jet...................................3	B3	
Oast House................................4	D3	
Old Colony Inn...........................5	B3	
Pulpit Rock Lookout......................6	C2	
St Matthew's Church.....................7	C4	
Willow Court Historic Site..............8	B4	

SLEEPING		
All Saints & Sinners B&B.................9	C4	
Bush Inn..................................10	B4	
Junction.................................11	C3	
New Norfolk Esplanade Caravan Park....12	C3	
Old Colony Inn.......................(see 5)		
Rosie's Inn..............................13	A3	
Tynwald.................................14	D3	
Willow Court Inn Budget Accommodation...15	B4	

EATING		
Banjos..................................16	B4	
Bush Inn............................(see 10)		
New Norfolk Hotel......................17	B4	
Oast House Crêpe Restaurant........(see 4)		
Old Colony Inn......................(see 5)		
Tynwald..........................(see 14)		
Woolworths Supermarket................18	B4	

TRANSPORT		
Buses to Hobart.........................19	B4	

the valley (used for drying the plant). Hops, which give beer its bitterness, are sensitive to wind, so banks of trees were planted as wind barriers; today, distinctive rows of tall poplars mark the boundaries of former hop fields.

Through the 20th century, New Norfolk was sculpted (and stigmatised) by two forces: the insane asylum Willow Court and the Boyer newspaper print mill just downstream. Hobart viewed New Norfolk as mainland Australians viewed Hobart: somehow lesser, reduced, utterly working class and morally debased. These days the asylum is no more, and the town is a weird mix of colonial remnants and slow-poke sensibility: locals say 'G'day' as they shuffle along the beleaguered main street.

Information

Derwent Valley visitors centre (☎ 6261 3700; www.riversrun.net.au; Circle St; ☺ 10am-4pm) is behind the courthouse, and handles accommodation bookings and local low-down. The free brochure *Historic Walks of New Norfolk* will guide you around the old-time sights.

See also www.newnorfolk.org and www.derwentvalley.net.au, both of which are useful for finding accommodation.

Sights & Activities
HISTORIC BUILDINGS

The jauntily designed **Oast House** (☎ 6261 4723; Tynwald Park; adult/child $5/3; ☺ 9am-4.30pm) on the perimeter of Tynwald Park, off the highway on the Hobart side of town; was built in the

1820s and served as a piggery before selflessly devoting itself to hops from 1867 to 1969. The timber building's kilns were used to dry and package hops for delivery to breweries. Take a self-guided tour of the museum, following the story of how hops were processed. Also here are a local craft gallery and a creperie (p116).

St Matthew's Church (☎ 6261 2223; www.newnorfolk .org/~st_matthews; 6 Bathurst St; admission free; ☒ service 9.30am Sun), built in 1824, is Tasmania's oldest Anglican church. It's been extensively altered since it first rose from the ground – its best features today are the impressive stained-glass windows. In the adjacent St Matthew's Close is a sporadically staffed **Craft Shop** that raises money for the church's restoration – on one wall is a massive clock face from the tower (long since demolished) of Willow Court asylum, around which the town evolved in the 1850s.

The infamous **Willow Court Historic Site** (www .newnorfolk.org/~willow_court; George St; ☒ daylight hr) itself dates from the 1820s, and housed invalid convicts before it became part of the state's mental-health program. In 1968 it housed 1000 patients, but by the 1980s asylums began to be phased out in favour of community-based treatment and housing. In 2000 the asylum was finally closed. Big plans are underway to redevelop the stately old buildings, slated to include gardens, restaurants, residential units, and even a five-star boutique hotel. Until then, it remains a mildly unnerving place to wander around.

The **Old Colony Inn** (☎ 6261 2731; www.newnorfolk .org/~old_colony_inn; 21 Montagu St; adult/child $2/50c; ☒ 10am-5pm) is a higgledy-piggledy, black-and-white-striped museum full of colonial furnishings and artefacts, built in 1815 as a hop shed. It's on a one-way street, so prepare to make a tight U-turn at the top end of the road division on Montagu St if you're approaching from Hobart. There's also accommodation here (see opposite).

OTHER ATTRACTIONS

For camera-conducive views over New Norfolk and a sweeping Derwent River bend, take the road along the northern side of the river eastward for 1km, then up a steep, unsealed side road to **Pulpit Rock Lookout**.

Devil Jet (☎ 6261 3460; www.deviljet.com.au; Esplanade; trips per adult/child $55/30; ☒ 9am-4pm) offers 30-minute jet-boat rides on the river, propelling you 10km upstream and back. Be prepared for 80km/h over shallows, traversing rapids and

360-degree spins. Trips depart on the hour; bookings recommended.

NEW NORFOLK TO MT FIELD

As you head west from New Norfolk towards Mt Field, you leave the Derwent River behind and slip into the folds of the narrow Tyenna River Valley.

In 1864, rainbow and brown trout were bred for the first time in the southern hemisphere at **Salmon Ponds Heritage Hatchery & Garden** (Map p110; ☎ 6261 5663; www.ifs.tas.gov.au; Salmon Ponds Rd, Plenty; adult/child/family $7/5/20; ☒ 9am-5pm), 9km west of New Norfolk at Plenty. You can feed the fish in the display ponds, visit the hatchery and check out the angling museum. The restaurant here, **Pancakes by the Ponds** (meals $8-17) specialises in sweet and savoury crepes, plus island wines and decent coffee.

About 5km further west is **Kinvarra Estate Wines** (☎ 6286 1333; www.kinvarra.com.au; 1211 Glenora Rd, Plenty; ☒ by appointment), with wine tastings and sales in a lovely 1827 homestead. Riesling, point noir and sparkling white are the tipples of choice. It tends to open and close on a whim, so call for an appointment.

Further west, in the three historic rural towns of **Bushy Park**, **Glenora** and **Westerway**, you can see old barns, a water wheel and rambling hop fields. The shingled buildings hereabouts are typical of the local farms built in the 19th century. Hop-growing has vanished from much of Tasmania, but it's still pursued commercially around Bushy Park – the largest hops-producing town in the southern hemisphere. In late summer and autumn you can see hops vines winding up thin leader strings. For food in Westerway, try the Possum Shed (opposite); for accommodation try the Platypus Playground (opposite) and Duffy's Country Accommodation (opposite).

On the Tyenna River 4km before Mt Field is **Something Wild** (☎ 6288 1013; 2080 Gordon River Rd; www.somethingwild.com.au; adult/child/concession/family $13/6.50/11/39; ☒ 10am-5pm), a wildlife sanctuary that rehabilitates orphaned and injured wildlife, and provides a home for animals unable to be released. Visit the animal nursery, see native wildlife (devils, wombats, quolls), and maybe spot a platypus sniffing around the grounds.

Sleeping
BUDGET
New Norfolk Esplanade Caravan Park (☎ 6261 1268; fax 6261 5174; Esplanade; unpowered/powered site $15/20,

on-site vans $45, cabins $65-95) Shady, poplar-studded grounds on the Derwent's south bank. There are only four cabins, which have toilets – everyone else uses the astonishingly well-renovated amenities blocks. Prices for two people.

Willow Court Inn Budget Accommodation (☎ 6261 8780; 15 George St; dm $20-25, s & d from $25-60; 🖳) Part of the ongoing Willow Court redevelopment is this newish hostel, offering affordable accommodation in bright, simple rooms. It's a rambling, immaculately maintained place, with TVs in most rooms, internet access, a pool table in the games rooms and asylum-strength metal bunks.

Bush Inn (☎ 6261 2256; www.thebushinn.com.au; 49 Montagu St; s/d incl breakfast $50/70) Established in 1815, the Bush Inn is one of many pubs around the country claiming 'Australia's oldest' status. Inside are serviceable pub rooms with shared facilities and guest lounge. Discuss boasts of longevity with the staff when you order dinner at the bar (see right).

Old Colony Inn (☎ 6261 2731; www.newnorfolk.org /~old_colony_inn; 21 Montagu St; s/d incl breakfast $70/90) Set in picture-perfect gardens patrolled by a nonplussed tabby cat, the Old Colony Inn has a snug cottage for the romantically inclined, plus a spacious suite (sleeps three) inside the main house. Dinner, bed and breakfast packages for two are a very reasonable $120. There's a tearoom here too.

MIDRANGE

All Saints & Sinners B&B (☎ 6261 1877; www.allsaints andsinners.com.au; 93 High St; s/d incl breakfast $100/120) Named for its equidistant location betwixt churches and pubs, this renovated 1833 inn has a handful of attractive, recently upgraded B&B rooms. Big cooked breakfasts. No kids.

Heimat Chalets (☎ 6261 2843; www.heimatchalets .com; 430 Black Hills Rd, Black Hills; powered sites $28, chalets d $125-140, extra person $35) About 9km out of town (signposted off Lyell Hwy west of the bridge) is Heimat, offering family-friendly accommodation in an amenable rural setting. There are two powered, en-suite sites, and two self-contained chalets, plus a playground, all-weather barbecue hut and chalet breakfast provisions. Dinner by arrangement; book ahead.

Platypus Playground (☎ 6288 1123; www.riverside-cottage.com; 1658 Gordon River Rd, Westerway; d $130) You can't miss this cute, red riverside cottage at Westerway, offering ecofriendly accommodation. Winning features include an outdoor deck over the river and the chance to spot a

platypus or hook a trout. The owners make it a priority to minimise guests' environmental impact: there's no stove as they'd prefer you didn't cook with oils and fats (but there is a toaster, kettle and microwave, and breakfast provisions for $20); ecofriendly toiletries and detergents are supplied; and the *piéce de résistance* is the outdoor, gas-operated toilet!

Duffy's Country Accommodation (☎ 6288 1373; www .duffyscountry.com; 49 Clark's Rd, Westerway; d $120, extra adult/ child $25/15) Overlooking a field of raspberry canes are two immaculate self-contained cabins – one a studio-style cabin for couples, the other a two-bedroom relocated rangers' hut from Mt Field National Park. Breakfast provisions provided: toast, eggs and homemade raspberry jam!

Other options:

Junction (☎ 6261 4029; www.junctionmotel.com.au; 50 Pioneer Ave; s/d from $95/110) Recently refurbished motel complex.

Rosie's Inn (☎ 6261 1171; www.rosiesinn.com.au; 5 Oast St; d $120-180) Quiet, motel-like B&B with rude red-and-purple carpets.

TOP END

[our pick] **Tynwald** (☎ 6261 2667; www.tynwaldtasmania .com.au; 1 Tynwald St; d incl breakfast $145-190; 🖳 🐕) Tynwald is a turreted, three-storey 1830s mansion overlooking the river, with six antique-furnished guest rooms (done utterly tastefully), a heated swimming pool, extensive gardens, tennis court and cooked breakfasts. There's also a self-contained stone cottage on the grounds. Tynwald is run with casual style by two chefs – the restaurant here is the best in Norfick (see p116). Wireless internet access too.

Eating

Banjos (☎ 6261 8766; cnr Burnett & High Sts; items $3-8; ☺ breakfast & lunch) Banjos seems to employ every teenager in town, and (not coincidentally) is the liveliest place in town. Locals scoff down pizza rolls, pies, quiches and laugh it up as Pat Benatar wails on the stereo.

Possum Shed (☎ 6288 1364; 1654 Gordon River Rd, Westerway; meals $7-29; ☺ breakfast & lunch Wed-Mon Oct-Mar, Thu-Sun Apr-Sep) At Westerway en route to My Field is this brilliant riverside foodie haunt, with outdoor seating, a resident platypus (sightings not guaranteed) and locally sourced lunches and snacks (salads, pancakes, wraps, BLTs). The coffee is great too, and service comes with a grin.

Bush Inn (☎ 6261 2256; 49 Montagu St; mains $10-20; ☺ lunch & dinner) This old pub has a classic menu of seafood- and meat-heavy pub favourites, including surf 'n' turf (steak topped with prawns), rump steak, roast of the day and chicken Kiev. There's a kids' menu too, plus an outdoor deck with dreamy river views.

Oast House Crêpe Restaurant (☎ 6261 4723; Tynwald Park; mains $14-20; ☼ lunch daily, dinner Fri & Sat) As well as its museum and craft shop, the Oast House offers up a great crepe restaurant, serving sweet and savoury varieties, plus all-day breakfasts, light lunches and Devonshire teas. You can sip a glass of wine here too.

New Norfolk Hotel (☎ 6261 2166; cnr Stephen & High Sts; mains $15-20; ☼ lunch & dinner) Amid the clash and bingle of the poker machines there's standard pub fare: fish and chips, steaks and chicken schnitzels, plus the odd oddity like flounder fillets. Big serves, and a kids menu.

Tynwald (☎ 6261 2667; Tynwald St; mains $27-33; ☼ dinner) In addition to its accommodation (p115), Tynwald has an outstanding, seasonally shifting menu, with French influences and an emphasis on game meats (rabbit, hare, quail, even reindeer!). Desserts raise the bar even higher. Bookings recommended.

There's a **Woolworths Supermarket** (☎ 6261 1320; cnr Charles & George Sts; ☼ 8am-8pm) for self-caterers.

Getting There & Away

Hobart Coaches (☎ 13 22 01; www.hobartcoaches.com .au) is the main operator between Hobart and New Norfolk (buses 130 and 134), and provides five services a day in both directions on weekdays, and three on Saturday ($7 one way, 50 minutes). In New Norfolk, the buses leave from Burnett St; in Hobart they depart from stop F on Elizabeth St.

MT FIELD NATIONAL PARK

☎ 03 / pop 170 (National Park township)

Mt Field, 80km northwest of Hobart (and 7km beyond Westerway), was declared a national park in 1916 and is famed for its mountain scenery, alpine moorlands, lakes, rainforest, waterfalls and abundant wildlife. To many locals it's simply known as National Park, a moniker given to the small town at its entrance. It's an accessible place to visit for a day, or to bunk down overnight with the kids.

Information

The **Mt Field National Park visitors centre** (☎ 6288 1149; www.parks.tas.gov.au; 66 Lake Dobson Rd; ☼ 8.30am-

5pm Nov-Apr, 9am-4pm May-Oct) houses a café and displays on the park's origins, and has reams of information on walks and ranger-led activities held from late December until early February. There are excellent day-use facilities in the park, including barbecues, shelters and a children's playground.

See p64 for national park entry frees.

Walks

Pick up a copy of the *Welcome to Mt Field National Park* brochure, which details walks in the park, from the visitors centre.

SHORT WALKS

The park's most touted attraction is the cascading, 40m-high **Russell Falls**, which is in the valley close to the park entrance. It's an easy 20-minute circuit walk from the car park along a wheelchair-suitable path. From Russell Falls, you can continue past **Horseshoe Falls** and **Tall Trees Circuit** to **Lady Barron Falls**, a two-hour return walk past mountain ash (*Eucalyptus regnans*, the world's tallest flowering plants).

The 15-minute **Lyrebird Nature Walk** starts 7km up Lake Dobson Rd. It's a pocket-sized introduction to park flora and fauna – great for kids – with numbers along the track corresponding to information in a brochure from the visitors centre.

For kids (and adults!) who don't mind a longer walk, there's the **Pandani Grove Nature Walk**, which traces the edge of Lake Dobson through magical stands of endemic pandani palms that grow up to 12m high before toppling over. This walk takes 40 minutes. Park at Lake Dobson car park, 16km from the park entrance.

HIGH-COUNTRY WALKS

There are some awesome walks at the top of the range, where glaciation has sculpted steep cliffs and bruised deep valleys into what was once a continuous plateau. Shimmering lakes perforate the valley floors; smaller tarns adorn the ridge-tops.

If you're setting out on a walk to the high country, take waterproof gear and warm clothing – the weather is mutable year-round – and check weather and track conditions with the visitors centre before you set out. Walks here include those to **Lake Nicholls**, **Seagers Lookout** and **Lake Seal Lookout** (all two hours return), the **Mt Field East Circuit** (four to five hours return) and **Lake Belcher** (five to six hours return).

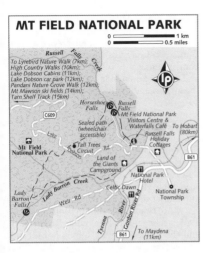

MT FIELD NATIONAL PARK

TARN SHELF TRACK

The **Tarn Shelf Track** is a brilliant walk year-round in clear weather. In summer the temperature is mild; in autumn deciduous beech leaves along the way turn golden. In winter you may need skis or snowshoes; in spring the sound of melting snow trickling beneath the boardwalk seems to somehow enhance the silence.

There's a 4WD gravel road from Lake Dobson to the ski fields and Tarn Shelf, but this is only open to authorised vehicles. Most mere unauthorised mortals walk from Lake Dobson car park along the Urquhart Track to its junction with the gravel road; both track and road are steep. Continue along the road to the ski fields, at the top of which is the start of the Tarn Shelf Track.

The track is fairly level, with a boardwalk protecting delicate vegetation and keeping walkers out of the mud. Either continue as far as you like along the track and then return via the same route, or take one of two routes branching off at Lake Newdegate then circle back to the ski fields. If you travel east past Twisted Tarn, Twilight Tarn and Lake Webster, the walk takes five or six hours return from the car park, while the wonderful Rodway Range circuit to the west takes six or seven hours return.

Skiing

Skiing was first attempted here on **Mt Mawson** in 1922. A low-key resort with clubby huts and rope tows has evolved, and when nature sees fit to offload some snow (infrequently in recent years) it makes a rootsy change from the commercial ski fields on mainland Australia. The ski field is open 10am to 4pm weekends and school holidays, weather permitting. The cost for a day's snowploughing is $30/15 per adult/child. Up-to-date snow reports are available online at www.ski.com.au/reports/mawson, or via a **recorded message service** (☎ 6288 1166).

There are no ski-equipment hire outlets here; hire ski and snowboard gear in Hobart at Skigia & Surf (below).

Sleeping & Eating

Land of the Giants Campground (☎ 6288 1526; unpowered/powered sites $16/25) A privately run, self-registration campground with adequate facilities (toilets, showers, laundry and free barbecues) just inside the park gates. Bookings not required. Site prices are additional to national park entry fees.

Lake Dobson Cabins (☎ 6288 1149; www.parks.tas .gov.au; Lake Dobson Rd; cabins up to 6 people $40) Get back to your pure mountaintop essence at these three simple six-bed cabins about 14km inside the park. All are equipped with mattresses, cold water, wood stove and firewood (there's no power), and have a communal toilet block. Visitors will need to bring gas lamps and cookers, plus utensils. Book at the visitors centre.

Russell Falls Holiday Cottages (☎ 6288 1198; fax 6288 1341; 40 Lake Dobson Rd; d $140, extra adult/child $20/15) In a super location next to the park entrance, these spotless, self-contained cottages have been the happy recipient of a slick makeover. Buy your food in New Norfolk before you arrive, or go hungry.

Celtic Dawn (☎ 6288 1058; www.celticdawn.com.au; 2400 Gordon River Rd; light meals $5-10; ☾ lunch Sat & Sun) About 600m west of the national park turn-off

---

WINTER ROAD WARNING

If you're staying in the Lake Dobson huts, skiing Mt Mawson or trampling the Pandani Grove Nature Walk or other high-country walks, you'll have to drive the 16km, unsealed Lake Dobson Rd. In winter, despite climate change's best efforts, you'll need chains and antifreeze for your car. Hire them in Hobart through **Skigia & Surf** (Map p82; ☎ 6234 6688; 123 Elizabeth St; ☾ 9.30am-6pm Mon-Fri, to 4pm Sat).

is this kooky little octagonal café with only a couple of tables. Tacos, soups, filo pastries and great coffee are the order of the day. There are also a couple of great-value rooms here: one double room ($70) and one room with two single beds ($25), both with bathrooms and a shared outdoor kitchen.

Waterfalls Café (☎ 6288 1516; 66 Lake Dobson Rd; meals $8-15; 🕑 lunch) Simple eatery next to the visitors centre, serving up reasonable café fare (burgers, nachos, soup and schnitzels).

National Park Hotel (☎ 6288 1103; Gordon River Rd; mains $15-27; 🕑 dinner)) This relaxed rural pub, 300m past the park turn-off, cooks up mixed grills, chicken dishes and steaks. The barmaid shakes her head and says, 'They love their meat 'round here…' Skip the ordinary pub accommodation (single/double $50/85) unless you're desperate.

There's also accommodation at Maydena (p300), 12km east of Mt Field.

Getting There & Away
The drive to Mt Field through the Derwent River Valley and Bushy Park is an absolute stunner: river rapids, hop fields, rows of poplars and hawthorn hedgerows. Public transport connections to the park are limited to **Tassielink** (☎ 1300 300 520; www.tassielink.com.au) services, running on Tuesday, Thursday and Saturday ($30, 3½ hours) from December to March. Some Hobart-based tour operators (see p93) offer Mt Field day trips, usually taking in Something Wild wildlife sanctuary (p114) as well as the national park.

SEVEN MILE BEACH
☎ 03 / pop 450
Out near the airport, 15km east of Hobart, is this brilliant, safe swimming beach (Map p110; seven miles long!), backed by shacks, a corner store and pine-punctured dunes. When the swell is working, the point break here is magic.

A two-minute walk from the beach, **Seven Mile Beach Cabin Park** (☎ 6248 6469; www.comfycabins .com.au; 12 Aqua Pl; unpowered/powered sites $15/25, cabins $120) is a spacey patch with blue-painted corrugated-iron cabins and free gas BBQs – as low-key as can be.

Follow Surf Rd out past the airport runway and around to the left for 2km and you'll come to **Barilla Bay Oyster Farm** (☎ 6248 5458; www.barilla bay.com.au; 1388 Tasman Hwy, Cambridge; tours adult/child $10/5, mains $28-35; 🕑 lunch daily, dinner daily Oct-Jun

& Tue-Sat Jul-Sep). Hit the slick restaurant, or grab a dozen shucked oysters ($10) washed down with some Oyster Stout, brewed on site. Tours most days; call for bookings and to confirm times.

To get to Seven Mile Beach, drive towards the airport and follow the signs. Local buses 191, 192, 291 and 293 also run here.

CHANNEL HIGHWAY
The convoluted Channel Hwy (Map p110) is the continuation of Sandy Bay Rd, mimicking the D'Entrecasteaux Channel coastline as it flows south. It was once the main southbound road out of Hobart, but was relegated to pleasant tourist drive once the Southern Outlet (Hwy A6) from Hobart to Kingston opened in 1985, stealing most of the traffic. Drive slowly and check out the views, hilltop houses and gardens en route south.

Taroona
☎ 03 / pop 2000
Ten kilometres from Hobart is snoozy Taroona, its name derived from an Aboriginal word meaning 'seashell'. It's a bush-meets-beach hippy 'burb that peaked during the '70s, but has since lost much of its feel-good community vibe. Taroona's main claim to fame is as the hometown of Mary Donaldson, now Crown Princess Mary of Denmark (see the boxed text, opposite).

On the suburb's southern fringe stands the **Shot Tower** (☎ 6227 8885; fax 6227 8643; Channel Hwy; adult/child $5.50/2.50; 🕑 9am-5pm), a 48m-high, circular sandstone turret – each block precisely curved and tapered – built in 1870 to make lead shot for firearms. Molten lead was dribbled from the top, forming perfect spheres on its way down to a cooling vat of water at the bottom. The river views from atop the 318 steps (we're pretty sure we counted them correctly…) are wondrous. The tower is surrounded by leafy grounds and has a snug **Tearoom** (light meals $4-8; 🕑 11am-3pm) downstairs. If it's sunny, devour a Devonshire tea on the stone rampart outside.

On the northern fringe of Taroona is Truganini Reserve and the bottom end of Truganini Track (p90), which leads up a wooded valley to Mt Nelson Signal Station.

Hillgrove (☎ 6227 9043; hill.bb@bigpond.net.au; 269 Channel Hwy; d $130), directly opposite the Shot Tower, is a 19th-century cream-and-green Georgian house with a steep, spooky-

CROWN PRINCESS MARY OF DENMARK (AKA MARY DONALDSON OF TAROONA)

A few Tasmanians have found themselves in the spotlight recently, but no-one has garnered more international attention than Mary Donaldson, the girl from Taroona now living a modern-day fairy tale in Europe. Mary was born in Hobart in 1972 to Scots who had emigrated to Australia a decade earlier. The youngest of four children, she attended Taroona High School before graduating from the University of Tasmania (commerce and law) in 1993. Mary moved to Melbourne and worked in advertising, then travelled through Europe and the US before returning to Australia to live in Sydney.

Mary met Denmark's Crown Prince Frederik in a Sydney pub during the 2000 Olympic Games; the prince was in Oz with the Danish sailing team. The pair sailed into a relationship that sent the gossip mags into a frenzy of speculation until Mary and Fred announced their engagement in 2003. They married in a lavish ceremony in Copenhagen in 2004 with a sea of well-wishers lining the streets, waving Danish and Australian flags. Interest in Tasmania as a holiday destination for the Danes has skyrocketed, and Tassie produce has found a new export market in Denmark.

'Our Mary' is never far from the covers of Danish and Australian gossip mags, as journos dissect every aspect of her life: is she too thin? Does she own too many shoes? How's her Danish coming along? Of course, the real show-stoppers have been Frederick and Mary's two kids: HRH Prince Christian, born October 2005, and HRH Princess Isabella, born April 2007.

looking mansard roof and beautiful gardens. Guests get the run of the two-bedroom, self-contained ground floor (sleeps three), plus a large veranda from which to absorb the leafy Shot Tower views.

To get to Taroona from Hobart, take **Metro Tasmania** (☎ 13 22 01; www.metrotas.com.au) bus 56, 61–3, 67, 68, 94, 162, 167 or 168 from Franklin Sq stop O. A one-way adult fare is $3.

Kingston

☎ 03 / pop 13,000

Sprawling Kingston, 12km south of Hobart, is a booming outer suburb of the city. It started to evolve from a sleepy beach enclave when the Southern Outlet roadway established a rocketshot route into town. The beach here is a super spot to laze away a sunny afternoon and reflect on how a long, clean, sandy beach so close to an Australian capital city has remained so lowkey and uncommercial (there are no high-rise apartment blocks here – for now).

SIGHTS & ACTIVITIES

As you branch off from the Southern Outlet and approach Kingston, continue straight ahead at the first set of lights instead of turning right onto the Channel Hwy; this road takes you down to the beach. If you're trundling down the Channel Hwy from Taroona, turn left at these lights.

Kingston Beach is a popular swimming and sailing spot, with steep wooded cliffs at each end of a long arc of sand. There's a picnic area

at the northern end, accessed by a pedestrian bridge over the pollution-prone, nonswimmable (and therefore aptly named) Browns River. Behind the sailing clubhouse at the southern end of the beach is a track leading to a beaut little swimming spot called **Boronia Beach**, which has a deep rock pool. Sections of this track are heavily eroded.

Blackmans Bay, about 3km from Kingston Beach, has another decent beach and a blowhole (down Blowhole Rd). The water at these beaches is usually quite cold, and there's rarely any surf.

Beside the Channel Hwy south of Kingston is the headquarters of the **Australian Antarctic Division** (☎ 6232 3209; www.aad.gov.au; 203 Channel Hwy; admission free; ☷ 8.30am-5pm Mon-Fri), the department administering Australia's 42% wedge of the frozen continent. Australia has a long history of exploration and scientific study of Antarctica – it's one of the original 12 nations that ratified the Antarctic Treaty in 1961. Visitors can check out the displays here, which feature Antarctic equipment, clothing and scientific vehicles, plus ecologic info and some brilliant photographs. The centre's cafeteria is open to the public.

SLEEPING & EATING

Kingston Beach Motel (☎ /fax 6229 8969; 31 Osborne Esplanade; s/d $85/120, extra person $20) Old-style motel opposite Kingston Beach that was undergoing a major overhaul when we visited. Only four rooms were available at the time, but there

---

DETOUR: TINDERBOX

Make time to drive through Blackmans Bay and a further 10km to **Tinderbox**. The views along the way are eye-popping, and at Tinderbox itself is a small beach bordering **Tinderbox Nature Marine Reserve** (www .parks.tas.gov.au/marine/tindbox). Here you can snorkel along an underwater trail running alongside a sandstone reef, marked with submerged information plates explaining the rich local ecosystem. Bruny Island is just across the water – locals often launch their outboards here and skim over to Dennes Point for a BBQ.

From Tinderbox, continue around the peninsula to Howden and back to Kingston via the Channel Hwy.

---

will be nine once the extravagant rebuild is finished (prices may rise too). Cheaper rates off season.

On the Beach (☎ 6229 3096; wilksey@bigpond.com; 38 Osborne Esplanade; d $100, 2br unit $150) Not quite on the beach, but directly across the road from it, with one self-contained unit attached to the rear of the owners' home. There's also a large two-bedroom unit upstairs under the steeply pitched roof that's perfect for two couples (no kids).

Citrus Moon Café (☎ 6229 2388; 23 Beach Rd; mains $10-16; ☺ breakfast & lunch) Bright, retro café with a predominantly vegetarian menu. Devour brekky until noon, then choose from burgers, bagels or salads for lunch, or swing by for coffee and homemade cake (vegan, flourless or regular options available). If you *must*, there's a few tasty beef, chicken and fish dishes too.

Beachside Hotel (☎ 6229 6185; 2 Beach Rd; mains $14-22; ☺ lunch & dinner) Good-quality traditional pub fare (the curried sausages are a coronary in disguise) right across the road from the beach, with an outdoor patio perfect for beery lunches. Cheap bar snacks and occasional live music in summer.

The Beach (☎ 6229 7600; Ocean Esplanade, Blackmans Bay; mains $20-27; ☺ lunch & dinner) On a sunny day there's no better spot than the outdoor terrace of this angular, metal-finned café-bar, south of Kingston opposite Blackmans Bay beach. Wood-fired pizzas, risotto, lamb shanks and pasta, all done with élan.

GETTING THERE & AWAY

To get to Kingston from Hobart take **Metro Tasmania** (☎ 13 22 01; www.metrotas.com.au) bus 61, 62, 63, 67, 68, 94, 162, 167 or 168 via Taroona, or bus 174, 184 or 185 via the Southern Outlet. Buses depart Hobart's Franklin Sq stop O; a one-way adult fare is $3.

Hobart Coaches (☎ 13 22 01; www.hobartcoaches.com .au) runs regular services (buses 89, 90, 92–4, 96 and 98) from Hobart to Kingston. Bus 89 continues to Blackmans Bay. The fare to both destinations is $3.10 one way.

Tasman Peninsula & Port Arthur

Just an hour from Hobart are the staggering coastal landscapes, sandy surf beaches and potent historic sites of the Tasman Peninsula. The *numero uno* ticket on the Tassie tourist trail is here – the Port Arthur Historic Site. There are boundless other attractions (natural and otherwise) down this way – enough to warrant a stay of at least a couple of days. If you're feeling active, bushwalking, surfing, sea-kayaking, scuba diving and rock climbing opportunities abound.

On the wild side of proceedings, don't miss a visit to the peninsula's legendary 300m-high sea cliffs, which will dose you up on natural awe. Most of the cliffs are protected by Tasman National Park, a coastal enclave that also embraces chunky offshore islands, magical underwater kelp forests, and heaths containing rare plants. The cliffs are a safe haven for innumerable seabirds, including wedge-tailed eagles, while the fertile waters below throng with seals, dolphins and whales. Waiting portentously at the end of Arthur Hwy is Port Arthur, the infamous and allegedly escape-proof penal colony of the mid-19th century. The crowds mill around the ruins – kids laugh and kick footballs while dads poke sausages on BBQs – but it's impossible to forget that this is a tragic place, both historically and more recently. Figures show that the downturn in regional tourism following the 1996 massacre has been reversed in recent years, and a number of tourism developments (new resort-style hotels and expansions of old ones) are leaping from architects' drawing boards into reality.

HIGHLIGHTS

- Paying your respects to the past, both distant and recent, at the **Port Arthur Historic Site** (p128)
- **Sea-kayaking** (p122) around the Tasman Peninsula's broken coastline
- Getting your hands dirty picking fresh raspberries, apricots and silvanberries at the **Sorell Fruit Farm** (p123)
- Spotting seals, dolphins and maybe even a whale on a cruise around **Tasman Island** (p129) from Port Arthur
- Battling vertigo atop the southern hemisphere's highest sea cliffs at Cape Pillar on the **Tasman Coastal Trail** (p124)
- Carving up the southern surf (or learning how to) at **Eaglehawk Neck** (p125)
- Chowing down on a canal-side burger at the **Waterfront Café** (p123) in Dunalley
- Pitching your tent at remote **Fortescue Bay** (p127) and falling asleep to the lull of the waves

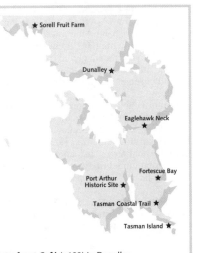

★ Sorell Fruit Farm

Dunalley ★

Eaglehawk Neck ★

Port Arthur Historic Site ★

Fortescue Bay ★

Tasman Coastal Trail ★

Tasman Island ★

| ▦ TELEPHONE CODE: 03 | ▦ www.tasmanregion.com.au | ▦ www.portarthur.org.au |

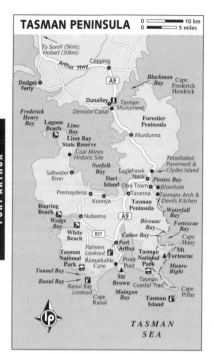

TASMAN PENINSULA

Getting There & Around

Take care driving down the peninsula to Port Arthur if you're behind the wheel, as plenty of gnarly accidents have occurred on the Arthur Hwy. It's a wiggly, narrow road in places, with exits hidden behind hills and around corners, and the usual idiots with lead feet.

Regional public-transport connections are surprisingly poor. **Tassielink** (☎ 1300 300 520; www .tassielink.com.au) runs a weekday evening bus from Hobart to Port Arthur ($25, 2¼ hours) during school terms, reducing to Monday, Wednesday and Friday mornings during school holidays. Buses stop at the main towns en route.

Redline Coaches (☎ 1300 360 000; www.redline coaches.com.au) also operates some weekday services between Hobart, Sorell and Dunalley, but no further south.

TOURS

If you don't have wheels, you can take a coach or ferry tour to the Tasman Peninsula from Hobart. Many operators run trips to Port Arthur. Some options:

Bottom Bits Bus (☎ 1800 777 103, 6229 3540; www .bottombitsbus.com.au; full-day tours $110) Small-group backpacker-focused day trips (every day except Tuesday and Thursday) including Port Arthur entry, evening ghost tour (Saturday only; additional cost) and visits to the peninsula's natural attractions (Tessellated Pavement, Tasman Arch, Devil's Kitchen).

Gray Line (☎ 6234 3336, 1300 858 687; www.grayline .com.au; full-day tour adult/child $90/45) Coach tours ex-Hobart, including a harbour cruise around the Isle of the Dead, Port Arthur admission and guided tour, and pit stops at Tasman Arch and the Devils' Kitchen.

Navigators (☎ 6223 1914; www.navigators.net.au; Brooke St Pier, Hobart; full-day tour adult/child $149/110) Cruises from Hobart to Port Arthur, returning on a coach, departing Wednesday, Friday and Sunday. Includes entrance to the historic site, guided tour and morning tea. Also running is a cruise around Tasman Island from Port Arthur (see p93).

Port Arthur Bus Service (☎ 6250 2200; www.tasman cruises.com.au; full-day trip adult/child $90/55) Meet Port Arthur on your own terms, with a ride there and back (including admission) from Tasman Island Cruises. Departs Hobart visitors centre at 8am; bookings required.

Roaring 40s Ocean Kayaking (☎ 6265 5000; www .roaring40stours.com.au; 1-/3-day tour $255/1150) Based in Kettering (p136), Roaring 40s also conducts epic sea-kayaking tours around the Tasman Peninsula, paddling past the monumental coastline. Prices include equipment, meals, accommodation and transfers from Hobart.

Tasman Island Cruises (☎ 6250 2200; www.tasman cruises.com.au; full-day tour adult/child $220/150) Take a bus to Port Arthur for a three-hour ecocruise around Tasman Island, then explore the Port Arthur Historic Site and bus it back to town. Includes morning tea, lunch and Port Arthur admission. Departs Hobart visitors centre at 8am; bookings required. You can also take just the cruise from Port Arthur (see p129).

SORELL

☎ 03 / pop 1730

Sorell is one of Tasmania's oldest towns, settled in 1808 primarily to supply locally processed wheat and flour to the rest of the colony, but its historic aura has tarnished over time. These days it's a T-junction service town with more petrol stations and fast-food joints than anything else, but it's still the gateway to the Tasman Peninsula. For maps and peninsula info, swing into the **Sorell visitors centre** (☎ 6265 6438; www.tasmanregion.com.au; 16 Main Rd; ☽ 9am-4pm May, 10am-4pm Jun-Sep, 9am-5pm Oct Apr). Pick up the *Tasman – The Essence of Tasmania* and the *Convict Trail* booklets, which cover the peninsula's key historic sites.

A handful of 19th-century buildings have survived near the centre of town and are worth a look. The 1841 **Scots Uniting Church** (Arthur St) is behind the high school. Also near the school are the **Sorell Barracks** (31 Walker St), now colonial accommodation, and the 1829 **Blue Bell Inn** (cnr Somerville & Walker Sts). On the main drag is the 1884 **St George's Anglican Church** (Gordon St), its adjacent **graveyard** propped with the headstones of early settlers.

The perfect pit stop is the **Sorell Fruit Farm** (☎ 6265 3100; www.sorellfruitfarm.com; 174 Pawleena Rd; pay per kilo, $6 minimum pick; ☒ 8.30am-5pm late Oct-May) where you can pick your own fruit from their intensively planted 12.5 acres. There are 15 different kinds of edibles on offer, including strawberries, raspberries, cherries, apricots, peaches and apples, and more exotic varieties like loganberries, tayberries and silvanberries. December and January are the best months for variety, but different fruits are in season at different times – check the website for a nifty chart. Afterwards, enjoy a snack or a mellifluous coffee in the **tearooms** (lights meals $5-9), or purchase a wide range of fruity jams, chutneys, sauces, wines and liqueurs. To get here, head east through Sorell towards Port Arthur. After exiting the town you'll see Pawleena signposted on your left.

Sleeping & Eating

Given its proximity to the airport, Sorell makes a handy overnight stop if you have an early flight.

Blue Bell Inn (☎ 6265 2804; www.bluebellinnsorell.com.au; 26 Somerville St; s/d incl breakfast from $100/130) A two-storey sandstone inn dating back to 1829, Blue Bell offers colonially furnished rooms and a barrage of cooked breakfasts in its elegant, plum-washed interior. The dining room (mains $20 to $29; open for breakfast and dinner) serves well-prepared meals (some with a Polish bent) to both guests and visitors, and will cater to vegans and coeliacs with prior notice. Book ahead. Quatro the Great Dane patrols the corridors.

Cherry Park Estate (☎ 6265 2271; www.cherryparkestate.com.au; 114 Pawleena Rd; d $120-140) Close to Sorell Fruit Farm, this property has three rooms with bathrooms, lots of surrounding open spaces, home-grown apricots (no cherries?) and creative (albeit *nouveau-riche*) flourishes like a Wild West–themed bar, and chandeliers and friezes. Cooked breakfast available with the higher tariff.

There's a slew of takeaways and cafés along the main street, and pubs serving farm-sized meals.

Getting There & Away

The **Tassielink** (☎ 1300 300 520; www.tassielink.com.au) service down the Tasman Peninsula from Hobart stops at Sorell ($7, 40 minutes).

DUNALLEY

☎ 03 / pop 290

The thickly timbered Forestier Peninsula – the precursor peninsula you'll cross en route to the Tasman Peninsula – is connected to mainland Tasmanian soil by the isthmus town Dunalley. Gouged-out in 1905, the **Denison Canal**, complete with a raiseable bridge, bisects the isthmus, providing a short cut for small boats. There's not much to see here, but there are a couple of good places to stay and eat.

Sleeping & Eating

Potters Croft (☎ 6253 5469; www.potterscroft.com.au; Arthur Hwy; s/d from $100/146, extra person $35) At Dunalley's northern end is this convict-brick, family-run estate, tripling as a craft gallery, local wine outlet and provider of snug accommodation. There are four en suite rooms sharing a large kitchen and lounge area, and a self-contained cottage sleeping four. Guided eco-expeditions (fishing, boating, walking, cycling, painting, photography – check the website) can also be arranged. Good winter rates.

our pick Waterfront Café (☎ 6253 5122; 4 Imlay St; meals $12-25; ☒ lunch daily, dinner Thu-Sat Oct-Apr) Dunalley's cultural and culinary hot spot is this fabulous hybrid antique store and elegant café, with a broad outdoor deck and views across the water. The menu lists interesting options like fish off the local pier, home-made cakes, brilliant coffee, Tassie wines and a world-famous sweet potato, spinach and cashew burger. Occasional live music (the estimable likes of Deborah Conway).

Dunalley Hotel (☎ 6253 5101; Arthur Hwy; mains $18-30; ☒ lunch & dinner) Traditionalists might prefer the town boozer, a friendly country pub serving lots of local seafood. Outdoor tables, a wide veranda and a seafood feast for two ($60) – life is good.

Getting There & Away

The **Tassielink** (☎ 1300 300 520; www.tassielink.com.au) Tasman Peninsula service will take you to Dunalley from Hobart ($18, one hour).

GONNA MAKE A JAILBREAK

In 1842 the notorious bushranger Martin Cash became one of the few felons to successfully flee Port Arthur and make it across Eaglehawk Neck to freedom. Cash and his cohorts George Jones and Lawrence Kavanagh busted out of Port Arthur easily enough, but the real test awaited at the Neck, with its ferocious Dogline. Shark attack must have seemed a lesser gamble – the three men swam around the Neck, losing only their clothes en route. On the other side they pilfered some clobber and bolted for the Midlands, where they successfully terrorised north–south travellers for several months before being recaptured. Cash and Kavanagh were banished to Norfolk Island for life; Jones was less fortunate, ending his days dangling from a noose.

EAGLEHAWK NECK
☎ 03 / pop 100

Eaglehawk Neck is the second isthmus you'll cross heading to Port Arthur, this one connecting the Forestier Peninsula to the Tasman Peninsula. In the days of convicts at Port Arthur to the south, the 100m-wide Neck had a row of ornery dogs chained across it to prevent escape – the infamous Dogline. Timber platforms were also built in narrow Eaglehawk Bay to the west, and stocked with yet more ferocious dogs to prevent convicts from wading around the Dogline. Rumours were circulated that the waters were shark-infested to discourage swimming – the occasional white pointer does indeed shimmy through these waters, but 'infested' overstates things a bit. Remarkably, despite these efforts, several convicts made successful bids for freedom (see the boxed text, above). The key convict sites are now protected as the **Eaglehawk Neck Historic Site** (☎ 1300 368 550; www.parks.tas.gov.au/fact sheets/parks_and_places/E aglehawkNeck.pdf).

There's an ATM and a handful of brochures at the Officers Mess (opposite).

Sights
As you approach Eaglehawk Neck from the north, turn east onto Pirates Bay Dr for the **lookout** – there's an astonishing view of Pirates Bay, the Neck and the rugged coastline beyond. Down on the isthmus, the only remaining structure from the convict days is the 1832

Officers Quarters (admission free; 9am-4.30pm), the oldest wooden military building in Australia. Sitting diagonally opposite the Officers Mess general store, its interior is fitted out with information boards on the history of the building and Eaglehawk Neck.

At the northern end of Pirates Bay is **Tessellated Pavement**, a rocky terrace that has eroded into what looks like tiled paving. At low tide you can walk along the foreshore to **Clydes Island**, where there are wicked coastline panoramas and several graves. You can see as far south as Cape Hauy.

Follow the signposted side roads to **The Blowhole**, **Tasman Arch** and the **Devil's Kitchen** for some close-up views of spectacular coastal cliffs. Watch out for sporadic blows at the Blowhole, and keep behind the fences at the other sites – the cliff edges are prone to decay. The Eaglehawk Neck Jetty is opposite the Blowhole car park.

On the road to the Blowhole is the signposted turn-off to the 4km gravel road leading to **Waterfall Bay**, which has yet more camera-conducive views (see Waterfall Bluff below).

Activities
BUSHWALKING
From the car park at Waterfall Bay, take the 1½-hour return hike to **Waterfall Bluff**. Much of the walk is through a forest of tall, slender trees that somewhat obscure the view, but the track stays close to the water and there are plenty of places to stop and gawp at the magnificent scenery from the clifftops (unfenced, except at the car park). Make sure you continue to the bluff itself before returning to the part of the walk that takes you down past the falls – if the bluff vista doesn't make you say 'Wow!', nothing will.

Waterfall Bay is also the start of the **Tasman Coastal Trail**, which climbs over Tatnells Hill then follows the coast to Fortescue Bay, out to Cape Hauy and on to Cape Pillar. Walkers should allow three to five days for the one-way trip; see www.parks.tas.gov .au/recreation/tracknotes/tasman.html for information.

If you'd rather tackle a one-day walk, traipse along the coast from Waterfall Bay to Bivouac Bay (six hours) or on to Fortescue Bay (eight hours), with camping available at both bays. If you need to return to your car, only walk as far as Tatnells Hill, from which there's an amazing view all the way from Eaglehawk Neck to the craggy rock formations of Cape Hauy.

Hit the bookshops for *Peninsula Tracks* by Peter and Shirley Storey ($18) – track notes for 35 walks in the area.

SURFING & DIVING
Pirates Bay (the ocean beach at Eaglehawk Neck) is one of southern Tassie's most reliable surfing spots. There are trusty beach and sandbar breaks around the bay, plus more challenging breaks around the cliffs near the Tessellated Pavement. If you're new to the ocean, you can take a surf lesson here with **Island Surf School** (☎ 6265 9776, 0400 830 237; www.islandsurfschool.com.au; 2hr group lessons $40). Boards and wetsuits are provided. Private lessons are available too.

Eaglehawk Dive Centre (☎ 6250 3566; www.eaglehawkdive.com.au; 178 Pirates Bay Dr; 1-/2-/4-day courses $200/395/550) conducts underwater explorations (sea caves, giant kelp forests, a sea lion colony and shipwrecks) and a range of PADI courses. A one-day introduction to scuba diving costs $199 (no experience necessary). Equipment rental is $85 per day; two boat dives with equipment costs $190. They provide free Hobart pick-ups, and dorm accommodation for divers for $25 per night.

Tours
Personalised Sea Charters (☎ 6250 3370; seachart@southcom.com.au; 322 Blowhole Rd, Eaglehawk Neck; trips per hr/day from $65/440) Takes small groups on game, deep sea, reef or bay fishing and sightseeing charter trips. All gear supplied.

Sealife Experience (☎ 6253 5325, 0428-300 303; www.sealife.com.au; 3½-hour cruises adult/child/family $95/50/260) Cruises taking in the peninsula's dramatic east coast from Eaglehawk Neck to Cape Hauy, with bountiful sea life along the way – bring your camera! Tours depart Eaglehawk Neck Jetty at 10am; bookings essential.

Sleeping
The advantages of staying at Eaglehawk Neck are that it's far more scenic than Port Arthur, relatively uncrowded and it's close to all the peninsula's major drawcards.

Eaglehawk Neck Backpackers (☎ 6250 3248; 94 Old Jetty Rd; unpowered sites/dm $16/20) A *very* simple, family-run hostel in a peaceful location signposted west of the isthmus. There are just four beds in the dorm, plus a couple of tent spots on the back lawn and a camp kitchen. Bike hire is $5 for the duration of your stay.

Lufra Hotel (☎ 6250 3262; www.lufrahotel.com; 380 Pirates Bay Dr; d $90-120, 2br apt $180) This chowder-coloured pub has a superb outlook over Pirates Bay above the Tessellated Pavement ('a bit of a view' – are they serious?). Rooms are modest but comfortable, all with bathrooms. A new wing of slick two-bedroom apartments should be finished by the time you read this. Chow down in the downstairs bistro (see below).

our pick Eaglehawk Café & Guesthouse (☎ 6250 3331; www.theneck.com.au; 5131 Arthur Hwy; d incl breakfast $110-130) Upstairs at this artsy little café (built in 1929) are three lovely B&B rooms, taking up the spaces once occupied by slumbering shipwrights. Two of the rooms have beaut French doors opening onto a balcony overlooking Eaglehawk Bay. Breakfast in the café (with its crankin' espresso machine).

Eaglehawk Hideaway (☎ 6250 3513; www.eaglehawkhideaway.com; 40 Ferntree Rd; s/d $120/140, breakfast $20) About 1km beyond Eaglehawk Neck is the turn-off to this big brick house, the ground floor of which is given over to guests. The bloom-filled gardens are great, but the house itself is nothing to write home about – stay for the location, not the accommodation. Dinner by arrangement.

Eating
Officers Mess (☎ 6250 3635; off Arthur Hwy; mains $10-22; breakfast, lunch & dinner;) A basic drive-up tourist-trap general store and café. There's not a lot to recommend it, but it does serve hot food and takeaways (including soup, roast beef and pizzas), it's good for kids and it's opposite the historic Officers Quarters (opposite).

Lufra Hotel (☎ 6250 3262; 380 Pirates Bay Dr; mains $15-34; breakfast, lunch & dinner) This hefty hotel aims to please all comers with its bistro serving fine local produce (seafood, quail, wallaby), and public bar with pool table where you can get traditional pub grub for a few dollars less.

Eaglehawk Café & Guesthouse (☎ 6250 3331; 5131 Arthur Hwy; mains $10-23; breakfast & lunch year-round, dinner Fri-Sun Dec-Feb) Arguably the peninsula's best dining option, just south of Eaglehawk Neck. Stylish décor, local art lining the walls, wines by the glass and a fine day-turns-to-night menu (try the Doo Town venison kebabs). Or just stop in for coffee and cake.

DOO TOWN

No-one is really sure how it all started, but the raggedy collection of fishing shacks at Doo Town (3km south of Eaglehawk Neck on the way to the Blowhole) all contain the word 'Doo' in their names. There's the sexy 'Doo Me', the approving 'We Doo', the unfussy 'Thistle Doo Me', the Beatles-esque 'Love Me Doo' and (our favourite) the melancholic 'Doo Write'. We doo hope the new breed of architecturally gymnastic beach houses here maintain the tradition.

Getting There & Away

Tassielink (☎ 1300 300 520; www.tassielink.com.au) can bus you from Hobart to Eaglehawk Neck in 1½ hours; the one-way fare is $21.

TARANNA

☎ 03 / pop 160

Taranna is a small town strung out along the shores of Norfolk Bay about 10km north of Port Arthur, its name coming from an Aboriginal word meaning 'hunting ground'. Historically important, it was once the terminus for Australia's first **railway**, which ran from Long Bay near Port Arthur to here. This public transport was powered by convicts, who pushed the carriages uphill, then jumped on for the ride down. In those days Taranna was called Old Norfolk. Not far offshore, **Dart Island** was used as a semaphore station to relay messages from Port Arthur to Hobart. Today, the waters near the island are used for oyster farming.

Taranna's main attraction (apart from a few good places to eat and sleep), is the **Tasmanian Devil Conservation Park** (☎ 6250 3230; www.tasmaniandevilpark.com; adult/child/family $24/13/59; Arthur Hwy; ☼ 9am-6pm), which functions as a quarantined breeding centre for devils to help protect against DFTD (see p51). It's also a breeding centre for endangered birds of prey. There are plenty of other native species here too, with feedings throughout the day: devils at 10am, 11am, 1.30pm and 5pm (4.30pm in winter), and kangaroos at 2.30pm. There's also a sea eagle show at 11.15am and 3.30pm. The park usually runs the much-touted **Devils in the Dark** nocturnal prowl, but it was on hold when we visited – call to see if it's been reinstated. The **Park Café** here was also closed when we visited,

but should be open again by the time you read this.

The **Federation Chocolate Factory** (☎ 6250 3435; fax 6250 3451; 2 South St; admission free; ☼ 9am-5pm Mon-Sat) sits alluringly close to Taranna. Check out chocolate being hand made and chew on some intriguingly flavoured delights (from favourites such as honeycomb or caramel nougat to the surprisingly good apple flavour, or perhaps liquorice or brandied apricot). Inside the factory is a ye-olde museum of blacksmithing and saw-milling equipment.

Sleeping & Eating

Teraki Cottages (☎ 6250 3435; fax 6250 3451; 996 Arthur Hwy, Taranna; s $70-80, d $80-90, extra adult/child $20/10) Perhaps the best-value accommodation on the peninsula, these three neat-as-a-pin, self-contained bushman's huts. At the southern end of Taranna they exude basic, rustic charm in a quiet bush setting with open fires. Breakfast provisions (free-range eggs, homemade jams) are a few dollars extra. No credit cards.

Norfolk Bayview B&B (☎ 6250 3855; norfolkbayviewbb@bigpond.com; 111 Nubeena Rd; s $85-100, d $120-135) Modern B&B on 45 rural acres just west of Taranna (past Teraki Cottages), with rates including a cooked breakfast and far-reaching views from the elevated verandas over Norfolk Bay. There's an open fire in the guest lounge.

Abs by the Bay (☎ 6250 3719; www.absbythebay.com; 5730 Arthur Hwy; d $88-110, extra person $20) Abalone? Abdominals? We suspect it's the former, and the water-view deck here affords the opportunity to relax the latter. Flexible configurations to accommodate two couples or two singles in suburbanite units.

Mason's Cottages (☎/fax 6250 3323; 5741 Arthur Hwy; d $90-100, extra person $20) On the highway at the northern edge of town, this place has a huddle of suburban-looking, two-bedroom brick units available for your self-contained discretion. Nothing flash, but you get what you pay for.

Norfolk Bay Convict Station (☎ 6250 3487; www .convictstation.com; 5862 Arthur Hwy; d incl breakfast $150-160) Built in 1838 and once the railway's port terminus (as well as the first pub on the Tasman Peninsula, the Tasman Hotel), this gorgeous old place is now a top-quality waterfront B&B. Eclectic rooms come with ripping cooked breakfasts. Complimentary port. Fishing gear for hire.

Fish Lips Café & Accommodation (☎ 6250 3066; www.fishlipstasmania.com.au; 5934 Arthur Hwy; r $66-180)

Between the highway and Little Norfolk Bay is this newish joint, offering fishy café lunches (mains $15 to $25), and a collection of affordable shared-bathroom rooms (sleeping up to three) and classier waterside double cottages. There's also a farmers market here on summer Sundays from 10am to 2pm.

Mussel Boys (☎ 6250 3088; 5927 Arthur Hwy, Taranna; mains $16-26; ☺ lunch & dinner) Open from noon, this bright, fresh café-restaurant has a mussel-bound menu worth screeching into the driveway for. Try the mussels in dill and coconut curry broth, or the expansive seven-course tasting menu (which might chew up your afternoon).

Getting There & Away

The **Tassielink** (☎ 1300 300 520; www.tassielink.com.au) Tasman Peninsula service calls in at Taranna ($21 one way, 1¾ hours) en route from Hobart to Port Arthur.

FORTESCUE BAY & TASMAN NATIONAL PARK

Sequestered 12km down a gravel road from the highway (the turn-off is halfway between Taranna and Port Arthur) is becalmed **Fortescue Bay**, with a sweeping sandy arc backed by thickly forested slopes. The sheltered bay was one of the semaphore station sites used during the convict period to relay messages to and from Eaglehawk Neck. Early last century a timber mill was in operation, and the boilers and jetty ruins are still visible near Mill Creek, as are the remains of some of the timber tramways used to collect the timber. The mill closed in 1952.

Fortescue Bay is one of the main access points for **Tasman National Park** (www.parks.tas.gov.au/natparks/tasman), encompassing the territory around Cape Raoul, Cape Hauy, Cape Pillar, Tasman Island and the rugged coast north to Eaglehawk Neck. Offshore, dolphins, seals, penguins and whales are regular passers-by. The usual national park entry fees apply at Fortescue Bay (see p64).

Sights & Activities

Apart from swimming and bumming around on the beach, most people come here to launch their fishing boats or do some **bushwalking**. Several walking tracks kick off at Fortescue Bay. To the north, a solid track traces the shoreline to **Canoe Bay** (two hours return) and **Bivouac Bay** (four hours return), continuing all the way to the Devil's Kitchen car park at **Eaglehawk Neck** (10 hours one way). To the east, a track meanders out to **Cape Hauy** (four to five hours return) – a well-used path leading out to sea cliffs with sensational views of the famous sea stacks **The Candlestick** and **Totem Pole**. To get into some rain forest, follow the same track towards Cape Hauy, then take the steep side track to **Mt Fortescue** (six to seven hours return). Another track extends all the way to **Cape Pillar** near **Tasman Island**, where the sea cliffs are 300m high – purportedly the highest in the southern hemisphere. You'll need two to three days return to knock off the Cape Pillar track. For track notes, see Lonely Planet's *Walking in Australia*.

Sleeping

You can dream the night away to the sound of gentle surf at **Fortescue Bay Campground** (☎ 6250 2433; www.parks.tas.gov.au; Tasman National Park; unpowered sites $24). There are no powered sites and showers are cold, but fireplaces and gas BBQs compensate. National park fees apply in addition to camping fees; book ahead during summer. There are no shops here so BYO food and drink.

PORT ARTHUR

☎ 03 / pop 200

Port Arthur is the name of the small settlement which has grown up around the Port Arthur Historic Site. In 1830 Governor Arthur chose the Tasman Peninsula to confine prisoners who had committed further crimes in the colony. A 'natural penitentiary', the peninsula is connected to the mainland by a strip of land less than 100m wide – Eaglehawk Neck (p124) – where ferocious guard dogs and tales of shark-infested waters deterred escape.

Between 1830 and 1877, 12,500 convicts did hard, brutal prison time at Port Arthur. For most it was hell on Earth, but those who behaved often enjoyed better conditions than they'd endured in England and Ireland. Port Arthur became the hub of a network of penal stations on the peninsula, its fine buildings sustaining thriving convict-labour industries, including timber milling, shipbuilding, coal mining, shoemaking and brick and nail production.

Australia's first railway literally 'ran' the 7km between Norfolk Bay at Taranna and Long Bay near Port Arthur: convicts pushed the carriages along the tracks. A semaphore

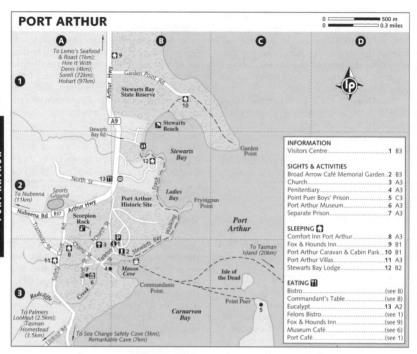

PORT ARTHUR

INFORMATION
Visitors Centre.....................................1 B3

SIGHTS & ACTIVITIES
Broad Arrow Café Memorial Garden..2 B3
Church..3 A3
Penitentiary...4 A3
Point Puer Boys' Prison........................5 C3
Port Arthur Museum............................6 A3
Separate Prison...................................7 A3

SLEEPING
Comfort Inn Port Arthur.....................8 A3
Fox & Hounds Inn................................9 B1
Port Arthur Caravan & Cabin Park....10 B1
Port Arthur Villas..............................11 A3
Stewarts Bay Lodge...........................12 B2

EATING
Bistro...(see 8)
Commandant's Table........................(see 8)
Eucalypt...13 A2
Felons Bistro.....................................(see 1)
Fox & Hounds Inn............................(see 9)
Museum Café....................................(see 6)
Port Café..(see 1)

telegraph system allowed instant communication between Port Arthur, other peninsula outstations and Hobart. Convict farms provided fresh vegetables, a boys' prison was built at Point Puer to reform and educate juvenile convicts, and a church was erected.

Despite its redemption as a major tourist site, Port Arthur remains a sombre, haunting place. Don't come here expecting to remain unaffected by what you see. There's a sadness here that's undeniable; a gothic sense of woe that can cloud your senses on the sunniest of days. Perhaps this is what brought a deranged young gunman here in April 1996. Unleashing an indiscriminate fusillade of bullets, he murdered 35 people and injured 37 more. After burning down a local guesthouse, he was finally captured and imprisoned north of Hobart, his file stamped 'Never to be Released'.

Port Arthur Historic Site

The **Port Arthur Historic Site** (☎ 6251 2310, 1800 659 101; www.portarthur.org.au; Arthur Hwy; ☼ tours & buildings 9am-5pm, grounds 8.30am-dusk) remains one of Tasmania's busiest tourist attractions. Inside the main entry building is a visitors centre, a café, restaurant and gift shop (which stocks some interesting convict-focused publications). Downstairs is an interpretative gallery where you can follow the convicts' journey from England to Tasmania. Buggy transport around the site can be arranged for people with restricted mobility – ask at the information counter. The ferry plying the harbour is also wheelchair accessible.

Beyond the main building are dozens of restored structures, most of which you visit on the guided tour (opposite). The **Port Arthur Museum**, containing numerous displays and a café, was originally an asylum, housing patients from throughout the colony. The **Separate Prison** was built as a place of punishment for difficult prisoners, following a decision to 'reform' prisoners by isolation and sensory deprivation rather than by flogging. The **Church** was built in 1836 but was destroyed by fire in 1884, while the **Penitentiary**, converted from a granary in 1857, was also damaged by fire in 1897. The **Broad Arrow Café**, scene of many of the 1996 shootings, was gutted following the massacre. Today, the shell of the building has been preserved and a **Memorial Garden** established around it.

ADMISSION PASSES

Admission to the site is via a fairly complex hierarchy of passes: either a Bronze, Silver, Gold or After Dark Pass. For details on the various tours and eating options included with the passes, see Guided Tours (below) and Eating (p130).

Bronze Pass (adult/child/concession/family $28/14/23/62) Includes admission to the site, a guided tour and a harbour cruise. Suits visitors here for half a day or so.

Silver Pass (adult/child/concession $66/48/61) Includes all of the above plus a tour of Isle of the Dead or Point Puer, an audio tour and lunch at either the Museum Café or Port Café. Suits visitors here for a full day.

Gold Pass (adult/child/concession $98/76/93) Includes all the Silver Pass offers, but you get to do both the Point Puer and the Isle of the Dead tour, and have morning and afternoon tea thrown into the mix. If you're staying overnight in the area, this is the pass for you (it's valid for two days).

After Dark Pass (adult/child $50/42) Gets you onto the Historic Ghost Tour and snares you a two-course meal at Felons Bistro.

GUIDED TOURS

A forty-minute guided tour of the historic site is included in the price of admission and leaves regularly from the visitors centre – an excellent intro to the site, visiting all the old buildings. Also included in the price of your ticket is a 25-minute commentated **Harbour Cruise** past Point Puer and the Isle of the Dead. When you buy your ticket you'll be told the times of the next tour and cruise.

More detailed guided tours include the **Isle of the Dead Cemetery Tour** (adult/child/family $12/8/34) through Port Arthur's old burial ground on an island in the harbour, and the **Point Puer Boys' Prison Tour** (adult/child/family $12/8/34), which visits the first reformatory in the British Empire built for juvenile male convicts (aged nine to 18). Book both these tours well in advance if you can.

Another humungously popular tour is the 90-minute, lantern-lit **Historic Ghost Tour** (☎ 1800 659 101; adult/child/family $20/12/55), which leaves from the visitors centre nightly at dusk (rain or shine) and visits a number of historic buildings, with guides relating spine-chilling occurrences. Bookings essential.

Activities

About 5km north of the Historic Site is **Hire it with Denis** (☎ 6200 9998, 0427 362 789; hirewithdenis@bordernet.com.au; 6 Andersons Rd). Denis offers reasonably priced rental of canoes (two hours $47), kayaks (two hours $36), bikes (half day $14), fishing gear (full day $8), tents ($19 per week) and more. Free delivery to Port Arthur; minimal charge to other areas. Denis also has accommodation available.

Tours

Take a cruise from Port Arthur out to Tasman Island:

Navigators (☎ 6223 1914; www.navigators.net.au; 1½hr cruise adult/child/concession/family $65/45/59/174) Monday and Thursday cruises from Port Arthur around the sea cliffs and seal colonies of Tasman Island.

Tasman Island Cruises (☎ 6250 2200; www.tasmancruises.com.au; Arthur Hwy; 3hr cruise adult/child/family $100/55/300) Run by the same folks as Bruny Island Charters (p139), this cruise chugs around the awesome sea cliffs of Cape Pillar and Tasman Island and up the coast to Cape Hauy. Plenty of seals and bird life en route.

Sleeping

Given the iconic status of Port Arthur to Tasmania's tourism, it's surprising to find few quality accommodation or dining offerings down here – bland, dated motel units and cheesy B&Bs prevail, with a few notable exceptions.

Port Arthur Caravan & Cabin Park (☎ 6250 2340, 1800 620 708; www.portarthurcaravan-cabinpark.com.au; Garden Point Rd; dm $18, unpowered sites $20, powered sites $22-28, cabins $95-105) Spaciously sloping with plenty of greenery, this well-facilitated park (including camp kitchen, wood BBQs and shop) is 2km before Port Arthur, not far from a sheltered beach. Port Arthur's best (and only) budget option.

Fox & Hounds Inn (☎ 6250 2217; www.foxandhounds.com.au; 6789 Arthur Hwy; d $100-190) *Ewww*, mock Tudor! Still, the rooms off to the side of the main building are the cheapest motel doubles south of Eaglehawk Neck (especially in winter), and it's a matter of seconds from the Port Arthur gates. You can get a bang-up pub meal here, too (p130).

Port Arthur Villas (☎ 6250 2239, 1800 815 775; www.portarthurvillas.com.au; 52 Safety Cove Rd; d $135-160) Not far from the Comfort Inn, this place has reasonable self-contained units sleeping up to four, horseshoeing around garden and outdoor barbecue area. Externally it's all faux-Victorian lace and brickwork, but inside things are a little more stylish. Walking distance to the historic site.

Comfort Inn Port Arthur (☎ 6250 2101, 1800 030 747; www.portarthur-inn.com.au; 29 Safety Cove Rd; d $145-185) A motel with flashy views over the historic site but unremarkable rooms. More impressive is the restaurant, Commandant's Table (right). Ask about packages including accommodation, dinner, breakfast and a Port Arthur ghost tour (from $236 for two).

Stewarts Bay Lodge (☎ 6250 2888; www.stewarts baylodge.com; 6955 Arthur Hwy; d $155-200, 2/3br cabin from $195/255) Not far from the Port Arthur Historic Site (you can walk there around the coast), this place offers one-, two- and three-bedroom self-contained, updated log cabins on a slope running down to swimmable Stewarts Bay. Tasty internet rates.

Sea Change Safety Cove (☎ 6250 2719; www.safety cove.com; 425 Safety Cove Rd; d $160-200) Whichever way you look from this guesthouse there are fantastic views – misty cliffs, sea-wracked beach or scrubby bushland. It's 4km south of Port Arthur, just off the sandy sweep of Safety Cove Beach. There's a beaut communal deck, a couple of B&B rooms inside the house, plus a large self-contained unit sleeping five.

Tasman Homestead (☎ 6250 3331; www.tasman homestead.com; off Safety Cove Rd; d $220, extra adult/child $40/30) Brilliant views extend from the wraparound veranda at this rangy, mudbrick-and-timber homestead, perfect for families and groups (sleeps up to nine). It's 3.5km off Safety Cove Rd (past Palmers Lookout), fully self-contained (breakfast provisions included) and totally private. Bookings are through the Eaglehawk Café & Guesthouse (p125) – be sure to specify that it's the homestead you're after.

Eating

There are a couple of daytime food options at the historic site: the Museum Café in the Old Asylum and the hectic Port Café inside the visitors centre, both serving the usual takeaway suspects.

Lemo's Seafood & Roast (☎ 6250 3403; 6555 Arthur Hwy; mains $8-36; ☺ lunch & dinner) Almost new when we visited, Lemo's first appears to be an unashamed money trap snaring passing tourists (they could fit 20 tour buses in the car park), but then you think, 'Where else am I gonna get some curried duck around here?' Affordable, authentic Asian food; fully licensed.

The Bistro (☎ 6250 2101; Comfort Inn Port Arthur, 29 Safety Cove Rd; mains $12-18; ☺ lunch & dinner) A less inviting companion to the Commandant's Table (below), this viewless bar serves pedestrian pub nosh (schnitzels, roasts, fish and chips, steak).

Eucalypt (☎ 6250 2555; 6962 Arthur Hwy; mains $12-22; ☺ breakfast & lunch Wed-Mon, dinner Fri) A relative newcomer to the peninsula, Eucalypt extols the virtues of the best things in life: 'Coffee, Art, Food'. Organic breakfasts, light Mod Oz lunches and casual dinners with a glass of wine. Perfect.

Commandant's Table (☎ 6250 2101; Comfort Inn Port Arthur, 29 Safety Cove Rd; mains $17-28; ☺ dinner) The better of the two dining options at the Comfort Inn (left), with wide historic site views and an unexpectedly worldly menu (try the fish of the day with Nonya sambal, ginger and lemon juice on basmati rice).

Fox & Hounds Inn (☎ 6250 2217; 6789 Arthur Hwy; mains $17-34; ☺ lunch Dec-Mar, dinner nightly) This restaurant at the Fox & Hounds does reputable meals in its backdated, ye-olde-themed dining room, mostly from the pub menu roll call of timeless classics (reef 'n' beef, mixed grill, lamb cutlets, curried scallops). It also has a children's menu, and oceans of cold Cascade on tap.

Felons Bistro (☎ 6251 2310, 1800 659 101; visitors centre; mains $20-28; ☺ dinner). In a wing of the visitors centre, Felons is a worthy choice before you head off on the Ghost Tour. Upmarket, creative dinners with a seafood bias reinforce their catchy slogan: 'Dine with Conviction'. Try the Cajun-style fish of the day. Reservations advised.

Getting There & Away

See p122 for information on public transport and tours to Port Arthur.

REMARKABLE CAVE

About 5km south of Port Arthur is Remarkable Cave, a long tunnel eroded from the base of a collapsed gully, under a cliff and out to sea. A boardwalk and stairs provide access to a metal viewing platform above the gully, a few minutes' amble from the car park. Believe it or not, hardcore surfers brave the turbulent swell surging in through the cave, paddling out through the opening to surf the offshore reefs beyond.

You can also follow the coast east from the car park to **Maingon Blowhole** (one hour return)

TASMAN PENINSULA & PORT ARTHUR &

DETOUR: SALTWATER RIVER & LIME BAY

At Premaydena, take the signposted turn-off (the C431) 13km northwest to **Saltwater River** and the restored ruins at the **Coal Mines Historic Site** (☎ 1300 369 550; www.parks.tas.gov.au; admission free; ☒ dawn-dusk), a powerful reminder of the colonial past. Excavated in 1833, the coal mines were used to punish the worst of the convicts, who worked in abominable conditions. The poorly managed mining operation wasn't economically viable, and in 1848 it was sold to private enterprise. Within 10 years it was abandoned. Some buildings were demolished, while fire and weather put paid to the rest.

A low-key contrast to Port Arthur, the old mines site is interesting to wander around, following a trail of interpretive panels. Don't go burrowing into any old mine shafts – they haven't been stabilised and are potentially dangerous. You can, however, snoop around the well-preserved solitary confinement cells, which are torturously small and dark.

Not far away is **Lime Bay State Reserve**, a beautiful area aflutter with rare birds and butterflies, and with some lazy coastal walks. From Lime Bay, the 2½-hour return journey to Lagoon Beach is an untaxing amble. There's free bush camping to the north along a sandy track. Camping is very basic, with pit toilets. BYO drinking water and fuel stoves.

---

or further on to **Mt Brown** (four hours return), from which there are awesome views. On the way back it's worth deviating to **Palmers Lookout** for majestic views of the entire Port Arthur and Safety Cove area.

KOONYA & NUBEENA
☎ 03

There's not a whole lot of shakin' going on in diminutive **Koonya** (population 100), apart from accommodation at Cascades (right) and the **Seaview Riding Ranch** (☎ 6250 3110; 60 Firetower Rd; 1-/2hr rides from $30/55), signposted off the main road from Taranna. On offer is horse riding for all ages and skill levels, with scenic rides led by long-time locals.

About 12km further along the road is charmless **Nubeena** (population 300), the largest town on the peninsula, fanned out along the shore of Wedge Bay. It's much more low-key than Port Arthur – it's really just a holiday destination for locals – but if all the other accommodation on the peninsula is booked out (trust us, it happens), you might be able to find a bed here.

The surrounding natural areas are much more appealing than Nubeena itself. The main things to do here are swimming and chilling out on **White Beach**, or fishing from the jetty or foreshore. Down a side route 3km south of town is some energetic walking to **Tunnel Bay** (five hours return), **Raoul Bay Lookout** (two hours return) and the exquisitely named **Cape Raoul** (five hours return). To the north is **Roaring Beach**, which gets wicked surf but isn't safe for swimming.

Sleeping & Eating
White Beach Tourist Park (☎ 6250 2142; www.white beachtouristpark.com; 128 White Beach Rd, Nubeena; unpowered/powered sites $24/26, cabins $85-100) Beachfront park in quiet, ghost gum–dotted surrounds south of Nubeena. Facilities include laundry, shop, petrol bowser, playground and barbecue areas with impossibly well-manicured lawns. Ask about local walks and cheaper off-season rates.

White Beach Holiday Villas (☎ 6250 2152; www .whitebeachholidayvillas.com.au; 309 White Beach Rd, Nubeena; d $100-140, extra person $15) At the other end of the beach from the tourist park, this holiday hub has seven rather dated, self-contained brick villas (one with spa) with plenty of space; the units up the hill are newer and pricier. New owners might shake things up (including a new name).

Storm Bay Guest House (☎ 6250 2933; www.storm bay.com.au; 91 White Beach Rd, Nubeena; guesthouse d $130-190, 2br cottage d $220, extra person $20) Getting rave reviews from readers – for value, quality and surrounds – this guesthouse on Hardy's Hill offers magical views across stormy Storm Bay to Bruny Island. Beaut breakfasts and glasses of wine (not necessarily at the same time) on the deck, plus tasteful interiors. Kids OK in the cottage (sleeps six) but not the guesthouse.

Cascades (☎ 6250 3873; www.cascadescolonial.com.au; 533 Main Rd, Koonya; d incl breakfast $160-320) This old property was originally an outstation for Port Arthur, with around 400 convicts working here at one time. Some of the buildings have been restored in period style to become snug, self-contained cottages (including one luxury option with spa). Full breakfast provisions and entry to a private museum included.

Nubeena Tavern & Restaurant (☎ 6250 2250; 1599 Main Rd, Nubeena; mains $12-25; ☒ lunch & dinner) There are a couple of takeaways in Nubeena – good for a pie or a pastie – but if you're after something meatier, try the local pub for a reef 'n' beef or chicken schnitzel and a glass of Norfolk Bay chardonnay (grapes grown at Koonya). Occasional live bands too.

Getting There & Away

Tassielink (☎ 1300 300 520; www.tassielink.com.au) will take you from Hobart to Koonya in 1¾ hours; the one-way fare is $22. The bus continues to Nubeena ($24, two hours).

The Southeast

The quiet harbours and valley folds of Tasmania's southeast have much to offer, particularly if you enjoy driving through green, undulating countryside and snacking from roadside produce stores. Once the apple-producing heart of the Apple Isle (in the 1960s there were 2000 orchards in the Huon Valley), the area has since diversified into cherries, apricots, Atlantic salmon, wines, mushrooms, cheese and even saffron, catering to the passing tourist trade. Here, the fruit-filled hillsides of the Huon Valley give way to the sparkling inlets of the D'Entrecasteaux Channel. Bruny Island awaits enticingly offshore, Hartz Mountains National Park is not far inland, and further south the South Coast Track kicks off at magnificent Recherche Bay.

Francophiles will detect a clear French lineage here. French explorers Bruni d'Entrecasteaux and Nicolas Baudin charted much of the region's coastline in the 1790s and early 1800s, d'Entrecasteaux arriving a good decade before the Brits hoisted the Union Jack at Risdon Cove near Hobart in 1803. The southeast has three distinct areas: the peninsula, including Kettering and Cygnet, Bruny Island, and the Huon Hwy coastal strip linking Huonville with Cockle Creek. The wide Huon River remains the region's lifeblood. Synonymous with the river is the famous Huon pine; sadly, only a few young specimens remain locally. The southeast is also known for its rainbows – the happy by-product of southern latitudes and abundant waterways. On cold, clear winter nights, you might also catch the *Aurora Australis,* the southern hemisphere's equivalent of the *Aurora Borealis* or Northern Lights.

THE SOUTHEAST

HIGHLIGHTS

- Forgetting the office, courtesy of a couple of days on **Bruny Island** (p136)
- Paddling a sea-kayak over the glassy swells of the **D'Entrecasteaux Channel** (p136)
- Conjuring up images of French explorers' tall ships anchored in remote **Recherche Bay** (p152)
- Tuning-in to the twang, shimmy and stomp of the **Cygnet Folk Festival** (p142), a jazzy January jamboree
- Inspecting a Huon pine hull under construction at Franklin's **Wooden Boat Centre** (p146)
- Smiling at your reflection in an alpine moorland tarn at **Hartz Mountains National Park** (p148)

Wooden ★ Boat Centre
Cygnet Folk ★ Festival
Hartz Mountains National Park ★
D'Entrecasteaux ★ Channel
Hastings Caves & ★ Thermal Springs
Ida Bay Railway ★
Bruny ★ Island
★ Recherche Bay

- Spelunking into the subterranean gloom at **Hastings Caves & Thermal Springs** (p151)
- Riding the **Ida Bay Railway** (p151) – Australia's southernmost railway – to the end of the line

▪ TELEPHONE CODE: 03 ▪ www.huontrail.org.au ▪ www.brunyisland.net.au

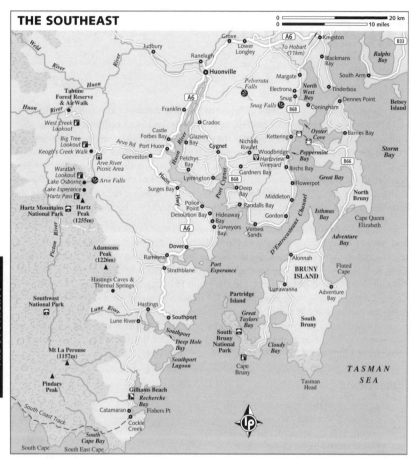

THE SOUTHEAST

Getting There & Around

BUS

Hobart Coaches (☎ 132 201; www.hobartcoaches.com
.au) runs several buses each weekday from
Hobart south through Margate, Snug and
Kettering to Woodbridge. A bus also runs
once each weekday from Hobart to Snug
and inland across to Cygnet. There are no
weekend services.

Tassielink (☎ 1300 300 520; www.tassielink.com
.au) runs buses along the Huon Hwy from
Hobart through Huonville, Franklin and
Geeveston to Dover. There are up to seven
services a day from Monday to Friday (five of
these terminate in Geeveston), and one each
on Saturday and Sunday (both terminating
in Geeveston).

At 9am on Monday, Wednesday and Friday
from December through March, a Tassielink
bus departs Hobart and continues south all
the way to the end of the road at Cockle Creek
(bookings essential).

CAR

The views from the Channel Hwy between
Hobart and Woodbridge are lovely, particularly on sunny days when the contrast between lush pastures and the deep-blue channel
waters is dazzling. If you then take the road
from Woodbridge to Gardners Bay en route
to Cygnet, you'll be rewarded with improbably
alluring views on both sides of the ridge. You
can also follow the coast from Woodbridge
through Verona Sands to Cygnet, occasion-

ally passing very close to the channel – an impressive detour.

Further south, some sections of the side route from Surges Bay through Police Point are surfaced with coarse gravel, which will shake up your spine if you're in an older vehicle. Check your tyres before you leave, and make sure your spare is in good shape.

TOURS

If you're *sans voiture* (as Bruni d'Entrecasteaux certainly was), you might want to join a southbound tour from Hobart (see p139 for information on getting to and around Bruny Island on a tour):

Gray Line (☎ 6234 3336, 1300 858 687; www.grayline .com.au; tours adult/child $130/65) Huon Valley day tours visiting Huonville, Franklin, Geeveston and the Tahune Forest AirWalk.

Peppermint Bay Cruise (p142) A five-hour cruise down the D'Entrecasteaux Channel to Woodbridge.

Tassielink (☎ 1300 300 520; www.tassielink.com.au; tours adult/child $16/8) Six-hour bus trips to Huonville on weekdays.

MARGATE
☎ 03 / pop 745
About 23km south of Hobart (beyond Kingston, covered on p119) is small-town Margate. Train spotters might like to scrutinize the **Margate Train** (☎ 6267 1020; www.view.com.au/margate train; 1567 Channel Hwy; admission free; ☺ 9am-4.30pm), the last passenger train used in Tasmania. It stands idly on a redundant section of track by the highway on the northern side of town, and houses craft shops, antique dealers, the **Pancake Train Café** (mains $10-19) serving pancakes and light meals, and even a barber and masseuse!

Behind the train is **Inverawe Native Gardens** (☎ 6267 2020; www.inverawe.com.au; 1565 Channel Hwy; adult/child $8/4; ☺ 9.30am-sunset Sep-May), a private, 9.5-hectare property with landscaped native gardens, trails, water views and 80 species of blow-through birds, including the 12 species endemic to Tassie.

Closer to town is the fabulous **Brookfield Vineyard** (☎ 6267 2880; www.brookfieldvineyard.com; 1640 Channel Hwy; admission free, mains $9-15; ☺ 9am-6pm, to midnight Fri), Margate's multifaceted hub of all things good: wine, gourmet fare, live music and artsy design. Breakfast until 4pm (nachos, pides, pasta, pies, crepes), Wednesday afternoon craft market, Friday night hootenanny.

Hobart Coaches (☎ 13 22 01; www.hobartcoaches .com.au) offers several bus runs from Hobart through Kingston to Margate ($6.50, 20 to 30 minutes) Monday to Friday, plus two services on Saturday.

SNUG
☎ 03 / pop 770
Early Euro explorers decided this area was a safe, sheltered anchorage, which spawned the heart-warming name Snug. The town was levelled by bushfires in 1967, when 80 houses burnt down. A temporary caravan village was established beside the oval, which eventually became the present-day caravan park.

Oyster Cove, off Manuka Rd 5km south of Snug, was a traditional camp for indigenous people, who called it Mena Loongana or Mannina. In 1847 it became the next destination for the Tasmanian Aborigines who survived Wybalenna on Flinders Island (see p26). In 1995, Oyster Cove was returned to the Tasmanian Aboriginal community.

Snug Falls are 3.5km off the highway (signposted). An easy 45-minute return walk, complete with seats and picnic shelters, leads to the foot of the falls. If the weather's hot, just south of Snug at **Coningham** is a safe swimming beach.

One kilometre south of Snug is the **Channel Historical & Folk Museum** (☎ 6267 9169; 2361 Channel Hwy; adult/child $5/1; ☺ 10am-4pm Wed-Sun), a historical showcase of local timber, fishing and shipbuilding industries, as well as the destructive 1967 fires. A move to Margate was mooted – look for them there if they're not here.

Sleeping & Eating
Snug Beach Cabin & Caravan Park (☎ 6267 9138; 35 Beach Rd; powered/unpowered sites from $23/18, cabins $75-120; ☐ ☑) Grass-sprung, sheltered sites and faux-cedar cabins near the beach. Nearby are man-made distractions like a tennis court, playground and parakeet aviary.

Aside from the decent-value pub fare plated up at low-slung **Snug Tavern** (☎ 6267 9238; 2236 Channel Hwy; mains $15-20; ☺ lunch & dinner) – steaks, crumbed scallops, roasts – there are slim pickings in Snug come meal time. A trip north to Margate will broaden your options.

Getting There & Away
Hobart Coaches (☎ 132 201; www.hobartcoaches.com.au) runs seven weekday buses from Hobart through Margate to Snug ($7.50, 30 minutes).

KETTERING
☎ 03 / pop 300

Blessed with photogenic looks, the lethargic port of Kettering shelters fishing boats and yachts in Oyster Cove Marina, next to the Bruny Island ferry terminal. Most folks just blow through here en route to Bruny, but it's an essential stop for sea-kayakers.

The **Bruny D'Entrecasteaux visitors centre** (☎ 6267 4494; www.tasmaniaholiday.com; 81 Ferry Rd; ☼ 9am-5pm), by the ferry terminal, has information on accommodation and services on Bruny Island, including walk notes and a self-guided driving tour.

At the marina is **Roaring 40s Ocean Kayaking** (☎ 6267 5000; www.roaring40skayaking.com.au; Oyster Cove Marina, Ferry Rd; ☼ closed Jun-Aug), Tassie's leading sea-kayaking tour operator. The company offers gear rental to kayakers, and organises a smorgasbord of kayaking trips to suit all levels of experience. A half-day paddle around Oyster Cove costs $90; a full day on the D'Entrecasteaux Channel costs $155, including lunch. A full day around the Tasman Peninsula costs $255. Overnight trips at venues such as Lake St Clair, Lake Pedder and Freycinet Peninsula are also available, plus night trips around the southwest wilderness (p303).

Sleeping & Eating
Oyster Cove Inn (☎ 6267 4446; www.view.com.au/oyster; 1 Ferry Rd; s/d without bathrooms from $40/70) A cream-coloured monolith presiding over the boat-cluttered harbour, this large pub has budget singles, twins and doubles upstairs. Kooky carpet, ill-matched linen, raggedy bathrooms – talk about no-frills! The restaurant (mains $10 to $25; open for dinner) raises the standards a little, with an extensive menu, local wines, a casual bar and outdoor deck.

Old Kettering Inn (☎ 6267 4426; ebaldwin@rezitech .com.au; 58 Ferry Rd; d incl breakfast $125) On the road to the ferry terminal, this 1894 property amid flower-festooned gardens and offers one commodious suite – bedroom, bathroom, lounge and outdoor deck – with a private entrance. Cooked breakfast included.

Tulendena (☎ 6267 4348; www.tulendena.com.au; 29 Bloomsbury La; d $150, extra person $30) Just north of Kettering, signposted off the highway, is this quality self-contained abode, sleeping four in mod-con comfort. The house squats in spacious gardens with birds all a-twitter and views from the private terrace. Two-night minimum; discounts for longer stays.

Herons Rise Vineyard (☎ 6267 4339; www.heronsrise .com.au; 1000 Saddle Rd; d $160, extra person $30) Just north of town, Herons Rise has two upmarket, self-contained cottages set among the vines (a third being built above the pinot-stacked wine cellar), each with a log fire. Breakfast provisions supplied.

Mermaid Café (☎ 6267 4494; 81 Ferry Rd; light meals $8-16; ☼ breakfast & lunch daily, dinner Fri & Sat) Inside the Bruny D'Entrecasteaux visitors centre is this informal licensed café, offering everything from a quick coffee and toasted sandwich to a bang-up meal.

Farm Gate Café & Providore (☎ 6267 4997; cnr Channel Hwy & Saddle Rd; lunch $8-20, dinner $24-27; ☼ breakfast & lunch Wed-Sun, dinner Fri & Sat) A new addition to the Channel food scene is this bright modern room, serving breakfast (omelettes, French toast or bircher muesli), lunch (chicken, pea and bacon pie; mushroom and thyme risotto) and dinner (twice-cooked duck salad; aged sirloin). Classy stuff.

Getting There & Away
Four weekday-only buses from Hobart run by **Hobart Coaches** (☎ 132 201; www.hobartcoaches .com.au) stop at Kettering. The 50 minute ride from Hobart costs $9.

BRUNY ISLAND
☎ 03 / pop 600

Bruny Island is almost two islands, joined by a narrow, 5km sandy isthmus called the Neck. Renowned for its wildlife (fairy penguins, echidnas, mutton birds), it's a windswept, sparsely populated retreat, blown by ocean rains in the south, and dry and beachy in the north.

Bruny's coastal scenery is magical. There are countless swimming and surf beaches, plus good sea and freshwater fishing. South Bruny is home to the steep, forested South Bruny National Park, which has some beaut walking tracks, especially around Labillardiere Peninsula and Fluted Cape.

The island was spied by Abel Tasman's beady eyes in 1642, and between 1770 and 1790 was visited by Furneaux, Cook, Bligh and Cox. It was named after Rear-Admiral Bruni d'Entrecasteaux, who explored the area in 1792. Strangely, confusion reigned about the spelling – in 1918 it was changed from Bruni to Bruny.

Tasmanian Aborigines of the Nuennone band called the island Lunawanna-Alonnah, a name given contemporary recognition (albeit broken in two) as the names of two island towns. Among their numbers was Truganini, daughter of Mangana, chief of the Nuennone band. Truganini left Bruny in the 1830s to accompany George Robinson on his infamous state-wide journey to win the trust of all the Tasmanian Aborigines. Many of Bruny's landmarks, including Mt Mangana, are named after the isle's original inhabitants. For more on Truganini, see p27.

The island has endured several commercial ventures. Sandstone was mined here and used for the Post Office and Houses of Parliament in Melbourne, and coal was also exhumed here. Both industries gradually declined due to lofty transportation costs. Only farming and forestry have had long-term viability.

Tourism is becoming increasingly important to the island's economy but remains fairly low-key. There are (as yet) no homogenised resorts, just plenty of interesting cottages and houses, most self-contained. Too many visitors try unsuccessfully to cram their Bruny experience into one day. If you can handle the peace and quiet, plan to stay a few days.

Information

The Bruny D'Entrecasteaux visitors centre (opposite) by the ferry terminal can help with accommodation bookings, books and information on walks, camping and driving tours. You can also buy national park passes for South Bruny National Park here. Online, check out www.brunyisland.net.au.

South Bruny has three **general stores**, open 9am to 5pm seven days, all with Eftpos facilities, and all selling petrol, takeaway food and provisions (though not everything your stomach desires adorns the shelves). The largest is at **Adventure Bay** (712 Main Rd) and has a multicard ATM. The store at **Alonnah** (☎ 6293 1424; 3 William Carte Dr) is also the post office. The third store is at **Lunawanna** (☎ 6293 1297; 10 Cloudy Bay Rd). There are no stores on North Bruny.

There's internet access in Adventure Bay at the Penguin Café (p141) or at the **Online Access Centre** (☎ 6293 2036; School Rd) at Alonnah School (signposted). The centre has complex opening hours – phone ahead.

Sights & Activities
MUSEUMS

The curiosity-arousing **Bligh Museum of Pacific Exploration** (☎ 6293 1117; www.brunyisland.net.au /Adventure_Bay/blighmuseum.html; 876 Main Rd, Adventure Bay; adult/child/family $4/2/10; ☺ 10am-4pm) details the local exploits of explorers Bligh, Cook, Furneaux and, of course, Bruni D'Entrecasteaux. The engaging collection includes maps, charts and manuscripts – many of them originals or first editions – plus globes and information on early Antarctic explorations.

At the council offices in Alonnah is the wee, volunteer-run **Bruny Island History Room** (☎ 6260 6366; www.brunyisland.net.au/Alonnah/historyroom.html; Main Rd, Alonnah; admission free; ☺ 10am-3pm), displaying newspaper clippings, photos and records of the island community's past, plus info on walks and attractions around Bruny.

LIGHTHOUSE

Worth visiting is the 1836 stone **Cape Bruny Lighthouse** (☎ 6298 3114; tours adult/child $5/2) on South Bruny – the second-oldest lighthouse in Oz! Take a tour (one day's advance booking required) or wander the surrounding **reserve** (☺ 10am-4pm), which has impressive panoramas of the rugged coast.

SOUTH BRUNY NATIONAL PARK & THE NECK

Fluted Cape, one of the disparate extremities of **South Bruny National Park** (www.parks.tas.gov.au /natparks/sthbruny), is east of the small Adventure Bay township. The easy trail leading here from the main beach passes **Grass Point** (1½ hours return), a brilliant breakfast spot on a sunny morning. From here you can walk along the shore to **Penguin Island**, accessible at low tide, or complete a more difficult circuit climbing the cape itself (2½ hours return).

The park's southwestern portion comprises the **Labillardiere Peninsula**, which features jagged coastal scenery and a lighthouse. Walks here range from leisurely beach meanderings to a seven-hour circuit of the entire peninsula (starting and finishing at Jetty Beach camping ground).

For up-to-date information on the national park walks plus other walks around the island, consult the Bruny D'Entrecasteaux visitors centre or check out www.brunyisland.net.au /Walks/brunywalks.html. For national park entry fees, see p64.

Bruny Island Neck Game Reserve (www.brunyisland .net.au/Neck/neck.html), on the isthmus between North and South Bruny, is home to mutton birds and little (fairy) penguins that nest in

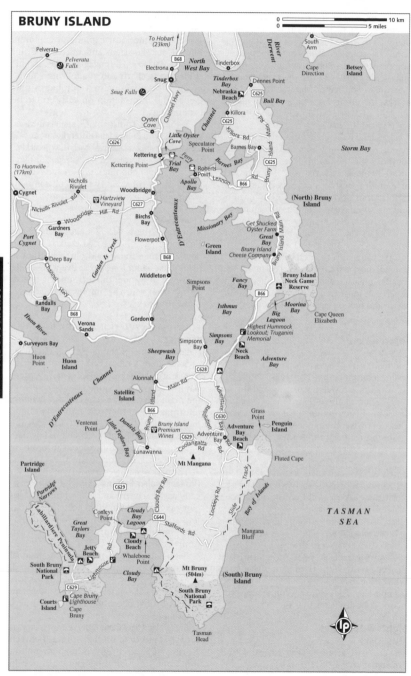

BRUNY ISLAND

0 _____ 10 km
0 _____ 5 miles

THE SOUTHEAST

Pelverata

Pelverata Falls

To Hobart (23km)

B68

North West Bay

Tinderbox

River Derwent

South Arm

Cape Direction

Betsey Island

Electrona

Snug

Snug Falls

Tinderbox Bay

Nebraska Beach

Dennes Point

C625

Bull Bay

Killora

Oyster Cove

Little Oyster Cove

C626

Channel Hwy

Channel

Killora Rd

Storm Bay

Kettering

Kettering Point

Ferry

Trial Bay

Speculator Point

Barnes Bay

Barnes Bay

Bruny Island Main Rd

C625

To Huonville (17km)

Nicholls Rivulet

Roberts Point

Apollo Bay

Lennon Rd

B66

C625

Cygnet

Nicholls Rivulet Rd

Woodbridge

Hartzview Vineyard

C627

Woodbridge Hill Rd

Birchs Bay

D'Entrecasteaux

Missionary Bay

(North) Bruny Island

Gardners Bay

Flowerpot

Green Island

Get Shucked Oyster Farm

Great Bay

Bruny Island Cheese Company

Bruny Island Main Rd

Port Cygnet

Gordon Creek

Deep Bay

Middleton

B68

Simpsons Point

Fancy Bay

Bruny Island Neck Game Reserve

Randalls Bay

B68

Gordon

Isthmus Bay

Big Lagoon

Moorina Bay

Cape Queen Elizabeth

Huon River

Verona Sands

Channel Hwy

Simpsons Bay

Highest Hummock Lookout; Truganini Memorial

Surveyors Bay

Huon Point

Huon Island

Sheepwash Bay

Simpsons Bay

Neck Beach

Adventure Bay

Channel

Alonnah

Main Rd

D'Entrecasteaux

Satellite Island

B66

C628

Resolution Rd

Grass Point

Penguin Island

Ventenat Point

Daniels Bay

Little Taylors Bay

Bruny Island Premium Wines

C629

Adventure Bay Rd

Adventure Bay

Adventure Bay Beach

Fluted Cape

Lunawanna

Coolangatta Rd

Mt Mangana

Lockleys Rd

Slide Track

Bay of Islands

TASMAN SEA

Partridge Island

Partridge Narrows

Partridge

C629

Cloudy Bay Rd

Staffords Rd

Mangana Bluff

Labillardiere Peninsula

Conleys Point

Cloudy Bay Lagoon

C644

Great Taylors Bay

Jetty Beach

Lighthouse Rd

Cloudy Beach

Whalebone Point

South Bruny National Park

Cloudy Bay

Mt Bruny (504m)

(South) Bruny Island

C629

Cape Bruny Lighthouse

South Bruny National Park

Courts Island

Cape Bruny

Tasman Head

the dunes. The best time and place to see the penguins is at dusk in the warmer months at **Highest Hummock Lookout**. Park at the Bruny Island Neck Game Reserve sign and climb the 273 steps to the **Truganini Memorial** for broad views of both ends of the island. Another timber walkway crosses the Neck to the beach on the other side. Keep to the boardwalk in this area – mutton birds dig deep holes in the sand that can be hard to see (a broken ankle is a sure-fire holiday bummer).

Bird-nerds can also visit the national park for glimpses of endangered species like the forty-spotted pardalote. During summer there are ranger-led park activities; for details, contact the **Parks & Wildlife Service** (☎ 6293 1419; www .parks.tas.gov.au/natparks/sthbruny).

TASTES OF BRUNY

If you're hankering for a quivering sliver of goat's milk cheese (or cow's, for that matter), the **Bruny Island Cheese Company** (☎ 6260 6332, 0428 606 332; 1087 Main Rd, Great Bay) is for you. Opening hours vary – call to confirm they're not knee-deep in curds out the back when you visit.

Get Shucked Oyster Farm (☎ 6293 1131; www.get shucked.com.au) is another brilliant Bruny business, cultivating the 'fuel for love' in these chilly southern waters. For a taste, visit the Hothouse Café (p141).

If you're workin' up a thirst, **Bruny Island Premium Wines** (☎ 6293 1008, 0409 973 033; wayaree@ clearmail.com.au; 4391 Main Rd, Lunawanna) offers cellar door sales at Australia's most southerly vineyard. Opening hours are irregular – call ahead to guarantee your tasting (pinot noir and chardonnay rule the roost).

Tours
FROM HOBART

From October to April, **Bruny Island Charters** (☎ 6293 1465; www.brunycharters.com.au) operates highly recommended three-hour tours of the island's awesome southeast coastline, taking in rookeries, seal colonies, bays, caves and towering sea cliffs. Trips depart Adventure Bay jetty at 11am daily from October to May, and cost $95/50 per adult/child. You can also take the tour as part of a full-day trip from Hobart ($155/110), including lunch and transfers.

Alternatively, travellers without a car could try Bruny Island Charters' **Bruny Island Bus Service** ($45; ☺ 8am) – a return bus trip from Hobart to Adventure Bay, with admission to the Bligh Museum of Pacific Exploration and

four hours' exploring time (hike the Fluted Cape Walk or bum around on the beach). Call for bookings.

Bruny Island Ventures (☎ 6229 7465; www.bruny island.net.au/Services/brunyislandventures.html) runs small-group Bruny day tours that cost $130/90 per adult/child. Tours depart Hobart four times a week and peruse the island's prime features, including the Neck, Adventure Bay and Cape Bruny Lighthouse, with meals included.

ON THE ISLAND

See left for details on the excellent cruise out of Adventure Bay operated by Bruny Island Charters.

Inala Nature Tours (☎ 6293 1217; www.inalabruny .com.au; 320 Cloudy Bay Rd) runs highly regarded personalised walking and 4WD tours of the island (from half a day to three days), focused on flora and fauna. The tour leader is a botanist, zoologist and conservationist; her 250-hectare property is home to almost 140 bird species (and one- and three-bedroom cottages for rent). A three-hour walking tour around the property costs $110 per person; a five-hour 4WD island tour costs $175 per person.

Other options include fishing charters, with all equipment provided, run by **Ol' Kid** (☎ 6293 1128; www.capcookolkid.com.au), operating from Captain James Cook Memorial Caravan Park in Adventure Bay (p140). Three-hour charters start at $90 per person (minimum two people).

Sleeping

Self-contained cottages abound on Bruny, most suitable for midsized groups and offering economical one-week rates. Bookings are essential, as owners/managers and their keys aren't always easily located – the Bruny D'Entrecasteaux visitors centre (p136) is a good starting point. Adventure Bay has the lion's share of accommodation, but there are places at Alonnah (the other main settlement on South Bruny), and at Barnes Bay and Dennes Point (pronounced 'Denz') on North Bruny.

There are no hostels on Bruny.

BUDGET
South Bruny

If you have a vehicle and a tent, the cheapest island accommodations are the free bush camping grounds. Camping on Bruny is restricted to these places to prevent the foreshore being

THE SOUTHEAST

damaged by indiscriminate tent placement. There are sites within South Bruny National Park (national park passes required) at **Jetty Beach**, a beautiful sheltered cove 3km north of the lighthouse, and at **Cloudy Bay**. There's also a campsite outside the national park at **Neck Beach**, at the southern end of the Neck. All sites have pit toilets and fireplaces; BYO firewood and water.

Captain James Cook Memorial Caravan Park (☎ 6293 1128; www.capcookolkid.com.au; 786 Main Rd, Adventure Bay; unpowered/powered sites $16/20, on-site vans $42-50, cabins $120) Right by the beach, this grandly named park could do with a few trees, but has decent facilities (including wheelchair-accessible cabins) and welcoming owners who go out of their way to ensure you have a happy stay. Fishing charters are available (see p139).

Adventure Bay Eco Village (☎ 6293 1270; www.adventurebayholidayvillage.com.au; 1005 Main Rd, Adventure Bay; powered sites $20, cabins $70-130) Beside the beach at the end of Adventure Bay Rd (3km past the general store), with cabins to suit all budgets and wildlife-filled grounds (white wallabies!). No late-night rabble-rousing, no tent sites, no pets, no boats (no fun?).

Hotel Bruny (☎ 6293 1148; brunypub@bigpond.com; Main Rd, Alonnah; d $70) There are two squat roadside units on offer at the pub – this doesn't sound too enticing, but they pass muster if all you're after is a clean room and comfy bed for the night.

MIDRANGE
South Bruny

Lumeah (☎ 6293 1265; www.lumeah-island.com.au; Adventure Bay Rd, Adventure Bay; d $140, extra person $20) Lumeah, an Adventure Bay sawmiller's cottage knocked up 115 years ago, offers accommodation perfect for two couples or two families: two double rooms, two bathrooms and a bunk room sleeping six (maximum 10 guests). It's fully self-contained, 50m from the beach, and has a barbecue area and spa. Nice one.

Explorers' Cottages (☎ 6293 1271; www.brunyisland.com; 20 Lighthouse Rd, Lunawanna; d $140, extra person $25) Just south of Lunawanna on the way to the lighthouse, these bright, beachy, self-contained cottages sleep four with lounge areas, log fires, board games and outdoor decks.

Mickeys Bay Eco Retreat (☎ 1300 889 557; www.mickeysbay.com; 736 Lighthouse Rd, Lunawanna; d $140, extra person $25) About 12km south of Lunawanna en

route to the lighthouse is this self-contained, open-plan studio apartment, sleeping up to six. It's a hip, modern design, with polished floorboards, handmade furniture, a BBQ and private beach. Perfect for families.

North Bruny

Bruny Beach House (☎ 5243 8486, 0419 315 626; www.brunybeachhouse.com; 91 Nebraska Rd, Dennes Point; d $135, extra person $20) Above the sandy sliver of Nebraska Beach in the north is this large, good-value beach house sleeping four. It's got all the requisite facilities, a wood heater and a super deck on which to sip and scan. BYO supplies; two-night minimum stay.

Wainui B&B (☎ 6260 6260; www.wainuibandb.com; 87 Main Rd, Dennes Point; r $150) Two large, attractive rooms and outdoor deck views are main selling points of this modern B&B at Dennes Point in the island's north. The owner is ex–Merchant Marine, and keeps things ship-shape. He'll sell you a BBQ pack for $35 to cook on the barbie.

292 Apollo Bay (☎ 6293 1271; www.brunyisland.com; 292 Apollo Bay Rd, Apollo Bay; d $175, extra person $25) This is the closest accommodation to the Roberts Point ferry terminal, which will make life easier if you're contemplating the 7am ferry! Sleeps six in self-contained, view-infused splendour.

TOP END
South Bruny

Morella Island Retreats (☎ 6293 1131; www.morella-island.com; 46 Adventure Bay Rd. Adventure Bay; d $170-270) For an extra-spesh occasion, book one of these unique, sequestered cottages 6km north of Adventure Bay (they also have beachfront cottages down by The Neck). Cottages range from sexy retreats for couples (complete with garden bath and hammock for two) to family-sized holiday homes. All are self-contained; design and décor could be described as 'classic castaway'. Prices drop by up to $50 for stays longer than one night.

The Tree House (☎ 0405-192 892; www.thetreehouse.com.au; Alonnah; d $180, extra person $25) This is a good-lookin', open-plan timber place overlooking the agriculturally named Sheep Wash Bay. It has two bedrooms, all the mod cons and super-dooper views. The price drops to $160 for stays of two nights or more. It's a 15-minute walk to the pub.

St Clairs (☎ 6293 1300; www.stclairs.com; Lighthouse Rd; d $210) On the road to the lighthouse (just past the Explorers' Cottages) is this plush (but not pretentious) getaway cottage built for two, surrounded by bushland. Renting it nets you a spa and cooked breakfast provisions; dinner by arrangement. The tariff drops to $190 for two nights; $180 for subsequent nights.

Eating

Pick up provisions and takeaways at the island's general stores (see p137).

Hothouse Café (☎ 6293 1131; 46 Adventure Bay Rd, South Bruny; meals $9-23; ☺ breakfast & lunch, dinner by arrangement) This café at Morella Island Retreat occupies a converted hothouse (sit inside on a sunny day and you'll start to sprout). Isthmus views and flappy bird life distract you from the menu of interesting snacks and mains (omelettes, steaks, flatbread wraps). Dinner is usually an option in January.

Bruny Island Smoke House (☎ 6260 6344; 360 Lennon Rd, North Bruny; mains $12-20; ☺ lunch Sat & Sun, dinner Fri) Managed with pizzazz, 'BISH' is a winner – gourmet pizzas, smoked fish and meats, cakes, decent coffee and astounding views from the deck. If only they were open more often!

Hotel Bruny (☎ 6293 1148; Main Rd, Alonnah; mains $18-25; ☺ lunch & dinner) An unassuming pub in Alonnah, with outdoor water-view seating to help you unravel, plus a reasonable menu heavy on local seafood. We suspect the smile-free barman was just having a bad day…

Penguin Café (☎ 6293 1352; 710 Main Rd, Adventure Bay; 2 courses $28; ☺ dinner) Next to the Adventure Bay store, Penguin Café serves fixed-price dinners (soup of the day, beef in red wine, fillet of ocean trout etc) in a cosy wooden room. Wines by the glass or bottle. Ask about their gourmet picnic hampers. Bookings essential. Reduced winter hours.

Getting There & Away

Access to the island is via **car ferry** (☎ 6272 3277) from Kettering across to Roberts Point on the north of the island. There are at least 10 services daily, taking 20 minutes one-way. The first ferry from Kettering is at 6.30am (7.45am on Sunday), the last at 6.30pm (7.30pm on Friday). The first ferry from Bruny is at 7am (8.25am on Sunday), the last at 7pm (7.50pm on Friday). The timetable may vary, so double-check departure times. Return fares: cars $25 ($30 on public holidays and public holiday weekends), motorcycles $11, bicycles $3 and foot passengers free.

The Roberts Point terminal on Bruny is a long way from anywhere. If you don't have your own wheels, see p139 for info on how to get to Bruny on a tour.

Getting Around

You'll need your own wheels to get around – there are no buses. A bicycle is a great option, but be prepared for long rides between destinations. Bruny has some narrow, winding gravel roads, the slippery, logging truck–infested road over Mt Mangana being the prime case in point. Not all car rental companies are cool with this concept.

WOODBRIDGE

☎ 03 / pop 250

Established in 1874 as Peppermint Bay (after the area's peppermint gums), Woodbridge was eventually renamed by a landowner nostalgic for his old home in England. It's a quiet village sitting squarely on the tourist trail thanks to the sexy Peppermint Bay development (p142), which has consumed the old Woodbridge pub.

About 3km south of Peppermint Bay is another stop for foodies: **Grandvewe Cheeses** (☎ 6267 4099; www.grandvewe.com.au; 59 Devlyns Rd, Birchs Bay; tastings free; ☺ 10am-5pm daily Sep-Jun, 10am-4pm Wed-Mon Jul-Aug), a farm churning out organic cheese from both sheep and cow's milk. Sample some tasty produce, snack on a cheese platter (the pecorino is perfection) or quaff some pinot noir from the owners' nearby Grandvewe Vineyard.

A little further south is **Fleurtys** (☎ 6267 4078; www.fleurtys.com.au; 3866 Channel Hwy, Birchs Bay; ☺ 11am-4pm daily), a cool little glass-fronted providore in the trees where you can take a bushwalk, inspect the essential-oil distillery and stock up on homemade jam, vinegar, honey, chutney, herbs, fudge and oils. The café here is great for lunch too (mains $10 to $16).

Hartzview Vineyard (☎ 6295 1623; www.hartzview .com.au; 70 Dillons Rd, Gardners Bay; tastings $2 refunded with purchase; ☺ 10am-5pm) is 7km up the hill from Woodbridge, off the road to Gardners Bay. For your palate's pleasure are a range of fortified wines, fruit liqueurs, a peppery pinot noir and a mellifluous mead. Lunch here is also a goer (salads, focaccia, smoked quiches, cheese platters – mains $10 to $18). There's also accommodation here (p142).

THE SOUTHEAST

Sleeping & Eating

Telopea (☎ 6267 4565; www.telopea-accommodation
.com.au; 144 Pullens Rd; s/d $88/99, extra adult/child
$22/11) A rural property with two wheelchair-
accessible (but unremarkable) self-contained
brick units on offer. Pullens Rd intersects with
the Channel Hwy on the northern outskirts
of Woodbridge.

Old Woodbridge Rectory (☎ 6267 4742; www
.rectory.alltasmanian.com; 15 Woodbridge Hill Rd; d $110-130)
At the start of the Gardners Bay road is this
friendly place with flower-filled gardens and
two large en suite rooms in a 1905 rectory.

Hartzview Vineyard (☎ 6295 1623; www.hartzview
.com.au; 70 Dillons Rd, Gardners Bay; d $160-200, extra adult/
child $40/20) This secluded hilltop vineyard of-
fers a fully equipped three-bedroom house
endowed with antiques, a log fire, breakfast
provisions and fine views over Gardners Bay.
Dinners by arrangement.

our pick **Peppermint Ridge Retreat** (☎ 6267
4192; www.peppermintridge.com.au; 290 Woodbridge Hill
Rd; d $160-220, extra person $25) Two amazing handmade straw bale and stone studios, complete
with composting toilets, recycled timbers,
spa baths, huge lofty spaces and brilliant
D'Entrecasteaux Channel and Bruny Island
views. Each sleeps five; breakfast supplies
included. The local wallabies aren't shy.

Peppermint Bay (☎ 6267 4088; www.pepper
mintbay.com.au; 3435 Channel Hwy) On a mesmeric
D'Entrecasteaux Channel inlet, Peppermint
Bay houses a provedore, an art gallery, the
upmarket à la carte Dining Room (mains
$25 to $30; open daily for lunch, and for dinner on Saturday), and the casual Local Bar
(mains $15 to $20; open daily for lunch, and
for dinner Tuesday to Saturday). The emphasis is on local produce: seafood, fruits, meats,
cheeses and other foodstuffs from just down
the road, used to fantastic effect. Reduced
winter hours. Bookings advised. You can also
take a cruise here from Hobart (see Getting
There & Away, below).

See also Grandvewe Cheeses, Fleurtys and
Hartzview Vineyard (p141).

Getting There & Away

Hobart Coaches (☎ 13 22 01; www.hobartcoaches.com
.au) has four weekday services; the trip from
Hobart takes one hour and costs $9.

Another option from Hobart is the
Peppermint Bay Cruise (Map p82; ☎ 1300 137 919;
www.peppermintbay.com.au/cruises; Brooke St Pier,
Hobart; cruises noon daily Oct-Apr, Mon, Wed & Fri-Sun

May-Sep), which runs a five-hour float down
the D'Entrecasteaux Channel to the sassy
Peppermint Bay development. Prices start at
$78/48 per adult/child including lunch at the
Peppermint Bay dining room of the restaurant, or prepared at the restaurant and eaten
on board. Cruise-prices only from $48/28.

CYGNET

☎ 03 / pop 930

Groovy Cygnet was originally named Port
de Cygne Noir (Port of the Black Swan) by
Bruni d'Entrecasteaux (swans proliferate on
the bay). Youthfully reincarnated as Cygnet
(a baby swan), the town has evolved into a
dreadlocked, artsy enclave, while still func-
tioning as a major fruit-producing centre.
Weathered farmers and banjo-carrying hippies chat amiably in the main street and prop
up the bars of the town's three pubs. To the
south, **Randalls Bay** and **Verona Sands** beaches
aren't far away.

January's ever-popular **Cygnet Folk Festival**
(www.cygnetfolkfestival.org) is three days of words,
music and dance, attracting talent like Jeff
Lang and Monique Brumby. The warmer
months also provide abundant fruit-picking
work for backpackers.

The **Cygnet Living History Museum** (☎ 6295 1602;
37 Mary St; admission by donation; 10am-3pm Tue & Wed,
12.30-3pm Fri & Sat) is a quaint history room next
to the church on the main street, stuffed full
of old photos, documents and curios.

Inside a converted Methodist church is
the **Living History Museum of Aboriginal Cultural
Heritage** (☎ 6295 0004; cnr Cross Rd & Nicholls Rivulet Rd,
Nicholls Rivulet; adult/child $4.50/2; 10.30am-2.30pm),
out of town at Nicholls Rivulet (5km from the
turn-off south of Cygnet). The small museum
contains historical information and displays
of southeast Tasmanian Aboriginal arts, crafts,
artefacts and stories, plus a garden and wetlands filled with plants significant to the local
Melukerdee Aboriginal band.

Sleeping

Cygnet Holiday Park (☎ 6295 1267; contact@cygnettophotel
.com.au; 3 Mary St; unpowered/powered sites $15/25) A bog-
basic camping ground accessed via the side road
next to the Cygnet RSL. Enquiries and check-in
at the Cygnet Hotel, opposite the park.

Huon Valley (Balfes Hill) Backpackers (☎ 6295
1551; www.balfeshill.alltasmanian.com; 4 Sandhill Rd, Cradoc;
unpowered sites/dm/d/f $15/25/50/75;) Off the
Channel Hwy 4.5km north of Cygnet, this

TOP 10 DEEP SOUTH FOODIE EXPERIENCES

The southeast is emerging as a real gourmet zone, with plenty of rainfall and sunshine sparking a feeding frenzy! Here are some of our favourite deep-south eating encounters:

- Munching into the quintessential Tasmanian apple, fresh from a roadside stall between Huonville and Cygnet (p146)
- Sipping a late-afternoon pinot noir or two at Home Hill (p145), Hartzview (p141) or Panorama Vineyard (p144)
- Sniffing out some peppery pecorino and smooth goat's cheese at Grandvewe Cheeses (p141) south of Woodbridge
- Getting agitated after a few oysters ('fuel for love') from Get Shucked Oyster Farm (p139) on Bruny Island
- Winding down from a lazy lunch at the fabulous Peppermint Bay (opposite) restaurant in Woodbridge
- Shucking mussels straight from the rocks along the Esperance Coast Rd (p150)
- Swilling apple cider at the Welcome Swallow Cyderworks (p144) behind Cygnet
- Blowing the steam off a hot, city-worthy espresso from Red Velvet Lounge (below) in Cygnet
- Picking blueberries at the farms along the Cygnet Coast Rd (p144)
- Transcending the average pub meal at the far-flung Dover Hotel (p151)

place has decent rooms, good facilities, extensive grounds and super views from the large communal area (despite all of which, some reader reports are negative). It's especially busy from November to May, when the host helps backpackers find fruit-picking work. A courtesy bus runs to/from Cygnet bus stop. Bike hire is $15/25 per half/full day.

Cygnet Hotel (☎ 6295 1267; www.cygnettophotel.com.au; 77 Mary St; dm/s/d $30/90/95) The big, red-brick 'Top Pub' on the upper slopes of Cygnet's main drag has lifted its game to provide heritage pub accommodation that's a rung or two above the rest. Budget bunk rooms serve as two-bed dorms. Downstairs you can grab a cold Cascade and a hot dinner at the bar, bistro or more upmarket Black Swan Restaurant.

Commercial Hotel (☎ 6295 1296; 2 Mary St; s/d with shared bathroom $45/60) Upstairs at the rambling old Commercial are decent pub rooms – not a bad option if you're just blowing through town. The bathrooms could use an overhaul.

Cygnet Bay Waterfront Retreat (☎ 6295 0980; www.cygnetbay.com.au; 11 Crooked Tree Point; d $150, extra person $30) Occupying the ground floor of a fairly bland-looking house is this self-contained apartment, 3km south of town. But forget the architecture – this is *absolute* waterfront, with a private entry, terrace, BBQ area and lawns rolling down to the bay.

Eating

School House Coffee Shop (☎ 6295 1206; 23a Mary St; meals $5-16; ⊙ breakfast & lunch Tue-Sun) Cute coffee shop with geranium-filled window boxes, serving hefty homemade pies, Turkish bread sandwiches, pasta, soups, all-day breakfasts and tempting cakes.

our pick **Red Velvet Lounge** (☎ 6295 0466; 24 Mary St; mains $8-12; ⊙ breakfast & lunch; 🖳) A new breed of hip cafés populates the main street, the best of which is this funky wholefood store and coffee house serving deliciously healthy meals (asparagus, olive and goats' cheese tart, beef rendang curry) to a diverse clientele. Good-looking staff, piles of music mags, mellow tunes, urbane without being yuppie, hippy without being feral – Cygnet has arrived!

Commercial Hotel (☎ 6295 1296; 2 Mary St; mains $10-24; ⊙ lunch & dinner) Our favourite Cygnet pub has turned its dining room into an all-day café, serving up a respectable range of light meals (focaccia, salads, pasta), plus hearty plates-full for pub-goers (steaks, roasts, mixed grills and what-not).

Cygnet Central Hotel (☎ 6295 1244; cnr Mary St & Garthfield Ave; mains $12-21; ⊙ lunch & dinner) Behind Cygnet's newest pub is a vast dining room overlooking a paddock: veal schnitzels, beer-battered scallops, disquieting carpet design and little joy for vegetarians.

DETOUR: CYGNET COAST ROAD

If you're not in a hurry (and why would you be?), don't miss the scenic coast road (the C639) between Cradoc and Cygnet. The direct route along the Channel Hwy (the B68) between these two towns is about 7km (this is the route for **roadside apple stalls**!) but the coastal route is a meandering 27km, past Petcheys Bay and Glaziers Bay.

The C639 heads south from Cygnet main street to Lymington. In January and February you can pick fruit at one of the **blueberry farms** along the way. The farms are also worth seeing in autumn when the bushes turn a spectacular russet-red.

In the backcountry about 15km from Cygnet, the **Welcome Swallow Cyderworks** (☎ 6295 1214; www.southcountrycyder.com; 113 Sunday Hill Rd, Petcheys Bay; ❧ 11am-3pm Wed-Mon), offers tastings and sales.

Further around the coast (6km from the northern end) is the **Scented Rose** (☎ 6295 1816; www .thescentedrose.com; 1338 Cygnet Coast Rd, Glaziers Bay; adult/child $7.50/3; ❧ 11am-5pm Fri-Mon Oct-Mar), a bloomin'-great garden display specialising in David Austin roses.

One kilometre from the Cradoc junction is the impressive **Panorama Vineyard** (☎ 6266 3409; www.panoramavineyard.com.au; 1848 Cygnet Coast Rd, Cradoc; tastings free; ❧ 10am-5pm Wed-Mon), where you can nose into its acclaimed pinot noir, plus chardonnay, merlot and riesling.

If you want to stay along the coast road, there are a few options:

Arundel Cottage (☎ 6295 1577; 643 Silver Hill Rd, Glaziers Bay; d $125, extra person $25) Unsophisticated (but homely) self-contained 1960s cottage sleeping four.

Riverside (☎ 6295 1952; www.huonriverside.com.au; 35 Graces Rd, Glaziers Bay; d $200, extra adult/child $50/35) Deluxe contemporary abode (perfect for two couples) with amazing Huon views from the wide verandas. Fresh flowers, quality linen and homemade breakfast provisions.

Beaupre Cottage (☎ 6295 1542; www.beaupre-farm.com; 3 Cygnet Coast Rd, Lymington; d incl breakfast $210) Gorgeous upstairs-downstairs timber cottage, each level a self-contained double. Bikes, rowboat and BBQ available; three-course dinner with a bottle of wine $95 for two.

Getting There & Away

Hobart Coaches' (☎ 13 22 01; www.hobartcoaches.com .au) bus 98 travels to Cygnet via Snug only once each weekday (with extra services on Thursdays). The trip takes one hour and costs $10.

HUONVILLE & AROUND
☎ 03 / pop 1530

The biggest town in the southeast, agrarian Huonville sits on the banks of the Huon River 35km south of Hobart, not far from some lovely vineyards and small villages. Having made its name as Tasmania's apple-growing powerhouse, it remains a functional, working town – low on charm but with all the services you need (banks, cafés, supermarkets, petrol, post office).

The Huon and Kermandie Rivers were named after Huon d'Kermandec, second-in-command to explorer Bruni d'Entrecasteaux. Prior to that, the area was known by Tasmanian Aborigines as Tahune-Linah. The region was originally steeped in tall forests – timber milling quickly became a major industry, focusing on the coveted soft-wood Huon pine. The initial plundering of Huon pine groves nearly wiped the tree out, as it's extremely slow-growing. Today, only immature trees survive along the river. Once the forest was levelled, apple trees were planted and the orchard industry blossomed – it's still the region's primary money spinner.

Information

Huon Valley Environment Centre (☎ 6264 1286; www.huon.org; 3/17 Wilmot St; ❧ 9.30am-4.30pm Tue-Fri) Excellent resource for anyone interested in Tasmanian environmental issues.

Huon visitors centre (☎ 6264 1838; www.huonjet .com/trips/viscentre1.html; The Esplanade; ❧ 9am-5pm; 🖳) By the river on the road to Cygnet (also the Huon Jet office).

Parks & Wildlife Service (☎ 6264 8460; www.parks .tas.gov.au; 22 Main Rd; ❧ 9am-4.30pm Mon-Fri) Main street office.

Sights & Activities

Take a frenetic, 35-minute jet-boat ride through the local rapids with **Huon River Jet Boats** (☎ 6264 1838; www.huonjet.com; The Esplanade; adult/child $62/40; ❧ 9am-5pm) – bookings recommended. You can also nudge out onto the river in a **pedal boat** ($14 for 30min).

At nearby Ranelagh (3km west of Huonville) is the super-stylish winery **Home Hill** (☎ 6264 1200; www.homehillwines.com.au; 38 Nairn St; tastings free; 🕑 10am-5pm), producers of award-winning pinot noir, chardonnay and dessert wines. There's also an excellent restaurant here (right).

About 13km from Huonville at Judbury is **Huon Valley Horsetrekking** (☎ 6266 0343; www.horsehavenfarmstay.com; 179 Judds Creek Rd) running horse treks from one hour to two days; a short ride costs $50. There's also a lovely cottage for rent here ($120 for a double).

Hooking fish proving problematic? Visit **Snowy Range Trout Fishery** (☎ 6266 0243; www.snowyrangetrout.com.au; Denison River; admission adult/child $5/2.50; 🕑 9am-5pm) for a guaranteed catch (equipment $25). It's 28km west of Huonville, past Judbury (signposted). Besides the admission, you also pay by weight for the rainbow or brown trout or salmon you snare.

At Grove, 6km north of Huonville, the **Huon Apple & Heritage Museum** (☎ 6266 4345; appleheritagemuseum@yahoo.com.au; 2064 Main Rd; adult/child/concession/family $6/3/5/15; 🕑 9am-5pm) has displays on 500 varieties of apples (count 'em) and 19th-century orchard life. Skip the tacky gift shop.

Sleeping

Grand Hotel (☎ 6264 1004; grandhot@bigpond.net.au; 2 Main St; s/d $30/50) The only accommodation in Huonville itself is this stoic old red-brick pub beside the bridge, with plenty of basic budget rooms (shared facilities). Predictable pub meals, too (mains $13 to $20).

Huon Bush Retreats (☎ 6264 2233; www.huonbushretreats.com; 300 Browns Rd, Ranelagh; d tepees $115, d cabins from $240, tent & campervan sites $24) Gay-friendly, disabled-friendly, wildlife-friendly retreat in a habitat reserve on miserable Mt Misery. On site are modern, self-contained cabins, a larger disabled-access cabin, luxury tepees, tent and campervan sites, plus walking tracks and barbecue shelters. Meals by arrangement. Check the website for directions – it's 10km from Huonville but not well signposted.

Matilda's of Ranelagh (☎ 6264 3493; www.matildasofranelagh.com.au; 2 Louisa St; s/d from $165/195 incl breakfast) At Ranelagh 2km northwest of Huonville is the 1865 Matilda's, one of Tasmania's finest heritage B&Bs (the Queen once stopped here for tea and a pee).

Eating

Café Motó (☎ 0400-315 533; 4 Wilmot St; mains $10-14; 🕑 breakfast & lunch Mon-Fri) The best eatery in Huonville itself is this hip little BYO off the main street, serving Hobart-quality coffee, cakes, quiches, pies and pastries – all homemade, all delicious.

Huon Manor Bistro (☎ 6264 1311; cnr Main & Short Sts; lunch from $15, dinner $24-28; 🕑 lunch Tue-Sun, dinner Tue-Sat) A gracious century-old home with a menu showcasing local produce (the emphasis is on seafood – pray the scallops and crayfish are in season). Full menu or cheaper lunchtime and café-style options. Garden seating and wines by the glass.

Home Hill Winery Restaurant (☎ 6264 1200; 38 Nairn St; mains $28-30; 🕑 lunch daily, dinner Fri & Sat) Home Hill vineyard (left) has a fab restaurant in a slick-looking, rammed-earth building with pasture views. The seasonal menu stars Tassie produce: Bothwell goats' cheese, Huon Valley mushrooms, King Island cream. Morning and afternoon tea, too.

For a quick bite on the riverside tables, try the following:
Banjo's Bakehouse (☎ 6264 8755; 8 Main Rd; items $3-8; 🕑 breakfast & lunch) Picnic fodder.
Boat House Café (☎ 6264 1133; The Esplanade; light meals $5-15; 🕑 lunch & dinner Wed-Sun) Burgers and fish and chips from a floating punt.

Getting There & Away

Tassielink (☎ 1300 300 520; www.tassielink.com.au) buses depart from Banjo's Bakehouse on the main street. The trip from Hobart takes one hour and costs $10.

FRANKLIN & AROUND
☎ 03 / pop 465
The Huon Hwy traces the Huon River south, passing the settlements of Franklin, Castle Forbes Bay and Port Huon. These were once important shipping ports for apples, but nowadays the old wharves and packing sheds are rotting like old fruit.

Strung-out Franklin is the oldest town in the Huon Valley – the wide, reedy riverscape here is one of Australia's best rowing courses. The town has seen a crop of cool new eateries spring up in the last five years, but not much has changed here architecturally for the last century. An example is the **Palais Theatre** (☎ 6266 3350; www.ds.tas.nu/palais; Huon Hwy; tickets $2; 🕑 6.30pm 1st Sun of month), begun in 1911 and ultimately an amalgamation of Federation and Art Deco styles. Classic movies screen here once a month.

The town's much-touted attraction is the **Wooden Boat Centre** (☎ 6266 3586; www.wooden boatcentre.com; Huon Hwy; adult/concession/child/family $6/5/4.50/18; ⌚ 9.30am-5pm). It's part of the School of Wooden Boatbuilding, a unique school running accredited 12-month courses in traditional boat-building using Tasmania's timbers. Stick your head in the door to learn about boat-building, watch boats being cobbled together and hear a sea shanty or two.

Online, check out www.franklintasmania .com.au.

Sleeping & Eating
FRANKLIN
Whispering Spirit Holiday Cottages (☎ 6266 3341; www.whisperingspirit.com.au; 253 Swamp Rd; d $95-140) We're not convinced a spirit can actually whisper (it's probably more telepathic than that), but we get what these guys are trying to say: their homy self-contained cottage and fantastic new two-bedroom, crimson strawbale unit have soul! Cheaper rates for longer stays. Miniature ponies on site.

Huon Franklin Cottage B&B (☎ 6266 3040; www .huonfranklincottage.com.au; 3554 Huon Hwy; d $100-120) Mustard-yellow house set high above the road to catch the river views, getting good feedback from readers. Offers two cottagey B&B rooms plus an outdoor spa at affordable rates. Dinner by arrangement. The owners have another cottage in the middle of town, sleeping six (double $115).

Kay Creek Cottage (☎ 6266 3524; www.kaycreek cottage.com; 17 Kay St; d $110-130; 💻) A characterladen, self-contained timber cabin, 1km south of Franklin above the main highway. Bonuses include Baltic pine floorboards, stereo, CD collection, games, wood fire, beautiful linen, bucolic setting and magic views. Breakfast extra.

Franklin Lodge (☎ 6266 3506; www.franklinlodge .com.au; 3448 Huon Hwy; d incl breakfast from $140) A two-storey building begun in the 1850s and eventually extended into the current grand Federation edifice. Inside are four en suite rooms, one with spa. Your cooked breakfast might involve feta and spinach pancakes, lemon ricotta pancakes or smoked salmon scrambled eggs.

Aqua Grill (☎ 6266 3368; 3419 Huon Hwy; meals $6-16; ⌚ lunch & dinner) Mighty fine takeaway fish and chips and other underwater snacks (try the

curried scallop crepe with white wine and cream sauce).

Franklin Tavern (☎ 6266 3205; Huon Hwy; mains $10-22; ⌚ lunch & dinner Wed-Sun) As well as cold beer and a long history, this two-storey, characterful pub (erected 1853), offers simple pub meals and all-day snacks, including toasted sandwiches and Devonshire tea. Sunday's $10 roast is a steal.

Franklin Woodfired Pizza (☎ 6266 3522; Huon Hwy; pizzas $14-21; ⌚ dinner daily, lunch Sun) This tiny tin shack bakes fantastic takeaway pizzas inside a kooky corrugated-iron oven. Try the 'Smoke on the Water' (garlic, salmon, brie, red onion, sour cream, capers and dill). Everybody sing: '*Smoooke on the waaater…*'

Petty Sessions (☎ 6266 3488; 3445 Huon Hwy; mains $17-32; ⌚ lunch & dinner) A picket fence and picture-perfect gardens enshroud this likeable café, inside an 1860 courthouse. Head for the deck and order classic café fare (salads, BLT, tandoori chicken burgers and seafood fettuccine), or try the house special: abalone chowder.

CASTLE FORBES BAY
Castle Forbes Bay House (☎ 6297 1995; www.castle forbesbayhouse.com.au; 27 Meredith Rd; s/d $60/85, house d $100) A 1928 schoolhouse with apple orchards for neighbours. On offer are two B&B rooms (bathrooms down the hall), guest lounge, affable owners, wonderfully overgrown gardens and cooked breakfasts. Next door is a familysized house for self-caterers, with a huge backyard to cavort in.

Camellia Cottage (☎ 6297 1528; www.camellia cottagebandb.com; 119 Crowthers Rd; d $100, extra person $20) Charming 1882 farm cottage with an open fire, nestled into flower-crowded gardens. The cottage sleeps three with limited cooking facilities; breakfast provisions included (juice, breads, jams, free-range eggs). A lazy dog, a couple of chooks and Zach the cockatoo patrol the BBQ area.

Donalea B&B (☎ 6297 1021; www.donalea.com .au; 9 Crowthers Rd; s/d from $100/140) Another CFB B&B with welcoming hosts, chill-the-hell-out views and petal-filled garden. Donalea has two bright rooms (one with spa), a new four-berth apartment, a guest lounge with rampaging log fire, and shelves of trashy romance novels to weep into.

PORT HUON

Kermandie Lodge (☎ 6297 1110; www.kermandielodge .com.au; Huon Hwy; motel s/d $80/88, unit s/d $100/110, extra adult/child $25/15) Roadside complex offering utterly unremarkable (but comfortable enough) two-bedroom units (with kitchen and washing machine), plus cheaper motel rooms. Bring binoculars to watch the tiny TVs.

Kermandie Hotel (☎ 6297 1052; fax 6267 0064; Huon Hwy; r $90) Next to Kermandie Lodge is this 1932 pub with refurbished rooms (all with en suite), plus an outdoor deck with water views – there are worse spots for a few cold jars of Cascade and steak sandwich for lunch or dinner (mains $11 to $24).

Getting There & Away

Tassielink (☎ 1300 300 520; www.tassielink.com.au) services do the one-hour trip from Hobart to Franklin for $12 ($14 to Castle Forbes Bay). They pull up at the takeaway shop on Franklin's main street.

GEEVESTON

☎ 03 / pop 830

Long stigmatised (justifiably) as a redneck logging town, Geeveston, 31km south of Huonville, is battling to become a tourist centre, offering some decent accommodations and eateries close to the Hartz Mountains and Tahune Forest AirWalk.

Geeveston was founded in the mid-19th century by the Geeves family, whose descendants still have fingers in a lot of local pies. In the 1980s the town was the epicentre of an intense battle over logging the Farmhouse Creek forests. At the height of the controversy, some conservationists spent weeks living in the tops of 80m-tall eucalypts to prevent them being felled. The conservation movement ultimately

won – Farmhouse Creek is now protected from logging.

See Sights (below) for info on the town's visitors centre. There's a multicard ATM inside the **Geeveston One-Stop Shop** (☎ 6267 1459; cnr School & Arve Rds; ⏰ 7am-late) on the road out to the AirWalk. Online, see www.geeveston .com.au.

Sights

In the town centre is the **Forest & Heritage Centre** (☎ 6297 1821; www.forestandheritagecentre.com; 15 Church St; ⏰ 9am-5pm), which acts as the local visitors info hub. It's a prolumber kind of establishment (in fact, the whole town has taken on the scent of rampant Forestry Tasmania PR), with a **Forest Room** housing forestry displays, and regular wood-turning demonstrations. Upstairs the **Hartz Gallery** (admission adult/child & concession/family $5/3/12) showcases the talents of local woodworkers. The centre also handles accommodation bookings, and you can buy Tahune Forest AirWalk and Hastings Caves tickets here (as well as at the venues themselves). Collect a map detailing short walks en route to the AirWalk (see p148).

Another place to browse over local crafts (ceramics, paintings, knits) and timber furniture is the **Southern Design Centre** (☎ 6297 0039; www.southerndesigncentre.com; 11 School Rd; ⏰ 10am-5pm).

Sleeping & Eating

Bob's Bunkhouse (☎ 6297 1069; www.bobsbunkhouse geevestonbackpackers.com.au; cnr Huon Hwy & School Rd; unpowered sites/dm $20/22, s, d & tw $49; 🖳) It's impossible miss this bright-blue, gay-friendly hostel just south of town, next to a colossal swamp gum log taken from the Arve Valley in 1971 (displayed like a trophy without a hint of remorse). Bob's roadside rooms are clean and comfy with shared facilities.

Cambridge House (☎ 6297 1561; www.cambridge house.com.au; cnr School Rd & Huon Hwy; s/d shared facilities $70/110, s/d with bathroom $110/140) A photogenic 1930 B&B offering upstairs accommodation in three bedrooms with shared facilities (ideal for families), or a downstairs en suite room. Baltic pine ceilings and the timber staircase are wonders.

Bears Went Over the Mountain (☎ 6297 0110; www.bearsoverthemountain.com; 2 Church St; d from $130; 🖳) Right in the middle of town, Bears has four rooms decorated in a whimsical bear theme (with the odd stuffed tiger) – kids will be in heaven. Complimentary port for cold southern nights.

Contented Bear (☎ 6297 0099; 6 Church St; lunch $9-20, dinner $24-27; ☽ lunch & dinner) A rustic café run by the Bears Went Over the Mountain owners. Try a homemade scallop pie or beer-battered barramundi for lunch; for dinner it's gotta be the Tassie salmon with king prawns and sesame-and-hollandaise sauce. Eat by the log fire or in the garden (ignore the awful commercial FM rock).

Kyari (☎ 6297 1601; 13 Church St; mains $10-15; ☽ breakfast & lunch) A streamlined eatery in a converted bank, with all-day breakfasts, enticing café fare, a kids' menu and an outdoor deck. Hours are subject to wild variations – call in advance before you get your hopes up.

Getting There & Away
Tassielink (☎ 1300 300 520; www.tassielink.com.au) buses arrive at and depart from the car park behind the Forest & Heritage Centre. The 1½-hour trip from Hobart costs $15.

ARVE ROAD & TAHUNE FOREST RESERVE
The sealed **Arve Rd**, constructed to extract timber from the local forests, trucks west from Geeveston through rugged, tall-timber country to the Hartz Mountains, the Tahune Forest Reserve and the Tahune Forest AirWalk.

Pick up a map from the Geeveston Forest & Heritage Centre (p147) detailing some easy short walks along the Arve Rd, including the following:

Arve River Picnic Area Has picnic tables and a ferny forest walk (10 minutes' round trip); 12km from Geeveston.
Big Tree Lookout A sub-five-minute walk leading to a timber platform beside a giant 87m-high swamp gum; turn-off is 14km from Geeveston.
Keogh's Creek Walk Fifteen-minute streamside circuit, 14km from Geeveston.
West Creek Lookout Provides views from a bridge extending out onto the top of an old tree stump; 21km from Geeveston.

About 29km west of Geeveston is the **Tahune Forest Reserve**, its name derived from Tahune-Linah, the Aboriginal name for the area around the Huon and Kermandie Rivers. Here you'll find the hugely successful **Tahune Forest AirWalk** (☎ 6297 0068; www.tasforestrytourism.com.au; adult/child/family $22/10/45; ☽ 9am-5pm) – 600m of see-through steel mesh walkways suspended 20m above the forest floor. One 24m canti-

levered section is designed to sway disconcertingly with approaching footsteps. Vertigo? There are a couple of ground-level walks here too, including a 20-minute riverside stroll through stands of young Huon pine.

The AirWalk is accessible for people with disabilities, and there is a **café** (mains $6-15; ☽ lunch) and gift shop here too. Drive here under your own steam or take a day trip from Hobart (p135). There are plenty of picnic spots around the reserve, and limited unpowered campervan spots (no tents). There's a free (unofficial) camp site at the Arve River Picnic Ground about halfway to the AirWalk.

You can assess the Tahune forest from even further above with the **Tahune Eagle Glide** (☎ 6297 0068; www.tasforestrytourism.com.au; adult/child $33/22; ☽ 9am-5pm). Wannabe eagles are strapped into a hang-glider, which in turn is latched to a 220m cable 30m above the Huon River and forest – a flying fox on steroids! You get two crossings for the price. Eagle Glide is 400m from the AirWalk car park.

HARTZ MOUNTAINS NATIONAL PARK
If you prefer your wilderness a little less pre-packaged than the Tahune Forest Reserve, head for the **Hartz Mountains National Park** (www.parks.tas.gov.au/natparks/hartz). A century ago, the Hartz plateau was a logging hotspot – stocks of small varnished gums were harvested for eucalyptus oil, which was distilled in Hobart for medicinal applications. But eventually the area was declared a national park, and in 1989 became part of the Tasmanian Wilderness World Heritage Area. For national park entry fees, see p64.

The 65-sq-km Hartz Mountains National Park is only 84km from Hobart – within striking distance for weekend walkers and day-trippers. The park is renowned for its jagged peaks, glacial tarns, gorges and wonderful alpine moorlands where fragile cushion-plant communities grow in the cold, misty airs. Rapid weather changes bluster through – even day-walkers should bring waterproofs and warm clothing.

There are some great hikes and isolated, sit-and-ponder-your-existence viewpoints in the park. **Waratah Lookout**, 24km from Geeveston, is an easy five-minute shuffle from the road. Other well-surfaced short walks include **Arve Falls** (20 minutes return) and **Lake Osborne** (40 minutes return). The steeper **Lake Esperance** walk (two hours return) takes you through

ED PARKER

Hobart-based environmentalist Ed Parker, 31, is a big fan of Tassie's old-growth forests, and is keen to see a more sustainable approach taken towards their management.

Are Tasmanians keyed-in to environmental issues? Apparently South Hobart is the greenest-voting suburb in Australia – it's a little world unto itself – but it's actually really polarised here. You'll see five cars with 'Protect Old-growth Forests' stickers on them, then see another couple with 'Greens Tell Lies' and 'I'm a Logger and I Vote' stickers. What's sad is that the state government isn't trying to end this polarisation by promoting genuinely sustainable industries. Forestry employs less people now than it used to, but clears more forest through mechanisation. It shouldn't be called the 'timber industry', because it's all about pulp – a lot of small timber mills around the state have gone out of business. It's not a good direction for the state when we've got booming tourism, hospitality and little boutique industries. To support old-school, polluting industries like the proposed pulp mill (see p47) goes against the trend.

Are ecotourism and forest-based tourism growing? Ecotourism should and will grow here. People want to see the forests, the beautiful beaches, the alpine areas – it's what attracts visitors to Tasmania. On the activity front there's recently been funding for trails through the state forests. Personally, I'd like to see more development of mountain bike trails to generate tourism dollars.

Are there any volunteering, carbon-offset or tree planting programs here that travellers can engage with? There's a national organisation that travellers can get involved with called **Conservation Volunteers Australia** (CVA; www.conservationvolunteers.com.au). They take volunteers for various projects: tree planting, weed control, translocating threatened starfish. They're great if you want to get your hands dirty. If you're interested in offsetting carbon emissions, check out Greening Australia's program **Breathe Easy** (www.breatheeasynow.com.au).

Are you optimistic about the future of Tassie's old-growth forests? I'm hopeful more than optimistic. If you look at forestry history over the last 15 years, there's not much reason for optimism. It's often cited that much of Tassie's wilderness is already protected – it's true that over 40% is in public reserve, but the majority of this is buttongrass plains or alpine mountaintops. A statistic that gets misused is that 60% of this remaining forest type or another is in reserve… but when you've logged all the rest, you can say that 100% of what's left is in reserve! It doesn't really hold up.

The recent project **Tasmania Together** (www.tasmaniatogether.tas.gov.au) undertook a massive survey of opinions on a whole range of things. Out of it came a number of recommendations. The government adopted most of them, but not the one that found the majority of Tasmanians want an immediate stop to the felling of old-growth forests. They completely ignored that one.

As related to Charles Rawlings-Way

high country even agnostics would proclaim as 'God's own'. You'll need to be fairly fit and experienced to tackle the steep, rougher track that leads to **Hartz Peak** (five hours return), which is poorly marked beyond **Hartz Pass** (3½ hours return).

There's no camping within the park, just basic day facilities (toilets, shelters, picnic tables, barbecues). Collect a *Hartz Mountains National Park* brochure from the Geeveston Forest & Heritage Centre (p147) or Huonville visitors centre (p144).

DOVER

☎ 03 / pop 570

Dozy Dover – a Port Esperance fishing town with a pub, a beach and a pier to dangle a line

from – is a chilled-out spot to while away a few deep-south days. Dover was originally called Port Esperance after a ship in Bruni d'Entrecasteaux's fleet, but that moniker now only applies to the bay. The bay's three small islands are called Faith, Hope and Charity.

In the 19th century this was timber territory. Huon pine and local hardwoods were milled and shipped from here (and also nearby Strathblane and Raminea) to China, India and Germany for use as railway sleepers. Today the major industries are fruit-growing and fish-farming, harvesting Atlantic salmon for export throughout Asia.

There's not much by way of attractions in Dover itself, but if you're heading further south, buy petrol and food supplies here. The

---

DETOUR: ESPERANCE COAST ROAD

The main road (the A6) from Geeveston to Dover heads inland at Surges Bay – an uninteresting but quick 21km dash. The more scenic alternative is to leave the highway at Surges Bay and follow the Esperance Coast Rd through Police Point and Surveyors Bay. Some of this road is unsealed, but it's in good condition. With panoramic water views, the road tracks through Desolation Bay and Hideaway Bay, past mussel-encrusted rocks and the waterlogged pens of commercial salmon farms.

Huon Charm Waterfront Cottage (☎ 6297 6314; www.huoncharm.com; 581 Esperance Coast Rd; d $115, extra person $25) is actually two rustic cottages (one studio-style sleeping two, the other with two bedrooms) literally on the water's edge at Desolation Bay (ignore the name, it's actually a beaut secluded little bay). There's quirky décor, with limited cooking facilities.

Online Access Centre (☎ 6298 1552; Old School, Main Rd; ⏰ 10am-2pm Mon-Fri, 11am-2pm Sat & Sun) is near the wood-fired pizza restaurant.

Sleeping
DOVER

Dover Beachside Tourist Park (☎ 6298 1301; www .dovercaravanpark.com.au; 27 Kent Beach Rd; unpowered/ powered sites $20/28, on-site caravans/cabins from $45/85) Opposite a sandy beach, this proudly maintained park features spotless cabins, a bookshelf full of beachy, raised-gold-font novels and ACTUAL GRASS (the drought hasn't made it this far south).

Dover Hotel (☎ 6298 1210; www.doverhotel.com .au; Huon Hwy; pub s/d $45/70, motel d $95) Whopping great pub with basic budget rooms above the bar (a tad noisy when bands are rockin' out), motel units out the back, and an adjacent self-contained unit sleeping up to seven ($190 for four adults). Water views from some rooms, mountain views from others. Pub meals downstairs (see Eating, opposite).

Smuggler's Rest (☎ 6298 1396; www.smugglersrest .info; Station Rd; d $85-105, extra person $15) Externally this place looks like an old SoCal nightclub (*the* Hotel California?), but there are no disco balls inside, just immaculate self-contained studios and two-bedroom units. The owners have bikes, fishing rods and old golf clubs for guests to play with.

Anne's Old Rectory B&B (☎ 6298 1222; www.annes oldrectory.com.au; 6961 Huon Hwy; s $70-90, d $90-100, incl breakfast) On the way into town (from the north), offering two über-floral B&B rooms, each with private bathroom down the hall, in a 1901 rectory surrounded by colourful gardens. Sooty the grey cat is too friendly for his own good.

Driftwood Holiday Cottages (☎ 6298 1441, 1800 353 983; www.driftwoodcottages.com.au; 51 Bayview Rd; d $160-220, f $190-240) offers modern, self-contained studio-style units or two large, family-friendly houses sleeping four to eight. Sit on your veranda, sip something chilly and watch fishermen rowing out to their boats on Port Esperance.

STRATHBLANE
Strathblane is 5km south of Dover.

Far South Wilderness Lodge & Backpackers (☎ 6298 1922; www.farsouthwilderness.com.au; Narrows Rd; dm/d/f $25/65/100; 🖳) On the Esperance River 5km south of Dover, Far South provides some of Tasmania's best budget accommodation, with a bushy waterfront setting, cosy lounge piled high with *National Geographic* mags, quality accommodation and a strong environmental focus. Mountain bikes and kayaks for rent ($15/35 per day).

Riseley Cottage (☎ 6298 1630; www.riseleycottage.com; 170 Narrows Rd; s $95, d $115-130, incl breakfast) The garden here is a labour of love, the perfect dressing for this elegant, gay-friendly guesthouse overlooking the water and bushland reserve. Cooked breakfast might entail salsa free-range eggs, gourmet smallgoods from the local butcher, fruits, breads and strong coffee. Three-course dinners (by arrangement) are fair value at $40 per person. No kids under 12.

Eating

Gingerbreadhouse Bakery (☎ 6298 1502; Main Rd; items $4-13; ⏰ breakfast & lunch) On the main bend as you curve down into town, this small Germanic bakery dishes out cooked breakfasts, stuffed croissants, homemade pies and tasty cakes, all made on site.

Dover Woodfired Pizza (☎ 6298 1905; Main Rd; mains $9-19; ⏰ lunch & dinner Wed-Sun) A snug, wood-panelled eatery offering traditional and gourmet wood-fired pizzas, baked spuds and filling pasta dishes. Eat in or takeaway.

Dover Hotel (☎ 6298 1210; Huon Hwy; mains $16-22; ⊙ lunch & dinner) This far-flung pub makes a real effort to depart from the deep fries, schnitzels and steaks omnipresent on Tasmanian pub menus. Nigh-on-gourmet selections include Hastings oysters, Huon Valley honeybrown mushrooms, local scallops and the fresh catch of the day from the local fishing fleet. Kids' menu, tempting desserts and a great wine list too.

Self caterers can stock up at the **Dover Grocer & Newsagency** (☎ 6298 1201; Main Rd; ⊙ 6.30am-6.30pm Mon-Fri, 7am-6.30pm Sat, 7am-6pm Sun), a fully stocked store with beaut deli produce, Tassie wines, and fresh fruit and veggies.

Getting There & Away
Tassielink (☎ 1300 300 520; www.tassielink.com.au) buses arrive at and depart from the Dover Store on the main street. The trip from Hobart takes 1¾ hours and costs $20. There are two services each weekday from Hobart, except from December through to March when an extra service runs every Monday, Wednesday and Friday (en route further south to Cockle Creek).

SOUTHPORT
☎ 03 / pop 300
Originally Southport was called Baie des Moules (Bay of Mussels), one of several names it's had over the years. Many travellers don't take the 2km detour off the main road to visit the town, but it's a worthy diversion if only to stay in the B&Bs here, which make good use of the waterside slopes. Unfortunately, public transport won't get you here.

Known as **Burying Ground Point**, the bluff south of town was once a convict cemetery; it's now a public reserve. There's also a memorial to the 1835 shipwreck of the *King George III* in which 35 people bubbled below.

Sleeping & Eating
Southport Tavern (☎ 6298 3144; southport.settlement@bigpond.com; Main Rd; unpowered/powered sites $16/20, cabins/motel d $65/120) A sprawling, faux-colonial pub, general store and caravan park. The weary can bunk down for the night in the caravan park or adjacent motel units; the hungry can nosh up in the dining room (mains $15 to $20; open for dinner Wednesday to Monday) or with takeaways (burgers, fish and chips et al) from the store (open 8am to 6pm).

Jetty House (☎ 6298 3139; www.southportjettyhouse .com; Main Rd; s/d incl breakfast $100/140, extra person $25)

Tailor-made for relaxation (or post–South Coast Track recovery), this rustic, family-run guesthouse down near the wharf is a rambling, veranda-encircled homestead built in 1875. Rates include full cooked breakfast and afternoon tea; dinner by arrangement. Minimum two nights; cheaper rates for longer stays.

Southern Forest B&B (☎ 6298 3306; www.southern forest.com.au; 30 Jager Rd; s/d/tr incl breakfast from $75/110/145) Up the hill opposite Southport Tavern is this hospitable B&B in native bush – simple and Euro-stylish, with plenty of wood and not a hint of twee floral excess. Accommodation is in a wing sleeping six (three bedrooms, two bathrooms and lounge) – ideal for families and groups. No kitchen, but breakfast included.

HASTINGS CAVES & THERMAL SPRINGS
☎ 03
Signposted 10km inland from the Huon Hwy, the excellent Hastings Caves & Thermal Springs facility attracts visitors to the once-thriving logging port of Hastings, 21km south of Dover. The only way to explore the caves (which are within the Hastings Caves State Reserve) is via guided tour. Buy tickets at the **Hastings visitors centre** (☎ 6298 3209; www.parks .tas.gov.au/reserves/hastings; adult/concession/child/family $22/18/11/55; ⊙ 9am-5pm Mar, Apr & Sep-Dec, 9am-6pm Jan & Feb, 10am-4pm May-Aug). Tours leave on the hour, the first an hour after the visitors centre opens, the last an hour before it closes. Admission includes a 45-minute tour of the amazing dolomite Newdegate Cave, plus entry to the **thermal swimming pool** behind the visitors centre, filled with 28°C water from thermal springs (pool-only admission adult/child/concession/family $5/2.50/4/12). The wheelchair-accessible **Hot Springs Trail** does a big loop from the pool area, taking 20 minutes to navigate (note that the pool is also wheelchair-accessible).

There's a decent **café** (light meals $6-15; ⊙ breakfast & lunch) at the visitors centre, which also sells barbecue and picnic hampers.

From the visitors centre, the cave entrance is a further 5km drive. No public transport runs out this way.

LUNE RIVER
☎ 03
A few kilometres southwest of Hastings is the diminutive enclave of Lune River. Here, Australia's southernmost railway, the **Ida Bay Railway** (☎ 6298 3110; www.idabayrailway.com.au;

FRENCH CONNECTIONS

Five years ago it seemed the pristine Tasmanian south was about to change for the worse. In 2004 the Tasmanian government gave private landowners permission to log the forests of the northeast peninsula of Recherche Bay – a decision that stirred up controversy in Tasmania and as far away as France.

In 1792 two French ships under the command of explorer Bruni d'Entrecasteaux, *La Recherche* and *L'Espérance*, anchored in a harbour near Tasmania's southernmost point and called it Recherche Bay. More than a decade before British settlers arrived in Tasmania, the French met the Lyluquonny Aborigines here and were carrying out the first significant scientific studies on the continent. There are two heritage sites at Recherche Bay with protected status (relics of the French observatory and garden, not accessible to the public), but the explorers' journals record them venturing far into the bush. With the government's announcement, historians, scientists and conservationists became concerned that the area earmarked for clearfelling was home to yet more sites of historic interest to both Australia and France. Needless to say, tensions between the anti- and prologging groups escalated – the prospect of the kinds of protests seen in Tasmania when the Franklin River was under threat in the mid-1980s loomed large.

Fortunately, in 2006 the land owners agreed to sell the northeast peninsula to the Tasmanian Land Conservancy, and it's now protected as a significant site. Read more at www.recherchebay .org and www.tasland.org.au.

In other southern developments, a Melbourne property developer plans to build a $15-million tourist complex at Cockle Creek East (an area which, interestingly, is inside the Southwest National Park, but not part of the World Heritage area). The developer has been negotiating approval with the Tasmanian government since the late '90s. Construction was slated to begin in 2005, but as yet the bulldozers haven't arrived.

---

328 Lune River Rd; rides adult/concession/child/family $25/20/12/60; ☺ 9am-5pm daily Oct-Apr, Wed, Sat & Sun only May-Sep) tracks a scenic 14km, 1½-hour narrow-gauge course through native bush to Deep Hole Bay. Take a picnic lunch and explore the beach, then catch a later train back to Lune River. Trains depart Lune River at 9.30am, 11.30am, 1.30pm and 3.30pm during summer, and 10am, noon and 2pm during winter. There's a café (light meals $4-10; ☺ breakfast & lunch) at the Lune River end of the line serving cakes, sandwiches, burgers and bacon and eggs.

COCKLE CREEK
☎ 03

Australia's most southerly drive is the 19km gravel stretch from Ida Bay past the soft-lulling waves of Recherche Bay to Cockle Creek. A grand grid of streets was once planned for Cockle Creek, but dwindling coal seams and whale numbers poured cold water on that idea.

The area features craggy, clouded mountains, sigh-inducing beaches, and (best of all) hardly any people – perfect for camping and bushwalking. The challenging **South Coast Track** starts (or ends) here, taking you through to Melaleuca in the Southwest National Park.

Combined with the **Port Davey Track** you can walk all the way to Port Davey in the southwest (see p303). Lonely Planet's *Walking in Australia* has detailed track notes. Shorter walks from Cockle Creek include ambles along the shoreline to the lighthouse at **Fishers Point** (two hours return), and a section of the South Coast Track to **South Cape Bay** (four hours return). National park entry fees apply to all these walks; self-register at Cockle Creek.

There are some brilliant free **camping grounds** along Recherche Bay, including at Gilhams Beach, just before Catamaran. You can also camp for free at Cockle Creek itself, but national park fees apply as soon as you cross the bridge. Bring all your own provisions, including fuel or gas stoves. There are pit toilets (no showers) and some tank water (boil before drinking).

Getting There & Away
Tassielink (☎ 1300 300 520; www.tassielink.com.au) buses arrive at and depart from the Cockle Creek ranger station. The service runs three times a week (Monday, Wednesday and Friday) from December through March. The 3½-hour trip from Hobart costs $65, returning to Hobart on the same days.

Midlands & Lake Country

Baked, straw-coloured plains, hawthorn hedgerows, fertile river valleys lined with willows and poplars, roadside mansions: Tasmania's Midlands have a distinctly English-countryside feel. The area's agricultural potential fuelled Tasmania's settlement. Coach stations, garrison towns, stone villages and pastoral properties sprang from the dirt as convict gangs hammered out the road between Hobart and Launceston. The course of the Midland Hwy (aka the Heritage Highway) has veered from its original route. Many old towns are now bypassed, so it's worth making a few detours to explore their Georgian main streets, rose-filled gardens, antique shops and country pubs. Pick up a free *Heritage Highway* touring map at visitors centres around the state. Of all the towns, Ross is probably your safest bet for accommodation and eateries.

The under-populated Lake Country atop Tasmania's Central Plateau is about as far from the well-worn tourist track as Tassie gets – reason enough to visit its subalpine moorlands and trout-filled lakes. On the southern fringe of the highlands is the fertile Derwent Valley, a fecund fold studded with vineyards, hop fields, orchards and old oast houses. If you consulted a dictionary for the definition of 'sleepy backwater', you'd probably find a list of Derwent Valley towns.

The region's three major highways are the Lyell Hwy, between Hobart and Queenstown; the Lake Hwy, which ascends the lofty Central Plateau; and the Midland Hwy, a sinewy umbilical between Hobart and Launceston.

HIGHLIGHTS

- ■ Arcing a fly across a highland steam and snaring a trout in the **Lake Country** (p161)
- ■ Trying to find the carving of Jorgen Jorgenson, former king of Iceland, on the **Ross Bridge** (p156)
- ■ Reading the heinous convict histories in the red bricks along the main street of **Campbell Town** (p158)
- ■ Questioning your moral direction at the **Four Corners of Ross** (p157)
- ■ Haunting yourself silly on a ghost tour of **Kempton** (p155) or **Oatlands** (p155)
- ■ Pondering the quiet, middle-of-nowhere beauty of the **Steppes Sculptures** (p161)
- ■ Watching the mist descend on **Great Lake** (p161) in winter
- ■ Touring through the hop fields, hedgerows and hamlets of the **Derwent Valley** (p162)

MIDLANDS & LAKE COUNTRY

| ■ TELEPHONE CODE: 03 | ■ www.tasmaniacentral.tas.gov.au | ■ www.centralhighlands.tas.gov.au |

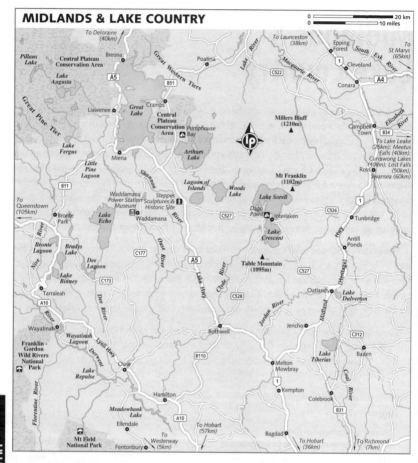

MIDLANDS & LAKE COUNTRY

MIDLANDS & LAKE COUNTRY

MIDLAND (HERITAGE) HIGHWAY

Hobart was founded in 1804 and Launceston in 1805. By 1807, the need for a land link between the two prompted surveyor Charles Grimes to map an appropriate route. The road was constructed by convict gangs, and by 1821 was suitable for horses and carriages. Two years later a mail cart operated between the two towns, which became the first coach service (it sometimes carried passengers). The main towns on this road were established in the 1820s as garrisons for prisoners and guards, protecting travellers from the menace of bushrangers.

Getting There & Around

Redline Coaches (☎ 1300 360 000; www.tasredline.com .au) powers along the Midland Hwy two to four times daily; you can jump off at any of the main towns – Kempton, Oatlands, Ross or Campbell Town – except on express services. The Hobart to Launceston one-way fare is $35 (about 2½ hours). For info on individual towns, see the Getting There & Away sections under each town.

KEMPTON

☎ 03 / pop 340

Pipsqueak Kempton, about 50km north of Hobart, was founded in 1838, making it one of the state's earliest settlements. Originally known as Green Ponds, it's notable for its an-

---

THE FATHER OF TASMANIA

Anthony Fenn Kemp (1773–1868) was a charismatic character: one half egotistical bankrupt with scant moral fibre, one half progressive patriot who was critical in Tasmania's evolution from convict dump to independent colony. Fleeing debts in England, he became embroiled in the 1808 ousting of Governor Bligh in NSW, then shifted focus to commercial opportunities in Van Diemen's Land in 1816. In the heady days of the new colony, he became a dedicated pastoralist, merchant and political sabre-rattler. Never far from controversy, he made as many friends as enemies, and left behind more than a dozen children – a fact that has seen him dubbed the 'Father of Tasmania'. For a critical (and comical) look at Kemp's exploits, read Nicholas Shakespeare's excellent *In Tasmania*.

---

tiques stores and breezy bucolic surrounds, and as the one-time residence of notorious rabble-rouser Anthony Fenn Kemp (see the boxed text above), after whom the town was named.

Chase Kemp's ghost up and down the long main street on **Kempton Historic & Ghost Tours** (☎ 0411-120 138; www.kempton.com.au; 1½hr tours per person $15; ☿ sunset), a mystery-soaked stroll around the old town's haunts. Bookings essential.

Hospitable **Wilmot Arms Inn** (☎ 6259 1272; wilmotarms@trump.net.au; 120 Main Rd; s/d from $90/110) is a former coaching inn with authentically aged B&B rooms and a flower-filled garden. Across the street is the faux-colonial **Huntington Tavern** (☎ 6259 1292; 121 Main St; mains $17-25; ☿ 11am-9pm Mon, to 10pm Tue-Sat, noon-7pm Sun), serving classic pub fare in the bar (with pool table) or bistro out the back.

OATLANDS
☎ 03 / pop 550

More tidy-town than twee, Oatlands contains Australia's largest collection of Georgian architecture. On the stately main street alone (which feels like a film set) there are 87 historic buildings, many of which are now galleries and craft shops.

The town's site was chosen in 1821 as one of four military posts on the Hobart–George Town road, but was slow to develop. In 1832 an optimistic town surveyor marked out 50 miles (80km) of streets on the assumption

Oatlands would become the Midlands capital. Many folks made the town home in the 1830s, erecting solid buildings with the help of former convicts and soldiers who were skilled carpenters and stonemasons. Alas, Oatlands never grew into the hoped-for capital. Today the town is soporifically rural – lonesome dogs and utes plastered with Bundaberg Rum stickers cruise the wide streets, and nothing's open after 8pm.

Information

The keen-to-assist **Oatlands visitors centre** (☎ 6254 1212; oatlands@tasvisinfo.com.au; 85 High St; ☿ 9am-5pm) proffers general info and handles accommodation bookings. There's a post office and a couple of banks on the main street, but the banks have restricted opening hours. There's a multicard ATM inside the **BP Service Station** (☎ 6254 1533; 52 High St; ☿ 8am-8pm).

Sights & Activities

Much of the sandstone for Oatlands' early buildings came from the shores of adjacent **Lake Dulverton**, an aquatic reserve that climate change has rendered bone dry.

Behind the visitors centre is a sandstone **History Room** (admission free; ☿ 9am-5pm) full of photos, relics and old knickknacks. While you're here, pick up the free handouts *Welcome to Historic Oatlands*, which includes self-guided town tour directions, and *Lake Dulverton Walkway Guide*, for ex-lake explorations.

Peter Fielding's Oatlands Tours (☎ 6254 1135; departs from 7 Gay St; tours $10) offers a one-hour town tour departing on demand from 9am to 5pm daily. Peter also runs 90-minute candle-lit ghost tours, starting at 8pm from May to September, and at 9pm from October to April, taking in the old gaol, courthouse and other spirited convict sites. Book via phone or the visitors centre.

Callington Mill (☎ 6254 0039; fax 6254 5014; Mill Lane; admission free; ☿ 9am-5pm), off High St, was built in 1837 and ground flour until 1891. Restoration work has begun after a century of neglect. The eerie sounds of chickens and laughing children are piped through restored outbuildings, including the 15m-high mill tower (climb the wobbly stairs to the top). Also here is **Dolls at the Mill** (admission $2), a collection of over 2000 dolls from around the world.

Sleeping

There's free **camping** (one night maximum) in the picnic area beside Lake Dulverton, at the northern end of the Esplanade. There are toilets and barbecues here.

The town's two pubs, the **Kentish Hotel** (☎ 6254 1119; www.view.com.au/kentishhotel; 60 High St; s/d $55/75) and **Midlands Hotel** (☎ 6254 1103; fax 6254 1450; 91 High St; s/d $50/65), offer reasonable rooms. The Kentish gets a better recommendation for its en suite facilities, DVD players, fresh coat of paint and Licorice Allsort linen.

Blossom's Cottage (☎ /fax 6254 1516; 116 High St; d incl breakfast $110) Behind Blossom's cute cottage tearooms (see below) is a near-new self-contained garden studio. It's bright and cheerful, with a cast-iron bed, blackwood timber floors, leadlight windows and a small kitchenette. Great value.

Oatlands Lodge (☎ 6254 1444; fax 6254 1456; 92 High St; s/d incl breakfast $100/120) Warm and inviting in two-storey, hen-pecked sandstone splendour, Oatlands Lodge is the cream of the town's accommodation. Rates include a huge breakfast spread (dinners by arrangement).

Waverley Cottages (☎ 6254 1264, 0408 125 049; waverleycottages@bigpond.com; s/d $130/160, extra person $25) This is a fully equipped, thoroughly colonial collection of cottages: Amelia Cottage (104 High St), opposite the Midlands Hotel; Forget-me-not Cottage (17 Dulverton St), directly behind Amelia; and Waverley Cottage and Waverley Croft, both 7km west of town. Stand-by rates sink to $125 per double.

Eating

Blossom's Georgian Tea Rooms (☎ 6254 1516; 116 High St; light meals $4-12; ☾ lunch Thu-Mon) At the northern end of the main street, Blossom's exudes old-fashioned warmth, and is a great place for a Devonshire tea, some raisin toast or a light meal (like Tassie smoked salmon with homemade bread and salad).

The Stables (☎ 6254 0013; 85 High St; light meals $4-12; ☾ breakfast & lunch) Next door to the visitors centre is this low-key café with office furnishings and wailing Cold Chisel, but reasonably priced snacks like toasted focaccias, wraps, fish and chips, and sandwiches.

Kentish Hotel (☎ 6254 1119; 60 High St; mains $14-22, bakery items $3-8; ☾ bistro lunch & dinner, bakery breakfast & lunch) Our pick for lunch and evening dining in Oatlands. Favourites include steak, fish and chips, seafood crepes, smoked salmon salad and daily specials. There's usually a few sly locals sipping frothies at the bar from opening time, and the bakery next door sells pies, pasties, rolls, coffee and fabulously quivering 'snot blocks' (vanilla slices for the uninitiated).

Self-caterers can head to the **Oatlands Foodmarket** (☎ 6254 1246; cnr Church & High Sts; ☾ 8am-6.30pm Mon-Thu, to 7pm Fri, to 5pm Sat & Sun).

Getting There & Away

Redline Coaches (☎ 1300 360 000; www.tasredline.com .au) services Oatlands from Hobart ($19, one hour) and Launceston ($25, 1¼ hours), with buses arriving at and departing from Oatlands Roadhouse at 47 High St, 500m from the visitors centre.

ROSS

☎ 03 / pop 300

Another tidy (nay, immaculate) Midlands town is Ross, an ex-garrison town 120km north of Hobart. Established in 1812 to protect Hobart–Launceston travellers from bushrangers, Ross became an important coach staging post at the centre of Tasmania's burgeoning wool industry, and, before the famous Ross Bridge was built in 1836, a fording point across the Macquarie River.

These days Ross' elm-lined streets are almost gagging on colonial charm and history. Accommodation owners charge like wounded bulls, but strict rules on development restrain the possibility of overcommercialisation. Soak up the ambience on foot – assess the architecture, check out the craft and antiques stores, and scoff down a Devonshire tea at one of the town's cafés.

Information

The **Ross visitors centre** (☎ 6381 5466; www.taswool centre.com.au; Church St; ☾ 9am-5pm) is inside the Tasmanian Wool Centre (see opposite). Pick up a brochure (purchased by donation) detailing the town's historic buildings. There are no ATMs or banking facilities in town.

Sights & Activities

The oft-photographed 1836 **Ross Bridge** is the third-oldest bridge in Australia. Its graceful arches were designed by colonial architect John Lee Archer, and it was built by two convict stonemasons, Colbeck and Herbert, who were granted pardons for their efforts. Herbert chiselled out the 186 intricate carvings decorating the arches, which include Celtic symbols, animals and the faces of notable people (including Governor Arthur and Anglo-Danish convict Jorgen Jorgenson, the farcical ex-king of Iceland). At night the bridge is lit up and the carvings shimmer with spooky shadows.

The crossroads in the middle of town is known as the **Four Corners of Ross**, leading your soul in one of four directions: temptation (represented by the Man O'Ross Hotel), salvation (the Catholic church), recreation (the town hall) or damnation (the old gaol).

Other notable historic edifices include the 1832 **Scotch Thistle Inn** (Church St), now a private residence; the 1830 **Barracks** (Bridge St), restored by the National Trust and also a private residence; the 1885 **Uniting Church** (Church St); the 1868 **St John's Anglican Church** (cnr Church & Badajos Sts); and the still-operating 1896 **Post Office** (26 Church St).

Off Bond St, the **Ross Female Factory** (☎ 6278 7398; www.femalefactory.com.au/FFRG/ross.htm; admission free; ☼ 9am-5pm) was one of Tasmania's two female convict prisons (the other was in Hobart; see p87). Only one building remains, but archaeological excavations among the sunburnt grass are underway, and descriptive signs and stories provide insight into these women's lives. Pick up a copy of the *Ross Female Factory* brochure from the visitors centre, then walk along the track near the Uniting Church at the top of Church St to get here. Nearby is the wind-blown **Old Ross Burial Ground**, with headstones carved by the same stonemasons who worked on the bridge.

The **Tasmanian Wool Centre** (☎ 6381 5466; www.taswoolcentre.com.au; Church St; ☼ 9am-5pm) houses a wool exhibition, **museum** (admission by donation) and craft shop – pick up a beanie if you have a cold head. The museum focuses on convict times and the Australian wool industry – there are hands-on bales of wool and a woolly audiovisual display. If you've got a group of eight or more, the centre also runs guided **town tours** (adult/child $5/free). Bookings essential.

Sleeping

Ross Caravan Park (☎ 6381 5224; http://caravanpark.rosstasmania.com; Bridge St; unpowered/powered sites $17/20, cabin s/d $45/60) This is an appealing patch of green near Ross Bridge on the banks of the fish-filled Macquarie River. Utilitarian, barracks-style cabins sleep two to four people, have cooking facilities and offer the cheapest accommodation in town. Bathrooms are shared, and you'll need your own linen. Reception is at Ross Motel.

Man O'Ross Hotel (☎ 6381 5445; www.manoross.com.au; 35 Church St; s/d without bathroom incl breakfast $70/85) Accommodation prices at this gracious old pub are a bit steep given the shared bathrooms, but the sunny, modernised rooms are better than average, there's a roomy guest lounge and continental breakfast is included.

Ross Motel (☎ 6381 5224; www.rossmotel.com.au; 2 High St; d/f incl breakfast from $120/160) Barely old enough to have a minibar, the independently owned Ross Motel offers spic-and-span Georgian-style cottage units, each with microwave, fridge, TV and DVD (prices include breakfast provisions). Family units sleep four.

Willowbank Cottage (☎/fax 6381 5219; 28 Church St; d $120-140, extra person $20) There's plenty of elbow room at this two-bedroom, two-bathroom, two-TV cedar house, which is perfect for families (the kids won't mind the naff carpet). Check in at the adjacent Antiques & Treasures at Ross store.

Ross B&B (☎ 6381 5354; www.rossaccommodation.com.au; 12 Church St; d $125-130) B&B rooms are in a 1927 house, managed by the same folks that run Colonial Cottages of Ross. Choose from two en suite rooms, both queen-sized (how big is a queen?), or a two-bedroom retreat in a separate wing. Plenty of peachy colours; garden setting with warbling birds.

Ross Bakery Inn (☎ 6381 5246; www.rossbakery.com.au; 15 Church St; s/d incl breakfast from $70/140) Wake up to breakfast fresh from a 100-year-old wood-fired oven when you stay in this 1830s coaching house, adjacent to the Ross Village Bakery (p158). Small, cosy rooms are offset by a guest lounge with an open fire and complimentary bakery treats. Groups of five or six can bed down in Kirsty's Cottage, a three-bedroom self-contained cottage across the street ($175).

Colonial Cottages of Ross (☎ 6381 5354; www.rossaccommodation.com.au; reception at 12 Church St; d $145-154, extra person $25-33) This organisation manages three carefully restored, self-contained abodes: **Captain Samuel's Cottage** (Church St), **Hudson Cottage** (High St) and **Church Mouse Cottage** (cnr High & Bond Sts). Sizes vary from one to three bedrooms (sleeping up to six people). Continental breakfast provisions provided.

Somercotes (☎ 6381 5231; www.somercotes.com; off Mona Vale Rd; d $170, extra person $25) Off the Midland Hwy about 4km south of Ross is this rambling estate with a Georgian homestead and B&B in four restored cottages. Each cottage is self-contained (breakfast provisions provided) and sleeps two or four people. Guided tours of the estate's historic buildings (including homestead) are available by appointment.

Eating

Ross General Store, Bakery & Tearooms (☎ 6381 5422; 31 Church St; light meals $4-10; ☿ breakfast & lunch) This jack-of-all-trades store has an olden-days vibe, an open fire and a fuss-free menu of breakfast, pies, soups, homemade cakes and sandwiches, plus the omnipresent Devonshire tea. People have travelled from North Dakota specifically for the scallop pies.

Ross Village Bakery (☎ 6381 5246; 15 Church St; items $4-14; ☿ breakfast & lunch) Overdose on carbs at the legendary Ross Bakery (the caramel slice is a cardiac arrest in disguise). They also do savoury stuff: wood-fired pizzas, soups, salads and pies of all denominations.

Man O'Ross Hotel (☎ 6381 5445; 35 Church St; mains $15-24; ☿ lunch & dinner) Dinner options in Ross are thin on the ground, so you may end up eating bangers and mash or a chicken schnitzel at the pub. The rose- and birch-dappled beer garden is ideal for lunch and Plenty O'Beer, and there's a kids' menu too.

Getting There & Away

Redline Coaches (☎ 1300 360 000; www.tasredline.com .au) services Ross, with buses pulling up to Ross Newsagency at 38 Church St. The 1½-hour trip to Hobart costs $25; the one-hour ride to Launceston is $17.

CAMPBELL TOWN

☎ 03 / pop 900

Campbell Town, 12km north of Ross, is another former garrison settlement. Unlike Oatlands and Ross, the Midlands Hwy still trucks right on through town. The local catch-cry 'Campbell Town is reaching out to you!' overstates things just a little – the vibe here is more introspective and agrarian – but the town does make a handy pee-and-pie stop between Hobart and Launceston (or between Cradle Mountain and the east coast). Along the main drag are a couple of hotels, a supermarket, pharmacy, bank, post office and general shops.

The first white settlers here were Irish timber-workers who spoke Gaelic and had a particularly debauched reputation. Today, Campbell Town is ground zero for Tassie's cattle and sheep farming industries. In late May/early June every year, the showgrounds

behind the high school host the annual **Campbell Town Show** (www.campbelltownshow.com.au), aka the Midlands Agricultural Show. Running strong since 1839, it's the oldest show in Australia.

Information

Pick up a free brochure detailing a self-guided Campbell Town tour at the **Campbell Town visitors centre** (☎ 6381 1353; www.campbelltowntasmania .com; 103 High St; ☿ 10am-3pm Mon-Fri, occasional weekends). It's beside the post office in the old courthouse, a 1905 building still used occasionally for judicial proceedings. Also here is the Heritage Highway Museum (below). The opening hours listed here are a rough guide – the centre is volunteer-run so hours vary. If you're looking for info outside of opening hours, the takeaway shop two doors down (next to the police station) stocks useful brochures.

There's a multicard ATM inside the Festival IGA Supermarket (opposite), and internet access at Zeps restaurant (opposite).

Sights & Activities

The curio-strewn **Heritage Highway Museum** (☎ 6381 1353; 103 High St; admission free; ☿ 10am-3pm Mon-Fri, occasional weekends) features histories of figures like John Batman and Martin Cash (a local bushranger), and artefacts like a 1930s film projector, old toys, coins and books. The museum is volunteer-run and has unpredictable opening hours.

Be sure to look down as you wander along High St. Rows of **red bricks** set into the footpath detail the crimes, sentences and arrival dates of convicts like Ephram Brain and English Corney, sent to Van Diemen's Land for such crimes as various as stealing potatoes, bigamy and murder.

Campbell Town has a crop of buildings in the over-100-years-old category, mostly along High and Bridge Sts. Highlights include the 1835 **St Luke's Church of England** (High St); the 1840 **Campbell Town Inn** (100 High St); the 1834 **Fox Hunters Return** (132 High St); **The Grange** (High St), an impossible-to-miss 1847 mansion, now a conference centre; and the 1878 **Old School** (Hamilton St), in the current school's grounds.

The bridge across the Elizabeth River here was completed in 1838, making it almost as archaic as the Ross Bridge. Locals call it the **Red Bridge** because it was convict-built from more than 1.5 million red bricks baked on-site. There's a comprehensive booklet on the bridge available at the visitors centre.

DETOUR: LAKE LEAKE

The secondary B34 road from Campbell Town heads east through the excellent fishing and bushwalking area around Lake Leake (33km from Campbell Town) to Swansea (69km) on the east coast. Redline buses ply this route once a day from Monday to Friday, and can drop you at the Lake Leake turn-off, 4km from the lake.

The shimmering surface of Lake Leake itself is punctuated by ghostly tree stumps, and is encircled by holiday shacks. For passers-by there's a **camping area** (powered/unpowered sites $8/5) and a rough-and-tumble, shingle-covered pub, the **Lake Leake Hotel** (☎ 6381 1329; www.lakeleakechalet .com.au; 340 Lake Leake Rd; s/d $40/75). The hotel offers lunch and dinner daily (mains $14 to $20) and basic accommodation, plus boat hire ($90 per day) and guided fishing trips (from $600).

After checking out the lake and maybe casting a fly or two across the water, those with their own wheels can explore further east to the **Meetus Falls** and **Lost Falls** forest reserves. Meetus Falls is the pick of the two – it's 10km from the signposted turn-off and has a sheltered picnic area, barbecues and toilets.

If you're really into trout fishing, **Currawong Lakes** (☎ 6381 1148; www.troutfishtasmania.com.au; 1204 Long Marsh Rd, Lake Leake; d $175) is the place for you. It's a private trout fishery 12km west of the Lake Leake turn-off along an unsealed road. The property is home to trout-filled lakes, a handful of good-quality self-contained cabins, and plenty of peace and quiet. Fly fisherman can fish for a full day for $150, with no licence required. Equipment hire (rod, waders, flies) costs $50.

Sleeping & Eating

Campbell Town Hotel (☎ 6381 1158; www.goodstone .com.au; 118 High St; s/d $65/75) It seems unlikely from the outside, but part of this building predates all the other hotels in town. This pub offers 10 down-at-heel and anonymous (but clean enough) motel units out the back, and reasonably priced meals (mains $8 to $18) for lunch and dinner.

St Andrews Inn (☎ 6391 5525; standrewsinn@ southcom.com.au; Midland Hwy, Cleveland; s/d incl breakfast $90/120) Convict-built in 1845, this National Trust–classified roadside coaching inn is 16km north of Campbell Town at Cleveland. Upstairs are two large en suite B&B rooms (with TVs and complimentary port); downstairs is a bubbly little café (meals $10 to $24) with an outdoor deck. It's open for breakfast and lunch Tuesday to Sunday and for dinner by arrangement. Walking up and down the stairs, you might rub shoulders with Juicy Lucy, the friendly resident ghost.

Fox Hunters Return (☎ 6381 1602; www.foxhunters .com.au; 132 High St; s/d from $130/150) On the left as you enter town from Hobart is this pukka establishment, built with convict labour in 1833 as a coaching inn and now offering spacious rooms, each with private bathroom and sitting area. The cellar under the main building housed convicts during the construction of the neighbouring Red Bridge.

our pick **Zeps** (☎ 6381 1344; 92 High St; meals $7-22; breakfast, lunch & dinner;) Easily the best choice in town to refuel is hyperactive Zeps, serving brekky, *panini*, pasta, fat pies and good coffee throughout the day, plus pizza and Mod Oz mains in the evening. Takeaways and internet access is available too.

Tassie Thai (☎ 6381 1020; 80 High St; mains $11-16; lunch & dinner Wed & Sat) What a surprise! Chilli-laced Thai classics like pad Thai, *tom yum gung* and Massaman curry are served in a brick booth shop amid the pie-and-burger highway wastelands. Tartan placemats pay homage to Campbell Town's Celtic roots. Takeaways available.

Self-caterers can stock up at the **Festival IGA Supermarket** (☎ 6381 1311; 113 High St; 8am-6pm Mon-Fri, 9am-5.30pm Sat & Sun).

Getting There & Away

Redline Coaches (☎ 1300 360 000; www.tasredline .com.au) buses run to Campbell Town, chugging up to the milk bar at 107 High St, next to the police station. The 1¾-hour Hobart run costs $29; the 45-minute journey to Launceston costs $15.

LAKE COUNTRY

The people-free Lake Country on Tasmania's Central Plateau is spiked with steep mountains and perforated with glacial lakes, waterfalls, abundant wildlife and unusual flora, including the ancient pencil pine. The plateau's northwestern sector, roughly one-third of its total area, is part of the Tasmanian Wilderness World Heritage Area. The region is also known for its world-class trout fishing and for its socially divisive hydroelectric schemes, which have seen the damming of rivers, the creation of artificial lakes, the building of power stations (both above and below ground), and the construction of massive pipelines arcing over rough terrain like giant metal worms. If you want to see the developments first-hand, check out the active Tungatinah, Tarraleah and Liapootah power stations on the extensive Derwent scheme between Queenstown and Hobart.

On the western edge of the Central Plateau is the Walls of Jerusalem National Park (see p243), a perennial fave of mountaineers, bushwalkers and cross-country skiers. Experienced hikers can walk across the Central Plateau into 'The Walls', and also into Cradle Mountain–Lake St Clair National Park.

BOTHWELL
☎ 03 / pop 340

Encircling a village green, Bothwell is a lowkey (some would say catatonic) historic town 74km north of Hobart in the Clyde River Valley. Standout National Trust–acknowledged buildings include an old **Bootmaker's Shop** (☎ 6259 5649; High St), open by appointment; the 1820s **Thorpe Mill** (Dennistoun Rd); the **Castle Hotel** (14 Patrick St), first licensed in 1821, and the endearing 1831 **St Luke's Church** (Dennistoun Rd).

The **Bothwell visitors centre** (☎ 6259 4033; www.bothwell.com.au; Market Pl; ☾ 10am-4pm Sep-May, 11am-3pm Jun-Aug) doubles as the Australasian Golf Museum (see below). Pick up the free leaflet *Let's Browse in Bothwell* and check out the wee map, marked with locations of historic buildings.

Bothwell is best known for it's proximity to Trout Heaven, but the town also lays claim to Australia's oldest golf course, known as **Ratho** (☎ 0409-595 702; www.rathogolf.com; Highland Lakes Rd; greens fees $15; ☾ 8am-dusk). The course was rolled out of the dust in 1822 by the Scottish settlers who built Bothwell. It's still in use today, and is open to all golfers. You can hire clubs from the **Australasian Golf Museum** (☎ 6259 4033; www.ausgolfmuseum.com; Market Pl; admission adult/child $4/2; ☾ 10am-4pm Sep-May, 11am-3pm Jun-Aug), set up in Bothwell's 1887 schoolhouse (this is also the visitors centre).

DAISY CHAIN, ANYONE?

Adjacent to St Luke's Church in Bothwell is the age-old St Luke's Cemetery. Botanists marvel over the fact that here, dotted among the crumbling tombstones, grows the ultrarare Lanky Button Daisy (*Leptorhynchos elongatus*). It's a diminutive native flower, and this obscure boneyard is one of only four known places it grows in Tasmania. Just the right mix of nutrients in the soil, perhaps?

Bothwell is also home to **Thorpe Farm** (☎ 6259 5678), which produces sensational goat's milk cheese under the label Tasmanian Highland Cheese (often available at the visitors centre, the Fat Doe Bakery and select Hobart delicatessens). The farm also makes *wasabi* and stone-ground flour. Visits by appointment; call ahead for directions.

Sleeping & Eating

Bothwell Caravan Park (☎ 6259 5503; http://bothwell.50webs.com/caravanpg.htm; Market Pl; unpowered/powered sites $10/15) This isn't exactly a park, more a small patch of gravel behind the visitors centre. Check in at the Central Highlands Council on Alexander St (9am to 4.30pm Monday to Friday), or after hours at the Bothwell Garage (☎ 6259 5599) on Patrick St. Site prices are for two people.

On Alexander St there are a couple of decent, self-contained houses for rent. An unremarkable 1950s red-brick number, **Park House** (☎ /fax 6259 5676; 25 Alexander St; d $80, extra person $20) sleeps six; inquire at 28 Elizabeth St. Next door is the far more appealing but more expensive **Batt's Cottage** (☎ 6265 9481, 0409 659 480; 23 Alexander St; d $115, extra person $20), a symmetrical National Trust–registered cottage with warped brick walls, dating from 1840.

Bothwell Grange (☎ 6259 5556; bothwell_grange@skyoptic.com.au; 15 Alexander St; d $99 incl breakfast) A highway hotel built in 1836, the oncegrandiose Grange has a snug Georgian atmosphere and comfortable B&B accommodation. There are six rooms, all with bathrooms, antique beds and timber ceilings. Evening meals by arrangement. Mind your head – the doorways were built for diminutive 19thcentury bumpkins.

Castle Hotel (☎ 6259 5502; fax 6259 4021; 14 Patrick St; mains $14-19; ☾ lunch daily, dinner Fri & Sat) The affable, country-aired Castle has been continually licensed since 1829. The Cascade and Boag's continue to flow, washing down better-than-average meals (heavy on the meat and local produce). There are a couple of surprisingly good en suite rooms upstairs, with bathrooms, TVs and DVDs ($90 per double).

Fat Doe Bakery & Coffee Shop (☎ 6259 5551; 12 Patrick St; items $3-8; ☺ breakfast & lunch Mon-Fri) Make the unpretentious Doe a quick pit stop for a sandwich, lamington, fresh-from-the-oven cake or one of the tasty range of pies on offer (as always, we recommend the scallop version).

Getting There & Away

Metro Tasmania (☎ 132 201; www.metrotas.com.au) runs bus 140 from stop F on Elizabeth St at 4pm each weekday to Bothwell (one-way adult/child $15/8, 1½ hours).

BOTHWELL TO GREAT LAKE

On the dirt road looping off the Lake Hwy between Bothwell and Great Lake is the hydroelectric ghost town of Waddamana, and the **Waddamana Power Station Museum** (☎ 6259 6158; www.townsoftasmania.com/waddamana; admission free; ☺ 10am-4pm). Originally a private venture, the hydroelectric station was built between 1910 and 1916. Financial difficulties resulted in a government takeover and the creation of a Hydro-Electric Department, which today is the omnipotent Hydro Tasmania. Check out displays on Tassie's hydro history, and the massive operational turbines.

Signposted off the highway 35km north of Bothwell (25km south of Miena) are the ethereal **Steppes Sculptures**, a ring of 12 stones with affixed iron representations of Midlands life – wildlife, cattle drovers and Tasmanian Aborigines – created by Tassie sculptor Stephen Walker in 1992. A 900m track leads north from the stones to the ruins of the **Steppes Historic Site**, the homestead of the locally notable Wilson family for 112 years from 1863. For detailed info see the Parks & Wildlife Service brochure *The Steppes Historic Site* from visitors information centres.

THE LAKES

Levelling out at 1050m above sea level on the Central Plateau, **Great Lake** is the largest natural freshwater lake in Australia. The first European to dip his toe here was John Beaumont in 1817; his servant circumnavigated the lake in three days. In 1870 brown trout were released into

the lake and it soon became a fishing fantasia. Rainbow trout were added in 1910 and also thrived. Attempts were made to introduce salmon, but this recalcitrant species refused to multiply. Trout have now penetrated most of the streams across the plateau; some of the best fishing is in the smaller streams and lakes west of Great Lake.

In the seminal days of hydroelectric ambition, a small Great Lake dam was constructed to raise water levels near Miena. Great Lake is linked to nearby Arthurs Lake by canals and a pumping station, and supplies water to the Poatina Power Station on its northeastern shore.

For lake and bushwalking info, try the sporadically staffed **Parks & Wildlife Service Ranger Station** (☎ 6259 8148; www.parks.tas.gov.au) at Liawenee, 10km north of Miena on the western side of Great Lake.

Public transport services to the area is non-existent.

Fishing

There's brilliant fishing right across the Central Plateau, with good access to most of the larger lakes. Great Lake, Lake Sorell, Arthurs Lake and Little Pine Lagoon are all popular haunts. The plateau itself actually contains thousands of lakes; many are tiny, but most still contain trout. You'll have to walk to most of the smaller lakes, which means carrying lightweight camping gear, as the region is prone to snowfalls.

A long list of regulations apply to fishing in the area, aimed at ensuring fish continue to breed and stocks aren't depleted. On some parts of Great Lake, for instance, you can use only artificial lures, and you're not allowed to fish in streams flowing into the lake. On the Central Plateau, some waters are reserved for fly-fishing. Bag, size and seasonal limits apply to all areas. The **Inland Fisheries Service** (www.ifs.tas.gov.au) website offers priceless advice. See p59 for more fishy business.

Sleeping & Eating

Campers can try the basic camping ground at **Dago Point** (camping per adult/child $3.30/1.65), beside Lake Sorell. A better bet for families is the camping ground on Arthurs Lake at **Pumphouse Bay** (camping per adult/child $3.30/1.65), which has better facilities including hot showers. Campers self-register at both sites and fee payments rely on an honour system. Bring

---

SHOUT ABOUT TROUT

Catching a trout in Tasmania should be as easy as getting your feet wet – most of the state's rivers and lakes have been stocked with brown and rainbow species – but you still need to be in the right place at the right time. There are also restrictions on the types of tackle permitted in various areas in different seasons.

Live bait is tried-and-true (impaling a grasshopper, grub or worm on a hook), but bait fishing is banned in most inland Tasmanian waters – it's too effective to give the fish a sporting chance! Artificial lures are more acceptable, coming in myriad shapes, sizes, weights and colours. Depending on the season, a 'Cobra' wobbler or Devon-type 'spinner' might work for you in lakes, while your preferred stream lure might be a 'Celta'. Other winners include claret dabblers, brown bead head buggers and yum-yum emergers.

The most artful form of trout fishing is of course fly-fishing, which often involves wading through rivers and lakes in the early morning. Fly-fiends tie their own flies, but a huge variety is available in fishing shops. In Hobart try Spot On Fishing Tackle (p107). Many areas in Tasmania are dedicated fly-fishing reserves.

When fishing in the Lake Country, prepare for Tasmania's riotously changeable weather – bring warm, waterproof clothing, even in summer. Engaging a professional guide for lessons or a guided trip is a stellar idea: try **Fish-Wild Tasmania** (☎ 6223 8917, 0418 348 223; www.fishwildtasmania.com), **Rod & Fly Tasmania** (☎ 6266 4480, 0408 469 771; www.rodandfly.com.au), or check out **Trout Guides & Lodges Tasmania** (www.troutguidestasmania.com.au).

---

all your supplies. It's recommended that you boil tap water.

Great Lake Hotel (☎ 6259 8163; www.greatlakehotel .com.au; Swan Bay, Miena; dm $35, d from $95, f $135) From Miena, take the turn-off to Bronte Park and you'll soon come across this small-town pub, offering a accommodation from bog-basic anglers' cabins with shared facilities to self-contained motel-style units. The meat-based meals in the bar (mains $10 to $23; open lunch and dinner) will reduce vegetarians to tears.

Central Highlands Lodge (☎ 6259 8179; www .centralhighlandslodge.com.au; Haddens Bay, Miena; s/d $108/136) On the southern outskirts of Miena, this jaunty, rough-sawn timber lodge offers clean, comfortable cabins. The Eagles twang over the sound system in the lodge restaurant (mains $13 to $26; open lunch and dinner) – a great place to rejuvenate with a cold beer and a hot meal (try the venison hot pot) and talk about the one that got away.

The **Great Lake General Store** (☎ 6259 8149; Swan Bay, Miena; ⊙ 8am-5pm Sun-Thu, 8am-7pm Fri & Sat), next door to the Great Lake Hotel, sells petrol, fishing supplies and takeaway food.

DERWENT VALLEY

Lake St Clair is the head of the Derwent River, which flows southeast towards Hobart through the fertile Derwent Valley.

New Norfolk, the valley's lynchpin town, is covered in the Hobart chapter (see p112). The Lyell Hwy largely mimics the flow of the Derwent River to the Central Plateau, continuing past Derwent Bridge west to Queenstown.

HAMILTON
☎ 03 / pop 150

National Trust–classified Hamilton was planned with great expectations, but it never evolved beyond a small, soporific village. Historic sandstone buildings adorn the main street, with photo-worthy views of mountain ranges and peaks to the west. Lyell Hwy rolls through town – it's called Franklin Pl along this short stretch.

Hamilton was settled in 1808 when New Norfolk was established, and was a mid-19th century boomtown. By 1835 it had 800 residents, well watered by 11 hotels and two breweries. Grids of streets were surveyed, but the dry local soils defeated many farmers. The town stagnated, and several buildings were eventually removed. There's a lonesome sense of abandon to the place these days – even the pub was closed when we visited.

Hamilton's history is documented in the **Hamilton Heritage Centre** (☎ 6286 3218; Cumberland St; admission adult/child $1/50c; ⊙ 9am-5pm), set up in an 1840 Warder's Cottage. It is a DIY arrangement: keys are available from the adjacent council chambers or Glen Clyde House (right).

Take a fascinating tour of the locally owned, 300-hectare working **Curringa Farm** (☎ 6286 3332; www.curringafarm.com; 5831 Lyell Hwy; 45min tour per person $35), 3km west of Hamilton. The owners aim to strike a balance between business and sustainability, an approach applied to the 3000 sheep, poppies, oats and cabbage seed farmed here. Alternatively, take a woolly angle on things with a sheep shearing tour. Bookings required (call the night before).

Sleeping

Cherry Villa (☎ /fax 6286 3418; 38 Arthur St; d $110-150) The 1834 Cherry Villa offers two attractive rooms amid bee-buzzing rose gardens. Straight out of an architectural textbook, it's a classically symmetrical Georgian house, with twin dormer windows and chimneys. It's also Hamilton's only traditional, hosted B&B (continental breakfast). Dinners by arrangement.

Emma's, George's, Victoria's and **Edward's** (☎ 6286 3270; www.newnorfolk.org/~hamilton_cottages; reception Uralla House, 33 Franklin Pl; d $120, extra adult/child $35/25) are old sandstone cottages with authentic furnishings, strung out along the main road in the town centre and nestled in cute-as-can-be country gardens. They sleep between two and five slumberers.

Olde School House (☎ 6286 3292; www.hamiltonschoolhouse.com; 39 Franklin Pl; d $150, extra adult/child $50/30) Pay attention class! This educational edifice was built in 1856 and served as the school until 1935. Two self-contained units sleep up to five, and the owners have managed to restrain themselves just enough to the frilly-doyley-floral decoration front. Full breakfast provisions supplied.

ourpick **Over the Back** (☎ 6286 3333; www.curringafarm.com.au; 5831 Lyell Hwy; d $175, extra person $30) You feel a long way from anywhere at Over the Back, but that's the appeal. About 3km west of Hamilton, it's a fully self-contained log cabin sleeping five, offering a secluded slice of rural life on the 300-hectare Curringa Farm. The spa cottage is a further 3km from the farmhouse, beside Meadowbank Lake (good for fishing and swimming) – the lake and gum tree views from the deck are quintessentially Australian. The owners are active in preserving local ecosystems, and run tours of their property (above). There's also a three-bedroom house available, sleeping up to eight.

Jackson's Emporium (below) also provides accommodation around town.

Eating

Platter Pie Café (☎ 6286 3206; 32 Franklin Pl; items $4-6; ⓨ breakfast & lunch) This roadside pull-in has little external appeal, but redeems itself with sensational homemade pies (curried steak, corn and bacon, steak and kidney), fresh burgers, quiches, coffee and sandwiches.

Glen Clyde House (☎ 6286 3276; 2 Grace St; meals $7-22; ⓨ breakfast & lunch) On a sharp bend at the town's northern end is this hefty 1840 sandstone house: part licensed café (Devonshire teas, pies, steaks, smoked trout pâté), part Tasmanian craft gallery. The outdoor deck is a top spot for a snack.

Jackson's Emporium (☎ 6286 3258; www.jacksonsemporium.com.au; 13 Franklin Pl; mains $10-15; ⓨ breakfast, lunch & dinner; 💻) Ramshackle Jackson's (an emporium since the 1850s) cleverly caters to visitors staying in Hamilton's self-contained accommodation, proffering a range of chef-prepared frozen meals (spaghetti bolognaise, beef stroganoff, Thai chicken), desserts, wine and beer. Ask about their three accommodation options – McCauley's, Kelleher's and Arcadia (doubles from $130).

You might also want to try the 1826 convict-built **Hamilton Inn** (☎ 6286 3204; Tarleton St) to see if anything's cookin' in the kitchen.

Getting There & Away

Tassielink (☎ 1300 300 520; www.tassielink.com.au) runs buses once daily (except Monday and Wednesday) between Hobart and Queenstown via Hamilton, Ouse and Lake St Clair. The 1¼-hour trip from Hobart to Hamilton costs $13. Buses stop at Hamilton Newsagency.

ELLENDALE

☎ 03 / pop 470

Hamlet-sized Ellendale rests on a narrow link road between Lyell Hwy and Westerway – a nifty shortcut to Mt Field National Park (p116). Ellendale was once a hop-growing area, though few remnants of the industry remain. There's little here apart from a creekside picnic shelter, a general store and some accommodation, but it's a quiet base for day trips to Mt Field or the southwest.

Not far along Ellendale Rd (off Lyell Hwy midway between Hamilton and Ouse, not serviced by bus), you cross **Meadowbank Lake**, part of the Derwent River hydroelectric scheme.

Sleeping

Platypus Cottage (☎ 0419-875 890, 0427-881 281; nigel tomlin@bigpond.com; 38 The Avenue; d $90-120) This magic wee weatherboard cottage comes as sweet relief – not a colonial curlicue or floral bedspread in sight! It's fully equipped with kitchen, washing machine, TV and video, plus light breakfast provisions and a verdant rural setting.

Hamlet Downs (☎ 6288 1212; www.users.bigpond.com /hamletdowns; 50 Gully Rd; d incl breakfast from $140, extra adult/child from $10/35) Amid spectacular flower beds 6km south of Ellendale at Fentonbury, Hamlet Downs sleeps up to nine in self-contained comfort. Take a walk down to Fentonbury Creek to look for a platypus. Light or cooked breakfast included. Off-season rates as low as $100.

Hopfield Cottages (☎ 6288 1223; hopfieldcots@ trump.net.au; 990 Ellendale Rd; d $140-145, extra person $25) Main street Hopfield offers two self-contained abodes under the one conjoined, corrugated-iron roof, including full breakfast provisions and lots of quaint touches. Hollyhocks and roses succeed to raspberry canes out the back, running down to the river.

OUSE
☎ 03 / pop 160

Ouse (pronounced, rather deliciously, 'Ooze') was proclaimed early in Tassie's colonial saga, but for a long time there was just a river crossing here. Most of the town's ordinary weatherboard buildings were knocked up more recently, but Ouse remains a popular highway food stop, with a pub, takeaway (renowned for its pies) and supermarket. The riverside picnic ground is a serene spot.

Lachlan Hotel (☎ 6287 1215; ousepub@bigpond.com; Lyell Hwy; s/d $45/65) The rough-as-guts Lachlan offers serviceable, sunny pub rooms with shared facilities, plus bar lunches and dinners daily (mains $12 to $19).

Sassa-del-Gallo (☎ 6287 1289; fax 6287 1289; cnr Ticknell St & Lyell Hwy; d $90, extra person $25) Shamelessly suburban, Sassa-del-Gallo (Spanish for 'No Style'?) fails to deliver the Mediterranean flair suggested by its name. Still, it's clean and serviceable if all you're after is a bed. Room for six.

TARRALEAH
☎ 03 / pop 10

Halfway between Hobart and Queenstown, **Tarraleah** (☎ 6289 3222; www.tarraleah.com) is a surreal place. It was built in the 1920s and '30s as a residential village for hydroelectric workers, and at its peak it had a population

BLACK BOBS

You won't find it on any maps, but somewhere around the upper Derwent Valley was once the notorious town of Black Bobs. Tasmania has only recently shaken off its 'two-headed Tasmanian' tag, a throw-away insult used by mainlanders who viewed Tasmanians as hopeless inbreds wading through the shallow end of the gene pool. Isolated in the backwoods for decades, Black Bobs was allegedly rife with cousin-love; a place of evil, depraved men and their questionable spouses, existing in unnatural harmony. It seems Black Bobs has been lost to myth and history – no-one's really sure where it was, or it if ever actually existed – but keep an ear out for lonesome banjos on the back roads while you're passing through…

of hundreds, complete with police station, town hall, shops, church, golf course and 100 houses. Once the hydro work dried up, the village declined and the population plummeted. Hydro sold off most of the houses for removal in the 1990s, and then put the remainder of the village up for sale.

In 2002 Tarraleah (pronounced 'Tarra-lee-uh') was purchased by a family from Queensland ('The Family that Bought a Town', as the tabloids tagged them). They poured buckets of cash into the place, but recently sold the whole shebang to private interests who've spent further millions. It still feels like a ghost town if you visit outside peak season, but there's a full range of accommodation here, including **campsites** (unpowered/powered sites $12/26), rooms in the **Scholars House** (d from $130), self-contained one- to three-bedroom **cottages** (d from $190), and ritzy rooms in the luxury Art Deco **Lodge** (☎ 6289 1199; www.tarraleahlodge.com; Wild River Rd; d from $590).

On the food front there's a pub called the **Highlander Arms** (mains $15-25; ☽ dinner), the casual **Teez Café** (light meals $5-15; ☽ breakfast & lunch) and **Wildside Restaurant** (4-course degustation menu $85; ☽ dinner) in the Lodge (bookings essential).

Activities include mountain biking, bushwalking, golf, bird-watching, fishing, kayaking and squash – whatever floats your boat.

Hobart-to-Strahan **Tassielink** (☎ 1300 300 520; www.tassielink.com.au) buses stop here on request daily (except Monday and Wednesday). The two-hour jaunt from Hobart costs $26; from Strahan it's 3½ hours and $43.

East Coast

Tasmania's glorious east coast is an idyllic domain of sea, sand and serenity. The coastline is fringed with powder-white beaches and lapped by water that's impossibly clear and blue. It's a land of quiet bays and long, sandy shores, punctuated by granite headlands splashed with flaming orange lichen. If you want to be active there's endless hiking and water sports. Otherwise, this is the perfect setting for a relaxed and sun-soaked beach holiday.

Some of Tasmania's most beautiful national parks are found in this part of the state. There's Freycinet National Park, which encompasses picture-perfect Wineglass Bay; Maria Island, as rich in history as it is in wildlife; and often-overlooked Douglas-Apsley National Park, with its emerald forests and waterholes – a tranquil place for a swim. If your idea of an ideal holiday revolves more around joys of the palate, you'll find this part of Tasmania a particularly rich foraging ground. There's ultra-fresh seafood, berry farms overflowing with berry waffles and sundaes, and some of the best vineyards in the state.

The small seaside towns are well set up for visitors. There's plenty of good accommodation – but prices rise considerably in summer. In December and January you'd be unwise to travel here without prebooking somewhere to stay. In the depths of winter the east coast is always warmer than the rest of Tasmania, and even when a stormy surf pounds its beaches, the region is particularly atmospheric.

HIGHLIGHTS

- Slurping down briny-fresh oysters at **Freycinet Marine Farm** (p179)
- Plunging into the ice-blue waters at exquisite **Wineglass Bay** (p179)
- Absorbing the natural beauty of the Freycinet Peninsula from a **sea kayak** (p178)
- Swimming in the clear turquoise waterholes and wandering the gorge at **Douglas-Apsley National Park** (p185)
- Feasting on all things berry and sweet ice-cream delights at **Kate's Berry Farm** (p174)
- Getting up early to watch an **east coast sunrise** turn the sea to molten gold
- Hiking or biking in **Maria Island National Park** (p168) for some of the best up-close wildlife spotting anywhere
- Doing a **wine-crawl** (p173) between tasting rooms and cellar doors, savouring the fruits of the east coast's vines

Douglas-Apsley ★
National Park

East Coast ★
Wineries   Freycinet
              ★ Marine Farm
Kate's Berry ★
Farm   ★ Wineglass Bay
              ★ Freycinet
                Peninsula

              ★ Maria Island
                National Park

Getting There & Around

BICYCLE

East-coast Tasmania is ideally suited to cycling. The route is blessed by wonderful views, little traffic, few daunting hills and towns perfectly spaced to ride between. You're also less likely to get rained on here than in other parts of Tasmania.

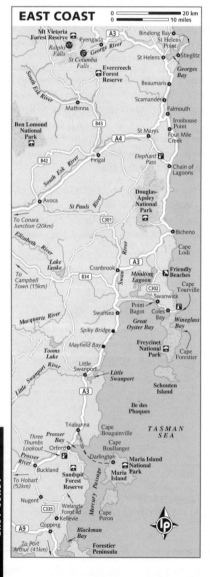

For cyclists travelling between Swansea and Coles Bay, there's an informal **boat service** (☎ 6257 0239) between Point Bagot and Swanwick, which costs $15 per person and saves approximately 46km of riding. The boat runs on request in both directions, between October and April, weather permitting.

BUS

The east coast is served by **Redline Coaches** (☎ 6336 1446, 1300 360 000; www.tasredline.com.au) and **Tassielink** (☎ 6230 8900, 1300 300 520; www.tassielink .com.au). Redline runs one service each weekday from Launceston to Swansea ($29.60), the Coles Bay turn-off ($36.20) and Bicheno ($36.90) and return, via the Midland Hwy and the inland B34 linking road. Services from Hobart connect with these services – you change buses at Campbell Town, where there's a wait of five minutes to three hours depending on the day. Redline also runs daily services (except Saturday) from Launceston to St Helens (and vice versa) along the A4 via Fingal, St Marys and Scamander. Hobart buses connect with this service at Conara on the Midland Hwy.

Tassielink runs one bus on weekdays from Hobart to Swansea during the school term, and only on Tuesdays, Wednesdays and Saturdays during school holidays ($24.90). Tassielink's Hobart–Bicheno service runs Wednesday to Friday and Sunday ($31.70).

For getting to the Freycinet Peninsula, **Bicheno Coaches** (☎ 6257 0293, 0419-570 293; www .wineglassbay.com, click on 'Getting here') connects with Redline and Tassielink buses at the Coles Bay turn-off daily except Saturday when there's still a Bicheno–Coles Bay Service (see p181).

ORFORD

☎ 03 / pop 500

The seaside village of Orford was once a seaport for the east coast whaling fleet, and the convict and military settlement on Maria Island, just across Mercury Passage. Today, Orford is mostly a holiday village where Hobartians have their seaside 'shacks' and spend summer holidays on the beach.

The Prosser River flows through **Paradise Gorge** as it approaches town: it's often a mirror-calm spot with perfect reflections. On the north side of the river is a convict-built road that once reached all the way to Hobart, and is now a peaceful riverside **walking track**.

EAST COAST

Another, coastal walking track of about 5km leads from Raspins Beach, along Shelly Beach and around the Luther Point cliffs to beautiful **Spring Beach**, which has crystal-clear water and, in the right conditions, surfing. The walk passes a convict-era **quarry**, which provided the sandstone for many buildings in Melbourne and Hobart.

The Prosser River is a good fishing and boating spot and you can hire paddle boats from **Sun Smart Paddle Boats** (☎ 0419-196 737) to explore. There's also diving in the clear waters offshore. The recently sunk **Troy D** has provided an artificial reef near Orford that's already attracted plenty of sea life. **Island Ocean Charters** (☎ 6257 1275; mail@islandoceancharters.com.au) can take you there and to dive sites around Maria Island.

Just off the highway opposite the Ampol service station is **Darlington Vineyard** (☎ 6257 1630; Holkham Court; ☺ 10am-5pm daily Jan-Feb, Fri-Mon Mar-Nov), which produces an award-winning riesling (tastings free).

Sleeping

Blue Waters Motor Inn (☎ 6257 1102; 28 Tasman Hwy; d $75-110, extra person $15) This place, with its brightly painted exterior, is more pub-and-gaming than accommodation oriented. It does have several different types of motel rooms, which are clean but unremarkable.

Prosser Holiday Units (☎ 6257 1427; cnr Tasman Hwy & Charles St; d $95; extra adult/child $20/10) These family-friendly, self-contained units are just off the highway on the edge of the Prosser River. The two-storey units have views of the water, and accommodate up to five.

Sanda House (☎ 6257 1527; www.orfordsandahouse .com.au; 33 Walpole St; d $100-120) A colonial B&B, it occupies Orford's oldest house, a pretty 1840s stone cottage surrounded by lovingly tended gardens on the south side of the river. Continental breakfasts are served in front of the fire in the dining room.

Spring Beach Holiday Villas (☎ 6257 1440; 314 Rheban Rd; d $100-145, extra adult/child $30/25) Just 150m from Spring Beach, this is the perfect spot for children. The two-bedroom self-contained units have a wood-fired stove, private outdoor area with BBQ, and water views.

Orford Riverside Cottages (☎ 6257 1655; www .riversidecottages.com.au; Old Convict Rd; d $150-190, extra adult/child $40/20) These pretty timber cottages are set in trees overlooking the Prosser River and have spas, fully equipped kitchens and an ex-

tensive DVD library. You can borrow a fishing line and catch your dinner from the deck.

Eating

Gateway Café (☎ 6257 1539, 1 Charles St, lunch mains $7.50-15.50, dinner mains $15-22; ☺ summer 7am-9pm, winter 7am-6pm) By the bridge over the Prosser River, this excellent café does all-day breakfast, lunches and dinners as well as great pies, cakes, wraps and rolls. They also sell Tasmanian gourmet provisions in the shop section.

Scorchers on the River (☎ 6257 1033; 1 Esplanade; mains $11-23; ☺ 11am-8pm Thu-Tue). Scorchers is known for superior eat-in or takeaway wood-fired pizzas, of which the garlic prawn and Spring Bay seafood number is tops. There's also good lasagne and salads.

Blue Waters Motor Inn (☎ 6257 1102; Tasman Hwy; mains $16-26; ☺ lunch & dinner) The recently revamped dining room has wide river views and does big meals that are better-than-pub. Try the bourbon-marinated T-bone or the wallaby schnitzel.

Getting There & Away

Tassielink (☎ 1300 300 520; www.tassielink.com.au) coaches stop at Coffee on Prossers (the old roadhouse just north of the river) en route from Hobart to Swansea and Bicheno (and vice versa). The trip from Hobart takes 1½ hours and costs $17.20.

TRIABUNNA

☎ 03 / pop 900

Triabunna, 8km north of Orford, is set on an inlet of Spring Bay that shelters a small cray- and scallop-fishing fleet. On the northern side of the bay, there's also an enormous pile of woodchips from the mill of Gunns Ltd, which processes Tasmania's forests into matchbox-sized pieces for export to Asia for paper making.

There's not much here of great interest to tourists, except that this is the jumping-off point for beautiful **Maria Island**. There's a pub and tearooms, and also a good **visitors centre** (☎ 6257 4772; cnr Esplanade & Charles St; ☺ 10am-4pm) that will ply you with information on the east coast.

Seawings (☎ 6257 1163, www.seawingsecotours.com .au; Waterfront, Triabunna), which operates the Maria Island Ferry (see p171), does three-hour ecotours leaving daily at 10.30am, visiting the Ile des Phoques seal colony and Maria

EAST COAST

DETOUR: WIELANGTA FOREST ROAD

There's a short cut that leads from the Tasman Hwy at Copping and pops you out on the east coast at Orford. It's a beautiful forest drive of 29km on a gravel route that's known as the **Wielangta Forest Road**. Road conditions are generally good – though you may need to look out for log trucks – and there are walks that lead into the heart of the forest.

The Wielangta Forest has recently been the focus of a high-profile logging debate. It's the habitat of 34 endemic species of plant – 11 of which are threatened – as well as 47 bird species including the Tasmanian wedge-tailed eagle and the swift parrot, and rare fauna including the eastern barred bandicoot, the spotted tail quoll and the Wielangta stag beetle. Despite this, it's largely unprotected and vulnerable to logging. Since 2005, when logging began in Wielangta, Senator Bob Brown has been fighting a court case to prevent the forest's destruction. This was successful until, in November 2007, a court decision removed the moratorium. At the time of research, the decision lay with the High Court, and the future of the Wielangta forests still hung in the balance. You can read more about the case at Bob Brown's website www.on-trial.info.

Walks in the forest include the 20-minute stroll through beautiful rainforest at **Sandspit Forest Reserve**, where there's also a picnic area, and a 90-minute return hike called the **Wielangta Walk**, which follows the river valley. There's also the **Three Thumbs Lookout**, 6km from Orford, where a (rougher) side road leads up to a high point, giving wonderful views of Maria Island. The two-hour return walk to the open, rocky summit of the highest 'thumb' rewards you with even better panoramas of the coast.

There are no bus services along this road. If you've driven from Orford, you'll reach a give-way sign at the southern end of the forest road – turn right and head past nearby Kellevie to reach the turn-off to either Buckland or Copping. Some cyclists consider the road too steep and rough to be enjoyable, but if you're used to gravel and hills, you should breeze it.

Island's soaring Fossil Cliffs. Passengers can be dropped on the island after the tour.

Sleeping & Eating

Triabunna Cabin & Caravan Park (☎ 6257 3575; www.mariagateway.com; 4 Vicary St; unpowered/powered sites $16/18.20, on-site vans $44-54, cabins $77-110) This small, cheek-by-jowl compound opposite the sports fields has all the usual caravan park facilities.

Spring Bay Hotel (☎ 6257 3115; 1 Charles St; s/d $40/70) This pub is often filled with salty characters from the local fishing fleet – a bit rough around the edges, but welcoming. Rooms have shared facilities and a continental breakfast is included. Reasonable pub food is served nightly except Sunday.

Tandara Motor Inn (☎ 6257 3333; Tasman Hwy; d $125, extra person $10) Recently refurbished, this is now a decent place to stay with light, bright, well-decorated motel rooms, each with an attractive en suite. There's a pool when water restrictions allow.

Girraween Gardens & Tearooms (☎ 6257 3458; 4 Henry St; light meals $4-12; ⏰ 9.30am-4pm daily, closed Sat Jun-Aug) Giraween has a rigorously manicured garden and tearooms serving sandwiches, cake and light restaurant meals. A good place for afternoon tea if you're early for the ferry.

Getting There & Away

Tassielink (☎ 1300 300 520; www.tassielink.com.au) coaches stop at the visitors centre. The 1¾-hour trip from Hobart costs $18.20.

MARIA ISLAND NATIONAL PARK

Beautiful Maria (pronounced ma-*rye*-ah) Island, with its high craggy peaks, rises up like a fairytale castle across the waters of Mercury Passage, which separates it from the mainland. It's a peaceful haven, blissfully free of cars, that's a top spot for walking, wildlife-watching, biking and camping – and soaking in the peace.

Maria has some gorgeous natural scenery: soaring cliffs, fern-draped forests, blond-white beaches and azure seas. Forester kangaroos, wombats and wallabies wander about, and there's bountiful bird life, including the grey-plumed Cape Barren goose. Below the water there's also lots to see, with good snorkelling and diving in the clear, shallow waters of the Marine Reserve.

Maria became a national park, as much for its history as for its natural assets, in 1972 and at time of research, the island was also being assessed for Unesco World Heritage status.

History

Maria Island has a rich history that has seen various incarnations as a penal settlement, an industrial site and a farming community. The island was originally home to the Oyster Bay tribe of Tasmanian Aborigines, who called it Toarra Marra Monah. They lived primarily on shellfish, and made the crossing to the mainland in bark canoes.

Dutch explorer Abel Tasman landed here in 1642, and named the island in honour of Anthony Van Diemen's wife. The island became Tasmania's second penal settlement in 1821 and, for the next 10 years, the convicts were set to work to develop the island. Many of the surviving buildings such as Commissariat Store (1825) and the Penitentiary (1830) survive from this era. By the early 1830s Maria Island was becoming too expensive to be viable, so the convicts were shipped back to settlements on the Tasmanian mainland. For the next 10 years, the island was the domain of whalers, farmers and smugglers.

In 1842 Darlington reopened as a probation station and a road was built to a second settlement at Long Point (Point Lesueur). At one stage there were some 600 convicts on Maria, but when convict transportation to Tasmania slowed, convict numbers dwindled and Darlington was again closed in 1850. The whole island was leased for grazing the following year.

Then, with the arrival of enterprising Italian businessman Diego Bernacchi in 1884, Maria Island began a new era of development. Darlington's buildings were renovated and structures like the Coffee Palace added (1888). The town of 260 was renamed San Diego. Over the next 40 years a cement factory and wine and silk-growing industries were developed. This industrial era ended with the advent of the Great Depression in the 1940s and the island reverted to farming.

In the 1960s the government bought the properties on the island, and reintroduced animals like Forester kangaroos, Bennetts wallabies and Cape Barren geese that had been wiped out since European occupation. In 1972 the island became a national park.

Information

The visitors centre in Triabunna (p167) can answer any questions you have about the island, or you can inform yourself ahead of time with online information at www.parks .tas.gov.au/natparks/maria.

There's a **visitors reception area** in the old Commissariat Store, just a short walk from where the ferry docks, where you can get detailed information on walks, biking routes, wildlife, camping and the island's history. There's a **public telephone** near the ranger station in Darlington.

The island has no shops, so you need to bring all your food and gear with you. Bring clothing for cool, wet weather as well as hot sun: a hat and sunscreen are essential. A current national park pass is also required (p64).

Sights & Activities

The township of **Darlington** is the place to start your time on the island. There's **The Penitentiary**, which once housed convicts (and is now bunk-house-style accommodation – see p171) as well as the restored **Coffee Palace**, and **Mess Hall**.

From Darlington it's a short walk (under two hours return) to the **Painted Cliffs** at the southern end of Hopground Beach. Here the sculpted sandstone cliffs are stained with iron oxide in a kaleidoscope of colours. It's best to visit at low tide – ask when that is in the Commissariat Store.

On the northern tip of the island there's circuit walk of 1½ hours to **Cape Boullanger**, the **Fossil Cliffs** and the old brickworks. If you have more time (allow four hours return from Darlington), climb **Bishop & Clerk** (599m) and marvel at the soaring bird's-eye views while you eat your packed lunch on the exposed, rocky slabs at the top. **Mt Maria** (711m) is the island's highest point. It's a seven-hour return hike through the eucalypt forests from Darlington. The summit gives good views over the isthmus that connects the island's northern and southern parts.

The seas around Maria, from Return Point to Bishop & Clerk, are a designated marine reserve, so there's no fishing allowed, including in the Darlington area. The reserve encompasses the giant kelp forests and caves around **Fossil Bay**, and has excellent scuba diving and snorkelling. Two good spots for snorkelling are under the ferry pier and at the Painted Cliffs. You'll need a wetsuit if you plan to stay in long.

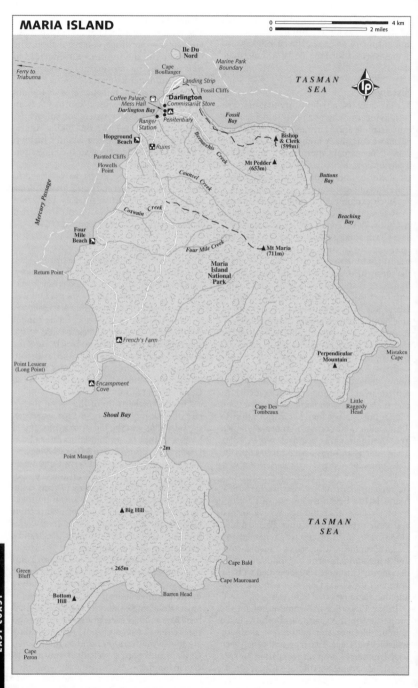

MARIA ISLAND

0 ——————— 4 km
0 ——————— 2 miles

Ile Du Nord

Cape Boullanger

Marine Park Boundary

Ferry to Triabunna

Landing Strip

Coffee Palace; Mess Hall
Darlington Bay

Darlington
Commissariat Store

Fossil Cliffs

TASMAN SEA

Ranger Station

Penitentiary

Hopground Beach

Ruins

Fossil Bay

Bernacchis Creek

Bishop & Clerk (599m)

Mt Pedder (653m)

Painted Cliffs

Howells Point

Counsel Creek

Buttons Bay

Mercury Passage

Coxwain Creek

Beaching Bay

Four Mile Beach

Four Mile Creek

Mt Maria (711m)

Return Point

Maria Island National Park

French's Farm

Point Lesueur (Long Point)

Perpendicular Mountain

Mistaken Cape

Encampment Cove

Shoal Bay

Cape Des Tombeaux

Little Raggedy Head

2m

Point Mauge

Big Hill

TASMAN SEA

Green Bluff

265m

Cape Bald

Cape Maurouard

Bottom Hill

Barren Head

Cape Peron

Bird-watchers will love the abundant bird life on Maria Island. If you're lucky, you might spot the endangered forty-spotted pardalote.

You can hire bicycles on Maria Island for $15 per day. Ask at the **ranger station** (☎ 6257 1420), where the ranger on duty will also be able to give you advice about where to cycle.

Tours

If like the idea of a multiday bush walk but don't much fancy a soggy tent and noodles from the campstove at dinner, then the **Maria Island Walk** (☎ 6227 8800; www.mariaislandwalk.com.au) might be your thing. Between October and the end of April, this four-day walk takes a gentle, guided wander through the most lovely parts of Maria. The first two nights are spent under canvas at secluded bush camps, and the third at the historic former home of Diego Bernacchi in Darlington. There's amazing food and fine Tasmanian wines to go with it. The walk costs $1950, including all meals, accommodation and transport from Hobart.

Sleeping

There are **camping grounds** (d/f $12/15, extra person $5) on the island at Darlington, French's Farm and Encampment Cove. Bookings aren't required. Gas BBQs are provided close to the Darlington site only, so camping stoves are essential. Fires are allowed in designated fireplaces but are often banned over summer. French's Farm and Encampment Cove have limited tank water supplies.

Penitentiary Accommodation Units (☎ 6257 1420; d $15, d $40, 6-bed r $80) The brick rooms of the penitentiary that once housed the island's convicts are now a good, simple place to stay – if you don't mind the ghosts. There are six bunks in each room, a table and a wood heater, and shared bathrooms with coin-operated hot showers nearby. There's no linen provided, and no electricity. The Penitentiary is often fully booked over summer, so plan well ahead.

Getting There & Away

The Maria Island ferry service has undergone some upheavals recently, and at the time of research there was just one small-scale ferry operating, though others were applying for the licence. If you're planning to visit, Triabunna visitors centre (p167) will give you the most up-to-date information.

The **Seawings** (☎ 6257 1163; www.seawingsecotours .com.au; adults/kids/bikes $50/$25/$10) ferry service to

Maria Island departs the docks at Triabunna at 9am and 3.15pm daily in summer. The return ferry departs Maria 9.30am at 4pm daily in summer. The service may be limited to about four days a week in winter – call ahead to check which days. The trip takes 20 to 25 minutes and is weather-dependent. Arrive 20 minutes before scheduled departure times. Seawings will also drop passengers on Maria after one of its eco-tours (p167).

It is also possible to land on the grass airstrip near Darlington by light plane, chartered from Coles Bay, Hobart or Launceston.

SWANSEA

☎ 03 / pop 580

Swansea has thrived on Tasmania's growth in tourism, and this once-sleepy seaside town is now an energetic and attractive holiday haven, with plenty to see and do, good beaches and some wonderful wineries and restaurants on its doorstep.

Swansea lies on the western shore of beautiful Great Oyster Bay, and has sweeping views of the Freycinet Peninsula over often-calm blue waters. Founded in 1820 and originally known as Great Swanport, Swansea also has some historic streetscapes and an absorbing museum.

There are plenty of lovely places to stay here, with a particular abundance of good B&Bs, as well as some less-inspiring motel blocks where the best feature is the view of the water. Swansea can get busy in summer. That means accommodation prices rise and vacancies are hard to come by, so as with the rest of the east coast in summer, ensure you book ahead. Prices generally fall in winter.

Information

Online Access Centre (☎ 6257 8806; Franklin St; ⓨ 10am-3pm Mon-Tue & Thu-Fri, 10am-5pm Wed, 10am-1pm Sat & Sun) Adjacent to the town's primary school.

Swansea Corner Store (cnr Victoria & Franklin Sts; ⓨ 7am-7pm) Has a multicard ATM.

Swansea has been having troubles with the quality of its water supply for some time, and all water must be boiled before drinking. Most accommodation supplies preboiled drinking water for guests.

Sights & Activities

HISTORIC BUILDINGS

The best of Swansea's historic buildings are easily seen on foot accompanied by a *Swansea*

EAST COAST

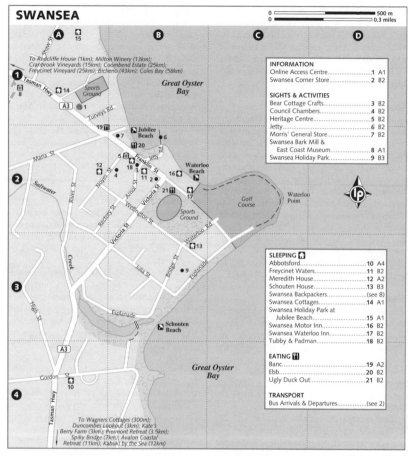

SWANSEA

0 ___ 500 m
0 ___ 0.3 miles

To Redcliffe House (1km); Milton Winery (13km);
Cranbrook Vineyards (15km); Coombend Estate (25km);
Freycinet Vineyard (25km); Bicheno (43km); Coles Bay (58km)

Great Oyster Bay

Tasman Hwy

Sports Ground

Turveys Rd

Jubilee Beach

Maria St

Franklin St

Waterloo Beach

Saltwater

Noyes St

Arnol St

Victoria St

Wellington St

Waterloo Point

Golf Course

Sports Ground

Rectory St

Victoria St

Waterloo Rd

Creek

Julia St

Bridge St

Esplanade

High St

Esplanade

Schouten Beach

Gordon St

Tasman Hwy

Great Oyster Bay

To Wagners Cottages (300m);
Duncombes Lookout (3km); Kate's
Berry Farm (3km); Piermont Retreat (3.5km);
Spiky Bridge (7km); Avalon Coastal
Retreat (11km); Kabuki by the Sea (12km)

INFORMATION	
Online Access Centre...................1	A1
Swansea Corner Store.....................2	B2

SIGHTS & ACTIVITIES	
Bear Cottage Crafts........................3	B2
Council Chambers............................4	B2
Heritage Centre..............................5	B2
Jetty...6	B2
Morris' General Store......................7	B2
Swansea Bark Mill &	
East Coast Museum.....................8	A1
Swansea Holiday Park......................9	B3

SLEEPING 🏠	
Abbotsford...................................10	A4
Freycinet Waters...........................11	B2
Meredith House..............................12	A2
Schouten House.............................13	B3
Swansea Backpackers..................(see 8)	
Swansea Cottages.........................14	A1
Swansea Holiday Park at	
Jubilee Beach............................15	A1
Swansea Motor Inn.........................16	B2
Swansea Waterloo Inn....................17	B2
Tubby & Padman............................18	B2

EATING 🍴	
Banc...19	A2
Ebb...20	B2
Ugly Duck Out...............................21	B2

TRANSPORT	
Bus Arrivals & Departures..............(see 2)	

Heritage Walk booklet ($2.50) available from **Bear Cottage Crafts** (☎ 6257 8091; 18 Franklin St). Most of the best buildings are along the waterfront on Franklin Street. **Morris' General Store** (13 Franklin St), built in 1838, is a Swansea landmark, as are the attractive 1860 **council chambers** and imposing Meredith House (now a hotel; see p174), both up on Noyes Street.

There's also a surprisingly good display at the **Heritage Centre** (☎ 6257 8215; Franklin St; adult/child $3/1; ✆ 9am-5pm Mon-Sat) located in the old Swansea Schoolhouse. Here there's an eclectic collection of Aboriginal artefacts, convict paraphernalia, war memorabilia – and an enormous billiard table that can be hired for games ($2 per person) outside of museum hours.

SWANSEA BARK MILL & EAST COAST MUSEUM

This complex on the edge of Swansea has a **museum** (☎ 6257 8382; 96 Tasman Hwy; adult/child/family $10/6/23; ✆ 9am-5pm) explaining the processing of black wattle bark to obtain tannin for tanning leathers. The mill was one of the few industries that operated in Swansea through the Great Depression, and it helped keep the town alive. There's also an interesting display on the early exploration by French explorers of Tasmania's east coast. At the time of research, a bakery/café was in the pipeline.

OTHER ATTRACTIONS

When Swansea's old wooden jetty began to succumb to rot, ingenious townspeople came up with a solution: a new **jetty** (Jetty Rd) made of milk bottles. The jetty, a great spot for fishing or simply admiring the views, used over a million compressed plastic milk bottles – and is guaranteed to outlast its predecessor.

Duncombes Lookout, 3km south of town, provides panoramic views of Oyster Bay and the Freycinet Peninsula. A further 4km south is **Spiky Bridge**, which was built by convicts in 1843 using thousands of local fieldstones but no mortar. The nearby beach and headland are popular for picnics and fishing.

In town, a 30- to 50-minute stroll between Waterloo Beach and the Esplanade passes through the rookeries of mutton birds (short-tailed shearwaters) that burrow here in the breeding season from September to April. The adults return at dusk in a flurry of wings from feeding at sea. The route is known as the **Loon.tite.ter.mair.re.le.hoin.er Walk**, named for the Tasmanian Aboriginal tribe that lived in this area.

If you prefer to cruise around on two wheels, you can hire mountain bikes from **Swansea Holiday Park** (☎ 6257 8148; per half/full day $15/25) at Schouten Beach.

WINE TASTING & WINERIES

On the Tasman Hwy north of Swansea there are several wineries, most with free tastings and cellar door sales. **Milton Winery** (☎ 6257 8298; off Tasman Hwy; ☽ 10am-5pm), 13km north of Swansea, has tastings in an attractive pavilion overlooking a lake and the vineyards. Try the sparkling pinot noir chardonnay.

Spring Vale Vineyards (☎ 6257 8208; www.springvale wines.com; 130 Spring Vale Rd; ☽ 10am-4pm) is at Cranbrook, about 15km north of town and has a wonderful pinot gris, which is one of Tassie's hottest wines. Nearby is **Craigie Knowe Vineyard** (☎ 6257 8252; 80 Glen Gala Rd; ☽ 9am-5pm), which produces outstanding cabernet sauvignon and pinot noir. Opening hours can vary, so call first. About 10km further north, just past the Great Oyster Bay lookout, an enormous expanse of vines heralds the domain of Gunns Ltd, controversial timber and woodchip conglomerate (see p47) and the owners of **Coombend Estate** (☎ 6257 8881; off Tasman Hwy; ☽ 9am-5pm). There are tastings and cellar door sales here, but you are better to continue up the same driveway to the acclaimed **Freycinet Vineyard** (☎ 6257 8574; off Tasman Hwy; ☽ 9am-5pm) where winemaker Claudio Radenti makes an exquisite Radenti sparkling. The tasting room also serves great coffee.

Sleeping

BUDGET

Swansea Holiday Park at Jubilee Beach (☎ 6257 8177; www.swansea-holiday.com.au; 27 Shaw St; unpowered/powered sites for two $24/28, cabins d $90-160; 🖳 🐾) This neat, family-friendly park is close to the shallow, protected waters of Jubilee Beach and has 180-degree water views. The best camping sites are beachside. Some self-contained cabins have a spa and ocean vistas.

Swansea Backpackers (☎ 6257 8650; www.swansea backpackers.com.au; 96 Tasman Highway dm/d $34/75; 🖳) This top-notch new backpackers at the Swansea Bark Mill is sure to be a crowd pleaser. It has smart and spacious public areas and a shiny stainless steel kitchen. The rooms surround a shady deck and are clean and peaceful.

MIDRANGE
Guesthouses & B&Bs

Freycinet Waters (☎ 6257 8080; www.freycinetwaters .com.au; 16 Franklin St; s $120-140, d $130-160) This brightly decorated B&B has friendly owners and a real seaside ambience. There's a sunny breakfast room with water views, and also a brand-new self-contained apartment, with its own deck and entrance.

our pick **Abbotsford** (☎ 6257 9092; www.swansea bedandbreakfast.com.au; 50 Gordon St, d $130-170) This delightful stone house has been lovingly refurbished by its Scottish owners, and is one of the nicest places to stay in Swansea. There are three double bedrooms with a shared bathroom and guest lounge, so it's perfectly suited to couples or families travelling together. The owners put up the No Vacancy sign as soon as one of the rooms is occupied, however, so if you're first in, you'll have the whole house to yourself. Breakfasts are divine.

Redcliffe House (☎ 6257 8557; www.redcliffehouse .com.au; 13569 Tasman Hwy; s $130, d $145-160) This restored heritage farmhouse, built in 1835, is just north of town. The rooms are beautifully decorated and a guest lounge is equipped with books and a decanter of port. There's also an excellent DVD library. For those that prefer complete privacy, there's a self-contained apartment with breakfast provisions supplied.

Schouten House (☎ 6257 8564; www.schoutenhouse .com.au; 1 Waterloo Rd; d $150-180) This convict-built brick-and-sandstone mansion was presented as a wedding gift to a Swansea couple in 1844. Its huge rooms, with their original timbers, now house this atmospheric, antique-filled

EAST COAST

B&B. You can't go past the pancakes with bacon and maple syrup for breakfast.

Motels

Swansea Motor Inn (☎ 6257 8102; www.swanseamotorinn .com; 1c Franklin St; d $68-160) This salmon-coloured motel has a range of rooms – the standard level of which are, frankly, hospital-like. If you're after something more swanky, ask for room 20, which has a spa and good water views.

Swansea Waterloo Inn (☎ 6257 8577; 1a Franklin St; d $77-150) You can't miss this red-brick block on the beach side as the road bends through Swansea. It's aesthetically uninspiring, but some of the rooms do have good water views. Check out the pub/restaurant for curiosity value: there's a log truck Hall of Fame behind the bar.

Self-Contained Apartments & Cottages

Swansea Cottages (☎ 6257 8328; www.swanseacottages .com.au; 43 Franklin St; d $140-240, extra adult/child $40/30) These neat and appealing cottages are right by Jubilee Beach. Fully equipped and air-conditioned, they sleep up to seven – some have spas. There's a DVD library, and fishing rods and bikes are available for hire, as well as racquets and balls for the tennis court next door.

Wagners Cottages (☎ 6257 8494; www.wagners cottages.com.au; Tasman Highway; d $180-270) Wagners has five lovely stone cottages set in lush gardens a couple of kilometres south of town. Each has a deep spa bath, and there are open fires, fresh flowers, a movie library and complimentary port. Breakfasts feature fresh eggs from Wagners' hens and just-out-of-the-oven bread.

TOP END

Meredith House (☎ 6257 8119; www.meredith-house .com.au; 15 Noyes St; d $130-220) Meredith House, built in 1853, now houses one of Swansea's nicest places to stay. Furnished with antiques, some of the pretty B&B suites look over Great Oyster Bay, and others the burgeoning green gardens. There's also a row of modern studio spa apartments adjacent.

Kabuki by the Sea (☎ 6257 8588; www.kabukibythe sea.com.au; Tasman Hwy; d $180, extra person $40) This is as close as you can get to a traditional Japanese *ryokan* in Tasmania. Set on clifftops 12km south of Swansea with endless sea views, this is a row of self-contained apartments adorned with 'a touch of Japan'. Even more of an attraction is the excellent Japanese restaurant (opposite).

Tubby and Padman (☎ 6257 890; www.tubbyand padman.com.au; 20 Franklin St; cottage ste $165-185, units $155-165, extra person $35; ☐) This snug Georgian cottage – that takes its name from its original owners – was once Swansea's department store, and is now a classy B&B. The thoughtfully decorated suites have spas and log fires, and come with breakfast provisions. There are also two stylish self-contained apartments that sleep four to five guests.

Piermont Retreat (☎ 6257 8131; www.piermont.com .au; Tasman Hwy; d $245-295) Piermont is just the spot for a romantic hideaway holiday or just a great place to relax to the sound of the waves. Set in gardens and bushland close to the shores of Great Oyster Bay are 12 stone cottages, with fireplaces and spas, close to a secluded beach. There's a pool, a tennis court, bikes for hire and a new restaurant that serves plenty of fresh east-coast seafood nightly (except Wednesday).

Avalon Coastal Retreat (☎ 1300 36 11 36, www .avaloncoastalretreat.com.au; Tasman Highway; house sleeping 6 adults $770) This is the kind of place that makes you feel you're in a movie about the lives of the rich and famous. All glass and steel and ocean views that go on forever, this is possibly the most luxurious beach house in Tasmania. The kitchen and cellar are well stocked, and the beach is nearby – though you'll hardly want to leave the house.

Eating

The east coast is a new top of the list for Tasmanian epicures, and a few establishments in Swansea are highlights. Be sure to make bookings in summer.

Kate's Berry Farm (☎ 6257 8428; Addison St off Tasman Highway; teas & desserts $4-9; ☒ 10am-4.30pm) Sit under the wisteria-draped pergola and absorb sweeping views over Great Oyster Bay while you indulge in Kate's berries. She does them in a range of ice creams, jams and sauces, and in handmade berry chocolate. The Belgian waffles with berry compote are to die for.

Ugly Duck Out (☎ 6257 8850; 2 Franklin St; meals $8-26; ☒ 8.30am-9pm) This casual diner was named as a play on Swansea's Swan Inn, which burned down some years ago. The *Sydney Morning Herald* has proclaimed it the home of the best fish and chips in Tasmania – they also do a great salads, gourmet burgers, curries and pastas. The whole menu is available as takeaway.

our pick **Banc** (☎ 6257 8896; cnr Franklin & Maria Sts; lunch mains $8-26, dinner mains $26-40; ☒ dinner Wed-Mon, brunch & lunch Sun & Mon, closed Tue & Wed Jun-Aug) The

Banc is becoming known as one of Tasmania's top restaurants. Using the freshest east-coast produce, it serves up wonderful dishes like venison steaks, slow-roasted suckling pig, and abalone confit with fresh lime mirin. Lazy late breakfasts are served Sunday and Monday.

Kabuki by the Sea (☎ 6257 8588; Tasman Hwy; mains $22-26; ☼ lunch daily, dinner Tue-Sat Dec-Apr, Fri & Sat May-Nov) The smiling Japanese clientele here is a good sign that Kabuki is serving its Japanese food just right. Try the marinated *una ju* (eel) or the baby east-coast abalone. Incongruously, good Devonshire teas are also available.

Ebb (☎ 6257 8088; 11 Franklin St; dinner mains $27.50-32.50; ☼ 11.30am-3pm & 6pm-late, closed Mon) This new restaurant right on the waterfront serves fresh, light lunches and a sophisticated dinner menu that's big on fresh east-coast seafood. One house speciality is oysters done seven ways: perfect with a good local chardonnay.

Getting There & Away

Buses arrive at and depart from the Swansea Corner Store, on the corner of Franklin and Victoria Sts. The fare for the 2¼-hour **Tassielink** (☎ 1300 300 520; www.tassielink.com.au) bus journey to/from Hobart is $25.90; the **Redline Coaches** (☎ 1300 360 000; www.tasredline.com.au) fare from Hobart/Launceston is $28/29.60. See p166 for more about bus routes.

COLES BAY & FREYCINET NATIONAL PARK

☎ 03 / pop 150

The township of Coles Bay is set on a beautiful sweep of sand and clear sea at the foot of the dramatic orange granite peaks of the Hazards. It's a laid-back, salt-tousled holiday town with plenty of accommodation (though book well ahead in summer), good places to eat and some fun, active tour options. The gorgeous Freycinet National Park is the reason that most people come here. It's a wild domain of sugar-white beaches and waters that are Bombay Sapphire clear. In the coastal heathland and forests, wildflowers and native birds and animals are abundant. The park encompasses the whole of the peninsula south of Coles Bay, including Schouten Island to the south, and a stretch of coastal bushland around Friendly Beaches further north.

History

The first inhabitants of the Coles Bay area and the Freycinet Peninsula were the Oyster Bay Tribe of Tasmanian Aborigines. Their diet was rich in the abundant shellfish of the bay, and there are shell middens as evidence of this all over the peninsula.

Dutch explorer Abel Tasman visited in 1642 and named Schouten Island. In 1802, Baudin's French expedition explored and named the Freycinet Peninsula, as well as having encounters with Aboriginals. When other expeditions noted the presence of seals, sealers arrived from Sydney and quickly plundered them.

A whale 'fishery' was established at Parsons Cove by Coles Bay in 1824 – the area is still known as the Fisheries. Here southern right whales that were hunted on their migration down the peninsula were processed; the sparkling waters and blond sands soon became polluted with rotting whale remains. The station was closed by the 1840s, when most of the whales had gone.

Coles Bay was named after Silas Cole, who arrived in the 1830s and burnt shells from Aboriginal middens to produce lime for the mortar that was used in many of Swansea's early buildings. Since the early field naturalists' expeditions here, in the late 1800s, the bay has been a popular holiday spot. In the 1920s the first holiday homes were built and the area has been a much-loved holiday idyll ever since.

In the early days of the colony both the Freycinet Peninsula and Schouten Island were farmed, but in 1906 both became game reserves. In 1916 Freycinet shared the honours with Mt Field in becoming Tasmania's first national park; Schouten Island was added in 1977. Friendly Beaches (north of Coles Bay) was added to the park in 1992.

Information

Coles Bay lies 31km from the turn-off on the Tasman Hwy and is the gateway to the Freycinet National Park. When travelling this stretch between dusk and dawn, it's essential to take it slowly: there's plenty of wildlife around and you don't want to be flattening any of it in your hurry to get to the park.

Park information is available from the helpful **Freycinet visitors centre** (☎ 6256 7000; frey cinet@parks.tas.gov.au; ☼ 8am-5pm May-Oct, 8am-6pm Nov-Apr) at the park entrance just past Coles Bay. Standard national park fees apply (see p64) to enter the park. From late December to February, inquire here about free ranger-led activities such as walks, talks and slide shows.

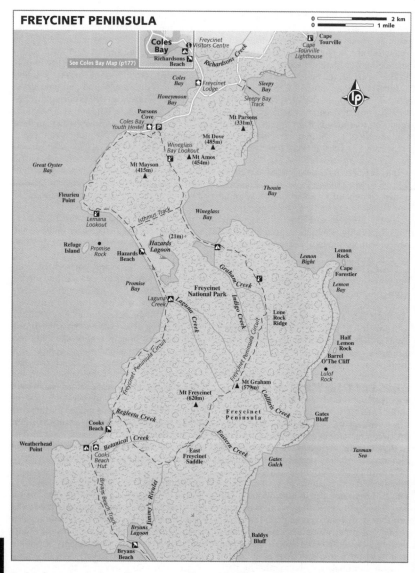

FREYCINET PENINSULA

0   2 km
0   1 mile

Park information is also online at www.parks.tas.gov.au/natparks/freycinet.

Town maps and general tourist information are available from most stores in Coles Bay. **Coles Bay Trading** (☎ 6257 0109; 1 Garnet Ave; ⊙ 8am-6pm Mar-Nov, 7am-7pm Dec-Feb) is the general store, newsagency and post office. It also has an ATM and sells petrol, as well as essentials like fishing rods, tackle and bait, and buckets and spades. There's a takeaway too, and at time of research it was being renovated to include a café-restaurant.

The **Iluka Holiday Centre** (☎ 6257 0115; Coles Bay Esplanade), opposite Muirs Beach, has a takeaway food outlet, pub and petrol, plus a **mini-market** (⊙ 8am-6.30pm) that also houses

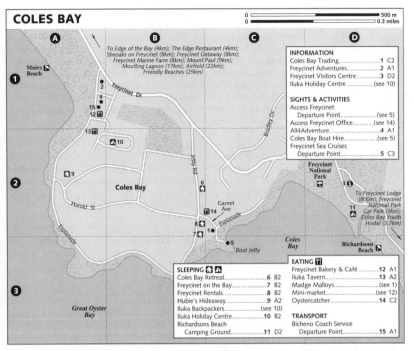

COLES BAY

0 — 500 m
0 — 0.3 miles

Muirs Beach

To Edge of the Bay (4km); The Edge Restaurant (4km);
Sheoaks on Freycinet (8km); Freycinet Getaway (8km);
Freycinet Marine Farm (8km); Mount Paul (9km);
Moulting Lagoon (17km); Airfield (22km);
Friendly Beaches (25km)

Freycinet Dr

Bradley Dr

Jetty Rd

Coles Bay

Harold St

Esplanade

Garnet Ave

Esplanade

Great Oyster Bay

Coles Bay

Boat Jetty

Richardsons Beach

Freycinet National Park

To Freycinet Lodge (800m); Freycinet National Park Car Park (3km); Coles Bay Youth Hostel (3.7km)

INFORMATION
Coles Bay Trading....................**1** C2
Freycinet Adventures.................**2** A1
Freycinet Visitors Centre............**3** D2
Iluka Holiday Centre ....(see 10)

SIGHTS & ACTIVITIES
Access Freycinet
  Departure Point...................(see 5)
Access Freycinet Office...........(see 14)
All4Adventure......................**4** A1
Coles Bay Boat Hire.................(see 5)
Freycinet Sea Cruises
  Departure Point...................**5** C3

SLEEPING
Coles Bay Retreat......................**6** B2
Freycinet on the Bay..................**7** B2
Freycinet Rentals......................**8** B2
Hubie's Hideaway.....................**9** A2
Iluka Backpackers...................(see 10)
Iluka Holiday Centre................**10** B2
Richardsons Beach
  Camping Ground..................**11** D2

EATING
Freycinet Bakery & Café **12** A1
Iluka Tavern...........................**13** A2
Madge Malloys......................(see 1)
Mini-market........................(see 12)
Oystercatcher.......................**14** C2

TRANSPORT
Bicheno Coach Service
  Departure Point...................**15** A1

an ATM. Internet access is available at the Freycinet Bakery & Café (p180).

Freycinet Adventures (☎ 6257 0500; www.freycinet adventures.com; 2 Freycinet Dr) hires out essential camping equipment and also runs a water taxi service that can deliver you to Hazards Beach, Cooks Beach and Schouten Island.

An online guide to the area can be found at www.freycinetcolesbay.com.

Sights & Activities
BEACHES & LAGOONS
The beach that most people come here to see is the heart-stoppingly perfect curve of **Wineglass Bay**, with its white sands and ice-blue waters. A dip in the clear (but decidedly cool) sea here necessitates a walk of about three hours return on steep tracks with sublime views.

There's also gorgeous, tiny **Honeymoon Bay** – a short walk from Freycinet Lodge – most beautiful at sunset when the orange rocks and east coast lichen are lit a deep umber.

Friendly Beaches is a magnificent ocean beach, signposted from the main road about 26km north of Coles Bay. A five-minute walk leads from the car park to a vantage point for uninterrupted views of tumbling surf and an endless stretch of sand.

Moulting Lagoon, the estuary of the Swan River (which the road to Coles Bay from the turn-off skirts around), is a large expanse of shallow water that's an important waterbird breeding ground. It's home to black swans, wild ducks and oyster farming.

BUSHWALKING
If you want to get to the heart of Freycinet National Park – and to quieter spots away from the Wineglass Bay–admiring crowds – then the way to do this is on foot. It's about 7km from Coles Bay to the walking tracks car park. Drive or bus here, or follow the shoreline via Honeymoon Bay (1½ hours one way).

The Wineglass Bay walk is deservedly one of the most popular in Tasmania. You can make the steep climb to the **Wineglass Bay Lookout** to get superb views over the bay and peninsula, a 1½-hour return walk, but if you want to hear the squeak of those white sands beneath your feet, you're in for a longer walk. The steep decent from the lookout to the bay takes at least another 30 minutes, making the

EAST COAST

out-and-back trip from the car park some 2½ hours. Alternatively, you can make this walk a circuit by continuing from Wineglass Bay across the shady Isthmus Track to Hazards Beach and back along the coast (about four hours return). Another superb walk, if you're fit, is the trek to the spectacular views from the summit of **Mt Amos** (three hours return).

The **Freycinet Peninsula Circuit** is a two-day, 31km trek around the peninsula, from Hazards Beach south to Cooks Beach (there's an optional extension to beautiful Bryans Beach at the south end of the circuit), then across the peninsula over a heathland plateau before descending to the water at Wineglass Bay. The trek can also be done in the opposite direction, avoiding the very steep ascent from Wineglass Bay with your heavy pack. Details of the walk can be found in Lonely Planet's *Walking in Australia*.

For those with less time, inclination and/or mobility, worthwhile shorter walks include beautiful granite-framed **Sleepy Bay** (10 minutes), just off the Cape Tourville Rd, and the easy boardwalk track at **Cape Tourville**, a 20-minute circuit that affords inspiring panoramas of the peninsula's eastern coastline and is suitable for some wheelchair-users and prams. You'll also see **Cape Tourville Lighthouse** and gaze towards the northeast coast of Tasmania. It's particularly spectacular at sunrise.

For all national park walks, remember to get a parks pass and, for longer walks, to sign in (and out) at the car park registration booth.

GUIDED WALKS

For those who prefer to experience their wilderness in more comfort, **Freycinet Experience** (☎ 6223 7565, 1800 506 003; www.freycinet.com.au) offers a four-day, fully catered traverse of the entire length of the peninsula. Walkers return each evening to the peacefully secluded Friendly Beaches Lodge to enjoy splendid meals, local wine and comfortable beds. The walk covers a total of 37km, with departures between November and May. It costs $2075 per person.

FISHING

You can be taken on a charter to where the fish are by those in the know, or hire a tinny (aluminium dinghy) to get out onto the water independently. **Access Freycinet** (☎ 0408 146 833) offers inshore fishing charters (and walker

drop-offs on request). All tackle and bait is supplied, and your skipper will clean the fish.

For fishing trips under your own steam, **Coles Bay Boat Hire** (☎ 0419-255 604; Garnett Ave boat ramp, per 2-/3-hr $75/95) hires dinghies with outboards and all safety equipment. They also rent fishing equipment ($10 for tackle box) separately and can advise on good land-based fishing spots. You can hire snorkelling equipment here too.

SEA-KAYAKING

Coles Bay is often sheltered from the wind and is a great spot for sea-kayaking. **Freycinet Adventures** (☎ 6257 0500; www.freycinetadventures.com.au; 2 Freycinet Dr) offers three-hour paddles ($90) twice daily (morning and afternoon – times vary seasonally) that allow you to get a glimpse of the peninsula from the water. Alternatively, embark on a four-day expedition ($990) down the whole length of the peninsula. All instruction, equipment and food are included.

CRUISES

Freycinet Sea Cruises (☎ 6257 0355; freycinetseacruises.com) offers a four-hour cruise to Wineglass Bay ($110) – including a champagne and oyster lunch – a three-hour cruise to Schouten Island ($75) and a six-hour cruising and walking trip ($170). You're likely to see dolphins, sea eagles, seals, penguins and perhaps even migrating whales in the right season. It's a superb way to experience the peninsula if you're not going to do so on foot.

ROCK CLIMBING & ABSEILING

There's some excellent rock climbing on the Freycinet Peninsula. Experienced climbers head to Whitewater Wall on the peninsula's eastern side for challenging climbs. With prior notice, **Freycinet Adventures** (☎ 6257 0500; www.freycinetadventures.com.au; 2 Freycinet Dr) can arrange some thrilling abseiling here. Half-day trips cost $125 per person. Contact them in advance.

QUAD BIKING

You can get off the beaten track into parts of the national park few others access with **All4Adventure** (☎ 6257 0018; www.all4adventure.com.au; Coles Bay Esplanade) quad biking tours. Two-hour tours (with 30 minutes' training beforehand) depart daily at 9am, 1pm and 3.30pm and cost $114. Half-day tours to Friendly Beaches and lovely Bluestone Bay depart at 8am and cost

WINEGLASS BAY

The hype surrounding Wineglass Bay is quite remarkable. You've no doubt seen the iconic images of this perfect arc with its stunning clear waters and pure white sand. It's also been voted one of the top 10 beaches in the world (by US-based magazine *Outside*). The images of Wineglass Bay are definitely reaching the public, and travellers no doubt visit Tasmania's east coast planning to see this magnificent beach for themselves – and yet somehow the reality of how the beach is accessed is not quite reaching the same audience!

So it bears repeating here: the return walk to the Wineglass Bay lookout takes one to 1½ hours and involves climbing about 600 steep steps each way. To frolic on the sand and/or swim in the bay's pristine waters involves walking for 2½ to three hours return, with the initial part of the walk following the same path as to the lookout. Don't despair if that sort of physical exertion is beyond you – other options for seeing the bay do exist. Take a scenic flight over it, or get right in amongst it by boat.

Interestingly, Freycinet National Park is now the second-most popular national park in Tasmania (after the Cradle Mountain–Lake St Clair National Park, p289), and it receives close to 250,000 visitors annually. This has put pressure on the park's infrastructure, necessitating a large new paved car park at the head of the walking tracks. There's also been extensive work on the path to the lookout recently. Track workers haven't managed to smooth out the hill, but the path is much wider in parts than it was before – avoiding the tourist-jams that used to occur in peak season.

$195. A driver's licence is essential. They also have ATV passenger vehicles, ideal for kids, for which prices are $65 (two-hour tours) and $105 (half-day tours.)

SCENIC FLIGHTS
Thirty-minute scenic flights over the peninsula are available for $95 per person from **Freycinet Air** (☎ 6375 1694; www.freycinetair.com.au); longer flights as far afield as Maria Island are also on offer. The airfield is close to Friendly Beaches, signposted off the main road.

FREYCINET MARINE FARM
Just off the Coles Bay road is **Freycinet Marine Farm** (☎ 6257 0140; 1784 Coles Bay Rd; ☼ 9am-5pm daily Sep-May, 11am-3pm Mon-Fri Jun & Jul, closed Aug), which grows huge, succulent oysters in the tidal waters of Moulting Lagoon. They now have a fancy new sales room where you can try and buy their wares, including freshly shucked oysters, mussels and rock lobsters. There's a large deck where you can BYO wine and enjoy a seafood picnic.

Sleeping
Accommodation is at a premium at Christmas, in January and at Easter – and prices are higher. Book well ahead for these periods.

BUDGET
There are walkers' camping grounds at Wineglass Bay, Hazards Beach (two to three

hours' walk from car park), Cooks Beach (4½ hours) and Bryans Beach (5½ hours). Further north, there are two basic camp sites with pit toilets at Friendly Beaches. There are no camping fees here, but national park entry fees apply. The park is a fuel-stove-only area and campfires are not permitted. There's usually water in tanks at Cook's Beach, in Jimmy's Rivulet between Mount Graham and Cook's Beach, and at Laguna Creek behind Hazards Beach. Check water availability with a ranger before departing.

There's free bush camping outside the national park at the River & Rocks site at Moulting Lagoon. Drive 8km north of Coles Bay, turn left onto the unsealed River & Rocks Rd, then turn left at the T-junction. Bring your own water.

There are pretty beachside camping spots all along **Richardsons Beach** (☎ 6256 7000; fax 6256 7090; freycinet@parks.tas.gov.au; unpowered sites for two/family $12/15, extra adult/child $5/2.50, powered sites $15/7, extra adult/child $3.50/20). There are powered sites, toilets and running water – just yards from the beach. Camping here is deservedly popular, especially during the summer holiday period. Between 1 December and after Easter, allocation of sites is by a ballot system. Applications must be made on a form downloadable from the **national parks** (www.parks.tas.gov.au) website or by calling the **Freycinet visitors centre** (☎ 6256 7000), and must be submitted by 31 October. There's sometimes the odd tent spot left over, even during the peak season, so it's worth calling to see if they can squeeze you in. Outside the ballot period, bookings can be made in advance for these sites at the visitors centre. National park entry fees apply.

Coles Bay Youth Hostel (dm $12-15, r $50-70, 2 person minimum booking) Right on the waterfront at Parson's Cove, this rustic, unstaffed hostel has two basic five-person cabins and a kitchen area with fridge and stove. There are pit toilets and only cold water on tap. Entire cabins can be rented for $50 ($70 for non-YHA members) via a ballot system from mid-December to mid-February and at Easter (call before mid-September to register for the summer ballot, and by mid-January for the Easter ballot). Book through Tasmania's **YHA head office** (Map p82; ☎ 6234 9617; yhatas@yhatas.org.au; 1st fl, 28 Criterion St, Hobart). Keys and bed linen are obtained from the Iluka Holiday Centre.

Iluka Holiday Centre (☎ 6257 0115, 1800 786 512; www .ilukaholidaycentre.com.au; Coles Bay Esplanade; unpowered/powered sites for 2 $23/28, dm $27, on-site vans $65, cabins & units d $95-160, additional adult/child $20/15) Illuka is a big, friendly holiday park that's a favourite with local holiday makers, so book ahead. There's a shop, bakery and pub/bistro adjacent. Iluka Backpackers has six four-bed dorms ($27 per person) and just one double ($67), as well as a large kitchen. Discounts for YHA members.

MIDRANGE
Hubie's Hideaway (☎ 0419-255 604; 33 Coles Bay Esplanade; d $120-160, extra adult/child $25/15) At this cute timber cabin, close to the shops and bakery, you'll fall asleep to the sound of the sea. Sleeps up to seven.

Freycinet Rentals (☎ 6257 0320; www.freycinetrentals .com; 5 Garnet Ave, Coles Bay) Freycinet Rentals has a range of good holiday cottages in Coles Bay. Prices vary from $130 to $170 in summer for two people (extra adult/child $15/10), with price for doubles about $20 lower in winter. Minimum stays apply for long weekends and Christmas holidays.

Coles Bay Retreat (☎ 0418-132 538, 8660 2446; 29 Jetty Rd; www.colesbayretreat.com; d unit/house $130/240) A contemporary, well-appointed three-bedroom house with amazing views over the Hazards. There's also a one-bedroom cottage.

our pick Freycinet Getaway (☎ 0417-609 151; www .freycinetgetaway.com; s $135-230) Freycinet Getaway has the funky Cove Beach Apartments (97 The Esplanade) and Azure Beach House at Swanwick – all fully self-contained and decorated in better-than-beach-house style.

TOP END
Sheoaks on Freycinet (☎ 6257 0049; www.sheoaks .com; 47 Oyster Bay Crt; B&B d $165-180, cottage d $150-200, extra person $20) Thought B&Bs were all chintz and lace? Think again. Stylish Sheoaks is housed amid fine contemporary architecture, and has glorious views (inside and out). Great breakfasts (and packed lunches on request) will keep you fuelled throughout the day. Sheoaks also manages five nearby beach houses with the same panache.

Freycinet on the Bay (☎ 6257 0034, 0417-157 886; www .freycinetonthebay.com.au; 35 Jetty Rd; d $200, extra person $50) This older-style, wood-lined house sleeps up to eight. You can barbecue on the deck overlooking Richardsons Beach.

Edge of the Bay (☎ 6257 0102; www.edgeofthebay .com.au; 2308 Main Rd; ste d $198-292, cottage d $180-236, extra person $24) This peaceful, small resort is right on the beach, 4km north of Coles Bay. It has stylishly decorated waterside suites, and cottages sleeping up to five. There are mountain bikes, dinghies and two artificial grass tennis courts for guests' use. There's also a good restaurant on site (see opposite).

Freycinet Lodge (☎ 6257 0101; www.freycinetlodge.com .au; cabin d $182-319, extra person $55, 2-bedroom cabins $214-384) Freycinet Lodge is in a gorgeous location right in the national park, and just steps from Richardsons Beach. It has smart cabins, some with enormous spas and enticing views, and several with disabled access. There are guided activities and two restaurants on site (see opposite). However, recent traveller feedback tells us this is not the beachside nirvana it once was: it's gone just a touch downmarket of late.

Mount Paul on Freycinet (☎ 6257 0300, 0408-504 414; www.mtpaul.com.au; d $240-270) To really get away from it all at Freycinet, retreat up to Mount Paul, where two timber ecolodges offer wonderful panoramas of the peninsula and only the wildlife for neighbours. This is a magically peaceful spot – you'll want to stay for days.

Eating
Dining options in Coles Bay are somewhat limited; dinner bookings are advised for the restaurants.

Freycinet Bakery & Café (☎ 6257 0272; Shop 2, Coles Bay Esplanade; meals $3-15; ⏱ 8am-5pm; 🖥) This bakery has fuelled many a Freycinet walking epic. Pick up hearty sandwiches here or enjoy a lazy all-day breakfast outside. They do good cakes and pastries, and a commendable curried scallop pie.

Oystercatcher (☎ 6257 0033; 6 Garnet Ave; meals $6-15; ☽ lunch & dinner Nov-Apr) You can sit on the deck here, or grab a quick takeaway. They serve excellent fish and chips, wraps, salads and rolls.

Richardsons Bistro (☎ 6257 0101; Freycinet Lodge; mains $18-24; ☽ from 10am daily, dinner Nov-Apr only) There's nothing fancy about this casual dining option at Freycinet Lodge, but it does good seaside dishes like crayfish, chips and salad, oysters lots of ways, and decent beer-battered fish. Grab a table on the deck and eat outside, drenched in the glorious view.

Iluka Tavern (☎ 6257 0429; Coles Bay Esplanade; mains $18-29; ☽ lunch & dinner) This popular, friendly pub gets packed with tourists and locals. They offer excellent pub nosh: look past the reef 'n' beef and the ubiquitous chicken parmigiana and you'll find things like Thai green prawn curry and seafood linguine.

Bay (☎ 6257 0101; Freycinet Lodge; mains $21-40; ☽ dinner) At night the Lodge puts on the Ritz with Freycinet's finest dining in the Bay restaurant. Forget beer batter: here the catch of the day might be coated in chermoula and served with caramelised pumpkin and cherry tomatoes. Try the magnificent seafood platter for two, with everything out of the bay. There's a good Tasmania-heavy wine list to boot. Bookings essential.

Edge (☎ 6257 0102; Edge of the Bay, 2308 Main Rd; mains $23-31; ☽ dinner) Get to the Edge of the Bay resort early to enjoy the water views. The chefs serve up fresh east-coast produce and plenty of seafood. Try the lobster pasta, or stripy trumpeter with seafood risotto. There are also meaty options and vegetarians are catered for.

our pick **Madge Malloys** (☎ 6257 0399; 7 Garnet Ave, Coles Bay; mains $28-33; ☽ dinner Tue-Sat) At Madge's the menu depends on what Mother Nature provides to the fishing boat each day. That might mean steam-baked bastard trumpeter, wrasse with crab stuffing, or poached calamari that melts in the mouth. Bookings and hungry tummies essential.

Getting There & Away
Bicheno Coaches (☎ 6257 0293, 0419-570 293) runs buses between Bicheno, Coles Bay and the national park's walking tracks car park, connecting with east-coast Redline Coaches and Tassielink services at the Coles Bay turn-off. The Hobart–Coles Bay turn-off fare with Tassielink is $30.80, and the Launceston–Coles Bay turn-off fare with Redline is $36.20.

From May to November there are usually three Bicheno–Coles Bay services on weekdays and at least one Saturdays and Sundays. Extra services run, on demand, in peak season. The Bicheno–Coles Bay fare is $11, and from Bicheno direct to the walking tracks it costs $25. They will pick up from accommodation if requested. Buses depart Bicheno from the **Blue Edge Bakery** (55 Burgess St) and in Coles Bay from in front of the Iluka Tavern and shops.

Getting Around
It's almost 7km from Coles Bay to the national park walking tracks car park. **Bicheno Coaches** (☎ 6257 0293, 0419-570 293) does the trip three times each weekday and once on Saturday and Sunday; bookings are essential. The one-way/return cost from Coles Bay to the car park is $5/9. Your park entry fee is in addition to this.

BICHENO
☎ 03 / pop 750

Bicheno is blessed with the kind of idyllic coastal scenery that was always going to make it a hit with seaside holiday makers. The Gulch, Bicheno's curvaceous natural harbour, is filled with water of the clearest blue, its foreshore is edged with granite and fine white beaches, and the whole town is fringed with the startling green of eucalypts under an often deep-blue sky. The fishing boats that shelter in the harbour are this town's mainstay – as are the tourists in the summer holiday season. The style here is more fish and chips (and buckets and spades) than upmarket Swansea for example, but its still a hugely popular holiday spot. Book accommodation ahead if you intend to stay overnight here in summer.

History
European settlement began here when whalers and sealers made the Gulch their port as early as 1803. The town became known as Waubs Bay Harbour, after an Aboriginal woman, Waubedebar (one of many who were kidnapped and enslaved by the sealers) rescued two drowning men when their boat was wrecked offshore. After her death in 1832 her body was buried here, and the settlement bore her name until the 1840s when its name was changed to honour James Ebenezer Bicheno, once colonial secretary of Van Diemen's Land (and reportedly most famous for his girth).

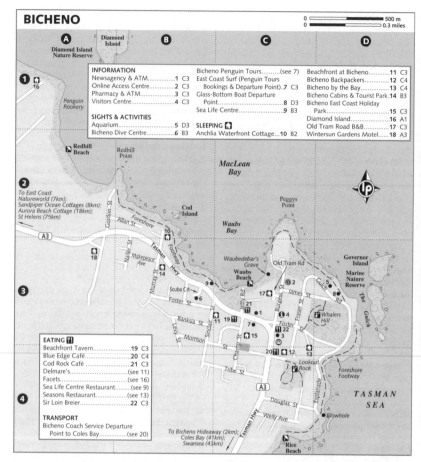

BICHENO

0   500 m
0   0.3 miles

INFORMATION
Newsagency & ATM..............1 C3
Online Access Centre..........2 C3
Pharmacy & ATM..................3 C3
Visitors Centre......................4 C3

SIGHTS & ACTIVITIES
Aquarium..............................5 D3
Bicheno Dive Centre............6 B3

Bicheno Penguin Tours.........(see 7)
East Coast Surf (Penguin Tours
   Bookings & Departure Point).7 C3
Glass-Bottom Boat Departure
   Point...............................8 D3
Sea Life Centre.....................9 B3

SLEEPING
Anchlia Waterfront Cottage...10 B2

Beachfront at Bicheno...........11 C3
Bicheno Backpackers............12 C4
Bicheno by the Bay...............13 C4
Bicheno Cabins & Tourist Park.14 B3
Bicheno East Coast Holiday
   Park..................................15 C3
Diamond Island.....................16 A1
Old Tram Road B&B...............17 C3
Wintersun Gardens Motel......18 A3

EATING
Beachfront Tavern...................19 C3
Blue Edge Café......................20 C4
Cod Rock Café 21 C3
Delmare's.............................(see 11)
Facets..................................(see 16)
Sea Life Centre Restaurant.....(see 9)
Seasons Restaurant...............(see 13)
Sir Loin Breier......................22 C3

TRANSPORT
Bicheno Coach Service Departure
   Point to Coles Bay.............(see 20)

In 1854, Bicheno became a coal-mining port, but mining fortunes here declined after the discovery of gold in Victoria on the mainland, so Bicheno evolved into a quiet fishing town, and eventually the seaside holiday spot it is today.

Information

There are multicard ATMs outside the pharmacy on Burgess St (close to the post office), and by the newsagency on the town's main strip.

Bicheno visitors centre (☎ 6375 1500; 69 Burgess St; ☼ 9am-5pm Mon-Fri, 9am-1pm Sat, 11am-4pm Sun, winter hours vary, closed Sunday in winter) The helpful volunteer staff at this centre can assist with all the sights (and beds) in the area and can make bookings.

Online Access Centre (☎ 6375 1892; The Oval, Burgess St; ☼ 9.30am-12.30pm Mon, 10am-2pm Tue-Thu, noon-4pm Fri) Behind the public loos at the oval.

Sights & Activities
WILDLIFE CENTRES

The **Sea Life Centre** (☎ 6375 1121; 1 Tasman Hwy; adult/child/family $6.50/4/20; ☼ 9am-5pm) is a little aquarium that feels like it's stepped out of the 1970s, fish tanks and all. There are some interesting things on display – including all manner of sea-theme tack in the gift shop – but it's not as enthralling as the price would lead you to expect. The on-site restaurant, also specialising in sea creatures, is a better deal (see p185).

In an unassuming shed on the waterfront, there's a second **aquarium** (☎ 0418-300 620; Gulch

Rd; adult/child $3/2; 10am-4pm). Here there are changing displays of sea creatures including seahorses, giant crabs and crayfish. There's also a touch tank – but little fingers will be kept well away from the crabs.

About 7km north of Bicheno is a place both kids and adults can enjoy. **East Coast Natureworld** (6375 1311; www.natureworld.com.au; adult/child/concession/family $16/8.50/13.50/43; 9am-5pm) is a varied menagerie of native and non-native wildlife including Tasmanian devils, wallabies, quolls, snakes, wombats and enormous roos. There are devil feedings daily at 4pm, and a devil house where you can get up close to these creatures. Other animals are fed at 10am. The tea rooms serve Devonshire teas and the like.

WALKS
The 3km **Foreshore Footway** extends from Redbill Point to the **Blowhole**, right around the **Gulch** and wandering its length is the best way to see Bicheno's pretty coastline. When the seas are rolling in just right, huge columns of foamy seawater spurt spectacularly into the air through the granite rock formations at the Blowhole. Don't get too close: even on calm days you can be unexpectedly drenched. You can return along paths through the she-oaks at **Whalers Hill**, which has panoramic views over town. In whaling days, passing whales were spotted from here.

WATER SPORTS
Waubs Beach and Rice Beach are fairly safe ocean beaches for swimming on calm days. Redbill Point often has good surfing breaks: there's usually a **surf carnival** here in January. For surfboard, boogie board and kayak hire, talk to the friendly people at Bicheno Backpackers (right).

The clear waters off Bicheno are known for their excellent temperate water diving and **Bicheno Dive Centre** (6375 1138; www.bichenodive.com.au; 2 Scuba Court; 9am-5pm) organises underwater trips, mainly to dive sites in the Governor Island Marine Reserve. One-day charters including all equipment and one/two boat dives cost $112/152. There is also budget accommodation in a basic self-contained unit available to divers (single $30).

If you prefer to stay above water, there's a fun and informative 45-minute **glass-bottom tour** (6375 1294, 0407-812 217; adult/child $15/5, children under 4 free) that can show you some of Bicheno's underwater wonders. Tours leave

from the Gulch at 10am, 1pm and 2pm in summer, weather and minimum numbers permitting (bookings advised).

And if you find the most interesting fish the one wriggling on the end of a fishing line, then **Go Fish** (6375 1581, 0419-750 757) can help you catch it. They take three-hour charters with all fishing gear included, costing from $75 per person.

Tours
Bicheno is one of the top spots in Tassie to view penguins. **Bicheno Penguin Tours** (6375 1333; www.bichenopenguintours.com.au; East Coast Surf; adult/child $20/10) takes nightly tours at dusk as the birds are heading back to their burrows. The one-hour tour with an expert guide will take you as close to the little birds as you can get anywhere. This is a wonderful and pure nature experience: no grandstands or souvenirs. Departure times for the tours vary year-round, dependent on when dusk falls. Enquire at the East Coast Surf.

Cruising along through all those views on the back of a trike has long been *the* way to see Bicheno, but Bertrand Cadart, your charismatic French chauffeur at **Le Frog Trike Rides** (0407 511 454), is now the busy Freycinet Coast mayor. If you book well in advance, however, you may just be able to call him away from his civic duties to give you a spin. Price on application.

Sleeping
Bicheno has scores of holiday homes and motel rooms, but lacks the more sophisticated B&B options that are available in Swansea.

BUDGET
Bicheno Backpackers (6375 1651; www.bichenobackpackers.com; 11 Morrison St; dm $23-25, d $60-70) This friendly backpackers stretches across two mural-painted buildings. The double rooms are quite plush (the sea view one's the pick) and there's a good communal kitchen. It's the fun equipment for rent here that's the highlight though. They have bikes, kayaks, surfboards, boogie boards, fishing rods and tennis gear. There's also luggage storage, and the friendly owners can help with bookings.

Bicheno East Coast Holiday Park (6375 1999; www.bichenoholidaypark.com.au; 4 Champ St; unpowered/powered sites $20/25, d $85, cabin d $98-108, extra adult $15-20, extra child $13-15) This neat, friendly park with plenty of green grass and shady tent spots is centrally located and has a BBQ, camp kitchen, laundry facilities and kids' playground. They also do showers for non-stayers for $2. Cabins sleep up to seven.

MIDRANGE

Bicheno Cabins & Tourist Park (☎ 6375 1117, 1800 789 075; www.bichenocabins.com.au; 30 Tasman Hwy; d $70-139, extra person $9-18; 💻) This place eschews the greenery of a standard park for concrete and gravel, but its range of cabins are new and mod-con-filled (including wireless internet) and can sleep up to six. Note that there are no camping sites here.

Wintersun Gardens Motel (☎ 6375 1225; www.wintersunbicheno.com.au; 35 Gordon St; d $104-122; 🔊) This motel just on the edge of town has an attractively old-fashioned feel with rose-filled gardens, clipped box hedges and hanging baskets. The spic-and-span units are modest but well equipped – opt for the newer Room 11 if it's available.

Beachfront at Bicheno (☎ 6375 1111; www.beachfrontbicheno.com.au; Tasman Hwy; d $115-145; 🔊) This recently renovated property has several grades of rooms, but the ones that look out over the pool and the lawns are the pick. There's a playground and a BBQ area, as well as a pub with a bistro (open for lunch and dinner) and a good à la carte restaurant (dinner only) with views over the bay (see right).

Sandpiper Ocean Cottages (☎ 6375 1122; www.sandpiper.com.au; Tasman Hwy; d $120-155, extra adult/child $30/20) These three secluded, wood-lined cottages are 8km north of Bicheno on Denison Beach. Each sleeps five and has a full kitchen, laundry, BBQ facilities and a big deck from which to admire the views.

Anchlia Waterfront Cottage (☎ 6375 1005; www.anchliawaterfront.com.au; 2 Murray St; d $130-200, extra person $20) Anchlia is one large house, divided into two separate self-contained cottages, set among the gum trees right by the sea. Cod Rock Terrace is a timber-lined two-storey, two-bedroom home; Penguin Nook is a spacious one-bedroom unit. You can sometimes watch penguins play in the garden.

Bicheno Hideaway (☎ 6375 1312; www.bichenohideaway.com; 179 Harveys Farm Rd; d $135-180, extra person $25) These architecturally interesting chalets are set in wildlife-rich bushland, close to the sea and with glorious views. The recently done-up Boathouse has great, quirky décor and even four-poster beds. There are options to suit just a couple, or up to 6 people. There's a

minimum stay of two to three nights, depending on the cottage. Books and fishing gear can be borrowed.

Old Tram Road B&B (☎ 6375 1298; www.oldtramroad.com.au; 3 Old Tram Rd; d $150-160) This is old-world B&B is set in pretty gardens from which a private track leads to Waubs Beach. There are just two rooms, both with sparkling en suites. The gourmet breakfasts should keep you going for a whole day of beachcombing.

Bicheno by the Bay (☎ 6375 1171; www.bichenobythebay.com.au; cnr Foster & Fraser Sts; 1-bedroom units $140-175, 2-bedroom $170-210; 🔊) There are 20 cabins in a bushland setting here, some of which sleep up to six people. The sea-view cabins are best. Facilities include an outdoor heated pool, a tennis court, communal fire pit and kids' pirate boat playground. The on-site restaurant, Seasons, is probably the best in Bicheno. See opposite).

TOP END

Diamond Island (☎ 6375 0100; www.diamondisland.com.au; 69 Tasman Hwy; d $190-300, extra person $25; 🔊) About 2km north of Bicheno, this complex of 26 sun-soaked apartments surrounded by green lawns has wonderful views north along the coast. Recently renovated and stylishly furnished with luxury linens, spa baths, DVD players and the like, the resort has a solar-heated pool and private beach access. You can wander over to Diamond Island when the tide is low. There's also a good restaurant (opposite) on site.

our pick Aurora Beach Cottage (☎ 6375 1774; www.aurorabeachcottage.com.au; 207 Champ St, Seymour via Bicheno; d from $230) For somewhere totally secluded and away from it all, gorgeous Aurora Beach Cottage has to be the pick. This timber and stone cottage is 18km north of Bicheno in a beautifully quiet spot, right on the beach. You can sit out on the deck and watch the waves, or stroll on the sand for miles. Breakfast provisions on request. A top spot for peace-lovers.

Eating

If you're visiting outside the peak summer season, your evening dining options are restricted, with some places closing or considerably reducing their opening hours. Ask at your accommodation for recommendations.

our pick Sir Loin Breier (☎ 6375 1182; 57 Burgess St; 🕙 9am-5pm Mon-Sat) This superior butcher's shop has an amazing range of deli items, and you can stock up here for picnics. The shop burgeons with cooked local crayfish, smoked trout, oysters, gourmet pies, cheeses and smoked quail sausages. Divine.

Blue Edge Café (☎ 6375 1972; 55 Burgess St; meals $3-10, ☺ 7am-5.30pm daily summer; ▱) Blue Edge does good sandwiches, wraps, pies, cakes and salads, and you can enjoy the aromas of the freshly made breads, all baked on the premises. The Tasmanian smoked salmon pie is heavenly.

Cod Rock Café (☎ 6375 1340; 45 Foster St; meals $7.50-18.50; ☺ 9am-8.30pm) Pumps out lots of local seafood in various takeaway guises, with fish and chips cooked to order, and fresh crayfish in season. It also does burgers for those suffering seafood-overdose.

Sea Life Centre Restaurant (☎ 6375 1121; 1 Tasman Hwy; meals $13-30; ☺ lunch & dinner, closed August) The best thing about the restaurant here are the views over the startlingly blue waters of the Gulch. The menu offers a variety of sea morsels (choose your crayfish – fresh from the tanks – natural, char-grilled or mornay) as well as steaks, and even a good vegetarian lasagne. The seafood chowder is said to be worth travelling the world for.

Beachfront at Bicheno (☎ 6375 1111; Tasman Hwy) This crowd-pleasing complex has two eateries: Delmare's (mains $16 to $30; open for dinner October to April), offering Mediterranean fare such as pizza, pasta, seafood and salads; and the laid-back Beachfront Tavern (mains $14 to $25; open for lunch and dinner), which serves standard pub fare – lots of grilled meats, plus fish of the day, schnitzels and salads.

Seasons Restaurant (☎ 6375 1521; Bicheno by the Bay, cnr Foster & Fraser Sts; ☺ dinner) This little restaurant in an appealing wooden cabin at the Bicheno by the Bay resort has an open kitchen and unpretentious service. You can sit on the deck and order from a great menu that, predictably, has plenty of marine fare. If you're all seafooded out, you could try the finger-licking honey-and-soy-coated pork cutlets.

Facets (☎ 6375 0100; 69 Tasman Hwy; mains $22-28; ☺ lunch Dec-March, dinner nightly) This breezy restaurant at Diamond Island has a smart, nautical feel and serves up equally sophisticated fare. Have an aperitif on the deck outside so you can absorb the views, then come in for a menu that's a feast of fresh seafood. The herb-crusted Tasmanian trevalla is a highlight. Bookings advised.

Getting There & Away

Redline Coaches (☎ 1300 360 000; www.tasredline.com .au) and **Tassielink** (☎ 1300 300 520; www.tassielink .com.au) serve the town. Tassielink's trip from Hobart costs $31.70. The Redline fare from Launceston is $36.90.

Bicheno Coach Service (☎ 6257 0293, 0419-570 293) runs between Bicheno and Coles Bay, departing from Blue Edge Café (left). The fare is $11/20 one way/return to Coles Bay, and $13/25 to the national park walking tracks car park.

DOUGLAS-APSLEY NATIONAL PARK

This stretch of intact dry eucalypt forest is the kind of environment that existed over much of the east coast before European settlement. The area was declared a national park in 1989 after a public campaign expressed concern over woodchipping of local forests.

Douglas-Apsley is often overlooked, but it's a wonderful park, cut through at one end by a river gorge that has deep, inviting swimming holes, and plenty to explore. There are rocky peaks, waterfalls and abundant bird and animal life – and best of all, you won't encounter the midsummer hordes that you do at Freycinet.

Access to the park is by gravel roads. To reach the southern end, turn west off the highway 4km north of Bicheno and follow the signposted road for 7km to the car park. A basic camping ground with a pit toilet is provided, and you can throw yourself into the **Apsley Waterhole** for refreshment. To access the northern end, at **Thompsons Marshes**, turn west off the highway 24km north of Bicheno onto the rough E Rd. This is a private road, so obey any signs as you follow it to the car park and boom gate at the park border (4WD is recommended for the final section). You won't find suitable places to camp near this car park.

National park entry fees apply (p64). Open fires are not permitted here from October to April, when cooking is only allowed on fuel stoves.

Bushwalking

There's an easy 10-minute stroll along a wheelchair-standard track leading to the **Apsley Lookout**, where you can get a great view over the river. A three- to four-hour return walk leads to **Apsley Gorge**.

At the park's northern end is the walk to **Heritage and Leeaberra Falls**, which takes five to seven hours return. There's camping near the falls.

For experienced walkers, the major walk is the three-day **Leeaberra Track**. The walk should be done from north to south to prevent the spread of the *Phytophthora* plant disease present in the south. There can be little adequate drinking water on this walk, so you may need to carry your own. Check with Parks & Wildlife before you undertake it. Water from the Apsley River also needs to be boiled for three minutes before drinking it.

ST MARYS
☎ 03 / pop 800

St Marys is a peaceful little town in the Mt Nicholas range, surrounded by forests and cattle farms. Visit for the quiet, small-town atmosphere and the craggy heights around town, which you can climb for breathtaking views over the area.

e.ScApe Tasmanian Wilderness Café & Gallery (☎ 6372 2444; Main Rd) has information leaflets and can give walking advice.

The top of **South Sister** (832m), towering over Germantown Rd, 6km north of town, is a 10-minute walk from the car park. To get to **St Patricks Head** (683m) turn down Irish Town Rd, just east of town. This long, steep 90-minute (one-way) climb with some cables and a ladder is a true challenge, but the top is a spectacular vantage point for views right along the coast.

Sleeping & Eating

St Marys Seaview Farm (☎ 6372 2341; www.seaview farm.com.au; German Town Rd; dm with linen $30, d units $75) Yes, 'Seaview' is right: the coastal panoramas from here are unbelievable. This beef and blueberry farm is a quiet hilltop retreat – the kind of place you'll want to stop and stay for a while. You'll find Seaview Farm at the end of a dirt track 8km from St Marys – Germantown Rd opposite St Marys Hotel. Bring all your own food.

St Marys Hotel (☎ 6372 2181; Main Rd; s/d $40/70) There's basic accommodation upstairs at this corner pub. They also do good dinners in the restaurant ($10 to $25.50) nightly, including a great local venison pie with native pepperberry chutney.

ourpick Addlestone House (☎ 6372 2783; addle stone@bigpond.com; 19 Gray Rd; d $100-120; 🖳) This immaculate B&B is as good as they get. The rooms are beautifully decorated, there's a cosy

guest lounge, and the hosts are charming. Highly recommended, and the top place to stay in these parts.

Purple Possum Wholefoods (☎ 6372 2655; 5 Story St; light meals $4.95-9.50; ☽ 9am-6pm Mon-Fri, 9am-2pm Sat) An unexpected find in a little country town, this place has wonderful homemade soups, vegetarian wraps, fabulous coffee and cakes to die for. You can't go past the rhubarb cake.

Happy Belly Deli (☎ 6372 2044; 54 Main St; meals $5-15; ☽ 11am-6pm Tue-Sun) This new deli in the old butcher's shop does fab delicatessen items for your picnics, as well as café lunches and early dinners. It uses lots of local produce and has the most amazing sourdough breads that alone are worth visiting for.

Mt Elephant Pancake Barn (☎ 6372 2263; Mt Elephant Pass; savoury pancakes $14.90-19.90, sweet pancakes $7.90-9.90; ☽ 8am-6pm) This place, 9km south of town off the highway to Bicheno, is a bit of an institution, but it may just be a tad overrated and over-priced. Cash payment only.

Getting There & Away

By bus, St Marys is best accessed from Launceston, St Helens or Bicheno. **Redline Coaches** (☎ 1300 360 000; www.tasredline.com.au) runs a daily service (except Saturday) between Launceston and St Helens that calls at St Marys (buses from Hobart connect with this service at Conara on the Midlands Hwy). The fare for the 1¾-hour journey from Launceston is $23.40; from St Helens it costs $5.90 and takes 30 to 40 minutes.

On weekdays you can also catch a lift on the postal run with **Broadby's** (☎ 6376 3488) between St Helens and St Marys, departing the Mobil service station in St Helens around 7.30am, and leaving St Marys for the return journey at 8.20am from outside the post office. The fare is $5 each way. Ring to confirm.

WARNING

Cyclists riding Elephant Pass must be careful. The road is steep, narrow and winding, and it's difficult for vehicles to negotiate their way around bicycles.

SCAMANDER & BEAUMARIS
☎ 03 / pop 990 (combined)

Low-key Scamander and Beaumaris probably aren't much of an attraction in themselves, but they do have beautiful, long white-sand beaches where the surf rolls in and you feel like you can wander forever. There are good

---

DETOUR: FINGAL VALLEY

To get off the main east coast tourist route, you can head west from St Marys on the A4 and drive through beautiful, rolling country to Fingal, Mathinna and the Evercreech Forest Reserve.

Sleepy **Fingal**, 21km west of St Marys, was one of the larger agricultural settlements from the early days of the colony and has many fine 19th-century buildings in the main street. It holds the quirky annual **Fingal Valley Festival** in early March, which includes World Roof Bolting and World Coal Shovelling Championships.

For amazing tree-scapes, visit **Evercreech Forest Reserve**, 34km north of Fingal, near Mathinna. A 20-minute circuit walk through blackwood and myrtle takes you to the White Knights, a group of the world's tallest white gums (*Eucalyptus viminalis*); the loftiest branches reach 91m. You can also visit **Mathinna Falls** (follow signs from the Mathinna junction on the B43), a spectacular 80m-high, four-tier waterfall. There's an easy 30-minute return stroll to the base.

The 1844 **Fingal Hotel** (☎ 6374 2121; 4 Talbot St; s with/without bathroom $50/40, d with/without bathroom $70/60) has good, no-frills rooms and serves lunch and dinner daily. Or stay in the colonial B&B at **Mayfield Manor** (☎ 6374 2285, www.mayfieldmanor.com.au; d $75-125), set in gorgeous cottage gardens near the centre of town. There are spa suites and a self-contained cottage. There's camping at the Griffith Camping Area (signposted off the C423 just after you turn off for Mathinna Falls).

---

surfing spots around Four Mile Creek. Fishers can toss in a line for bream from the old bridge over the Scamander River, or try catching trout further upstream. Shelley Point, just north of town, has rock pools to explore and shells to collect.

Sleeping & Eating

Scamander Tourist Park (☎ 6372 5121; Scamander Ave; unpowered/powered sites d $20/25 on-site vans $50, cabins $85, extra person $10) There are shady sites at this simple park and it's close to the beach. Pets are allowed and kids under five are free.

Carmens Inn (☎ 6372 5160; 4 Pringle St; d $77, extra adult/child $22/11) Opt for newly renovated unit number 1 here if you can. Other rooms are spotless but outdated. There's a wheelchair-friendly unit, and the owners are super-helpful.

Pelican Sands (☎ 6372 5231; www.pelicansands scamander.com.au; 157 Scamander Ave; dm $30, unit d/f $100/180; 🖭) If you want to stay on the water-

front, you can't get closer to the beach than this. Some units have been recently renovated and are top-notch. There's a dorm for back-packers too.

Scamander Beach Resort Hotel (☎ 6372 5255; www .scamanderbeach.com.au; Tasman Hwy; d $110; 🖭) This large hotel doesn't look too appealing from the outside, but the rooms are decent – most have great sea views. There's also the new Asian-influenced Spice Restaurant on site (mains $20 to $25; open for dinner) and the pub here does lunches (mains $18 to $22.50).

Eureka Farm (☎ 6372 5500; 89 Upper Scamander Rd; breakfast & light meals $7.50-12; ☺ 8am-5pm Oct-Jun) A couple of kilometres south of Scamander is a sign for this fruit-lover's paradise, and it's worth the short detour. Try a smoked salmon omelette for breakfast, or get stuck into the all-day fruit wonders: berry crepes, the fruiti-est ice creams, smoothies, summer puddings or the amazing choc-raspberry pavlova.

The Northeast

If you dream of endless beaches, where you're the only soul about – of picture-perfect clear-blue waters, powder-white sands and peace – then Tasmania's northeast is the place to head. This part of the state has the dazzling natural beauty of the east coast, but gets far fewer visitors and still feels quite wild. The northeast corner is also the sunniest part of Tasmania, so you're likely to be overarched by blue skies, summer and winter.

Fishers love Tasmania's northeast. There's outstanding game fishing off St Helens, or you can cast a line off the beach at gorgeous Binalong Bay. Divers can take to underwater worlds here, and snorkellers can explore the coast's rocky gulches. For walkers there are endless beach strolls in the Bay of Fires. Wildlife-rich Mt William National Park is perhaps the best spot for beachside camping in Tasmania. Seafood, of course, is top of the menu: the crayfish, abalone and deep-sea fish are just-off-the-boat fresh. There are several great food experiences worth travelling a long way for here: arrive on an empty stomach.

The northeast is not all about surf and sand either. The hills and valleys behind the coast are coloured in deepest green. This is rainforest, waterfall and prime pasture country. At Pyengana you can sample handmade cheeses and ice creams, feed beer to a famous imbibing pig or stand in awe at the amazing St Columba Falls. There's the purple geometry of lavender farming near Scottsdale, the historic tin-mining town of Derby, and sinuous, scenic routes that connect it all.

HIGHLIGHTS

- Being awe-inspired by the remote beauty of the **Bay of Fires** (p194)
- Detouring to the green fields and forests of **Pyengana** (p193)
- Throwing in a line and **catching your dinner** (p191)
- Hiking to waterfalls like **Ralphs Falls** and **St Columba Falls** (p193)
- Wandering through the wildlife at **Mt William National Park** (p196)
- Kayaking the placid waters of Ansons River and floating in your boat on the mirror-calm lagoon with the **Bay of Fires Walk** (p195)
- Smelling the heady scent of lavender at **Bridestowe Lavender Estate** (p198)
- Being a water baby (or beach babe) at **Binalong Bay** (p194)

- TELEPHONE CODE: 03
- www.northeasttasmania.com.au
- www.parks.tas.gov.au/reserves/bayoffires

GETTING THERE & AROUND
Bicycle
Cyclists who take on the challenge of the northern part of the A3 (Tasman Hwy) will love its winding, narrow passes and scenic lookouts, but need to be traffic-aware. Alternatively, take the secondary roads like the gravel C843, where there's little traffic and fewer hills. Pack a tent to enjoy camping at Mt William National Park (p196), the Weldborough Hotel (p196), Tomahawk (p198) and Bridport (p198).

Bus
Redline Coaches (☎ 6336 1446, 1300 360 000; www.tasredline.com.au) runs daily, except Saturday, from Launceston to Conara Junction. Here you transfer onto a **Calows** (☎ 6372 5166; ticketing through Redline) coach and continue through Fingal ($19.70, 1½ hours) and St Marys ($23.40, 1¾ hours) to St Helens ($29, 2½ hours). Redline services from Hobart connect with this service in Conara daily except Saturday. There's a daily Redline service (except Saturday) from Launceston to Scottsdale ($15.80, 1½ hours), Derby ($22.30, 2½ hours) and Winnaleah ($25.10, 3½ hours), from where you can continue with Broadby's to St Helens.

Broadby's (☎ 6376 3488) makes a weekday postal run – with an informal lift-share system – between St Helens and St Marys, departing the Mobil in St Helens at 7.30am and leaving St Marys post office at 8.20am for

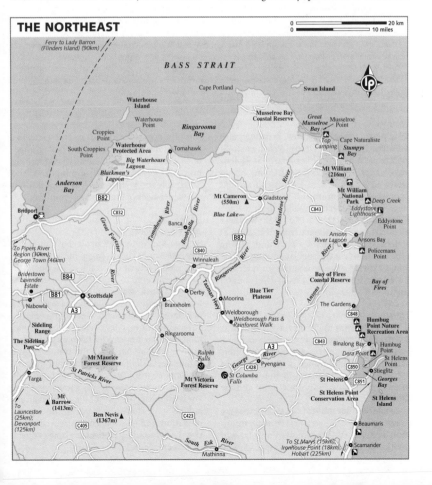

THE NORTHEAST

THE NORTHEAST

THE TRAIL OF THE TIN DRAGON

There's an interesting piece of history in Tasmania's northeast, and it's one with an unexpected twist. Tin was discovered in these hills in the late 1800s, attracting thousands of miners. Many came from the goldfields of Victoria, and many were Chinese.

At its peak, the Chinese community in and around Derby, Weldborough and Moorina numbered a thousand people. The Chinese were allocated the smaller workings further away from the central mines, and they developed their own settlements and mining practices, of which there are many remnants today. There's currently a major project underway here to document this Chinese mining heritage and to map it in a route that tourists can follow called the **Trail of the Tin Dragon**.

The route – with interpretative attractions along the way – is scheduled for completion in 2009. It will lead between Scottsdale and St Helens, its centrepiece being the new **Tin Centre** (☎ 6354 1062; ☒ 9am-5pm; adult/child/family $16/8/40) in Derby. Set in an architecturally innovative building on the edge of the Ringarooma River, the centre has an informative exhibition, 'Life, the Universe and Tin', with detailed stories from the lives of Chinese and European miners, as well as a strong environmental message about restoration and regeneration after mining. At Moorina, visitors can see a **Burning Tower**, inscribed with Chinese characters where paper offerings were burnt for good fortune. Chinese miners congregated for recreation at Weldborough, where there was once a **Daoist temple** (currently in the Queen Victoria Museum & Art Gallery in Launceston; see p205. There's the remains of a second burning tower here, and interpretation including a new offering wall is planned: visitors will be able to get offering tokens to speed their own journeys. The trail will be book-ended with snazzy holographic displays at the visitors centres in Scottsdale (p198) and St Helens (opposite). There are currently all sorts of Chinese mining artefacts on display in the latter. Ask at either centre for a map/brochure on the trail from early 2009.

See also www.trailofthetindragon.com.

$5 in petrol money each way. Broadby's also does the St Helens–Derby–Winnaleah–St Helens postal run. This departs St Helens post office weekdays at 10.15am, leaves Derby at 12.30pm and Winnaleah around 1pm; the contribution is $7 to $10 one way to/from either Derby or Winnaleah.

Tassielink (☎ 6230 8904, 1300 300 520; www.tassie link.com.au) runs the service from Hobart to St Helens via the Midlands Hwy and Epping Forest. There's a transfer at Epping Forest onto Calows Coaches to continue to St Helens. Buses go Monday to Thursday (four hours) costing $46 one way.

Tours

If you really want to get off the beaten track, **Beach to Bush Adventures** (☎ 6372 5468; www.beachto bushadventures.com.au; day trip adult/child $220/66) offers catered 4WD and guided walking tours of the northeast, taking in out-of-the-way spots in the Bay of Fires, Eddystone Point and the Blue Tier.

Pepper Bush Adventures (☎ 6352 2263; www.pep perbush.com.au; from $375 per person) runs premium tours in a luxury 4WD to give you a taste of the Tasmanian back country in style. Choose the Wilderness and Wildlife Tour with the Gourmet Bush Tucker experience for an afternoon/evening of creature-spotting and feasting on game like venison, wallaby and trout. The Waterfalls and Wilderness Day Tour takes in the wilder sides of the northeast rainforest.

ST HELENS
☎ 03 / pop 2000
Set on the wide and protected sweep of Georges Bay, St Helens began life as a whaling and sealing settlement in the 1830s. Soon the 'swanners' came to plunder here, harvesting the bay's black swans for their downy underfeathers. By the 1850s, the town was a permanent farming settlement, which burgeoned in 1874 when tin was discovered. St Helens has long been an important Tasmanian fishing port and today harbours the state's largest fishing fleet. All that fish means there's plenty of excitement for anglers: charter boats will take you out to where the big game fish swim. For landlubbers this sweet little town is a lively holiday spot. There's good eating and accommodation, and good beaches nearby. There's also the outstanding **Suncoast Jazz Jamboree** held each year in June.

Information

The **St Helens visitors centre** (☎ 6376 1744; 61 Cecilia St; ☼ 9am-5pm), just off the main street behind the library, will ply you with brochures and help with bookings. It also houses the town's interesting History Room, which gives a good insight into St Helens' past.

Services, including the post office, supermarkets and banks (with ATMs) can be found along Cecilia St. There's internet access at the **Online Access Centre** (☎ 6376 1116; 61 Cecilia St; ☼ 9am-5pm Mon-Fri, 10am-noon Sat & Sun).

Visit **Service Tasmania** (☎ 1300 135 513; 23 Quail St; ☼ 8.30am-4.30pm Mon-Fri) for national parks passes.

Sights & Activities

Both sides of the entrance to Georges Bay are state reserves and have some gentle walking tracks. A good track circles around **St Helens Point** (one hour return; take St Helens Point Rd out). On the north side, Skeleton Bay (10km north) and Dora Point (11km north), both in **Humbug Point Recreation Area** off Binalong Bay Rd, offer hours of walking on well-marked tracks.

There are some beautiful rainforest walks and overgrown ruins of the area's mining past on the **Blue Tier** plateau, northwest of St Helens. You can purchase a map outlining walks in the Tier at the visitors centre.

Because it's set on a muddy, tidal bay, St Helens' beaches aren't tops for swimming. **Stieglitz** (7km east at St Helens Point) and the beaches at St Helens and Humbug Points are better options, though check surf conditions as there can be rips. Also on St Helens Point are the spectacular **Peron Dunes**.

The calm waters of Georges Bay are excellent for water sports. **East Lines** (☎ 6376 1720; 28 Cecilia St; ☼ 9am-5pm Mon-Fri, 10am-2pm Sat & Sun) hires equipment (surfboards, wetsuits, snorkelling gear and fishing rods) and also has bikes for rent ($5/15/25 per hour/four hours/day). For diving, contact Bay of Fires Dive (p195) at Binalong Bay. To get out onto the water you can hire sea kayaks and aluminium dinghies at the St Helens Youth Hostel (right).

If you are at all into the sport of fishing, then St Helens – Tasmania's game-fishing capital – is the place to collect stories about the big one that didn't get away. The following operators offer game-fishing charters:
Keen Angler (☎ 0409 964 847)
Professional Charters (☎ 6376 3083; www.gamefish .net.au)

Roban Coastal Charters (☎ 6376 3631; www .robancoastalcharters.com.au)

Tours

Barefoot Adventures (☎ 0408-018 088; www.bare footadventures.com.au) Got a yen to get out on the water for a bit of hunter-gathering? These guys can take you to the top spots for snorkelling, abalone hunting, cray fishing and gourmet beach picnics. Shoes not required.

Johno's 'Quicky' 4WD Tas Tours (☎ 6376 3604, 0418-132 155; www.johnos4wdtours.com.au) Venture up dry riverbeds, make wet river crossings and climb steep hills around St Helens for sublime views on one of Johno's 'quickies' (1½ hours, $35). Half-day tours ($80, including lunch) discover the Bay of Fires or Pyengana, taking in secret spots along the way, and full-day excursions visit both coast and rainforest ($145). Night spotlight tours in search of native wildlife are $30.

Sleeping

You can sleep much more affordably St Helens than in other popular parts of the state. There's little of the top-notch variety here though.

BUDGET

There are free camping sites in bushland north of St Helens at Humbug Point Nature Recreation Area. The turn-off is 7km out of town, en route to Binalong Bay. The camping area is a further 5km through the reserve, at Dora Point.

St Helens Youth Hostel (☎ 6376 1661; 5 Cameron St; non-members dm $22-27, d $55-70, 10% member discount; ▣) This YHA has bunk and double rooms, but the highlight here is all the gear for hire. Bikes ($25 per day), kayaks ($15 to $20 per hour), tinnies ($80 to $90 for two hours) will get you out onto the water and into the bush, and there's even camping gear for rent, so that you can go walkabout at the breathtaking Bay of Fires.

Kellraine Units (☎ 6376 1169; 72 Tully St; d $70, extra adult/child 40/20) Just north of St Helens' centre, on the route out of town, these spic-and-span units (one with wheelchair access) are incredibly good value. Each has a full kitchen, laundry and spacious living area. The friendly owners tend a good video library, too.

St Helens Caravan Park (☎ 6376 1290; reception@ sthelenscp.com.au; Penelope St; unpowered sites for two $23-27, powered sites for two $22-28, cabin d $75-110, villa d $100-120) This park has a pleasant, green

THE NORTHEAST

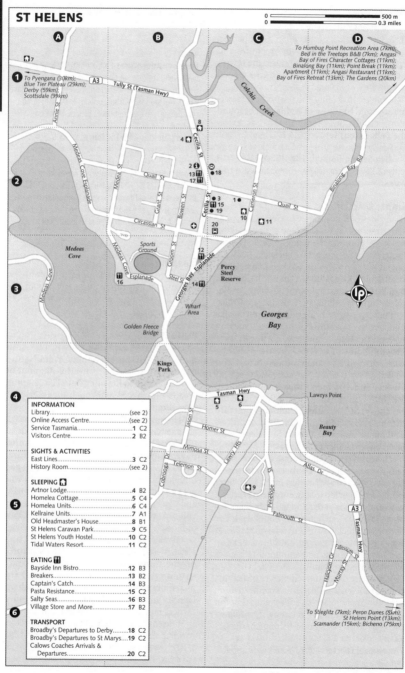

ST HELENS

0 _____ 500 m
0 _____ 0.3 miles

To Pyengana (30km);
Blue Tier Plateau (29km);
Derby (59km);
Scottsdale (99km)

To Humbug Point Recreation Area (7km);
Bed in the Treetops B&B (7km); Angasi
Bay of Fires Character Cottages (11km);
Binalong Bay (11km); Point Break (11km);
Apartment (11km); Angasi Restaurant (11km);
Bay of Fires Retreat (13km); The Gardens (20km)

Tully St (Tasman Hwy)

Colchis Creek

Cecilia St

Medeas St

Quail St

Grant St

Bowen St

Cecilia St

Cameron St

Quail St

Circassian St

Binalong Bay Rd

Medeas Cove Esplanade

Medeas
Cove

Sports
Ground

Groom St

Steel St

Georges Bay Esplanade

Percy
Steel
Reserve

Medeas Cove
Esplanade

Medeas Cove

Wharf
Area

Georges
Bay

Golden Fleece
Bridge

Kings
Park

Tasman Hwy

Lawrys Point

Homer St

Beauty
Bay

Jasons St

Mimosa St

Lawry Hts

Cobrooga Dr

Telemon St

Penelope St

Atlas Dr

Falmouth St

A3

Tasman Hwy

Hillyards Gr

Murray St

Falmouth St

To Stieglitz (7km); Peron Dunes (8km);
St Helens Point (13km);
Scamander (15km); Bicheno (75km)

DETOUR: PYENGANA

About 26km west of St Helens the turn-off to tiny Pyengana (pie-en-*ga*-na) leads to an impossibly emerald-green valley with three great attractions you simply shouldn't miss.

'Pyengana' is derived from an Aboriginal word describing the meeting of two rivers and it's these, together with the high rainfall here, that make ideal dairy pasture. In the 1890s, European pioneers recognised this and brought in dairy cattle which thrived on the lush grass. Exporting milk from this isolated valley was impractical, but once converted into cheese and butter the produce could survive the slow journey to market.

Today, cheddar cheese is still produced using century-old methods at the **Pyengana Dairy Company** (☎ 6373 6157; St Columba Falls Rd; ☯ 9am-5pm Sep-May, 10am-4pm Jun-Aug). Here you can taste and purchase cheddars in kaleidoscopic flavours, then take a seat in the **Holy Cow! Café** (meals $8-30) for dairy delights like ploughman's lunch, cheese on toast, milkshakes and heavenly, rich ice creams. Try the pepperberry version, flavoured with berries from the nearby Blue Tier plateau.

Pyengana's **Pub in the Paddock** (☎ 6373 6121; St Columba Falls Rd; s/d/tw $40/55/60; mains $11-25; ☯ lunch & dinner) is world-famous for Priscilla, Princess of the Paddock, the beer-imbibing pig, but it's worth a visit just as much for its old-world country atmosphere and great home-cooked meals. It's also a lovely place to stay: rooms are prettily decorated and peaceful. You'll wake up to views of the cow pastures and thoroughly country sounds.

Further down the valley there's also **St Columba Falls**. They take a spectacular 90m plunge off the hillside and are particularly impressive after rain. An easy 20-minute walk from the car park (where there are loos and picnic tables) leads to a platform at their base. If you loved this you'll also appreciate **Ralphs Falls** (take the turn off to the right signed shortly before St Columba Falls.) There's a 20-minute return walk or a 50-minute circuit taking in the falls and sweeping views across astoundingly green farmland. Note: it's not recommended to continue on the rough road past Ralphs Falls to Ringarooma unless you have a 4WD with good clearance.

---

setting to the south of town and good, family-friendly amenities including a games room and playground.

MIDRANGE

Artnor Lodge (☎ 6376 1234; 71 Cecilia St; s with/without bathroom $85/65, d with/without bathroom $95/75) Just back off St Helen's leafy main street, this neat little complex has off-street parking, clean rooms and shared laundry/kitchen facilities.

Old Headmaster's House (☎ 6376 1125; www.theold headmastershouse.com.au; 74 Cecilia St; r $115-125) You'll get a real Tassie welcome in this slightly eccentric household. Don't expect this to be your blandly anonymous motel-room experience, and embrace the owners' quirks. The rooms are prettily antique decorated, and breakfasts cooked to order. There was a home-grown apple pie just out of the oven when we visited.

Homelea (☎ 6376 1601; homelea.bookingtools.com; 16 & 22 Tasman Hwy; cottage d $140-150, unit d $95-135, extra adult/child $15/10; ⬜) Just over the road from the water, Homelea is a neat, brightly-painted complex with comfortable units, some recently renovated. There's plenty of space for kids to tear about and a playground where they can burn energy. There's also a spa cottage. Both accommodation types sleep up to six.

TOP END

Tidal Waters Resort (☎ 6376 1999, 1800 833 980; www .tidalwaters.com.au; 1 Quail St; r incl breakfast $165-240, extra person $40; ⬜ ☯) On the tidal lagoon at Georges Bay, this large complex has 60 rather generic rooms (some with disabled facilities) and echoingly large public areas. There's an à la carte restaurant (mains $19-29; open for breakfast and dinner) and a deck for casual dining (mains $15 to $20; open for lunch and dinner) right on the water's edge.

Bed in the Treetops B&B (☎ 6376 2238; www.bed inthetreetops.com.au; 701 Binalong Bay Rd; s $190-210, d $240-270, extra person $75-90) Some 7km out of St Helens en route to Binalong Bay, you drive up and up through the trees to reach this secluded, stylish wooden home. There are two luxurious apartments here, immaculately furnished and with spas and views. Rates include afternoon tea or predinner drinks and a full breakfast.

Eating

Breakers (☎ 6376 2665; 57a Cecilia St; meals $3-12; ☯ 8am-4pm Tue-Sun) Eat outside under the umbrellas at this little place, just off the main street, or take away good, simple fare including Caesar salad, lamb korma and butter chicken.

Pasta Resistance (☎ 6376 2074; 22 Cecilia St; mains $5-15.50; ✆ 8am-9pm summer, 11am-7pm winter) This little eatery serves abundant dishes of pasta that's freshly made daily. They do a killer chilli gnocchi, carbonara that'll have you ordering seconds, and there's gelati to finish.

our pick **The Village Store & More** (☎ 6376 1666; 55 Cecilia St; $7.90-15; ✆ breakfast & lunch; 🖳) This great deli/café serves what it calls 'peasant food' on big wooden tables among funky décor. There are wood-fired organic breads, gourmet Tassie titbits to take away, scrumptious breakfasts and lunch items like focaccias, rotis and homemade meat pies. Try the Salmon Mardi Gras: 'like a party in your mouth'.

Captain's Catch (☎ 6376 1170; Wharf Area; takeaway meals $9-14; ✆ lunch daily) At the time of research, this popular fish-and-chip spot on the water had just received the go-ahead for a major expansion to include a new restaurant. If their usual formula is anything to go by, this will the best spot for consistently good food in St Helens. Our mouths are watering.

Bayside Inn Bistro (☎ 6376 1466; 2 Cecilia St; mains $15-28; ✆ breakfast, lunch & dinner) A big, crowd-pleasing menu is on offer here, with lots of the expected meat and fish dishes (roast of the day, schnitzel, steak, and fish and chips), but also crayfish at market prices and a few veg options.

Salty Seas (☎ 6376 1252; 16 Medeas Cove Esplanade; mussels/crayfish per kg $7/50; ✆ daily) Crayfish are the special here – you can choose them right out of the tanks – but there are also oysters, mussels and fish fresh off the boat. You can feast on this marine abundance on their deck overlooking a bird sanctuary.

Getting There & Away

The Redline/Calows depot is at 2 Circassian St, while Broadby's depart from the United service station or the post office, depending on the route. See p189 for detailed bus info.

BAY OF FIRES

The Bay of Fires is a 29km sweep of powder-white sand and crystal-clear seas that's been called one of the best beaches in the world. In 2005 *Condé Nast Traveller* named it second, behind only Anse Du Grand Colombier in the French West Indies. The word is out about this unspoiled spot so if you're after beachside solitude, go now.

To call the Bay of Fires one beach is really a misnomer. The Bay itself is made up of a string of superb beaches, punctuated by lagoons and rocky headlands, and backed by coastal heath and bush. There are gulches full of crayfish and abalone, and there's great recreational diving in the bay's clear waters (see opposite). The ocean beaches provide some good surfing but are prone to rips. Check conditions with locals before swimming, or plunge into one of the tiny rock-protected coves.

There's no road that runs the length of the bay. The C850 heads out of St Helens to the gorgeous beachside holiday settlement of **Binalong Bay** (see below), which marks the southern end of the Bay of Fires. The road (C848) continues north to holiday 'shacks' at **The Gardens**, but stops here. There are some deliriously beautiful bush camping sites behind the beaches all along this stretch; **Swimcart Beach** and **Cosy Corner** are the most popular and have pit toilets. **Seatons Cove** and **Sloop Beach** are generally quieter. Bring your own water and firewood: fires are allowed outside fire ban periods.

The bay's northern end is reached via the gravel C843, which leads to **Ansons Bay** and then Mt William National Park. Pretty Ansons Bay is a quiet holiday village that's a popular fishing, boating and swimming spot: if you have kayaks, **Ansons River Lagoon** is perfect for sheltered paddling. **Policemans Point** has free camping spots. There are no petrol stations or shops at Ansons Bay, so fill up at either St Helens or Gladstone.

Eddystone Point, just north of Ansons Bay, marks the Bay of Fires' northern extremity. Since 1889 the imposing granite tower of **Eddystone Point Lighthouse** (37m) has warned ships off this rocky shoreline. The complex, which includes historic lighthouse keepers' cottages, is worth a visit. There's bush camping at nearby **Deep Creek** within Mt William National Park.

BINALONG BAY
☎ 03 / pop 200

Set on a sheltered gulch, and drenched in picture-perfect views of sea and sand, Binalong Bay is the only permanent settlement on the Bay of Fires. It was first used by fishermen and farmers around 1900, and only by the 1940s were there any permanent residents. Now, this quiet spot is growing in popularity as a beachside holiday idyll. There's not much

FIRE WALKING Tony Wheeler

Stretching south of Mt William National Park is the Bay of Fires, a long sweep of white sand named in 1773 by French explorer Tobias Furneaux after the Aboriginal fires spotted along the coastline. Middens (piles of discarded mollusc shells and bones) are mute evidence of the area's Aboriginal history.

From November to May the **Bay of Fires Walk** (☎ 6391 9339; www.bayoffires.com.au) conducts a four-day, three-night Bay of Fires experience, where a maximum of 10 people embark on a well-catered journey of natural discovery. It costs $1950 per person.

Perched on a ridge top high above the bay's blue waters is the stunning Bay of Fires Lodge. Architecturally it's good enough to grace the title page of *Australian Architecture Now*, a weighty coffee-table book featuring some of the 1990s' most noteworthy Australian buildings. But the lodge is far more than simply a beautiful design. It's also built according to the very best eco-logical principles, right down to composting toilets, and showers for which water has to be hand-pumped up to a holding tank.

To ensure prospective guests really appreciate the environmentally sensitive luxury, the su-perb views and the fine food and wine, they have to pass a test before reaching it: they have to walk for two days.

The first day sees participants do a 9km walk to a permanent tented camp hidden in dunes behind the beach. The second day's exertions alternate between beachside and inland walks, and include fording Deep Creek, lunch near Eddystone Point lighthouse, and, finally, crossing a series of headlands and dramatic coves before climbing up to the lodge.

The next morning, guests can do a spot of kayaking on Ansons River or simply laze around enjoying the views while working up an appetite for dinner. The final day comprises a short walk out to a waiting minibus, which whisks you back to Launceston.

here – no shops, just some holiday cottages, a dive operator and one fabulous restaurant – but it is precisely this quiet, low-key atmos-phere that most people come for.

Swimming, snorkelling and surfing draw water babies. There's good surf in and around the bay, and great swimming on calm days. Snorkellers head to **Binalong Gulch** where they can pick up abalone (with a licence). This is one of the best spots in Tasmania for diving: the elusive weedy seadragon is often spotted here. **Bay of Fires Dive** (☎ 6376 8173; 0419-372 342; www.bayoffiresdive.com.au) rents out scuba equip-ment and does boat dives and sub-aqua train-ing. They also rent out kayaks, body boards, wetsuits, snorkelling gear and mountain bikes. They'll even take you on a boat cruise to catch your own crayfish.

Sleeping & Eating

Bay of Fires Character Cottages (☎ 6376 8262; www .bayoffirescottages.com.au; 64-74 Main Rd; d $150-250, extra person $30) These well-kitted-out cottages have a million-dollar location overlooking the bay. All have mesmerising views, in which you can absorb yourself as you hang out and have a BBQ on the deck. There are full kitchen and laundry facilities in each.

Point Break (☎ 6331 1224; www.pointbreakbinalong .com; 20 Beven Heights; d 180-190, extra person $30) Surely the coolest beach house at Binalong Bay. All timber floors, high ceilings and bright, nauti-cal white, this beautifully furnished house is a place to chill with friends after a day in the surf. It has every possible mod con, and sleeps up to eight.

Angasi Apartment (☎ 6376 8222; www.angasi.com .au; Main Rd; d $220, extra person $50) From the outside this looks like a humble little fisherman's cot-tage, but inside it's been funkily modernised to make it a cool beachside apartment: per-fect for romantic escapes. The price includes breakfast at wonderful Angasi restaurant (below) next door.

Bay of Fires Retreat (☎ 0418-145 984; Jeanneret Beach, up to 6 people $220-260) Thirty minutes' stroll along the beach from Binalong Bay, this breezy, private beach house sleeps up to six in classy surroundings with Tasmanian art on the walls.

Angasi (☎ 6376 8222; www.angasi.com.au; Main Rd; mains $27-38; ⏰ breakfast, lunch & dinner) People come for miles to eat at Angasi, and it's not just because of the sublime views. This little restaurant is making a name for itself as one of the best in the state. Try the oysters six ways – chilled and grilled – or the rock lobster medallions with coriander lime custard. Meat eaters also well catered for.

WELDBOROUGH

☎ 03 / pop 50

As the Tasman Hwy approaches the Weldborough Pass, an arabesque cutting that is famously popular with motorcyclists, it follows a high ridge with vistas of surrounding forests and mountains. Near the top, stop at the **Weldborough Pass Rainforest Walk** for a 15-minute interpretative circuit through moss-covered myrtle rainforest.

Tiny Weldborough is almost a ghost town today, compared with the bustling settlement it must have been in the midst of the tin rush here in the late 1800s. In mining days Weldborough had 800 inhabitants, mostly Chinese, and there are still remains of their culture here. See boxed text, p190.

In a quiet, forest setting, the characterful **Weldborough Hotel** (☎ 6354 2223; Tasman Hwy; d/f $60/75; meals $12-22; ☽ lunch & dinner Mon-Sat) is a wonderful lunchtime or overnight stop. Painted in deep colours and decorated in period style, it serves up hearty pub food and has comfortable rooms. There's also free camping, with hot showers, in an attractive setting out back. The only condition is that you order a main meal in the pub. It's a favourite spot with cyclists.

GLADSTONE

☎ 03 / pop 100

About 25km north of Weldborough, off the Tasman Hwy between St Helens and Scottsdale, is the tiny town of Gladstone. It was one of the last tin-mining centres in northeastern Tasmania, and when the mine closed in 1982 its inhabitants were forced to look for new ways to eke out a living. Gladstone also had a large Chinese population, evidence if which can be seen in the historic cemetery. There's a general store selling supplies, takeaways and fuel. The **Gladstone Hotel** (☎ 6357 2143; Chaffey St; s/d $40/70; ☽ lunch daily, dinner Mon-Sat) does pub meals and has simple accommodation (shared facilities).

MT WILLIAM NATIONAL PARK

Beautiful Mt William in Tasmania's far northeast corner is one of the state's most gloriously unvisited national parks. It's the kind of place to come and camp for a few days, stroll the beaches, fish, swim or surf, and let the wildlife come to you. It's a land of shimmering turquoise waters, dazzling white beaches, coastal woodlands and heath that's abundant with native animals, birds and flowers. The area was declared a national park in 1973 to protect the endangered Forester kangaroo, which now flourishes here.

The high point of the park is 216m **Mt William**. It's an easy, gradual climb (two hours return) and affords wide views of the coastline and the islands of the Furneaux group. These were the high points of the Bassian Plane that formed the land bridge linking Tasmania to what's now the mainland, via which the first inhabitants crossed to Tasmania. Aboriginal habitation of the area is illustrated by the large shell midden at **Musselroe Point**. To the south, the lighthouse at **Eddystone Point** (see p194) is clearly visible, its night-time beam a beacon to ships entering dangerous Banks Strait.

There's idyllic (free) beachside **camping** under the she-oaks at Stumpys Bay, at Top Camp near Musselroe Bay and also beside lovely tannin-stained Deep Creek in the park's south. Campground 4 at Stumpys has a shelter, picnic tables and gas BBQs that are free to use. All the sites have pit toilets but no drinking water. Fires are allowed in designated fire spots, but bring your own firewood and beware of fire restrictions.

National park entry fees apply. You can register and pay at the kiosk on the northern access road or, if approaching from the south, buy a pass from the general store in Gladstone or **Service Tasmania** (☎ 1300 135 513; 23 Quail St; ☽ 8.30am-4.30pm Mon-Fri) in St Helens.

Getting There & Around

The northern end of Mt William is 17km from Gladstone and the southern end is around 60km from St Helens. From Bridport, take the road towards Tomahawk and continue to Gladstone. The nearest petrol stops to the park are in Gladstone or St Helens. There's no petrol station at Ansons Bay. Be careful driving at night as there's always wildlife on the road.

DERBY

☎ 03 / pop 170

Today little Derby (pronounced *dur*-bee) is a quiet, attractive town set in the valley of the peaceful Ringarooma River. One hundred years ago this was a large, thriving mining centre, which began when tin was discovered here in 1874. The northeast's tin rush attracted thousands and several mines operated in Derby and its surrounds. At its boom-time height, it numbered 3000 souls. In 1929, after heavy rains, a mining dam burst in Derby and 14 people died in the resulting flood. The mines closed for five years after this tragedy, then reopened in 1935 but closed again after WWII, causing an exodus. Today, Derby sells itself on this mining history and has an appealing streetscape that's a pleasure to wander and browse.

Sights & Activities

The new **Tin Centre** (☎ 6354 1062; adult/child/family $16/8/40; ⏱ 9am-5pm) is in an architecturally striking building by the Ringarooma River. The centrepiece of Derby's tale of tin, it has an interesting multimedia presentation on the mining history of the area (see boxed text, p190).

In the historic Old Schoolhouse building adjacent, the **Derby History Room** (admission by donation) has a display on the social history of Derby, as opposed to its mining past. Opening hours vary as it's staffed by volunteers, and the Tin Centre can tell you when.

Next door to the Old Schoolhouse is **Bankhouse Manor** (☎ 6354 2222; 51 Main St), a restored timber bank building dating from 1888. It's owned by an artist and houses a gallery showcasing local arts and craft, as well as a collection relating to Chinese history here. It may offer B&B rooms, though at time of research the manor's future was uncertain. They also sell wonderful homemade ice cream.

Derby gets as many as 10,000 visitors in late October for its annual **Derby River Derby**. The derby sees around 500 competitors in all sorts of inflatable craft, with the emphasis on the distinctly homemade, racing down a 5km river course. The primary goal in this good-humoured contest is not so much to reach the finish line, but to sabotage your neighbours' vessels and be the last one still floating. As a free-for-all spectacle, it's hard to beat.

If you're driving from the north, check out the gigantic trout mural splashed across the riverside cliffs as you cross the bridge into Derby.

Sleeping & Eating

There's not much accommodation in Derby. Free short-term **camping** is allowed in Derby Park by the Ringarooma River, including

caravan spots, but there are but no powered sites. Facilities include toilet blocks, a kids' playground, gas BBQs, picnic tables and a tennis court nearby. Washing is *au naturel*: you can swim in the river.

Cloverlea Gardens Bed & Breakfast (☎ 6354 6370; 27 Legerwood Lane; d $88-110) The Gardens' pretty Camelia Cottage at Branxholm is the best accommodation option near Derby. The glorious gardens here are reason enough to visit, and the cute, cosy cottage (that comes with breakfast provisions) is a peaceful spot to stay.

Cobbler's Cottage (☎ 6354 2145; 63 Main St; d $120, extra person $20) This old timber miner's cottage in the main street is pretty low key, but if you don't mind a basic overnight stop, it's a good self-contained option. It's run by Federal Tavern, just up the street.

Berries Café (☎ 6354 2520; 72 Main St; meals $5-14.50; ⏱ 10am-5pm summer, reduced hr winter) This welcoming café is housed in a pretty mining-era weatherboard cottage where you can sit on the veranda in summer or beside the log fire in winter. Try the smoked salmon and King Island brie quiche, homemade with free-range eggs, or the great pavlovas with home grown berries.

The old mining-era pubs in the area offer budget accommodation and pub meals. There's the lovely 1907 **Imperial Hotel** (☎ 6354 6121; Stoke St; s/d $35/55; ⏱ lunch & dinner) in nearby Branxholm and the **Winnaleah Hotel** (☎ 6354 2331; Main St, s $45, d with/without bathroom $70/50; ⏱ lunch & dinner) in Winnaleah, north of Derby. The **Dorset Hotel** (☎ 6354 2360; Main St; s/d $35/75) in Derby sometimes offers very basic rooms, and does decent pizzas of an evening.

Getting There & Away

See p189 for buses servicing Derby.

SCOTTSDALE

☎ 03 / pop 2000

Scottsdale is the largest town in Tasmania's northeast and services the farming communities that work the rich agricultural here. The town was named for surveyor James Scott, who opened the area to European settlement from 1855. Potato, poppy and dairy farming are now mainstays, as are forestry operations in the pine and eucalypt forests nearby. Scottsdale and surrounds are recently most famous for being the base of a 2006 smear campaign by members of the conservative

Exclusive Brethren religious sect against the Australian Greens. Exclusive Brethren members are successful businesspeople in the town.

Information

The architecturally innovative **Forest EcoCentre** (☎ 6352 6466; King St; admission free; ۞ 9am-5pm), run by Forestry Tasmania, houses an interactive forest interpretation centre (and also a café and gift shop selling local handicrafts). In the same building is the **Scottsdale visitors centre** (☎ 6352 6520; scottsdale@tasvisinfo.com.au), which stocks plenty of good handouts on drives, walks and places to stay. It can also make tour and accommodation bookings.

There are services and banks with ATMs located along King St, the main road through town.

Sights & Activities

Near Nabowla, 22km west of Scottsdale, is the turn-off to the **Bridestowe Estate Lavender Farm** (☎ 6352 8182; www.bridstowelavender.com.au; 296 Gillespies Rd; ۞ 9am-5pm daily Nov-April, 10am-4pm Mon-Fri rest of year). This is the largest lavender farm in the southern hemisphere, and the deep purple display here in the flowering season (mid-December to late January) is unforgettable. The farm produces lavender oil for the perfume industry, and you can take a tour of the operation, including the farm and distillery in the flowering season (adult/child under 16 $5/free). There's also a café and gift shop that sell everything lavender, from drawer scenters to lavender fudge and honey to lavender-flavoured muffins and ice cream.

The road from Scottsdale to Launceston crosses a pass called the **Sideling** (about 15km south of Scottsdale). Outfitted with toilets, picnic tables and outstanding views as far as Flinders Island on a clear day, it makes a great respite from the winding road.

Sleeping & Eating

Lords Hotel (☎ 6352 2319; 2 King St; s/d $30/50; ۞ lunch & dinner) Lord's has been a Scottsdale landmark since 1911 and is still known for better-than-counter pub meals ($10 to $23.50) like its signature chicken Oscar, as well as good roasts and steaks. There's recently refurbished accommodation with shared facilities.

Scottsdale Hotel-Motel (☎ 6352 2510; 18-24 George St; s/d $47/59) This hotel describes itself as a working man's pub, and doesn't try to be

anything fancy, but it does have budget rooms and bistro meals ($12 to $19.50) for lunch and dinner daily (no lunches on Saturdays).

Willow Lodge (☎ 6352 2552; 119 Kings; s $70-90, d $90-125, extra person $30) Surely one of the most lovely places to stay in the northeast, this wonderful B&B in a Federation home is presented with absolute attention to detail. The bright, colourful rooms look over lovely gardens. They spoil with you traditional Devonshire tea on arrival and after-dinner liqueurs.

Beulah (☎ 6352 3723; 9 King St; s $95, d $125-145; ☐) This elegantly decorated 1878 home has three luxurious rooms decked out in heritage style. To be completely spoilt, pick the spa and sauna suite with an open fireplace. There's also a cosy guest lounge, where you can enjoy a good port by the fire or an indulgent afternoon tea.

Anabel's of Scottsdale (☎ 6352 3277; www.vision.net .au/~anabels; 46 King St; s/d $110/130, extra adult $15; mains $20-28; ۞ dinner Tue-Sat) Anabel's is a National Trust–classified home with accommodation in spacious modern motel-style units (some with cooking facilities) overlooking a woodland garden. There's relaxed fine dining in the restaurant with seafood, game, great eye fillet and quality Tasmanian wine.

Pop into the **Cottage Bakery** (☎ 6352 2273; 9 Victoria St; ۞ 6am-5.30pm Mon-Fri) to pick up picnic fodder – they do fine pies, too.

TOMAHAWK
☎ 03 / pop 12

The small holiday settlement of Tomahawk is out on an isolated bit of the north coast, 40km from Bridport on a sealed road. For most of the year its beaches are largely deserted, so it's a good place to get away from your travelling peers. It has excellent fishing for keen anglers; particularly good is the trout fishing at **Blackman's Lagoon** in the Waterhouse Protected Area, about 10km west of Tomahawk.

Tomahawk Caravan Park (☎ 6355 2268; Main Rd; unpowered/powered sites $18/23, on-site vans & cabins $65-75) is the only place to stay in these parts. The basic vans and cabins use the communal amenities block. BYO linen. There's petrol, a small shop and café serving a limited range of food.

BRIDPORT
☎ 03 / pop 1235

This well-entrenched holiday resort is on the shore of Anderson Bay. Just 85km from Launceston, it's popular with Tasmanians seeking leisure and there are plenty of holiday houses lazing about town. This is also a good base from which to explore the wineries of the Pipers River region, 30km west of here (p221).

Sights & Activities

Bridport has safe swimming beaches and its sheltered waters are also ideal for water skiing. Sea, lake and river fishing are key attractions here, and there's trout fishing in nearby lakes and dams.

The area is renowned for its native orchids, which flower from September to December. The **Bridport Wildflower Reserve** (Richard St; admission free) is 2km past the caravan park and protects a swathe of largely virgin coastal bush and heathland. There are walking tracks here, and you might spot endangered flora like the juniper wattle (*Acacia ulicifolia*), some of the 49 bird species, or threatened species like the eastern barred bandicoot, spotted-tail quoll or wedge-tailed eagle.

Golfers rave about **Barnbougle Dunes** (☎ 6356 0094; www.barnbougledunes.com) golf course, just 5km east of Bridport. It's been variously named the number-one public golf course in Australia, the world number-seven public-access course, and overall 35th-best course in the world – quite some praise for a course in this remote spot that only opened in 2004. Barnbougle is a par-71 links course, in rolling sand dunes right on the edge of Bass Strait. There are also attractive self-contained timber cottages (single/double $140/160) and villas (sleeping up to eight, $750) on site, and a bar and restaurant in the clubhouse, serving breakfast, lunch and dinner daily. Green fees for nine holes/18 holes/all day are $60/98/120; golf set hire is from $55.

Sleeping & Eating

Bridport Caravan Park (☎ 6356 1227; Bentley St; unpowered/powered sites $16/20) Strung out for three kilometres of foreshore, this must be the longest caravan park in Tasmania. It fills up quickly during summer's tourist high tide, so book ahead if your heart's set on staying here. There's no camp kitchen, but there are BBQs nearby, as well as a kids' playground and a tennis court.

Bridport Seaside Lodge Backpackers (☎ 6356 1585; www.bridportseasidelodge.com; 47 Main St; dm/tw/d $22.50/25/50, en suite d $77) There are great water views from this friendly hostel, and it feels more like a beach house than a backpackers. You can hire bikes and canoes too, or just hang out on the deck and have a BBQ. The dorms and comfortable doubles have shared facilities, and one has its own en suite.

Bridport Hotel (☎ 6356 1114; Main Rd; s/d $25/50) This probably isn't the kind of place you'd escape to for a quiet romantic weekend, but it does have cheap rooms with shared facilities to crash in after a full day on the beach. Lunch and dinner (mains $13 to $24) are available in the hangar-like dining room with the usual suspects in pub dining well represented: surf 'n' turf, chicken schnitzel, calamari and seafood plates.

Platypus Park Country Retreat (☎ 6356 1873; www .platypuspark.com.au; Ada St; d $90-165) In a quiet spot beside the Brid River, Platypus Park has a range of appealing self-contained cottages and units, overseen by the friendly owners who are fifth-generation Tasmanians and can tell you all about the area. There's trout fishing in well-stocked dams nearby.

Bridport Bay Inn (☎ 6356 1238; 105 Main St; s/d $100-110, cottage d $130, extra person $15; mains $17-28; ☾ lunch & dinner) There's row of simple, comfortable motel units behind this restaurant–bar. Inside they serve a satisfying menu including good fresh locally caught seafood, trevalla, roasts, fillet mignon, Atlantic salmon and delicious wood-fired pizzas.

Bridport Resort (☎ 6356 1789; www.bridport-resort .com.au; 35 Main St; 1-/2-/3-bedroom villa $150/180/210; ☐) A low-key little complex set in bushland right by the sea, this place has a range of pin-neat, timber-lined cabins. Kids will love the resort's play areas, games room and heated indoor pool. There are also a tennis court, BBQs and a great restaurant on site

The Flying Teapot (☎ 6356 1918; 1800 Bridport Rd; light meals $7-20; ☾ 10am-4pm Sat & Sun, closed in inclement weather) Want to get up close and personal with light planes – and perhaps watch some land and soar off as you sip on your afternoon tea? Then visit this café on the side of a private airstrip that's a meeting point for pilots and aviation enthusiasts. They serve wholesome, homemade food, including quiches, frittatas, smoked salmon stacks and enticing crepes of both the savoury and sweet variety. Ultralight joy flights can be taken from here by prior arrangement.

Joseph's (☎ 6356 1789; 35 Main St; mains $21-35; ☾ dinner Tue-Sat) Have a predinner drink on the deck and then take a seat by the windows here to savour dishes big on fresh local produce. There's an amazing Harvest of the Sea platter, overflowing with seafood, spicy New Orleans gumbo or tender Flinders Island lamb.

Getting There & Away

There is a **bus service** (☎ 0409-561 662) that runs twice a day Monday to Friday between Scottsdale and Bridport ($5 one way). The service connects with Redline coaches in Scottsdale and does door-to-door pickups/drop-offs on request.

See p314 for details of the weekly ferry service connecting Bridport to Flinders Island (which occasionally calls at Port Welshpool in Victoria too).

Launceston & Around

If you wanted to create the perfect pocket-sized city, you'd probably start by making it small enough to stroll around. You might add agreeable old architecture, interspersed with parks, and you'd probably place it somewhere near the water. Downtown you'd give it art galleries, a great museum, plenty of enticing places to shop and, of course, some excellent eateries. Finally you might arrange some gentle countryside around it. If you did all that, you might have just created Launceston. The city really is a bit of a gem; it has shed its former stolid, country-bumpkin air and is now surprisingly artsy and sophisticated. It's still got a relaxed, rural sort of feel – rush hour lasts barely 10 minutes – and it's only 10 minutes out into the country. And remarkable Cataract Gorge brings the wilds into the heart of town. Midweek you may find few signs of a rollicking nightlife, but you can hang out in the cool cafés and restaurants on Charles St, get your museum fix at the fabulous Queen Victoria Museum & Art Gallery, or romantically wander the waterside boardwalks of the Seaport at dusk.

The vines of the Tamar Valley are a wine-bibber's Valhalla: the tastings and cellar doors will keep you merry. You'll want to take in the reed-fringed banks of the gorgeous Tamar River and the wide horizons bounded by craggy Ben Lomond National Park to the east. There's lots of the past to absorb too: historic towns like Evandale; Clarendon and Woolmers homesteads; and the lighthouses and maritime instalments of George Town and Low Head.

HIGHLIGHTS

- Finding the wild within the city at Launceston's magnificent **Cataract Gorge** (p202)
- Swooshing down the slopes at **Ben Lomond National Park** (p226)
- Strolling the 'Paris end' of **Launceston's Charles St** (p210) and settling in at one of its hip cafés for a latte
- Quaffing some fine wines and stocking up at the cellar doors in the **Tamar Valley Vineyards** (p213)
- Feeling like you've stepped onto the set of *Gone with the Wind* as you admire the neo-classical stately home at **Clarendon** (p225)
- Watching the world's tiniest penguins emerge from the sea at **Low Head** (p221)

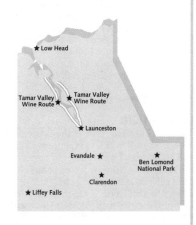

- Walking through the myrtle and sassafras rainforest to exquisite, multi-tiered **Liffey Falls** (p223)
- Cheering on the riders as they career dangerously around town at Evandale's **National Penny Farthing Championships** (p225)

...u'll want to do ...on. This is a city ...green spaces of the ...Cataract Gorge, to ...re lined with superb ...got a few days, you'll want to ... of its great restaurants and cafés, vis... ...seums, and perhaps take a cruise on the Tamar River to see the city and surrounds from the water. Be sure to take it slow here, though. When in Rome...

HISTORY

Bass and Flinders were the first Europeans to sight Launceston's Tamar River when they sailed in here on their 1798 voyage of discovery. The first settlement was established in 1804, when the British, intent on beating the French in claiming this island, built a military post at what's today George Town. Not long after, an expedition scouted south and found the present-day site of Launceston, naming it for the English seaside town in Cornwall – although this version came to be pronounced *Lon-ses-ton*. Early Launceston was both a port and a military headquarters. By 1827 it already had a population of 2000, and was shipping wool and wheat from the surrounding districts. By the 1850s the town was Tasmania's second major centre and was proclaimed a municipality. In 1871 tin was discovered at Mt Bischoff, which further cemented Launceston's fortunes as a trading hub and a decade later it opened its own stock exchange. In the 20th century it has been an important service town for the rich agricultural region that surrounds it.

ORIENTATION

The city grid forms around the Brisbane St Pedestrian Mall, which runs between Charles and St John Sts. Flanking the old seaport on the Tamar are a string of contemporary riverfront eateries and a resort hotel. West of the city is Cataract Gorge, a rugged ravine that's one of the city's major tourist drawcards. Charles St south of the CBD is emerging as a caffeinated, bohemian enclave.

INFORMATION
Bookshops
Angus & Robertson (Map p204; ☎ 6334 0811; 80-82 St John St) A popular bookery.

Birchalls (Map p204; ☎ 6331 3011; 118-120 Brisbane St) Considered Australia's oldest bookshop (c 1844).

Internet Access
Cyber King Internet Lounge (Map p204; ☎ 6334 2802; 113 George St; per min 15c, per hr $5; 8.30am-7.30pm Mon-Fri, 9.30am-6.30pm Sat & Sun)

Medical Services
Launceston General Hospital (Map p203; ☎ 6348 7111; 287-289 Charles St)
St Vincent's Hospital (Map p204; ☎ 6332 4999; 5 Frederick St)

Money
ATMs are installed at most banks in the city centre, which are mainly on St John St or Brisbane St near the Mall.

Post
Main post office (Map p204; ☎ 13 13 18; 111 John St; 9am-5pm Mon-Fri, 9.30am-1pm Sat)

Tourist Information
Visitors centre (Map p204; ☎ 1800 651 827, 6336 3133; www.ltvtasmania.com.au; cnr St John & Cimitiere Sts; 9am-5pm Mon-Fri, 9am-3pm Sat, 9am-noon Sun & public holidays) The centre houses racks of pamphlets and handles statewide accommodation, tour and transport bookings.

SIGHTS
Cataract Gorge
Ten minutes' wander west of the city centre, edging the residential suburb of Trevallyn, is the magnificent **Cataract Gorge** (Map p203; www.launcestoncataractgorge.com.au; 9am-dusk). It's amazing to have such a wild area cut right into the core of the city: the bushland, cliffs and tumbling waters of the South Esk River here really feel a million miles away from town.

Two walking tracks straddle the gorge, leading from Kings Bridge up to the Cliff Grounds Reserve and First Basin, where there's an outdoor **swimming pool** (admission free; Nov-Mar), picnic spots and fine dining at the **Gorge Restaurant** (☎ 6331 3330; meals $18-32; lunch Tue-Sun, dinner Tue-Sat) with sociable peacocks loitering outside. There's also a **kiosk** serving snacks and afternoon teas. Trails lead from here up to the Cataract and Eagle Eyrie Lookouts. The gorge walk takes about 30 minutes; the northern trail is the easier, while the southern Zig Zag Track has some steep climbs as it passes along the cliff tops. The whole scene is impressively

LAUNCESTON

0 ——————— 500 m
0 ——————— 0.3 miles

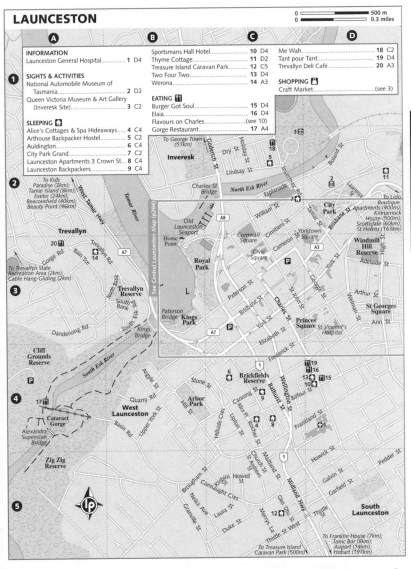

INFORMATION
Launceston General Hospital............... 1 D4

SIGHTS & ACTIVITIES
National Automobile Museum of
  Tasmania.. 2 D2
Queen Victoria Museum & Art Gallery
  (Inveresk Site)............................... 3 C2

SLEEPING
Alice's Cottages & Spa Hideaways..... 4 C4
Arthouse Backpacker Hostel.............. 5 C4
Auldington.. 6 C4
City Park Grand.................................. 7 C2
Launceston Apartments 3 Crown St.. 8 C4
Launceston Backpackers..................... 9 C4

Sportsmans Hall Hotel........................ 10 D4
Thyme Cottage................................... 11 D2
Treasure Island Caravan Park............ 12 C5
Two Four Two..................................... 13 D4
Werona.. 14 A3

EATING
Burger Got Soul.................................. 15 D4
Elaia.. 16 D4
Flavours on Charles......................(see 10)
Gorge Restaurant.............................. 17 A4

Me Wah.. 18 C2
Tant pour Tant.................................... 19 D4
Trevallyn Deli Café............................. 20 A3

SHOPPING
Craft Market.................................(see 3)

LAUNCESTON & AROUND

floodlit at night. You can also access First Basin from the main car park by following the signs from York St to Hillside Crescent, Brougham St, then Basin Rd. The **Basin Café** (6331 5222; breakfast, lunch & dinner, reduced hr in winter) has wide views over the river and greenery from fold-back windows and is just the spot for a lazy, late weekend breakfast.

At First Basin, the world's longest single-span **chairlift** (6331 5915; adult/child one-way $10/7, return $12/8; 9am-dusk) makes the 10-minute crossing over the parkland and river (you can board the chairlift at either end). Just upstream is the Alexandra Suspension Bridge. Another walking track (45 minutes one way) leads further up the gorge to Second Basin

CENTRAL LAUNCESTON

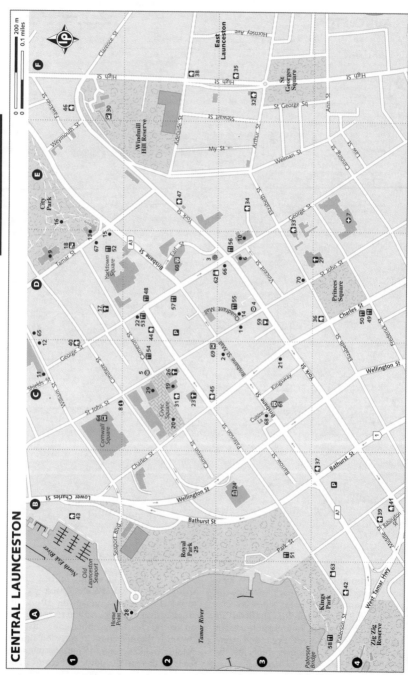

and further still to Duck Reach, the earliest municipal hydroelectric power station in Australia (established in 1895).

Queen Victoria Museum & Art Gallery

There are major changes on the cards at the wonderful **Queen Victoria Museum & Art Gallery's** two sites (☎ 6323 3777; www.qvmag.tas.gov.au; admission free; ⏰ 10am-5pm) in the remodelled **Inveresk railyards** (Map p203; 2 Invermay Rd) and at **Royal Park** (Map p204; 2 Wellington St). Previously, both sites have housed both art and museum collections, but at time of research, that was about to be turned on its head. Royal Park was due to close in mid-2008 for major renovations and reopen in 2010 housing exclusively fine and decorative arts – including the collection from Inveresk, which will be transferred here. The Inveresk site will take on a more natural-sciences and history focus and will be the new home of the **Planetarium**, previously at Royal Park. All this means that there will be a period from mid-2008 until 2010 when Launceston's much-loved museums will be in flux.

In the meantime you'll still be able to see aspects of the major collections on display (however, one of the museum's favourite treasures, the Chinese Joss House – see p190 –

will be closed during renovations.) Ask at the visitors centre and at the museum's Inveresk site for information on progress and expect knock-out new displays when the whole change is complete.

Boag's Brewery

The ubiquitous Boag's beer (preferred by most northern Tasmanians – southerners are loyal to Hobart's Cascade) has been brewed on William St since 1881. You can see this alchemy in action on a tour from the irresistibly named **Boag's Centre for Beer Lovers** (Map p204; ☎ 6332 6300; www.boags.com.au; 39 William St; ⏰ tours at 10am, 11am & 2pm Mon-Thu, 10am, 11am & 1pm Fri) Tours range from one hour (adult/child $18/14) to 90 minutes ($25/22) and take in the brewery and a tasting (with soft drinks for kids). The on-site museum also sheds some light on brewing history.

Historic Buildings

Launceston has a fascinating architectural heritage and, as it was built over a more extended period than some of the other towns in Tasmania, has a diversity of building styles. Some of the private homes here are simply beautiful: wander the hillsides of Trevallyn to sticky-beak.

LAUNCESTON & AROUND

LAUNCESTON & AROUND

LAUNCESTON & AROUND FOR CHILDREN

- Squealing with delight at City Park's **Japanese macaques** (right)

- Floating through the air on the **Cataract Gorge chairlift** (p203)

- Burning energy with hours of creative play at **Kids Paradise** (opposite)

- Being entranced by the weird and wonderful critters at **Seahorse World** (p217)

- Getting outdoor-energetic at the activity centre at **Tamar Valley Resort** (p214)

Notable public edifices include **Macquarie House** (Map p204) on Civic Sq, built in 1830 as a warehouse but later used as a military barracks and office, and the **Town Hall** (Map p204), erected in 1864 in Victorian Italianate style. Opposite is the **old post office** (Map p204; Cameron St) with its unique round clock tower.

One corner of City Park is the site of **Albert Hall** (Map p204), erected in 1891 for a trade fair and housing the unusual Brindley water-powered organ.

The National Trust–classified **Old Umbrella Shop** (Map p204; ☎ 6331 9248; 60 George St; ☼ 9am-5pm Mon-Fri, to noon Sat) is a rare example of a largely intact early-20th-century store. It sells all kinds of period knick-knacks, including, of course, an amazingly large range of brollies.

Launceston also does a large range in churches – most built between 1830 and 1860. On the Civic Sq block are the **Pilgrim Uniting** (Map p204) and the **St Andrews Presbyterian** (Map p204) churches and opposite Princes Sq is **St Johns Anglican Church** (Map p204), all dating from this era.

Signposted 8km south of town, **Franklin House** (☎ 6344 7824; 413 Hobart Rd, Franklin Village; adult/child/concession/family $8/free/6/16; ☼ 9am-5pm Mon-Sat, 12-4 Sun) is one of Launceston's most attractive Georgian homes. Built in 1838, it's now beautifully restored, furnished and passionately managed by the National Trust. Franklin Village–bound Metro buses 40 and 50 from the city stop here.

Parks & Gardens

Wonderful, green **City Park** (Map p204) has enormous oaks and plane trees, an el-
egant fountain, a fern-filled conservatory, a Victorian bandstand and a playground and mini train for kids. A glass-walled enclosure of **Japanese macaques** (☼ 8am-4pm Apr-Sep, to 4.30pm Oct-Mar) will also fascinate little ones for hours.

Princes Sq (Map p204; btwn Charles & St John Sts) features an enormous bronze fountain purchased at the 1855 Paris Exhibition.

Other public spaces include **Royal Park** (Map p204), at the North Esk and Tamar River junction, where there's a river-edge boardwalk leading to the Cataract Gorge Reserve, Ritchies Mill, Home Point and the new Seaport development; and **Windmill Hill Reserve** (Map p204), to the city's east, which has a great swimming pool.

A 10-minute drive north of the city is **Tamar Island Wetlands** (☎ 6327 3964; West Tamar Hwy; adults/children & concession/family, $3/2/6; ☼ 10am-4pm April-Sep, 9am-5pm Oct-March), where there is a 2km wheelchair-friendly boardwalk through a significant wetlands reserve teeming with bird life (including brown falcons and white-bellied sea eagles).

Further upstream from Duck Reach is the **Trevallyn State Recreation Area** (☼ 8am-dusk), on the Trevallyn Dam. This is Launcestonians' favourite spot for watersports like rowing. You can take a picnic and a splash in the shallows on a warm day. To get to the reserve, follow Paterson St west (after crossing Kings Bridge it becomes Trevallyn Rd and then Gorge Rd), then turn right into Bald Hill Rd, left into Veulalee Ave and veer left into Reatta Rd to the reserve.

Other Attractions

The **Design Centre of Tasmania** (Map p204; ☎ 6331 5506; www.twdc.org.au; cnr Brisbane & Tamar Sts; ☼ 9.30am-5.30pm), on the fringe of City Park, is the place to browse for the products of creative Tasmania. There's top-notch work by craftspeople here – great for classy Tassie gifts. In the same building, the **Wood Design Collection** (adult/child/concession $5/free/4) showcases local designs, with more sassafras, Huon pine and myrtle than your average southwest forest.

The oxymoronic **National Automobile Museum of Tasmania** (Map p203; ☎ 6334 8888; www.namt.com .au; 86 Cimitiere St; adult/child/family $9.50/5.50/24.50; ☼ 9am-5pm Sep-May, 10am-4pm Jun-Aug) will excite rev-heads – this is one of Australia's best presentations of classic and historic cars and motorbikes. The '69 Corvette Stingray will burn tyre tracks into your retinas.

On rainy days, **Kids Paradise** (☎ 6334 0055; www .kidsparadise.net.au; 1 Waterfront Drive; adult/toddler/child/ family $12/$5/$9/$22) is the place to let the little ones loose. In this rapturous treasure-trove of fun, there's a pirate ship and four interactive playrooms. They'll be soaked to the bone and giggling with delight in the Wetzone.

ACTIVITIES
Hang-gliding
Who hasn't looked at a bird and marvelled at its swooping, soaring flight? You can do the same with a spot of **cable hang-gliding** (☎ 0419 311 198; Reatta Rd; www.cablehanggliding.com.au; adult/ child $20/15, tandems $30; ☽ 10am-5pm Dec-Apr, to 4pm May-Nov & school holidays). You'll hurtle over the edge of a cliff and glide down a 200m long cable, suspended under wide wings. It's great stomach-in-your-mouth fun. Head west along Paterson St and from King's Bridge follow the signs.

Biking
You can get on two wheels and get off the beaten track with **Mountain Bike Tasmania** (Map p204; ☎ 6334 0988; www.mountainbiketasmania.com.au; in Mountain Designs, 120 Charles St) It guides rides by the North Esk River ($75) and through the Trevallyn Reserve ($90), as well as a thrilling descent of Ben Lomond ($150) – a downhill adrenaline rush losing 1050m in altitude as fast as you can say 'Marzocchi shocks'. For more sedate biking, you can hire a battery-powered model from **Ecoride** (☎ 0409-700 655; shop 33 Quadrant Mall) for $15 for a half-hour to $70 for a full day. The rechargeable batteries give you over 600km of effortless travel. How green!

Roman Baths
You just can't go to Launceston without spending a few hours at **Aquarius Roman Baths** (Map p204; ☎ 6331 2255; 127-133 George St; adult $26, no children under 16; ☽ 8.30am-8pm Mon-Fri, 9am-6pm Sat & Sun) Go a good shade of beetroot in the Caldarium, chill out in the Tepidarium, or simply soak in the Salubre Thermae (warm healing baths). Steam rooms, spas and mud or seaweed massages will make you walk out of here feeling born again.

TOURS
Get your historical bearings with a 1½-hour **Launceston Historic Walk** (☎ 6331 2213; adult/child/ concession/family $15/11/15/40), a journey through the Georgian, Victorian and modern architecture of the city. Departing 10am Tuesday to Saturday and 4pm Monday.

As the sun goes down, get spooked on a 90-minute **ghost tour** (☎ 0421 819 373; www.launcestoncity ghosttours.com; adult/child/concession/family $25/10/20/55) around the city's back alleys and lanes. You'll hear spine tingling stories of ghoulish spectres and severed heads. Tours depart from the **Royal Oak Hotel** (Map p204; ☎ 6331 5346; 14 Brisbane St) – where Cyril is the resident ghost – at dusk. Bookings essential.

Coach Tram Tours (☎ 0419 004 802; coachtramtour@ vision.net.au) offers three-hour bus-based tours of the city's key attractions (adult/child/family $37/18.50/90). In addition, it runs excursions around the Tamar Valley and Beauty Point (adult/child $55/25). Tours used to be in an old tram – not any longer.

Tamar River Cruises (Map p204; ☎ 6334 9900; www .tamarrivercruises.com.au; Home Point Pde; adult/child/con-cession/family $19/10/17/48) conducts 50-minute explorations of the Gorge on the 1890s-style *Lady Launceston*. If you're on for more extended cruising, try its **Batman Bridge Luncheon Cruise** (adult/child/concession/family $98/49/90/254). There's also an extended afternoon trip and an evening voyage with dinner.

FESTIVALS & EVENTS
Festivale (www.festivale.com.au) Three days in February feverishly devoted to celebrating eating, drinking, arts and entertainment, staged in City Park. The event involves over 70 Tasmanian food and wine stalls, dancing, theatre and bands twanging through electric and acoustic gigs.
Launceston Cup Held in February; horses work up a sweat on the track.
Australian Three Peaks Race (www.threepeaks.org .au) A four-day nonstop nautical rush in March to sail from Beauty Point (north of Launceston) to Hobart, pausing long enough for teams of runners to jump ashore and scale three mountains along the way.
Easter Pacing Cup Over Easter the trotting track gets pounded.
Royal Launceston Show In October – all candy floss and bumper cars with pedigree livestock thrown in for good measure.

SLEEPING
Budget
Launceston Backpackers (Map p203; ☎ 6334 2327; www.launcestonbackpackers.com.au; 103 Canning St; 4-/6-bed dm $19/18, tw/tr $24/20, d with/without bathroom $60/50; ☐) The insides of this large Federation house have been gutted to make way for the

LAUNCESTON & AROUND

cavernous interiors of this hostel. It's in a leafy, green location looking over Brickfields Reserve, but it's not the most inspiring hostel you'll ever visit. Rooms are decently clean and fresh, though.

Lloyds Hotel Backpackers (Map p204; ☎ 1300 858 861; www.backpackers-accommodation.com.au; 23 George St; dm $22, s/d/f $55/70/120; 💻; wi-fi) Lloyds stakes a claim as Launceston's happening-est pub. Downstairs the place goes nuts, but above things remain relatively calm, with clean en suite rooms, kitchen, capacious communal areas and wi-fi internet.

our pick **Arthouse Backpacker Hostel** (Map p203; ☎ 6333 0222; www.arthousehostel.com.au; 20 Lindsay St, 4-/6-/8-bed dm $27/25/23; 💻) Housed in a beautiful old heritage home, the Arthouse has spacious, airy dorms, a welcoming shared sitting room with a huge plasma TV, a wide upstairs veranda for shooting the breeze on and a courtyard with BBQ out back. You can also hire bikes or camping equipment, store gear…and the young owners are friendly to boot. It's even set up for disabled travellers and is also Australia's first carbon-neutral backpackers.

HOTELS, MOTELS & PUBS
Irish Murphy's (Map p204; ☎ 6331 4440; cnr Brisbane & Bathurst Sts; dm/d $21/45; 💻) This corner pub is just two blocks from the city centre and has reasonable bunk and double rooms, kitchen, common room and clean bathrooms. The bar/restaurant downstairs gets thumpin' when bands are on.

Sportsmans Hall Hotel (Map p203; ☎ 6331 3968; www.maskhospitality.com.au; cnr Charles & Balfour Sts; s/d from $50/65) In the most salubrious part of Charles St, 'Sporties' is a bit of an institution. It's been done up recently and the rooms are really decent – without en suites but each with its own private bathroom. Whatever you do, don't get a room over the bar – if you intend to get any sleep that is.

Hotel Tasmania (Map p204; ☎ 6331 7355; www.saloon.com.au; 191 Charles St; s $60, r $80) This place has spacious rooms – all with en suites – that fortunately forgo the Wild West kitsch of the bar/bistro downstairs. Benefits include continental breakfast and tea- and coffee-making facilities.

Star Bar (Map p204; ☎ 6331 6111; www.starbarcafeandhotel.com.au; 113 Charles St; s $80, d $100, family $150) Another bar/bistro with accommodation upstairs, Star Bar is right in the heart of the CBD and has better-than-pub rooms upstairs.

It's all spick-and-span and each room has a sparkling en suite.

CAMPING & CABINS
Treasure Island Caravan Park (off Map p203; ☎ 6344 2600; treasureislandlaunceston@netspace.net.au; 94 Glen Dhu St; unpowered/powered sites d $22/26, onsite vans $50, cabins $75-82) If you turn your back to the highway, you could forget that the city is so close (2.5km) – you won't be able to ignore the highway noise, however, though this does die down at night. There are pretty camping spots among the trees.

Midrange
COTTAGES & SELF-CONTAINED APARTMENTS
Launceston Apartments (Map p203; ☎ 6344 6953; www.launcestonapartments.com.au; d from $100-190) A collection of cottages and older-style apartments is available through this agency. If you can get it, gorgeous Three Crown St is the pick: it's a little workers' cottage with three bedrooms that's been fabulously renovated and is downright cool. Stay here one night and you'll wish you could move in permanently.

Thyme Cottage (Map p203; ☎ 6331 1906; www.thymecottage.com.au; 31 Cimitiere St; d $140, extra adult/child $25/15) A delightful 1880s cottage providing self-contained heritage accommodation. With cottage furniture and antiques, it exudes warmth and charm. Modern facilities and full breakfast supplies provided. Sleeps up to seven in three bedrooms.

Quest Launceston Serviced Apartments (Map p204; ☎ 6333 3555; www.questlaunceston.com.au; 16 Paterson St; d $170-190; 💻) Set in the beautifully restored Murray Building in the heart of town, these apartments are everything you could want in an upmarket home-away-from-home: spacious, comfortable, fully self-contained and decorated with style. They also have facilities for disabled travellers.

Launceston Historic Cottages (Map p204; ☎ 0437-008 336; www.launcestonhistoriccottages.com; 1 Babington St; d $180, extra person $10) This smartly decorated two-bedroom Victorian workers' cottage is a cosy place for an overnight stay, and has all you'd need to spend much longer. There's a cute veranda for sunny outdoor breakfasts.

GUESTHOUSES & B&BS
Kilmarnock House (Map p203; ☎ 6334 1514; www.kilmarnockhouse.com; 66 Elphin Rd; s from $95, d $130-150, f $170) This National Trust–listed 1905 Edwardian

mansion provides gracious accommodation in elegantly antique-furnished rooms. Lovebirds will enjoy the romantic Honeymoon Spa Suite. The rate includes a generous breakfast and children are welcome.

Airlie on the Square (Map p204; ☎ 6334 0577, 0427-480 008; www.airlielodge.com.au; Civic Sq; s/d $95/125, extra person $30; 🖳) Airlie is truly a rose among thorns. It's housed in the last of the beautiful old buildings on Civic Square – the others were demolished to make way for concrete horrors in the 1970s. Wonderfully peaceful Airlie has been thoughtfully decorated and the friendly owner serves scrumptious breakfasts. A real haven in the city's heart.

Ashton Gate (Map p204; ☎ 6331 6180; www.ashton gate.com.au; 32 High St; s $115, d $135-170, cottage d $170) This thoroughly welcoming and refreshing Victorian B&B exudes a sense of home, and each en suite room is immaculately decorated in period style. There's also a self-contained apartment in the Old Servants' Quarters.

Kurrajong House (Map p204; ☎ 6331 6655; www .kurrajonghouse.com.au; cnr High & Adelaide Sts; d $130-170) From the scented rose garden outside to the crackling log fires when you come in, you'll love the home-but-smarter feel of this welcoming B&B. The cooked breakfasts are a sumptuous affair.

Fiona's B&B (Map p204; ☎ 6334 5965; www.fionas .com.au; 141a George St; d $140-165, extra guest $20) Fiona's has beautifully stylish rooms, some with great panoramas over Launceston. There are fine touches like luxury linens and claw-foot baths, and most rooms have their own private courtyard or access to the leafy, green garden.

HOTELS & MOTELS

Old Bakery Inn (Map p204; ☎ 1800 641 264, 6331 7900; www.oldbakeryinn.com.au; cnr York & Margaret Sts; d $90-135) You can almost smell freshly baked bread aromas coming from the ovens, which are still a feature of this 130-year-old building. There are 24 appealingly decorated rooms here with cons like minibars and electric blankets. Rates don't include breakfast.

Motel & Apartments (Map p204; ☎ 1800 060 954, 6331 6699; www.leisureinnhotels.com; 147 Paterson St; d $120-198, extra adult/child $30/15) Originally an old coaching inn on the banks of the Isis River in Tasmania's Midlands, this hotel was moved to its present location bang next to Cataract Gorge, brick by painstaking brick. It's been swankily refurbished, but has man-

aged to retain the wooden beams and the old-world feel.

Colonial on Elizabeth (Map p204; ☎ 1800 060 955, 6331 6588; www.colonialinn.com.au; 31 Elizabeth St; d $125-250; 🖳) Formerly the Launceston Church & Grammar School, today this 1847 building houses boutique colonial rooms all done up in leather sofas and dusky-rose hues. Attached is the exceedingly praiseworthy café-wine bar, Three Steps on George (p210).

City Park Grand (Map p203; ☎ 6331 7633; www .cityparkgrand.com.au; 22 Tamar St; d $140-275; 🖳) This building has been a hotel since 1855 so staff know just how to make you feel at home. The expansive rooms have recently been redecorated in the best of taste. There's also Q22 bar/restaurant here which does à la carte dinner nightly.

Top End
COTTAGES

Alice's Cottages & Spa Hideaways (Map p203; ☎ 6334 2231; alices.cottages@bigpond.com; 129 Balfour St; d $170-206) Alice's bills itself as the place for 'wickedly wonderful romantic retreats' – and why not indeed? It has several sumptuously decorated B&B cottages, including 'Camelot' and 'The Boudoir', where it's all spas, four-post beds, open fires and self-contained privacy.

GUESTHOUSES & B&BS

Werona (Map p203; ☎ 6334 2272; www.werona.com; 33 Trevallyn Rd; d $120-230; 🖳) This opulent B&B is in a Queen Anne Federation home with unsurpassed views. There are amazing decorative mouldings, *trompe l'oeil* murals and beautiful leadlighting. The Joan suite is top-of-the-line here – with a fairy-tale four-poster and spa en suite. On the ground level there's a billiards table and a guest lounge, and there's a pretty garden out back.

Waratah on York (Map p204; ☎ 6331 2081; www .waratahonyork.com.au; 12 York St; d $202-288, extra person $48) The Waratah is set in an 1862 Victorian Italianate mansion and is an opulent and unashamedly old-fashioned gay-friendly B&B. Its rooms – some with four-post beds – are luxuriously 'heritage' and the executive spa suites have panoramic views.

Hatherley House (Map p204; ☎ 6334 7727; www .hatherleyhouse.com.au; 43 High St; junior deluxe ste from $260, deluxe ste from $310) Veritably hip Hatherley has won a string of awards and it's not hard to see why. Set in an 1830s mansion overlooking expansive lawns, this sophisticated small hotel is decked out with the best furnishings, art and ultra-modern fittings money can buy, and yet the effect is pleasingly low-key cool. Leave the kiddies at home.

HOTELS & MOTELS

Peppers Seaport Hotel (Map p204; ☎ 6345 3333; www .seaport.com.au; 28 Seaport Blvd; d $187-320; 🖳) Right on the waterfront in the swanky new Seaport development, this glam hotel is big on design in natural timbers and muted tones. The Mud Club day spa offers all manner of massages and beauty treatments, and when you've worked up an appetite you can hang out at the Mud bar (see right) next door.

Auldington (Map p203; ☎ 6331 2050; www.auldington .com.au; 110 Frederick St; d from $210, extra person $48; 🖳) This small private hotel has a historic exterior complete with lacy wrought-iron balconies which belies the funkily modern fitout inside. It's plum in town in a quiet spot, has a wheelchair friendly suite and the kind of cheerful, personal service that you don't get in the larger hotels.

SELF-CONTAINED APARTMENTS

Lido Boutique Apartments (Map p203; ☎ 6334 5988; www.thelido.com.au; 47-49 Elphin Rd; apt $190-420) The eight spacious and wonderfully decorated apartments here exude 1930s style. They all have the most comfortable queen-sized beds and expansive living areas. For pure indulgence, reserve the exotic three-bedroom 'Japanese Imperial' suite with an enormous spa and every imaginable mod con.

Two Four Two (Map p203; ☎ 6331 9242; www.two fourtwo.com.au; 242 Charles St; d incl breakfast $198-220, extra adult/child $50/25) Now *this* is a cool renovation! Alan the furniture maker has channelled his craft into three self-contained apartments, each with blackwood, myrtle or Tasmanian oak detailing. Flat-screen TVs, stainless-steel kitchens, coffee machines and spa baths complete the experience.

York Mansions (Map p204; ☎ 6334 2933; www.york mansions.com.au; 9-11 York St; apt $216-352) Yearning to spend a night as the Duke or Duchess of York? Stay in one of the five opulent, historically themed apartments in the 1840 Georgian, National Trust–classified York Mansions.

EATING
Restaurants

Izakaya (Map p204; ☎ 6331 0613; 25 Yorktown Sq; sushi $4-12, mains $19-26; 🕑 lunch Wed-Fri, dinner Tue-Sat) Be wooed by chef Caesar Woo and his masterful sushi (using trevalla, flathead, salmon or tuna – whatever's fresh) and superior mains. The interior and location are nothing flash, but the food transcends place and time. The *ika izakaya huu* (squid slivers marinated in black vinegar and sweet soy) are sensational.

Three Steps on George (Map p204; ☎ 6334 2084; 158 George St; mains $17-26; 🕑 dinner) Part of the Colonial on Elizabeth complex (p209), this wonderful restaurant/wine bar not only has great décor (check out the convict bricks), but friendly service and slap-up bistro fare. There's plenty to keep meat-eaters happy, including the aged Fillet Wellington and the Three Steps Burger.

Northern Club (Map p204; ☎ 6331 3568; 61 Cameron St; mains $15-32; 🕑 lunch & dinner) The Northern Club goes pub Mondays and Tuesdays with a $12 menu all day. At other times it's the place for laid-back sophisticates to eat, drink and play. All the meat and fish is local. The lamb shanks are so tender they'll make you go weak at the knees.

Me Wah (Map p203; ☎ 6331 1308; 39-41 Invermay Rd; mains $15-80; 🕑 lunch Tue-Sun, dinner daily) This is hands down Launceston's best Chinese restaurant and serves all sorts of old favourites as well as innovative dishes heavily influenced by fresh Tasmanian seafood. The abalone with shitake mushrooms in oyster sauce ($80) may blow your budget – but might also just blow your mind.

Pickled Evenings (Map p204; ☎ 6331 0110; 135 George St; mains $18-24; 🕑 dinner) In India, the word 'pickled' is often used to mean drunk: that's the explanation for the topsy-turvy décor in this restaurant. But there's nothing higgledy-piggledy about the service or food here. The heady aromas that greet you at the door confirm this'll be the best Indian you've had in a while.

Fee & Me (Map p204; ☎ 6331 3195; cnr Charles & Frederick Sts; per course 3 courses $19.50, 4 courses $17.50, 5 courses $15.50; 🕑 dinner Tue-Sat) The awards plastered all over the wall here are testament to Fee & Me's semilegendary status. The menu is structured so that you can have three, for or five courses, all of which are entrée sized. There are delights like hare pie with parmesan soufflé topping and an ambrosial lemongrass rice pudding for desert.

Mud (Map p204; ☎ 6345 3340; 28 Seaport; lunch mains $21.90-29.90, dinner mains $17.90-38; 🕑 lunch & dinner)

You can hang out on the cool leather sofas or at the bar here, then migrate to the tables where you can order such sophisticated fare as slow cooked duck leg with red cabbage and hazelnut, or simply a good old porterhouse from the grill with roasted garlic and potatoes. Trendy and relaxed – and food that's consistently great.

Hallam's Waterfront (Map p204; ☎ /fax 6334 0554; 13 Park St; mains $23-34; ☑ lunch & dinner) Adjacent to the Tamar Yacht Club and decked out in a requisite nautical theme, this place has friendly service and specialises in exquisite crayfish dishes. The hot-and-cold seafood platter ($79 for two people) gets a thumbs-up. There's also a takeaway attached, catering to gourmet fish-and-chip lovers.

ourpick Luck's (Map p204; ☎ 6334 8596; 70 George St; mains $24-37; ☑ lunch Tue-Fri, dinner daily) This classy new restaurant was once a butcher's shop, but now it's all ornate gilded wallpaper, spanking white tablecloths and an definite air of retro-cool. Luck's serves fancy food in a French-bistro atmosphere. There's *chateaubriand* with *chasseur* sauce, or closer to home, a Flinders Island lamb rack. For afters try the dark chocolate and Turkish delight tart.

Stillwater (Map p204; ☎ 6331 4153; Ritchies Mill, 2 Bridge Rd; dinner 2/3 courses $70/85, 6-course tasting menu $105; ☑ breakfast, lunch & dinner) Set in the stylishly renovated 1840s Ritchies flour mill beside the Tamar, Stillwater does laid-back breakfasts, relaxed lunches – and then puts on the Ritz for dinner. There are delectable seafood, meaty and vego mains. Try the incredible Asian *assiette* of sweets.

Pubs

Irish Murphy's (Map p204; ☎ 6331 4440; cnr Brisbane & Bathurst Sts; mains $13.50-26.50; ☑ lunch Tue-Sun, dinner daily) This popular pub offers a better-than-average take on the humble counter meal. The menu consists of delicious Irish fare – stew may be involved.

Flavours on Charles (Map p204; ☎ 6331 3968; 252 Charles St; mains $17.50-26-50; ☑ breakfast, lunch & dinner Tue-Sun) This restaurant in the Sportsmans Hall Hotel does great bistro fare: hearty staples like thick beef sausages with creamy herb mashed potato. Leave room for a wicked liquid centre chocolate pudding afterwards.

Royal on George (Map p204; ☎ 6331 2526; 90 George St; mains $18-24; ☑ breakfast Sat & Sun, lunch & dinner) There's a fantastic, inventive menu – that includes kids' and gluten-free options – here.

Cafés & ...

Café Rossilli (... $7-22; ☑ breakfa... is homemade ... ing little café on ... chicken, eggs and ... wherever possible. Lu... ...y salads and wraps. You can fi... a latte done just right and an almon... ...onut cake that's to die for.

Pasta Resistance Too (Map p204; ☎ 6334 3081; 23 Quadrant Mall; lunch meals $7-9; ☑ lunch Mon-Sat) The 20-year success story of this popular eatery says it all for the food. There's wonderful fresh pasta with lashings of mouthwatering sauces: try the creamy chicken pesto with sundried tomatoes or the unbeatable spinach and ricotta ravioli with mushroom and tomato. You can also bulk-buy pasta and sauces for around $12 per kg.

Fresh (Map p204; ☎ 6331 4299; 178 Charles St; mains $8-16; ☑ breakfast & lunch daily, dinner Fri) Retro-arty (and now licensed) Fresh offers an all-vegetarian/vegan menu that's both deliciously tempting and environmentally aware. It does energising breakfasts, linger-over lunches and coffees and cakes in between. The food's organic as much as possible and it works hard to recycle waste, as well as supporting green community issues.

Burger Got Soul (Map p203; ☎ 6334 5204; 243 Charles St; $9.90-14; ☑ lunch & dinner) Hands down the best burgers in Launceston, served in a funky atmosphere by happy staff. They're all into healthy too: it's good, lean meat, the freshest bread, crunchy salads – and it even does Soul Veggie Burgers for those of the nonmeat eating persuasion.

Elaia (Map p203; ☎ 6331 3307; 240 Charles St; mains dinner $17.20-27; ☑ breakfast, lunch & dinner except Sun nights; ☐) You'll love the Mediterranean atmosphere in this great spot on Charles St. It does inventive pizzas, delicious pastas and risottos, steaks and good salads. You can also occupy the soft leather wall benches for all-day breakfast or coffee and cake.

ourpick Tant pour Tant (Map p203; ☎ 6334 9884; 226 Charles St; ☑ 7.30am-6pm Mon-Fri, 8.30am-4pm Sat & Sun) Your eyes will surely be bigger than your stomach at this wonderful French patisserie. As well

…s, it serves a jaw-
…ants, cakes and pastries;
…s and light lunches too. You'll
…e in Paris as you savour your *mille*
…nd coffee at a streetside table.

Trevallyn Deli Café (Map p203; ☎ 6334 9588; 1-3 Osborne Ave; mains $12-26; ☼ breakfast & lunch Sun-Wed, breakfast, lunch & dinner Thu-Sat) This little foodie enclave on the hill at Trevallyn does organic as much as possible and can cater to gluten-free eaters. There are also man-sized meals: gourmet pizzas, pastas, local salmon and steak. Everything's delicious and good for the conscience too – even the coffee is of the Fair Trade variety.

DRINKING & ENTERTAINMENT

Most of Launceston's entertainment options are advertised in the *Examiner* newspaper daily.

Royal Oak Hotel (Map p204; ☎ 6331 5345; 14 Brisbane St; ☼ 11am-late) We can almost guarantee you won't get beaten up at Launceston's friendliest and most laid-back pub. There are heaps of brilliant beers on tap, open mic nights (last Wednesday of the month) and live acoustic rock Wednesday to Sunday.

James Hotel (Map p204; ☎ 6334 7231; www.james hotel.com.au; 122 York St; nightclub $5-7; ☼ 3pm-midnight Mon-Wed, 5pm-5.30am Thu-Sat) The James hosts a steady stream of local and interstate acoustic and full-blown rock acts (Sarah McLeod, AC/DC tribute bands etc), plus DJs in Reality nightclub out the back (Thursday to Saturday from 11pm).

Tonic Bar (off Map p203; ☎ 6335 5777; Country Club Av, Prospect Vale; ☼ daily until late) Launceston's new super-cool bar at the Country Club (8km out of town) is the latest place to see and be seen. There are cocktail specials on Friday evenings and free live music gets the place thumping Thursday to Saturday. Tapas and bar snacks also available.

Irish Murphy's (☎ 6331 4440; cnr Brisbane & Bathurst Sts; admission free; ☼ noon-midnight Sun-Wed, to 2am Thu-Sat) This low-lit watering hole (see p208), stuffed full of Emerald Isle predictabilia, has live music every night (usually free), including Sunday arvo jam sessions.

Princess Theatre (Map p204; ☎ 6323 3666; 57 Brisbane St) Built in 1911 and including the smaller Earl Arts Centre, this theatre stages an eclectic mix of drama, dance and comedy, drawing acts from across Tasmania and the mainland.

Village Cinemas (Map p204; ☎ 6331 5066; 163 Brisbane St; adult/child/concession $14.50/10/11.50) Big-budget

flicks and Hollywood blockbusters offer cinematic escapism.

SHOPPING

Mill Providore + Gallery (Map p204; ☎ 6331 0777; Ritchies Mill, 2 Bridge Rd; ☼ 9am-6pm) Above Stillwater Restaurant in the Ritchies Mill complex, you'll find this treasure-trove of everything for the home, kitchen, stomach and soul! There's a brilliant delicatessen and chocolatier for picnic goodies. The gallery upstairs will keep you browsing for hours.

Pinot Shop (Map p204; ☎ 6331 3977; 135 Paterson St; ☼ 10am-6pm Mon-Thu, to 7pm Fri & Sat) Close to Ritchies Mill, this boutique specialises in Pinot Noirs and fine wines – particularly of the Tasmanian variety. It also does premium international and 'big-island' vintages. Tastings of selected wines available – and it can freight wine Australia-wide.

Paddy Pallin (Map p204; ☎ 6331 4240; 110 George St; ☼ 9am-5.30pm Mon-Fri, to 4pm Sat, 10am-2pm Sun) sells (and hires out) all the gear you need for a camping adventure. **Mountain Designs** (Map p204; ☎ 6334 0988; 120 Charles St, ☼ 9am-5.30pm Mon-Fri, to 4pm Sat, 11am-3pm Sun) also does gear sales and hire, fuel sales, MTB hire and park passes.

Craft markets (Map p203) are held every weekend near Launceston showground off Forster St, just past the **Aurora Stadium** (Map p203; off Forster St; ☼ 9am-2pm Sun).

GETTING THERE & AWAY
Air

There are regular flights between Launceston and both Melbourne and Sydney, connecting with other Australian cities. For flight details see **Qantas** (☎ 13 13 13; www.qantas.com.au), **Jetstar** (☎ 13 15 38; www.jetstar.com), **Virgin Blue** (☎ 13 67 89; www.virginblue.com.au) or **Tiger Airways** (☎ 9335 3033; www.tigerairways.com).

For details of the daily flights from Launceston to Flinders Island see p314. Light plane charter flights also can be arranged.

Bus

Redline Coaches (☎ 1300 360 000; www.tasredline.com.au) and **TassieLink** (☎ 1300 300 520; www.tassielink.com.au) operate out of Launceston. The depot for services is at **Cornwall Square Transit Centre** (Map p204; cnr St John & Cimitiere Sts), behind the visitors centre.

Redline runs buses to Burnie ($31.30, two hours 20 minutes), Deloraine ($11.70, 45 minutes), Devonport ($23.30, 1½ hours), George

Town ($11.10, 45 minutes), Hobart ($33.20, 2½ hours), Stanley ($49.50, four hours), Bicheno ($36.90, 2½ hours), St Helens ($29, 2¾ hours) – operated by Calows Coaches – and Swansea ($29.60, two hours). There are also services to the East Tamar on weekdays.

TassieLink (☎ 1300 300 520, 6336 9500; www.tassie link.com.au) has a regular city express service to Devonport ($21, 1¼ hours), tying in with the ferry schedules and to Hobart ($30.20, 2½ hours). It also services the northwest, including Sheffield ($27.00, two hours), Gowrie Park ($35.60, 2¼ hours), Cradle Mountain ($53.30, three hours), Tullah ($46.10, 4¾ hours), Rosebery ($48.10, five hours), Zeehan ($55.80, 5½ hours), Queenstown ($64.70, six hours) and Strahan ($73.90, seven hours).

Manion's Coaches (Map p204; ☎ 6383 1221) services the West Tamar region from Launceston. For details see right.

Car

Many of the major car rental firms have desks at the airport or in town. There's **Europcar** (Map p204; ☎ 13 13 90, 6331 8200; 112 George St) and **Thrifty** (Map p204; ☎ 6333 0911, 1300 367 227; 151 St John St), and cheaper operators like **Economy Car Rentals** (Map p204; ☎ 6334 3299; 27 William St), with prices starting at $37 per day (older cars and rentals of at least seven days). **Lo-Cost Auto Rent** (Map p204; ☎ 6334 3437, 1800 647 060; www.rentforless.com.au; 80 Tamar St) have starting rates from $30 daily for multiday hire.

GETTING AROUND
To/From the Airport

Launceston airport is 15km south of the city. A **shuttle bus** (☎ 6343 6677) runs a door-to-door airport service costing $12/6 per adult/child. A taxi to the city costs about $40.

Bicycle

Arthouse Backpackers Hostel (see p208) rents out bikes on an hourly and daily basis, as does **Mountain Designs** (see opposite). There's also **Ecoride** (see p207), which hires battery powered bikes.

Bus

The local bus service is run by **Metro** (☎ 13 22 01; www.metrotas.com.au); the main departure points are on the two blocks of St John St between Paterson and York Sts. For $5 you can buy a Day Rover pass for unlimited travel after 9am Monday to Friday and all day Saturday and Sunday. Most routes don't operate in the evening and Sunday services are limited.

AROUND LAUNCESTON

TAMAR VALLEY

Funnelling north from its higher reaches around Launceston to its ocean mouth on the Bass Strait, the Tamar River and the valley that cradles it are among Tasmania's greatest natural beauty spots. This wide, tidal stretch of water is often glassy-calm. Fringed with deep-green reeds and framed with emerald hills, it can be picture-postcard perfect. From Launceston the Tamar River stretches 64km, separating the east and west Tamar districts. On the east side is the river's ocean port, Bell Bay near George Town. The Batman Bridge – an architectural and engineering wonder – unites the Tamar's two banks near Deviot.

The hillsides of the Tamar Valley and the nearby Pipers River region are covered in a geometry of vines. This is among Tasmania's key wine-producing areas, and the dry premium wines created here have achieved international recognition.

At the time of writing the Tamar Valley was under the cloud of the proposed Gunns Pulp Mill: community opposition was quite clear from the ubiquitous red 'Stop the Mill' stickers and placards and the adamant anti-mill graffiti all over the Tamar Valley. See p47.

Getting There & Around
BICYCLE

The ride north along the Tamar River is an absolute gem. On the west bank, it's possible to avoid most of the highway and follow quiet roads with few hills through small settlements. On the eastern shore, follow the hilly minor roads inland through stunning landscape to Lilydale. The only way to cross the lower reaches of the Tamar River is either via Batman Bridge or by ferry (p214).

BUS

On weekdays **Manion's Coaches** (Map p204; ☎ 6383 1221; 72 Shore St, Beaconsfield) services the west Tamar Valley from Launceston stopping at Legana ($4.90), Grindelwald/Rosevears ($6.60), Exeter and Gravelly Beach ($8.60), Deviot and Sidmouth ($8.90), Beaconsfield ($9.40) and Beauty Point ($10.25). In Launceston, buses

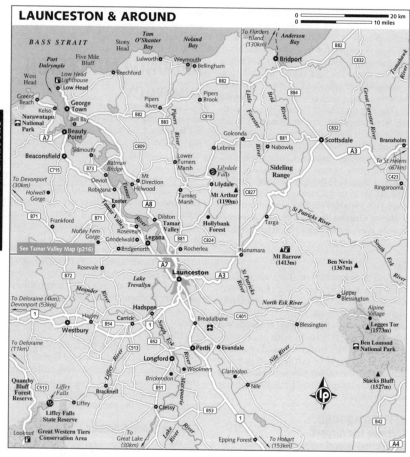

LAUNCESTON & AROUND

leave from 165 Brisbane St opposite the Village Cinemas. Southbound you'll need to hail the bus at the stop in Beaconsfield's main street (Weld St) near the IGA Supermarket.

Redline Coaches (☎ 1300 360 000, 6336 1446; www .tasredline.com.au) runs two buses every weekday (no weekend services) along the eastern side of the Tamar from Launceston to Hillwood ($7), the Batman Bridge turn-off ($8.50) and George Town ($11.10, 45 minutes). There's also a daily Redline service between Launceston and Deloraine ($11.70, one hour), via Carrick ($4.90) and Westbury ($6.90).

FERRY
The little **Shuttlefish ferry** (☎ 6383 4479, 0412 485 611; www.shuttlefishferry.com.au; ☼ Wed-Mon Nov-Apr)

makes trips across the Tamar between Beauty Point and George Town three times a day in summer. It departs the public pontoons on Wharf Rd at Beauty Point and in George Town it leaves from the pier at the end of Elizabeth St. The 25-minute journey costs $11/7 per adult/child one way, $20/11 return. The ferry also carries bikes – cyclists appreciate the shortcut.

Legana
☎ 03 / pop 1990
The main feature of Legana, a Launceston satellite suburb 12km north of town, is **Grindelwald**, a Swiss 'village' that inexplicably emigrated to Tasmania to start a new life as a residential suburb and resort. The **Tamar**

Valley Resort (☎ 6330 0400; www.tamarvalleyresort .com.au; 7 Waldhorn Dr; 🖳 🐾) has quite smart accommodation, a restaurant, some slightly twee shops and an activity centre with water bikes, boats, canoes, pedal carts, a playground with a giant jumping pillow, minigolf and full-sized golf.

Further down Waldhorn Drive is **Rosevears Estate** (☎ 6330 1800; www.rosevearsestate.com.au; 1A Waldhorn Dr; tastings $2; 🕙 10am-5pm). This top winery was acquired by controversial timber and woodchipping giant Gunns Ltd (see p47) in its recent expansion into the wine business (and may soon be enjoying breathtaking views of the latter's proposed pulp mill, just across the Tamar River). There are wine tastings, cellar door sales and a flash restaurant, **Estelle** (🕙 breakfast & lunch daily; mains $16-24.50). There's also on-site accommodation in studio apartments from $250 for two people (see below).

SLEEPING & EATING

Launceston Holiday Park (☎ 6330 1714; www.island cabins.com.au; 711 West Tamar Hwy; powered sites d from $28-30, cabins d from $70-115; 🖳) Conveniently located, this park has a range of cabins (two with spas), from basic stuffy budget versions to deluxe spa units. There's a guest laundry, BBQ and games room.

Tamar Valley Resort (☎ 6330 0400; www.tamarvalley resort.com.au; 7 Waldhorn Dr; hotel ste d $170-240, chalets $214-260, apt $214-259, extra person $15) There are neat hotel rooms and some quite luxurious chalets and apartments here. The alpine theme is carried right through the hotel with the giant flower canvases on its walls.

Rosevears Estate (☎ 6330 1800; www.rosevearsestate .com.au; 1A Waldhorn Dr; 1-/2-bedroom cottages $250/350) There are 20 modern cottages on the hillside here overlooking the river – just the place to hang out on the balcony with a glass of the local drop. The restaurant's tasting plates (mains $16.50 to $24.50; open lunch and dinner Wednesday to Saturday) are good when savoured with this estate's wine.

Food-wise, try **Alpenrose Restaurant & Lounge Bar** (☎ 6330 0444; Waldhorn Dr; lunch mains $8.50-19.90, dinner mains $19.50-31.50; 🕙 breakfast, lunch & dinner). Despite being part of Grindelwald village, it fortunately avoids references to 'Swiss cheese'. Lunches are quick and casual, but it's finer dining at dinner: it does a great ocean trout with seared cherry tomatoes. There's a kiddies' menu and the play area is adjacent.

Rosevears
☎ 03 / pop 160

Get off the main highway (A7) onto narrow Rosevears Dr that follows the waterside past moored yachts and swaying reed-beds to the pretty riverside settlement of Rosevears. Vines climb all over the hills here and several good wineries make this a favourite haunt of wine lovers.

Even if you're no wine buff, you should drop into glorious **Ninth Island Vineyard Strathlynn** (☎ 6330 2388; 95 Rosevears Dr; tastings $3; 🕙 10am-5pm). The vines and views are achingly beautiful here – especially when they turn golden in autumn. Go inside to taste the vino or pop into the popular restaurant.

our pick Daniel Alps at Strathlynn (mains $18.90-$29.90; 🕙 12-3pm) is great for a long lazy lunch. Head chef Daniel (who's just a notch off celeb-chef) whips up seasonal regional food for a daily-changing menu. As much as possible, the fruit and veg is organic and locally sourced.

Along the scenic riverbank drive, you'll come across **Rosevears Waterfront Tavern** (☎ 6394 4074; 215 Rosevears Dr; mains $20-25; 🕙 lunch & dinner). One of Tasmania's oldest pubs, it was opened in 1831 and now serves all sorts of deliciously tempting upmarket fare. Don't mind the obligatory chicken parmigiana: you can also have your chook done with honey and macadamia, crunch on crumbed scallops or savour salt-n-pepper squid. The laid-back beer garden does bar snacks.

Nearby is the fully self-contained **Conmel Cottage** (☎ 6330 1466; www.conmelcottage.com.au; 125 Rosevears Dr; s/d $130/140). Prices include breakfast that's supplied for you to cook and there's a veggie garden and orchard with more than 40 fruit and nut trees to raid.

On Craythorne Rd, off to the left just after Conmel if you're travelling north, is the highly browse-worthy **Treeform Gallery** (☎ 6330 3646; www.treeform.com.au; 110 Craythorne Rd; 🕙 10am-4pm) where talented local craftsmen create beautiful pieces of furniture and ornaments from native timbers, much of it salvaged from 'waste' left by forestry operations. It ships nationally and internationally.

You can also stay at **SummerSett** (☎ 6394 3882, 0427-943 882; 259a Rosevears Dr; d $95, extra person $10) about 1km past the Rosevears Hotel, heading north. This self-contained unit on the ground floor of a riverbank home sleeps up to four and comes with breakfast provisions.

LAUNCESTON & AROUND

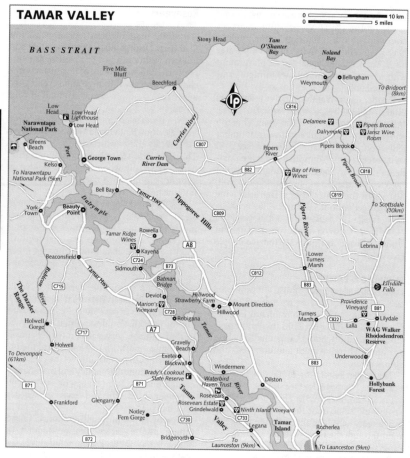

TAMAR VALLEY

From here, you can follow Brady's Lookout Rd (left off Rosevears Dr if you're travelling north) and follow the signs to the nearby **Brady's Lookout State Reserve**. The well-known bushranger Brady used this rocky outcrop to spy on travellers on the road below, so the views are of course spectacular.

Exeter & Around

☎ 03 / pop 400

This is predominantly an orchard and mixed farming area. The local **Tamar visitors centre** (☎ 6394 4454; www.ltvtasmania.com.au; West Tamar Hwy; ☼ 8.30am-5pm May) will inform you.

There are few places to stay here now since the **Exeter Hotel** (☎ 6394 4216; Main Rd) closed its rooms for renovation, but they should be

swanky when the work's complete. Counter meals are served here from Wednesday to Saturday. Another food option is the **Exeter Bakery** (☎ 6394 4069; Main Rd; ☼ 7am-5pm Jun-Aug, to 6pm Sep-May). Its century-old wood-fired oven produces all manner of pies – from seafood to tender wallaby. It also serves up cakes, bread and slices, and filled rolls to take away.

South of Exeter, Gravelly Beach Rd will take you to **Koukla's** (☎ 6394 4013; 285 Gravelly Beach Rd; mains $17.50-22.50; ☼ lunch Wed-Sun, dinner Sat & Sun), a BYO café serving huge portions of sensational Greek-influenced cuisine. Try the amazing *kleftiko* – slow baked lemon lamb with roasted vegetables – or the sensational Greek custard pie. The same road will take you to Robigana (derived from the Aboriginal word for swans), where the road crosses the Supply River. From here there's a marked walking track (one hour return) beside the Tamar River to **Paper Beach**. There's also a pleasant 400m walk along the river to the meagre ruins of Australia's first water-driven **flour mill**. Further along the **Artisan Gallery** (☎ 6394 4595; www.artisangallery.com.au; 32 Deviot Rd, Robigana; ☺ 10am-5pm Sep-May, to 4pm Fri-Mon Jun-Aug), showcases crafts of well-known and local artisans, including some unusual water-etched porcelain bowls and vases. It also has a strong collection of boutique Tasmanian wines from around the region.

Next you can visit **Marion's Vineyard** (☎ 6394 7434; Foreshore Drive, Deviot; ☺ 10am-5pm for tasting & cellar door sales) run by an endearingly eccentric Californian who's called Tasmania home for 30 years. You can buy good wines from the 'straight range' – but more fun is the Giggleskins 'deranged range' with creative labels and names like 'Afterglow' and 'Seducer Guaranteed'. If the wine's got to you, you can always stay here in their cute timber **chalet** (d $146) looking over the vineyard and water.

BATMAN BRIDGE

Opened in 1968 as one of the world's first cable-stayed truss bridges, the Batman Bridge has an eye-catching design that resulted not so much from creative inspiration as from foundation problems. The Tamar's east offered poor support for a large bridge, so it holds up just a minor part of the span. Most of the bridge is actually supported by the 100m-tall west tower that leans out over the river. There are good views from the east side.

Passing underneath the bridge on the western bank is a gravel road leading to **Sidmouth**. Here the long-worshipped local institution is Auld Kirk ('old church'), built in 1843 from 'freestone' by convict and free labour. Proceed north on the C724 to the Auburn Rd junction at Kayena. Turning left on Auburn road and travelling for about a kilometre leads you to **Tamar Ridge Wines** (☎ 6394 1114; Auburn Rd, Kayena; ☺ 10am-5pm), another Gunns Ltd (see p47) wine venture, which offers tastings and cellar door sales.

Beaconsfield & Around
☎ 03 / pop 1015
This little town set in apple-growing country has had two great moments of glory. The first was when gold was discovered here in 1877 and

the second when a mining accident killed one miner and kept two trapped deep underground – and under unwavering national attention – for two weeks in 2006 (see p218). This accident kept the mine closed for some time and Beaconsfield in the doldrums, but now the excitement's died down, this slightly shabby town has gone back to what it always was: a quiet rural backwater, presiding over historically one of the richest small gold mines in Australia.

Most visitors come to Beaconsfield to see the **Grubb Shaft Gold & Heritage Museum** (☎ 6383 1473; West St; adult/child/concession/family $9/4/7/24; ☺ 10am-4pm). To tell the history of what was once Australia's biggest gold mine, the museum has hands-on interactive exhibits, including old mining machinery, a waterwheel and a display on life as a miner. You can see the working mine headshaft right behind the museum and wherever you walk in Beaconfield, you can imagine the miners hard at work in the ground right beneath your feet. Note: you can get a three-attraction pass to the Grub Shaft Museum, Platypus House and Seahorse World (see below) for $40 per adult and $105 for a family (two adults and up to three kids four to 16. Children under four go free).

If you want to stay in town, **Beaconsfield Backpackers** is the pick. Set in the attractive **Exchange Hotel** (☎ 6383 1113; 141 Weld St, dm/s/d $22/20/30), this friendly place is often frequented by seasonal fruit-picking travellers. All the clean rooms have TVs and there's a communal kitchen/sitting room and laundry facilities. Downstairs the **pub** (☺ lunch daily, dinner Mon-Sat) does decent counter meals and also serves up cones of Tassie's favourite Valhalla ice cream.

Nine kilometres south of Beaconsfield is **Holwell Gorge** reserve, containing sections of original forest, giant trees and three waterfalls. The walking track linking the southern and northern gorge entrances takes around two hours one way.

Beauty Point
☎ 03 / pop 1500
Though the surrounding landscape is certainly bonny, the town's name actually derives from pulchritude of the bovine variety: a now-immortalised bullock called Beauty.

The main attractions here are two nature-based displays in wharf sheds down on the water. At **Seahorse World** (☎ 6383 4111; www.seahorseworld.com.au; Beauty Point Wharf; adult/child/concession/family $20/9/16/50; ☺ 9.30am-4.30pm, last tour

LAUNCESTON & AROUND

TODD, BRANT & LARRY

The Beaconsfield mine disaster of April 2006 will be remembered for many reasons, not least for the media circus that surrounded the incident. On Anzac Day, a rock fall killed miner Larry Knight and trapped Todd Russell and Brant Webb in a cage 1km underground. After an exhaustive two-week rescue operation that made global headlines (further sensationalised by the heart-attack death of a TV reporter on the surface), Todd and Brant emerged to a media feeding frenzy. Magnates quaffed beer at the Beaconsfield pub, rock stars flew in to perform, Oprah was mentioned. Weathering the storm, Todd and Brant signed lucrative deals for their story, but to everyone's great disappointment, they turned out to be regular blokes – short on charisma, patience and eloquent summations of their ordeal. Oprah never called; the mine reopened in April 2007. Tony Wright's *Bad Ground: Inside the Beaconsfield Mine Rescue* is the definitive account of the tragedy.

3.30pm) you can view specimens of these astounding sea creatures from all round the world – from Tasmania's own weedy sea dragons to the strange pot-bellied seahorse (*Hippocampus abdominalis*), which you can see in various stages of development from the tiniest shrimpy critters to portly full grown. There's even a touch-tank where the little horses will swim up and wrap their tails around your fingers.

In the wharf shed opposite, **Platypus House** (☎ 6383 4884; www.platypushouse.com.au; Inspection Head Wharf; adult/child/concession/family $18/9/15/46; ☷ 9am-4pm, last tour 3pm) has the world's only two monotremes: the platypus and the echidna. While you do actually get to see the platypus gambol in their glass-sided tanks and transparent 'burrows', it's not a hugely inspiring presentation. The echidna room is fun as you get to walk among several of these trundling creatures and cheerful guides give you the lowdown on it all.

For information on a three-attraction pass to the above spots, combined with Beaconsfield's Grubb Shaft Museum, see p217.

SLEEPING & EATING

Beauty Point Tourist Park (☎ 6383 4536; www.beauty pointtouristpark.com.au; Redbill Point; powered sites $25, onsite vans $70, cabins $99-119) There's camping on the grass by the water here, comfortable vans and good cabins that are all kitted out even for longer stays. A tennis court and river swimming will keep you busy.

Tamar Cove (☎ 6383 4375; 4421 Main Rd; motel d from $95; ☷) What an appealing little enclave you'll find here! Attractive, recently done-up motel rooms front a well-manicured landscape with a pool to dip in. The restaurant (meals $16 to $28; open breakfast in summer, lunch and din-

ner year-round) gets rave reviews. You can't go past its signature seafood chowder. Yum!

Beauty Point Cottages (☎ 6383 4556, 0428 768 790; 14 Flinders St; d $144-188) You can stay in the historic homestead here, or in a self-contained spa cottage. Great decoration with attention to detail makes it look good inside, but even better is looking outdoors – the river views are sensational.

Pomona Spa Cottages (☎ 6383 4073; www.pomona spacottages.com.au; 77 Flinders St; d from $230, extra person $40, discounts for longer stays) There are three spa cottages in the grounds of this heritage homestead, masterfully built in the same genre as the old home itself and so comfortably kitted out you could move right in. There are decks with rotundas and, naturally, great views.

Carbone's Café (☎ 6383 4099; 225 Flinders St; mains $13.90-21.90; ☷ breakfast & lunch) On sunny days at Carbone's the windows wrap right back and the water feels so close you could touch it. The menu tempts with fresh local fare – we liked the smoked salmon with zucchini fritters – and the chai lattes are just about perfect too.

Seahorse World Café (☎ 6383 4964; Beauty Point Wharf; mains $9.50-17.50; ☷ breakfast & lunch) Upstairs at Seahorse World and privy to unbeatable views over the Tamar, this restaurant-café serves good meals and snacks that draw heavily on the sea. Try the Malibu – jumbo prawns poached in coconut, rum and garlic sauce. Is that a chocolate seahorse on my cappuccino froth?

Greens Beach

☎ 03 / pop 200

This little holiday settlement, founded in 1828, is the favourite getaway of Launcestonians and it's not hard to see why: there are miles of beach and headland to stroll and protected waters to fish and swim in. It's also right next to Narawntapu National Park, so there's great camping and hiking on the doorstep.

Get your supplies at **Greens Beach Shop** (☎ 6383 9228; Greens Beach Rd; ☺ 8.30am-6pm), where there's also a basic takeaway. The shop manages hire of the **tennis courts** that are right next door ($15 per day). **Greens Beach Golf Club** (☎ 6383 9102; ☺ 6am-6pm, green fees per day $15) is also adjacent. It's a nine-hole, par 72 course with plenty of trees and sea views from the eigth tee.

Opposite the shop is the departure point for the **Greens Beach West Head Coastal Trail**. It's about 10km return, passing between waterside holiday shacks and the shoreline and entering the national park about half way along. National park fees apply. The walk leads through dense stands of she-oaks and paperbark, rich with wildlife and Aboriginal heritage, to spectacular West Head Lookout. If you don't have time to walk, you can drive to just below the lookout on Gardners Rd and take a five-minute stroll up to the views.

You can camp or take a cabin at friendly **Greens Beach Caravan Park** (☎ 6383 9222; Main Rd; unpowered/powered sites $15/14, cabins d $220, extra person $10) right behind the beach. For somewhere more fancy try **Beaches n Greens** (☎ 0438-344 436; 2 Tamar Crescent; d $95-140, extra guest $15). All decked out in yellow and blue, these pretty weatherboard houses, sleeping up to five, have Bass Strait views and are encircled with timber decks. Just the spot for a postbeach barbie. Truly top notch is **Greens Beach Luxury Escape** (☎ 0408-376 211; www.luxuryescapestas.com.au; 19 Pars Rd; house $250), a glam beach house sleeping four with views to die for.

Narawntapu National Park

Located 25km east of Devonport (12km off the B71), the Narawntapu (formerly Asbestos Range) National Park is a reserve of coastal heath, dunes and bushland that's astoundingly abundant in wildlife. Visit just on dusk and you'll see Forester kangaroos, foraging wombats, wallabies and pademelons.

The park can be accessed near Greens Beach at two points via the C721 and C741. However, the main entrance, where there's a **ranger station and information centre** (☎ 6428 6277; ☺ 8am-4pm Dec-April, 9am-3pm May-Nov) is off the B71 near Port Sorell (see p238). **Discovery rangers** provide guided walks and activities

from here in summer. If you're entering the park from the Greens Beach side, you can buy your parks pass from the Greens Beach shop, or self-register on entry.

Horse riding is allowed and the park has corrals and a 26km trail; bookings with the ranger are required. **Bakers Beach** is the safest swimming area and water-skiing is permitted here in summer.

There are some engaging walking trails in the park. You can hike round **Badger Head** in around six to eight hours (via Copper Cove), while the **Archers Knob** (114m) walk (around two hours return) has good views of Bakers Beach. The one-hour **Springlawn Nature Trail** includes a boardwalk over wetlands to a bird hide. The beach from Griffiths Point to Bakers Point is good for beachcombing and sunset-watching.

The park has four **camp sites**. Caravans can drive to **Springlawn Beach** (powered sites d/family $15/20) and there are unpowered sites at **Koybaa**, **Bakers Point** and **The Horseyard** (d/family $12/15), which has a corral for horses. There are tables and toilets at all sites. Firewood is sometimes provided but there's not always reliable water, so check with rangers before setting off or bring your own.

George Town

☎ 03 / pop 5550

George Town sits sentinel on the Tamar River's Eastern shore, close to where it empties into Bass Strait. The town was founded in 1804 by Lieutenant Colonel Paterson, as part of the British attempt to stave off settlement by the French who had been reconnoitring the area. The town's older buildings date from the 1830s and 1840s, when it prospered as the port linking Tasmania with Victoria. Though today it's perhaps not the most appealing of towns, it's still got a historic maritime feel and a couple of attractions worth visiting.

INFORMATION

Commonwealth Bank (Macquarie St) Has an ATM.
Post office (Macquarie St)
Visitors centre (☎ 6382 1700; Main Rd; ☺ 9am-5pm) On the main road as you enter from the south.

SIGHTS

Ask at the visitors centre for a map detailing the **George Town Heritage Trail**, which walks you interestingly through the town's history, starting at the **Old Watch House** (1843) on Macquarie

LAUNCESTON & AROUND

MANNA OR MADNESS? GEORGE TOWN & THE PULP MILL

It's been said you can gauge Tasmania's political and environmental persuasions by the messages on its bumper stickers, and while the West Tamar appears – from the stickers and placards at least – to be vociferously anti-mill, in George Town it's another story altogether. George Town would be the closest town to the proposed $2 billion Gunns Pulp Mill (see p47) and hopes to benefit from jobs created during its construction, as well as rising house prices amid a general mill-related boom. For this quiet seaside town (that's been rather in the doldrums since the Devil Cat Bass Strait ferry was scrapped) it seems like a boon. But ask people around town about the pulp mill – and if they'll talk to you about it at all – the mood is not so clear. Sure, people would like to see new jobs and investment in town, but it's become increasingly evident that the majority of contractors will be brought in from outside. There are concerns about dangerous construction traffic and an on-going flow of heavy log trucks on the roads nearby. The issue of pollution has people worried too. So although the most widespread bumper sticker you might see in George Town is the succinct judgement 'Greens Tell Lies', dig a little deeper here and you'll find a town that's not entirely happy about the mega-mill that appears about to be built on its doorstep.

St, which houses a small museum. Just outside town there's **Mt George**, which (now among modern communications towers) retains the semaphore equipment once used to relay signals via Mt Direction to Launceston. There's a wheelchair-accessible ramp from the car park to the mountain top.

Bass & Flinders Centre

Undoubtedly the highlight of a visit to George Town, even for committed landlubbers, is the great new **Bass & Flinders Centre** (☎ 6382 3792; 8 Elizabeth St; ☺ 10am-4pm, adult/child/family $10/8/24) housing a replica of the *Norfolk*, the little yacht used by Bass and Flinders for their 1897 circumnavigation of Van Diemen's Land. Built for a historic re-enactment of the voyage in 1998, the red-sailed replica *Norfolk* now rests here, together with several other historic wooden vessels and an excellent interpretive display.

TOURS

Seal & Sea Adventure Tours (☎/fax 6382 3452, 0419-357 028; www.sealandsea.com) cruises out to the Australian fur seal colony at Tenth Island, with an enthusiastic and knowledgeable guide at the helm. Trips cost $121 per person for two people and $98 per person for groups of three or more. River trips, fishing, diving and PADI instruction are also available.

North of town at the airport (heading towards Low Head, turn right down North St for about 2km) you can take ultralight-plane flights over the hills with **Freedom Flight** (☎ 6382 4700). These cost from $85 per person for 30 minutes; book well in advance.

SLEEPING & EATING

There are camping and caravan sites at Low Head – see opposite.

George Town Heritage Hotel (George Town Hotel; ☎ 6382 2655; 75 Macquarie St; d $100) Built in 1845, this historic pub with ornate wrought-iron balconies offers basic but comfortable accommodation with en suites, and includes a decent bistro (mains $15 to $24) serving the usual steaks and seafood.

Pier Hotel Motel (☎ 13 24 00, 6382 1300; www.pier hotel.com.au; 5 Elizabeth St; d $155-180; 🖳) There are clean-and-tidy motel rooms here, but the star attraction is the recently refurbished and deservedly popular bistro (mains $18 to $25; open lunch and dinner). It serves excellent pizzas, porterhouse steaks, snacks and salads. Fold-back doors are opened onto the water in warm weather.

Charles Robbins (☎ 6382 4448; www.thecharles robbins.com.au; 3 Esplanade North; d $240-360, extra person $76) Done up all modern in leather sofas and glass, these spa suites are George Town's take on luxury. One is equipped with disabled facilities.

Signature Cafe (☎ 6382 1748; 48 Macquarie St; mains $8-12; ☺ 8am-5pm Mon-Fri) This is a cheerful place with a good range of light meals such as focaccias and salads.

our pick **York Cove** (☎ 6382 9900; www.yorkcove.com .au; 2 Ferry Blvd; d $225-265; 🖳 🐾) This new waterfront resort is making waves on the Tamar. There are upmarket motel-style rooms and apartments, and a funky bar-restaurant (dishes $15 to $32; open breakfast, lunch and dinner), which does contemporary café food and excellent coffees.

GETTING THERE & AWAY
The George Town agent for Redline is the **Shell Service Station** (Main Rd).

Low Head
☎ 03 / pop 465

Low Head and George Town are barely divided – you won't notice leaving one before arriving in the other. It's in a spectacular setting, though, looking out over the swirling – and treacherous – waters of the Tamar as it empties into the sea.

The historic **Low Head Pilot Station** was established in 1805 with the current buildings erected between 1835 and 1962. The Tamar pilot boats are still based here. The **Pilot Station Maritime Museum** (☎ 6382 2826; Low Head Rd; adult/child/pensioner/family $5/3/4/15; 10am-4pm) has a great display of maritime clutter – from whalebones to diving bells to shipwreck flotsam and jetsam. Even landlubbers will love it

At the head itself visit the 1888 **lighthouse** (grounds to 6pm) to get a perspective over the great torrent of the Tamar as it spills into the strait. Bring your earmuffs if you plan to be here on a Sunday at noon: this is when the **foghorn** sounds with an earsplittingly deafening bellow.

Little penguins live around the lighthouse and you can view them with **Low Head Penguin Tours** (☎ 0418 361 860; www.penguintours.lowhead.com.au). Tours cost $15/9 per adult/child and take place nightly from dusk, departing from a signposted spot beside the main road just south of the lighthouse.

There's good surf at **East Beach** on Bass Strait and safe swimming at most beaches around the head.

SLEEPING & EATING
Low Head Tourist Park (☎ 6382 1573; www.lowhead touristpark.com.au; 136 Low Head Rd; unpowered/powered sites $22/27.50, cabins $80, cottages $95) This river's-edge park has comfortable timber-lined cabins as well as caravan and camping spots – water views included.

Pilot Station (☎ 6382 2826; Low Head Rd; d from $100) Low Head's historic precinct offers a range of pleasant, fully self-contained, waterfront colonial cottages for up to eight people.

Belfont Cottages (☎ 0418 300 036; www.cottages ofthecolony.com.au; 178 Low Head Rd; d $135) These cottages once housed the caretakers of the leading light next door and now offer accommodation in period-style interiors. Watch out for the rising damp!

Coxwain's Cottage Café (Low Head Rd; Pilot Station; 10am-4pm) On a cold winter's day you'll be glad of the hearty warm soups ($7.50) and snacks served up in this snug café overlooking the water.

Pipers River Region
This region's most famous vineyard is **Pipers Brook** (☎ 6382 7527; 1216 Pipers Brook Rd; tastings $3; 10am-5pm) where you can try Pipers Brook, Ninth Island and Krieglinger wines in an architecturally innovative building that also houses the **Winery Café** (mains from $22; lunch), which serves a changing menu of light snacks and a delectable tasting plate.

Also within the Pipers Brook estate, but signposted up a different drive, you can visit the separately run **Jansz Wine Room** (☎ 6382 7066; 1216B Pipers Brook Rd, Pipers Brook; 10am-4.30pm) where you can taste damn fine sparklings, including a delightful pink fizz of a rosé. Self-guided tours clarify some of the 'méthode Tasmanoise' wine production. You can enjoy cheese platters with the sparkly, and take a spell on the lakeside terrace contemplating the vines.

Some 15km away, south of Pipers River, **Bay of Fires Wines** (☎ 6382 7622; 40 Baxters Rd, Pipers River; tastings free; 10am-5pm) is the home of recently prestigious Arras Sparkling and a fine Tigress Riesling. Other local vineyards worth a visit include the friendly **Delamere** (☎ 6382 7190; 4238 Bridport Rd, or B82 Hwy, Pipers Brook; 10am-5pm), which offers superb unwooded chardonnay and pinot noir varieties; and **Dalrymple** (☎ /fax 6382 7222; 1337 Pipers Brook Rd; 10am-5pm) for good French-style pinot noir and award-winning sauvignon blanc.

Lilydale
☎ 03 / pop 345

Quiet Lilydale is little more than a main street with a few stores and services – and some brightly painted utility poles. You can stock up for a picnic at National Trust–listed **Bardenhagen's General Store** (Main Rd; 7am-7pm Mon-Fri, 7.30am-6pm Sat) and then take a walk to **Lilydale Falls**, 3km north of town. If you're feeling energetic, you could tackle **Mt Arthur** (five to seven hours return), which towers dramatically above Lilydale.

On the road to Lalla is the **WAG Walker Rhododendron Reserve** (admission per vehicle $2; 9am-6pm Apr, May & Sep–mid-Dec, 9am-6pm Sat & Sun mid-Dec-Mar), where

LAUNCESTON & AROUND

there are over 100 varieties of rhododendron and exotic tree. The rhodos make an unbelievable display September to December.

Nearby is Tasmania's oldest working vineyard, **Providence Vineyard** (☎ 6395 1290; www.provi dence.com.au; 236 Lalla Rd; tastings free; ☽ 10am-5pm) which has a fine chardonnay and pinot, and also sells wines from other boutique vineyards.

The latest attraction in these parts is Forestry Tasmania's newest tourism venture **Hollybank Treetops Adventure** (☎ 6395 1390; www .treetopsadventure.com.au; adult/child $99/66; ☽ 9am-5pm) about 6km south of Lilydale. Here, harnessed to a cable-mounted swing-seat, you can skim through the treetops at stomach-churning heights, in the care of an experienced guide who will interpret the surrounding forest. There are short walks and forest picnic spots for nonadventurers.

SLEEPING & EATING

Camping is possible for $6 (for up to two people) at Lilydale Falls Reserve. You need to pay a $50 deposit at **Lilydale Takeaway** (☎ 6395 1156; Main Rd) to get a key to the amenities block where there ere even hot showers; $14 is refunded on return of the key (two-night stay limit).

Lilydale Tavern (☎ 6393 1230; Main Rd; d $79; ☽ bakery 9am-5pm) Simple motel-style rooms and a fabulous bakery/café offering light meals, cakes and pastries. People come from miles around to eat its famous pies.

Cherry Top & Eagle Park (☎ 6395 1167; cherrytop@big pond.com; 81 Lalla Rd; cottage d $120) This is a place you can pause for a while. There are two sweet self-contained cottages here on a farm that grows most of its own food. Share a yarn around the fire pit and be guided on a farm walk, and enjoy fresh farm produce for your breakfast. Take the C822 out of Lilydale and follow the signs.

Plovers Ridge Host Farm (☎ 6395 1102; fax 6395 1107; 132 Lalla Rd; s/d from $95/130) An organic property growing apples, berries, nuts veggies and garlic, Plover Ridge offers sun-soaked self-contained accommodation with cooked breakfast in two snug timber units with fantastic valley and mountain views. Filling evening meals are also available (two courses from $25 per person).

SOUTH OF LAUNCESTON

To the south of Launceston lie Hadspen and Carrick, once small historic villages. They incorporate some landmarks, historic buildings

and one of the richest historic homesteads in Tasmania.

Hadspen & Carrick
☎ 03

Hadspen is an outlying residential suburb about 15km southwest of Launceston. Most visitors who come here do so to visit nearby **Entally House** (☎ 6393 6201; www.entally .com.au; adult/child/family $9/7/20; ☽ 10am-4pm). Built in 1819 by shipping entrepreneur Thomas Haydock Reibey, it is one of Tasmania's oldest – and loveliest – country homesteads and gives a vivid picture of the affluent rural life of that period. You can inspect the antique-filled house or stroll under the magnificent English trees in the garden. Entally has been leased from the National Trust by woodchipping giant Gunns Ltd (see p47) since 2005, when the company committed $500,000 to restore the estate. It's also to become a showcase for Gunns' wines.

Just 4km from Hadspen, on the old highway to Deloraine, is Carrick. The village's most prominent feature is the 1846 four-storey, ivy-smothered **Carrick Mill** (67 Bass Hwy). At the time of research this was closed for renovations, but was thought to be opening by the end of 2008 as an upmarket restaurant. Behind the mill is the crumbling 1860 ruin known as **Archers Folly** (Bishopsbourne Rd), twice burnt down. Next door is the **Tasmanian Copper & Metal Art Gallery** (☎ 6393 6440; www.tascoppermetalart.com; 1 Church St; ☽ 9.30am-5pm), where there's an Aladdin's Cave of imaginative metalwork for sale.

SLEEPING & EATING

Hawthorn Villa (☎ 6393 6150, 0427 936 150; cnr Meander Valley Hwy & Church St, Carrick; s/d from $90/130) Encircled by the well-tended gardens here are four mud-brick cottages providing comfortable B&B accommodation with thoughtful touches like crisp white linen and extra thick bath towels. All have wood fires and generous breakfast provisions.

Carrick Inn (☎ 6393 6143; Meander Valley Rd; mains $9.50-19.50; ☽ lunch & dinner) has been offering hospitality here since 1833 and does better-than-average pub meals in the welcoming Sammy Cox Bistro, with plenty of meat and seafood.

Westbury
☎ 03 / pop 1300

This languid country town, with its tree lined streets and **village green**, has a feast of historic buildings and a decidedly English feel. Westbury's best known for the **White House** (☎ 6393 1171; King St; adult/child under 16/concession/family $8/free/6/16; 🕙 10am-4pm Tue-Sun), a property built by Thomas White in 1841–42 as a general store, which now features all sorts of collections and oddities including a 1.8m-high, 20-room doll's house. The on-site **White House Bakery** (right) will get your taste buds craving.

Pearn's Steam World (☎ 6393 1414; 65 Bass Hwy; adult/child $5/2; 🕙 9am-4pm) comprises two huge sheds filled with the world's largest collection of antique steam engines and relics. This place will appeal most to old-machinery enthusiasts. If that's not enough to oil your engines then head on over to the **Vintage Tractor Shed Museum** (☎ 6393 1167; 5 Veterans Row; adult/child $3/free; 🕙 9am-4pm) which has 93 farm tractors from 1916–52, as well as 600 scale models of tractors: in short, everything pertaining to these beasts of the field.

If you're more of the artistic persuasion, you shouldn't miss the **John Temple Gallery** (☎ 6393 1666; 103 Bass Hwy; admission free; 🕙 10am-5pm), which exhibits inspiring photographs by this top Tasmanian photographer.

There is 1km of paths among 3000 privet hedges at the **Westbury Maze** (☎ 6393 1840; 10 Bass Hwy; adult/child/family $6/5/22; 🕙 10am-5pm Sep-Jul, to 6pm Jan). Make your way to the centre to climb a viewing platform and get a bird's-eye view of this gigantic riddle. The tearoom serves Devonshire teas and light lunches, and there's a gift shop selling – of course – puzzles.

SLEEPING

Andy's Bakery (☎ 6393 1846; 45 Bass Hwy; 🕙 24hr; 🖳) There are free caravan spots behind Andy's. Shower/toilet facilities cost $5 and you can hang out inside at any hour of the day.

Olde Coaching Inn (☎ 6393 2100; 54 William St; s/d $70/100) Dating from 1833, this place was the original inn of the village. This B&B option comprises comfortable and spacious quarters set in beautiful English garden surrounds.

Fitzpatricks Inn (☎ 6393 1153; www.fitzpatricksinn .com.au; 56 Meander Valley Rd; d $100) This grand 1833 building set in lovely gardens has been extensively refurbished, but retains all of its period charm. There are eight spacious en suite rooms, and a continental breakfast is served in the restaurant. There's also an à la carte restaurant and a bar menu for snacks.

our pick Gingerbread Cottages (☎ 6393 1140; 52 William St; d from $160-180, extra adult/child $30/20)

These little cottages alone are worth staying in Westbury for. Decked out with antiques, a cosy, country feel and absolute attention to detail, they are fully self-contained with all mod-cons. Our favourite is the cute timber-lined Gingerbread Cottage (c 1880).

EATING

White House Bakery (☎ 6393 1066; King St; 🕙 9am-4pm Tue-Sun) Nestled into the side of the White House historic estate, this bakery creates magic with dough using a wood-fired oven (dating from 1840) to give you the freshest and tastiest hot bread this side of the Bass Strait. There are also tarts, cakes and incredible biscuits.

Serendipi Tea House (☎ 6393 2544; 34 William St; snacks $5-14; 🕙 10am-4pm Wed-Sat) There are delicious homemade cakes and meals at these friendly tea rooms. Leaf teas are served in bone china and it does takeaways for the weary traveller.

Westbury Hotel (☎ 6393 1151; 107 Bass Hwy; mains $14-21.50; 🕙 lunch & dinner) This pub isn't doing accommodation until after renovations are finished in early 2009, but it serves good meals: roasts, chicken kiev and a parmigiana that's up there with the best of them.

Hobnobs (☎ 6393 2007; 47 William St; mains from $32.50; 🕙 lunch Sun, dinner Thu-Sat) The atmosphere in this inviting restaurant is casually delicious – and the chefs are top-notch. Book in for a traditional Sunday roast (complete with Yorkshire pud), or save yourself for dinner – the mouthwatering slow-braised venison shanks are a treat on a cold winter's evening. There's wheelchair access too.

Liffey Valley

This valley at the foot of the Great Western Tiers (Kooperona Niara or 'Mountains of the Spirits') is famously the spiritual home of conservationist and politician Dr Bob Brown. The natural centrepiece of **Liffey Falls State Reserve** (34km southwest of Carrick) is **Liffey Falls**. There are two approaches to the falls, which are actually four separate cascades. From the upstream car park (reached by steep and winding road) it's a 45-minute return walk on a well-marked track. You can also follow the river upstream on foot to the Gulf Rd picnic area; allow two to three hours return. The area has some fine fishing.

Longford

🕿 03 / pop 2830

Another small historic town, dating from the early days of settlement, Longford was

---

TALL POPPIES

As you travel Tasmania's agricultural heartlands, you may see fields of purple poppies. Tasmania grows 40% of the legal global poppy crop and extracts the opiate alkaloids for use in the production of painkillers and other medicines. You may notice the large Tasmanian Alkaloids production plant near Westbury.

The growing and harvesting of poppies in Tasmania is strictly controlled by the state government and the Poppy Advisory and Control Board, but because poppies are grown in rotation with a range of farm crops, accidents can happen. A local horse trainer was surprised to learn that some of his steeds had ingested poppy seeds that had stowed away in horse feed – disqualifying three from racing after testing positive for opium 'use'. Never try to enter a poppy field, it's illegal and most are protected by electric fences. Believe the warning signs on fences: the unrefined sap from opium poppies can kill.

---

founded in 1807 when a number of free land-holding farmers were moved to Van Diemen's Land from Norfolk Island. It's one of the few Tasmanian towns not established by convicts.

The village is proud of its gardens, hosting the **Longford Garden Festival** each November. Well known to brown trout–fishing enthusiasts, Longford is also a popular base for fishing in the nearby rivers and streams, and at Cressy 13km to the south.

There's an **online access centre** (☎ 6391 2200; Wellington St; ☯ 10am-5 Mon-Fri), just behind the library, costing around $5.50 per hour and you'll find a Commonwealth Bank ATM next to the BP service station on Marlborough St.

SIGHTS & ACTIVITIES

Longford is spread out around **Memorial Park** and is known for architectural gems such as the bluestone **Anglican Church** (Goderich St), the **Town Hall** (Smith St), the **library** (Wellington St) and the **Queens Arms Hotel** (Wellington St).

The streets of this little town are also known for something quite different: their stint in the 1950s and '60s as an Australian Grand Prix track. The **Country Club Hotel** (19 Wellington St) is a shrine to this racy past with racing photos and paraphernalia all over the walls. Nowadays the town's main event is the **Blessing of the Harvest Festival** in March, with a street parade and country-fair stalls.

There are two wonderful historic estates around Longford, both established by the Thomas Archer family in the colony's early days. **Woolmers** (☎ 6391 2230; www.woolmers.com.au; Woolmers Lane; adult/child/senior/family from $18/5/15/41.50; ☯ 10am-4.30pm, tours 11am, 12.30am, 2pm, 3.30pm) dates from 1819 and you'll feel like you've stepped back in time, wandering through the antique-

filled rooms. Here there's also the **National Rose Garden** – two hectares of headily scented blooms. At **Brickendon** (☎ 6391 1383; www.brickendon.com.au; Woolmers Lane; adult/child/concession/family $12/4.50/11/35; ☯ 9.30am-5pm Tue-Sun, closed Jul & Aug), the homestead is still lived in by the Archer family, so you can't visit that but you can spend time in the gorgeous old gardens and the farm village. Kiddies will love the animal feeding, and there's trout fishing in the lake. Both properties offer accommodation (see below). To reach both, follow the signs from Wellington St in Longford.

SLEEPING & EATING

Longford Riverside Caravan Park (☎ /fax 6391 1470; 2a Archer St; unpowered/powered sites d $18/22, dm $40, d $40-60) You can fish and kayak right from the green riverbanks of this park. There are some cheap bunks, decent rooms and cabins, and the amenities block is disabled-friendly. Under-control dogs welcome.

Country Club Hotel (☎ 6391 1155; 19 Wellington St; s/d $40/50) This busy pub is a bit of a shrine to Longford's car racing days and you can dine in the Chequered Flag bistro here among the fast-car memorabilia. It's good food including all the usual pub suspects (bistro is open lunch and dinner).

Racecourse Inn (☎ 6391 2352; www.racecourseinn .com; 114 Marlborough St; d $155-195) There's welcoming (and gay-friendly) hospitality in this restored Georgian inn. The rooms are beautifully antique decorated and the à la carte breakfasts are distinctly gourmet: think eggs Benedict, eggs with smoked salmon, and berries and fruits from the property. Meals are served most nights in the restaurant too.

Brickendon (☎ 6391 1383; accommodation@brickendon.com.au; Woolmers Lane; B&B historic cottage d $160, farm cottage d $150) Brickendon has two well-equipped, early-19th-century cottages (one each for 'coachman' and 'gardener' wannabes), furnished with antiques and family collectables, plus three much newer self-contained cottages with old-style trimmings.

Woolmers (☎ 6391 2230; fax 6391 2270; www.woolmers.com.au; Woolmers Lane; d from $170) There are seven little cottages set in the grounds of Woolmers. Most once housed servants and free settlers on the estate and they are now all done up for visitors. The Gardeners Cottage is heartbreakingly beautiful.

Servants Kitchen Restaurant (☎ 6391 1163; Woolmers Lane; ☺ lunch) You can take Devonshire teas and lunches in front of the roaring log fire at this little restaurant on Woolmers Estate. If you're staying in the cottages it can arrange a two- or three-course dinner hamper ($25/30) to take away.

JJ's Bakery & Old Mill Cafe (☎ 6391 2364; 52 Wellington St; mains $10-20; ☺ 7am-5.30pm Mon-Fri, to 5pm Sat & Sun) There are delectable bakery offerings at this happening place in the Old Emerald flour mill. Pizzas here include the legendary satay chicken and mango variety and it also does various bruschettas, pies and quiches. You can finish off with all things sweet and heavenly: pavlovas, mud muffins and a fine custard tart.

Evandale
☎ 03 / pop 1035

Walk down the main street in Evandale and you'll feel like you've stepped back a century, which is why the whole town is National Trust–listed. It's such an attractive place you'll want to take time to wander its sweet, quiet streets, browse its galleries and market stalls and hang out in cafés. The highlight of the year here is February's National Penny Farthing Championships, when one-wheel warriors race the town's streets at alarming speed.

INFORMATION
At the informative **visitors centre** (☎ 6391 8128; 18 High St; ☺ 10am-3pm) you can pick up the pamphlet *Evandale Heritage Walk* ($3), which will guide you around the town's historic features. The history room here has a display on famous locals including painter John Glover and highly decorated WWI soldier Harry Murray. Both are commemorated with statues on Russell St: Glover, 18 stone and club-footed and Murray hurling a grenade.

SIGHTS & ACTIVITIES
As you enter town travelling from the airport to the north, there's a castle-like **water tower** (High St) which encloses a convict-dug tunnel designed to supply water to Launceston. Evandale's two historic **churches** – both St Andrews – face off across High St, one Uniting and the other Anglican. There are also stately homes like **Solomon House** (High St), **Fallgrove** (Logan Rd) and **Ingleside** (Russell St). Also on Russell St is **Brown's Village Store**, which still has the original Victorian wooden shop-fitout (and seemingly some of its wares).

The highlight of Evandale's constellation of historic properties (south of town via Nile Rd) is **Clarendon** (☎ 6398 6220; 634 Station Rd; adult/child/concession/family $10/free/8/20; ☺ 10am-4pm). Built in 1838 in neo-classical style, it looks like it's stepped straight out of *Gone with the Wind* and was long the grandest home in the colony. The antique-graced home is set in seven park-like hectares on the South Esk River bank and you can tour both. For accommodation here, see p226.

Evandale Market (Falls Park; ☺ 9am-1pm) is held each Sunday, and is an exuberant mix of happy locals selling fresh fruit and veg (much of it organic), kids' pony rides (and occasionally a mini train) as well as stalls selling crafts and bric-a-brac.

Foodies shouldn't miss the **Tasmanian Gourmet Sauce Co** (☎ 6391 8437; www.gourmetsauce.com.au; 174 Leighlands Rd; ☺ 10am-5pm Oct-Apr, to 4pm Wed-Sun May-Sep), 3km west of Evandale. Here local fruits and berries are wizarded into delicious jams, sauces, chutneys and relishes. Taste and buy to your heart's content. You can stroll the fabulous topiary-laden gardens too.

FESTIVALS & EVENTS
February's **Evandale Village Fair & National Penny Farthing Championships** (www.evandalevillagefair.com; adult/child $7/free) is when the town comes out to play. There are Penny Farthing races at breakneck speed, a market and the occasional pipe-band parading the streets.

SLEEPING
Stables Accommodation (☎ 6391 8048; evandalestables@bigpond.com; 5 Russell St; B&B s/d $100/140, extra adult/child $30/25) The Stables has three comfortable self-contained units set back off the street behind Browns Village Store (above). Ask for the one with the countryside mural behind the bed.

Solomon Cottage (☎ 6391 8331; 1 High St; s/d $100/130) This cottage was built in 1838 as a

LAUNCESTON & AROUND

bakery. Joseph Solomon would never have envisaged his oven taken up by a queen-sized bed (note the brick-vaulted ceiling!). The cottage has two bedrooms and the price includes a cooked breakfast with fresh croissants and fruit.

Clarendon (☎ 6398 6190; 634 Station Rd; d $110) This comfy, cottagey accommodation is in an idyllically quiet setting on the estate. TV, microwave and tea- and coffee-making facilities are included and breakfasts can be, on request. Otherwise, wander over to Menzies Restaurant (open for breakfast and lunch) for a cooked breakfast feast.

Arendon Cottage (☎ 6391 8093; 30 Russell St; d 120, extra person $10) You can sit out on the veranda here and watch the world go by through the white roses. The beautifully kitted-out cottage sleeps up to four. You can get cosy by the wood-burning stove. The breakfast provisions are abundant.

ourpick Wesleyan Chapel (☎ 6331 9337; 28 Russell St; $120) Built in 1836, this tiny brick chapel has been used as a druids' hall, an RSL hall and a meeting place for Scouts. Now, under the high ceiling, it's eminently stylish accommodation for two.

Farthings Village Accommodation (☎ 6391 8251; bookings@farthingsvillageaccommodation.com.au; 16 Russell St; d $140, extra person $20) Sleeping up to four, this cute cottage has been lovingly restored in old-world style. The master bedroom has a king-sized four-poster and the bathroom has a spa. Inquire at the Evandale General Store.

Other recommendations:

Clarendon Arms Hotel (☎ 6391 8181; 11 Russell St; s/d $45/80) This pub has decent budget rooms with shared facilities, and does lunch and dinner daily.

Prince of Wales Hotel (☎ 6391 8381; cnr High & Collins Sts; d $55-70, f $70-80) Less salubrious than the other pub in town, the Prince of Wales also offers cheap accommodation.

EATING

Muse Coffee Bar (☎ 6391 8552; 14 Russell St; mains $7-18; ☽ 10am-5pm, Fri & Sat 6-8pm) This cool little eatery does morning and afternoon teas and delicious lunches using plenty of fresh local produce. Try the Tasmanian smoked salmon on sourdough with figs. Fridays and Saturdays are pizza nights.

Ingleside Bakery Café (☎ 6391 8682; 4 Russell St; mains $15-20; ☽ breakfast & lunch) Sit in the beautiful walled courtyard or under the high ceiling inside these atmospheric former council chambers. Fresh baking smells waft from the

wood oven, making the bakery wares quite irresistible. They do delectable pies and pasties ($6), a swagman's lunch for the hungry ($20) and all manner of sweet treats.

Clarendon Arms Hotel (☎ 6391 8181; 11 Russell St; mains $13-20; ☽ lunch & dinner) This pub serves up commendable bistro meals and has an outdoor beer garden where you can dine under the trees. Try the homemade beef-and-Guinness pie.

Ben Lomond National Park

This 165-sq-km park takes in the whole of the Ben Lomond massif: a craggy alpine plateau some 14km long by 6km wide. The plateau reaches heights of 1300m and its peaks are above 1500m. Legges Tor (1573m) is the second-highest peak in Tasmania and in fine weather affords amazing 360-degree views. A feature of the park is the tumbled landscape of dolerite columns (popular with rock climbers) and chunky scree slopes.

Ben Lomond has long been Tasmania's St Moritz – well not quite, but when the snow does fall the lifts grind into action and there is skiing here. The park's also magnificent in the summer when alpine flowers run riot.

Ben Lomond was named after its Scottish namesake by the founder of Launceston, Lieutenant Colonel Paterson, in 1804. From 1805 to 1806 Colonel Legge explored the plateau and named its features after explorers of the Nile River in Africa and members of the fledgling Van Diemen's Land colony.

SIGHTS & ACTIVITIES

In summer, there's easy walking here. It's two hours each way to **Legges Tor** from Carr Villa, about halfway up the mountain. You can also climb to the top from the alpine village on the plateau, which takes about 30 minutes each way on marked tracks. (All walkers and cross-country skiers should register at the self-registration booth at the alpine village.)

If you're happy to go off track, you can walk across the plateau in almost any direction. This is easy enough in fine weather but not recommended in less-than-complete visibility. Unless you're well equipped, walking south of the ski village isn't advised.

The snow can be fickle here but the ski season is generally from early July to mid September. Full-day ski-lift passes cost $50/45/35/25 per adult/student/teenager 13 to17/child, while half-day passes cost

$30/25/20/15. Under sevens and over 70s ride free! There are three T-bars and four poma lifts. **Ben Lomond Snow Sports** (☎ 6393 6105; ◔ from 9am) runs a kiosk selling takeaway fare and a shop doing ski rental package deals. Skis, boots, poles, a day lift pass and a lesson cost $90/78/65 per adult/teenager 13-17 years/ child under 13.

SLEEPING & EATING

There's accommodation year-round at Tasmania's highest pub, **Creek Inn** (☎ 6390 6199; d in summer/winter $90/180, extra child in summer/winter $5/25). There are cosily heated en suite rooms here and the best thing is – snow conditions permitting – you can ski right to the door. There's also a fully licensed **restaurant** (mains $20; ◔ 10am-4pm in summer, breakfast lunch & dinner in winter) where you can top up your skiing or hiking energy.

There's also a good **camping** area, 1km along from the park entrance, which offers secluded, cleared, unpowered sites, flushing toilets, drinking water and a fantastic lookout.

GETTING THERE & AWAY

In the ski season **McDermotts Coaches** (Map p204; ☎ 6394 3535; 40 St John St, Launceston; adult/concession/family return $27/21/87) runs a service departing from the back entrance of the Launceston Sport & Surf store (the Birchalls car park) at 8.30am daily, departing the mountain at 4pm. An additional shuttle service runs between the rangers station ($14/11 per adult/concession return) and the alpine village throughout the day. Park entrance fees are $11 per person – you can buy them on the bus. Book a day in advance.

Outside the ski season, driving is your only transport option. Note that the track up to the plateau is unsealed and includes Jacob's Ladder, a very steep climb with six dramatic hairpin bends and no safety barriers. During the snow season chains are standard equipment. Don't forget antifreeze in winter.

LAUNCESTON & AROUND

Devonport & the Northwest

There's a rule of thumb in this part of Tasmania: the further west you go, the remoter it gets. Start in the countryside around the port city of Devonport and you'll see a land of rich, red earth chequered by an agricultural patchwork of fields. This is prime farming country: Tasmania's dairy, beef and vegetable heartland, framed by the jagged peaks of the island's alpine core.

As you work your way west along the shores of Bass Strait, the seaside towns become smaller, the beaches more rugged, the inland forests more dense. Rich farmland gives way to windswept cattle paddocks bounded by groves of the northwest's emblematic, papery-barked tea tree. If you make it to the furthest northwest reaches, you'll discover an isolated territory, excoriated by the buffeting winds of the Roaring 40s, with an excitingly world's-end feel.

There's plenty to attract the traveller to Tasmania's less-visited quarter. You may arrive right into the heart of it if you voyage here on the *Spirit of Tasmania*. Close by you'll find such varied diversions as the magical caves near Mole Creek, the mountain highs of the Walls of Jerusalem and the arty little towns of Deloraine and Sheffield. Explore along the coast and you'll find the idyllic beach of Boat Harbour, rugged Rocky Cape National Park and historic, seaside Stanley. From here you can plunge into the remotest west of all: the mysterious, deep rainforests of Tasmania's Tarkine; the fierce beaches of Marrawah, with their gigantic western waves; or Woolnorth, where they farm the wind and you can breathe the cleanest air on earth.

DEVONPORT & THE NORTHWEST

HIGHLIGHTS

- Watching Mexican-waving glow worms in the limestone caves at **Mole Creek Karst National Park** (p242)

- Meeting the eclectic Paper People and browsing the handmade paper display at **Creative Paper Tasmania** (p253) in Burnie

- Camping at the dramatic **Walls of Jerusalem National Park** (p243), especially snow-blanketed in winter

- Tiptoeing through the tulips in the ancient volcano of **Table Cape** (p257)

- Feeling the power of the Roaring 40s at **Stanley** (p260) as you stand victorious atop the Nut

- Driving – or better, cycling – the achingly remote **Western Explorer** (p268) on a true backblocks adventure

- Marvelling at the phenomenal reflections in the black waters of the **Pieman River** (p269)

- Hiking the deep forests and savage beaches of the **Tarkine Wilderness** (p268)

■ TELEPHONE CODE: 03   ■ www.devonporttasmania.travel   ■ www.tasmaniasnorthwest.com.au

Getting There & Around

AIR

QantasLink (☎ 13 13 13) connects Devonport to Melbourne and **Regional Express** (Rex; ☎ 13 17 13) services Burnie/Wynyard airport at Wynyard.

BICYCLE

The main (A1) route west from Launceston is best avoided due to heavy traffic, but there's plenty of good cycling on the minor routes in this area: the B54 is better for travel to Deloraine. There's less traffic on the A2 west of Burnie and it makes for pleasant cycling. There are plenty of meandering backroads throughout the northwest region where you can really get off the beaten track into rural Tasmania. The absolute highlight of cycling here is the remote gravel of the Western Explorer (C249) connecting Arthur River and Corinna. This traverses the glorious Tarkine Wilderness and is about as wild a region as it's possible to access by bike in Tasmania.

BUS

Redline Coaches (☎ 1300 360 000, 6336 1446; www.red linecoaches.com.au) services the north and northwest coasts daily, with buses from Launceston to Devonport ($24.40, 2½ hours), via towns including Deloraine ($16.60, 45 minutes) and Latrobe ($5.40, 15 minutes). This service picks up passengers at the *Spirit of Tasmania* ferry terminal. From Devonport buses continue west along the Bass Highway to Ulverstone ($6.70, 25 minutes), Penguin ($8.80, 40 minutes), Burnie ($13, one hour), Stanley ($32, two hours) and Smithton ($32, 2½ hours).

Tassielink Coaches (☎ 1300 300 520, 6336 9500; www.tassielink.com.au) work their way west from Launceston two to three times a week, depending on the season, ending up in Strahan. These buses stop in Devonport ($21.20, 1½ hours) Sheffield ($27, two hours 10 minutes), Gowrie Park ($35.60, 2½ hours) and Cradle Mountain ($53.30, three hours). From here they head southwest to Rosebery, Zeehan, Queenstown and Strahan. For further details, see p283. Tassielink also operates a daily express service, picking up passengers from Devonport's *Spirit of Tasmania* ferry terminal and running them to Launceston ($21.20, 1½ hours) and Hobart ($51.40, 4 hours). This service also runs daily in reverse from Hobart, reaching Devonport in time for the nightly ferry sailing.

There's a local bus operated by **Merseylink** (☎ 1300 367 590; www.merseylink.com.au) from

Monday to Saturday, running between Devonport and Latrobe ($3.10), and a separate service also run by Merseylink between Devonport and Port Sorell ($4) Monday to Friday. Both services depart from the Rooke St interchange in Devonport.

DEVONPORT

☎ 03 / pop 25,122

Devonport is best known to visitors to Tasmania as the port of the *Spirit of Tasmania I* and *II*, the smartly red-and-white ferries that connect the island state with the mainland. It's quite an evocative sight to see them, all lit up at night; when after three deep burps of the horn they cruise past the end of the main street to begin their voyage north. Devonport is a waterside city: it straddles the Mersey River and seascapes stretch out from it to either side. One of the landmarks in town is the Mersey Bluff Lighthouse, built in 1889 to warn ships off the rocky coastline and guide them safely into port. The protected Mersey River mouth still serves as an important harbour for exporting agricultural produce from surrounding fertile lands. Many visitors get off the ferry in Devonport, jump in their cars and scoot. This quiet little port town is possibly not the most glamorous spot in the state, but take your time to ground your feet on Tasmanian soil here: walk along the Mersey and up to the lighthouse for unmissable views over the coastline and Bass Strait.

Orientation

Devonport is spread about the banks of the Mersey River. East Devonport is the location of the docks and the Spirit of Tasmania (italics) ferry terminal, while the west bank of the river is where you'll find the centre of town. Formby Rd, alongside the Mersey, and Rooke St are the main thoroughfares, and Rooke St becomes a pleasant pedestrian mall in the heart of town.

Information

Most banks have branches and ATMs in or near the Rooke Street Mall.

Visitors centre (☎ 6424 4466; tourism@devonport .tas.gov.au; 92 Formby Rd; ☽ 7.30am–9pm or 9pm) This friendly and efficient visitors centre has smiling faces to meet all ferry arrivals – the 9pm closure is when there are day crossings of the ferry, which arrive at 7pm.

Post office (88 Formby Rd)

DEVONPORT & THE NORTHWEST

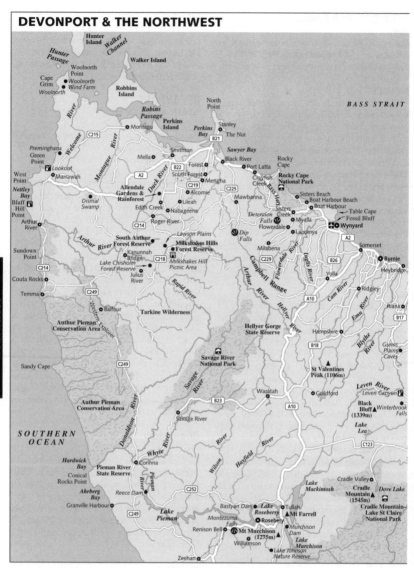

BASS STRAIT

SOUTHERN OCEAN

Online access centre (☎ 6424 9413; 21 Oldaker St; ⏱ 9.30am-5.30pm Mon-Fri, to 1.30 Sat; per 15 min $2) This centre is located in Devonport's library.

Backpacker's Barn (☎ 6424 3628; 10-12 Edward St; ⏱ 8am-6pm Mon-Fri, to 4pm Sat) This is *the* spot in Devonport to buy or hire outdoor gear and get advice on outdoor adventures. They also have showers for weary travellers ($4) and storage lockers ($2 per day).

Sights & Activities
TIAGARRA

Get your grounding in Tasmania's Aboriginal history at **Tiagarra** (☎ 6424 8250; Bluff Rd; adult/child/family $4/2.50/10; ⏱ 9am-5pm) on the Mersey Bluff headland close to the lighthouse. The absorbing displays here tells the story of Aboriginal culture in Tasmania, from the time humans

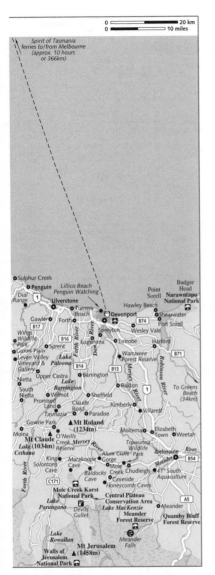

first crossed over the land bridge that's now under Bass Strait. There's a soberingly frank assessment of the decimation of Aboriginal society and culture at the time of European invasion. Outside, you can follow the marked trail around the headland to see some of Tiagarra's collection of aboriginal rock carvings (petroglyphs); some are thought to be more than 10,000 years old. At time of research, Tiagarra was in the planning process for a brand new building and enhanced displays.

DEVONPORT MARITIME MUSEUM

This excellent **museum** (☎ 6424 7100; 6 Gloucester Ave; adult/child/family $4/1/8; ☒ 10am-4.30pm Tue-Sun Oct-Mar, to 4pm Tue-Sun Apr-Sep) is in the former harbourmaster's residence (c 1920) and pilot station near the foreshore. It has an extensive collection of flags and other maritime paraphernalia, including a superb set of models from the ages of sail through steam to the present seagoing passenger ferries.

DON RIVER RAILWAY

You don't have to be a trainspotter to love this collection of locomotives. The **railway** (☎ 6424 6335; www.donriverrailway.com.au; Forth Main Rd; adult/child/pensioner/family $10/6/8/25; ☒ 9am-5pm) is 4km west of town, just off the Bass Highway. Trainheads will go crazy over the brightly painted rolling stock. The entry price includes a half-hour ride in a diesel train (between 10am and 4pm), and you can hop on the puffing steam train on Sundays and public holidays.

DEVONPORT REGIONAL GALLERY

This excellent **gallery** (☎ 6424 8296; 45-47 Stewart St; admission free; ☒ 10am-5pm Mon-Sat, 2-5pm Sun) houses predominantly 20th-century Tasmanian paintings, contemporary art by local and mainland artists, plus ceramics and glasswork.

HOME HILL

The National Trust–administered **Home Hill** (☎ 6424 8055; 77 Middle Rd; adult/ under 18/concession $8/free/6; ☒ 1.30-4pm Tue-Thu, Sat & Sun, Jul-Aug by appointment) was the residence of Joseph Lyons (Tasmania's only prime minister of Australia; 1932–39). Lyons lived here with his 12 children and his wife Dame Enid Lyons, who was the first woman to be sworn in as a member of the House of Representatives (1943) and as a federal cabinet minister (1949).

HOUSE OF ANVERS

You could wander through the museum here and learn about how the delights of the cocoa bean were first discovered by the Aztecs, but you might as well give in: everybody knows you're here for the chocolate. **House of Anvers** (☎ 6426 2958; www.anvers-chocolate.com.au; 9025 Bass Hwy, Latrobe; ☒ 7am-5pm) is a chocolate factory that creates a range of sweet treats: fudges,

DEVONPORT

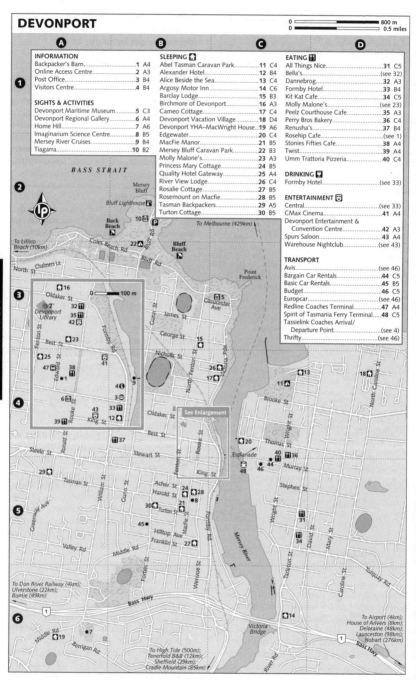

0 — 800 m
0 — 0.5 miles

INFORMATION

Backpacker's Barn	**1**	A4
Online Access Centre	**2**	A3
Post Office	**3**	B4
Visitors Centre	**4**	B4

SIGHTS & ACTIVITIES

Devonport Maritime Museum	**5**	C3
Devonport Regional Gallery	**6**	A4
Home Hill	**7**	A6
Imaginarium Science Centre	**8**	B5
Mersey River Cruises	**9**	B4
Tiagarra	**10**	B2

SLEEPING

Abel Tasman Caravan Park	**11**	C4
Alexander Hotel	**12**	B4
Alice Beside the Sea	**13**	C4
Argosy Motor Inn	**14**	C6
Barclay Lodge	**15**	B3
Birchmore of Devonport	**16**	A3
Cameo Cottage	**17**	C4
Devonport Vacation Village	**18**	D4
Devonport YHA–MacWright House	**19**	A6
Edgewater	**20**	C4
MacFie Manor	**21**	B5
Mersey Bluff Caravan Park	**22**	B3
Molly Malone's	**23**	A3
Princess Mary Cottage	**24**	B5
Quality Hotel Gateway	**25**	A4
River View Lodge	**26**	C4
Rosalie Cottage	**27**	B5
Rosemount on Macfie	**28**	B5
Tasman Backpackers	**29**	A5
Turton Cottage	**30**	B5

EATING

All Things Nice	**31**	C5
Bella's	(see 32)	
Dannebrog	**32**	A3
Formby Hotel	**33**	B4
Kit Kat Cafe	**34**	C5
Molly Malone's	(see 23)	
Peelz Courthouse Cafe	**35**	A3
Perry Bros Bakery	**36**	C4
Renusha's	**37**	B4
Roseship Cafe	(see 1)	
Stonies Fifties Cafe	**38**	A4
Twist	**39**	A4
Umm Trattoria Pizzeria	**40**	C4

DRINKING

Formby Hotel	(see 33)	

ENTERTAINMENT

Central	(see 33)	
CMax Cinema	**41**	A4
Devonport Entertainment & Convention Centre	**42**	A3
Spurs Saloon	**43**	A4
Warehouse Nightclub	(see 43)	

TRANSPORT

Avis	(see 46)	
Bargain Car Rentals	**44**	C5
Basic Car Rentals	**45**	B5
Budget	**46**	C5
Europcar	(see 46)	
Redline Coaches Terminal	**47**	A4
Spirit of Tasmania Ferry Terminal	**48**	C5
Tassielink Coaches Arrival/ Departure Point	(see 4)	
Thrifty	(see 46)	

BASS STRAIT

Mersey Bluff

Bluff Lighthouse

Back Beach

To Lillico Beach (10km)

Coles Beach Rd

Bluff Beach

To Melbourne (429km)

Point Frederick

Gloucester Ave

James St

George St

Nicholls St

Brooke St

Oldaker St

Best St

Thomas St

Esplanade

Murray St

Stephen St

Acher St

Harold St

Turton St

Hilltop Ave

Franklin St

King's St

Steele St

Stewart St

Tasman St

Greenway Ave

Valley Rd

Middle Rd

Forbes St

Wenvoe St

Mersey River

Victoria Bridge

River Rd

Bass Hwy

To Don River Railway (4km); Ulverstone (22km); Burnie (49km)

To High Tide (500m); Tenerfold B&B (12km); Sheffield (29km); Cradle Mountain (85km)

To Airport (4km); House of Anvers (8km); Deloraine (48km); Launceston (98km); Hobart (276km)

Middle Rd

Berrigan Rd

See Enlargement

Oldaker St

Devonport Library

Fenton St

Best St

Edward St

Rooke St

King St

Ronald St

William St

Gunn St

North St

Chalmers La

North Fenton Rd

Formby Rd

0 — 100 m

truffles, and the most amazing chocolate-orange slices. You can also come here for your breakfast *pain au chocolat* washed down with what's surely one of the best hot chocolates known to man. The factory is 8km southeast of town on the Bass Hwy.

IMAGINARIUM SCIENCE CENTRE

This unexpected find in Devonport is a hit with kids. The **Imaginarium Science Centre** (☎ 6423 1466; 19-23 MacFie St, access via Wenvoe St carpark; adult/4-17 yr/concession/family $8/5.50/6.50/26; ☺ 10am-4pm Mon-Thu, 12-5pm Sat & Sun) has all sorts of hands-on scientific displays: you won't be able to tear the young ones away from the tower puzzles, echo tube and air-message contraption. There are magnetic trains in the area for kids aged three to seven, and a dressing-up wardrobe that will transform your little darling into anything from police officer to pirate.

PENGUIN-WATCHING

Between late August and March at Lillico Beach, off the Bass Hwy on the western edge of town, you can watch little penguins emerge from the sea and return to their burrows at dusk. There's a special viewing area where you can get up close, and volunteers are usually on hand to explain the secrets of these creatures, the smallest penguins on earth.

Tours

Mersey River Cruises (☎ 6424 4466) operates the cruise vessel *Centurion*, which departs from the pontoon opposite the visitors centre. You'll head upriver towards Latrobe and views of Mt Roland, then edge out through the mouth of the river onto Bass Strait in search of dolphins. There are 1½-hour cruises daily at 1pm and 3pm (adult/child $22.50/11) and a three-hour dinner cruise at 6.30pm ($60/30).

You can swoop over the beauties of northern Tasmania in a light plane on a sightseeing flight with **Tasair** (☎ 6427 9777; www.tasair.com .au). For a snapshot of Devonport's environs there's the Northern Experience, which will take you over Lake Barrington, Mt Rowland and Port Sorell ($77 per person). See Tassie's Alpine heart with the Cradle Experience flight ($121 per person).

To be shown some of Tasmania by an entirely passionate and charming Tasmanian, consider taking a tour with **Murray's Day Out** (☎ 6424 5250; www.murraysdayout.com.au; day trips per person from $110). Murray offers 'service with humour' and can take you all over the place in his comfortable van (seating up to seven). Go all the way west to Marrawah, drop in on Cradle Mountain or just tool around the back lanes near Devonport.

Sleeping

BUDGET
Hostels

Tasman Backpackers (☎ 6423 2335; www.tasmanback packers.com.au; 114 Tasman St; dm/tw per person $16/18, d $50, without bathroom $40) This recently renovated hostel was once a sprawling nurses' quarters but it's now a friendly place to stay with a great, international feel. The en suite doubles all have TV/DVD player – and there's an in-house movie theatre for the rest. They offer free ferry/bus station pick-ups, and can make tour and bus bookings.

Devonport YHA–MacWright House (☎ 6424 5696; 115 Middle Rd; dm/s from $18.50/25.50) This YHA hostel in a large old house offers simple, clean accommodation and a friendly vibe. It's 3km from the city centre, about a 40-minute walk or a five-minute bus ride (bus 40). There's a discount for YHA members. A good share kitchen and laundry complete the facilities.

Pubs/Hotels

Molly Malone's (☎ 6424 1898; mollymalones@vantage group.com.au; 34 Best St; dm/d $20/50, d without bathroom $35; ▣) Even Devonport has a go at your ol' Irish pub – and they do a pretty good job. This place has an excellent reputation for its bar food. Upstairs it's not quite as salubrious. There are basic (bordering on grungy) dorms and doubles. Still, it's a good place to crash cheaply and there's a lively atmosphere on Friday and Saturday when the pub below (see p236) gets thumpin'.

Alexander Hotel (☎ 6424 2252; 78 Formby Rd; dm/s/d $25/49/59) The rooms here are no great shakes, but it's a cheap and simple place to stay, close to the centre of town. The pub downstairs is the kind of place where you're sure to get talking to locals.

Formby Hotel (☎ 6424 1601; fax 6424 8123; 82 Formby Rd; dm/s/d $45/69/79, extra person $20) There are clean and simple rooms above this pub, some of which have superb views of the river – you can watch the *Spirit of Tasmania* voyage past your window. There's also great food downstairs (see p235). Note that the dorm room is men only.

Camping & Cabins

Mersey Bluff Caravan Park (☎ 6424 8655; mbcp1@ bigpond.net.au; Bluff Rd; unpowered/powered sites d $15/18, on-site vans d $40, cabins d from $62) In a seaside setting on Mersey Bluff, this pleasantly treed park is just steps from the beach. There's a campers kitchen and BBQ facilities, a takeaway shop on site and walks nearby.

Abel Tasman Caravan Park (☎ 6427 8794; www .tigerresortstas.com.au; 6 Wright St; unpowered sites $20, powered sites $23-26, on-site vans $45-60, cabins $75-120) Right by East Devonport Beach and only 800m from where the *Spirit of Tasmania* docks, this friendly park has neat cabins, clean amenities, BBQ areas and a campers kitchen.

Devonport Vacation Village (☎ 6427 8886; fax 6427 8388; 20-24 Nth Caroline St; unpowered/powered sites/en suite sites d $22/26/30, cabins d $62-92) This large village is another budget option and its location in East Devonport makes it a convenient place to stay if you need to hop on or off the ferry.

MIDRANGE
Cottages

`ourpick` **Cameo Cottage** (☎ 6427 0991, 0439-658 503; www.devonportbedandbreakfast.com; 27 Victoria Pde; d $140-160, extra person $30) Tucked away in quiet back streets, this ultra-neat two-bedroom cottage was built in 1914, but is now thoroughly up-to-date. It's got a well-equipped kitchen, cozy lounge where you can watch DVDs to your heart's content, a laundry, and a quiet garden where you can cook up a storm on the BBQ.

Devonport Historic Cottages (☎ 1800 240 031; www .devonportcottages.com; d $150) manages three attractive weatherboard cottages: **Rosalie Cottage** (66 Wenvoe St), **Turton Cottage** (28 Turton St) and **Princess Mary Cottage** (42 MacFie St). All date from the late 1800s, and have been beautifully refurbished as fully equipped accommodation and are only a short stroll from the city centre. There are ample breakfast provisions and log fires to doze in front of. Extra touches include an old gramophone in Rosalie and hand-stencilled walls in Turton.

Guesthouses & B&Bs

Alice Beside the Sea (☎ /fax 6427 8605; www.alicebeside thesea.com; 1 Wright St; d $99-130) Located close to the ferry terminals, this compact B&B offers comfortable, two-bedroom, self-contained accommodation across the road from the beach and close to supermarkets.

River View Lodge (☎ 6424 7357; www.riverviewlodge .com.au; 18 Victoria Pde; s with/without bathroom $103/90, d with/without bathroom $120/100) This friendly lodge is just across green parkland from the waters of the Mersey, only minutes' walk from town. It's clean, bright and homely: there's a piano and roaring log fire in the guest lounge, and scrumptious cooked breakfasts are laid on.

Rosemount on Macfie (☎ 6424 7406; www.rose mountonmacfie.com; 47 MacFie St; d $100-145) A heritage home set in rose-filled gardens awaits you here. Rosemount offers spacious, two-room apartments, with queen sized beds and period décor. Some rooms have spas and include ample continental breakfast provisions.

MacFie Manor (☎ 6424 1719; www.macfiemanor .com.au MacFie St; s $100, d $110-130) The beautiful wrought-iron tracery on this handsome Federation home tells you you've found one of Devonport's nicest place to stay. The comely decoration continues inside, with four-poster beds, carved timber fireplaces and a Scottish theme: you can choose from the Edinburgh, Kilmarnock or Stewart rooms. Fully cooked breakfasts are part of the deal.

Tenerfold B&B (☎ /fax 6427 3170; www.tenerfold bandb.com.au; 84 Melrose Dr, Aberdeen; d $140) Just a 10-minute drive south of the CBD, this luxuriously appointed two-bedroom apartment is good value, with rural views in a secluded and private setting surrounded by a tranquil garden. To get here take the Devonport Main Rd (B14) south continuing on Sheffield Rd, turning right at the C146. There's a fully cooked breakfast included in the rate.

Birchmore of Devonport (☎ 6423 1336; www.bedsand breakfasts.com.au/Birchmore; 10 Oldaker St; s $145, d $170-190) This old Federation dame has spacious, well-appointed rooms and is just a minute away from the city centre. A good cooked breakfast is served each morning in the conservatory.

Motels & Hotels

Argosy Motor Inn (☎ 1800 657 068, 6427 8872; Tarleton St; s $80-120, d $80-129) It can't be said that this brick establishment is a thing of great beauty, but the rooms are clean and tidy, ranging from standard to 'executive' suites with spa, and the views over the Mersey are lovely. There's also a bistro on site.

Edgewater (☎ 6427 8441; www.edgewater-devonport .com.au; 4 Thomas St; d $90-230; ▣) This once-dowdy motel has been snazzed up recently and is now a good place to stay in East Devonport, in a better-than-motel sort of way. Some rooms have spas and pleasant water views, and there's a popular restaurant on site. It's just a hop and a skip from where the *Spirit of Tasmania* docks.

Barclay Lodge (☎ 1800 809 340, 6424 4722; 112 North Fenton St; d $105-130, units $135-165, extra person $25; 🖭) This may not be your most architecturally rewarding stay in Tasmania but you'll find all sorts of good facilities, including a tennis court, swimming pool and tourist information. All units have a kitchen, and one unit is equipped for disabled travellers.

Quality Hotel Gateway (☎ 6424 4922; www .gatewayinn.com.au; 16 Fenton St; d 155-250; 🖳) The standard accommodation here is of the rather ordinary motel variety, but if you are after somewhere really top-notch to stay in Devonport, check out the hotel's deluxe spa rooms: these are swanky and super-stylish and feel like they belong to an entirely classy establishment.

Eating
RESTAURANTS
Renusha's (☎ 6424 2293; 132 William St; mains $9-18; ☺ lunch Wed-Fri, dinner Tue-Sat) The gaudy décor here may be what first catches your attention, and you'll be glad it did: the food is sensational. It serves superb Indian food and a fine Italian pasta too, and has earned a local reputation for being consistently great.

Umm Trattoria Pizzeria (☎ 6427 7055; 13 Murray St; mains $12-20; ☺ dinner Wed-Sun) There's fine Italian fare at this friendly little place in East Devonport. The pizzas, straight out of the wood oven, are simply superb – light, crispy and delicious. Try the blackboard specials for a new take on your pizza favourites.

Bella's (☎ 6424 7933; 159 Rooke St; mains $15-25; ☺ 7am-10pm Tue-Sat) Don't be put off by the slightly daggy décor and the faux olive trees. Bella's has a reputation for its traditional Italian pizzas and great pastas, with a range of lip-smacking sauces. They serve good cooked breakfasts and light lunches too.

High Tide (☎ 6424 6200; 17 Devonport Rd; mains $15-30; ☺ lunch, dinner Mon-Sat, breakfast Fri-Sun) The panoramic views over the Mersey River, Mt Roland and the Great Western Tiers aren't the only excellent thing here. There's a varied and frequently changing menu that sports choices such as marinated venison fillet, Moroccan prawns, curried scallops and a famously good seafood chowder. To get here, follow Formby Rd south towards Quoiba. The restaurant is off to the left on the river bank shortly after crossing under the Bass Highway.

Dannebrog (☎ 6424 4477; 161 Rooke St; mains $16-35; ☺ lunch & dinner) There's nothing Scandinavian about this restaurant, but it's named after the Danish flag in honour of Tasmanian Crown Princess Mary of Denmark (see p119). If you're a committed carnivore you'll feel at home here amid all the steaks. There's a highly recommended 800g rump steak served with salad, chips and a sauce of your choice ($35).

Twist (☎ 6423 2033; 5 Rooke St; mains $22-27; ☺ lunch & dinner Tue-Fri, dinner Sat, brunch & lunch from 10am Sun) This smart new restaurant with a lime green 'twist' to its décor is getting rave reviews from locals. Try the pan-fried wallaby sirloin served with pepperberry sauce.

PUBS
Molly Malone's (☎ 6424 1898; 34 Best St; mains $9-27) Hungry for some down-home fare with the occasional Irish twist? Then you can't go wrong at Molly's. There's a fine seafood platter for two ($55), with enormous king prawns; excellent bangers and mash; and, of course, a fine Belfast Beef and Guinness pie.

Alexander Hotel (☎ 6424 2252; 78 Formby Rd; mains $17-25; ☺ lunch & dinner) This local favourite does all the standard pub fare. The roast is the hit in the friendly dining rooms, and the steaks and seafood have a good reputation among Devonport's townsfolk.

Formby Hotel (☎ 6424 1601; 82 Formby Rd; mains $19-27; ☺ lunch & dinner) The refurbed dining room here offers slap-up bistro meals including pizza, pastas, salads, steaks and seafood. There are excellent fresh juices and smoothies at the café bar, and coffee and cakes between meal times.

CAFÉS & QUICK EATS
All Things Nice (☎ 6427 0028; 175 Tarleton St; ☺ 24hr) This bakery and café is located near the ferry terminal. It offers all manner of bakery items: gourmet chunky pies, including that Tassie icon, scallop pie ($5); cakes and other sweets; and a good strong cuppa.

Perry Bros Bakery (☎ 6427 8706; 67 Wright St; ☺ 6am-8pm Mon-Fri, 6am-1pm Sat) specialises in excellent curry scallop pies ($3.60), great lunchtime menus and good cakes for in between. After an early-morning ferry arrival you can fill up here: the excellent gourmet breakfasts come with hash browns, baked beans and the lot.

Kit Kat Cafe (☎ 6427 8437; 175 Tarleton St; ☺ breakfast from 5.30am, lunch & dinner) This welcoming café offers hungry arrivals off the ferry big bacon-and-egg breakfasts ($7) and eat ins or take-aways including juicy, delicious burgers, fish and chips, wraps and sandwiches. There's a play corner where the little tackers can keep busy while you break your fast.

Rosehip Cafe (☎ 6424 1917; 10-12 Edward St; meals $6.50-10.50; ☼ breakfast & lunch Mon-Sat) This café next to the Backpacker's Barn (p230) is the healthiest option in town. It prepares wholesome food and light snacks using plenty of organic produce. The spinach and sweet potato frittata is fantastic. Also available are delicious breakfasts and plenty of good salads.

Stonies Fifties Cafe (☎ 6424 2101; 77 Rooke St; meals $8-18; ☼ breakfast & lunch Mon-Sat) You can eat hearty all-day breakfasts at this classic Devonport diner, or choose from a good range of burgers: the Chubby Cheeser is its renowned cheese burger. The coffees here are the standout: they have 18 different types – all named after '50s music stars: say 'Little Richard' for an espresso.

Peelz Courthouse Cafe (☎ 6423 5373; 145-151 Rooke St; meals $9-17; ☼ 8.30am-4pm) There are freshly squeezed juices, smoothies, great coffees and fine chai lattés here. On Sundays you can enjoy a big brekky ($10.50) under the umbrellas outside. There are also good gourmet baguettes, burgers and pastas.

Drinking & Entertainment

Check the *Advocate* newspaper for entertainment listings.

Central (☎ 6424 1601; 82 Formby Rd; ☼ 3pm-midnight Wed, 3pm-1am Thu & Fri, 1pm-1am Sat, 1pm-9pm Sun, closed Mon & Tue) Set in the Formby Hotel, locals regard this as Devonport's best bar. It's all done in leather sofas and laid-back cool, and they fold the concertina windows open onto the river on warm nights. There are live bands Friday nights, Saturday nights are huge, and Sunday afternoons see acoustic sessions and a sophisticated crowd.

Warehouse Nightclub (☎ 6424 7851; 18 King St; admission $6-10; ☼ 10pm-late Thu-Sat) This is one of Devonport's few clubbing hangouts and draws a young crowd to boogie to up-and-coming bands a few times a month and Saturday-night DJs.

Spurs Saloon (☎ 6424 7851; 18 King St; ☼ 5pm-late Thus-Sat) Serves you drinks in a Wild West setting with barrels for tables and the requisite stuffed animal-head menagerie on the walls. There's karaoke here Thursday night, and the eight-ball tables are popular with the young blokes.

Molly Malone's (☎ 6424 1898; 34 Best St) An expansive, wood-panelled Irish den that gets big crowds guzzling its beer and watching live music on Friday and Saturday nights.

Cmax cinema (☎ 6420 2111; 5-7 Best St; adult/child $12/9) The Cmax hosts blockbusters and teen flicks. The plusher cinemas have deep sink-into seats.

Devonport Entertainment & Convention Centre (☎ 6420 2900; 145-151 Rooke St; ☼ box office 10am-4pm Mon-Fri) This venue stages everything from children's concerts to ABBA impersonators.

Getting There & Away
AIR

There are regular flights to/from Melbourne with QantasLink while Tasair flies between Devonport and King Island via Burnie/Wynyard.

BOAT

The **Spirit of Tasmania** (☎ 1800 634 906, 13 20 10; www.spiritoftasmania.com.au; ☼ telephone bookings 6.30am-9.30pm) sails ferries between Station Pier in Melbourne and the ferry terminal on the Esplanade in East Devonport. For details of services, see p336.

BUS

Redline Coaches (☎ 1300 360 000, 6336 1446; www.redlinecoaches.com.au; 9 Edward St) has its terminal opposite the Backpacker's Barn and will also stop at the ferry terminal when the ferry is in. For details of services to and from Devonport, and for information about **Tassielink** (☎ 1300 300 520; 6230 8900, www.tassielink.com.au) services to Strahan (via Cradle Mountain), Launceston and Hobart, see p229. In Devonport, Tassielink coaches pull up outside the visitors centre and the ferry terminal.

If none of the scheduled services suit your bushwalking needs, charter a minibus from **Maxwells** (☎ 6492 1431, 0418-584 004) to take you exactly where you want, when you want. Prices are for a group of up to four people (for groups of more than five people the price is per person). Devonport to Cradle Mountain costs $160 (or $40 per person). Devonport to the Walls of Jerusalem National Park costs $185 (or $45 per person), Devonport to Lake St Clair via Great Lake $289 (or $70 per person). Importantly they also do the Lake St Clair–Cradle Mountain run at the time you specify for $360 (or $90 per person). They can also arrange trips to Launceston and Hobart.

CAR

Budget (☎ 13 27 27, 6427 0650), **Avis** (☎ 136 136, 6427 9797), **Europcar** (☎ 6427 0888) and **Thrifty** (☎ 1800 030 730, 6427 9119) have representatives at the airport and ferry terminal, while **Hertz** (☎ 6424 1013; 26 Oldaker St) is in town. **Bargain Car Rentals** (☎ 1300 729 230; 25 Murray St, in Dockside Food & Coffee) and **Basic Car Rentals** (☎ 6424 4757; 50 Forbes St) offer cheaper cars.

Getting Around

The airport is 5km east of town. A **shuttle bus** (☎ 0400-035 995) runs between the airport or ferry terminal, the visitors centre and your accommodation for $10 per person. Bookings are essential. A **taxi** (☎ 6424 1431) will cost approximately $15.

Serenity Shuttles (☎ 6424 9251; 0424-596 370) operates services between the northwest coast and Launceston Airport. The Devonport–Launceston Airport fare is $45.

To get across the Mersey other than by the road bridge, you can take the **ferry** ($2.50 one way) from opposite the visitors centre to the eastern side of the river, beside the ferry terminal. This ferry runs on demand between 7.30am and 6pm, Monday to Saturday.

LATROBE

☎ 03 / pop 2770

Only 10km south of Devonport on the Bass Highway, Latrobe exudes an entirely different flavour to its larger neighbour. It's an attractive historic town, with heritage buildings housing some commendable restaurants, cafés and antique shops. Once a busy shipping port on the Mersey River, Latrobe was built on mining and agricultural fortunes: it's no surprise there are 75 National Trust–registered buildings on the main street alone. There are beautiful riverside forest walks here, and you have an excellent chance of spotting a platypus. The town also has the distinction of being the home of that most Tasmanian of sports: competitive wood-chopping.

Information

The Latrobe **visitors centre** (☎ 6421 4699; tourism@ latrobe.tas.gov.au; 48 Gilbert St; ⏱ 9.30-4.40pm Mon-Fri, to 4.30pm Sat & Sun) sits just in front of Kings Creek, adjacent to Lucas' Hotel.

Sights

Warrawee Forest Reserve (⏱ gates 9am-dusk) is a fantastic Mersey-side 2.3-sq-km recreational area. Walks here include a 10-minute, wheelchair-accessible Pond Circuit, a 20-minute walk downstream to Farrell Park, and a one-hour return Forest Circuit. However, the area's star attractions are the resident platypuses. Warrawee is 4.5km south of town down Hamilton St; turn off Gilbert St at the ANZ bank. **Platypus-spotting tours** ($10; 2 hours) are organised through the visitors centre, usually at dawn and dusk; be sure to book ahead. Pick-up is from the visitors centre.

The town's history is depicted through the 600 prints and original architectural drawings on display in the **Court House Museum** (Gilbert St; adult/child $2/1; ⏱ 1-5pm Fri & Sun), next to the post office in the centre of town.

The **Australian Axeman's Hall of Fame** (☎ 6426 2099; www.australianaxeman.com.au; 1 Bells Pde; adult/child/ concession/family $10/5/8/25; ⏱ 9am-5pm) honours the legendary axemen of the northwest, who dominate the sport of competitive wood-chopping. The roof of the main competition arena is held up by 14 massive timber columns representing native Australian timbers from each state. The hall exhibits logging memorabilia and includes displays of wood-chopping trophies. Included in the entry fee here is the **Platypus & Trout Experience**, which sheds much light on the breeding life and habits of this shy monontreme. There are no live examples in the display – but they're often spotted in the Mersey River just over the road. There are live trout in display tanks, and you can get information on trout fishing in nearby waters and fishing licences here. A café–restaurant serves light snacks and refreshments.

Adjacent to Axeman's is **Sherwood Hall** (☎ 6426 2888; Bell's Pde; adult/ under 15 $2/free; ⏱ 10am-2pm Tue & Thu, 1-4pm Sat, Sun & public hols, or by appointment), a historic cottage built by a remarkable pioneer couple, ex-convict Thomas Johnson and his half-Aboriginal wife Dolly Dalrymple Briggs.

If you're visiting Latrobe in the summer months, you also shouldn't miss the **Cherry Shed** (☎ 6426 2411; cnr Gilbert St & Bass Highway; ⏱ 9am-6pm December 20–mid-April). Here, you can sample and buy the plump red cherries that grow around these parts. Also on offer are cherry wines and liqueurs, jams, pies and a divine cherry ice cream.

Festivals & Events

Henley-on-the-Mersey carnival Held on Australia Day (January 26) at Bells Pde in Latrobe, site of the town's former docks.

Latrobe Wheel Race Annual bicycle race held on Boxing Day, attracting professional riders from around Australia.

Sleeping & Eating

Lucas' Hotel (☎ 6426 1101; www.lucashotellatrobe.com .au; 46 Gilbert St; s/d $95/105, without bathroom $70/80, with spa $115/130) This excellently restored pub has superb rooms with the feel of thoroughly upmarket accommodation. There's fantastic food on offer (mains $10 to $30) in an elegant old-world dining room too, including such meaty specials as filet mignon and beef vindaloo. They also have a kids menu and some wickedly good deserts. The dining room is open for breakfast, lunch and dinner. Out back, adjacent to the tourist information office, Lucas' also has a licensed coffee shop (open 9am to 3.30pm) serving all-day breakfasts, cakes and snacks. Any meal over $10 includes a free glass of vino.

Latrobe Motel (☎ 6426 2030; latrobemotel@ozemail .com.au; 8 Palmers Rd; s/d $80/90; 🖳) These standard (but fastidiously neat and roomy) ground-floor brick lodgings are a decent option for a night. The motel sits just off the Bass Hwy roundabout, opposite the hospital.

Lucinda (☎ 6426 2285; www.lucindabnb.com.au; 17 Forth St; s $85-105, d $105-140) Lucinda provides handsome accommodation in a National Trust–classified home, set in parklike grounds. A couple of its heritage rooms have spectacularly intricate moulded ceilings: see if you can spot the one red rose in the plasterwork as you lie in your four-poster bed.

Bicci Blue (☎ 6424 1622; 147 Gilbert St; mains $9.45-11.50; ☽ 6.30am-5pm Tue-Fri, to 4pm Sat & Sun) Speciality breads, pastries and delicious homemade pies are served here, and all are made using natural ingredients where possible.

Café Zeta (☎ 6426 1622; 20 Gilbert St; mains $9.45-11.50; ☽ lunch Tue-Sat) This stylish new establishment serves beautifully presented café food and heartier meals, including melt-in-your-mouth salmon penne and some exquisitely tender lamb shanks. Friday and Saturday evenings things get pretty fancy here: try the chicken breast stuffed with spinach, almond and pecorino, or the superb seafood platter ($27), which diners are said to travel miles for.

Glo Glo's (☎ 6426 2120; 78 Gilbert St; mains $22.50; ☽ dinner Mon-Sat) Glo Glo's is housed in Latrobe's

grand 1880s bank building, and in the elegant dining room you can sample food that's equally sophisticated. There's a fine Chateaubriand, prime aged eye fillet, exquisite duck and local venison. The accompanying vegetables are of the just-plucked, home-grown variety. All this is accompanied by one of the best wine lists in Tasmania, served from the wine cellar in the original bank vault.

PORT SORELL

☎ 03 / pop 1820

Port Sorell, just east of Devonport, is much lauded as a place for seaside holidays, but, despite its attractive rural location, it's rather barren and treeless and feels like it's sprung up overnight. Set along Hawley Beach and the tidal flats of the Rubicon River, it has some large holiday conglomerates such as Shearwater, and several retirement villages.

There are walks at low tide on the muddy tidal flat nearby, and also to Point Sorell, 6km north along the shoreline. Hawley Beach has sandy, sheltered swimming beaches, and is a popular fishing spot. It's just a 20-minute drive from here to Narawntapu National Park (p219).

Sleeping & Eating

Port Sorell Lions Caravan Park (☎ 6428 7267; fax 6428 7269; 44 Meredith St, Port Sorell; unpowered/powered sites d $12/20, on-site vans d $40, cabins $60) This friendly camping ground has sites sprawled along the enticing waterfront. There's a laundry, a big camp kitchen and a kids playground.

Shearwater Cottages (☎ 6428 6895; shearwater cottages@vision.net.au; 7-9 Shearwater Blvd, Shearwater; $90-130) This incredibly neat little enclave is set around a manicured garden and has simple, attractive rooms with all the mod cons. A breakfast basket or BBQ pack is available on request.

Sails on Port Sorell (☎ 6428 7580; www.sailsonport sorell.com.au; 54 Rice St, Port Sorell; d/apt $120/135, villa d $150, extra person $30) These boutique apartments are just a hop and a skip from the beach and have been kitted out with stylishly contemporary décor in a nautical theme: there are sails and a minilighthouse, plus a stranded boat for kids to play in. The villa sleeps up to six people.

Hawley House (☎ 6428 6221; www.hawleyhousetas .com; Hawley Esplanade, Hawley Beach; d $150-200) Hawley House is a white Gothic 1878 mansion set in beautifully landscaped gardens with wide ocean views. It offers luxury accommodation in the main house or the stables/lofts (some with spa). Candle-lit dinners in the home's grand dining room are possible by arrangement.

Ghost Rock (☎ 6428 4005; 1055 Port Sorell Rd, ☾ 11am-5pm Wed-Sun, daily Jan & Feb) Just off the road between Devonport and Port Sorell is this attractive vineyard and cellar door that serves antipasto platters, teas, coffees and cakes in stylish surroundings.

The area's other gastronomic options are restricted to the various takeaways around town and the busy bistro at the **Shearwater Resort** (☎ 6428 6205; Shearwater Blvd, Shearwater; mains $15-22; ☾ lunch & dinner).

DELORAINE
☎ 03 / pop 2500

You could hardly go wrong if you decided to establish a town in such beautiful rural surroundings as stretch out around Deloraine. At the foot of the Great Western Tiers, the town has wonderful views just about wherever you look. Wisely, they've made the streetscapes here pretty lovely, too. Georgian and Victorian buildings, ornate with wrought-iron tracery, crowd together along the main street that leads to green parkland on the banks of the Meander River. The town has an artsy, vibrant feel, with several cool little eateries, some bohemian boutiques and secondhand shops. The strong artistic community here celebrates annually with the Tasmanian Craft Fair (p240), drawing tens of thousands of visitors in late October/early November: bear in mind that accommodation is tight if you're visiting at this time.

With Deloraine as a base you can bushwalk the Great Western Tiers, explore the caves of the Mole Creek Karst National Park or get acquainted with Tasmanian devils at the nearby Trowunna Wildlife Park (p242).

Information

Bushwalkers can pick up food supplies in Deloraine, but for specialised gear you're better off buying in Devonport or Launceston.
ANZ Bank (54 Emu Bay Rd) Has an ATM.
Commonwealth Bank (24 Emu Bay Rd) Has an ATM.
Great Western Tiers Visitor Centre (☎ 6362 3471; 98-100 Emu Bay Rd; ☾ 9am-5pm) Shares premises with the Deloraine Folk Museum & YARNS: Artwork in Silk and has information on antique, arts and crafts, and gallery outlets. Internet access is also available ($2 per 15 minutes).

Online access centre (☎ per 30min/hr $3/5; ☾ 10am-4pm Located down the steps behind the Library
Post office (10 Emu Bay Rd)

Sights & Activities
MUSEUMS & GALLERIES

The **Deloraine Folk Museum & YARNS: Artwork in Silk** (☎ 6362 3471; 98 Emu Bay Rd; adult/child/concession/family $7/2/5/15; ☾ 9.30-4pm) The centrepiece of the museum here is an exquisite four-panel, quilted and appliquéd depiction of the Meander Valley through a year of seasonal change. It's an astoundingly detailed piece of work that was a labour of love by 300 creative local men and women. Each of the four panels entailed 2500 hours of labour and the whole project took three years to complete. It's now housed in a purpose-built auditorium, where you can witness a presentation explaining the work: it's fascinating and truly worth seeing. Also on display at the museum are slightly moth-eaten local history exhibits.

ASHGROVE FARM CHEESE

Journey 10km north of Deloraine to find **Ashgrove Farm Cheese** (☎ 6368 1105; www.ashgrovecheese.com.au; 6173 Bass Hwy, Elizabeth Town; ☾ 9am-5.30pm), a cheese factory specialising in award-winning traditional varieties such as Rubicon red, smoked cheddar and creamy Lancashire. You can watch the cheeses being made and then taste the fine results in a crumbly vintage cheddar or an adventurous *wasabi*-infused sample. It's also a great place to purchase deli fare for a picnic.

BUSHWALKING

Dominating the southern skyline are the Great Western Tiers (their Aboriginal name is Kooparoona Niara, 'Mountain of the Spirits'), which provide some excellent walking and feature waterfalls, exceptional forest and some long climbs. The **Meander Forest Reserve** is the most popular starting point. From the swing bridge over the Meander River here – where there are bowers of man ferns and tall trees – you can walk to **Split Rock Falls**. This route takes about three hours return, or you can walk to **Meander Falls** – five to six hours return.

Other good walks on the Great Western Tiers include those to **Projection Bluff** (two hours return), **Quamby Bluff** (five hours return) and **Mother Cummings Peak** (three to five hours return). Note that several tracks on the tiers

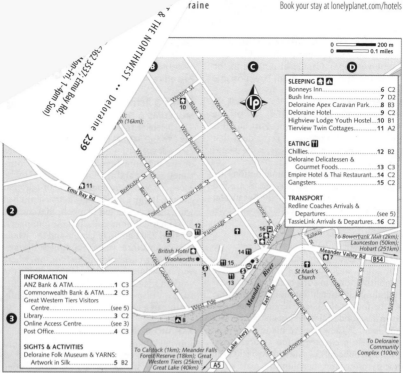

SLEEPING
Bonneys Inn...........................**6** C2
Bush Inn.............................**7** D2
Deloraine Apex Caravan Park....**8** B3
Deloraine Hotel....................**9** C2
Highview Lodge Youth Hostel...**10** B1
Tierview Twin Cottages............**11** A2

EATING 🍴
Chillies...............................**12** B2
Deloraine Delicatessen &
   Gourmet Foods..................**13** C3
Empire Hotel & Thai Restaurant...**14** C2
Gangsters.............................**15** C2

TRANSPORT
Redline Coaches Arrivals &
   Departures.........................(see 5)
TassieLink Arrivals & Departures...**16** C2

INFORMATION
ANZ Bank & ATM...................**1** C3
Commonwealth Bank & ATM....**2** C3
Great Western Tiers Visitors
   Centre...............................(see 5)
Library................................**3** C2
Online Access Centre..............(see 3)
Post Office..........................**4** C3

SIGHTS & ACTIVITIES
Deloraine Folk Museum & YARNS:
   Artwork in Silk....................**5** B2

that require the crossing of private land have been closed due to public liability issues, including Montana Falls, Westmoreland Falls and the South Mole Creek Track.

41° SOUTH AQUACULTURE

About 6km out of town in the direction of Mole Creek (well-signed down Montana Rd) is **41°South Aquaculture** (☎ 6362 4130; 323 Montana Rd; adult/child/concession/family $10/5/7/25; 🕙 9am-5pm Nov-Mar, 10am-4pm Apr-Oct). You don't have to be a fish-lover to visit this interesting farm where salmon are reared in raised tanks and a wetland is used as a natural biofilter. This no-waste, no-chemical fish farming is the cleanest way of raising fish: 10,000 to 15,000 salmon are growing here art any one time, without any negative impact on the environment. This also makes for superb smoked salmon, which you can taste and buy in the tasting room, or you can lunch on smoked salmon sandwiches, salmon roulettes and snack platters in the café.

Festivals & Events

The impressive **Tasmanian Craft Fair** is held in annually in Deloraine and runs for four days,

ending on the first Monday in November. Up to 30,000 people visit 200 stalls at 10 venues around town, the main one being the Deloraine Community Complex.

Sleeping
BUDGET

Deloraine Apex Caravan Park (☎ 6362 2345; West Pde; unpowered/powered sites d $11/14) At the bottom of the main street and on the banks of the Meander River is this simple camping spot with basic facilities. Don't be alarmed if an almighty thundering disturbs your slumber here in the middle of the night: there are train tracks right beside the park. Just block your ears as the freight train rolls through.

Highview Lodge Youth Hostel (☎ 6362 2996; 8 Blake St; dm/d from $21/49, f $49-84) It's a bit of a steep climb up to this hilltop YHA, but you'll be rewarded by the expansive views over the Great Western Tiers. It has a cosy, homely atmosphere, and when the wood heater is roaring, you could just imagine you're out in a bushwalking hut, somewhere in the wilds. Travellers not staying overnight may use the shower facilities for $5 per person.

Bush Inn (☎ 6362 2365; fax 6362 2329; 7 Lake Hwy; r per person $25) There's spacious pub accommodation here, and although there are no en suites there are just seven rooms – and there's rarely a full house – so you won't be sharing the bathroom with too many others. The price includes a self-serve continental breakfast.

Deloraine Hotel (☎ 6362 2022; www.delorainehotel .com.au, Emu Bay Rd; r $30 per person) This 1848 pub is veritably *draped* in wrought-iron lace, and its pubbish interior is being renovated bit by bit into what will eventually be an altogether salubrious establishment. In the meantime you can get one of the simple rooms upstairs for the night, and dine on fair pub grub (mains $12 to $13) in the restaurant below.

MIDRANGE

Bonney's Farm (☎ 6362 2122; 76 Archer St; d from $90-100, extra person $15) Set on a working farm among the crops and the cattle are three fully self-contained two- or three-bedroom units, with excellent views of the Great Western Tiers. To get here, head some 4km out of town towards Devonport and take the turn-off to Weetah.

Tierview Twin Cottages (☎ 6362 2377; 125 Emu Bay Rd; 4-person cottage d $115, 6-person cottage d $135, extra person $20) These identical twin cottages are just off the main street, and offer comfortable self-contained accommodation. One cottage has an open fire and sleeps up to four in two bedrooms, the other sleeps up to six and has a spa bathroom. Get your keys from the Shell service station opposite.

Bonney's Inn (☎ 6362 2974; www.bonneys-inn .com; 19 West Pde; s/d/tw $120/148/168) Built by John Bonney, son of a convict, in the 1830s, this was Deloraine's original coaching inn: horses were tied up out the back, and servants camped in the garden. Inside, travellers still stay in an old-world atmosphere in attractively modernised rooms. The days begin with hearty cooked breakfasts including homemade pastries and fresh, local fruit.

Bowerbank Mill (☎ 6362 2628; www.bowerbankmill .com.au; 4455 Bass Hwy; s/d without bathroom $125/155, cottage $195) This fantastic B&B is set in a historic 1853 flour mill some 2km east of the town centre. It's thoughtfully furnished, with beautiful antiques throughout, and the cottage has an amazing six-storey high bluestone chimney and a great fireplace to toast by. Substantial continental breakfasts are provided and there are reduced rates for longer stays.

TOP END

Calstock (☎ 6362 2642; www.peppers.com.au/calstock; Lake Hwy; d $305-475) On this 80-hectare property just south of Deloraine, parklike grounds filled with mature trees surround a Georgian mansion, which now houses a much-awarded boutique hotel. There are seven bedrooms (one wheelchair accessible) and two magnificent suites decorated in French provincial style, as well as grand lounges, gourmet breakfasts, and a three-course set menu dinner ($80) by arrangement. Leave the kiddies at home.

Eating

Deloraine Delicatessen & Gourmet Foods (☎ 6362 2127; 36 Emu Bay Rd; mains $5.50-11.50; ☺ breakfast & lunch Mon-Sat) A fine place for late-morning baguettes, bagels and focaccias, with a variety of tasty fillings. Its coffee is pungently superb, and it does dairy- and gluten-free meals too.

Christmas Hills Raspberry Farm Cafe (☎ 6362 2186; www.raspberryfarmcafe.com; Christmas Hills Rd, Elizabeth Town; meals $9.50-29; ☺ 7.30am-5pm) There are 16 acres of raspberries grown here, and you can take a short walk to see them in all their glory – before indulging in everything raspberry at the lakeside café. Think raspberry sundaes piled high with the ruby-coloured fruits, homemade raspberry ice cream, raspberry waffles, baked raspberry cheesecake, pavlovas, smoothies and even a shocking pink raspberry latte. The farm is 8km north of Deloraine on the Bass Highway.

Gangsters (☎ 6362 3882; 53-55 Emu Bay Rd; mains $9.50-18.50; ☺ lunch & dinner Wed-Sun) The roomy dining room here is decked out with gangster-theme touches, but the menu will keep you on the straight and narrow: there are pizzas, burgers, sandwiches, focaccias, soups and excellent smoky pork ribs.

Chillies (☎ 6362 3669; 81 Emu Bay Rd; mains around $10; ☺ breakfast & lunch Mon-Fri) Brightly painted and terracotta tiled in a faintly Mexican theme, this place across the road from the visitors centre serves good light meals and the best seafood chowder ever. There's also great coffee and cake for just $6.

Empire Hotel & Thai Restaurant (☎ 6362 2075; 19 Emu Bay Rd; mains $10-20; ☺ 7.30am-9.30pm summer, 11.30am-3pm winter, dinner 5.30-9-30pm year-round) The newly renovated café in this heritage hotel serves breakfasts, cakes and coffees, while the adjacent Thai restaurant serves up fine lunches and dinners. There's also a bar next door that has live entertainment a few nights a week. There are plans to open an upmarket backpackers upstairs by late 2008.

Getting There & Away

See p229 for details of the Redline Coaches service from Launceston to Deloraine, which arrives at and departs from outside the visitors centre.

Tassielink (☎ 1300 300 520, 62 72 7300; www.tassielink .com.au) Tassielink does ply the route from Launceston to Deloraine, but (for complicated reasons) can only pick up passengers here who are travelling further than Devonport, and can't drop people off. This means you can only travel with Tassielink from Deloraine if you are heading to Sheffield ($27, two hours 10 minutes), Cradle Mountain ($53.30, three hours), or further along their west coast service to Strahan. See p229 for more information.

CHUDLEIGH
☎ 03

Make a beeline (sorry...) for Chudleigh's **Honey Farm** (☎ 6363 6160; www.thehoneyfarm.com.au; 39 Sorell St; ☼ 9am-5pm Sun-Fri) where you can get sticky fingers lingering over the free tastings of some of their range of over 50 different types of honey, or sample some of the superb honey ice cream. In the shop you can browse through all things bees and honey – from beeswax boot polish to propolis supplements, to honeycomb, to bee cuddly toys. Less cuddly – but much more fascinating – are the 1000 bees you can watch hard at work in a glass-walled hive in the museum display corner.

Two kilometres west of Chudleigh is the **Trowunna Wildlife Park** (☎ 6363 6162; adult/child/ concession/family $16/8.50/14/44; ☼ 9am-5pm Feb-Dec, to 8pm Jan), which specialises in Tasmanian devils, wombats and koalas. The park operates an informative 75-minute tour where you get to pat, feed or even hold the critters. Tour start at 11am, 1pm and 3pm. The park also has many birds, including rosellas, geese, white goshawks and two wedge-tailed eagles.

MOLE CREEK
☎ 03 / pop 260

About 23km west of Deloraine and just around the bend from Chudleigh is pretty Mole Creek, a tiny rural town with beautiful mountain views and a couple of good places to stay and eat. It's also a great jumping-off point for spelunking and bushwalking. There's a **Parks and Wildlife Visitors Centre** (☎ 6363 1487;

☼ 9am-5pm Tue-Fri; ▯) here, which can help with info on bushwalking in the area – particularly at the Walls of Jerusalem – and on visiting the nearby caves.

Sights & Activities
MOLE CREEK KARST NATIONAL PARK

The word 'karst' refers to the scenery characteristic of a limestone region, including caves and underground streams. The Mole Creek area contains over 300 known caves and sinkholes. The park itself is in a number of small segments, including the public caves which you can tour. For bookings contact **Mole Creek Caves** (☎ 6363 5182, fax 6363 5124; mccaves@parks.tas.gov.au).

Public Caves

The national park's two public caves are **Marakoopa** (its name derives from an Aboriginal word meaning 'handsome'), and **King Solomons Cave**. Visits to Marakoopa can be made on two different tours, which run several times each day between 1 October and 31 May. The first tour shows you underground rivers and an incredible display of glow worms, as well as sparkling crystals and beautiful reflective pools. These easy tours leave at 10am, 12pm, 2pm and 4pm and are suitable for all age groups. A more demanding tour involves climbing a steep stairway and visits the Great Cathedral, with delicate limestone gardens of shawls and straws and glow worm clusters. It leaves at 11am, 1pm and 3pm daily. (In winter, from 1 June to 30 September, there's no 4pm tour.) Tours of King Solomons Cave will show you lavish colours and formations in this more compact cave. Tours depart at 10.30am, 11.30am, 12.30pm, 2.30pm, 3.30pm and 4.30pm daily from 1 December to 30 April. Prices for admission and tours are adult/child/concession/family $15/8/12/38. (In winter, from 1 May to 30 November, the 10.30am and 4.30pm tours are dropped). The caves are a constant 9°C so wear warm clothes and good walking shoes. Snappers beware: there's no flash photography allowed in the glow worm chamber as this affects their natural luminescence. Entry to King Solomons Cave is payable only by credit card or Eftpos – no cash. Cash payments for entry to both caves can be made at Marakoopa, 11km away. When you come back up into the light you can hang out at the picnic grounds or use the free electric BBQs.

Wild Caves

Cyclops, Wet, Honeycomb and Baldocks are among the better-known wild caves in the Mole Creek area that are without steps or ladders. If you're an experienced caver who wants to take on some vertical rope work, you'll need to make arrangements with a caving club. Alternatively you can take one of the excursions offered by **Wild Cave Tours** (☎ 6367 8142; www.wildcavetours.com; 165 Fernlea Rd, Caveside), which provides tours for $85/170 per half/full day, including caving gear (not for children under 14 years). Your guide is an environmental scientist and her love of the caves really shines through. She'll show you a host of endangered species in the caves, and knows of species yet to be described. Book ahead on the tours and bring spare clothing and a towel – if the drought ever breaks, you could get very wet.

R STEPHENS LEATHERWOOD HONEY FACTORY

At this **factory** (☎ 6363 1170; 25 Pioneer Dr; admission free; ❧ 9am-4pm Mon-Fri Jan-Apr), you can watch leatherwood honey extraction and bottling plant in operation. (Leatherwood trees – *Eucryphia lucida* and *Eucryphia milligani* – are endemic to Tasmania.) There are also honey sales here and if you ask nicely, they might give you a low-key guided tour of the factory.

DEVILS GULLET

Those with transport should head for the Western Tiers. The only road that actually reaches the top of the plateau is the gravel road to Lake Mackenzie. Follow this road to **Devils Gullet**, where there's a 40-minute return walk leading to a platform bolted to the top of a dramatic gorge: looking over the edge isn't for the faint-hearted.

BUSHWALKING

There are a number of popular short walks in the area, including **Alum Cliffs Gorge** (one hour return), a short scenic walk along a sloping spur to an impressive lookout. Alum Cliffs (or Tulampanga, as it's known to the tribal custodians, the Pallittorre people) is a sacred celebration place where tribes met for corroborees. Note that the South Mole Creek Track crosses private land and remains closed to walkers due to public liability issues. For information about walking in the Walls of Jerusalem National Park, see right.

Sleeping & Eating

Mole Creek Caravan Park (☎ 6363 1150; cnr Mole Creek & Union Bridge Rds; unpowered/powered sites $15/17, extra person $3) This is a thin sliver of a park about 4km west of town beside Sassafras Stream, at the turn-off to the caves and Cradle Mountain.

Mole Creek Hotel (☎ 6363 1102; tigerbar69@hotmail .com; Main Rd; s/d $50/90, extra adult/child $25/15) This attractive pub was built with breezily high ceilings in 1907 and has clean better-than-pub rooms – some with good views – upstairs. The restaurant here (mains $12 to $21, open lunch and dinner) does great, meaty meals like lamb shanks in red wine and rosemary sauce. If you're tiger-curious, you should pop into the Tiger Bar here, where you can see a life-sized model of the Tasmanian tiger, jaws dramatically agape, and a collage of tiger sighting articles from the local paper.

Mole Creek Guest House & Laurel Berry Restaurant (☎ 6363 1399; 100 Pioneer Dr; s $105, d $135-150; 🖳) This place is a real find. There are beautifully renovated, spacious rooms and a little private cinema upstairs. Downstairs Laurel Berry restaurant serves really excellent food all day – from the hearty walkers' breakfasts to the homemade quiche and salad at lunch (mains $11 to $26), to the fantastic steaks at dinner (mains $18 to $27). You can't go past the bread-and-butter pudding with laurel berry syrup.

Blackwood Park Cottages (☎ 6363 1208; www.black woodparkcottages.com; 445 Mersey Hill Rd; cottages $125-165), this place offers two lovely self-contained cottages set among well-maintained gardens in a rural setting, with views to the surrounding mountains. There's handcrafted furniture, heated floors, and breakfast is homemade bread, muffins, real coffee and free-range eggs. Children are most welcome. It's well signed off a side road just to the Deloraine side of Mole Creek.

WALLS OF JERUSALEM NATIONAL PARK

This compact national park is one of Tasmania's most beautiful. It's a glacier-scoured landscape of spectacularly craggy dolerite peaks, alpine tarns, a diverse array of flowering plants and forests of ancient, gnarled pines. The park adjoins the lake-spangled wilderness of the Central Plateau and is part of the Tasmanian Wilderness World Heritage Area. Several walking tracks lead through it, and also join the park with hikes in the Cradle Mountain–Lake St Clair National Park.

The park is reached from Mole Creek by taking the Mersey Forest Rd to Lake Rowallan. The last 11km is on well-maintained gravel roads. The most popular walk here is the full-day trek to the 'Walls' themselves. A steep path leads up from the car park on Mersey Forest Rd to Trappers Hut (two hours return), Solomon's Jewels (four hours return), through Herod's Gate to Lake Salome (six to eight hours return), then Damascus Gate (nine hours return). If you plan to visit historic Dixon's Kingdom hut and the hauntingly beautiful pencil pine forests that surround it (10 hours return from the carpark) or climb to the top of Mt Jerusalem (12 hours return), you are far better to camp up in the Walls for at least one night. There are tent platforms and a composting toilet at Wild Dog Creek. You'll need to be fully equipped and prepared for the harsh weather conditions: it snows a substantial amount here particularly – but not only – in winter, and it's not unheard of to be snowed in here in a tent for days. Walks across the park are described in *Cradle Mountain Lake St Clair and Walls of Jerusalem National Parks*, by John Chapman and John Siseman, and in Lonely Planet's *Walking in Australia*.

Tasmanian Expeditions (☎ 1800 030 230, 6334 3477; www.tas-ex.com) has a six-day Walls of Jerusalem circuit ($1390) taking in the park's highlights as well as some of the more out-of-the-way spots such as Lakes Adelaide, Myrtle and Mt Rogoona.

Getting There & Away
BUS
For buses on demand contact **Maxwells** (☎ 6492 1431), which runs from Devonport to the Walls of Jerusalem ($185 for up to four people or $45 per person for larger groups) and from Launceston to Cradle Mountain via the Walls of Jerusalem ($240 or $60 per person).

CAR
The quickest access to the Walls is from Sheffield or Mole Creek. From Mole Creek take the B12, then the C138 and finally the C171 (Mersey Forest Rd) to Lake Rowallan; remain on this road, following the C171 and Walls of Jerusalem signs to the start of the track.

MOLE CREEK TO SHEFFIELD
Head north on the C137 some 4km after Mole Creek and you'll traverse the Gogg Range before passing through the little settlement

of Paradise – surrounded by emerald green fields and forested hills. Shortly after Paradise there's a T-intersection at which you can follow signs right to Sheffield or left to Gowrie Park and Cradle Mountain.

Gowrie Park
Situated at the foot of Mt Roland just 14km from Sheffield, Gowrie Park makes an excellent base for mountain walks or for a rural retreat. There are walks to the summits of Mts Roland (1234m), Vandyke (1084m) and Claude (1034m), and shorter walks in the cool, shady forests of the lower slopes, such as the pleasant meander through the bush at nearby O'Neills Creek Reserve. Bird lovers take note: there are 94 species in the Mt Roland area.

SIGHTS
Mt Roland is a comb of rock that's the prominent mountain backdrop to the picturesque rural views here. This steep-sided mountain looks spectacularly difficult, but it can be climbed by confident walkers: just don't attempt it when its icy in winter.

There are two access points. The first is from Claude Rd village, a short distance towards Gowrie Park from the T-junction at Paradise. To use this access, turn off at Kings Rd and head south for about 1.5km to the start of the Mt Roland Track, which is 6.5km long and takes 3½ hours return (this track is very steep and awkward in places, necessitating clambering up and over boulders). The other access point is at Gowrie Park itself, where you turn off the main road just near the sports ground and travel 2km to the start of the track. The track itself is 10km and takes approximately four hours return.

SLEEPING & EATING
Mt Roland Budget Backpackers (☎ 6491 1385; www .weindorfers.com; 1447 Claude Rd; powered sites d $5, dm, tw & d per person $10; ☐) Tucked into the foothills of Mts Roland, Vandyke and Claude, this place is an ideal hiking base. It will also give new meaning to the idea of camping with wildlife: you'll have pademelons, possums and wallabies visiting every night. They also have simple, hostel-style accommodation with a well-equipped kitchen, free laundry and internet use.

Gowrie Park Wilderness Cabins (☎ 6491 1385; 1447 Claude Rd; d from $72; ☐) Adjacent to the backpackers and run by the same people are these four comfortable self-contained cabins. In winter (May to the end of September) you get a second night for free. When we visited, we noted that the complex was for sale. The settlement here is also home to the much-loved restaurant Weindorfers.

Silver Ridge Wilderness Retreat (☎ 6491 1727; www.silverridgeretreat.com.au; 46 Rysavy Rd; apt $125-250; ⛽) Right at the foot of Mt Roland, these cottages are about as peaceful as you can get, and have fantastic mountain views. You can soak in the heated indoor pool, climb mountains, watch the birds and the beasts, or go horse riding on Mustang Sally, Misty or Mac.

Weindorfers (☎ 6491 1385; Cradle Mountain Main Rd, Gowrie Park; mains $10-26.50; ⏰ 10am-late Nov-April) This rustic wooden cabin is the place to sample wonderful home cooking in front of a roaring fire. Come here with a post-bushwalk appetite and start with a steaming soup and fresh bread, then try the house special of smoked trout or the divine lamb mushrooms. Leave room for the legendary golden-syrup ice cream. Weindorfers also caters of vegetarians, gluten-free and other special diets. Reservations are essential. Open by prior arrangement in winter.

C140 & Lake Barrington

Approximately 6km down the road from Gowrie Park to Cradle Mountain, turn off onto the C140, which will take you northwest back towards Sheffield. From the southern end of this road, there are heartstoppingly panoramic views of Mt Roland. Two kilometres along you'll pass **Highland Trails Horse Riding** (☎ 6491 1533, 0417-145 497; www.highland-trails.com.au; 1st hr $40, then per hr $30) which can take you out on horseback into the foothills of Mts Roland, Van Dyke and Claude on rides ranging form one hour to several days. Longer trips involve overnight camping.

Slightly closer to Sheffield is **Cradle Vista** (☎ 6491 1129; www.cradlevista.com.au; 978 Staverton Rd; d $130), where you can get your first wonderful views over Cradle Mountain on a clear day. There's comfortable, bright B&B accommodation here in a couple of en suite rooms in the main house and a large, open-plan unit.

The **Granary** (☎ 6491 1689; www.granary.com.au; 575 Staverton Rd; s $110-120, d $120-180; ⛽) has half a dozen well-equipped timber cottages featuring the windows produced at the **stained-glass workshop** (⏰ 9am-5pm Wed-Fri, to noon Sat) here.

Linen and electric blankets are supplied. This is the perfect spot for families as there's oodles for the kids to do: from the treehouse to the games room and the video library. Mum and dad can soak in the spa or sweat it out in the sauna.

Just 400m from the Granary, and well signed from every direction, is **Tasmazia** (☎ 6491 1934; www.tasmazia.com.au; 500 Staverton Rd; adult/child $16/9; ⏰ 10am-4pm April-Nov, 9am-5pm Dec-March) and the **Village of Lower Crackpot.** This whimsical complex of hedge mazes, a colourful miniature village and a lavender farm is well meaning in tongue-in-cheek, crazy pantomime style. Adults don't scoff: the kids will love it. Look out for such waggish touches as Nancy the witch, who appears to have crashed her broomstick, or the sword in the stone: if you can retrieve it, King Arthur style, it will win you this whole fanciful kingdom for yourself. When you're famished from all the fun, you can retreat to the large **pancake parlour** (pancakes $8.95-17.95; ⏰ 10am to 4pm) to feast on sweet and savoury pancakes – possibly the best is a sweet nutty concoction known, rather appropriately in the context, as the Nutcase.

The approach road from the turn-off near the maze leads to the section of **Lake Barrington** that has been marked out for international, national and state rowing championships. Other access roads lead to picnic areas and boat ramps; camping is also available.

Further along the C140 road, and flanked by a hedge the size of Texas, is **Carinya Farm Holiday Retreat** (☎ 6491 1593; www.carinyafarm .au; 63 Staverton Rd; d $115, extra person $20). Staying in pine-lined loft-bedroom chalets overlooking peaceful farmland and Mt Roland, guests receive homemade bread and freshly laid farm eggs. Dinner can be arranged.

Lovers of fine food and wine should visit **Barringwood Park Vineyard** (☎ 6492 3140; 60 Gillams Rd, Lower Barrington; ⏰ 10am-5pm daily Jan-Feb, 10am-5pm Wed-Sun March-Dec), where there are tastings and cellar-door sales of handcrafted cool-climate wines. You can sit out on their deck, savour a gourmet platter with your vino, and be awe-inspired by the glorious views.

Wilmot

☎ 03

Wilmot, on the western side of Lake Barrington, is worth staying at if you're visiting Cradle Mountain and don't mind a drive (note the amusing trail of novelty letter boxes all along the C132). You can fill up on petrol and diesel here, and there's an ATM.

The township boasts the first **Coles store** (☎ 6492 1335; ✆ 7.30am-6pm) – the Coles name is now part of one of Australia's largest supermarket chains.

Set in the 1893 Wilmot bakery, the **Old Wilmot Bakehouse** (☎ 6492 1117; www.oldwilmotbakehouse.com.au; Cradle Mountain Rd; s/ste $55/145, extra person $35) offers lovely country accommodation. There are just four rooms – ranging from backpacker to king-sized suite, all with en suites. You'll be tempted into the adjacent **bakery** (✆ 10am-4pm) by the wonderful aromas of baking bread. The pies here are renowned, as are the enormous cooked breakfasts that go for $15. There are dinners for house guests and pizza nights on weekends. Bookings are essential.

Five kilometres north of Wilmot is the turn-off to **Lake Barrington Garden Café** (☎ 6492 1394; Lake Barrington Rd; meals $8.50-32.50; ✆ 10-4pm Oct-Apr), a further 3km down a gravel side road in a beautiful garden setting beside Lake Barrington. Sit outside and you can listen to native birdsong and gaze over to Mt Roland and the lake, and savour all things yummy from the excellent menu, including the Garden Gourmet Platter ($32), delicious deserts like the plum teacake, and fine wines, coffees and smoothies. The two-hour return walking track to beautiful **Forth Falls** starts in the café's car park.

SHEFFIELD
☎ 03 / pop 1020

The lovely 'Town of Murals' wasn't always the thriving rural hub it is today. In the 1980s Sheffield was a typical small Tasmanian town in the doldrums of rural decline. That was until some astute townsfolk came up with an idea that had been applied to the small town of Chemainus in Canada, with some surprisingly wonderful results. The plan was to paint a few large murals on walls around town, depicting scenes from the district's pioneer days. What started with these humble beginnings has been a roaring success: Sheffield is now a veritable outdoor art gallery with over fifty fantastic large-scale murals, and an annual painting festival to produce more. People come from all over the world to wander its streets and appreciate what's now a collection of really excellent artwork – and the influx of visitors has allowed the town to thrive way beyond those early mural-painting dreams.

Information

Newsagency (Main St) Acts as a Westpac agent; also has a multibank ATM. There's also a Commonwealth Bank with an ATM on Main St.

Slater's Country Store (☎ 6491 1121; 52 Main St; ✆ 8.30am-5.30pm Mon-Sat, 9am-5pm Sun) Has an ATM.

Visitors centre (☎ 6491 1036; 5 Pioneer Cres; ✆ 9am-5pm) Supplies information on the Kentish region, and provides internet access ($2 per 15 minutes). Also makes accommodation and tour bookings.

Sights & Activities
MURAL AUDIO TOURS

You can now grab a headset from the visitors centre and take a thoroughly informative **audio tour** of Sheffield's alfresco art. Headsets cost $7 or you can get two for $10. It's the perfect way to see the murals, and the interpretation is first class. The tour takes about 90 minutes with strolling time between murals, but you can keep the headset all day. You'll hear all about the best-known paintings like *Stillness and Warmth*, which features Gustav Weindorfer of Cradle Mountain fame (see p295); *Butlers Mail Coach 1910*, a huge, magnificent depiction of a coach and horses against the backdrop of Mt Roland; and *Cradle Mountain Beauty*, a wide panorama of Cradle Mountain in snow. Spot the park ranger carrying a bathtub to one of the Overland Track huts! The audio tour takes you to some 20 of the best of the murals in town and also leads you through the **Working Art Space** (✆ 11am-3pm Fri-Tue), where you can see local artists at work and buy some of their oeuvre.

KENTISH MUSEUM

This **museum** (☎ 6491 1861; 93 Main St; entry by donation; ✆ 10am-noon & 1-4pm Mon & Wed, 10-3pm Tue, Thu & Fri) has all sorts of historic clutter on display: an early telephone exchange, old organs, military paraphernalia, and the world's first automatic petrol pump, invented by a local Sheffield boy.

MURAL HOUSE

The odd little **Mural House** (☎ 6491 1784; 100 High St; adult/child/student $2/50c/$1; ✆ 1-5pm Tue, Thu, Sat & Sun) contains interpretations of native art of various cultures in the form of internal wall murals. You may be better off with the outdoor art in town – but if you want to actually buy some art, you can do so here.

AUNTY IRIS'S MUSEUM

This **doll museum** (☎ 6491 1559; 44 Main St; adult/child $2/1; ✆ 9am-5pm) bills itself as one of Australia's

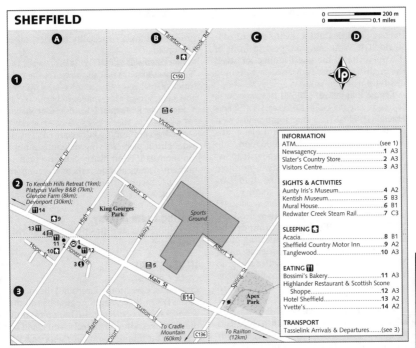

SHEFFIELD

DEVONPORT & THE
NORTHWEST

most comprehensive and boasts over 1500 dolls from the 1800s to the present day. If you can bear all those glassy eyes googling at you, it's the kind of place where the kids will be fascinated.

REDWATER CREEK STEAM RAIL
Departing from the original Sheffield train station at the eastern end of town, the **Steam Rail** (☎ 6491 1613; cnr Main & Spring Sts; adult/child/concession/family $5/3/4/12) offers rides on locomotives running on a narrow-gauge track from 11am to 4pm on the first weekend of each month, for two weeks in early January and on some public holidays – dependent on volunteer train-driver availability. Train buffs will ooh and ahh at the rare A Krauss 10 locomotive here. There's also **Steam Fest**, a grand three-day occasion on the long weekend of March that's a true celebration of steam and bygone days, and a must (not just for trainspotters). The tractor pulling competitions are a hoot!

Festivals & Events
Mural Fest, Sheffield's celebration of outdoor art is held late March to early April each year.

It's a massive paint-off; a theme is set and artists from all over Australia descend upon the town to compete for a cash prize, and to add another nine murals to the town's walls. The best thing about all this is that you get to watch some incredibly skilled artists at work on their creations. If you plan to visit at this time, be sure to book accommodation well ahead.

Sleeping
There's an overnight parking facility for caravans and campervans next to the recreation centre on Albert St. Water and toilets are available, but there are no showers and no other facilities. There's a shower at the information centre (three minutes for $1).

Sheffield Country Motor Inn (☎ 6491 1800; fax 6491 1966; 49-53 Main St; motel s/d $85/95, units d $90-100, extra adult/child $20/15) There are neat and well-equipped motel rooms here, one with three bedrooms, set just back off main street. Some of the towns best murals are immediately adjacent.

Tanglewood (☎ 6491 1854; www.tanglewoodtasmania.com; 25 High St; s from $90, d $95-110, extra person

$10) There are three large bedrooms here, all with en suites, delicious feather doonas and electric blankets, and a great sense of old-world style. You can sip a port in front of the open fire in the guest lounge, or stroll the English gardens. They also serve evening meals by arrangement.

Kentish Hills Retreat (☎ 6491 2484; www.kentish hills.com.au; 2 West Nook Rd; d $100-130, apt $130-150, extra adult/child $25/20; 🖳) In a quiet location just west of town with superb views of Mt Roland, this option offers a range of accommodation from double rooms to apartments sleeping up to six. It's more motel than hotel in style, but there are good facilities, including spas, minibars, queen-sized beds and a guests' laundry.

Acacia (☎ 6491 2482; www.acaciabbtas.com.au; 113 High St; s from $80, d $110-135; 🖳) This welcoming B&B is set in a 1906 home surrounded by attractive gardens and has appealing guest rooms, excellent breakfasts and friendly hosts. You can make yourself tea or coffee and grab a homemade biscuit, or perhaps relax in the guest lounge by the cosy fire with a board game or a DVD.

Platypus Valley B&B (☎ 6491 2260; www.platypus valley.com.au; 10 Billing Rd; s $99-130, d $110-150, extra adult/child $60/30) Tucked away in green country just outside Sheffield (off the C141; take the turn-off onto the B141 about 1km outside town), this beautiful spot is somewhere you're almost guaranteed to see platypuses gambolling. This is a beautiful timber home with attractive guestrooms, in an environment where the key ingredient is peace.

our pick Glencoe Farm (☎ 6492 3267; www.glencoe ruralretreat.com.au; 1468 Sheffield Rd; d $165-185) Just north of Sheffield on the B14 at Barrington, this gorgeous property, owned by celebrated French chef Remi Bancal, is making a great name for itself. You can stay in its romantic and eminently stylish rooms, and you just mustn't miss the superb three-course dinners ($50) – available by prior arrangement.

Eating

Yvette's (☎ 6491 1893; 43 Main St; mains $9.90-18.90; 🕑 lunch Thu-Mon) This French-style café has cool red-leather sofas, an upmarket bistro feel and friendly service. There's an excellent mezze tasting plate with warm Turkish bread ($18), and there's a popular Cajun chicken burger ($9.90). Try Yvette's cob sandwich: a three-layered wonder of chicken, bacon, tomato, egg and mayo ($9.90).

Bossimi's Bakery (☎ 6491 1298; 44 Main St; 🕑 breakfast & lunch Mon-Fri) This bakery does the industry proud with lots of speciality pastries, cakes and bread.

Hotel Sheffield (☎ 6491 1130; 38 Main St; mains; $10-16; 🕑 lunch & dinner) You can always try the pub, which offers good-value counter-meal options and a lively local atmosphere to boot.

Highlander Restaurant & Scottish Scone Shoppe (☎ 6491 1077; 60 Main St; mains $18-20; 🕑 breakfast, lunch & dinner Wed-Sun) No kilt required! This is a delightful place serving delicious pumpkin scones ($5) and hearty café fare such as homemade pies and desserts by day, and an à la carte menu including traditional roasts by night.

Getting There & Away

Tassielink buses stop directly outside the visitors centre.

ULVERSTONE

☎ 03 / pop 9800

Quiet little Ulverstone sits around the mouth of the Leven River, and though it has all the services visitors expect, it also has a pleasantly old-fashioned rural town feel – you could be forgiven for thinking you have stepped back in time 30 years.

The commanding feature in town, which you can't miss as you drive in (at the intersection of Reibey St and Alexandra Rd) is the vastly imposing **Shrine of Remembrance**, built in 1953 and incorporating an older WWI memorial. It's rich in symbolism: look for the laurel wreath, the chain links of togetherness, and the torch of remembrance – or at least set your watch by the clock on top.

The Ulverstone **visitors centre** (☎ 6425 2839; 13 Alexandra Rd; 🕑 9am-5pm) is a treasure-trove of local knowledge. The internet is available at the **online access centre** (☎ 6425 7579; 15 King Edward St; per hr $2; 🕑 9.30am-12.30am & 1.30pm-4.30pm Mon-Thu, 9.30am-12.30pm Fri) in the local library.

The **Ulverstone Local History Museum** (☎ 6425 3835; 50 Main St; admission $4; 🕑 1.30-4.30pm) concentrates on the area's early farmers, displaying tools, manuscripts, an extensive photographic collection, and assorted artefacts behind a mock-pioneer façade.

Ulverstone is a pleasant, quiet place to stop if you're touring this part of the world. You may not want to hang around for ages, but it's certainly worth ducking into for its friendly, old-fashioned country-town feel.

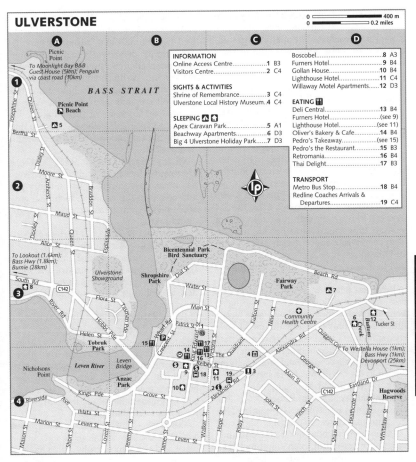

ULVERSTONE

INFORMATION
Online Access Centre.................1 B3
Visitors Centre..........................2 C4

SIGHTS & ACTIVITIES
Shrine of Remembrance.............3 C4
Ulverstone Local History Museum.4 C4

SLEEPING
Apex Caravan Park.....................5 A1
Beachway Apartments................6 D3
Big 4 Ulverstone Holiday Park......7 D3

Boscobel......................................8 A3
Furners Hotel..............................9 B4
Gollan House.............................10 B4
Lighthouse Hotel.......................11 C4
Willaway Motel Apartments......12 D3

EATING
Deli Central..............................13 B4
Furners Hotel.......................(see 9)
Lighthouse Hotel.................(see 11)
Oliver's Bakery & Cafe.............14 B4
Pedro's Takeaway................(see 15)
Pedro's the Restaurant.............15 B3
Retromania...............................16 B4
Thai Delight..............................17 B3

TRANSPORT
Metro Bus Stop........................18 B4
Redline Coaches Arrivals &
    Departures............................19 C4

Sleeping
BUDGET
Apex Caravan Park (☎ 6425 2935; Queen St; unpowered/powered sites $14/16) There's not much shade here but you can hardly be more seaside than this location off Picnic Point Beach on the western side of the mouth of the Leven River.

Big 4 Ulverstone Holiday Park (☎ 6425 2624; fax 6425 4654; 57 Water St; sites d $31, on-site vans $68, 3-bunk cabins from $95, units $105-140; 🖳) Set in grassy, treed surroundings just behind East Beach, this park, close to the town centre, is friendly and has good facilities, including a campers kitchen, playgrounds and plenty of adjoining parkland to run free in.

Furners Hotel (☎ 6425 1488; 42 Reibey St; s/d $60/80) It's all grand wooden staircases and flowery carpets here, and the rooms are comfortable in a pleasingly old-fashioned way. Each has its own bathroom. The meals downstairs are excellent (see p250).

Beachway Apartments (☎ 6425 2342; 1 Heathcote St; s/d from $72/80, extra adult/child $20/15, 1-/2-/3-bed apt $185/220/320; 🖳 🖳) This complex has some motel-style rooms as well as recently upgraded self-contained apartments. There's an outdoor heated pool and spa, and a satisfying restaurant on site, serving breakfast and evening meals (mains $25 to $27).

MIDRANGE
Westella House (☎ 6425 6222; www.westella.com; 68 Westella Dr; s $80-110, d $110-128) This Gothic Revival home looks as pretty as a gingerbread house.

Inside you'll find just three beautifully decorated rooms, and friendly hosts who serve a slap-up breakfast. The highway has encroached since the house was built in 1865, but there's not much traffic at night and the bedrooms' windows are double glazed.

Boscobel (☎ 6425 1727; www.boscobel.com.au; 27 South Rd; d $95-160; 🐾) Boscobel has rather old-fashioned accommodation in a National Trust–listed home. The frills extend from the bedrooms through to the alfresco-dining tablecloths. There's a heated indoor pool in summer, but you may opt instead to go swimming in your bathroom: the deluxe room has the biggest spa you've ever seen.

Willaway Motel Apartments (☎ 6425 2018; www .willaway.southcom.com.au; 2 Tucker St; d $100-130; 🖳) You can't go wrong with this collection of generic, tidy self-contained modern units. They're opposite a nice stretch of lawn with BBQ facilities, only a minute to the beach, and have wireless internet for communications junkies.

Lighthouse Hotel (☎ 6425 1197; lighthouse@good stone.com.au; 33 Victoria St; d $109-129) The faux lighthouse crowning the central well here feels a little like a circus tent, but the motel-style rooms are neat and clean. All have mini bars and tea- and coffee-making equipment. A rather minimalist continental breakfast is included in the tarriff. Meals are served in the central dining area daily (see right).

Moonlight Bay B&B Guest House (☎ 6425 1074; www.moonlightbay.worldstays.com; 141 Penguin Rd; d $140-165) With absolute beach frontage, this luxury (and gay-friendly) boutique B&B commands views over Bass Strait. Both suites include a lace-canopy four-poster bed (one king-sized). The rate includes full English buffet-style brekky and the use of a spa. The guesthouse is 5km northwest of town and is unsuitable for children.

Gollan House (☎ 6425 3613; 58 King Edward St; d $150; 🖳) Built in 1910 for a Dr Gollan and his family, this attractive mansion has been meticulously restored and houses boutique accommodation in expansive rooms with fireplaces, spas, and high ceilings. Breakfast is delivered to your room.

Eating

Pedro's Takeaway (☎ 6425 5181; Wharf Rd; mains $4-9; ☻ 11am-8pm) Next door to Pedro's Restaurant, this place does superb fish 'n' chips, as well as fresh fish and seafood to take away.

Deli Central (☎ 6425 5205; 48b Victoria St; meals $5-13; ☻ 8am-5pm Mon-Fri, to 12.30pm Sat) You'll find Ulverstone's best breakfasts here: try the chewily delicious French sourdough with poached free-range eggs and homemade relish. At lunch you can't go past the roast pumpkin and caramelised-onion tart. The food is organic and locally grown as far as possible. Stock up for picnics at the impressive deli here. It's slightly tricky to find: ask for the car park off Edward St, behind Thai Delight.

Oliver's Bakery & Cafe (☎ 6425 4118; 41 Reibey St; sandwiches from $5.60; ☻ 6am-6pm) Oliver's has inventive focaccias, tasty savoury pies and crispy all things sweet, including great apple pies, cream buns, caramel slices and custard tarts.

Retromania (☎ 6425 1900; 31 King Edward St; $7-15; ☻ breakfast & lunch Mon-Sat) This little café sells retro gifts and memorabilia and serves fine Italian coffee as well as sandwiches, soups and jacket potatoes. There's also a 1950s meal deal: a hamburger with corn chips, salsa and milkshake ($13.50).

Furners Hotel (☎ 6425 1488; 42 Reibey St; mains $10-21; ☻ lunch & dinner) Furners is set in an ornate Federation building – perhaps Ulverstone's best – with a wide veranda and liberal wrought-iron lace. Inside they serve a hearty menu that includes all sorts of carnivorous fare from the wood-fired grill. You can get all your greens at the salad bar. Save room for some commendable deserts.

Thai Delight (☎ 6425 3055; 25 King Edward St; mains from $10; ☻ dinner Tue-Sat) Locals rave about this place and you can tell why: the Thai chef in the kitchen whips up everything from scratch, to order, and it's perfectly, pungently spicy. If you can't tell your *Tod Mon Gai* from your *Peek Gai Tod*, the friendly servers will explain.

Lighthouse Hotel (☎ 6425 1197; 33 Victoria St; mains $18-25; ☻ lunch & dinner Mon-Sat) You can get the usual pubby fare here: roasts, fish, steaks, chicken schnitzels, chips and salad to overflow your plates.

Pedro's the Restaurant (☎ 6425 6663; Wharf Rd; mains $24-29; ☻ lunch & dinner) Grab a table right by the water at this top-notch restaurant, perched on the banks of the Leven River where it empties into Bass Strait, and savour tastes of the sea as the sun goes down. What a view! The paradise seafood platter for two ($89) is the most popular offering here. Make sure you arrive on an empty stomach. The menu caters to both carnivores and vegetarians.

Getting There & Away

Redline Coaches arrive at and depart from Alexandra Rd, near the War Memorial clock, outside the IGA Supermarket, opposite Gunns/Mitre 10. For further details of transport services in the region, see p229.

During the week, **Metro** (☎ 13 22 01, 6431 3822) operates regular local buses from Burnie to Ulverstone ($3.40). Buses heading to Burnie leave from the corner of King Edward and Reibey Sts.

AROUND ULVERSTONE
Penguin
☎ 03 / pop 4040

Penguin feels like one of those pretty little English seaside towns where its all ice creams, buckets and spades, salt-tousled hair, and the occasional sneaky breeze as you try to brave it out on the beach. But there's one very un-English thing about this place. You guessed it: penguins! The beaches and dunes around town are some of the spots were the world's smallest penguin (*Eudyptula minor*) comes ashore during its breeding season, and even if you don't see any of them in the feather, you can get acquainted with the model penguins around town: perfect for photo ops. The town also attracts visitors for its glorious roadside garden displays, as well as its sandy beaches and azure shallows.

Staff at the friendly Penguin **visitors centre** (☎ 6437 1421; 78 Main Rd; 🕑 9am-4pm Oct-Mar, 9.30am-3.30pm Apr-Sep) will ply you with the local lowdown, including details on the little-known 80km Penguin-to-Cradle walking trail that starts at Dial Range just outside town (see p252).

The **online access centre** (☎ 6337 0771; 125 Ironcliffe Rd; 🕑 8am-3pm Mon, Wed & Fri, 8am-9pm Tue & Thu, 9am-noon Sat) is located on the grounds of the Penguin High School.

From September to March, real penguins return from their daytime ocean foraging at dusk at **Penguin Point**. You can view them independently, but ask at the visitors centre about any tours being offered when you're in town. Note that flash photography of the penguins is prohibited.

Hiscutt Park, beside Penguin Creek, has good playground equipment and a scaled-down working **Dutch windmill**. In September, the tu-

lips surrounding the Wipmolen mill are so abundant, you might suddenly feel like you're in Holland.

Every Sunday the popular **Penguin Market** (🕑 9am-3.30pm) takes place. There are over 300 browse-worthy stalls here selling everything from fresh local produce to art and crafts, gifts and trinkets. Foodies will love the gourmet grub and Tassie wines.

SLEEPING & EATING

Neptune Grand Hotel (☎ 6437 2406; 84 Main Rd; s/d/ tw without bathroom $39/49/49) Right in the heart of Penguin, this friendly pub has clean but basic accommodation: rooms have sinks, but facilities are shared. The dining room serves some cheap staples (mains $5 to $26): there's a parmi (chicken parmigiana) special from $5 to $7, and the surf 'n' turf is only $15 for weekday lunches.

Glenbrook House B&B (☎ 6437 1469, 0417-293 275; glenbrookhouse@bigpond.com; 89-91 Browns Lane; d $85-110) Want to really get away from it all? Then come to Glenbrook. It's only 3kms from Penguin, but surrounded by 50 peaceful acres of natural bush, orchard and trout-filled creeks. There's B&B accommodation in the house or a self-contained cottage. Continental breakfast is included in the tariff.

Madsen (☎ 6437 2588; www.themadsen.com; 64 Main St; d $148-195; 🖳) This boutique hotel is housed in a truly grand edifice right on the waterfront. Many of the rooms have breathtaking views of Bass Strait, and the views of the interior aren't half bad either. Decorated in meticulous good taste, with a touch of the antique and a good measure of contemporary cool, this is a particularly pleasurable place to stay. Don't book just one night.

Groovy Penguin Café (☎ 6437 2101; 74 Main Rd; mains $8-13; 🕑 breakfast & lunch Wed-Sun; 🖳) This lesbian- and gay-friendly retro-gallery café sports melamine tables, crazy-coloured walls, and a menu that's strong on organic. You can't go wrong with a zesty veggie burger, a huge, creamy smoothie or a potent coffee from the hands of some mightily skilled baristas. The sea views come free.

Wild Café Restaurant (☎ 6437 2000; 87 Main Rd; lunch mains $12-19, dinner mains $20-29; 🕑 lunch & dinner Wed-Sun) The whole northwest coast is talking about this upmarket addition to Penguin's dining scene. The cuisine includes Thai-inspired char-grilled calamari, and five-spice brioche with marinated duck, orange and Grandmarnier. Wow!

DETOUR

The forested hinterland near Ulverstone is perfect off-the-beaten-track exploring territory. There's a circuit using the B17 from either Ulverstone or Penguin known as the **Coast to Canyon Circuit**. Start by driving to Penguin along the picturesque coast road, then delve south to Riana. In the **Dial Range**, just behind the Penguin, there are some good walking tracks, including the start of the little-known **Penguin Cradle Trail**: an 80km, six-day bushwalk through rugged backblocks to Cradle Mountain. It's for experienced walkers only. Ask for a route guide at Penguin's visitors centre (p251).

From Riana, a scenic drive brings you to the **Woodhouse Lookout**, with excellent views over the Leven Valley. More winding road leads to **Wings Wildlife Park** (☎ 6429 1151; www.wingswildlife .com.au; 137 Winduss St; adult/child $17/8; ☺ 10am-4pm) which has an eclectic collection of creatures, native and exotic, ranging from devils to camels, crab-eating macaque monkeys and even bison. There's a **camping ground** (unpowered/powered sites d $10/13.30; dm s/d $15/20, cabins $85-139), and light meals in the **café** (☺ 10am-4pm).

Close by are **Gunns Plains Caves** (☎ 6429 1388; adult/child/concession/family $12/6/10/35; ☺ 10am-4pm), filled with magical limestone formations and glow worms. There are guided tours between 10am and 3.30pm that involve some clambering and ladder work.

Back on the B17 you can complete the circuit back to Ulverstone or take the C127 and C125 to the Leven Canyon. On the C124 at Gunns Plains is **Leven Valley Vineyard & Gallery** (☎ 6429 1186; www.levenvalleyvineyard.com.au; 321 Raymond Rd; ☺ 10am-5pm Wed-Mon Nov-April, Fri-Mon May-Oct), a boutique vineyard where you can taste and buy wine, and browse pottery, wood turning and jewellery. Signposted just off the road near the vineyard are lower and upper **Preston Falls**: all cascading water and primeval man ferns.

Continue via Nietta to **Leven Canyon**. A 15-minute track leads to the sensational gorge-top lookout, a sky platform peering 275m down to the Leven River below. From the Leven Canyon picnic ground you can drive approximately 1km down Loongana Rd to the car park for a 20-minute walk to the canyon floor. There's a 10-hour walk through the canyon for experienced walkers. Nearby day walks lead to **Winterbrook Falls** (four hours return) and **Black Bluff** (six hours return).

There's B&B accommodation and visits to the gorgeous gardens (adults $5) at **Kaydale Lodge** (☎ 6429 1293; www.kaydalelodge.com.au; 250 Loongana Rd, Nietta; s/d $80/120). The tearoom here serves morning and afternoon teas, and home-cooked meals by arrangement.

GETTING THERE & AWAY

During the week, **Metro** (☎ 13 22 01, 6431 3822) runs regular local buses from Burnie to Penguin ($4.50) and return (see p256). The main stop is at (the now defunct) Penguin Station on Crescent St.

BURNIE

☎ 03 / pop 19,335

Try as you might, you can't exactly call Burnie an outrageously attractive town. It's certainly in a dramatic natural setting – tumbling down steep hillsides to the shores of Emu Bay – but Burnie has long been an industrial stronghold for paper making, heavy-machinery manufacturing, agricultural services and shipping. Perhaps the biggest features in town are the shockingly gigantic piles of woodchips on the dockside – the fate of much of Tasmania's forests – most of it being readied for export to Asia. It has plenty of services for visitors, though, and is a handy jumping-off point for Cradle Mountain and the far reaches of the northwest coast. Lovers of architecture will appreciate the abundance of fine Art Deco buildings around town.

Information

North West Regional Hospital (☎ 6430 6666; Brickport Rd) A few minutes west of the city centre: take Brickport Rd off the Bass Hwy just east of Cooee.

Online access centre (☎ 6431 9469; 2 Spring St; per hr/30 mins $6/3, ☺ 9am-5pm Mon-Fri, 9.30-12pm Sat) Internet access is also available at the visitors information centre.

Visitors centre (☎ 6431 4391; Little Alexander St; ☺ 9am-5pm Mon-Fri, to 4pm Sat, 10am-2pm Sun) Located in the same building as the Pioneer Village Museum. Offers several interesting brochures about walks, including a 17km-long circuit that will take you to parks, creeks and beachside boardwalks. If you're an art and architecture fan, ask for maps of the public art and Art Deco walking trails around Burnie.

Sights & Activities

PIONEER VILLAGE MUSEUM

This absorbing **museum** (☎ 6430 5875; Little Alexander St; adult/child $6/2.50; ☺ 9am-5pm Mon-Fri, to 4pm Sat, Sun & public hols), is a re-creation of a 1900s village streetscape – including a blacksmith, wash house, stagecoach depot and boot-maker – complete with appropriate soundtrack.

BURNIE REGIONAL ART GALLERY

This **art gallery** (☎ 6431 5918; gallery@burnie.net; Civic Centre Precinct, Wilmot St; admission free; ☺ 10am-4.30pm Mon-Fri, 1.30-4.30pm Sat, Sun & public hols) has excellent exhibitions of contemporary Australian artworks, including photography, sculpture and painting.

PARKS & GARDENS

Burnie Park (☺ car access sunrise-sunset) features rose-filled flower beds and the oldest building in town, **Burnie Inn**. This National Trust–classified inn was built in 1847 and later moved to the park from its original location. You can admire it from the outside only. The adjacent oval is home to New Year's Day Burnie Athletics Carnival, and also the revered Burnie Dockers Aussie Rules football team.

The serene **Emu Valley Rhododendron Garden** (☎ 6433 0478; Breffny Rd; adult/child $5/3; ☺ 10am-4pm Aug-Feb), 8km south of Burnie (on the B18) via Mount St and then Cascade Rd, has 20,000 rhodos that flower in riotous colour from mid-September to mid-November. For more green, visit **Annsleigh Gardens & Tearooms** (☎ 6435 7229; 4 Metaira Rd; adult/child $4.50/free; ☺ 9am-5pm Sep-April), 9km south of Burnie on the B18. The lovingly manicured outdoors here features gazebos, water features and cottage garden beds.

Just outside the city centre, **Round Hill Lookout** and **Fern Glade** are the best places for views and peace. Round Hill is accessed by a side road off Stowport Rd, which departs the Bass Hwy on the eastern fringe of suburban Burnie. Fern Glade is also east of the city centre – turn off the Bass Hwy into Old Surrey Rd, just past the old Australian Paper Mill, then take Fern Glade Rd to the left. Fern Glade is renowned as a top spot for platypus spotting at dawn and dusk.

CHEESE TASTING

Down Old Surrey Rd, on the way to Fern Glade, you'll find the cheesemaker **National Foods Australia** (☎ 6433 9255; 145 Old Surrey Rd; ☺ 9am-5pm Mon-Fri, 10am-4pm Sat & Sun) and its cheese-tasting centre. There's usually a range of brie, cam-embert and hard cheeses to try here. Light meals like – you guessed it – ploughman's lunch – are also available.

CREATIVE PAPER TASMANIA

Just beside the large Australian Paper Mill is **Creative Paper Tasmania** (☎ 6430 7717; www.creative papertas.com.au; East Mill Studios, Old Surrey Rd; entry by gold coin donation, tours adult/child/concession/family $15/8/12/40; ☺ 9am-5 Mon-Fri, to 4pm Sat & Sun), where you can meet the Paper People – life-sized models in paper – and browse the shop and gallery for some incredible paper creations. Half-hour tours here explain the process of making paper with personality, using all sorts of recycled and ecofriendly material including jeans, cotton and even roo poo!

HELLYERS ROAD WHISKY DISTILLERY

About 1km further up Old Surrey Rd is this **whisky distillery** (☎ 6433 0439; www.hellyersroaddis tillery.com.au; 153 Old Surrey Rd; tours adult/child under 16 $10/free; ☺ 9.30am-5.50pm, reduced opening in winter). You can tour the distillery here to see how this golden single-malt whisky is made, and afterwards take a tasting of whisky or Southern Lights vodka, which is also made here (nips $2 to $4). The on-site café serves snacks and lunches.

PENGUIN-WATCHING

A boardwalk on Burnie's foreshore leads from Hilder Pde to the western end of West Beach, where there's an **penguin observation centre**. Over summer you can observe the birds for free at dusk as they emerge from the sea and waddle back to their burrows. Volunteer wildlife guides are usually present to talk about the penguins and their habits.

Sleeping

BUDGET

Burnie Holiday Caravan Park (☎ 6431 1925; www.burnie beachaccommodation.com.au; 253 Bass Hwy, Cooee; unpowered/powered sites d $18/25, dm $25, on-site vans d $50, cabins d $88-98, extra person $15; ☒) Located 4km west of the city centre, this park has two backpacker rooms (four and six bunks) equipped with fridge and stove, some grassy camping sites at the property's rear, vans with kitchenettes and a range of cabins.

Regent Hotel (☎ 6431 1933, 26 North Terrace; d $45, s without bathroom $30) Not a flashpacker's by any means, but there are basic rooms above the pub here: the ones at the front have sea views.

DEVONPORT & THE NORTHWEST

lonelyplanet.com

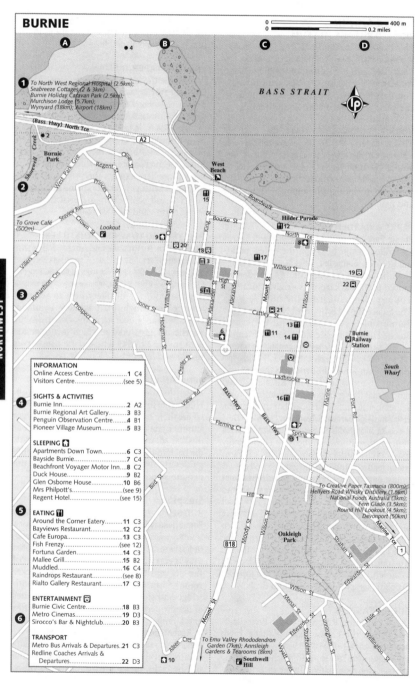

BURNIE

BASS STRAIT

West Beach

Hilder Parade

Burnie Park

Burnie Railway Station

South Wharf

Oakleigh Park

Southwell Hill

To North West Regional Hospital (2.5km);
Seabreeze Cottages (2 & 3km);
Burnie Holiday Caravan Park (2.5km);
Murchison Lodge (5.7km);
Wynyard (18km); Airport (18km)

To Grove Café (500m)

To Creative Paper Tasmania (800m);
Hellyers Road Whisky Distillery (1.5km);
National Foods Australia (3km);
Fern Glade (3.5km);
Round Hill Lookout (4.5km);
Devonport (50km)

To Emu Valley Rhododendron Garden (7km); Annsleigh Gardens & Tearooms (8km)

INFORMATION
Online Access Centre...............1 C4
Visitors Centre........................(see 5)

SIGHTS & ACTIVITIES
Burnie Inn.................................2 A2
Burnie Regional Art Gallery.........3 B3
Penguin Observation Centre........4 B1
Pioneer Village Museum..............5 B3

SLEEPING
Apartments Down Town.............6 C3
Bayside Burnie...........................7 C4
Beachfront Voyager Motor Inn....8 C2
Duck House...............................9 B2
Glen Osborne House.................10 B6
Mrs Philpott's.......................(see 9)
Regent Hotel.......................(see 15)

EATING
Around the Corner Eatery..........11 C3
Bayviews Restaurant.................12 C2
Cafe Europa.............................13 C3
Fish Frenzy.........................(see 12)
Fortuna Garden........................14 C3
Mallee Grill.............................15 B2
Muddled..................................16 C4
Raindrops Restaurant..............(see 8)
Rialto Gallery Restaurant..........17 C3

ENTERTAINMENT
Burnie Civic Centre..................18 B3
Metro Cinemas.........................19 D3
Sirocco's Bar & Nightclub..........20 B3

TRANSPORT
Metro Bus Arrivals & Departures.21 C3
Redline Coaches Arrivals &
  Departures...........................22 D3

Double rooms have showers but other facilities are shared.

MIDRANGE

Duck House (☎ 6431 1712; www.ozpal.com/duck; 26 Queen St; s/d $100/140, extra adult/child $30/20) Salvation Army stalwarts Bill and Winifred Duck lived here for 30 years, and have been immortalised in this charming little two-bedroom cottage that bears their name. The decoration, predictably, has an emphasis on ducks.

Mrs Philpott's (☎ 6431 1712; www.ozpal.com/philpotts; 28 Queen St; s/d $100/140, extra adult/child $30/20) Managed by the same people as Duck House, this equally attractive cottage next door is enhanced by leadlight, a claw-foot bath, brass bedsteads and an unusual keyhole-shaped entry.

Murchison Lodge (☎ 6435 1106; fax 6435 2778; 9 Murchison Hwy, Somerset; r/units $105/145; 💻) At Somerset, just west of Burnie, this motel has good, clean rooms, a decent restaurant (open for dinner Monday to Saturday) and free wi-fi. You can't beat the location: it's right on the edge of the crystal-clear Cam River, where you can swim and fish to your heart's content.

Bayside Burnie (☎ 6431 4455; ciburnie@southcom.com.au; 139 Wilson St; d $115-150) This large hotel right in town keeps changing its name, but it's also had a recent change of décor, which is all for the better. The rooms here are decent, but the pick of the place is Maginty's Irish Bar downstairs – one of Burnie's better-loved watering holes.

Glen Osborne House (☎ 6431 9866; fax 6431 4354; 9 Aileen Cres; s/d from $120/160) It may be set in the suburban hills in Burnie's south (off B18), but there's nothing suburban about this establishment. It provides high-standard hospitality in a lavish, National Trust–listed 1885 Victorian house with established gardens. The rate includes a home-style cooked breakfast.

Beachfront Voyager Motor Inn (☎ 1800 355 090, 6431 4866; www.beachfrontvoyager.com.au; 9 North Tce; r $129-160; 💻) Right across the road from West Beach, this motel has spacious rooms – many recently renovated. Those on the waterfront are the pick, with superb ocean views. The on-site Raindrops Restaurant (see right) is much loved by Burnie-ites.

Apartments Down Town (☎ 6432 3219; www.apartmentsdowntown.com.au; 52 Alexander St; apt $145-190) Didn't we say Burnie was big on Art Deco? This 1937 building is Deco through and through, and has been thoroughly modernised

to house spacious and well-equipped two- and three-bedroom serviced apartments.

our pick **Seabreeze Cottages** (☎ 6435 3424; www.seabreezecottages.com.au; s/d $130/170, extra adult/child $40/20) These cottages west of the city centre may just be Burnie's best. There's the cool, contemporary Beachhouse (243 Bass Highway, Cooee) just a stroll across the road from the beach; the romantic heritage three-bedroom Somersby (82 Bass Highway, Cooee); and cute Number Six (6 Mollison St), all kitted out with modern chic décor, juke box and all. We love them!

Eating

RESTAURANTS

Fortuna Garden (☎ 6431 9035; 66 Wilson St; mains $10-23; ☽ lunch Mon-Fri, dinner) This is a licensed and BYO Chinese restaurant serving great garlic prawns, Mongolian beef, and piles of stir-fry veg to keep vegetarians happy. Eat-in or takeaway.

Muddled (☎ 6431 9393; 104 Wilson St; lunch mains $10-33, dinner mains $24-33; ☽ lunch Tue-Fri, dinner Tue-Sat until 10pm) There's nothing muddled about the international cuisine served up here. There is a fine seafood paella, and unusual delicacies such as BBQ ox tongue, periwinkles and char-grilled quail. This is the only place in Burnie where you can order until 10pm or later.

Rialto Gallery Restaurant (☎ 6431 7718; 46 Wilmot St; mains $14-25; ☽ lunch Mon-Fri, dinner Mon-Sat) It's no wonder that this restaurant is such a well-loved Burnie institution: it's been doing a roaring trade for 28 years with its mouthwatering Italian fare. Dishes include tortellini in butter and sage, meltingly delicious ravioli with a pungent four-cheese sauce and fine wood-oven pizzas.

Raindrops Restaurant (☎ 6431 4866; 9 North Tce; mains $19-32; ☽ lunch & dinner) This eatery at the Beachfront Voyager Motor Inn serves up a good range of locally sourced surf and turf in a convivial atmosphere. Vegetarians are also catered for.

Bayviews Restaurant (☎ 6431 7999; 1st fl, 2 North Tce; mains $16-34; ☽ breakfast Sat & Sun, lunch & dinner). This new upmarket establishment is right on the beach and serves a brief menu of excellent café-style dishes, from shitake risotto to ocean trout blini and roast lamb. The wraparound views are sublime.

CAFÉS & QUICK EATS

Around the Corner Eatery (☎ 6431 5963; 53 Mount St; meals $4-16.50; ☽ 8am-5pm Mon-Fri) Aaah...this is a place to relax on the soft furnishings with a hot choc and the newspaper. They do fab wholesome breakfasts, lunches and afternoon teas, including great homemade burgers and delicious cakes.

Cafe Europa (☎ 6431 1897; cnr Cattley & Wilson Sts; mains $4.90-15.90; ☺ 8.30am-7pm Mon-Thu, 8.30-10pm Fri, 10am-6pm Sat) Step into this café-bar with its sky-blue walls and you'll feel you're somewhere on the Med. The bar sells Italian, French and Spanish wines, and all the likely suspects in European liqueurs. Food includes cooked breakfasts, excellent *pides* (Turkish bread) and salads for lunch, and a host of sweet treats including baklava and Greek biscuits.

Grove Café(☎ 6431 9779; 63 West Park Grove; mains $8.50-14.50; ☺ breakfast Sat & Sun, lunch) Next to a garden centre and sharing its outdoor ambience, this little café serves light lunches and morning and afternoon teas. The coffee here is excellent and you can accompany it with fresh mixed-berry muffins or a slice of Death by Chocolate. It's at the West Park Nursery (drive up West Park Grove alongside Burnie Park).

Fish Frenzy (☎ 6432 1111; 2 North Terrace; meals $9.50-24; ☺ 11am-9pm) Downstairs from Bayviews Restaurant, this gourmet fish 'n' chippery does all the usual takes on this seaside favourite, and also offers healthy options such as grilled fish with Greek salad.

Mallee Grill (☎ 6431 1933; 26 North Tce; mains $15-43; ☺ lunch Sun-Fri, dinner) In the Regent Hotel, the Mallee Grill is a meat showcase, specialising in steaks. The juicy large rump steaks go for $28, served with chips and potatoes, and there's also the carpetbag variety – steak stuffed with oysters. The all-you-can-eat salad bar ($4 at lunch and $6 at dinner) is the best bet for vegetarians.

Entertainment

Metro Cinemas (☎ 6431 5000; www.metrocinemas.com.au; cnr Marine Tce & Wilmot St) This is a shiny cinema showing shiny, mainly first-release Hollywood flicks, but it also serves up some marathon, all-night screenings of old classics.

Burnie Civic Centre (☎ 6431 5033; Wilmot St) This multifunctional complex sees everything from concert divas to comedy acts to readings. Entry is via King St.

Sirocco's Bar & Nightclub (☎ 6431 3133; 64 Wilmot St) This late-night venue entertains a mixed crowd with a regular line-up of live music and DJs pumping out the latest techno, dance, pop and rock.

Getting There & Away

AIR

The Burnie/Wynyard airport (known as either Burnie or Wynyard airport) is at Wynyard, 20km northwest of Burnie.

BUS

See p229 for details of Redline Coaches services to and from Burnie. These buses stop on Wilmot St opposite the Metro Cinemas.

From Monday to Friday, except public holidays, **Metro** (☎ 13 22 01, 6431 3822) has regular local buses to Penguin, Ulverstone, Wynyard ($4.50 each), departing from bus stops on Cattley St beside Harris Scarfe department store.

WYNYARD & AROUND
☎ 03 / pop 4200

Arranged around the wooded banks of the sinuous Inglis River, Wynyard is a quiet little town that's a service centre for all the agriculture that surrounds it. It's sheltered from westerly weather by prominent Table Cape and Fossil Bluff, and has a pleasant, sedate air. On its doorstep are unpeopled beaches, wind-blasted lighthouses, and the amazing spring display of tulips – spread like a giant coloured bar code across the rich red soils of Table Cape. There are lovely walking trails beside the Inglis River, accessed from several spots close to the centre of town.

Information

Visitors centre (☎ 6443 8330; info@wowtas.com; 8 Exhibition Link; ☺ 9am-5pm) The friendly and super-knowledgeable volunteers at this swanky new visitors centre preside over a real treasure-trove of tourist information. Ask them for the brochure *Scenic Walks of Wynyard and the Surrounding Districts* if you're keen to get out and about on foot. At the library, just behind the police station and ATMs on Goldie St, is the **Online access centre** (☎ 6442 4499; 21 Saunders St; per hr $5; ☺ 10am-5pm Mon-Fri). There's also internet access at the visitors centre.

Sights

FOSSIL BLUFF

Three kilometres west of the town centre is 275-million-year-old Fossil Bluff. It was created by an ancient tidewater glacier and is rich in fossils, including the remains of prehistoric whales and the oldest marsupial fossil found in Australia. The species was named *Wynyardia bassiana* in honour of the town. At low tide you can walk around the base of the bluff and fossick for some of the hundreds of different kinds of fossils preserved here. Ask at the visitors centre for the geological guide *Looking for Fossils*.

TABLE CAPE

An extinct volcano, right here in the verdant hills of Tasmania? Believe it or not, the rocky ramparts of Table Cape once encircled a lake of boiling lava. To visit the Cape in its present, more benign, condition, take the minor road (C234) 4km northwest out of Wynyard, and drive right up to the **lighthouse**, which began its seaside vigil in 1888.

With all that volcanic past, the chocolate-red soils of the cape are extraordinarily fertile. It's just the spot to grow tulips and there's a mesmerising array of colour at **Table Cape Tulip Farm** (☎ 6442 2012; 363 Lighthouse Rd; admission free; ✆ 10am-4.30pm late-Sep–mid-Oct) when the bulbs are in flower in October. A **Tulip Festival** is held usually on the first weekend of October, and is a fun family affair with food, song and dancing against the bright backdrop of the flowers. From March to August you can buy bulbs in the farm's shop.

WONDERS OF WYNYARD

Adjacent to the visitors centre is the **Wonders of Wynyard** (☎ 6443 8330; 8 Exhibition Link; adult/under 15 yr/concession/family $6/3/5/15; ✆ 9am-5pm), a veteran car collection owned and restored by a Wynyard local. There's a rotating collection of at least 15 ancient Ford cars and motorbikes, including the world's equal-oldest Ford.

FLOWERDALE LOBSTER HAVEN

Signposted west of Wynyard on the C229 is the **Flowerdale Lobster Haven** (☎ 6442 2800; 241 Robin Hill Rd, Flowerdale; adult/child $5/1; ✆ 10am-4pm Feb-May). Here you can get a close-up view of the giant freshwater crayfish. It's strangely deep-blue, grows up to 1m long, and is an endangered primeval inhabitant of the west coast's creeks and rivers. The tearoom provides light snacks.

Activities

Hire scuba gear from the **Scuba Centre** (☎ 6442 2247; 62 Old Bass Hwy; ✆ 9am-5pm Mon-Sat) for dives in Wynyard Bay and Boat Harbour.

South of Wynyard the hills of the Oldina State Forest Reserve feature the **Noel Jago Walk**, a short nature walk beside Blackfish Creek. Passing under man ferns and eucalyptus trees,

it takes 30 to 45 minutes to complete. There are reputed to be platypuses in the creek.

Scenic flights over Cradle Mountain ($140 per person, one hour) and the west ($250 per person, 2½ hours) can be arranged with **Western Aviation** (☎ 6442 1111), located next to the airport. They even offer a full-day trip around Tasmania, stopping in Hobart for lunch ($1200 per person).

Sleeping

Beach Retreat Tourist Park (☎ 6442 1998; 30b Old Bass Hwy; unpowered & powered sites d $24, backpacker s/d $30/45, s or d motel units/cabins $80/90) This has to be one of the prettiest caravan parks anywhere. It's in a peaceful spot right by the beach in grounds that are meticulously manicured and pleasingly green. The backpacker's accommodation is in simple double rooms – none of that dorm-sleeping nonsense. There's an excellently equipped kitchen to share.

Wharf Hotel (☎ 6442 2344; 10 Goldie St; s/d $49/75) The Wharf is slowly being upgraded throughout and the clean and pleasant rooms upstairs are really decent. Some have baths (baths!) and look out over the peaceful Inglis River. The bistro downstairs (p258) is excellent.

The Waterfront (☎ 6442 2351; www.waterfront.net .au; 1 Goldie St; s/d from $90/110; ▯) As motels go, this is a particularly satisfying one. As the name implies, this place is slap-bang on the water and has clean, stylish rooms with extras like wireless internet. The Riverview restaurant (p258) is quite a sophisticated affair.

our pick **Seaward** (☎ 6442 2657; www.seawardbb .com; 31 Old Bass Highway; d $135-165, extra adult/child $35/25; ▯) The guest book says staying here is 'like walking into a magazine' and it's really true. The owners have kitted out this swish self-contained apartment using exemplary taste and style. There's a corner spa bath, cool leather sofas, wireless internet, brekky provisions – and it's child friendly, too.

Eating

Buccaneers for Seafood (☎ 6442 4104; 4 Inglis St; lunch $7-15, dinner $18-27; ✆ lunch & dinner) This is a hugely popular seafood emporium – you won't ever be surrounded by more marine paraphernalia unless you're underwater. Diners sit around the clinker-built sailing boat and chow down on fresh catches; steaks, pasta and takeaways are also available. Inglis St angles off Goldie St at the roundabout in the town centre. Bookings are advised.

DEVONPORT & THE NORTHWEST

Wynyard Hotel (☎ 6442 2048; 1 Inglis St; mains $9-30; ☽ dinner Tue-Sat) The glass panel above the dining room door here says 'Dining Room and Cabaret' but we're sad to report you can no longer take in any high kicks here. There's good, solid pub fare to fill you – all the usual dishes represented, including (how many is it now?) that good old chicken parmigiana.

Riverview (☎ 6442 2351; 1 Goldie St; mains $18-32; ☽ dinner Mon-Sat) There's quite a stylish dining room here on the edge of the river, and it serves the kind of thing you wouldn't expect from a motel – from *char sui* pork stack with fried wontons to a steaming rabbit pie.

Wharf Hotel (☎ 6442 2344; 10 Goldie St; mains $19-26; ☽ lunch & dinner) There's bistro-style dining here, specialising in Tassie seafood and steak. It's a busy place right on the waterfront: judging by its popularity, you're bound to get a good feed. Blackboard specials daily.

Getting There & Away

AIR

The Burnie/Wynyard airport (often listed as Burnie airport) is just one block from Wynyard's main street. If you're looking to get a ride to or from Burnie, the **Burnie Airbus** (☎ 0439-322 466; adult $10) meets most flights and can pick up from prearranged points and from the visitors centre; bookings are advised.

Rex (☎ 13 17 13; www.regionalexpress.com.au) fly to Burnie/Wynyard from Melbourne.

Tasair (☎ 1800 062 900, 6248 5088; www.tasair.com.au) flies between Devonport and King Island via Burnie/Wynyard once a day. One-way flights from Burnie/Wynyard to either Devonport or King Island cost $165. Tasair also flies to Burnie/Wynyard from Hobart on weekdays for $165 one way.

BUS

During the week, **Metro** (☎ 6431 3822) in Burnie runs regular local buses from Burnie to Wynyard for $4.50. The main bus stop is on Jackson St.

BOAT HARBOUR BEACH

☎ 03 / pop 400

Picture-perfect Boat Harbour has the kind of blond-sand beach and sapphire-blue waters to make you feel like you've taken a terribly wrong turn off the Bass Hwy and ended up somewhere in the Caribbean. Not to worry: no pirates here – apart from a particularly Jolly Roger on the beach, that is.

You can take to the harbour's remarkable waters to swim and snorkel, discover the rockpools, or paddle in the shallows. The usually calm seas are perfect for kids, and it's a low-key family-friendly place, but get here quick: there are developers sniffing around to build resorts at Boat Harbour. The crowds are bound to follow.

Sleeping

Sunny Sands Holiday Units (☎ 6442 2578; www.sunnysands.com.au; 285 Port Rd; d $130-170) Fresh and simple, these well-thought-out self-contained units have balconies to relax on and wide views of the sea.

Boat Harbour Beach Houses (☎ 6445 0913; www.boathabourbeachhouse.com; d $150-200, extra person $30) There are two beach houses managed by the same owners: the View (12 Moore St) is set high on the hillside with endless panoramas, and the Waterfront (314 Port Rd), whose deck is so close to the water, you could fish off it. They're both excellently equipped.

Harbour Houses (☎ 6442 2135; www.harbourhouse.com.au; Esplanade; d $200, extra person $40) These perfect little waterfront cottages are open plan, brightly decorated and liberally doused with a good dose of cool. We love the surfboard tables and rugs.

ourpick Paradise House (☎ 6435 7571; 22 Azzure Beach Houses, 263 Port Rd; d $240, extra adult/child $30/20; 🖳) This supersmart beach house is part of a new complex and has absolutely top-notch accommodation in three bedrooms. The trendy living areas have mod cons including free wi-fi. Bikes, fishing gear, surfboards, boogie boards and all manner of beach gear come free. Standard rate is for up to two adults and two children.

Azzure Holiday Houses (☎ 0400-142 222; 263 Port Rd; d $280, extra adult $30; 🖳) It's all contemporary style at the beach houses in this complex. There's every convenience you could imagine: DVD/CD players, wi-fi, air conditioning, a swanky kitchen, and walls hung with contemporary art.

Eating

Jolly Rogers (☎ 6445 1710; 1 Port Rd; mains $10-25; ☽ breakfast, lunch & dinner) This laid-back beachside café serves real-hunger solutions: burgers, pastas and, of course, great fish and chips. Try the fabulous salt-and-pepper squid ($17). There's also a fenced play area where you can stow the little ones.

Getting There & Away

If driving from Wynyard, the best route from the cape is to follow C234 northwest; there are some great views of the cliffs and rocky coast along this road. By bus, the daily Redline Coaches service from Burnie will drop you at the turn-off to Boat Harbour (3km) or Sisters Beach (8km) for $6.

ROCKY CAPE NATIONAL PARK

This is Tasmania's smallest national park, stretching 12km along Bass Strait's shoreline. It was known to Aboriginal Tasmanians as Tangdimmaa and has great significance to the Rar.rer.loi.he.ner people, who made their homes in the sea caves along the coastline here 8000 years before European occupation.

Inland, the park is made up of coastal heathland and rare *Banksia serrata* forests. The rolling green hills are splashed bright with wild flowers in the spring and summer months; those fond of flowers will be thrilled by the orchid-hunting here. The rocky quartzite coastline has abundant rockpools brimming with seaweeds and brightly coloured anemones and sea stars.

There's good swimming in the park at Sisters Beach, Forwards Beach and Anniversary Bay. **Sisters Beach** has an 8km stretch of bleached-blond sand, picnic tables and a shelter. Close by is Sisters Beach village, reached via C233 from Boat Harbour.

On Rocky Cape itself, you can drive out to a stunted **lighthouse**, with the Nut (p260) floating distantly on the horizon.

Bushwalking

From Sisters Beach, the walk to **Wet Cave**, **Lee Archer Cave** and **Banksia Grove** takes 45 minutes (one way); to reach the start of this walk, follow the signs to the boat ramp. You can continue further along the coast to Anniversary Point (three hours return). It's also possible to follow the coast to Rocky Cape and return along the **Inland Track** (eight hours return).

From the western end of the park at Rocky Cape Rd (accessed from a separate entrance off the Bass Hwy, west of the turn-off to Sisters Beach), you can walk to two large Aboriginal caves, South Cave and North Cave, the latter off the road to the lighthouse. The caves are significant Aboriginal sites, so visitors are encouraged *not* to enter them. There's also a good circuit of the cape itself –

allow 2½ hours. There's no drinking water in the park, so carry your own, and watch out for snakes, particularly in summer.

Sleeping & Eating

There are no camping facilities inside the national park itself, only on the highway near the entrance to Western End (see below).

SISTERS BEACH

Sisters Beach General Store (☎ 6445 1147; Honeysuckle Ave; ♡ 7.30am-7pm winter, 7.30am-8pm summer), which sells supplies, takeaways and park passes, also runs Bamboo Beach House and Shifting Sands.

Sea Change (☎ 6445 1456; 6 Elfrida Ave; d $99, extra person $25) Billed as a B&B, it's actually more of a self-contained apartment, nicely decorated, and with all you need to stay a few days. There's a tannin-brown creek nearby where platypuses are frequently spotted.

Bamboo Beach House (☎ 6445 1147; 19 Kenelm Ave; cottage d $130-150, extra adult/child $25/15) A self-contained, low-key three-bedroom cottage that can sleep up to six people.

Shifting Sands (☎ 6445 1147; 119 Irby Blvd; cottage d $130-150, extra adult/child $25/15) This is a new two-bedroom unit with great sea views and a sunny deck. It can sleep up to six people.

WESTERN END

Rocky Cape Tavern & Caravan Park (☎ 6443 4110; Bass Hwy; unpowered/powered sites $11/22, motel d $70) Conveniently located on the highway just near the western end of the national park, this place has clean and tidy facilities. The tavern serves counter meals daily (mains $18 to $27.50).

CRAYFISH CREEK TO BLACK RIVER

This part of the coastline is a series of pretty little beaches and rocky coves marred by the heavy-industry complex at Port Latta, the terminus for the 85km iron-ore pipeline from the Savage River Mine. Fortunately there's only one factory located here, and away from the busy smokestack the coast is pleasant.

You can camp at **Peggs Beach Conservation Area** (camp sites per adult/child $2.50/1.50), where there are toilets, tables, fireplaces, water and an on-site caretaker with whom you register. This area is popular for fishing and is prime Australian salmon territory (October to March).

Camping is also available at the **Crayfish Creek Caravan Park** (☎ /fax 6443 4228, 0419-302 354; 20049 Bass Hwy; unpowered/powered sites $18/22, on-site

DEVONPORT & THE NORTHWEST

DETOUR

Head into the hills south of Rocky Cape (on C225) and you'll discover forests, waterfalls and timber-getting the way it used to be done. At **Water Wheel Creek Timber Heritage Experience** (☎ 6458 8144, www .waterwheelcreek.com.au; 1314 Mawbanna Rd; adult/child/family $10/5/25; ☺ 10am-5pm Nov-Apr, to 3pm May & Sep-Oct) there's a timber-working museum, interpretative forest walks, a working timber tramway and a warm, wood-lined café. Further south you can visit **Dip Falls**, where a short, steep walk will get you to the cascades' base. About 1km from the car park, you'll find the **Big Tree**, its circumference a whopping16m.

vans $40, cabins $75-140), in a quiet bush setting among the tea trees on the banks of Crayfish creek, or take one of their pretty timber cabins. There's also a delightful multilevel 'tree house' (double with spa from $140) for those who prefer lofty accommodation.

Gateforth Cottages (☎ 6458 3248; www.gateforth cottages.com; 40 Medwins Rd; d $180, with spa $220) Offering comfortable and very relaxed accommodation in self-contained cottages, and with fantastic views of Circular Head, Gateforth is also a terrific base from which to wander the farm lanes, pat the animals and go fishing. Kids are most welcome. To get here, travel about 6km west of Port Latta. Gateforth Cottages are signed to the left about 1km past the C225 to Mawbanna.

STANLEY
☎ 03 / pop 550

Get this far west in Tasmania and you begin to feel it: there's a whiff of something in the air that feels quite distinctly like the very end of the world. Little Stanley exudes more than a trace of this frontier, life-on-the-edge ambience. The town is a scatter of brightly painted cottages, sheltering in the lee of an ancient volcano, the Nut, that's been extinct for 13 million years. In Stanley's harbour bobs a fleet of fishing boats, piled high with cray pots and orange buoys, but beyond this shelter the ocean is often whipped into whitecaps. Stroll through town on a fine day and you may not feel that underlying edginess that comes from being on the world's rim; but when the Roaring 40s blast through, you'll feel it sure

enough, and that's part of the excitement of being here.

Information

There's an ATM located inside the town's minimart (on the corner of Wharf Rd and Marine Esplanade).

Newsagency (☎ 6458 1372; 17 Church St) You can make Eftpos withdrawals here.

Post office (Church St) Also serves as an agent for Commonwealth Bank and National Bank.

Visitors centre (☎ 6458 1330; info@stanley.com.au; 45 Main Rd; ☺ 9.30am-5.30pm Mon-Fri, 10am-4pm Sat & Sun, reduced hours in winter) Friendly and knowledgeable staff with extensive regional advice. Also offers internet access ($2 per 15 min).

Sights & Activities
THE NUT

This striking 152m-high volcanic rock formation can be seen for many kilometres around Stanley. It's a steep 20-minute climb to the top: worth it for the views. The best lookout is a five-minute walk to the south of the **chairlift** (☎ 6458 1286; adult/child/family $9/7/25; ☺ 9.30am-5.30pm Oct-May, 10am-4pm Jun-Sep), and you can also take a 35-minute walk (2km) on a path around the top. From here, in summer, you can wait to view mysterious short-tailed shearwaters (also called mutton birds) as they return to their burrows at dusk after a day's foraging in the ocean.

STANLEY DISCOVERY MUSEUM

To learn more about Stanley, visit the diminutive **folk museum** (Church St; adult/child $3/50c; ☺ 10am-4pm), filled with old Circular Head photos and artefacts, including marine curios. It also runs a genealogical service ($5, including museum entry).

STANLEY ARTWORKS

You don't have to be an art buff to enjoy the amazing skill and creativity that's on offer at this **gallery** (☎ 6458 2000; 29 Church St; ☺ 9am-6pm, reduced hours in winter). There's usually an artist in residence who you can watch at work.

SEAQUARIUM

Providing a great display of marine life, **Seaquarium** (☎ 6458 2052; Fisherman's Dock; adult/child/ family $8/5/23; ☺ 9am-5pm daily 7 Sep-14 May, 11am-3pm Sat & Sun 15th Jun-6 Sep) is a great place to bring the kids. It's educational fun: they'll be squealing over the touchy-feely tank.

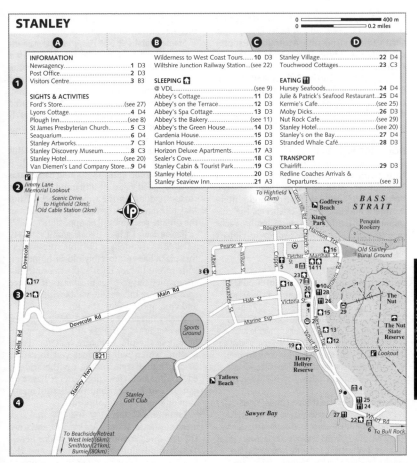

STANLEY

0   400 m
0   0.2 miles

Jimmy Lane
Memorial Lookout
Scenic Drive
to Highfield (2km);
Old Cable Station (2km)

To Highfield
(2km)

Godfreys
Beach

**BASS
STRAIT**

Kings
Park

Penguin
Rookery

Rougemont St

Harrison Tce

Green Hills Rd

Church Rd

Old Stanley
Burial Ground

Pearse St

Marshall St

Fletcher St

Dovecote Rd

Albert St

Wilson St

Cripps St

Main Rd

Edwardes St

Hale St

Victoria St

Marine Esp

Dovecote Rd

Wells Rd

Stanley Hwy

B21

Sports
Ground

Stanley
Golf Club

Tatlows
Beach

Henry
Hellyer
Reserve

Wharf Rd

**The
Nut**

**The Nut
State
Reserve**

Lookout

Sawyer Bay

To Beachside Retreat
West Inlet (6km);
Smithton (21km);
Burnie (80km)

To Bull Rock

HIGHFIELD

This impressive **homestead** (☎ 6458 1100; Green Hills Rd; adult/child/family $9/4/22; ⏰ 10am-4pm) was built in 1835 for the chief agent of the Van Diemen's Land Company, a wool-growing venture launched in 1824. The impressive home – with equally impressive views – is a rare example of domestic architecture of the Regency period in Tasmania. Highfield is 2km north of town. You can tour the house and outbuildings including stables, grain stores, workers' cottages and the chapel.

OTHER HISTORIC BUILDINGS

The bluestone warehouse on the seafront is the 1844 **Van Diemen's Land Company Store** (16 Wharf Rd), and while it once held bales of wool

for export, it now houses an exclusive boutique hotel, @VDL (p262). Also near the wharf is the particularly fine old bluestone **Ford's Store** (15 Wharf St), first used for grain storage and then as a bacon factory. It's believed to have been built in 1859 from stones brought here as ship's ballast. Today it's home to a top restaurant, Stanley's on the Bay (p263).

Next door to the Discovery Museum is the restored **Plough Inn** (Church St), a Georgian terrace that began life in 1854 as a hotel. It's now a private residence.

Other buildings of historical interest include **Lyons Cottage** (☎ 6458 1145; 14 Alexander Tce; admission by donation; ⏰ 10am-4pm Nov-Apr, 11am-3pm May-Oct), the birthplace of one-time prime minister Joseph Lyons (b 1879); the **Stanley Hotel**

(19 Church St), formerly the Union Hotel and dating from 1849; and **St James Presbyterian Church** (Fletcher St), possibly Australia's first prefabricated building, transported to Stanley from England in 1885.

The **Wiltshire Junction Railway Station** (Wharf Rd) was saved from demolition by being transported to Stanley, where it's now part of the Stanley Village accommodation complex (right).

DOCKSIDE FESTIVAL

On the weekend before the Melbourne Cup (which is held the first Tuesday in November), Stanley hosts the Dockside Festival. This annual feast of food, entertainment and jazz music celebrates the culmination of the Melbourne-to-Stanley yacht race (the precursor to the Sydney-to-Hobart yacht race).

Tours

Stanley Seal Cruises (☎ 6458 1294, 0419-550 134; www.stanleysealcruises.com.au; Fisherman's Dock) Provides 75-minute cruises to see some 50 to 500 Australian fur seals sunning themselves on Bull Rock, near Stanley. Cruises depart at 10am and 3pm from October to April, and at 10am in May and September, sea-conditions permitting. Tours cost $49/9/19/130 per adult/child under five/child/family. The same company also provides offshore fishing charters; these cost $200 for four people for two hours, all equipment supplied.

Wilderness to West Coast Tours (☎ 6458 2038, 0417-593 158; www.wildernesstasmania.com; 8 Church St) This operation has platypus- and penguin-spotting excursions (adult/child $50/25) from 1 September to the end of May, departing Stanley at dusk. During the same months they also offer full-day 4WD wilderness tours ($249 per person) to the Tarkine rainforests and to wild beaches near Arthur River. Your guide is a chef, and cooks a gourmet lunch in the rainforest. Longer, all-inclusive camping tours to Sandy Cape are available from November to April, costing $339 per person per day including chef-prepared meals.

Sleeping
TOWN CENTRE

Stanley Cabin & Tourist Park (☎ /fax 6458 1266; www.stanleycabinpark.com.au; Wharf Rd; unpowered sites d $22-24, powered sites d $24-26, dm $24-26, cabins d $75-105; 🖳) With wide views of Sawyer Bay in one direction, and towered over by the Nut in the other, this park is in a spectacular spot. There are waterfront camp sites and neat little cabins. There's also a backpackers hostel comprising six twin rooms. Linen is supplied, but it's BYO towels. A good share kitchen, BBQs, and an internet kiosk complete the facilities.

Stanley Hotel (☎ 6458 1161; www.stanleytasmania.com.au; 19 Church St; s $45, d from $65, without bathroom from $45) This historic pub has a rabbit warren of rooms upstairs. They're brightly painted and truly delightful – this has to be some of the nicest pub accommodation around. The shared bathrooms are superclean and the staff superfriendly. You can sit out on the upstairs veranda and spy down on the Stanley streetscape.

Sealer's Cove (☎ 6458 1414; fax 6458 2076; 2-4 Main Rd; d $95-110) There's simple, comfortable B&B accommodation here. It's nothing flash, but is certainly good value. Bear in mind this option closes its doors in the winter months, from May to August. You can roll right home from the on-site restaurant (see opposite).

Hanlon House (☎ 6458 1149; 6 Marshall St; s $100-145, d $160-185) Originally a Catholic presbytery, this place has comfortably old-fashioned en suite rooms ('Mary Ellen' is the spa suite) accompanied by generous breakfasts. It's a nice spot to enjoy the seaside views with victuals and vino in front of the log fire.

Stanley Village (☎ 6458 1404, 15-17 Wharf Rd, www.stanleyvillage.com.au; d $130-140; 🖳) The reception here is in the old Wiltshire Junction Train Station which will conduct you to rather bricky motel-style rooms on the water's edge, with good views over Sawyer Bay. You can dine at the excellent on-site restaurant Stanley's on the Bay (opposite).

Touchwood Cottages (☎ 6458 1348; www.touchwoodstanley.com.au; 31 Church St; d from $170, extra person $30) The three accommodation options here – Touchwood Cottage, the Studio and the Pines – have been painstakingly decorated in good old colonial style. There are pressed-metal ceilings, bluestone walls, roaring log fires and an abundance of frill. The largest (Touchwood Cottage itself) sleeps up to six.

Gardenia House (☎ 6458 1109; www.gardeniahouse.com.au; 44 Alexander Tce; d from $275 for 2 nights) This incredibly smart and luxurious cottage can be rented in part or in full. It's been beautifully renovated and is filled with a good mix of antique and contemporary furniture. There are expansive sea views, log fires and a claw-foot bath. If you want the whole house (sleeping six) you'll pay $675 for a two-night minimum stay.

our pick @VDL (☎ 6458 2032; www.atvdlstanley.com.au; 16 Wharf Rd; s $180-220; 🖳) What's been done

DEVONPORT & THE NORTHWEST

within the bluestone walls of this 1840s warehouse is quite incredible. This ultra-hip two-suite boutique hotel is frankly the coolest of the cool. Everything's top class, from the bedding to the artworks on the walls. If you've booked just one night you'll be disappointed.

There's a collective of 'Abbey' accommodation in town, all of which can be booked at the **Stanley Hotel** (☎ 1800 222 397, 6458 1161; 19-21 Church St). There's the period-style **Abbey's Cottage** (1 Marshall St; d $185), across the road from Hanlon House; the more modern **Abbey's on the Terrace** (34 Alexander Tce; d $185); the light-and-bright **Abbey's Spa Cottage** (46 Alexander Tce; d $185); **Abbey's the Green House** (26 Church St; d $185); and **Abbey's the Bakery** (1 Marshall St; d $150). The extra person charge is $30 for all cottages. Continental breakfast is included in the rates.

OUT OF TOWN

Stanley Seaview Inn (☎ 6458 1300; www.stanleyseaviewinn.com.au; 58 Dovecote Rd; s $95-150, d $96-166; 🖳) With million-dollar views of the Nut and the township, this welcoming option has a selection of motel rooms and self-contained accommodation. The on-site Nut View Restaurant is open for dinner from September to May, and has a great local seafood platter on its satisfying menu (mains $24 to $30).

Old Cable Station (☎ 6458 1312; www.oldcablestation.com.au; 435 Greenhills Rd, West Beach; d $110-160, spa cottage $220) Having maintained a telephonic link with the mainland for over 30 years from 1935, it now upholds a sophisticated guesthouse. Comprising private en suite accommodation (some rooms with spas) and a self-contained cottage (sleeping up to four), this option offers sea views, seclusion and peace. The on-site restaurant (see right) is sensational.

Beachside Retreat West Inlet (☎ 6458 1350; www.beachsideretreat.com; 253 Stanley Hwy; d $168-198, cabin $268-288, cabin with spa $338-368, 3-bedroom lodge $318) There's luxurious and ecofriendly accommodation in a Land-for-Wildlife property here (a voluntary scheme whereby landowners devote part of their property as a reserve for native species), just metres from a secluded beach. You'll enjoy magnificent sunsets, spot sea eagles, and thoroughly unwind in this natural haven.

Horizon Deluxe Apartments (☎ 0448-251 115; Dovecote Rd; www.horizonapartments.com.au; d $450; 🖳)

You can hardly beat the views from these luxurious new hilltop apartments, and inside they're kitted out with spas, surround sound, luxury toiletries, fluffy robes and touch-of-a-button climate control. Chocolate truffles and personal bar are provided: you bring the romance.

Eating

Nut Rock Cafe (☎ 1800 222 397, 6458 1186; The Nut State Reserve, Brown Rd; cakes $3; 🕙 9.30am-5.30pm) To keep your energy up as you conquer the Nut, or to restore you when you come down, this café offers coffees and frothy hot chocolates, soft drinks, Tassie's favourite Valhalla ice cream and a good range of cakes: the moist carrot cake is tops.

Stranded Whale Café (☎ 6458 1202; 6 Church St; mains $7-10; 🕙 lunch) Just down from the Town Hall, the Stranded Whale serves excellent homemade meals, including filling soups and seafood crepes.

Moby Dicks (☎ 6458 1414; 5 Church St; mains $8-12.50; 🕙 7.30-11.30am) This is where to tuck into an enormous breakfast before you go out and battle the wild west winds. Try the protein rush for power: scotch fillet, bacon and fried eggs on toast ($14.50); or the Canadian Breakfast: bacon and eggs on homemade waffles with maple syrup ($9).

Stanley Hotel (☎ 6458 1161; 19 Church St; mains $12-26; 🕙 lunch & dinner) This pub serves better-than-bistro fare, including year-round fresh seafood and servings the size of the Nut itself. The venison-and-cranberry sausages are juicily divine.

Sealer's Cove (☎ 6458 1234; 2-4 Main Rd; mains $13-20; 🕙 dinner Tue-Sun) Painted an attractive neptune-blue, and with laid-back, wooden-table style, this eatery not only serves beer-battered flathead, salt-and-pepper calamari, mussels, scallops and prawns; it also offers lip-smacking pastas and pizzas. Try the eclectic sassafras pizza: peanut satay sauce base, fresh local veggies and fetta cheese.

Stanley's on the Bay (☎ 6458 1404; 15 Wharf Rd; mains $18-30; 🕙 dinner Mon-Sat Sep-Jun) Set inside the historic Ford's Store, this fine-dining establishment specialises in steak and seafood. The wonderful seafood platter for two burgeons with local scallops, oysters, fish, octopus and salmon ($80).

Old Cable Station (☎ 6458 1312; 435 Greenhills Rd, West Beach; lunch mains $14.50-29.50, dinner 2 courses $44, 3 courses $55) This is a truly sophisticated dining option offering fine food in the salubrious surrounds of the Cable Station. Don't miss the Stanley Crayfish or the delectable Black River lamb.

Hursey Seafoods (☎ 6458 1103; 2 Alexander Tce; ☉ 9am-6pm) is awash with tanks of live sea creatures – including fish, crayfish, crabs and eels – for the freshest of (uncooked) seafood takeaways. The Hursey complex includes **Kermies Cafe** (mains $10-18; ☉ 9am-4pm), a café-takeaway serving battered prawns, crayfish salad and abalone patties, and upstairs, the licensed **Julie & Patrick's Seafood Restaurant** (mains $20-29; ☉ dinner), where you can dine on Thai crayfish salad or flathead in riesling sauce. Grab a table with a red gingham tablecloth by the window for dreamy views over the bay.

Getting There & Around
BUS
Redline Coaches offers a weekday evening service into Stanley (arriving 5pm) from Burnie ($19), but the next service out is in the morning departing 7.15am (heading to Burnie again). Buses stop at the visitors centre.

SMITHTON & AROUND
☎ 03 / pop 3361

A 22km stretch of rugged coast further west of Stanley, small-town Smithton is a bit of a backwater – in the nicest possible way. Set on the banks of the Duck River, it's a service centre for the beef farming and vegetable cropping that occur in the surrounding countryside, and is also the administrative centre for the Circular Head region. Forestry has always been big here, and Smithton is now the location of one of the biggest hardwood-timber mills in Australia, owned by Gunns Ltd (see p47).

You might not come to Smithton for Smithton's sake, but it's certainly a good place to stock up before you head off into the rainforests to the south and the wilds further west.

For insights into pioneer days here, visit the **Circular Head Heritage Centre** (☎ 6452 3296; cnr Nelson & King Sts; adult/child $2/1; ☉ 10am-3pm Mon-Sat, 12.30-3pm Sun). The most fascinating exhibit is the skeleton of the mysterious, wombat-like *Zygomaturus tasmanicum*. Few such complete examples of these have ever been found.

You'll find all the major banks here, and there are two ATMs on Emmett St.

Sights & Activities
WOOLNORTH
About 25km from Smithton, and sprawling across the northwestern tip of Tasmania, is the 220-sq-km cattle and sheep property of Woolnorth, still a holding of the Van Diemen's Land company, nearly 200 years since it was first founded. Today its commercial operation comprises over 4000 sheep, 12,000 beef and dairy cattle and 10 dairies that can each milk 1000 cows a day.

Also at Woolnorth, enormous wind turbines harness the power of the Roaring Forties, adding nearly 4MW of energy to the Tasmanian grid. You can view them up close with **Woolnorth Tours** (☎ 6452 1493; www .woolnorthtours.com) who offer informative one-hour excursions (adult/child $17.50/12) around the wind farm, as well as a half-day tour (adult/child $70/45) and full-day tour (adult/child $130/75). These visit Cape Grim, the Woolnorth property, and take you to see the shipwreck off Woolnorth Point, weather permitting.

Take deep lungfuls of the air here: the Baseline Air Pollution Station off Cape Grim declares this to be the cleanest air in the world.

DISMAL SWAMP
Thirty kilometres southwest of Smithton (just off the A2) is another of Tourism Tasmania's ventures, the dubiously named **Dismal Swamp** (☎ 6456 7199; www.tasforestrytourism.com.au/pages/site_ nw_dismal.html; adult/5-16 yr $20/10; ☉ 9am-5pm Nov-March, 10am-4pm April-October). There's a 110m-long slide here that provides a thrilling descent into a blackwood-forested sinkhole. To slide, kids must be over eight and at least 90cm tall. There's a café, retail and interpretation centre on the edge of the sinkhole, and boardwalks on the forest floor, 50m below. Among the sculpture and interpretation, look out for a frighteningly large replica of a giant wombat – imagine meeting that on a dark night in the forest!

SOUTH ARTHUR FOREST DRIVE
There are some ancient, dripping rainforests and tannin-brown rivers south of Smithton, which you can get into the heart of via the **South Arthur Forest Drive**. The drive was a circuit crossing the Arthur River in two places, at Kanunnah Bridge and Tayatea Bridge, until massive flooding washed away the latter. A new bridge is expected to be built in 2009: ask at Stanley visitors centre for updates. In the meantime, this is an out-and-back drive via the (part-gravel) C218. Highlights are the

DEVONPORT & THE NORTHWEST

roadside **Sumac River lookout**, and the incredibly still, forest-encircled **Lake Chisholm**, a flooded dolomite sinkhole that's a 30-minute walk from the car park through man fern and myrtle forest. There's also the **Milkshake Hills Forest Reserve**, where you can take a one-hour return walk and get Serengeti-like views over **Lawson Plains**.

Tours

Tall TimbersAdventure Tours (☎ 1800 628 476; 6452 2755; www.talltimbershotel.com.au; Scotchtown Rd) offers adventure tours to the Tarkine Wilderness in a 4WD OKA bus ($179 per person) and also helicopter sightseeing tours in several variations. Flight options include 20 minutes ($140 to $300 per person), 45 minutes ($275 to $635 per person) and romantic coastal sunset experiences ($259 to $575 per person). Prices vary according to the number of passengers.

Sleeping & Eating

Montagu Camping Ground (Old Port Rd; camp sites $10; ☽ Nov-Apr) This ground is just east of the diminutive Montague township, which is 16km west of Smithton.

   Bridge Hotel/Motel (☎ 6452 1389; bridgehotel@our .net.au; 2 Montagu Rd; hotel s/d $49/59, without bathroom $39/49, motel s/d $89/99) This place has comfortable rooms with shared facilities in the hotel proper and several dozen with en suite motel units round the back. Seafood, steak, roasts – your usual pub suspects – and platters are available nightly in the Colloboi restaurant.

   Tall Timbers Hotel/Motel (☎ 1800 628 476, 6452 2755; www.talltimbershotel.com.au; Scotchtown Rd; motel d/tr from $140/175, with suite d/tr $165/185, 1-/2-bedroom units $210/240; ☒) Some 2km south of Smithton, Tall Timbers has an impressive portico of massive timber beams and a reception area under an amazing timber cathedral ceiling. The rooms are comfortable and a reliable bistro serves lunch and dinner (mains $16.50 to $29). But perhaps the best thing about Tall Timbers is the tours they offer (see above).

   Rosebank Cottages (☎ 6452 2660; www.rosebank cottages.com; d 160-170) Comprises three charming and quaint B&B cottages, one in Smithton (42 Goldie St) and the other two set in sweetly perfumed gardens 6km east of town at Sedgy Creek (46 Brooks Rd), 500m off the highway. Breakfast is provided.

Getting There & Away

See p229 for details of bus services.

MARRAWAH

☎ 03 / pop 370

Untamed, unspoilt Marrawah is a domain of vast ocean beaches, mindblowing sunsets and green, rural hills. The power of the ocean here is astounding, and the wild beaches, rocky coves and headlands can have changed little since they were the homeland of Tasmania's first people. The coast here is abundant with signs of Aboriginal Tasmania – and somehow there's a feeling of lonely emptiness here, as if these original custodians had only just left this land.

   It's vast ocean waves that Marrawah is best known for today. Sometimes the Southern Ocean throws up the remains of long-forgotten shipwrecks here – things tumble in on waves that sometimes reach over 10m. Experienced surfers and windsurfers come here for the challenging breaks.

   Marrawah General Store (☎ 6457 1122; 800 Comeback Rd; ☽ 7.30am-7pm Mon-Fri, 8am-7.30pm Sat & Sun) sells supplies and petrol, and is an agent for Australia Post and Commonwealth Bank. Fill up on fuel here if you're planning to take the Western Explorer to Corinna (p269) as there's no other petrol outlet until Zeehan, some 200km away.

Activities
SURFING

The annual **West Coast Classic**, that most excellent round of the state's surfing championships, is regularly decided at Marrawah, as is a round of the state's windsurfing championships. Green Point, 2km from the town centre, has a break that's impressive in southerly conditions, and there's also good surfing further along the road at Nettley Bay.

   South of Marrawah, there's good surfing in an easterly at Lighthouse Beach (at West Point) and great reef surfing in similar conditions at Bluff Hill Point. West Point surf beach is reached by taking the left-hand branches of the road from the turn-off on C214, while Bluff Hill Point surf beach is to the right of the lighthouse off Bluff Hill Point Rd.

BEACH WALKS

There's a lengthy beach walk from Bluff Hill Point to West Point (four hours one way) and a coastal walk from Bluff Hill Point to the mouth of the Arthur River (two hours one way). There's also a highly scenic walk north along the beach from Green Point to

---

DETOUR

As you head south on B22 out of Smithton, just 3km north of Edith Creek you'll come upon **Allendale Gardens & Rainforest** (☎ 6456 4216; fax 6456 4223; Edith Creek; adult/5-16yr $10/3.50; ☼ 9am-5pm Oct-Apr), over two hectares of bird-filled exotic gardens.

This place is truly a wonder of green-fingered creativity, and it's the life's work and passion of Max and Lorraine Cross, who nurture it. You can wander through an incredible variety of trees and flowering plants here: there's the glorious birch walk, a spectacular dahlia-and-rose garden, a wisteria pergola, spring blossoms, autumn colours and a panoply of trees from Himalayan spruces to redwoods, tulip trees and the exquisite Chinese dove tree. Allen Creek ripples its way through the gardens, crossed by no less than six bridges.

On the garden's fringes there's a peaceful stand of rainforest. Here you can admire towering old-growth stringy-barks with girths of over 15m, spot a rare creeping fern and perhaps even see the platypus in the creek. Suitably well-walked, you should then indulge in tea, scones and cream in the teahouse, with lashings of Max's homemade raspberry and blackberry jams.

To head back to Stanley, take the scenic route (30 minutes) south through Edith Creek, along C219 towards Nabageena, which then traverses gravel back roads through Lileah, Alcomie, Mengha, South Forest and Forest. The view of the Nut as you approach Stanley is unforgettable.

Preminghana (around three hours return). For details of the indigenous significance of these areas, see opposite.

FISHING

In winter you can catch Australian salmon at Nettley Bay or off the rocks at West Point, while in summer you can catch black-backed salmon off the beach at the mouth of the Arthur River, or catch estuary perch in the river itself.

Tours

King's Run Wildlife Tours (☎ 6457 1191; www.kingsrun.com.au; per person $75) Geoff King is a local character who has become (deservedly) famous for his devil-spotting tours. He takes visitors on evening trips to an atmospheric old fishing shack in a remote spot on his 300-hectare property to watch devils tuck voraciously into a buffet dinner of road kill.

Sleeping & Eating

Camping is possible for free at beautiful Green Point, where there are toilets, water and an outdoor cold shower. You must pitch your tent by the toilets back from the beach, not on the foreshore.

Glendonald Cottage (☎ 6457 1191; www.kingsrun.com.au; 79 Arthur River Rd; d from $95) Just down C214 towards Arthur River, this is a spacious self-contained two-bedroom rural place with plenty of reading material on Aboriginal history and the ecology of the area.

our pick **Marrawah Beach House** (☎ 6457 1285; 19 Beach Rd, Green Point; d from $120, extra person$20) This must be close to the ultimate beach house! It's secluded, view-filled and brightly decorated with plenty of starfish and seahells, and the friendly owners set it up with treats like fresh flowers and local honey before you arrive. The beach house can sleep up to five people. Ring ahead, as the managers live elsewhere.

Ann Bay Cabins (☎ /fax 6457 1358; www.annbaycabins.com.au; Green Point Rd; d $120-140) These two superb, soporific wooden cabins are just the place to hang out and get away from it all. You can sit out on the deck and admire the views, or luxuriate in the deep spa bath, with bathing essentials and choccies supplied. Continental breakfast is provided.

You can get a good meal and a drink at **Marrawah Tavern** (☎ 6457 1102; Comeback Rd; mains $10-25; ☼ lunch & dinner). Choices include steak sandwiches, prawns, roasts, beef 'n' reef, and whole local flounders.

ARTHUR RIVER
☎ 03 / pop 110

There are only a few hardy souls who call Arthur River their full-time home – the rest of the population is made up of committed 'shackies', and fishers who love the wild remoteness of the country around here. There's a **Parks & Wildlife Service ranger station** (PWS; ☎ 6457 1225) on the northern side of the river, where you can get camping information and permits for off-road vehicles.

Gardiner Point, signposted off the main road on the southern side of the old, timber Arthur River bridge, is Tasmania's official **Edge of the**

World: the sea here stretches uninterrupted all the way to Argentina. There's a plaque at the point – a great place to take those leaning-into-the-wind, world's-end photos.

Activities

CANOEING

You can explore the amazing river and rainforest with watercraft from **Arthur River Canoe & Boat Hire** (☎ 6457 1312). This place offers information on river conditions and storage for your gear, and hires single and double Canadian canoes for $12 to $16 per hour and $50 to $70 per day. They also rent out aluminium dinghies with outboards for $25 an hour or $130 per day. Even better, they'll help you organise a down-river expedition from either Kanunnah Bridge (two-day trip) or the Tayatea Bridge site (four-day trip). They'll meet you at the launching site with the boats and drive your car back to Arthur River for you.

CRUISES

The reflections on the Arthur River have to be seen to be believed, and you can get out among them on board the MV *George Robinson*, operated by **Arthur River Cruises** (☎ 6457 1158; www .arthurrivercruises.com). Cruises depart daily at 10am from September to May (adult/child $74/30). You'll see sea eagles and kingfishers, stroll in the rainforest and enjoy a BBQ lunch.

An alternative cruise is offered by **ARReflections River Cruises** (☎ /fax 6457 1288; www .arthurriver.com.au; 4 Gardiner St). Its attractive MV *Reflections* departs at 10.15am daily for a 5½-hour return trip to Warra Landing, where you also get a guided rainforest walk and gourmet lunch (adult/child $77/44).

Sleeping & Eating

Camping grounds (unpowered sites per adult/pensioner/family $5/4.50/15, per week $20/18/60) in the area include Manuka, Peppermint and Prickly Wattle, the latter on the road to Couta Rocks. They have taps, cold showers and toilets, but no bins – take your rubbish out with you. Self-register at the PWS office. There's also basic camping in Arthur River opposite the kiosk.

Arthur River Holiday Units (☎ /fax 6457 1288; 2 Gardiner St; s from $88, d $95-110) These comfortable, self-contained units may not have the most stylish decoration you've even seen, but they're great for families and perfect for people less nimble on their feet, as they have level access. Accommodation and river-cruise packages are available.

Ocean View Holiday Cottage (☎ 6457 1100, 0419-537 500; Lot 80 Gardiner St; d $100, extra person $20) This is a pleasant three-bedroom house sleeping up to six people, with views of the river mouth. It also offers a cosy wood fire, electric blankets and satellite TV. Inquire at the house opposite.

TASMANIAN ABORIGINAL SITES

The Marrawah area, with its isolated beaches and cliffs, has seen minimal disturbance from European development, in direct contrast to the maximal disturbances visited by Europeans upon the area's former Aboriginal inhabitants – these include the massacre of an estimated 30 Aborigines in 1827 at euphemistically named Suicide Bay to the north. Some areas have now been proclaimed reserves to protect rock carvings, middens, hut depressions and seal hides.

There's a significant Aboriginal site along the road to Arthur River at West Point. Beyond the township at Sundown Point is a site containing several dozen mudstone slabs engraved with mainly circular motifs. The Arthur Pieman Conservation Area, further south, has been called one of the world's most important archaeological complexes, in particular because of its dense concentration of middens. There are also several important cave sites at Rocky Cape National Park.

Arguably the most significant site on the West Coast is 7km north of Marrawah at Preminghana (formerly known as Mt Cameron West). At the northern end of the beach are low-lying slabs of rock with geometric rock carvings dating back at least two millennia. Also in this area are remnants of stone tools, tool quarries and middens. There are also natural links with Tasmanian Aboriginal culture, such as boobialla, honeysuckle and tea-tree clusters – plants used to prepare food and traditional medicines.

Preminghana was returned to the Aboriginal people in 1995 – you can't visit the area independently. If you'd like to be authoritatively guided around this and other significant Aboriginal sites, contact the **Tasmanian Aboriginal Land and Sea Council** (TALSC; ☎ 6231 0288; fax 6231 0298; 4 Lefroy St, North Hobart), which keeps a list of heritage officers who can accompany you to the sites.

DEVONPORT & THE NORTHWEST

Sunset Holiday Villas (☎ /fax 6457 1212; 23 Gardiner St; d $100-120, extra person adult/child $25/15) There are two self-contained two-bedroom units here sleeping six people comfortably. They share a balcony and views of the beach, which can be stunning at sunset.

The town has a kiosk with limited supplies, and there are also **fresh crayfish** (☎ 6457 1212) available.

THE TARKINE WILDERNESS

The Tarkine is a 3500-sq-km stretch of wild, natural country between the Arthur River in the north and the Pieman River in the south. It encompasses the largest intact tract of temperate rainforest in the Southern Hemisphere, as well as tall eucalypt forests, endless horizons of buttongrass plains, savage ocean beaches, sand dunes and extensive coastal heathland. Because of its remoteness, ferocious weather and isolation, the Tarkine survived almost untouched well into the 20th century.

The area first entered the national psyche through the controversy over the building of the so-called Road To Nowhere in 1995 (see opposite), and conservation groups have been seeking full protection for it ever since. Part of the Tarkine was partly protected in the Arthur Pieman Conservation Area, but until 2005 its ancient myrtle rainforest was without protection. In 2003, the Tasmanian government gave the go-ahead to 'selectively log' the Tarkine's giant myrtle trees, sparking a campaign to save them. In May 2005, after an election in which Tasmania's forests became a national issue, the federal government declared 73,000 further hectares of the Tarkine rainforest safe from logging. Some conservation groups still call for a Tarkine National Park, to be added to the remote Savage River National Park (opposite), as unprotected parts of the Tarkine remain vulnerable to logging, mining, uncontrolled off-road driving and, unfortunately, arson.

You can get into the heart of the Tarkine with route notes from the **Tarkine National Coalition** (☎ 6431 2373; www.tarkine.org), the conservation group that's led the campaign to protect the area. Download a range of driving and walking brochures on its website (under 'guides').

The folks at **Tarkine Trails** (☎ 6223 5320, 0427-397 815; www.tarkinetrails.com.au) are busy proving that the Tarkine is worth much more protected, as a natural playground, than it would be reduced to woodchips. They can take you on guided six-day rainforest walking adventures ($1549), five-day boat and beachwalking tours, with 4WD connections ($1549) and six-day vehicle-based Tarkine explorations ($2499).

For some etherally beautiful photography from this region, buy *Tarkine,* put together by the World Wildlife Fund.

WESTERN EXPLORER (C249) & ARTHUR PIEMAN CONSERVATION AREA

The Western Explorer is probably Tasmania's most excitingly remote road journey. It delves deep into the buttongrass wilderness of the **Arthur Pieman Conservation Area** of the western Tarkine. It was controversially upgraded from a barely there 4WD track into a wide gravel road in 1995, to the cries of conservationists who saw it as further opening up this great western wilderness to damage and exploitation. It was dubbed The Road To Nowhere, and predictions about its damaging effects have unfortunately come true: mostly in the form of frequent fires, set both unintentionally and on purpose. The increased visitor traffic means that such fires are now able to strike deep into this area. A 2008 fire – started by a car accident – burnt out 17,000 hectares of the Tarkine's heart.

Now the road is there it's a wonderful means of traversing an incredibly rugged, remote part of Tasmania. Thanks to the barge over the Pieman River at Corinna (see opposite) you can travel from Arthur River right down the west coast to Zeehan and Strahan.

The road condition varies from season to season. Although it's regularly negotiated by vehicles without 4WD and is promoted as a tourist route, it's remote, unsealed and at times rough, rocky and steep, all of which justifies the 50km/h speed limit. Don't drive the road at night or in bad weather. For an up-to-date assessment on track conditions ask at the **Arthur River ranger station** (PWS; ☎ 6457 1225).

Fill up your car at Marrawah if you're travelling south or at Zeehan, Tullah or Waratah if heading north: there's no petrol in between.

The 1000-sq-km Arthur Pieman Conservation Area takes in features including the remote fishing settlement of **Temma**, the mining ghost town of **Balfour**, magnificent wild beaches like **Sandy Cape Beach**, the rugged **Norfolk Range**, the **Thornton** and **Interview Rivers** and savage **Pieman Heads**. Because it doesn't have national park status, this fragile environment is still threatened by indiscriminate off-road vehicle use, grazing, malicious damage to Aboriginal sites and fire. The wild beaches here are feared for their vehicle-swallowing quicksand.

CORINNA & THE PIEMAN RIVER
☎ 03

In rip-roaring gold-rush days Corinna was a humming town with two hotels, a post office, plenty of shops and a population in and around town that numbered 2500 souls. That's hard to believe now when you pull up on the forested edge of the Pieman, turn off your car's engine and absorb the unbelievable forest peace.

A wise bunch of tourism experts took over the remains of Corinna a few years ago, and have turned it, with utmost care, into a really pleasant little place to stop and stay, while retaining the deep-forest feel. There's no mobile phone reception, there are no TVs, and the most prevalent sound is birdsong.

While in Corinna you can't miss the **Pieman River Cruise** (☎ 6446 1170). You'll be awe-filled by the reflections and may appreciate this more rustic alternative to the crowded Gordon River cruises out of Strahan. Costing $79/39 per adult/child, the tour on the MV *Arcadia II* departs at 10am and returns at 2.30pm daily. Book well ahead.

Also on offer are canoe and kayak paddles on the Pieman, fishing trips, and boat trips to Lovers' Falls, where you can be dropped with a picnic hamper and sigh at the beauty of it all.

Bushwalking around here includes nearby Mt Donaldson (four hours return) and Philosopher's Falls (four hours return). The shorter Huon Pine Trail on the banks of the Pieman has some sections that are accessible by wheelchair. For details on all these activities, ask at the reception of Corinna Wilderness Experience (below).

Sleeping & Eating
Corinna Wilderness Experience (☎ 6446 1170; www .corinna.com.au; s $50, cottages d $175, houses d $150-200; extra person $25) Has a collection of newly built but suitably rustic looking self-contained timber cottages, with interiors all kitted out in contemporary style. There are three older-style houses, also comfortably self-contained, and the old pub, which houses really decent backpackers rooms. There are also all the usual shared backpackers facilities. One of the cottages is wheelchair accessible. Outside, there's also (unpowered) camping with toilets and showers for $15 per vehicle.

You can satisfy your hunger in the **pub-restaurant** which serves hearty homemade meals for lunch and dinner (mains $12 to $35) including gourmet pizzas, focaccias and delectable wallaby shank pies. Picnic hampers are also available for order.

The complex's reception area has a store selling basic produce, and also has a small deli section.

Getting There & Away
From the south, it's approximately a 45-minute drive from Zeehan and a 1½-hour drive from Strahan, while from the north it's a two- to three-hour drive from Arthur River. See opposite for more details.

The **Fatman ferry** (☎ 6446 1170; motorcycles & bicycles/standard vehicle/caravan $10/20/25; ◷ 9am-5pm Apr-Sep, to 7pm Oct-Mar) slides across the Pieman on demand. Note there's a 9m-length limit on vehicles with caravans.

SAVAGE RIVER NATIONAL PARK
A remote area of 180 sq km, this park sits in Australia's largest area of cool-temperate rainforest and contains a swathe of buttongrass on its central Baretop Ridge. Savage River was initially worked over for its alluvial gold, and there is still the large Savage River opencut iron ore mine close by. There are no roads into the national park, so it can't be visited – but it's good to know its there.

HELLYER GORGE
You can also approach Corinna from Somerset, just west of Burnie – a route that will take you on the Murchison Hwy through magnificent Hellyer Gorge. The picnic area by the Hellyer River makes for a pleasant roadside repose.

Parallel to the Murchison Hwy is the B18 from Burnie, an alternative road that's faster but less scenic. About 70km south of Burnie is the C132 turn-off to Cradle Mountain.

WARATAH
☎ 03 / pop 230

Waratah has two claims to fame. It's nearby tin mine at Mt Bischoff was once the world's richest, and the last verifiably breathing Tasmanian tiger was trapped here in 1936.

This is a pretty lakeside town sliced through by Happy Valley gorge and its cascading waterfall, and surrounded by wild hillsides. To get an impression of early days, visit the local **museum** (☎ 6439 1252; Smith St; ☼ 10am-4pm Oct-May, noon-3pm Mon-Fri Jun-Sep). Next door is **Philosopher Smith's Hut**, a reconstruction of the abode of one James Smith, the prospector who discovered tin in them-there hills. Also of interest is the historic **stamper mill**, once used to break up tin ore and now restored to its former glory. It's close to the town hall. You can watch things rattle and whirr at the touch of a button.

Behind the post office, **Waratah Camping & Caravan Park** (☎ 6439 7100; Smith St; unpowered/powered d $15/20) has lakeside caravan and camping sites. Keys to the amenities block are available at the post office or the roadhouse/general store. **Bischoff Hotel** (☎ 6439 1188; Main St; s/d $44/88, d without bathroom $66) offers rooms and counter meals for lunch and dinner (mains $10 to $18). There's also the attractive **O'Connor Hall Guesthouse** (☎ 6439 1472; 2 Smith St; d $110-160) with wrought-iron tracery and four-poster beds. Be sure to book ahead for accommodation – the Mt Bischoff mine has reopened for business, on the back of the metals boom.

DEVONPORT & THE NORTHWEST

The West

There are no two ways about it: Tasmania's west truly is its wilder side. We're talking endless ocean beaches where the surf pounds in from South America, ancient mossy rainforests dripping emerald green, whisky-tinted rivers, glacier-sculpted mountain peaks and boundless untamed horizons that make you feel you're the only soul in the world.

There's a rugged human side to this part of Tasmania too. The first inhabitants braved the west's ferocious weather indomitably; but convicts transported into aching isolation on Sarah Island suffered extreme privations, leaving behind desperate legends of mutiny and cannibalism. Later piners and miners ventured into rivers and forests here. Outdoor adventurers were the next to feel the lure of the wild west. Their depictions of this region's beauty helped win Australia's most intense environmental protest, the battle to save the Gordon and Franklin Rivers from a hydroelectric dam. Even today, west-coasters are different: they have a certain rough-at-the-edges, no-nonsense charm. The visitor will find a vast outdoor playground: multiday hikes, such as the Overland Track, to tackle and river rafting on the incredible Franklin River. There's sailing, jet-boating, sandboarding and helicopter flights, or more gentle outdoor pleasures like chasing the reflections on a mirror-calm Gordon River cruise, riding through the rainforests on a restored heritage railway or being driven to the heart of it all in a comfortable 4WD.

HIGHLIGHTS

- Sand-boarding on the towering sand dunes at **Henty Dunes** (p278)
- Waking up on a sailboat on the **Gordon River** (p279) to reflections so perfect, they'll have you puzzling which way is up
- Shouldering a backpack and striding out through Tasmania's breathtaking alpine heart on the **Overland Track** (p290)
- Getting some full wilderness immersion on a 10-day rafting journey down the wild **Franklin River** (p288)
- Watching the sun sink towards South America and feeling the awesome power of the waves on 33km-long **Ocean Beach** (p278)
- Riding the rails through the rainforest between Strahan and Queenstown on the **West Coast Wilderness Railway** (p286)
- Swooping low over the King River and landing on the forested Teepookana Plateau on a **scenic helicopter flight** (p281)
- Climbing from the mud to the quartzite peak of remote **Frenchmans Cap** (p288), one of Tasmania's more off-the-beaten-track bushwalks

★ Ocean Beach

Henty Dunes ★

Queenstown ★

Strahan ★ ★ West Coast
Wilderness
★ Railway

Teepookana
Plateau & Forest

The
★ Overland
Track

★ Frenchmans
Cap

★ Franklin-Gordon
Wild Rivers
National Park

THE WEST

■ TELEPHONE CODE: 03   ■ www.tasmaniaswestcoast.com.au

Getting There & Around

Tassielink (☎ 6230 8900, 1300 300 520; www.tassielink.com.au) operates two/five times a week in winter/summer from Hobart to Bronte Junction ($33.40 one way, 2¼ to 2¾ hours), Derwent Bridge ($39.90 one way), Lake St Clair ($46.40 one way, three to 3½ hours), the start of the Frenchmans Cap walk ($48.20 one way, four hours), Queenstown ($58.50 one way, 5½ to six hours) and Strahan ($67.70 one way, 6½ to 8½ hours), times varying due to Queenstown stopover); and return. From Launceston, Tassielink offers a return service to Deloraine ($10.60, 40 minutes), Sheffield ($27, two hours 10 minutes), Gowrie Park ($35.60, 2½ hours), Cradle Mountain ($53.30, 3¼ hours), Tullah ($46.10, five hours), Rosebery ($48.10, 5¼ hours), Zeehan ($55.80, six hours), Queenstown ($64.70, 6½ hours) and Strahan ($73.90, eight hours). This route is covered three to seven days a week, depending on the season, and includes a connection service from the ferry dock in Devonport to the bus station and vice versa.

For information about additional services for those walking the Overland Track, see p297.

Drivers heading north up the Western Explorer Rd should fill up at Zeehan, Tullah or Waratah, as there's no fuel at either Savage River or Corinna.

TULLAH
☎ 03 / pop 270

Long isolated in the dreaming rainforests of the West Coast Range, and wrapped around by deep, tannin-brown rivers, the little town of Tullah was established when mineral riches were discovered here in 1887. The lead-zinc-copper-silver-ore bearing body in nearby Mt Farrell sustained the town until the mine closed in the 1970s.

The name Tullah comes from an Aboriginal word meaning 'meeting of two rivers', and indeed, Tullah is almost an island: there are bridge crossings to enter and leave town, and seven dams in the vicinity. The town shelters in the nape of majestic Mts Farrell and Murchison, and the waters of Lake Rosebery lap close.

For most of its history, Tullah was only accessible to the outside world by horse or on foot. Later came a narrow gauge train and only in 1962, a road. In the 1970s and 1980s, Tullah was a 'hydro-town' accommodating workers building hydroelectric dams. It was a rollicking time: with 800 hardworking men

in town the pub regularly served 38 18-gallon beer kegs in one week.

Though posthydro Tullah has been a somnolent backwater, like much of the west coast it's currently experiencing a mining boom again, driven by the rise in metal prices. Old mines are reopening and there's an air of optimism about. It's still a quiet place though, offering visitors accommodation as well as trout fishing, boating and horseback riding.

Information

The friendly folks at the **Tullah Tavern Museum and Café** (☎ 6473 4141; Farrell St; ⏰ 9am-5pm; 🖥) dole out information on the area, as well as running an informative display on mining and hydro times. Pick up some of the mineral-bearing rocks to find out for yourself what a weighty issue mining is here.

Sights & Activities

At **Radford Woodcrafts** (☎ 6473 4344; ⏰ 9am-4pm most days) gallery and workshop you can breathe the woody aromas of Tassie timbers, stroke some smooth grains, and buy quality lamps, clocks and other woodware, including a wide range of colourful wooden genie's bottles!

There are several scenic drives alongside major hydroelectric dams and lakes. Three kilometres north of town you can follow a road west for 55km to **Reece Dam** and then a further 29km to Zeehan. Another scenic road, the **Anthony Rd**, starts 5km south of town and heads over the flanks of Mt Murchison towards Queenstown – providing good views as it crosses the West Coast Range. From town, a scenic minor road also leads to **Murchison Dam**.

The area's best **walks** include **Mt Farrell** (three hours return) and **Mt Murchison** (1275m; six hours return).

To commemorate the days of steam when Tullah's only link to the outside world was by train, local residents have restored **Wee Georgie Wood** (☎ 0417-142 724; Murchison Hwy; adult/child/pensioner/family $6/2/3/12), one of the narrow-gauge steam locomotives that operated on the town's original railway. From late September to early April, on Saturdays or Sundays, usually between 10am and 4pm, passengers can take 20-minute rides through the hills and rainforest, on part of the original track.

Tullah Horse-Back & Boat Tours (☎ 6473 4289, 0409-809 441; www.tullahhorseback.com.au; Mackintosh Track) provides a perfect way to discover the back

THE WEST

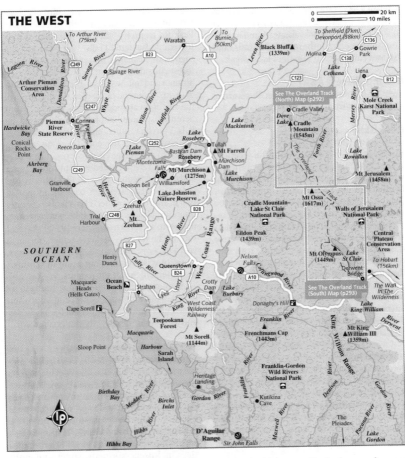

tracks and forests of this still-wild part of the world. A gang of characterful horses and their charming owners will take you on anything from hour-long rides ($40/200 per hour/day) to multiday explorations – combined with, or separate from boat and fishing trips ($30 per hour) on nearby waters, and trips in the carts drawn by their gentle-giant draught horses ($20 per half-hour). All prices per person.

Sleeping & Eating

Tullah Lakeside Chalet (☎ 6473 4121; www.tullahchalet .com; Farrell St; dm $25, backpackers tw $50, d $80-140) Set in ex-hydro workers' accommodation, this lake-edge hotel is being renovated bit by bit and has some well-decorated, comfortable rooms. Ask for one with a lake view. The backpackers' ac-

commodation is exceedingly clean, and rooms have en suites. The chalet can advise on boat/ mountain bike hire and local walks. It also has a pub and restaurant (mains $10 to $25, open breakfast, lunch and dinner) with glorious lake views. It also does very good food: the pumpkin and pistachio pie with sassafras and leatherwood honey jelly was our pick.

Tullah Tavern Museum & Café (☎ 6473 4141; Murchison Hwy; units $110; 💻) There are two upscale self-contained units here: clean and spacious with lovely mountain views. In the bright and welcoming café (mains $3 to $10, open 9am to 5pm) you can grab a light meal, sup on some of the on-tap beers or warm up by the log fire. There's wireless internet both here and in the accommodation.

THE WEST

Tullah Village Café (☎ 6473 4377; Farrell St; mains around $15-19; ☽ breakfast, lunch & dinner) You can get cooked breakfasts, snack takeaways and heavier fare and decent hamburgers, schnitzels, and fish and chips here. It also does kids' meals.

Getting There & Away

See p272 for transport information. Buses arrive at and depart from the BP service station.

ROSEBERY

☎ 03 / pop 1500

Rosebery's best asset is its beautiful location. It nestles in a valley of temperate rainforest with Mt Murchison to the east, imposing Mt Black (950m) to the north, and Mt Read (which has Tasmania's highest rainfall) to the south. Rosebery itself gets 3.5m of rainfall on average each year. The town was founded in 1893 when gold was discovered in the area; the mine here now extracts zinc, lead and copper from the earth, employing much of the populace. Rosebery is what you might call a rough diamond: unpolished on the outside but possessed of a good heart. You may not linger long here, but if you do you should find the locals friendly, and there's some wonderful nature nearby.

Information

Newsagency (☎ 6473 1142; Agnes St; ☽ 5.30am-5.30pm Mon-Fri, 6am-3pm Sat, 7am-1pm Sun) Also handles ANZ transactions and has a 24-hour ATM.

Online access centre (☎ 6473 1938; ☽ 9am or 10am-4pm or 5pm Mon-Fri, 10am-1pm Sat) In the District School on Morrisby St.

Post office (Agnes St) Also a Commonwealth Bank agent.

Sights & Activities

The high school has some interesting old **mine remnants** (Propsting St) along its front fence, including a water wheel and railway carriage for steep inclines. The school also contains a small **mining museum** (admission free) that displays artefacts and old photos; ask at the school's reception. There's a **heritage centre** next to the Pasminco Mine site containing pictures and other memorabilia of the town's history.

In late March or early April each year, the town comes alive with the **Rosebery Festival**. There's live music, horseback rides, a puppet theatre, food stalls, fireworks and, of course, that old Tassie favourite: wood-chopping.

With all that rain, Rosebery's naturally a top spot for waterfalls. The picnic area at the southern entrance to town is the start of a short (10-minute) walk along the Stitt River and over Park Rd to pretty **Stitt Falls**. And then there's incredible **Montezuma Falls**, 104m tall and the highest in Tasmania, that plume down a rainforest cliffside. Head out of Rosebery towards Strahan and follow signs to the falls 2km south of town. At the end of the road is Williamsford, the site of an abandoned mining town. From here an easy three-hour return walk leads to the falls. You can venture out onto the narrow (but safe) swing bridge suspended over the yawning chasm to get a great view.

If you prefer a guided walk to Montezuma Falls, **Hay's Adventure Tours** (☎ 6473 1247; www.hays tour.com; 10-12 Esplanade) runs trips for groups of two or more in summer. Hay's is also the only operator allowed into the **Lake Johnston Nature Reserve** to see an extraordinary 10,000-year-old stand of Huon pine. Its 4WD nature tours here cost $70 per person and take 2½ to three hours. Departure is usually about 11am in summer; in winter, whenever the fog lifts.

Additionally, Hay's offers trout fishing tours on Lakes Mackintosh, Rosebery and Murchison near Tullah for $165 per person for a half-day and $440 for a full day. All gear is supplied.

Sleeping & Eating

Rosebery Caravan Park (☎ 6473 1366; Park Rd; unpowered/powered sites $20/25, cabins $50-90) This park is surrounded by hills and has a small, grassy camping area, a gravel caravan area and basic cabins. It's so shady it can get quite cool once it loses the sun. Prices are for two people.

Rosebery Top Pub (☎ 6473 1351; Agnes St; s with/without bathroom $65/40, d $80/60, extra person $20) On Rosebery's main street and right in the centre of town, this pub has clean and quiet budget rooms over a friendly bar where you're sure to get chatting with locals. Counter meals are served in the restaurant nightly (mains $18 to $28).

our pick Mount Black Lodge (☎ 6473 1039; www .mountblacklodge.com; Hospital Rd; d $110-130) What a pleasure this rustic little lodge is. This cosy place run by friendly owners looks towards Mt Murchison and Mt Read, so ask for a mountain-view room. There's an appealing lounge where you can stay warm by the wood heater.

Blue Moon Restaurant & Gallery (mains $18.50-28; ☽ dinner) In Mount Black Lodge, serves excellent home-cooked food including such enticing dishes as Blue Moon beef with strawberry chilli jus, and fantastic fresh lasagne and ravioli.

Getting There & Away

Buses arrive at and depart from Mackrell's Milkbar at 24 Agnes St. See p272 for more information.

ZEEHAN

☎ 03 / pop 900

For Zeehan – as for much of the west coast – the big thing in town has always been mining. In 1882, Frank Long discovered silver and lead on the banks of Pea Soup Creek, marking the first days of a boomtown that became known as Silver City with a population of 10,000 and 27 pubs, the famous Gaiety Theatre – seating 1000 people – and even its own stock exchange.

When boom had evolved to bust, in the 1960s Zeehan revived its fortunes as dormitory town for the nearby Renison Bell Tin mine. In the 1980s, Renison Bell was Australia's largest underground tin mine and produced 46% of all the country's tin. Boom became bust again in the 1990s, but like much of the west coast, Zeehan is now feeding a minerals-hungry world again. In 2008 Zeehan Zinc expected to make $30 million from its open-cut zinc and lead mine in just six weeks, and the Renison Bell mine opened once again, hoping to ride high on the back of record tin prices.

Despite the present boom, Zeehan still has that quiet one-horse town feel where you could be forgiven for believing you just saw some tumbleweed roll down the main street. It's worth stopping, though, for the excellent museum complex, a couple of quirky private collections, or simply to wander Main St and appreciate the period architecture. In November each year the Zeehan Gem & Mineral Fair features gems, jewellery, minerals, crystals and fossils for sale or simply for wondering at; as well as gem-fossicking-related activities including gem-panning and crystal hunts.

Orientation & Information

The town is the administrative centre for the region and has branches of the ANZ and Commonwealth Banks. There's tourist information at the West Coast Pioneers Museum.

GETTING AWAY FROM IT ALL

Avoid the tourist hoards during peak season and head out to remote **Granville Harbour** (p276). A sometimes rough gravel road leads to this tranquil seaside haven northwest of Zeehan, making it the perfect respite from the hectic touring routes. Be sure to check the road conditions with a local before you go.

Online access centre (☎ 6471 7684; Zeehan Library, Main St; 2-4.30pm Mon, 3-7pm Tue, 3-7pm Wed, 2-4.30pm Thu, 11am-1pm Fri, 10am-noon Sat) Has internet access for $2 per 15 minutes.

Sights & Activities
WEST COAST PIONEERS MUSEUM

This excellent **museum** (☎ 6471 6225; Main St; adult/child & concession/family $10/9/22; 9am-5pm) is in the 1894 School of Mines building, and is one of the best regional mining museums in the nation. It also includes displays on the west's rail and shipping heritage. The ground floor features a world-class mineral display, including samples of bright orange crocoite, which is Tasmania's official mineral emblem and only found in this area. Upstairs there's a fascinating photographic history of the west coast. To one side of the museum is an exhibit of steam locomotives and carriages from the early west coast railways, and downstairs is a display of early mining equipment.

GAIETY GRAND

Just down the road from West Coast Pioneers Museum and covered by the same entry fee is the Gaiety Grand Complex. The Gaiety was one of the biggest, most modern theatres in the world when it opened in February 1898, and what a bonus it must have been for the miners to be able to move between the pub and the theatre through connecting doors. To mark the Gaiety's opening a troupe of 60 was brought to town from Melbourne and played to 1000 spectators every night for a week. Audiences came from as far afield as Queenstown, at that time a six-hour journey away. Such luminaries as Dame Nellie Melba were included on the billings.

The theatre has recently been beautifully restored to its former glory – complete with gorgeous red velvet drapes – and has occasional ballet and orchestra touring performances as well as local music hall gigs. There's

THE WEST

also a very worthwhile gallery collection by Tasmanian and local artists of the west coast. The friendly staff are a veritable (err….) mine of information.

HISTORIC WALK

Starting at the museum, this circuit walk follows Main St west, and turns left down Fowler St towards the golf course. The route leads through the **Spray Tunnel**, a former railway tunnel. Turn left again to follow the Comstock track (an old tramway) south to **Florence Dam**. Follow the right track at the fork, winding around Keel Ridge, then descend to the southern end of Main St. The walk takes two to three hours and passes a lot of old mine sites. More detailed information on this walk and others in the area can be obtained at the pioneers museum.

PRIVATE MUSEUMS

Zeehan has two off-beat private collections that are part of local lore and popular with visitors. There's **Shorty's Private Collection** (☎ 6471 6595; 22 Shaw St; admission by gold coin donation; 🕙 10am-5pm), an unusual and pleasingly tongue-in-cheek assemblage of minerals, mining odds and ends, and 'bushcraft oddities' – a display so all-encompassing it even includes a witches' coven! Near here you'll also find the eccentric **Dr Frankensteins Museum of Monsters** (☎ 6471 6580; 12 Whyte St; admission by donation). This local funhouse is open in the afternoon: ring the doorbell to alert the monster of your arrival. Look out for the sinister two-headed Tasmanian babies. Know the joke, don't you?

OTHER ATTRACTIONS

There are plenty of old mining relics outside town. Four kilometres south of Zeehan you'll find some old **smelters** beside the highway. For panoramic views you can follow the track starting near the smelters to the top of **Mt Zeehan**; the walk takes three hours return.

Northwest of Zeehan, the quiet C249 leads to the **Reece Dam**, part of the Pieman River hydroelectric scheme, that's known as a top spot for trout fishing. This road allows access to remote **Granville Harbour** on a rough dirt track (see boxed text, p275), one of the best spots in Tasmania for crayfish. The C249 also leads to peaceful Corinna, which is the jumping-off point for the Pieman River Cruise (see p269) and driving the Western Explorer (see p268). On the way to Reece Dam you can take a one-

---

> **WARNING**
>
> If walking off marked tracks in the bush close to Zeehan or at Trial Harbour, beware of abandoned mine shafts hidden by vegetation.

---

hour return walk to **Heemskirk Falls**, which is signposted off the road.

Directly west of Zeehan there's a gravel road to **Trial Harbour**. This was Zeehan's port and is now a ragged collection of holiday shacks and the odd permanent home. There are endless coastal walks here, good fishing and great free camping in the vicinity – but no shops or facilities. You can get your fix of the past at the local **history room** (🕙 opening times vary), run by volunteers, which gives an insight into the early days including tales of the ships that came in and the colourful local identities.

Driving south from Zeehan towards Strahan on the B27, you'll pass close to Ocean Beach and **Henty Dunes** (see p278).

Sleeping & Eating

Treasure Island Caravan Park (☎ 6471 6633; tiz@dodo .com.au; Hurst St; unpowered/powered sites d $19/25, on-site vans $45-65, cabins $77-90) This park is spread out alongside the Zeehan Rivulet on the northern edge of town. It has friendly management and plenty of greenery surrounds it.

Hotel Cecil (☎ 6471 6221; fax 6471 6599; Main St; s $55, d with/without bathroom $75/65, cottages $105) Characterful Hotel Cecil has spic-and-span pub rooms upstairs which come with their own ghost, Maud. The owners will tell you her story. If you're wary of otherworldly happenings, you might prefer the innocuous self-contained miners' cottages just outside.

Mt Zeehan Retreat (☎ 6471 6424; fax 6471 6430; 12 Runcorn St; d with shared bathroom $90, with en suite $100-120) Just out of town in a quiet setting, this neat B&B is run by a charming couple who cook up wonderful breakfasts including home-grown strawberries in season. The wood-lined rooms have nice views over the surrounding hills. There are no credit-card facilities.

Heemskirk Motor Hotel (☎ 6471 6107; fax 6471 6694; Main St; d $100-140) At the eastern entrance to town, this motel won't win any architectural design awards, but it does have large, clean motel rooms.

Coffee Stop (☎ 6471 6709; 110 Main St; 🕙 breakfast & lunch Mon-Fri) The light meals here include quiche, soups and sandwiches, and there are decent fish-and-chip takeaways. It also sells little ornaments made of west coast minerals.

Cribb Hutt Zeehan (☎ 6471 6122; 79 Main St; 5am-8pm winter, 5am-9pm summer) This friendly café/takeaway is the town's meeting place, and does pizzas, steaks, burgers and excellent homemade egg and bacon pies all day. In the evening it does takeaway meals catering to the young mining men in town, and you can also fill up on its chicken curry, spag bol, casseroles or roasts.

Infusion Restaurant (mains $15-22; lunch & dinner Mon-Sat) At Hotel Cecil, Infusion serves great, imaginative food – including a delicious eggplant parmigiana for vegetarians – in the atmospheric, old-fashioned dining room.

Abel Tasman Bistro (mains $15-25; lunch & dinner) Friendly dining at Heemskirk Motor Hotel that serves an excellent Moroccan chicken salad, salt and pepper squid and a super-spicy Thai green curry, among the usual steaks and fish and chips.

Getting There & Away

Buses arrive at and depart from the Coffee Stop on the main street. See p272 for more information.

STRAHAN

☎ 03 / pop 700

Strahan was once dubbed by an American travel writer 'the best little town in the world'. With its perfect location, nestled between the waters of Macquarie Harbour and the rainforest, it has faultless natural assets. Add to that the painstakingly restored pioneer buildings – the cutesy shops, hotels and cottages crowding up the slope from the compact waterfront – and you've got a scene that's almost Disney-Utopian. If you're more into rugged wilderness you might find Strahan just a bit sugary-sweet, but it certainly has all the services to help get you out easily into the wilds – and will wrap you in comfort when you return. It's no wonder that tourists flock here.

Strahan's present as the west coast's greatest tourist drawcard could have been very different had it not been for a turn of events in the early 1980s. When Tasmania's Hydro-Electric Commission (HEC; now Hydro Tasmania) began construction of a new mega-dam as part of the planned Gordon-below-Franklin power scheme, Strahan became the launching point for Australia's largest and most effective environmental protest. The Franklin River Blockade (see p287) lasted for months in 1982, and was eventually successful in saving from the floodwaters what's now one of the jewels of Tasmania's World Heritage Area: the mirror calm, tannin-brown waters of the lower Gordon River.

Several boats now ply these waters daily, from luxury catamarans to sailing yachts. There are also high-speed adventures to be had around Strahan in jet boats or helicopters, guided explorations by 4WD, or more slow-paced immersion in nature in the form of rainforest and beach walks. While you're here you'll hear about some of the incredible tales of mutiny and escape from the convict settlement on Sarah Island, and the swashbuckling stories of some of the early pioneers. You shouldn't miss Strahan's nightly theatrical performance (see p283) that's an entertaining primer on all this history.

Information

ATM Next to Banjo's Bakery.

Online access centre (per 30min $3) In the library, housed in the Customs House, a fine Federation structure on the Esplanade.

Parks & Wildlife Service (PWS; ☎ 6471 7122; 9am-5pm Mon-Fri) Also in the Customs House building, adjacent to the library.

Post office Also in the Customs House building; a Commonwealth Bank agent.

Strahan Activity Centre (☎ 6471 4300, 1800 084 620; www.puretasmania.com.au; Esplanade) Hotel conglomerate Pure Tasmania now owns much of Strahan, and has its own activity/information centre and gift shop on the water in the town centre. You can book its Gordon River Cruise (see p279), kayak tours (see p280), the West Coast Wilderness Railway (see boxed text, p286) and fishing charters (see p279) here. It also books (privately owned) 4WD quad-bike tours (see p280).

Strahan Clinic (☎ 6471 7152; Bay St) For health-related matters.

Strahan visitors centre (☎ 6472 6800; wcvibcs@westcoast.tas.gov.au; Esplanade; 10am-8pm summer, 9am-6pm winter) This architecturally innovative centre incorporates an insightful display on the area's history (see p278) and adjacent is the amphitheatre that shows *The Ship that Never Was* (see p283). Also doles out info and makes tour and accommodation bookings.

Supermarket/newsagent (Reid St) Also handles ANZ accounts.

STRAHAN

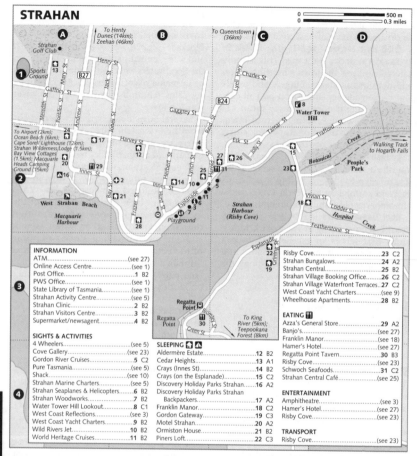

0 _____ 500 m
0 _____ 0.3 miles

Sights

MUSEUMS & GALLERIES

West Coast Reflections (☎ 6471 7622; Esplanade; ⏲ 10am-8pm summer, 9am-6pm winter) is the museum section of the Strahan visitors centre, installed beyond the Huon-pine reception desk. It's a creative and thought-provoking display on the history of the west coast, with a refreshingly blunt appraisal of the region's environmental disappointments and achievements, including the Franklin Blockade.

Nearby is **Strahan Woodworks** (☎ 6471 7244; 12 Esplanade; ⏲ 8.30am-5pm), where you can see Huon pine, sassafras and myrtle being turned, and then buy the end results, mainly kitchen knick-knacks, platters and ornamental objects. For more arts and crafts, check out the **Cove**

Gallery (☎ 6471 7572; Esplanade; ⏲ 8am-6pm summer, 10am-4pm winter), around the bay at Risby Cove.

OCEAN BEACH & HENTY DUNES

Six kilometres from town is **Ocean Beach**, awesome as much for its 33km length as for the strength of the surf that pounds it. This stretch of sand and sea runs uninterrupted from Trial Harbour in the north to Macquarie Heads in the south – and is *the* place to watch the orange orb of the sun melt into the sea. The water is treacherous: don't swim. The dunes behind the beach become a **mutton bird rookery** from October, when the birds return from their 15,000km winter migration. They remain here until April, providing an evening spectacle as they return to their nests at dusk.

Fourteen kilometres along the road from Strahan to Zeehan are the spectacular **Henty Dunes**, a series of 30m-high sugary-fine sand dunes backing Ocean Beach. Unfortunately, the peaceful beauty is marred by the strident, peace-shattering noises of off-road vehicles, which are permitted here. You can also sand-board down the slopes of these sandy giants. From the picnic area take the 1½-hour return walk through the dunes and out to Ocean Beach; remember to carry drinking water. You can have fun here playing Lawrence of Arabia crossing the Sahara.

TEEPOOKANA FOREST & KING RIVER

Although its condition is slowly improving, the **King River** has long served as a graphic example of that other west-coast feature: environmental degradation. It was used for many years as a waste sump for mining operations in Queenstown and has sterile, rust-coloured sludge along its banks. Nature is slowly healing itself here, however – it's thought that within a century, the King River could again run clean. You can see much of the length of the river from the West Coast Wilderness Railway (see boxed text, p286) which plies its steep banks. The gorgeous myrtle-rich forest that climbs the hillsides around the river is known as the **Teepookana Rainforest**. Through it, you can climb up to the Teepookana Plateau, which was once logged for fine-grained, blond, rot-resistant Huon pine. The timber is now so valuable that Huon limbs and stumps left behind by early piners are now salvaged. There are still a few gnarled trees standing, and you can walk through a young pine plantation which will be perfectly ripe for harvesting in a few thousand years. Climb the **Teepookana Tower** lookout for a magnificent view over the forests.

OTHER ATTRACTIONS

There's a lookout over the town at **Water Tower Hill**, accessed by following Esk St beside the Strahan Village booking office; it's less than 1km from the Esplanade.

Hogarth Falls is a pleasant 50-minute return walk through the rainforest beside the platypus-inhabited Botanical Creek. The track starts at People's Park.

The 45m-high **Cape Sorell Lighthouse**, at the harbour's southern head, is purportedly the second-highest in Australia. You'll need a boat to cross the heads unless you can find an accommodating fisher to take you over.

A return walk of two to three hours along a vehicle track from the jetty at Macquarie Heads leads to the lighthouse.

Activities

RIVER & HARBOUR CRUISES

A Gordon River cruise is what most visitors to Strahan come to do, and no matter how much wilderness beauty you've seen, you can't help but be inspired by the magic of this river: the perfect reflections in its treacle-darkness, the complete peace and the deeply green rainforest that surrounds it.

You can cruise the Gordon on a large, fancy catamaran in the company of a crowd of fellow river admirers (with plenty of comforts laid on) or be a bit more adventurous and visit with a small group by sailing boat. All cruises cross vast Macquarie Harbour before entering the mouth of the Gordon and proceeding to Heritage Landing for a rainforest walk. Most cruises visit Sarah Island – site of Van Diemen's Land's most infamously cruel penal colony – as well as Macquarie Heads and Hells Gates: the narrow harbour entrance. If you visit under sail, you can sneak a little further up the river than other cruise vessels are allowed to go, to beautiful Sir John Falls.

World Heritage Cruises (☎ 6471 7174, 1800 611 796; www.worldheritagecruises.com.au; Esplanade) is run by the Grining family, which has been taking visitors to the Gordon since 1896, and is Strahan's true river experts. You can join the Grinings aboard their new low-wash environmentally sensitive catamaran, the *Eagle,* for a morning cruise from 9am to 2.45pm year-round, or an afternoon cruise from 3pm to 8.30pm in the summer season (December to March) only. Prices, depending on whether you take a window seat (premium) or one in the centre of the boat (standard), are adult/child/family at $65/25/165 (standard) and $85/35/220 (premium). With the premium seats you can also purchase a Gold Pass for $105 per person, which includes a lunch or dinner buffet with wine, or you can simply pay an additional $15/8 per adult/child to graze on the buffet.

Also operating on the River is **Gordon River Cruises** (☎ 6471 4300, 1800 628 286; www.puretasmania .com.au; Esplanade), run by the conglomerate that now calls itself Pure Tasmania and seems to own half of Strahan (and other tourism concerns in Tasmania, for that matter). You'll cruise on the *Lady Jane Franklin II,* departing Strahan at 8.30am and returning 2.15pm, and in peak season only also departing at 2.45pm and returning at 8.30pm. There are three levels of service: the Captain's Premium Upper Deck ($195 for all tickets), a Window Recliner seat (adult/child/family $115/65/295) and Atrium seating in the centre of the vessel ($90/35/235). Lunch and your fill of tea and coffee are included in the fare.

If you'd like your Gordon River experience with a little soft adventure – and fewer people in the mix – then sailing on *Stormbreaker* with **West Coast Yacht Charters** (☎ 6471 7422; Esplanade) is the way to do it. There's a wonderful crayfish lunch, kayaking and fishing cruise that departs on demand most days at noon and returns at 3pm (adult/child $80/60). There's also an overnight trip up the Gordon River, so you can be first to see the undisturbed river reflections when you wake up on the water. The trip costs per adult/child $320/160. It departs Strahan at 2pm and returns at 1pm the following day. There's a visit to Sarah Island and all meals are included. The only cruise licensed to get a full 37km up the Gordon as far as magical Sir John Falls is *Stormbreaker*'s River Rafter Collection Trip (adult/child $250/125) that departs Strahan at 2pm and returns at 1pm the next day. You'll hear tales of rafting the west's wild rivers as you cruise back to Strahan. On all trips you can hook some of Macquarie Harbour's giant fish and take a short paddle in a sea kayak. Just for fun, you could also make this yacht your floating hotel for the night when it's docked in Strahan (see opposite).

Strahan Marine Charters (☎ 6471 4300, 0418-135 983) will do boat trips on demand for $145 per hour to Sarah Island, Hells Gates, the fish farms on Macquarie Harbour or anywhere else you'd like to visit – though if you do want to go as far as the Gordon River, it could cost you an arm and a leg. It will also pick up and drop off kayakers at remote spots on the harbour or river. Fishing gear and a BBQ can be provided.

SEA-KAYAKING

Pure Tasmania (☎ 1800 084 620, www.puretasmania .com.au; Strahan Activity Centre, Esplanade) combines its Gordon River trip with a spot of sea-kayaking on the river's mirror-calm waters for those who want to spend a little time away from the hubbub of the cruise vessels and enjoy the silence of the river. Between 1 January and the end of March, the full-day tours depart on the *Lady Jane Franklin* at 8.30am. The kayaks are launched on arrival at Heritage Landing and

you paddle upstream into the extreme peace of the river. You pull up for a rainforest lunch stop before drifting back downstream to the cruise boat – then return with the afternoon cruise boat back to Strahan via Sarah Island, arriving at 8.30pm. All meals are included in the cost of $345 per person.

JET-BOAT RIDES

Wild Rivers Jet (☎ 6471 7396; www.wildriversjet.com.au; 'The Shack', Esplanade) runs exhilaratingly speedy 50-minute jet-boat rides up the rainforested gorges of the King River, with Huon pine-spotting stops, for adult/child/family $65/38/175. Take the longer 1¾-hour combined boat/4WD trip (adult/child/family $85/46/220) and you'll also be able to visit the Teepookana Plateau with its ancient (and newly planted) Huon pines, and eagle's-eye forest lookout. Bookings recommended.

QUAD BIKING

4 Wheelers (☎ 6471 4300, 0419 508 175; $45) offers 45-minute guided hooning over the Henty Dunes on four-wheeled motorbikes. There's a 12km/h speed limit and participants must have a full drivers licence. Trips usually leave hourly in the summer season from the Henty Sand Dunes car park, 10 minutes' drive north of Strahan, and you can buy tickets here or from the Strahan Activity Centre. Kids can hop on a buggy (adult driver/first child/second child $50/30/20) as passengers.

SAND-BOARDING

Towering Henty Dunes are the spot to try your hand at a bit of sand-boarding. You climb the highest dune around, jump on your board and skid down at breakneck speed. 'The Shack' (☎ 6471 7396) and the **Strahan Activity Centre** (☎ 6471 4300) both rent boards for $35 for a half-day.

PINERS & MINERS EXPERIENCE

Immerse yourself in west coast history and get comfortably into the back blocks with these **luxury 4WD tours** (☎ 6471 4300, 1800 628 286) offered by Pure Tasmania. You ride in a Hi-Rail (a Landrover converted to ride on the rail tracks of the West Coast Wilderness Railway; see boxed text, p286) before the vehicle retracts its rail-riding wheels and proceeds deep into the bush. You hike to abandoned mining sites and settlements, and learn of the unique history and nature here, before cruising back to

Strahan on Macquarie Harbour. The tour costs $345 per person with gourmet food laid on.

SCENIC FLIGHTS

You can't help but be excited when you hear the distinctive buzz of a seaplane: it speaks of adventure and remoteness. In Strahan, you can get on one with **Strahan Seaplanes and Helicopters** (☎ 6471 7718; www.adventureflights.com.au; Strahan Wharf; ☼ 8.30am-5pm Sep-Jul) to take an 80-minute flight (adult/child $179/105, maximum four people) over Ocean Beach and Macquarie Harbour, landing on the Gordon River at Sir John Falls. There are also 15-minute helicopter joyrides taking in Ocean Beach, Hells Gates, Cape Sorell and Macquarie Harbour ($105/60, maximum three people), and 60-minute helicopter trips (including 25 minutes in the air) up to the Huon pines of the Teepookana Plateau, with hair-raising low flying over the King River ($199/105).

SWIMMING

Next to the caravan park is **West Strahan Beach**, with a gently shelving sandy bottom that provides safe swimming.

Sleeping

Much of the accommodation in the centre of town is now run by Pure Tasmania under the banner of **Strahan Village** (☎ 6471 4200, 1800 628 286; www.puretasmania.com.au; ☼ 7am-7pm May-Oct, 7am-9pm Nov-Apr), which has its booking office under the clock tower on the Esplanade. Book well ahead, particularly during the peak seasons.

BUDGET

Camping is possible at the basic **camping ground** (unpowered sites $5) at Macquarie Heads, 15km southwest of Strahan – follow the signs to Ocean Beach and see the caretaker. Prices are for up to two people.

Discovery Holiday Parks Strahan (☎ 6471 7239; cnr Andrew & Innes Sts; unpowered sites $20-35, powered sites $25-45, cabins $95-150; 💻) Right on Strahan's West Beach, this neat and friendly park has good facilities including a kiosk, a camp kitchen, BBQs and a kids' playground. Site prices are for up to two people.

Discovery Holiday Parks Strahan Backpackers (☎ 6472 6200; 43 Harvey St; dm $25-35, d $50-75, cottages $55-75) This place is in a nice bush setting some 15 minutes' walk from the town centre. It has very plain bunks and doubles, tiny, A-frame cabins and self-contained cottages.

There are shared facilities, a kitchen block and a laundry.

West Coast Yacht Charters (☎ 6471 7422, 0419-300 994; Esplanade; d $100, dm adult/child $50/25) If you're hankering to sleep in a floating bunk on a wharf-moored yacht, then this is a great option. Because the yacht is used for charters, it has late check-in and early check-out (be prepared to check in after 7.30pm and disembark before 9am). The yacht isn't moored every night, so you'll need to book ahead. Prices include continental breakfast.

Strahan Wilderness Lodge (☎ 6471 7142; www .bayviewcottages-cabins.com.au; Ocean Beach Rd; d without bathroom $70, tw with bathroom $80) A kilometre or two north of town, you can hear nothing but birdsong among 11 peaceful hectares of coastal vegetation. This old-style, laid-back place has spacious rooms and great views of gardens and harbour. Prices include continental breakfast.

MIDRANGE
Self-Contained Apartments

Bay View Cottages (☎ 6471 7142; www.bayviewcottages -cabins.com.au; Ocean Beach Rd; d $90, extra person $20) The same people who manage Strahan Wilderness Lodge run these private one-, two- and three-bedroom self-contained cottages. Each includes linen, tea- and coffee-making facilities, TV and heating.

Cedar Heights (☎ 6471 7717; cedarheights@vision.net .au; 7 Meredith St; d $100-120) These timber cabins with private courtyards are set back in a quiet street away from the hustle and bustle; the most you'll hear are the sounds of a golf ball being thwacked at the nearby golf course or a game of footy at the oval opposite. One apartment has a spa.

Strahan Bungalows (☎ 6471 7268; www.strahan bungalows.com.au; cnr Andrew & Harvey Sts; d $100-150, extra adult/child $25/20) Decorated with a nautical theme, these five lovely little bungalows are bright, light and friendly, and are equipped with everything you need for a self-contained stay. They're close to the beach and the golf course, and less than 15 minutes' walk from the centre of town.

Crays (☎ 6471 7422; www.thecraysaccommodation .com; 11 Innes St & 59 Esplanade; d $130-160, extra adult/ child $50/30) The Crays has two self-contained units on Innes St and six new bright, roomy architect-designed cottages on the Esplanade opposite Risby Cove. All units have harbour panoramas or views of beautiful bird-filled gardens. Guests who stay three nights are rewarded with a succulent Tasmanian crayfish on the house; and there are reduced prices for cruises on the yacht *Stormbreaker* (see p288).

Motels &Units

Motel Strahan (☎ 6471 7555; www.motelstrahan.com
.au; 3 Andrew St; d $110-170) This funky new complex is surely as good as motels get anywhere. The rooms are spic-and-span and decorated with care, the service is welcoming, and the whole effect is pleasingly clean, quiet and simple without compromising on style. It's also wheelchair-friendly.

Gordon Gateway (☎ 6471 7165, 1300 134 425; www
.gordongateway.com.au; Grining St; studios $155-180, chalets
$220-290, ste $180-290, extra person $35-55) In a scenic hillside location on the way to Regatta Point, this place has 10 modern, well-outfitted studio units and several larger A-frame chalets. All units have excellent views out to Macquarie Harbour and the township. Breakfast provisions supplied on request.

TOP END
Hotels, Guesthouses & B&Bs

our pick **Ormiston House** (☎ 6471 7077; www.ormiston
house.com.au; Esplanade; d $130-230; 🖳) This grand but informal historic house is the pick of the accommodation in Strahan. Built in 1899 by Frederick Ormiston, Strahan's founder, it's a genuine stately home, now beautifully refurbished and gracefully attended as a top-notch B&B. There are just five rooms, antique-furnished in Queen Anne style. Climb up to the widow's walk for some of the best harbour views in Strahan.

Risby Cove (☎ 6471 7572; www.risbycove.com.au;
Esplanade; d $151-233, extra adult/child $42/25) Once a waterfront sawmill complex, Risby Cove is now a smart little enclave all done up in corrugated-iron cool. There's a restaurant (see opposite), a gallery, and eight rooms and one- and two-bedroom spa suites, most with water views. Bike and kayak hire are also available here, and you can go for a row in the Cove's little wooden dinghy.

Franklin Manor (☎ 6471 7311; www.franklinmanor.com
.au; Esplanade; standard d $165, stables d $190, deluxe d $190-
210) On the Strahan waterfront, just out of town is this historic weatherboard mansion, nestled in lovely gardens. This was long one of Strahan's top spots to stay and it still has smart rooms, an enviable wine cellar and a restaurant (mains $32 to 35; open for dinner Monday to Saturday) with a fancy-looking menu. Since the Michelin star winning French chef/owner left here a few

years ago, though, things haven't been quite the same.

Strahan Central (☎ 6471 7612; fax 6471 7513; 1 Harold
St; d $168-190) Above Strahan Central Café, these attractive split-level suites are charmingly decorated in fittingly country style. There are good views over the water and the price includes continental breakfast.

Strahan Village Waterfront Terraces (☎ 6471 4200,
1800 628 286; fax 6471 4389; Esplanade; d $170-230) The heritage-listed Hamer's (formerly Hamer's Hotel) offers stylishly enhanced en suite accommodation, including a balcony room with superb views across the harbour.

Piners Loft (☎ 6471 7036, 1300 134 425; www.piners
loft.com.au; Grining St; d from $295, extra person $45) This handsome two-storey timber house (sleeping six) can be your own private lookout. It's built atop towering poles of King Billy and Celery-top pine, has good modern facilities, a sense of style and great views of the water.

Self-Contained Apartments

Aldermère Estate (☎ /fax 6471 7418; aldermereonhar
vey@bigpond.com; 27 Harvey St; d $160-220, spa apt $240,
extra person $40) Aldermère has several stylish and luxuriously modern fully self-contained two-storey apartments, with one- or two-bedroom configurations and a self-contained cottage. The apartments are serviced daily and include gas log fires and a hearty continental brekkie.

Wheelhouse Apartments (☎ 6471 7777; www.wheel
houseapartments.com.au; 4 Frazer St; d $320, extra adult/child
$65/35) Talk about a room with a view! Perched up high above the harbour, these smart and luxurious cottages have seamless acres of glass to give you jaw-droppingly good views of the harbour. Breakfast provisions are supplied, and its wheelchair-accessible.

Eating

Strahan Central Café (☎ 6471 7612; 1 Harold St; mains
$6.50-10.50; 🕒 7am-5pm) This unpretentious little café does reasonable breakfasts and better lunches proffering homemade quiche, focaccia with smoked salmon and pesto, toasted sandwiches and wraps. Of an afternoon, it also does fine scones and jam.

Banjo's (☎ 6471 7794; Esplanade; pizzas from $10;
🕒 6am-6pm) This popular central bakery next to Hamer's Hotel serves a decent breakfast menu along with snacks such as sandwiches, hot chunky pies and other savouries and pastries.

Schwoch Seafoods (☎ 6471 7157; Esplanade; mains $8-15; ☼ 9am-9pm daily) Run by a local cray fisherman, this little eatery serves up the freshest fish and seafood in town. Come for eat-in or takeaway and savour fish encrusted in incredibly light and golden batter that just melts in the mouth or oysters split fresh to order. Does a fine gourmet pizza too.

Hamer's Hotel (☎ 6471 7191; Esplanade; lunch mains $8-17, dinner mains $17-27; ☼ lunch & dinner) This done-up historic pub is now the casual eating hub in Strahan and serves a commendable menu of better-than-pub fare. Forget soggy pub roasts: starters here include such delicacies as grilled haloumi cheese with macadamia, rocket and zucchini salad, followed by steaming piles of black-lipped mussels. Hamer's is deservedly popular and often packed. Come here hungry.

Regatta Point Tavern (☎ 6471 7103; Esplanade; mains $15-32; ☼ lunch & dinner) If you want to eat with the locals away from the glitz, make your way to this down-to-earth pub near the railway terminus 2km around the bay from Strahan's centre. There are the usual steaks and burgers as well as good fresh fish, including Macquarie Harbour ocean trout. Check out the crayfish mornay ($80) if you're after something fancy.

Risby Cove (☎ 6471 7572; Esplanade; mains $22-33; ☼ dinner) People come from all over to dine at the Cove. The menu features such local delights as myrtle-infused blue eye trevalla. It's all classy and cool here with good, unpretentious service and consistently praiseworthy food. Perhaps the best place to dine in Strahan.

Franklin Manor (☎ 6471 7311; Esplanade; mains $30-35; ☼ breakfast & dinner) Franklin Manor has a grand menu available not only to house guests, but all comers. This is thoroughly fancy cuisine: menu items are the likes of hot smoked cured ocean trout on a port-glazed apple salad or chicken roulade filled with green chilli, prawn and coriander mousse. There's also a well-stocked wine room under the glass atrium that sometimes does tastings.

Drop by **Azza's general store** (Innes St; ☼ 6.30am-9pm) for basic food supplies and takeaways.

Entertainment

The Strahan visitors centre stages *The Ship That Never Was* in its **amphitheatre** (☎ 6471 7622; Esplanade; adult/concession/teenager or student $15/11/7.50, children under 13 yr free). The play is the entertainingly theatrical story of some convicts who escaped from Sarah Island in 1834 by building their own ship, and pleases all age groups. Performances are held at 5.30pm year-round, and also at 8.30pm in January.

Risby Cove (☎ 6471 7572; www.risbycove.com.au; Esplanade; adult/child $8.50/5.50) Risby Cove shows films nightly on the big screen in its newly refurbished theatrette. Ring for showing times and film details.

Hamer's Hotel (☎ 6471 4200; Esplanade) This pub sometimes stages live music entertainment. Watch the billboards for what's on.

Getting There & Around

Buses arrive at and depart from the visitors centre. **Strahan Taxis** (☎ 0417-516 071) can run you to surrounding attractions like Ocean Beach (about $15 each way) and Henty Dunes ($25 each way) and does hotel pick-ups and drop-offs for the morning river cruise departures. If you prefer to get around under your own steam **Risby Cove** (☎ 6471 7572) rents out bicycles (full-/half-day $30/20).

Those embarking on a cruise can park for free at the wharf car park. Spaces in front of the main shopping area have 30- to 60-minute time limits, and unbelievably, parking tickets do happen here!

QUEENSTOWN
☎ 03 / pop 3400

The winding descent into Queenstown from the Lyell Hwy is unforgettable for its moonscape of bare, dusty hills and eroded gullies, where once there was rainforest. The area is the clearest testimony anywhere to the scarification of the west coast's environment by mining. Copper was discovered here in the 1890s and mining has continued ever since, but today pollution is closely monitored and sulphur emissions controlled. Ironically, when green started to creep back to these barren hills, Queenstown residents were perplexed: they felt the town's identity was so closely tied to the surrounding barrenness that hills covered in green simply wouldn't do.

Although Queenstown is now getting in on the tourism trend, unlike overcommercialised Strahan it's still got that authentic, rough-and-ready pioneer town feel. You can spot miners in boilersuits wandering the streets and there's a rich social and industrial history that still feels alive. With the completion of the West Coast Wilderness Railway, Queenstown now

THE WEST

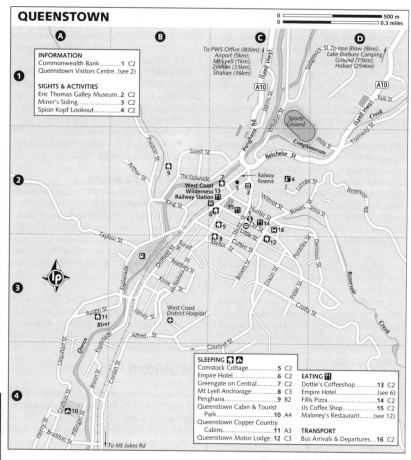

QUEENSTOWN

INFORMATION
Commonwealth Bank..........1 C2
Queenstown Visitors Centre..(see 2)

SIGHTS & ACTIVITIES
Eric Thomas Galley Museum..2 C2
Miner's Siding.....................3 C2
Spion Kopf Lookout............4 C2

To PWS Office (800m);
Airport (5km);
Mt Lyell (1km);
Zeehan (33km);
Strahan (36km);

To Iron Blow (8km);
Lake Burbury Camping
Ground (15km);
Hobart (254km);

SLEEPING
Comstock Cottage...............5 C2
Empire Hotel......................6 C2
Greengate on Central..........7 C2
Mt Lyell Anchorage..............8 C3
Penghana..........................9 B2
Queenstown Cabin & Tourist
Park...............................10 A4
Queenstown Copper Country
Cabins...........................11 A3
Queenstown Motor Lodge..12 C3

EATING
Dottie's Coffeeshop............13 C2
Empire Hotel.....................(see 6)
Fillis Pizza.........................14 C2
JJs Coffee Shop..................15 C2
Maloney's Restaurant........(see 12)

TRANSPORT
Bus Arrivals & Departures....16 C2

has a real tourist hub that is breathing new life into the town.

Orientation & Information

The main drag here is Orr St, which meets Driffield St almost directly opposite the West Coast Wilderness Railway station. Most shops, hotels and businesses are either on this street or close by. There's a Commonwealth Bank with ATM on Orr St.

Queenstown visitors centre (☎ 6471 1483; 1-7 Driffield St) A veritable treasure-trove of social and industrial history and run by volunteers with comprehensive information on the region. In the Eric Thomas Galley Museum.

Parks & Wildlife Service (PWS; ☎ 6471 2511; Penghana Rd; 8.30am-9.30am) Close to the mine entrance, this is the place to get advice on nearby walking tracks and to buy

national park passes if you haven't obtained them from the visitors centre. If you intend to use the Mt McCall Rd 4WD track from the southern end of Lake Burbury to the Franklin River, ask the ranger for a free permit and a key to the gate. Ring and book the key prior to coming to Queenstown.

Sights & Activities

ERIC THOMAS GALLEY MUSEUM

This **museum** (☎ 6471 1483; 1-7 Driffield St; adult/concession/pensioner/family $4/2.50/3/10; 9.30am-5pm Mon-Fri, 12.30-5pm Sat & Sun, winter hours vary) started life as the Imperial Hotel in 1898 and now houses an extensive photographic collection with wonderfully idiosyncratic captions showing the people and places of Tasmania's west coast, including an exposé of the Mount Lyell mining disaster which claimed 42 lives. There's also a clutter of old memorabilia, household items and clothing, right down to grandma's undies!

MINER'S SIDING
Opposite the museum, on the site of the original train station, is the Miner's Siding, a public monument with rail memorabilia and sculptures. The locomotive that was once parked here is now restored as part of the West Coast Wilderness Railway.

SPION KOPF LOOKOUT
Follow Hunter St uphill, turn left onto Bowes St, then do a sharp left onto Latrobe St to a small car park, from where a short, steep track leads to the summit of Spion Kopf (named by soldiers after a battle in the Boer War). The rhododendron-lined track features a rail adit near the car park and the top of the hill has a pithead on it. The panoramic views of town are excellent, particularly at sunset when the bare hills are flaming orange.

IRON BLOW
On top of Gormanston Hill on the Lyell Hwy, just before the final descent along hairpin bends into Queenstown, is a sealed side road leading to a lookout over the geological wound of Iron Blow. This is the now-deserted and flooded open-cut mine where the town's illustrious mining career began. Pay attention to signage on the road as the site's not always fully open due to changing conditions in the area.

MT JUKES RD
Continue south along Conlan St to Mt Jukes Rd, which will take you to side roads leading to sections of the West Coast Wilderness Railway. Further along this scenic road (9km south of Queenstown) is **Newall Creek**, where a platform provides access to a patch of superb King Billy and Huon-pine rainforest. The bitumen section of the road ends at **Lake Burbury**, a mountain-surrounded Hydro Tasmania lake that can be seen to magnificent effect from a lookout on the descent to its shores (see also boxed text, p287).

Tours
Douggies Mine Tours (☎ 6471 1472, 0407-049 612) An underground mine tour ($70 per person, 2½ hours). These are intensely worthwhile tours that take you right down into the working heart of Queenstown's copper mine with interpretation by characterful Douggie himself. Underground

tours leave at 10.15am and 1.15pm (and 7pm by demand). You're able to view the working machinery and get to chat with the miners themselves. There are also surface tours at 8.45am and 4.30pm. No kids under 14 years.
Mt Lyell Enviro Tours (☎ 0419-104 138) During the summer season this company offers three-hour tours ($55 per person) departing at 10am and 2pm, which interpret over 100 years of copper mining at Mt Lyell. The tours visit the mine's surface and tailings dam only, and consider especially the environmental impact of, and remediation after, mining. Can also arrange trips to Lakes Margaret and Burbury on request.

Sleeping
BUDGET
Lake Burbury camping ground, a 15-minute drive from Queenstown, is a scenic, quiet spot to put up a tent. Sites cost $5, payable to the caretaker. There are toilets but no showers.
Queenstown Cabin & Tourist Park (☎ 6471 1332; fax 6471 1125; 17 Grafton St; unpowered/powered sites $25/30, on-site vans d $50, d cabins $70-90, extra adult $10-15, extra child $5) You have to drive through run-down suburbs to get here, and though the park's set on gravel and is a bit bare, it has clean vans and cabins, a communal kitchen and a sheltered BBQ area.
Empire Hotel (☎ 6471 1699; empire@tassie.net .au; 2 Orr St; s $25, d with/without bathroom $60/45) The rooms here aren't as magnificent as the imposing Blackwood staircase that's a National Trust–listed treasure, but they are clean and tended by friendly staff who make you feel at home. It serves fine meals in the dining room downstairs; see p287.
Mt Lyell Anchorage (☎ 6471 1900; 17 Cutten St; s/d $50/$80) This friendly budget place in an old weatherboard home has clean singles and doubles with shared bathroom, as well as good kitchen and laundry facilities. It's just back from the main drag, making it quiet but central.
Queenstown Copper Country Cabins (☎ 0417-398 343; fax 6471 1086; 13 Austin St; s $70-80, d $80-100, extra person $15) This is a compact collection of modern, self-contained timber cabins, one of which is equipped for disabled travellers. The cabins are incredibly neat and tidy, and there are laundry facilities nearby.

MIDRANGE
Queenstown Motor Lodge (☎ 6471 1866; www.queens townmotorlodge.com.au; 54-58 Orr St; d $96-120, extra person $20; 💻) While it's no architectural gem, this compact little motel has friendly owners and

THE WEST COAST WILDERNESS RAILWAY

Love the romance of the days of steam? The old wood-lined carriages with shiny brass trimmings, the breathy puffing of steam engines and the evocative, echoing train whistle? Then you should hop on board Tasmania's newest restored railway, and make the breathtaking 35km rainforest rail journey between Strahan and Queenstown.

When it was first built in 1896, much as is the case today, this train and its route through torturously remote country was a marvel of engineering. It clings to the steep-sided gorge of the King River, passing through dense myrtle rainforest, over 40 bridges and on gradients that few other rolling stock could handle. Over 8km of its route the train uses the Abt rack and pinion system named after its inventor, Dr Roman Abt. In this arrangement, a third toothed rack rail is positioned between the two conventional rails. Locomotives are equipped with geared pinion wheels that lock into the rack rail, allowing trains to climb and descend gradients that would otherwise be too steep for them to negotiate.

The railway was the lifeblood of the Mt Lyell Mining & Railway Co in Queenstown, connecting it for ore and people haulage to the port of Teepookana on the King River, and later with Strahan. From 1896 the line ran along the Queen River and up the one-in-16 gradient Abt section to Rinadeena Saddle, before heading down the one-in-20 gradient Abt section through magnificent rainforest to the King River. Here it crossed a marvellously curved 400m-long bridge high above the water, before continuing to Teepookana and Regatta Point. The original railway closed in 1963.

Today the track is magnificently restored, and steam and diesel locomotives take passengers on a four-hour journey over its entire length. Trains depart from Queenstown at 10am and 3pm and Strahan at 10.15am and 3.15pm from the end of December to the end of March. Between April and September, there's a Strahan to Queenstown trip at 10.15am on Tuesday, Wednesday, Friday and Sunday, and a Queenstown to Strahan trip on Monday, Thursday and Saturday at 11am. Costs for riding the full length one way are $105/60 per adult/child, including lunch. Alternatively, for the same cost, you can ride halfway to the rainforest station at Dubbil Barrel and then hop on the train going back to where you boarded. If you've ridden one way and need to return to your embarkation point there's a bus service costing an additional $16/9 per adult/child. There's also a Premier Carriage 1st-class service ($195 per person) which includes extra special food, drinks and service. Inquiries and ticket purchases are at **Queenstown Station** (☎ 6471 1700; Driffield St) or the **Strahan Activity Centre** (☎ 6471 4300, 1800 628 286; Esplanade).

decent, clean rooms, and is on the quiet part of Queenstown's main street. There's also a good on-site restaurant.

Greengate on Central (☎ 6471 1144; fax 6471 2507; 7 Railway Reserve; apt from d $100, extra person $20, family of 4 $160) Set around with a shady veranda, this two-bedroom house sleeps up to five, and is pin-neat with polished boards and is fully self-contained. It's set just a hop and skip from the train station.

Comstock Cottage (☎ 6471 1200, 0409 711 614; 5 McNamara St; d $130-140, extra adult/child $40/25) This pretty miner's cottage set in attractive gardens has its original pressed-tin ceilings and sleeps up to four. The master bedroom has a romantic four-poster bed and the house is antique-decorated throughout. The price includes cooked breakfast provisions so you can cook up a morning storm.

TOP END

ourpick Penghana (☎ 6471 2560; www.penghana.com .au; 32 The Esplanade; d with/without bathroom from $150/140, ste $175; ☐) This National Trust–listed mansion was built in 1898 for the first general manager of the Mt Lyell Mining & Railway Co, and, as befits its managerial stature, is located on a hill above town amid a rare number of trees. The B&B accommodation here is first-rate and includes a billiards room and a grand dining room for enjoying chef-prepared à la carte meals nightly. Packed lunches on request. Entry is access via Preston St.

Eating

Dotties Coffeeshop (☎ 6471 1700; Queenstown Station, Driffield St; ☺ breakfast & lunch) Dotties is a good option if you're a bit of a train spotter. Serving smooth, creamy coffee and a selection of café delights, such as gourmet pies, pastries, cakes and biscuits, you can also sit alfresco on the train platform itself.

JJ's Coffee Shop (☎ 6471 1793; 13 Orr St; ◷ 7.30am-5.30pm) What a great place to hang out for breakfasts, lunches and good homemade snacks. JJ's does beautiful cakes, excellent soups, sandwiches, savoury crepes and a damn fine coffee too.

Filis Pizza (☎ 6471 2006; 21 Orr St; pizzas $8.90-23.90; ◷ 11am-10pm) This friendly place suggests over 40 different takes on the humble pizza – if you need a filling meal you can't go wrong with this fab option. Try the heavenly roast garlic and olive supreme with roasted chicken. It does good roast dinners ($10) at Sunday lunchtime, too.

Empire Hotel (☎ 6471 1699; 2 Orr St; mains $12-17; ◷ lunch & dinner) This old miner's pub has survived the ages and includes an atmospheric heritage dining room serving a changing menu of hearty pub standards, including roasts, pastas, including an excellent lasagne, and a divine seafood chowder.

Maloney's Restaurant (☎ 6471 1866; 54-58 Orr St; mains $22-24; ◷ dinner Mon-Sat) Who would expect such good food in a small-town motel? You can order the likes of garlic-infused chicken breast stuffed with roasted pine nuts, pesto and semi-dried tomatoes. There's also good steak, lamb, pork and seafood all cooked fresh to order.

Getting There & Away

Buses arrive at and depart from the milk bar at 65 Orr St. See p272 for more information.

FRANKLIN-GORDON WILD RIVERS NATIONAL PARK

The centrepieces of this environmentally awesome park are the wild, pristine rivers that twist their way through the infinitely rugged landscapes here and give the national park its name. The park is part of the Tasmanian Wilderness World Heritage Area and encompasses the catchments of the Franklin, Olga and Gordon Rivers. It was proclaimed in 1981 after the failed campaign to stop the flooding of precious Lake Pedder under the waters of the Pedder/Gordon hydroelectric dam scheme (see p301). The park is probably best known as the site of Australia's biggest-ever environmental battle, the Franklin Blockade, which drew national and international attention and was ultimately successful in saving the wilderness from further dams.

DETOUR: LAKE BURBURY

Heading south out of Queenstown along Conlan St to Mt Jukes Rd for about 15 minutes you'll come to the end of the bitumen road that leads to **Lake Burbury**. Built as a large hydroelectric dam, its construction flooded 6km of the old Lyell Hwy. The lake is surrounded by the Princess River Conservation Area, and the scenery around it is magnificent – especially when there's snow on the nearby peaks. There are impressive vistas from the attractive shoreline **camping ground** (unpowered sites for 2 people $5) just east of Bradshaw Bridge. Here there's also a public picnic area with sheltered electric BBQs and a children's playground. Fishermen say the trout in Lake Burbury make for some of the best fishing in Tasmania.

The battle to save the lower Gordon and Franklin Rivers was played out in Tasmania in the early 1980s. Despite National Park status and then World Heritage nomination, dam-building plans here by the then–HEC continued. In the aftermath of Lake Pedder's flooding, public opinion on the matter was clear: when a 1981 referendum asked Tasmanians to decide between two different dam schemes, 46% of voters scribbled 'No Dams' across their ballot papers. Politically, the state was in turmoil, and both the premier and opposition party leader were dumped over the dams issue. A state election resulted in a change of government, but no change in plans to go ahead with a new mega-dam. When the World Heritage Committee eventually announced the area's World Heritage listing and expressed concern over the proposed dam, the new state premier attempted to have the listing withdrawn.

Antidam and proconservation lobbyists then turned their attention to the federal arena. In May 1982, at a Canberra by-election, 41% of voters wrote 'No Dams' on their ballot papers, but the federal government still refused to intervene.

Dam construction began in 1982 and protesters from all over Tasmania set off from Strahan to stage what became known as the 'Franklin River Blockade'. Press pictures from the time show flotillas of blow-up dinghies stretched across the river, blocking the HEC boats' access to the dam work site. Despite the peaceful protests, the Tasmanian government passed special laws allowing protesters to be arrested, fined and jailed. In the summer of 1982–83, 1400 people were arrested in a confrontation so intense it received international news coverage.

The Franklin River became a major issue in the 1983 federal election, which was won partly on a 'No Dams' promise by the incoming Labor party, which then fully implemented the Franklin and Gordon Rivers' World Heritage assignation, finally protecting the rivers and rainforests fully.

The national park's most significant peak is **Frenchmans Cap** (1443m), with a magnificent white-quartzite top that can be seen from the west coast and from the Lyell Hwy. The mountain was formed by glacial action and has Tasmania's tallest cliff face.

The park also contains a number of unique plant species and major Aboriginal sites. The most significant is **Kutikina Cave**, where over 50,000 artefacts have been found, dating from the cave's 5000-year-long occupation between 14,000 and 20,000 years ago. The only way to reach the cave, which is on Aboriginal land in remote forest, is by rafting down the Franklin.

Much of the park consists of deep river gorges and impenetrable rainforest, but the Lyell Hwy traverses its northern end. Along this road are a number of signposted features of note, including a few short walks that you can take to see just what this park is all about:

Collingwood River This is the usual put-in point for rafting the Franklin River, of which the Collingwood is a tributary. You can camp for free here; there are pit toilets and fireplaces.

Donaghy's Hill Located 4km east of the bridge over the Collingwood River, this 40-minute return walk leads to the top of the hill above the junction of the Collingwood and Franklin Rivers. It has spectacular views of the Franklin and Frenchmans Cap.

Franklin River Nature Trail From the picnic ground where the highway crosses the river, a 25-minute return nature trail has been marked through the forest.

Frenchmans Cap Six kilometres further east is the start of the three- to five-day walk to Frenchmans Cap. There are two shelter huts along the way (though you'll need a tent) and much infamous mud, particularly on the plains known as the Sodden Loddens. Even if you don't intend doing the whole bush walk, you'll enjoy the initial 15-minute walk along the banks of the Franklin River. You can take a Tassielink-scheduled service to the beginning of this walk – see p272 for details.

Nelson River Just east of Lake Burbury, at the bottom of Victoria Pass, is an easy 20-minute return walk through rainforest to the excellent, 35m-high Nelson Falls. Signs beside the track highlight common plants of the area.

Rafting the Franklin

Rafting the Franklin River is about as wild and thrilling a journey as it's possible to make in Tasmania. This is really extreme adventure. Experienced rafters can tackle it independently if they're fully equipped and prepared, but for anyone who's less than completely river-savvy (and that's about 90% of all Franklin rafters), there are tour companies offering complete rafting packages. Whether you go with an independent group or a tour operator, you should contact the park rangers at the **Lake St Clair visitors centre** (☎ 6289 1172; Cynthia Bay; ☼ 8am-5pm winter, to 7pm or 8pm summer), which also has the latest information on permits and regulations, or the **Queenstown PWS** (☎ 6471 2511; Penghana Rd) for current information on permits, regulations and environmental considerations. You should also check out the detailed Franklin rafting notes on the PWS website at www.parks.tas.gov.au.

All expeditions should register at the booth at the junction of the Lyell Hwy and the Collingwood River, 49km west of Derwent Bridge. The trip down the Franklin, starting at Collingwood River and ending at Sir John Falls, takes between eight and 14 days, depending on river conditions. Shorter trips on certain sections of the river are also possible. From the exit point at Sir John Falls, you can be picked up by a **Strahan Seaplanes & Helicopters** (☎ 6471 7718) seaplane or by **West Coast Yacht Charters'** (☎ 6471 7422) *Stormbreaker* for the trip back to Strahan. You can also just do half the river. The upper Franklin takes around eight days from Collingwood River to the Fincham Track – it passes through the bewitchingly beautiful Irenabyss Gorge and you can scale Frenchmans Cap as a side trip. The lower Franklin takes seven days from the Fincham Track to Sir John Falls and passes through Great Ravine.

These tour companies offer complete rafting packages:

Rafting Tasmania (☎ 6239 1080; www.rafting tasmania.com) Has five-/seven-/10-day trips costing $1650/2000/2600.

Tasmanian Expeditions (☎ 6339 3999, 1800 030 230; www.tas-ex.com) An operator with nine-/11-day trips for $2450/2650.

Water By Nature (☎ 1800 111 142, 0408-242 941; www.franklinriver.com) This provides five-/seven-/10-day trips for $1740/2040/2660 and you get to fly out in a seaplane straight back to Hobart. Also climbs Frenchmans Cap.

MAPS

For adventures in this region, you'll need Tasmap's 1:100,000 *Olga and Franklin* and 1:25,000 *Loddon* maps, available from the Tasmanian Map Centre and Service Tasmania in Hobart (see Maps, p81).

CRADLE MOUNTAIN– LAKE ST CLAIR NATIONAL PARK

☎ 03

Cradle Mountain – that perfect new-moon curve of rock that photographers love to capture reflected in mirror-still waters – has become something of a symbol of Tasmania. It's perhaps the best-known feature of the island and is regarded as the crowning glory of the 1262-sq-km Cradle Mountain–Lake St Clair National Park. Its glacier-sculpted mountain peaks, profound river gorges, lakes, tarns and wild alpine moorlands extend from the Great Western Tiers in the north to Derwent Bridge in the south. The park encompasses Mt Ossa (1617m), Tasmania's highest peak, and Lake St Clair (200m), the deepest lake in Australia, brimming with the clear, fresh waters of this pristine environment.

The legendary adventure within the park is the celebrated Overland Track – a week-long hike that's become something of a holy grail for bushwalkers. The 80km track stretching from Cradle Mountain to Cynthia Bay on Lake St Clair (Leeawuleena or 'sleeping water' to Tasmania's indigenous people), is an unforgettable journey through Tasmania's alpine heart. For detailed information on the Overland Track, including a route description, see p290.

INFORMATION
Cradle Valley

There are now two visitor information centres: one outside the park boundary and one just within it. You'll find the first at the alarmingly named Cradle Mountain Transit Terminal – and unfortunately the crowds and the acres of car parking here do little for your sense of wilderness. Still, you'll find helpful staff at the **Cradle visitors centre** (☎ 6492 1110; Cradle Mountain Rd; ☼ 8.30am-4.30pm), who will ply you with park passes and bushwalking infor-

mation. Food and fuel are available. This is also the spot to jump on the bus shuttle service (p297) to Dove Lake at the foot of Cradle Mountain. Then there's the **Cradle Mountain visitors centre** (☎ 6492 1133; www.parks.tas.gov.au; ☼ 8am-5pm Jun-Aug, 8am-6pm Dec-March), where rangers provide detailed bushwalking information, weather condition updates, advice on bushwalking gear and tips on bush safety and etiquette. There's also an interpretative display here on the flora, fauna and history of the park. In summer there's a free ranger-run activity program, including guided nature walks. The centre has toilets, a small shop, drinking water and Eftpos (maximum withdrawal $50). It's also wheelchair-accessible and accepts major credit cards.

Dove Lake has flushing toilets, but no drinking water. Waldheim now has flushing toilets, drinking water and a very good day-use hut with gas heaters.

Whatever time of the year you visit, be prepared for cold, wet weather in Cradle Valley and on the Overland Track: it rains on seven out of 10 days, is cloudy on eight out of 10 days, the sun shines all day only one day in 10, and it snows in Cradle Valley on 54 days each year. You could find yourself camping in the snow at any time of year, but you also need to be aware of sunburn, not just in summer. Winds can be extreme. Be well prepared with warm and waterproof gear, and be weather savvy – check expected conditions and be prepared for these to change.

In mid-June you can come in from the cold and enjoy **Tastings at the Top**, a three-day festival of gastronomic delights held at Cradle Mountain Lodge (p295).

The top new attraction in Cradle Valley is the excellent **Devils@Cradle** (☎ 6492 1491; adult/child/family $25/10/45; ☼ 10am-4pm). This little Tasmanian devil park is the place to have close encounters with these fascinating creatures and learn about the facial tumour disease that's threatening their survival. There are feedings nightly at 5.30pm and 8.30pm.

Cynthia Bay

Cynthia Bay, on the southern boundary of the park, has the **Lake St Clair visitors centre** (☎ 6289 1172; ☼ 8am-6pm Dec & Jan, to 8pm Feb, to 5pm Mar-Nov). Apart from providing information on the Cradle Mountain–Lake St Clair National Park (and the Franklin-Gordon Wild Rivers National Park), the centre has displays on the

THE WEST

area's geology, flora and fauna, bushwalking and Aboriginal heritage. There's a display of woven reed handicrafts by three indigenous artists (for details of the indigenous cultural walk at Cynthia Bay, see p294), an eerie hologram of the thylacine, and a relief model of lake and mountains. If you've forgotten your rain gear you can pick up some waterproof attire in the Parks shop too.

At the adjacent, separately run **Lake St Clair Wilderness Resort** (☎ 6289 1137; www.lakestclair resort.com.au; ☼ 8am-8pm summer, 10am-3pm winter), you can book a range of accommodation (see p296), a seat on a ferry or cruise (p297), and there are also canoes for hire in the summer months.

THE OVERLAND TRACK
Information
A handy pocket-sized reference for the walk is the PWS *Overland Track: One walk, many journeys,* which has notes on ecology and history plus illustrations of flora and fauna you may see along the way. You can get all the latest on the track and walk-planning at www .overlandtrack.com.au. The reference map for the track and surrounds is the 1:100,000 Cradle Mountain–Lake St Clair map published by Tasmap.

Most hikers walk the Overland Track during summer when alpine plants are fragrantly in flower, daylight hours are long, and one can work up enough heat to swim in one of the frigid alpine tarns. The track's also most busy at this time and is subject to a crowd-limiting booked permit system from 1 December to 30 April; see boxed text, opposite. If you're well prepared and experienced, the track is quiet and icily beautiful in winter. Spring and autumn have their own charms, and fewer walkers than in summer.

The Track
Apart from in the peak time, when a north–south walking regulation is enforced, the track can be walked in either direction. The trail is well marked for its entire length and takes around six days. Side trips lead to features like **Mt Ossa**, and some fantastic **waterfalls** – so it's worth budgeting time for some of these. Apart from in the dead of winter, you can expect to meet many walkers each day: some 9000 people hike this path annually.

There are unattended huts with bare wooden bunks and coal or gas heaters spaced at a day's walking distance along the track: but don't count on any room inside in summer, and carry a tent. Camp fires are banned and you must carry a fuel stove for cooking.

The walk itself is extremely varied, negotiating high alpine moors, rocky scree, gorges and tall forest. A detailed description of the walk and major side trips is given in Lonely Planet's *Walking in Australia.* For further notes on the tracks in the park, read *Cradle Mountain–Lake St Clair and Walls of Jerusalem National Parks* by John Chapman and John Siseman.

CRADLE VALLEY TO WATERFALL VALLEY HUTS (3½ TO FIVE HOURS; 13KM)
From Ronny Creek, beyond the side road to Waldheim Chalet, follow the signs for the Overland Track past Crater Falls and Crater Lake to Marions Lookout. Avoid taking the track to Lake Lilla and Dove Lake (to the left of the Overland Track) and the Horse Track (to the right of the Overland Track).

Continue on the Overland Track past Marions Lookout to Kitchen Hut, a tiny emergency shelter. Follow the track to the west of Cradle Mountain to Cradle Cirque, where there are good views of Waterfall Valley, then continue down into the valley and take the signposted track to the Waterfall Valley Hut, sleeping 28. Tent sites are in the forest a short distance upstream of the original hut.

WATERFALL VALLEY HUT TO WINDERMERE HUT (THREE HOURS; 9KM)
Walk back to the Overland Track and follow it over an exposed plain and down to Lake Windermere. Follow the shore to some tent sites before turning southeast to the hut, which sleeps 40 people. Camping isn't allowed on the fragile moorland around the lake. Wombats are especially common here.

WINDERMERE HUT TO PELION HUTS (FIVE HOURS; 14KM)
Follow the track across a creek to Lake Curran and through Pine Forest Moor. Continue to Frog Flats, over the Forth River and on to Pelion Plains, where a muddy side track leads to the Old Pelion Hut. New Pelion Hut, which is indeed modern and sleeps 60, is further along the main track. Large sections of the track before and after these huts can be heavy going following rain. Less experienced walkers may find the combination of mud, leeches and exposed roots challenging.

LICENCE TO WALK

The Overland Track is struggling under the weight of its own popularity. Recent years have seen 9000 walkers tread its paths annually – that figure was less than 1000 in 1953. With all those feet on the ground, washing up scraps around camps, and human waste to deal with, there have been some big questions about environmental sustainability. There's had to be careful management of late to prevent this route and the wilderness it traverses from being loved to death. To help keep walker numbers manageable and the walking experience one of wilderness, not crowd-dodging, the following rules have been put in place:

■ There's a booking system in place from 1 November to 30 April, during which time a maximum of 34 walkers can depart each day.

■ There are fees of $150/120 per adult/child aged six to 16 and concession, to cover costs of the sustainable management of the track (these apply from November to April only).

■ The compulsory walking direction from November to April is north to south.

There's a web-based booking system for walking permits on the Overland Track website at www .overlandtrack.com.au.

PELION HUTS TO KIA ORA HUT (THREE TO FOUR HOURS; 8KM)

Follow the track south to Pelion Gap, from where you can climb to Mt Pelion East (1½ hours return) or Tasmania's highest mountain, Mt Ossa (three hours return). From Pelion Gap, the track descends into Pinestone Valley and crosses Pinestone Creek. Continue to cute, cosy Kia Ora Hut, which sleeps 24 people. There are tent platforms nearby.

KIA ORA HUT TO WINDY RIDGE HUT (THREE TO FOUR HOURS; 11KM)

Follow the track across Kia Ora Creek and on to shingled Du Cane Hut – only for emergencies and best used as a lunch stop. Continue about 2.5km to the signposted turn-off to Hartnett Falls, a thoroughly worthwhile 1½-hour side trip through the forest to a gorgeous cascade. Return to the Overland Track and climb to Du Cane Gap, then descend to Windy Ridge Hut, which sleeps 24. Camp sites are available a little to the north.

WINDY RIDGE HUT TO NARCISSUS HUT (THREE HOURS; 9KM)

There's easy cruising on lengthy sections of boardwalk here, and you should see plenty of wildlife in the open buttongrass plains. About halfway along, a track on the right leads to Pine Valley and onward to the Labyrinth and the Acropolis (1471m), a highly recommended side trip. To reach Pine Valley Hut takes 1½ hours, and from there you should allow another three to five hours to ascend

the Acropolis summit, where the views on a clear day are magnificent.

Continuing on the main track, you know you're near pretty Narcissus Hut at the northern end of Lake St Clair when you cross the swing bridge over Marion Creek. There are camp spots on the buttongrass plains nearby.

NARCISSUS HUT TO CYNTHIA BAY (FIVE HOURS; 16KM)

The last day of the Overland Track is a long, undulating walk through lakeside forest that's quite rough under foot due to exposed routes. You'll want to take a rest stop at the tiny hut at beautiful Echo Point before skipping along the last few kilometres to Cynthia Bay and a celebration of the end of your journey.

Alternatively, you can radio Lake St Clair Wilderness Resort from Narcissus Hut to reserve a place on one of its lake ferries; see p297. In peak season especially, it pays to have booked in advance, and always reconfirm by radio when you arrive at Narcissus.

OTHER BUSHWALKS
Cradle Valley

From the visitors centre you can take an easy but quite spectacular 10-minute circular **Rainforest Walk**. It's all on boardwalk and suitable for wheelchairs and prams. There's another boarded path nearby leading to **Pencil Pine Falls** and on to **Knyvet Falls** (25 minutes return), as well as the **Enchanted Nature Walk** alongside Pencil Pine Creek (25 minutes return). The boardwalk running the 8.5km-long

THE WEST

THE OVERLAND TRACK (NORTH)

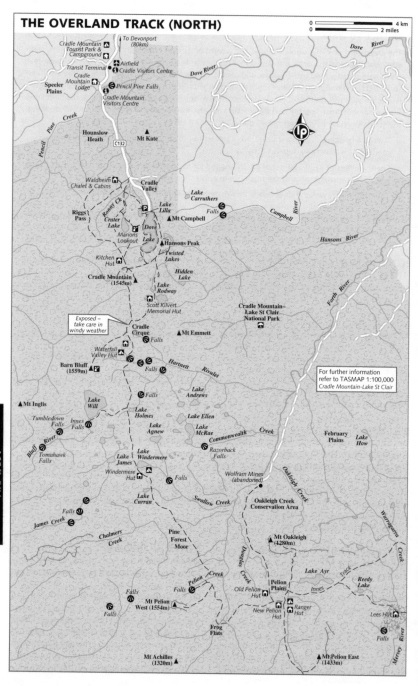

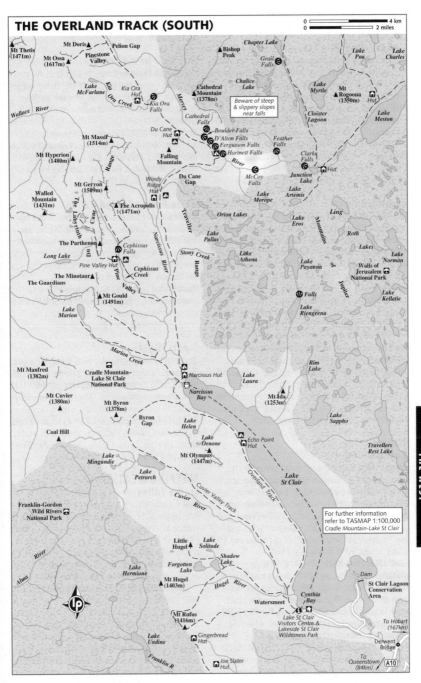

THE OVERLAND TRACK (SOUTH)

0 — 4 km
0 — 2 miles

Mt Thetis (1471m)
Mt Doris
Pinestone Valley
Pelion Gap
Mt Ossa (1617m)
Kia Ora Creek
Lake McFarlane
Kia Ora Hut
Kia Ora Falls
Mersey
Wallace River
Cathedral Mountain (1378m)
Chapter Lake
Bishop Peak
Grail Falls
Lake Poa
Lake Charles
Chalice Lake
Lake Myrtle
Mt Rogoona (1350m)
Hut
Lake Meston
Cathedral Falls
Cloister Lagoon
Du Cane Hut
Boulder Falls
D'Alton Falls
Fergusson Falls
Hartnett Falls
Feather Falls
Clarks Falls
Beware of steep & slippery slopes near falls
Mt Massif (1514m)
Mt Hyperion (1480m)
Falling Mountain
River
McCoy Falls
Junction Lake
Hut
Du Cane Gap
Lake Merope
Lake Artemis
Range
Windy Ridge Hut
Mt Geryon (1509m)
Walled Mountain (1431m)
The Acropolis (1471m)
Traveller
Orion Lakes
Lake Eros
Ling
Roth
Lakes
The Labyrinth
Du Cane
The Parthenon
Cephissus Falls
Pine Valley Hut
Lake Pallas
Lake Athena
Mountains
Lake Norman
Long Lake
Cephissus Creek
Stony Creek Range
Narcissus River
Lake Payanna
Walls of Jerusalem National Park
The Minotaur
The Guardians
Pine Valley
Mt Gould (1491m)
of
Jupiter
Lake Kellatie
Falls
Lake Marion
Lake Riengeena
Rim Lake
Marion Creek
Mt Manfred (1382m)
Cradle Mountain–Lake St Clair National Park
Narcissus Hut
Lake Laura
Mt Ida (1253m)
Mt Cuvier (1380m)
Mt Byron (1378m)
Narcissus Bay
Lake Sappho
Coal Hill
Byron Gap
Lake Helen
Lake Oenone
Echo Point Hut
Travellers Rest Lake
Lake Mingundie
Mt Olympus (1447m)
Lake St Clair
Lake Petrarch
Cuvier River
Cuvier Valley Track
Overland Track
Franklin-Gordon Wild Rivers National Park
For further information refer to TASMAP 1:100,000 Cradle Mountain–Lake St Clair
Little Hugel
Lake Solitude
Shadow Lake
Forgotten Lake
Dam
St Clair Lagoon Conservation Area
River
Alma
Lake Hermione
Mt Hugel (1403m)
Hugel River
Cynthia Bay
Watersmeet
To Hobart (167km)
Mt Rufus (1416m)
Lake St Clair Visitors Centre & Lakeside St Clair Wilderness Park
Derwent Bridge
Lake Undine
Gingerbread Hut
To Queenstown (84km)
A10
Franklin R
Joe Slater Hut

THE WEST

Cradle Valley walk between the visitors centre and Dove Lake is also wheelchair-friendly.

Crater Lake is a popular two-hour return walk from Ronny Creek. You can also make the spectacular climb to the summit of **Cradle Mountain**: the views are incredible in fine weather, but it's not advised in bad visibility or when it's snowy and icy in winter. Allow about eight hours.

Otherwise, marvel at Cradle Mountain from below – if the weather gods oblige – from the easy two- to three-hour circuit track around **Dove Lake**. Other walks in the area involve steep climbs. The **Twisted Lakes** walk via **Hansons Peak** provides great views of Cradle Mountain.

Cynthia Bay

The **Larmairremener tabelti** is an Aboriginal cultural-interpretative walk that winds through the traditional lands of the Larmairremener, the indigenous people of the region. This easy one-hour return walk starts at the visitors centre and loops through the lakeside forest before leading along the lake's shoreline back to the centre. From Watersmeet, near the visitors centre, you can also take the **Platypus Bay Circuit** (30 minutes return). Most other walks are fairly long: the circuit of **Shadow Lake** takes four hours return, while the highly worthwhile **Mt Rufus** circuit is at least seven hours return.

To take in just a little of the Overland Track magic, you can also catch the ferry to Echo Point (three hours back to Cynthia) or Narcissus Hut – five to six hours' walk back to Cynthia Bay along the lakeshore.

TOURS
Bushwalking

Craclair (☎ 6339 4488; www.craclair.com.au) Craclair was the pioneer of Tasmanian bushwalking and has been guiding walkers on the Overland Track longer than any other company. It offers eight-day classic Overland Track trips for $1950, as well as shorter circuits. They supply you with packs, sleeping bags, tents, waterproof jackets and over-trousers – and camp food cooked by their friendly guides. All you have to do is walk and smile.

Cradle Mountain Huts (☎ 6391 9339; www .cradlehuts.com.au) If camping isn't for you, then from October to May you can take a six-day guided walk in a small group (four to 10 people) along the Overland Track which includes accommodation on private huts. The $2500 fee includes meals, national park entry fees and transfer to/from Launceston. Gear hire is also available.

Tasmanian Expeditions (☎ 6334 3477, 1800 030 230; www.tas-ex.com) Between October and May Tasmanian Expeditions does an eight-day Overland Track trek for

$1850, and a six-day Cradle Mountain/Walls of Jerusalem walk for $1390 (see p243).

Bus/4WD-based Tours

Cradle Park Explorer Tour (☎ 6394 3535) You can take a Park Explorer tour (adult/child $15/10) that will get you conveniently to the park's bus-accessible highlights for a spot of walking, or a 4WD tour for evening wildlife-spotting ($25/12.50).

Grayline (☎ 6234 3336; www.grayline.com) Offers a day coach tour from Launceston to Cradle Mountain (adult/child $141/70.50) including a hike around Dove Lake on Mondays, Wednesdays, Fridays and Saturdays leaving at 8.30am and returning at 5pm.

Horse Riding & Quad Biking

Cradle Country Adventures (☎ 1300 656 069; www .cradlecountryadventures.com.au; 2hr trip $89, full-day from $220) The country around Cradle is perfect riding territory, and travelling on the back of one of this operator's friendly horses is a perfect way to see it. Half-day, full-day and multiday riding trips are available.

Quad Biking @ Cradle (☎ 1300 656 069; www .cradlemountainquadbikes.com.au; 2hr trip $89) For some muddy, wheel-spinning adventures, just outside the World Heritage Areas, these guys are the go.

Scenic Flights

You can get a spectacular bird's-eye view over Tasmania's alpine heart by taking a joy ride with **Cradle Mountain Helicopters** (☎ 6492 1132; www.adventureflights.com.au). The choppers leave from the airstrip next to the Transit Terminal, and half-hour flights cost $190/115 per adult/child. You can get all you postcard-perfect shots of sights like Cradle Mountain, Dove Lake and little-seen Fury Gorge.

SLEEPING & EATING
Cradle Valley

The Cradle Valley has heaps of accommodation options, but if you find yourself unable to secure a booking you could always try Gowrie Park (p244) or Tullah (p272). A lot of the accommodation here is self-catering but there's not much in the way of supermarket shopping, so bring your supplies with you.

Discovery Holiday Parks Cradle Mountain (☎ 6492 1395, 1800 068 574; Cradle Mountain Rd; unpowered/powered sites $25/35, dm $30, cabins $112-175; 💻) This is a bushland complex situated 2.5km outside the national park. It has well-separated sites (prices are for up to two people), a YHA-affiliated hostel, a camp kitchen and laundry and self-contained cabins.

THE WEINDORFERS' LEGACY

If not for the forward-looking vision of one Gustav Weindorfer, Cradle Mountain might never have been incorporated into a national park. Weindorfer, an Austrian immigrant, first came to Cradle in 1910 and built a wooden cabin, Waldheim (German for 'Forest Home'), in 1912 in this rugged and isolated wonderland. Weindorfer and his Australian wife, Kate, took their honeymoon at Waldheim and fell in love with Tasmania's alpine heart. Recognising its uniqueness, they lobbied successive governments for its preservation.

Kate Weindorfer had a passion for botany and became an expert in the area's bushland and flora, encouraging Gustav's appreciation of the landscape. Their spirit was tenacious: in those days a horse and cart could only get within 15km of Cradle Mountain, and from there they walked to Waldheim while packhorses carried supplies. The Weindorfers encouraged visitors to come to this remote place and share in its marvels.

Kate died in 1916 from a long illness, and Gustav moved to Waldheim permanently, devoting his life to preserving the mountain he loved. He died in 1932, and half a century later Cradle Mountain was finally declared a national park.

The original chalet burnt down in a bushfire in 1974, but was rebuilt using traditional carpentry techniques and stands as a monument to the Weindorfers. Just inside the doorway is Gustav's original inscription: 'This is Waldheim/Where there is no time/And nothing matters.'

Waldheim Chalet & Cabins (☎ 6492 1110; cradle@depha.tas.gov.au; cabins from $70) Set in the forest near the original Weindorfers' chalet (see boxed text, above) are some rustic wood-lined cabins with bunks sleeping eight, six and four. Each has kitchen facilities and there's a shared shower and toilet. Bookings are handled by Cradle Mountain visitors centre (see p289).

Cradle Mountain Highlanders Cottages (☎ 6492 1116; www.cradlehighlander.com.au; Cradle Mountain Rd; cabins $115-290) This genuinely hospitable place has a charming collection of self-contained timber cottages with wood or gas fires, queen-sized beds, electric blankets and hearty continental breakfast provisions. Three cabins include a spa; all cabins include linen and are serviced daily. The surrounding bush is peaceful and wildlife-filled.

Cradle Mountain Wilderness Village (☎ 6492 1500; www.cradlevillage.com.au; Cradle Mountain Rd; cottages d $180, chalets & villas sleeping up to 4 $260; ▯) When you walk into the reception here on a clear day, you'll be treated to some exceptional views of Cradle Mountain. There are some quite luxurious chalets and cabins set peacefully in the trees, but they're painted in such perfect eucalypt greys and greens that it feels almost like army-barrack camouflage.

Cradle Mountain Chateau (☎ 6492 1404, 1800 420 155; www.puretasmania.com.au; Cradle Mountain Rd; standard d $200-280, spa d $223-315, ste $230-351; ▯) This large complex is the first you come to on the way into Cradle Valley, and heralds its presence with a grand porticoed gate. Though the public areas

are pleasantly timbered and feature the obligatory log fires, the rooms are frankly rather motel-ish. Get one on the front side to be sure your morning view isn't one of the gravel car park. There's a bistro here serving good nosh (open lunch and dinner) and, not to be outdone by the Lodge, there's also the new Calm day spa where you can have relaxing treatments.

The highlight of this complex is undoubtedly the impressive **Wilderness Gallery** (☎ 6492 1404; www.wildernessgallery.com.au; Cradle Mountain Rd; admission $5, free for guests; ⏰ 10am-5pm) showcasing incredible environmental photography. There's also a well-stocked gift shop.

Cradle Mountain Lodge (☎ 6492 2100, 1300 134 044; www.voyages.com.au; Cradle Mountain Rd; d $260-620; ▯) When this mountain resort of wooden cabins emerges – pungent with woodsmoke – from the swirling mist on a cold winter's day, you can't help but be charmed by it. There are various standards of cabin here – the most luxurious are the King Billy Suites, privately secluded in the forest and with hot tubs on their decks. There is a little lake to fish in and plenty of short walks nearby, and the lodge puts on a plethora of guided activities to keep you busy. You can also be thoroughly pampered in the Waldheim Alpine Spa (☎ 6492 2133), which offers all sorts of massages and beauty treatments in a relaxing setting. Good, casual mountain fare is served in the Tavern (mains $8 to $24, open lunch and dinner), but the Highland Restaurant (two/three courses $55/64, dinner only) is the real culinary experience here, serving the likes

THE WEST

of prosciutto-wrapped wild rabbit saddle with mustard potato gnocchi – all accompanied by fine Tasmanian wines. The Lodge is also the venue for the renowned winter foodie event, Tastings at the Top (see p289).

Cradle Wilderness Cafe (☎ 6492 1400; Cradle Mountain Rd; mains $7-20; ☼ 9am-5pm Mar-Nov, 9am-8pm Dec-Feb) This café at the Cradle Mountain Transit Terminal is welcomingly warm and has a good range of drinks and snacks – you can pick up last-minute sandwiches for your walk here, too.

Road to Cradle Mountain

Lemonthyme Lodge (☎ 6492 1112; www.lemonthyme .com.au; Dolcoath Rd, Moina; lodge d from $120, cabins $190-375, extra adult/child $35/25; ☐) Off Cradle Mountain Rd at Moina is this secluded mountain retreat offering self-contained cabins, some with spa, and rooms in the main lodge (shared facilities). You can eat in the reputable restaurant (two/three courses $45/60, open breakfast and dinner). There's an animal feeding nightly at 8.30pm and there are some good walks on the property. Driving to Cradle Mountain from Devonport, turn onto the gravel Dolcoath Rd 3km south of Moina and follow it for a scenic 8km to get here.

Cradle Chalet (☎ 6492 1401; www.cradlechalet .com.au; 1422 Cradle Mountain Rd, Moina; d $198-280) There are attractive timber chalets in a bushland setting here. You can soak up the peace from your own private deck or chat with the friendly hosts, who are a mine of regional advice. The rooms include continental breakfast, and home-cooked evening meals are by arrangement (two/three courses $50/63).

Cynthia Bay

Lake St Clair Wilderness Resort (☎ 6289 1137; www .lakestclairresort.com.au; unpowered/powered sites per person/2 people $10/25, dm $28, cabins d $130-190, extra person $25) There are unpowered bush camping sites on the lakeshore here, and powered caravan spots. The backpackers lodge has two- to four-bunk rooms and kitchen facilities. There are also comfortably upmarket self-contained alpine cabins. In the main building opposite the Lake St Clair visitors centre there's a great café (mains $8 to $26, open 7.30am to 9pm summer, 10am to 3pm winter), serving a hearty menu to fill you up before or after a bushwalk, light snacks, and coffee that's been voted the best in Tasmania. There are a few basic food supplies, some outdoor gear and souvenirs in the shop.

You can camp for free at Fergy's Paddock, 10 minutes' walk back along the Overland Track. There are pit toilets, and fires are not allowed.

Derwent Bridge & Bronte Park

Derwent Bridge is just 2km from Lake St Clair and has a few good accommodation options, otherwise the nearest place to stay is Bronte Park, 30km from Lake St Clair, in the direction of Hobart. On your journey between Derwent Bridge and Bronte Park, don't miss the **Wall in the Wilderness** (☎ 6289 1134; www.thewalltasmania .com; adult/child $7.50/5; ☼ 9am-5pm Sep-May, 9am-4pm Jun-Aug). This amazing creation is a work of art in progress. Wood sculptor Greg Duncan is carving a panorama in wood panels depicting the history of the Tasmanian highlands. The scale is incredible: when it's finished the scene will be 100m long, which will take an estimated ten years to complete. Though the tableau is large-scale it's carved with breathtaking skill and detail: from the veins in the workers' hands, to the creases in their shirts, to the hair of their beards. The Wall is 2km east of Derwent Bridge, and is definitely worth making time for.

Bronte Park Holiday Village (☎ 6289 1126; www .bronteparkvillage.com.au; 378 Marlborough Hwy, Bronte Park; unpowered/powered sites $12/14, chalet d $100-110, cottage d $90-120) Just off the Lyell Hwy 30km east of Derwent Bridge, this place has a wide variety of accommodation, plus a bar and restaurant (mains $11.50 to $27.50, open breakfast, lunch and dinner) serving a changing menu featuring such favourites as beef 'n' reef ($27.50), good old chicken parmigiana, and rainbow trout with lemon and spinach, from the highland lakes nearby. The hotel can also help arrange a spot of fishing with Trout Adventures (☎ 6289 1009, 0418-139 048) or evening wildlife-spotting tours.

Derwent Bridge Wilderness Hotel (☎ 6289 1144; fax 6289 1173; Derwent Bridge; dm $25, d with/without bathroom $115/95) This chalet-style pub has a high-beamed roof and a pleasingly country feel. The lounge bar has a warm, expansive atmosphere in which to enjoy a beer and a meal in front of a massive log fire. The hostel and hotel accommodation is plain but comfortable, and the restaurant (mains $18 to $39.50, open breakfast, lunch and dinner) serves commendable pub fare, including excellent roasts, pasta dishes, steaks and daily fresh soups with inviting hot crusty bread.

Derwent Bridge Chalets & Studios (☎ 6289 1000; www.derwent-bridge.com; Lyell Hwy, Derwent Bridge; d $155-

230) Just 5km from Lake St Clair (500m east of the turn-off), this gay- and lesbian-friendly place has one-, two- and three-bedroom self-contained roomy cabins, some with spa but all with full kitchen and laundry facilities, and back-porch bush views.

Hungry Wombat Café (☎ 6289 1125; Lyell Hwy, Derwent Bridge; mains $5-10.30; ☺ 8am-6pm summer, 9am-5pm winter) Part of the Caltex service station, this friendly café is well placed to feed the famished, serving breakfasts to keep you going all day. For lunch there are soups, sandwiches, focaccias, wraps and burgers, and there's a range of all-day snacks, coffees and cakes. Everything's homemade and jolly good. There's a small grocery section too.

GETTING THERE & AWAY

See p272 for details of year-round services to Cradle Mountain and Lake St Clair. During summer, there are extra services.

Tassielink (☎ 6239 8900, 1300 300 520; www.tassielink .com.au) has services to Cradle Mountain Transit Centre from Launceston, every day in summer and twice a week in winter ($53.30, three to 3¾ hours). This service travels to Cradle Mountain via Devonport, and pick-up at the ferry terminal can be arranged (the fare from Devonport is $36.70).

Tassielink also has services to Lake St Clair from Hobart daily/four days weekly in summer/winter ($46.40, 2¾ hours). There's no direct service from Launceston to Lake St Clair any more, but you can get here by taking Tassielink's West Coast service to Queenstown, overnighting there, and hopping on its bus to Lake St Clair the following day ($92.50).

For Overland Track walkers, there's a Launceston–Cradle Mountain and Lake St Clair–Hobart package costing $90. It can also do baggage storage and transfers so you can go light on the track, at a cost of $10 per bag. A bushwalkers' package from Launceston to Cradle Mountain and Lake St Clair to Launceston costs $131.

Maxwells (☎ 6492 1431, 0418-584 004) runs services on demand from Devonport to Cradle Mountain (one to four passengers $160, five or more $40 per passenger), Launceston to Cradle Mountain ($240/60) via Walls of Jerusalem (p243), Devonport and Launceston to Lake St Clair ($280/70), and Lake St Clair to Bronte Park and Frenchmans Cap ($65/15).

If driving, fill up with petrol before heading out to Cradle Mountain – prices are significantly higher there than in the towns. The road north from Bronte Park to Gear Great Lake (35km) is mostly gravel. Though it's usually in a good condition, it's worth checking with a local before you depart.

GETTING AROUND
Cradle Valley
To avoid overcrowding on the narrow road into Cradle Mountain and gridlock at the Dove Lake car park, there's now a shuttle bus service to Dove Lake from the Cradle Mountain Transit Terminal at the new visitors centre outside the park. At peak times, travel to Dove Lake is *only* by bus and you must leave your car at the car park here. Shuttle buses (adult/child/family $7.50/3.75/18.75) leave at 10- to 20-minute intervals all day (mid-September to mid-May) and visitors can alight at stops along the way. There may be substantial queues at peak times. Contact the Cradle Mountain visitors centre (p289) for the shuttle's reduced winter timetable. Note: the bus is free if you have a holiday parks pass or a year's pass for your vehicle.

Cynthia Bay
Also run by **Maxwells** (☎ 6289 1125, 0418-328 427) is an on-demand service between Cynthia Bay/Lake St Clair and Derwent Bridge ($7 per person one way).

Lake St Clair Wilderness Resort (☎ 6289 1137; www .lakestclairresort.com.au) operates the all-important bushwalkers' ferry trips to and from Narcissus Hut at the northern end of Lake St Clair (45 minutes), and also offers the return trip as a lake cruise for nonwalkers. The one-way fare is adult/child $25/15, while the return cruise trip costs $35/18 and takes 1½ hours return. The boat departs Cynthia Bay three times daily from October to early May (9am, 12.30pm and 3pm) and collects bushwalkers at Narcissus Hut at 9.30am, 1pm and 3.30pm. If you're using the ferry service at the end of your Overland Track hike, you *must* radio the ferry operator when you arrive at Narcissus. Bookings are essential for both directions and there's a four-person minimum on any trip. In winter there's only one scheduled departure leaving Cynthia Bay at 11am and picking up walkers at Narcissus at noon. The service is based on demand and minimum numbers. Be sure to book and reconfirm. You can also ride the ferry one way to Echo Point (20 minutes) costing $18/15.

The Southwest

Tasmania's southwest corner is about as wild as it's possible to get in this plenty-wild state. It's an edge-of-the-world domain made up of primordial forests, rugged mountains and endless heathland, all fringed by untamed beaches and turbulent seas. This is among the last great wildernesses on Earth: a place for absorption in nature, adventure and isolation.

Much of the southwest is incorporated into the Southwest National Park, some 600,000 hectares of largely untouched country. Just one road enters the southwest, and this only as far as the hydroelectric station on the Gordon Dam. Otherwise, all access is by light plane to the gravel airstrip at Melaleuca, by sailing boat around the tempestuous coastline, or on foot. Despite its isolation, Tasmania's southwest has a human history. It was home to Tasmanian Aborigines for some 35,000 years, then became the territory of surveyors, miners and adventure-seekers. Apart from periodic burning here by the first inhabitants, which helped form the buttongrass plains, the southwest bore little human imprint before hydroelectric dams drowned a great swathe of it in 1972. Today, the logging of ancient forests continues controversially on its fringes, and the southwest has become known for antiforestry protests.

For the well-prepared visitor this part of Tasmania is an enticing adventure playground. There are challenging, multiday walks (as well as shorter wanders), remote sea-kayaking on the waterways of Bathurst Harbour and Port Davey, and ancient forests to explore. Those who prefer aerial pleasures can take a mind-blowing abseil down the curvaceous wall of the Gordon Dam, or swoop over the valleys and mountains on a scenic southwest joy flight.

HIGHLIGHTS

- Setting off for days of full immersion in nature on the **South Coast Track** (p303)
- Skimming over the perfect reflections on a sea-kayaking trip at **Bathurst Harbour** and **Port Davey** (p303)
- Flying over the southwest by light plane, then swooping down to land on the beach at **Cox Bight** or the gravel airstrip at **Melaleuca** (p303)
- Abseiling over the side of the **Gordon Dam wall** (p301)
- Sitting quietly in the **Melaleuca bird-hide** (p304) and watching for endangered orange-bellied parrots
- Wandering in awe among the tall trees in the ancient forests of the **Styx Valley of the Giants** and the **Upper Florentine Valley** (p302)
- Traversing one of Australia's hardest bushwalks through the **Western Arthurs Range** (p303)

Florentine Valley ★
Gordon Dam Wall ★
★ Styx Valley of the Giants
Western Arthurs Range ★
Port Davey ★
Bathurst ★ Harbour
Melaleuca ★ South Coast Track
★ Cox Bight

THE SOUTHWEST

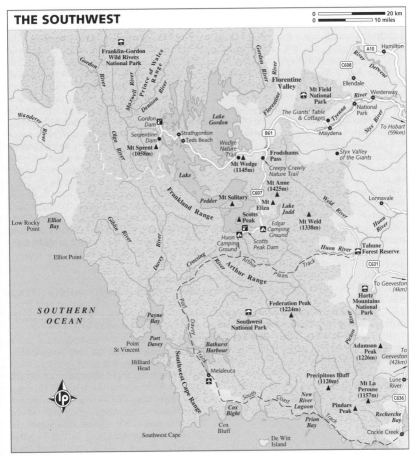

THE SOUTHWEST

0   20 km
0   10 miles

History

When the first humans came to this part of the world, they inhabited a planet in the grip of an ice age. The southwest was then covered in frigid open grasslands – ideal for hunting game and covering large distances on foot. Between 18,000 and 12,000 years ago, as the ice retreated, the landscape changed dramatically. Rising sea levels drowned river valleys and formed landlocked waterways like Bathurst Harbour. Warmer temperatures also brought more extensive forest cover, which Aboriginal Tasmanians burnt periodically to keep it open for hunting. Early European documentation of the original inhabitants here records them mostly around the coastline – though no doubt they ventured inland too for hunting game and meeting with other bands.

European explorers were at first appalled by the landscape. Matthew Flinders, the first to circumnavigate Tasmania, described the southwest thus: 'The mountains are the most dismal that can be imagined. The eye ranges over these peaks with astonishment and horror.' Other reports from those who climbed the peaks aptly described the interior as a series of rugged ranges that extended to the horizon.

Most of the early explorers were surveyors who cut tracks here and endured great hardships in the name of opening the region for development. But the acidic soils of the southwest, its remoteness and harsh weather

THE SOUTHWEST

conditions meant little farming ever got off the ground. Mineral deposits also proved less than anticipated, so although a road was cut as far as Gordon Bend in the 1880s, no permanent access to the southwest was established. Apart from the hardy few who came to Bathurst Harbour to hunt for Huon pine, and a few stalwart miners at Adamsfield and Melaleuca, early Tasmanians left the southwest well alone. They simply regarded it as uninhabitable.

The trials of early explorers make for interesting reading in *Trampled Wilderness: The History of South-West Tasmania* by Ralph and Kathleen Gowlland (out of print, it can be difficult to obtain). There's also *South-West Tasmania* by Ken Collins (Heritage Books), a fascinating natural history and field guide that identifies geology and glaciation, vegetation and the ecology of this region. An insight into the southwest's more recent human history can be glimpsed in *King of the Wilderness: the Life of Deny King* by Christobel Mattingley, a wonderful biography of Tasmania's best-loved bushman, who made Melaleuca his home.

Of these early developments, all that remains is the tiny tin mining lease still worked by the elderly Wilsons at Melaleuca, who, like the early pioneers, periodically sail their diggings out to Hobart by yacht. For most visitors – bushwalkers, kayakers and those flying in for a day trip – Melaleuca's most important feature is its small gravel airstrip built by Deny King, which gives access right to the heart of this great wilderness.

MAYDENA
☎ 03 / pop 250
Maydena is a quiet little town in the Tyenna Valley, surrounded by hills and eucalypt forests, just 12km west of the village National Park on the way to Strathgordon and the southwest. Take Junee Rd north out of town for about 10 minutes, and you'll come to the start of the 10-minute walk to the mouth of **Junee Cave**. Here, a waterfall cascades out of the cave mouth that is part of a 30km-long series of caverns known as the **Junee River karst system**. The system includes Niggly Cave, reputedly the deepest in Australia at 375m. Cave divers make hair-raising journeys through the flooded underground passageways, but other visitors can't enter.

Back in Maydena, employment has historically been in forestry. That's not

been sufficient to thrive on, however, and Forestry Tasmania has recently decided to jump on the tourism bandwagon and develop another of its forest attractions near Maydena (see the Tahune Forest AirWalk, p148, Hollybanks Treetops Adventure, p222 and Dismal Swamp, p264). The Maydena development has been on the cards in various guises since 2005, and by the summer season of 2008–09, there should be something up and running here. What's envisaged is a journey to nearby **Abbot's Lookout** that has panoramic views right over the southwest forests. This may be reached by 4WD bus. There may also be an activity centre here, in partnership with private enterprise, incorporating anything from a flying fox to mountain biking, horse riding and helicopter rides. The visitors centre in Hobart (see p84) will be able to update you on current developments.

Sleeping & Eating
Wren's Nest (☎ 6288 2280; 8 Junee Rd; d $120, extra adult/child $25/15) A well-equipped and homy three-bedroom cottage in a peaceful garden setting. It has all self-contained necessities including laundry and wood heating, and is just 20 minutes from the Styx Valley and an hour from Strathgordon.

Roydon Alpaca Stud & Accommodation (☎ 6288 2212; http://roydonalpacastud.com; 46 Junee Rd; r & cottage d $135, extra adult/child $20/15) There are cosy timber-lined one- and two-bedroom cabins here with glorious mountain views, and – something you don't expect in Tasmania – a small herd of friendly alpacas who are just dying to pose for a photo with you. There's also an in-house B&B option, and the friendly owners are a mine of information on the area.

ourpick **Giants' Table & Cottages** (☎ 6288 2293; www.giantstable.com.au; Junee Rd; cottage d $140-160, extra adult/child $30/15) Named for the nearby giant trees in the Styx, these were once simple workers' cottages – but you would never know. Now beautifully decorated in contemporary style, they're spacious, warmly wood-heated and come in various configurations: one sleeps up to 10. There's also an on-site restaurant (two/three courses $30/35, open for dinner Tuesday to Saturday in summer. Call for winter opening times, bookings essential) serving hearty fare to fill you after a day's adventuring. Platypuses are a frequent sight in the ponds on the property.

LAKE PEDDER IMPOUNDMENT

At the northern edge of the southwest wilderness lies the Lake Pedder Impoundment, a vast flooded valley system that covers the area that once cradled the original Lake Pedder, a spectacularly beautiful natural lake that was the region's ecological jewel. The largest glacial outwash lake in the world, its shallow, whisky-coloured waters covered 3 sq km and its wide, sandy beach made an ideal light-plane airstrip. The lake was home to several endangered species, and considered so important that it was the first part of the southwest to be protected within its own national park. But even this status ultimately failed to preserve it.

In the early stages of what was known as 'hydro-industrialisation', the government body responsible for Tasmania's electricity production – the Hydro-Electric Commission (HEC), now Hydro Tasmania – built dams, power stations and pipelines on the Central Plateau and Derwent River. These activities went largely unchallenged until the 1960s, when the HEC proposed flooding Lake Pedder to create a storage lake for electricity generation at the Strathgordon Hydroelectric power station, on the Gordon Dam, adjacent.

By this stage, Tasmania's fledgling conservation movement was stepping up a gear, and there were sustained, adamant protests with street marches in both Hobart and Melbourne. This did little to sway the HEC's all-consuming industrial agenda, despite the revelation that there were feasible engineering alternatives to flooding Lake Pedder for the Gordon Dam hydropower scheme.

The Tasmanian parliament collapsed under the weight of antiflooding protests, and a proconservation political movement called the United Tasmania Group – the world's first Green party – was formed. This polled 7% of the state vote in 1972, but failed to win a seat. Popular protest and political pressure were to no avail, however: the Scotts Peak and Serpentine Dams were built and Lake Pedder was lost under floodwaters in the winter of 1972. Next, the HEC turned its attention to the lower Gordon and Franklin Rivers. For details of the ensuing struggle to prevent new dams here – with a remarkably different outcome to the Lake Pedder campaign – see p287.

Together with Lake Gordon (to which Lake Pedder is connected via McPartlan Pass canal), the dams are the largest water catchment in Australia, with a surface area of 514 sq km, and a volume of 15.2 cubic kilometres – more than 20 times that of Sydney Harbour. The Gordon Power Station is the largest hydroelectric power station in Tasmania and generates 13% of the state's electricity.

Trout fishing is popular here. The lake is well stocked and fish caught range from 1kg to the occasional 20kg monster. Small boats or dinghies are discouraged because the lake is 55km long and prone to dangerously sizable waves. Boat ramps exist at Scotts Peak Dam in the south and near Strathgordon in the north.

There are two free camping grounds near the lake's southern end. The **Edgar Camping Ground** has pit toilets, water, fine views of the area and usually a fisherman or two – in wet weather it's less attractive as it's exposed to cold winds. There's also **Huon Camping Ground**, hidden in tall forest near Scotts Peak Dam with the same facilities as Edgar.

STRATHGORDON

☎ 03 / pop 30

Built to house HEC employees during construction of the Gordon Dam, Strathgordon still accommodates the few souls who operate the power station today. It's a quiet base for walking, fishing and water-skiing in summer.

About 2km past the township is the turn-off to the **Lake Pedder Lookout**, with good views over the lake. A further 10km west is the **Gordon Dam** itself. From the car park, walk down a flight of steps that takes you along the perfect curve of the dam wall. You can't go inside the underground power station any more, but you can plunge over the edge of the dam wall – all in the strictest safety of course – by spending a day with Hobart-based **Aardvark Adventures** (☎ 6273 7722, 0408-127 714; www.aardvarkadventures.com.au), which organises abseiling trips here ($180, suitable for beginners, minimum four people). You can do two different abseils, and then the big one: 140m right down the wall. It's the highest commercial abseil in the world.

There's a free camping ground at **Teds Beach** beside the Lake Pedder Impoundment (toilets and electric BBQs; no fires permitted), or ex-hydro **Lake Pedder Chalet** (☎ 6280 1166; www.lakepedderchalet.com.au; d with/without bathroom $90/55, units $120-150; 🏊), which offers various room standards: the cheapest are open only in summer (October to April) and the best have

STYX VALLEY OF THE GIANTS

The Styx: Even the name is evocative, speaking of the ancients and underworlds. Perhaps 'crossing the Styx' is not what you imagined doing on holiday, but if you come to the Tasmanian Styx, you'll be absorbed in a domain of ancient tall trees and forests so mysteriously beautiful you'd be forgiven for thinking you have indeed crossed to another world. Putting aside the intangible, Tasmania's Styx River Valley has also become known for something far more of this world: the logging of old-growth forests, and the fight to save them.

In the rich and heavily watered soils of the Styx River Valley, trees grow exceptionally tall. The *Eucalyptus regnans* (swamp gum) here are the loftiest trees in the southern hemisphere, and the highest hardwood trees on Earth. Trees of up to 95m tall have been recorded in the valley, and many of the trees in what's known as the **Valley of the Giants** reach over 80m above the ground.

Tasmania's powerful forestry industry has long been cutting these giants. Presently, 300 to 600 hectares are cut each year, and the region is the site of ongoing tussles between forestry operations and protesters. After Tasmania's forests became a national issue in the 2004 elections, 4000 additional hectares of the valley were added to reserves: an acknowledgement that intact forests are valuable for tourism. With new roads recently cut into previously wild territory, however, the loggers appear determined to clear-fell remaining old-growth forest here. On-site protests continue.

Conservationists and the Wilderness Society advocate a 150-sq-km national park in the Styx. Though this looks unlikely, you can visit the Styx to see for yourself what's threatened and be inspired by walking among some of the world's tallest trees. Southern visitors centres stock Forestry Tasmania's brochure on visiting the Styx and the Wilderness Society's *Styx Valley of the Giants* brochure and map with detailed driving directions and interpretation. You can also download this from its website at www.wilderness.org.au/campaigns/forests/tasmania/styx/. Note that the road here is unsealed and, though manageable by 2WD vehicles, can be slippery after rain. Watch out for log trucks.

In recent years, a similar battle to the one in the Styx has also been fought in the nearby **Upper Florentine Valley**. New logging roads have been pushed into previously undisturbed forest, and the Upper Florentine has also been a protest flashpoint that's attracted international attention. The Wilderness Society publishes a map with tour notes that will guide you to more soaring eucalypts, giant myrtles, treacle-coloured rivers and elegant man ferns. There are several walks varying from 15 minutes to two hours return. The Tiger Valley Lookout is one hour from the car park and has awe-inspiring views over the peaks and forests of the southwest. See www.wilderness.org.au/campaigns/forests/tasmania/upper-florentine-self-drive-guide.

lovely lake views. There's an on-site **restaurant** (lunch $7-13, dinner mains $14-25) serving three meals a day accompanied by wonderful water views. It also hires out boats, rods and fishing tackle. The hotel reception now also doubles as the Gordon Dam visitors centre, and has comprehensive information including two huge mock-up models of the power station and maps of the mountains and the lakes in 3D.

SOUTHWEST NATIONAL PARK

There are few places left in the world that are as isolated as Tasmania's southwest wilderness. The state's largest national park is made up of remote, wild country – forest, mountain, grassy plains and seascapes. Here grows the Huon pine, which lives for 3000 years, and the swamp gum, the world's tallest flowering plant. About 300 species of lichen, moss and fern – some very rare – festoon the rainforests, and the alpine meadows are picture-perfect with wildflowers and flowering shrubs. Through it all run wild rivers: rapids tearing through deep gorges and waterfalls plunging over cliffs.

Each year ever more people venture here in search of peace, isolation and challenge. Fit, experienced bush-walkers can undertake tough multiday walks (see opposite). One short walk is an easy 20-minute stroll through rainforest with child-friendly interpretive signage known as the **Creepy Crawly Nature Trail.** Its start is about 2km after the Scotts Peak turn-off from the Strathgordon Rd. Further south, the road leaves the forest near Mt Anne, revealing wonderful views of the surrounding mountains in fine weather. To the west lies the Frankland Range, while to the south is the jagged crest of the Western Arthur Range. The road ends at Scotts Peak Dam and there's free camping nearby (see p301).

Get your national parks pass and information about the southwest at the **Parks & Wildlife visitors centre** (☎ 6288 1149) at Mt Field National Park.

Sights & Activities

DAY WALKS

From Scotts Peak Rd you can climb to **Mt Eliza**, a steep, five-hour return walk, giving panoramic views over the Lake Pedder Impoundment and Mt Solitary. Continue on the same track to climb **Mt Anne**, a challenging walk with some difficult scrambling of at least 10 hours return. Another challenging eight-hour walk for experienced hikers is from Red Tape Creek (29km south of the main road, B61, along Scotts Peak Rd) to **Lake Judd**.

From the Huon Campground, the best short walk follows the start of the **Port Davey Track** through forest and buttongrass plain. **Mt Wedge** is a popular five-hour return walk (signposted off the main road), and has great views of the Lake Pedder Impoundment and Lake Gordon. If you're not up to that, there's the 15-minute **Wedge Nature Trail** from the car park.

LONG BUSHWALKS

The best-known walks in the southwest are the 70km **Port Davey Track** between Scotts Peak Rd and Melaleuca (four or five days duration), and the considerably more popular, 85km **South Coast Track** between Cockle Creek and Melaleuca (for information on Cockle Creek see p152).

The South Coast Track takes six to eight days to complete, and hikers should be prepared for weather that could bring anything from sunburn to snow flurries. Light planes fly bushwalkers into or out of the southwest, landing at Melaleuca, and there's vehicle access to Cockle Creek on the park's southeastern edge (see p304). Detailed notes to the South Coast Track are available in Lonely Planet's *Walking in Australia,* and there's comprehensive track information on the PWS website at: www.parks.tas.gov.au /recreation/tracknotes/scoast.html.

There are many other walks in the park, but you should first complete one of the better-known routes. The South Coast Track makes good preparation for the more difficult walks involving unmarked tracks – these require a high degree of bushwalking skill to complete

---

TOURS IN THE SOUTHWEST

There are a few tours available for those who'd like to tackle the southwest in a small group, with an experienced guide and someone else organising much of the gear and logistics.

Tasmanian Expeditions (☎ 1300 666 856, 6339 3999; www.tas-ex.com) offers three walking tour options in the southwest. The first is a nine-day trek on the South Coast Track ($2160), flying into Melaleuca and walking out along the coastline. For hard-core trekkers there's a 16-day trek along both the Port Davey and South Coast Tracks ($3280), and it also now offers the legendary Western Arthurs Traverse (12 days), one of Australia's hardest, remotest – and most spectacular – walks.

If you prefer your wilderness on water, consider a sea-kayaking adventure in the southwest. From December to March, **Roaring 40s Ocean Kayaking** (☎ 6267 5000; www.roaring40skayaking.com .au) offers kayaking and camp-based walking trips exploring Port Davey and Bathurst Harbour with access by light plane to and from Hobart. Costs vary from $2250 (seven days) to $1550 for a three-day trip, or $995 for a weekend.

You can also swoop over the southwest from the air on a scenic small-plane flight with Hobart-based operators **Par Avion** (☎ 1800 144 460, 6248 5390; www.paravion.com.au). On a clear day you can see the whole of this corner of Tasmania as you buzz over wild beaches and jagged peaks before landing at Melaleuca. Prices start from $180 (child $144) for a half-day trip, and $290 (child $236) for a full-day tour including a boat cruise on Bathurst Harbour.

Tasair (☎ 6248 5088; www.tasair.com.au) also offers flights. Its speciality is a two-hour flight ($243) that includes 30 minutes on the ground after an exciting beach landing at Cox Bight (if weather conditions are right). It also does a 'gourmet' flight into Melaleuca for $316 per person, which gives you time to get to a scenic spot and enjoy the picnic hamper provided.

safely and enjoyably. The shortest of these is the three-day circuit of the **Mt Anne Range**. The walk to **Federation Peak**, which has earned a reputation as the most difficult bushwalking peak in Australia, will take a highly experienced walker around seven days. The spectacular **Western Arthur Range** is an extremely difficult traverse, for which seven to 11 days are recommended.

Getting There & Away

From the end of October through March, **Tassielink** (☎ 1300 300 520; www.tassielink.com.au) operates an early morning bus to the start (and finish) of the Mt Anne Circuit, and to Scotts Peak, three days a week. It also runs a service to Cockle Creek during the same period. For the current season's departure days, times and fares, call Tassielink or look on its website from about September.

MELALEUCA

Melaleuca is little more than a couple of houses hidden in the bush and a white quartzite gravel airstrip with a wooden shed for an airport. As you fly in, you'll see the workings of the earth from the tin mining carried out by hardy bushmen over the years. In the trees by Moth Creek is the house lived in for over 40 years by the southwest's most legendary resident, Deny King (see p299). All around are buttongrass plains, mountains, water and wilderness. Walkers can overnight in a basic hut, and there's camping nearby. You can also visit the excellent bird-hide, where you might see the rare orange-bellied parrot.

One-way bush-walkers flights by Par Avion (one way $160, return $300) and Tasair (one way $176, return $330; for both see boxed text, p303) deposit walkers at the Melaleuca airstrip. They also pick up here by arrangement, and can leave food drops for hikers coming in to Melaleuca on the Port Davey Track. Tasair also drops walkers at Cox Bight on the coast. Flights run on demand, so book well ahead, especially in the summer season. Note: gas canisters and fuels like shellite and methylated spirits cannot be carried on the planes. You must purchase them at the airline offices and pick up at your destination.

Bass Strait Islands

Think Tasmania is relaxed? King Island and Flinders Islands, to Tassie's north, bring a new meaning to the word. If you're inclined to eat, sleep and suck down some fresh air, you'll be glad you made the effort. Even in January, the busiest month, you're unlikely to encounter many other cars on your explorations – be sure to raise a friendly hand from the driving wheel, because the locals will notice if you don't.

Apart from the remote freedom of these islands, the unmistakable highlight is the food, which lives up to its 'pure' reputation very well (the water that's bottled here is called 'Cloud Juice'). King Island's dairy products are ranked highly by cheese connoisseurs. There's excellent seafood, beef and lamb on Flinders Island, too. Walk it all off on great hiking tracks, or explore natural coastal beauty rich in marine and other wildlife. If privacy is what you're craving, you're almost guaranteed a beach to yourself. King Island is the largest island in the Hunter Group, planted at the western end of Bass Strait, and Flinders Island is the largest of the Furneaux Group in Bass Strait's east. Although they are quiet rural communities these days, both islands have troubled histories. Both served as the transient homes of prospectors, sealers and sailors, and as a long-term destination for Tasmanian Aborigines who were 'resettled' here (see p26).

You can access both islands by air from Melbourne (from Moorabbin, one hour southeast of the city), or from a number of locations in northern Tasmania.

HIGHLIGHTS

- Tasting the triple cream brie and chewing the cheddar at the splendidly generous **King Island Dairy** (p307)

- Dropping a line at **Trousers Point Beach** (p312), great for fishing, swimming and sunset costume changes

- Learning about King Island's tragic flotilla of **shipwrecks** (p306)

- Downing an ale with an ex-miner or two at **Grassy Club** (p309) on King Island

- Picking through whalebones and rusty shipwreck flotsam at the **King Island Historical Museum** (p307)

- Sipping sauvignon blanc at **Unavale Vineyard** (p312) – one of Australia's most isolated wineries

- Dawdling up to contemplate the well-deserved view from atop **Mt Strzelecki** (p312)

- Imagining untold wealth as you fossick for the misleadingly titled **Killiecrankie Diamonds** (p312) on Flinders Island

King Island Dairy ★

King Island ★
King Island Historical Museum ★
Grassy Club ★

Killiecrankie Diamonds ★

Trousers ★ ★ Mt Strzelecki
Point Beach ★ Unavale
Vineyard

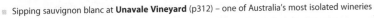

- TELEPHONE CODE: 03   - www.kingisland.org.au   - www.visitflindersisland.com.au

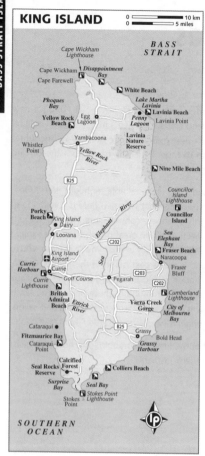

KING ISLAND
☎ 03 / pop 1570

A local website reads 'There are no traffic lights on King Island. There are several Policemen.' However, the only illegal thing here is the quality of the cheese. It seems unfair to farmers on Australia's arid mainland that such a small place could produce such bounty.

A skinny 64km long and 27km across at its widest point, King Island's wild beaches, rocky coastline, seafood and rustic atmosphere more than compensate for its size. In 1798 the island was named after Governor King of New South Wales (who, ironically, was born in Launceston, Cornwall). The main township is one-horse-town Currie, the local

harbour, which is close to the airport. Most of the island's facilities are located here.

Sealers and sailors, known collectively as 'Straitsmen', were attracted to these waters as a breeding ground for seals and sea elephants, which they hunted close to extinction. The surrounding seas proved perilous for many vessels (divers will note there are at least 57 shipwrecks nearby). The worst maritime disaster was in 1845, when the immigrant boat *Cataraqui* went down with 399 people aboard; all lives were lost.

King Island opened up for settlement and land selection in 1888. In addition to superb dairy produce, valuable exports include kelp and large crayfish. Another industry was the production of scheelite – used in the manufacture of armaments – until the mine and factory at Grassy closed in 1990. Rumours of it reopening surround the otherwise quiet little settlement to the southeast, which is well worth a drive: the views from here are some of the island's best. The other main settlement is Naracoopa, on the east coast.

Information

Most businesses on the island have Eftpos facilities.

King Island Tourism (☎ 1800 645 014, 6462 1313; www.kingisland.org.au; PO Box 269, Currie 7256) Provides information in person or via its comprehensive website. Also see www.kingisland.net.au for community news.

Main post office (☎ 6462 1792; www.auspost.com.au; 1 Main St, Currie; 🕑 9am-5pm Mon-Fri)

Online Access Centre (☎ 6462 1778; 5 George St, Currie; 🕑 10am-5pm Mon, 10am-7pm Wed, 1-5pm Thu, 10am-9pm Fri, 10am-noon Sat) Charges $5 per 30 minutes.

The Trend (☎ 6462 1360; 26 Edward St, Currie; trend@ kingisland.net.au; 🕑 8.30am-6pm Mon-Fri, 9am-5pm Sat, 9.30am-5pm Sun) Tourist information once you reach the island.

Westpac Bank (cnr Main & Edward Sts, Currie; 🕑 24hr) ATM.

Sights
LIGHTHOUSES & SHIPWRECKS

King Island has a treacherous coast and a disastrous record when it comes to shipwrecks and lives lost. If you're interested in this history, track down a copy of *The King Island Maritime Trail: Shipwrecks & Safe Havens,* a booklet with information on a dozen shipwreck sites around the island, complete with simple maps and details of the relevant coastal memorial cairns.

Alternatively, get information online from www.kingisland.net.au/~maritime/.

Four lighthouses guard the island. The one at Cape Wickham was built in 1861 and is the tallest in the southern hemisphere. Despite this, ship captains often mistook its light for that of the Otway Ranges in Victoria and sailed straight onto the coast. In response, the lighthouse at Currie was built in 1880. Neither is open but you'll find information on the lighthouse keepers at the museum. There's another lighthouse at Stokes Point, the southernmost point of the island, while Cumberland lighthouse is south of Naracoopa on the eastern side of the island.

KING ISLAND HISTORICAL MUSEUM
The island's **museum** (☎ 6462 1572; Lighthouse St, Currie; adult/child $4/1; 🕑 2-4pm Mon & Thu-Sun Dec-Feb, Sat & Sun only Mar-Nov), staffed by volunteers and located in the cottage that once housed the chief light-keeper, features many local-history displays with an emphasis on shipwrecks.

KING ISLAND DAIRY
An undisputed highlight, the low-key **King Island Dairy** (☎ 1800 004 950, 6462 1348; www.kidairy .com.au; North Rd, Loorana; 🕑 noon-4.30pm, Sun-Fri Oct-Apr, noon-4.30pm Sun-Tue, Thu & Fri May-Sep) is 8km north of Currie (just beyond the airport). Tuck into free tastings of the award-winning brie, cheddar, thick cream and yoghurt for which the island is renowned; keep a scorecard (ranging from 'delicious' to 'unrivalled') in case you want to make any purchases. The outstanding produce of the dairy is cheaper here and you can buy sizeable rounds of cheese, so you may want to bring an Esky to take home.

KELP INDUSTRY
Kelp Industries Pty Ltd (☎ 6462 1340; www.kelpind .com.au; 89 Netherby Rd, Currie; 🕑 8am-4pm Mon-Fri) was established in 1975 to commercially harvest the masses of bull kelp that wash up onto the island's rocks and beaches: if you're up early you might see the tractors hauling the seaweed in along the coast. The factory is the only kelp-processing plant in Australia. From the roadway next to Currie Golf Course you can see the kelp being air-dried on racks. It's left on the racks for about two weeks, kiln-dried, crushed, then shipped to Scotland where it's blended with kelp from other countries to create alginates, which are used in the manufacture of a va-riety of products including sauces, lotions and detergents.

CALCIFIED FOREST
A geological graveyard, the **Calcified Forest** has a sombre, almost eerie feel; some experts believe the tree remains to be up to 30 million years old. From Currie, head south to the **Seal Rocks Reserve** (off South Rd). A 20-minute stroll to the forest, 1km from the car park, leads to a viewing platform from where the ancient petrified tree trunks can be seen. There's a BBQ and shelter at the car park if you want to bring lunch.

Activities
Surf and freshwater **fishing** are popular here, especially from Naracoopa jetty. Do some **surfing** at the southern end of British Admiral Beach, Currie's main sandy stretch. You can **swim** at many of the island's unpopulated beaches and freshwater lagoons.

Diving among southern rock lobsters, dolphins, southern right whales and shipwrecks is recommended. **King Island Dive Charter** (☎ 6461 1133; www.kingislanddivecharter.com.au) provides single boat dives for $75, as well as good-value three- to seven-day packages (including dives on the *Cataraqui* wreck).

Golfing is popular on the island. The views are pretty spectacular at Currie Golf Course (☎ 6462 1126; arrange through King Island Golf and Bowling Club), near Boomerang by the Sea (see p308). So is **bushwalking**, particularly in the fern gullies of Yarra Creek Gorge, where you can see some of the island's 78 bird species (ten of which are confined to Tasmania, including the near-extinct orange-bellied parrot).

If you're keen on Australian **fauna**, King Island's decent-sized wildlife is plentiful and easy to observe and includes quails, wallabies, pademelons and platypuses. Tiger, copperhead and white-lipped snakes are also at large, and you'll see feral pheasants and flocks of wild turkeys. On the coast you may glimpse fur, elephant and leopard seals, and in the summer months a colony of little (fairy) penguins comes ashore just before dark at the end of the breakwater at Grassy.

Sleeping
CURRIE
Bass Caravan Park & Cabins (☎ 6462 1168; dinojohn@ bigpond.com; 100 Main St, Currie; on-site van $45, cabin $100)

BASS STRAIT ISLANDS

EVEREST IN A KAYAK

Kayaking across dangerously large stretches of water (read: 'the ditch' between Australia's East Coast and New Zealand) is quite the done thing by Australians at the time of writing, with two journeys completed in the last few months. Sydneysiders James Castrission, 25, and Justin Jones, 24, paddled over 3000km across the Tasman, for 62 days, from Forster in NSW to New Plymouth on New Zealand's North Island; at the same time two men and two women paddled back the other way and made it to the Australian shore in 31 days.

Remarkably, the stormy, bitterly cold, often treacherous waters of Bass Strait have also proved an irresistible attraction to occasional parties of the very hardiest sea-kayakers, battling strong currents and stronger winds to cross between the mainland and Tasmania. The first successful crossing was made, it's thought, in 1971 by a trio of Victorians in slalom kayaks. Since then a number of parties have attempted the crossing, although only about 50 kayakers (so far) have successfully made it across.

If you trace the usual route south on a map, kayakers run from Wilsons Promontory, the southernmost tip of the Australian mainland, to Hogan Island, Erith Island (Kent Group), Flinders Island, Preservation Island and Clarke Island. Landfall on Tasmanian terra firma is usually at Little Musselroe Bay in Tasmania's northeast.

It's 'only' a 250km trip measured on the map, but currents, tides and wind drift mean that the kayakers travel much further than that. Bass Strait crossings involve a two-week, or longer, itinerary with entire days often lost to bad weather. Overnight, kayakers stay huddled in tents on the bleak, windswept rocks that pass for islands in the Bass Strait. After a full day's paddling through often 3m-high waves, exhausted paddlers, who just want to crawl into a tent and collapse, are sometimes required to scour rugged island coasts for a safe landing spot where their kayaks won't be dashed to pieces against the rocks. This is the Mt Everest of sea-kayaking!

As affordable as KI gets, this small and somewhat desperate-looking park offers a handful of on-site caravans with en suite, plus relatively new two-bedroom cabins with kitchen and bathroom. Prices are based on two people. It's a few kilometres from the beach.

King Island Hotel (☎ 6462 1633; www.kingislandhotel .com.au; 7 Main St; d incl breakfast $125) Also known as Parer's, this double-storey number will never replace the grand old pub which burnt down in 1964, but it is clean and central (with easy access to shops, harbour and golf course), and has straightforward motel-style suites. There's a sports bar and pokies. The main bar has a large open fireplace and bang-up counter meals (mains $16 to $29).

Boomerang by the Sea (☎ 6462 1288; www.bythesea .com.au; Golf Club Rd; s/d $100/120) Time travel back to the pastel '80s. This block of decently equipped motel rooms all enjoy views across the golf course. It feels pleasantly isolated but it's only a short stroll into town, and there's an upstairs restaurant (opposite) on site for sunset vistas with your chardonnay.

ourpick **Devil's Gap Retreat and Craypot Cottage** (☎ 6462 1180, 0429-621 180; www.kingisland.net.au/~ devilsgap; Charles St, Currie; d $130) Retreat you will, like a devil into a gap (or a cray into a pot).

These weathered, one-bedroom cottages on the foreshore 1km northwest of Currie are a wild place to stay: self-contained, with ceiling-high stone hearths, open fires and tubs that spy the ocean. Owned by a local artist, the décor whispers 'rustic escape' (if you're listening) and the price includes breakfast provisions. Craypot Cottage, in central Currie, is another arty, comfortable option and better value than most.

Shannon Coastal Cottages (☎ 6461 1074; www .shannoncoastalcottages.com.au; Charles St; d $150-160, extra adult $30-40) These two windswept cottages (two-bed Shannon and one-bed Blencathra) are 3km northwest of Currie with rolling green and blue views, cosy gas fires, spa, and baby gear available. Walk back to the harbour via the beach.

NARACOOPA

Baudins Cottages (☎ 6461 1110; baudins@kingisland.net .au; The Esplanade, Naracoopa; d $140-175, extra person $40) Less 'French explorer' and more 'Australian retiree', these four clean, self-contained cabins (one- and two-bedroom) are across the road from the beachfront. There's an eatery on site, a veranda to relax on (sherry and cards in hand) and longsighted views across the bay.

Naracoopa Holiday Units (☎ 6461 1326; www.nara coopaholidayunits.com.au; 125 The Esplanade, Naracoopa; d $110, extra adult/child $25/15) In a seafront location on Sea Elephant Bay, these self-contained, one- and two-bedroom cottages are well equipped for self-catering and longer stays (read: games room including pool table).

GRASSY
King Island Holiday Village (☎ 6461 1177; kiholiday@ kingisland.net.au; 1a Blue Gum Drive; d $120-150, extra person $30-40) The more remote Grassy village maintains a slow, relaxed pace. This accommodation has a number of houses and units of varying sizes, some spa-equipped. Prices increase with ocean views and include breakfast provisions. The amenable host can arrange cheaper car hire and a 'penguin pack' for viewing the little creatures at dusk.

Eating
There are good eating options in Currie within walking distance of most accommodation, plus two supermarkets on Main St (both open daily). There's also a supermarket and a butcher in Grassy.

CURRIE
Boathouse (Currie Harbour; ☽ 24hr) A short scramble around the harbour, this 'restaurant without food' is the perfect chance to self-cater by the water in a tumbledown shack decorated by a local artist. The crockery, glasses and cutlery are in the cupboard – you bring the wine at any hour.

King Island Bakery (☎ 6462 1337; 5 Main St; snacks $3-6; ☽ breakfast & lunch daily, dinner Fri) Grab your picnic supplies here: freshly baked goods include gourmet pies with special KI fillings like crayfish and beef. Friday night is pizza night.

Nautilus Coffee Lounge (☎ 6462 1868; Edward St; mains $5-18; ☽ breakfast & lunch Mon-Sat) Downstairs, in a courtyard beside the roundabout, this café-gallery is your best bet for a big breakfast and an okay coffee. Try crayfish rolls, soup, burgers and other light meals. Croissant combos are rich and inventive ($16).

Boomerang by the Sea (☎ 6462 1288; Golf Club Rd; mains from $22; ☽ dinner from 6pm daily) Recognised as one of the island's best eating options, this roomy restaurant has fabulous ocean views and serves up locally sourced produce: beef, cheese and seafood.

NARACOOPA & GRASSY
Bert's Cafe (☎ 6461 1458; The Esplanade, Naracoopa; ☽ 10-6 Sat & Sun) Bert makes a mean toasted sandwich washed down with a lime spider milkshake. Also available on his veranda: Devonshire tea with a view of Sea Elephant bay.

Bold Head Brasserie and Grassy Club (☎ 6461 1341; 10 Main Rd, Grassy; mains $18-25; ☽ lunch Thu-Sun, dinner Wed-Mon, bar open daily) After a coldie at the traditional country bar (be sure to grab a souvenir stubby holder) wander next door for dim-lit, attentive service in this one-room restaurant. The chef is a fan of tapas dishes and the local cheeses (no complaints!), and his considered modern menu showcases local gourmet goodies, like Sea Elephant River oysters or rhubarb from Old Grassy Rd.

Getting There & Away
Flying is the only way to access King Island.

King Island Airlines (☎ 9580 3777; www.king islandair.com.au) flies to King Island daily from Melbourne's Moorabbin airport (45 minutes southeast from the city). Return flights cost around $300.

Regional Express (Rex; ☎ 13 17 13; www.regional express.com.au) flies from Tullamarine airport (Melbourne) to King Island, with return fares around $300.

Tasair (☎ 1800 062 900, 6248 5088; www.tasair.com .au) flies daily from Devonport and Burnie/ Wynyard to King Island (costing $385 return from both destinations).

You can usually save yourself some money through an airline package deal. King Island Airlines has deals starting at around $360 to $420 per person for two nights' accommodation and air fares (car hire is extra). Rex also has package deals.

Getting Around
There's no public transport on the island. Hire-car companies will meet you at the airport and bookings are highly recommended.

Most of King Island's 500km of roads are not sealed, so drive carefully. Unless you have a four-wheel drive, take extra care choosing which roads or tracks you take, or be prepared to dig yourself out of some sandy or muddy situations.

In Currie, you can rent cars from **Cheapa Island Car Rental** (☎ 6462 1603; kicars@kingisland.net .au; 1 Netherby Rd, Currie) from around $65 per day; you can reduce your excess from $800 to $330 by paying an extra $6 per day. **King Island Car Rental** (☎ 1800 777 282, 6462 1282; kicars@bigpond.com; 2 Meech St, Currie) has cars from $62 to $110 per day; you can reduce the excess from $1100 to $330 by paying an extra $8.80 per day.

The island's light traffic and flat roads make it straightforward for cycling. You can hire mountain bikes from **The Trend** (☎ 6462 1360; 26 Edward St, Currie; trend@kingisland.net.au; 8.30am-6pm Mon-Fri, 9am-5pm Sat, 9.30am-5pm Sun).

The island's **taxi service** (☎ 6462 1138) might also prove useful.

FLINDERS ISLAND
☎ 03 / pop 900

Coming in by light plane over these magnificent, bald grey granite peaks is a highlight in itself: think of it as an aerial tour, taking in what remains of the original land bridge to Australia. At the very least, be thankful you've been spared the kind of landing some vessels endured in the 1900s, when ships were beckoned onto rocks by the false lanterns of the sealers, or Straitsmen. These pirates were a rough group who eked out a living through the slaughter of tens of thousands of seals. The most tragic part of Flinders Island's history, however, was its role in the dismal treatment of Tasmanian Aborigines. Between 1829 and 1834, 135 indigenous people were transported to Wybalenna (an Aboriginal word that means 'Black Man's Houses') to be 'civilised and educated'. After 14 years, only 47 survived to make the journey to Oyster Cove, near Hobart, in 1847. See p26 for more.

These days, the remote, unassuming vibe and wild natural loveliness of the place make it appealing to travellers wanting a proper break (even mobiles are out of range). Activities on offer include outstanding fishing, great bushwalks, kayaking, photography and a safe family environment. There are gorgeous beaches (especially on the western side) and most are safe for swimming.

The largest of the 52 islands that make up the Furneaux Group (about 70km long and 45km wide), Flinders is also the richest in natural attractions. A protected habitat of between 800 and 900 species of plants support a wide variety of wildlife and more than 120 bird species, including the Cape Barren goose – the second-rarest goose in the world.

Beyond its brutal history, Flinders Island today is a rural community. Whitemark is the main administrative centre. Lady Barron, in the south, is the main fishing area and deepwater port. The island's main industries are sheep, farming and wool, cattle, milk-fed lambs, crayfish, abalone, poppies and seed cultivation. This makes for seasonal employment in shearing shed work, gumnut picking or as a deckhand.

Information

The best sources of information are the local tourism operators and shop managers on the island; see also www.focusonflinders.com.au. Note that regular mobile phones don't work here. Petrol can be purchased only in Whitemark and Lady Barron. There are no ATMs, but most businesses have Eftpos facilities.

Flinders Island visitors centre (☎ 1800 994 477, 6359 2380; 2 Lagoon Rd, Whitemark; www.visitflinders island.com.au; 10am-4pm Mon-Fri) Can help with bookings, packages and car hire.

Main post office (☎ 13 13 18; 7 Patrick St, Whitemark; www.auspost.com.au; 9am-5pm Mon-Fri) Agent for Westpac Bank.

Online Access Centre (☎ 6359 2396; cnr Patrick & Davies Sts, Whitemark; 4-7pm Mon, 10am-4pm Wed-Fri, closed Tue, Sat & Sun) At Flinders Island library, free half-hour net access.

Service Tasmania (☎ 6359 2201, ranger 6359 2217; www.servicetasmania.tas.gov.au; 2 Lagoon Rd, Whitemark; 10am-4pm Mon-Fri) Advice from Parks & Wildlife on maps, walking trails and national-park day passes ($22).

Sights
WYBALENNA HISTORIC SITE

Rated as one of the most important historic sites in the state, the **Wybalenna Historic Site** is all that remains of this unfortunate settlement set up to 'care for' the Aboriginal people. In truth, the opposite was achieved, with most of the people sent here succumbing to disease – including Mannalargenna and Tongerlongetter, the chiefs of the Portland and Oyster Bay groups. Close by are the cemetery (though no-one knows where the 100 or more Aboriginal people are buried) and memorial chapel. In 1999 Wybalenna was returned to the descendants of the indigenous people who lived there. For more information see p26.

FURNEAUX MUSEUM

In a slick new building not far from Wybalenna, the **Furneaux Museum** (☎ 6359 2010; furneauxmuseum@hotmail.com; 8 Fowlers Rd, Emita; adult/child $4/free; 1-5pm daily late Dec-Jan, 1-4pm Sat & Sun Feb-Nov) lies in grounds strewn with

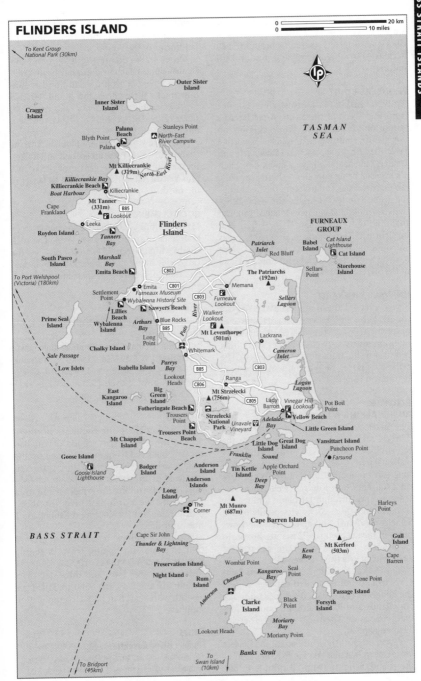

FLINDERS ISLAND

0   20 km
0   10 miles

To Kent Group
National Park (30km)

Outer Sister
Island

Craggy
Island

Inner Sister
Island

*TASMAN
SEA*

Stanleys Point
Palana
Beach
Blyth Point
North-East
River Campsite
Palana

Mt Killiecrankie
(319m)

North-East River

Killiecrankie Bay
Killiecrankie Beach
Boat Harbour
Killiecrankie

Cape
Frankland

Mt Tanner
(331m)
Lookout
B85

Leeka

Roydon Island

*Tanners
Bay*

**FURNEAUX
GROUP**

Babel
Island
*Cat Island
Lighthouse*
Cat Island

*Patriarch
Inlet*
Red Bluff

**Flinders
Island**

South Pasco
Island

*Marshall
Bay*
Emita Beach
C802

The Patriarchs
(192m)

Sellars
Point

Storehouse
Island

To Port Welshpool
(Victoria) (180km)

Emita
Furneaux Museum
Wybalenna Historic Site
Sawyers Beach

C801

Memana

*Sellars
Lagoon*

Furneaux
Lookout

C803

Settlement
Point

Prime Seal
Island

Lillies
Beach
Wybalenna
Island

Blue Rocks
*Arthurs
Bay*
B85

*Walkers
Lookout*

Mt Leventhorpe
(501m)

Lackrana

*Long
Point*

Chalky Island

Whitemark

*Cameron
Inlet*

Sale Passage

Low Islets

Isabella Island

*Parrys
Bay*
B85

Lookout
Heads

Ranga

C803

Pats River

C806

East
Kangaroo
Island

Big
Green
Island
Fotheringate Beach

Mt Strzelecki
(756m)

Lady
Barron
C805

*Logan
Lagoon*

Vinegar Hill
Lookout

Pot Boil
Point

*Trousers
Point*
Strzelecki
National
Park

Unavale
Vineyard
*Adelaide
Bay*

Yellow Beach

Little Green Island

Trousers Point
Beach

Mt Chappell
Island

Little Dog
Island
Great Dog
Island

Vansittart Island
Puncheon Point
Farsund

Goose Island

*Goose Island
Lighthouse*

Badger
Island

Anderson
Island

Tin Kettle
Island

Franklin   Sound

Apple Orchard
Point

*Harleys
Point*

Long
Island

Anderson
Islands

*Deep
Bay*

The
Corner

Mt Munro
(687m)

Cape Barren Island

BASS STRAIT

Cape Sir John
*Thunder & Lightning
Bay*

Preservation Island

Night Island

Rum
Island

Wombat Point

*Kent
Bay*

Mt Kerford
(503m)

Gull
Island

Cape
Barren

Anderson

*Kangaroo
Bay*

Seal
Point

Cone Point

Channel

Clarke
Island

Black
Point

Passage Island

Forsyth
Island

*Moriarty
Bay*

Lookout Heads

Moriarty Point

Banks Strait

To Bridport
(45km)

To
Swan Island
(10km)

whalebones, blubber pots and rusty wrecks. Staffed by volunteers, it displays a variety of Aboriginal artefacts (including beautiful shell necklaces), sealing, sailing and mutton-bird industry relics.

TROUSERS POINT

Aptly named after a trouserless escapee from the wreck of the *Sarah Anne Blanche* (a mutton bird oil boat), Trousers Point, on the island's southwestern tip, is well worth a peek. Explore the spectacular **Fotheringate** and **Trousers Point beaches**, have a quick dip, catch a sunset or bring supplies – there are picnic tables, barbecues and toilets in the free camping ground under the breezy she-oaks. Other native flora includes native tobacco (no, not that kind of tobacco), laurel, paperbark and bottlebrush. The colourful, accessible rocks surrounding the point are the perfect place to drop a fishing line and contemplate views of the Strzelecki peaks.

UNAVALE VINEYARD

Seven years old, the boutique **Unavale Vineyard** (☎ 6359 3632; unavale@bordernet.com.au; 10 Badger Corner Rd; tastings free; ⊙ by appointment) receives most recognition for its sauvignon blanc. Everything is done on site, right down to the labels. The cellar door is free, by appointment (or just call before you rock up).

Activities

BUSHWALKING & LOOKOUTS

The **Strzelecki Peaks Walk**, part of the annual Three Peaks Race, is a key route into the Strzelecki National Park. A medium-difficulty walk, it's four- to six-hours return and 5.6km long, starting about 12km south of Whitemark on Trousers Point Rd. The well-signposted track ascends through farmland and teatree scrub to emerge at rocky viewpoints on Mt Strzelecki (756m), and gives awesome views of the Furneaux group of 52 islands. Be sure to carry warm clothing, wet-weather gear, food and water at any time of the year.

The 3.4km circuit walk to **Trousers Point** (1½- to two-hours return) exposes you to the magnificent coast, its dunes, she-oak woodlands and kooky granite boulder formations. National park fees apply (see Service Tasmania, p310).

Ask at the visitors centre about the **Flinders Island Ecology Trail** that takes in five sites around the island, ranging from 20-minute to 60-

minute walks, each of which will teach you something new about the birds, wildlife and landforms of the region.

Other walks of varying length and difficulty along beach and coastal-heath trails can be linked with hinterland and mountain tracks throughout the island. Grab *A Walking Guide to Flinders Island and Cape Barren Island* by Doreen Lovegrove and Steve Summers ($11).

There are also a number of lookouts on the island, including **Furneaux Lookout** and **Walkers Lookout**, almost in the centre of the island, plus **Vinegar Hill** in the south and **Mt Tanner** in the north.

ROCK CLIMBING

Mt Killiecrankie (319m) has some very steep granite faces rising from sea level. The rock climbs within Strzelecki National Park and the ridge walk along the Strzelecki peaks should be attempted only by experienced walkers and climbers.

FOSSICKING

The elusive Killiecrankie 'diamond' is actually the semiprecious stone topaz. Most are clear, but some are pale blue or pink. **Killiecrankie Enterprises** (☎ 6359 8560; 7 Lagoon Rd, Whitemark; ⊙ 9.30am-4.30pm Mon-Fri, to 12.30pm Sat) stocks jewellery, hires shovels ($2) and sieves ($2), and will tell you where to look.

FISHING

Rock fishing along the southern, northern and northwestern coasts is good all year. Bait is easily obtained from the rocks and fishing tackle can be purchased from stores; however, you need to bring your own rod. Beach fishing is popular on the eastern coast and from Red Bluff. The North-East River (northeast of Killiecrankie) also has good fishing and a free campsite.

A number of local operators can arrange charter boats and fishing trips, including **Flinders Island Adventures** (☎ 6359 4507; www .flindersisland.com.au). Two- and three-day charters for six anglers costs $500 to $1000 per person, with gear, bait and accommodation supplied.

Tours

Flinders Island Adventures (☎ 6359 4507; www .flindersisland.com.au) Arranges fishing charters, evening mutton bird–viewing cruises (December to March, $35),

4WD tours (half- or full-day $100/166 per person) and other customised touring options.

Sleeping

The bulk of the options are in the island's south, but there's a spread of accommodation on the island – everything from laid-back camping to motel rooms, holiday houses and a retreat offering guaranteed rest and relaxation.

WHITEMARK

Interstate Hotel (☎ 6359 2114; interstatehotel@trump .net.au; Patrick St; s $22-65, d $38-95, incl cooked breakfast) In the centre of Whitemark is this amenable pub, built in 1911 and renovated in Federation green and burgundy, with no-frills budget rooms (shared facilities). Better rooms have private shower and TV.

Flinders Island Cabin Park (☎ 6359 2188; www .flindersislandcp.com.au; 1 Bluff Rd; camp sites for two people $14, cabin s $35, d $60-95, extra person $15) Close to the airport, this park is about 4km north of Whitemark. Eight family-sized, quality cabins are on offer, some with private bathroom, all with cooker and TV. The friendly owner also has cars ($66 per day) and bikes ($25 per day) for rent.

LADY BARRON

Furneaux Tavern (☎ 6359 3521; www.focusonflinders .com.au/tavern; Franklin Pde; s/d $80/110, extra person $30) The local drinking hole has 10 spacey, timber-panelled motel cabins with wrap-around decks, set in native gardens behind the bar-restaurant. Each has en suite, TV, fridge, kettle and toaster (continental breakfast provisions cost extra). Note that some road signage still refers to this place as the Flinders Island Lodge.

Silas Beach (☎ 6359 3521; Franklin Pde; d $130, extra person $35) The beach is a sprint away. You'll enjoy great views across the banksias from the big deck of this modern, three-bedroom holiday house (sleeping six). You can self-cater here and the contemporary, open plan, lofty living spaces are enhanced by the sound of the sea. Book through the tavern.

Partridge Farm (☎ 6359 3554; 310 Badger Corner Rd; d $130-135, extra person $27) Even locals take advantage of three options: the Bungalow B&B, the Top House three-bed abode or the Retreat, a self-contained one-bed unit. All have bush settings, lofty ceilings and views of Franklin Sound. Evening meals are

available on request. Watch out for roaming Cape Barron geese and guinea pigs.

Other holiday homes for rent here (usually with a two-night minimum stay):

Bucks at Lady Barron (☎ 0408-351 599; www .flindersisland.net; 15 Franklin Pde, Lady Barron; d/tr/q $122/126/140) Next to the tavern, this suburban brick option has a wood heater, leather couches, timber floors and sleeps six.

Lady Barron Holiday Home (☎ 6359 3555; www .ladybarron.com; 31 Franklin Pde; d $100, extra person $20) A homely, renovated 1940s place with three bedrooms (sleeps six), small deck and lawns.

TROUSERS POINT AREA

There is free camping in a lovely campground on Trousers Point, where facilities include toilets and gas barbecues (no powered sites, no showers).

Healing Dreams Retreat (☎ 6359 4588; www .healingdreams.com.au; 855 Trousers Point Rd; s/r $160/260) Even if you're not here to heal, join the locals and book in for a massage/spa/lunch combo ($80 for the full day). Dreamy dinners are also possible in the conservatory extension. This small retreat (maximum 14 guests) is in a great location at the foot of the Strzelecki Peaks, with Trousers Point beach close by. Guests can embrace the wilderness on 2km walks or mountain-bike rides through bush grounds shared with wallabies and wombats. The spacious, well-equipped rooms have eclectic décor. The rate listed here is for bed and breakfast only; there are 'spa' and 'outdoor' deals that include treatments, activities and all meals (certified organic) – see the website for more.

KILLIECRANKIE AREA

Killiecrankie Bay Holiday Houses (☎ 6359 8560; www .thecrayfishclub.com; 531 Killiecrankie Rd; d $120, extra person $30) Crayfish Club Holiday House is a two-storey, self-contained house in the island's north, close to lovely Killiecrankie Bay. It's perfect for groups and extended families, with five bedrooms that sleep up to ten people, including two bathrooms, two kitchens, laundry and barbecue. The two bedroom Killiecrankie Cottage, within cooee and owned by the same people, sleeps four people.

Killiecrankie also has a very basic and thus unbelievably cheap **camping** (504 Killiecrankie Rd, per site $5) but there's a much better (and free) option just 10km north at **North-East River Campsite** (Foochow Beach; free). Camp under the she-oaks behind the dunes. The tidal estuary of the river is a breeding ground for fish (salmon, flathead, prawns) and this brings in the sea birds. There are two toilets and a picnic table here.

Eating
WHITEMARK

Walkers Supermarket (☎ 6359 2010; Patrick St; 9am-5.30pm Mon-Fri, to noon Sat) Across from the pub, Flinders Island's IGA has a reasonable range of basic groceries, as well as fuel.

Flinders Island Bakery (☎ 6359 2105; 4 Lagoon Rd; sandwiches & pies $3-6; 8.30am-5pm Mon-Fri) The only decent coffee on the island is at the only bakery – try a wallaby and red-wine pie or pick up some preservative-free bread made with rainwater. Two words: lemon tart. Open on weekends in summer.

Sweet Surprises (☎ 6359 2138; 5 Lagoon Rd; snacks & meals $3-12; 7.30am-4.30pm Mon-Fri, 9am-1pm Sat) Mostly savoury and deep fried, you'll find fish and chips, toasted sandwiches and burgers at this friendly, low-key coffee shop opposite the bakery.

Interstate Hotel (☎ 6359 2114; Patrick St; lunch $10-12, dinner mains $16-27; lunch noon-1.30pm Mon-Fri, dinner 6-7.30pm Mon-Sat) A rockin' jukebox, pool table, Boag's on tap and the biggest ocean catches up on the wall: this country pub in the centre of Whitemark is the hub of island life. Its dining room serves a range of well-priced lunches and dinners, with the usual array of pub grub on offer and a natural emphasis on local seafood. Call to see if Sunday dinner is available.

LADY BARRON

This township's **store** (☎ 6359 3503; 11 Henwood St; 9am-5.30pm Mon-Fri, 9am-3pm Sat, 10am-5pm Sun) has chemist basics, magazines and newspapers, fruit and veg, plus fuel.

Furneaux Tavern (☎ 6359 3521; Franklin Pde; bar meals $10-15, restaurant mains $22-35; bar lunch & dinner daily, restaurant lunch & dinner Wed-Sun) A first-name-basis oasis, this is your only option for meals in Lady Barron. The tavern has beaut views over Franklin Sound to Cape Barron Island and the wharf, where you can watch the fishing boats chugging in as you sip a cold Boag's. Filling bar meals include the wallaby burger (no kidding!) or a solid steak sandwich, and the Shearwater restaurant menu has daily specials for the locavore: fish (perhaps ling), scallops or lamb.

Getting There & Away
AIR

Airlines of Tasmania (☎ 1800 144 460, 6359 2312; www.airtasmania.com.au) offers daily scheduled services between Launceston and Flinders Island ($300 return), as well as services to Moorabbin in Victoria three times a week ($404 return).

Flinders Island Travel (☎ 1800 674 719; www.flindersislandtravel.com.au) can help arrange tailor-made package deals (including flights, accommodation and car rental). Most accommodation on the island has signed up; see the website for comprehensive details.

FERRY

Southern Shipping Company (☎ 6356 3333; www.southernshipping.com.au; Main St Bridport; 8am-4.30pm Mon-Fri) operates a weekly ferry (departing Monday) from Bridport in Tasmania's northeast to Flinders Island; the ferry continues to Port Welshpool in Victoria on demand. A return trip to Flinders Island costs $97 per person (transporting a vehicle costs from $515 to $930 (including driver). The journey takes 8½ hours one way. Bookings essential (at least four weeks in advance).

Getting Around

There is no public transport on the island. Hire-car companies will meet you at the airport and bookings are essential. **Flinders Island Car Hire** (☎ 6359 2168), based in Whitemark, rents vehicles for between $70 and $80 per day. The Flinders Island Cabin Park (p313) has cars for similar rates ($66 per day), as well as bikes.

There is one **taxi** (☎ 6359 2112) for hire on the island (if you've been having drink at Whitemark and need to get back to Lady Barron, phone Jim).

Unsealed roads make it necessary to drive carefully, particularly around the more remote areas. Unless you have a four-wheel drive, try not to end up in sandy or slippery places.

OTHER ISLANDS
Cape Barren Island

Cape Barren Island is around 10km to the south of Flinders Island and is the only other island in the Furneaux Group to have a permanent settlement, which started when the sealers and their Aboriginal wives moved here in the early 19th century. The community adopted a mix of European and Aboriginal ways and some traditions, like mutton-birding and shell-necklace making, are practised today. Kent Bay, on the island's southern side, was the first settlement south of Sydney.

The main settlement on Cape Barren Island, known as the **Corner**, has a small school, church and medical centre. Today's islanders number about 70.

For experienced bushwalkers, the circuit walk of the shoreline offers great coastal views, including the wreck of the *Farsund,* lovely beaches and interesting rock formations. Ask at the Flinders Island visitors centre if you are interested in visiting.

Kent Group National Park
Named by Matthew Flinders after a fellow naval officer in 1798, this 27.5-sq-km region qualified for park status partly due to its cultural heritage, which includes human occupation dating back at least 8000 years, the presence of seal hunters in the 19th century and an old lighthouse on Deal Island. It also qualified because of its outstanding wildlife, such as the sizable fur seal colony at Judgement Rocks and roosting sea birds – short-tailed shearwaters, oystercatchers, petrels and penguins. The waters surrounding the islands are a marine reserve.

In 2001, the half-dozen tiny land masses of the Kent Group, located 55km northwest of Flinders Island, and with only Deal, Dover and Erith big enough to qualify as islands (the other three are islets), became Tasmania's 19th national park.

Swan Island
Fancy hiring out your own island with five mates? The owners live in one house here and rent out the other house. The island has eight beaches and the immediate area has decent fishing, but the main attraction is a get-away-from-it-all experience.

Just 3km off the northeast coast of Tasmania (a mere fifteen minutes by plane), this island is 3km long and is dominated by its lighthouse, built in 1845 and automated in 1986 when the government sold the island. Many sea birds nest in its environs and you can watch the mutton birds and penguins returning to their nests around sunset.

Swan Island Retreat (☎ /fax 6357 2211; s/d $55/77, extra adult $55) is a self-contained cottage that sleeps up to six (no cygnets under 16). There's an open fire and the cottage is well equipped. Discuss charter-flight possibilities with the owners when making your booking.

Three Hummock Island
Aboriginal people once swam the 5km across from Hunter Island to use this as a summer hunting ground. A reserve since the 1970s, this place 25km off Tasmania's northwestern tip is home to over 90 species of birds, including thousands of mutton birds in the summer. Family-owned **Eagle Hill Lodge** (☎ 6452 1405; www.threehummockisland.com.au; $80 per person) is the only accommodation here, sleeping up to 10 people. It has a fully equipped kitchen, lounge and ocean views. Guests must bring their own food.

Charter flights to Three Hummock Island are possible leaving from Burnie/Wynyard airport in Tasmania, and from Melbourne's Moorabbin airport. Roaring 40s Ocean Kayaking (p136), basing itself at Kettering in Tasmania's southeast, organises an annual five-day trip to Three Hummock Island, which involves circumnavigating the island by kayak.

Directory

CONTENTS

ACCOMMODATION

Tasmania offers everything: serene camping grounds, grungy hostels, gourmet breakfasts in guesthouses, ecoresorts, colonial high-ceilinged hotels and clean motel lodgings. It's worth noting that despite this variety, main tourist centres are often fully booked in summer, at Easter and during other public holidays, so it's wise to book ahead.

More and more, mainland Australians are embracing the idea of the weekend escape, which means that accommodation from Friday night through to Sunday can be in greater demand (and pricier) in major tourist centres. If you have the luxury of time, be on the lookout for midweek packages.

High-season prices are quoted in this book unless otherwise indicated. Use our prices as a guide and remember that stand-by (walk-in) rates and low-season rates (not to mention weekend specials and the like) can be lower than anything quoted in this book. Walk-in rates are best queried late in the day; also check websites such as www.wotif.com for last-minute deals.

The listings in the Sleeping sections of this guidebook are ordered from budget to mid-range to top end. We generally treat any place that charges up to $50/100 per single/double as budget accommodation. Midrange facilities are $100 to $180 per double, while the top-end tag is applied to places charging more than $180 per double.

In most areas you'll find seasonal price variations. Over summer (December to February) and at other peak times, particularly school and public holidays, prices are usually at their highest. The cooler winter months (June to August) experience significantly less tourist traffic and there can often be decent savings on accommodation prices.

A few notes about facilities: if you're travelling around Tasmania in the cooler months, you may find your accommodation very cold when you arrive, particularly if you're staying in a cottage or self-contained unit. Ask about heating when you make your booking, and if you know your arrival time, ask your hosts to light a fire or turn on the heating in advance. The good news is that many establishments have electric blankets on their beds. Conversely, air conditioning is rare apart from in big-city hotels. Most accommodation in Tasmania offers nonsmoking rooms (many places, especially hostels and guesthouses, are entirely nonsmoking). If you have a car, ask about parking when booking accommodation for central Hobart and Launceston.

BOOK YOUR STAY ONLINE

For more accommodation reviews and recommendations by Lonely Planet authors, check out the online booking service at www.lonelyplanet.com/hotels. You'll find the true, insider lowdown on the best places to stay. Reviews are thorough and independent. Best of all, you can book online.

If you are interested in eco-accommodation, the 'Natural State' has a growing number of options. These green-friendly businesses are listed in the GreenDex in the back of this book (p368).

The **Royal Automobile Club of Tasmania** (RACT; ☎ 13 27 22, 6232 6300; www.ract.com.au) has an annual statewide accommodation directory *Experience Tasmania* ($8) that suits all budgets. It's available from the club shop (and its affiliates, such as the RACV in Victoria or NRMA in New South Wales). Alternatively, check the online listings on the useful website **Travelways** (www.travelways.com.au). **Tourism Tasmania** (www.discovertasmania.com) also lists myriad options, from apartments to camping (click on Accommodation).

Camping & Caravan Parks

There are plenty of magical places in Tasmania where you can camp for free or at little cost. For details of over 145 camp sites in reserves, conservation areas and roadside bays, check out the *Camping Guide to Tasmania* (3rd edition), compiled by Craig Lewis and Cathy Savage (about $15), or go online to the website of the **Parks & Wildlife Service** (PWS; www.parks.tas.gov.au) – click on Outdoor Recreation, then Camping and Caravanning. Camping in most national parks requires you to purchase a park pass (see p64) and then pay a small (unpowered) site fee ($15/10/5 per family/couple/child, additional adult $5). Quite a few parks don't have site fees, though this can mean they have minimal facilities.

Tasmania has a large number of camping and caravan parks (sometimes calling themselves 'tourist parks'), which generally comprise the state's cheapest form of accommodation and are conveniently close to town centres (with the notable exception of

Hobart). Nightly costs for two campers are anywhere between $15 and $26, slightly more for a powered site. In general, caravan parks are well maintained and represent good value, with almost all of them equipped with hot showers, kitchens and laundry facilities. Some parks offer cheap dormitory-style accommodation and more expensive on-site cabins. Cabin sizes and facilities vary, but expect to pay $70 to $140 for two people in a cabin with kitchenette.

If you intend to do a lot of caravanning/camping, consider joining one of the major chains such as **BIG4** (☎ 9811 9300, 1800 632 444; www.big4.com.au), which offers 10% discounts for members at its six Tasmanian parks including Hobart, Bicheno and Coles Bay.

A good general resource for campers and caravanners is the free *Caravan and Holiday Park Guide to Tasmania* brochure (available from most large visitors centres), and the website www.caravantasmania.com.au, which lists the majority of sites around the state.

Guesthouses & B&Bs

Tasmania is the land of the B&B. New places are opening all the time, with everything from restored convict-built cottages, rambling old houses, upmarket country manors and beachside bungalows. Note that some places advertise themselves as B&Bs but are in fact self-contained cottages with breakfast provisions supplied, or (beware) a suburban home with a room set aside, a decanter of oxidised port and a chocolate from last Easter.

Only in the cheaper B&Bs are you likely to have to share the bathrooms and the toilets. Breakfast might be 'continental' (think cereal and toast), 'hearty' (add muffins or fruit) or

DIRECTORY

'full cooked' (eggs and bacon, sausages or ham) and is often supplied in the form of provisions that you cook and serve yourself. Some B&B hosts, especially in isolated locations or in small towns where restaurants are limited, may cook dinner for guests (usually 24 hours' notice is required). Rates can range anywhere from $90 to $280 per double, although there is a dearth of B&B accommodation at the lower end of this price range.

The best online information is at **Bed & Breakfast and Boutique Accommodation of Tasmania** (www.tasmanianbedandbreakfast.com), with links to over 140 B&Bs; if you want to go upmarket, try www.beautifulaccommodation.com /tasmania.

Hostels

The YHA network in Tasmania has shrunk a little bit, but youth hostels and/or backpackers facilities can be found in major towns.

To stay in a hostel you often need to supply your own bed linen – for hygiene reasons, a regular sleeping bag will not do. If you haven't got sheets they can be rented at many hostels (for around $3 to $5).

INDEPENDENT HOSTELS

Tasmania has plenty of independent hostels and the standard can vary enormously. Look out for ones that are purpose-built, as these often have the best facilities. Other good places tend to be smaller, more intimate hostels where the owner is also the manager (this is the norm in Tasmania). Some places are run-down hotels or pubs trying to fill empty rooms (the unrenovated ones are often gloomy and depressing); others are converted motels where each four-to-six-bed unit has a fridge, TV and bathroom, but communal areas and cooking facilities may be lacking.

Independent backpackers establishments typically charge $22 to $29 for a dorm bed and $50 to $80 for a twin or double room (usually with shared bathroom).

YHA HOSTELS

At the time of research, Tasmania had 10 hostels as part of the **Youth Hostels Association** (YHA; www.yha.com.au). YHA hostels provide basic accommodation, usually in small dormitories (bunk rooms), and often also have twin and double rooms. They usually have 24-hour access, cooking and laundry facilities, and a communal area with a TV. Many have in-

formative noticeboards (including rideshare) and lots of brochures.

Nightly charges start at $24 for members; most hostels also take non-YHA members for an extra $3. Australian residents can become full YHA members for $32 for one year; join online, at the Hobart or any state office, or at any YHA hostel. Families can also join and kids under 18 receive free membership.

The YHA is part of the **International Youth Hostel Federation** (IYHF; www.hihostels.com), also known as Hostelling International (HI), so if you're already a member of that organisation in your own country, your membership entitles you to YHA rates in the relevant Tasmanian hostels. Visitors to Australia should purchase an HI card preferably in their country of residence, but can also buy one at major local YHA hostels at a cost of $37 for 12 months; see the HI website for further details.

Hotels & Motels

Hotels in Tasmania's cities are generally comfortable and anonymous, in a multistorey block. Aimed at business travellers and tourists, they tend to have a restaurant/café, room service, gym and various other facilities. The exception is pubs (see opposite), which often have a little more character. We quote 'rack rates' (the official advertised rates) throughout this book; ask about discounts.

For comfortable midrange accommodation, motels (or motor inns) are the places to stay. These places tend to be squat structures that congregate just outside the CBD or on the highways at the edge of town. Most are modernish (though the décor can sometimes be stuck in a 1970s time warp) and have similar facilities (tea- and coffee-making, fridge, TV, bathroom). Prices vary and there's rarely a cheaper rate for singles, so they're a better option if you are travelling as a couple or a group of three. The price will indicate the standard, but you'll mostly pay between $90 and $140 for a room.

Some useful accommodation groups and websites:

Best Western (☎ 13 17 79; www.bestwestern.com.au) A midrange chain with eight properties (predominantly motels) throughout the state.

Federal Hotels & Resorts (☎ 1800 130 002; www .federalresorts.com.au) Upmarket hotels and resorts in Hobart, Launceston, Strahan, Cradle Mountain and Freycinet National Park.

Grand Hotels International (www.ghihotels.com) Operates the swish Hotel Grand Chancellor in Hobart and Launceston; also has less ritzy Chancellor Inns in places such as Scamander, Burnie and Queenstown.

Innkeepers Collection (☎ 1300 130 269, 6224 3579; www.innkeeper.com.au) Large, Tasmania-wide accommodation group that includes hotels, motels, lodges and apartments.

Pubs

In many smaller towns, staying at a pub means that you'll be in the social heart of the community. Pub rooms are invariably cheap, upstairs, small, older in style and plain, with a long amble down the hall to the (shared) bathroom. That said, plenty of ageing hotels have been renovated in recent times.

You can sometimes rent a single room at a pub for not much more than you'd pay for a bed in a hostel dorm. Standard pubs have singles/doubles with shared facilities starting at around $35/70; a minimal continental breakfast (instant coffee, white bread and Vegemite) is often included in the price. Few pubs have a separate reception area – just ask in the bar whether there are rooms available. But if you're a light sleeper, never book a room above the bar, especially on Friday and Saturday nights.

The useful website www.tassiepubs.com .au has details of hotels offering pub accommodation.

Self-Contained Apartments & Cottages

Holiday units are largely self-contained, with many rented on either a daily or weekly basis. They often have two or more bedrooms, making them cost-effective for groups. The prices given in this guide are for single-night stays and are mostly in the range from about $120 to $150 a double – the larger units (which are often referred to as 'villas' or 'chalets') regularly cost over $150 per double, while historic cottages can be anything up to about $200 a double, higher in the pricier parts of Hobart or historic towns such as Richmond. Unlike prices for holiday units, prices for historic cottages usually include breakfast (with cook-your-own provisions supplied).

TasVillas (☎ 6344 3222; www.tasvillas.com) is a network of self-contained, self-catering accommodation throughout the state. **Cottages of the Colony** (www.cottagesofthecolony.com.au) has links to self-contained historic cottages.

Other Accommodation

In country areas, farmers may be willing to rent out a room in exchange for some labour or just to supplement their income (see p331).

If you want to stay a bit longer in Tasmania, noticeboards in universities, hostels, bookshops and cafés are good to check out. In the cities, it's sometimes possible to stay in the hostels and halls of residence normally occupied by university students, though you'll need to time your stay to coincide with the longer uni holiday periods (from November to February). Another place to look for a shared flat or a room is in the classified advertisements section of the daily newspapers: Wednesday and Saturday are usually the best days.

ACTIVITIES

See the Tasmania Outdoors chapter, p56.

BUSINESS HOURS

Most shops and businesses are open from 9am to 5pm or 5.30pm Monday to Friday, and to either noon or 5pm on Saturday. Sunday trading is becoming more common but is limited to the major cities. In most large towns there is usually one late shopping night each week (normally Friday), when traders keep their doors open until 9pm. You'll find milk bars (general stores) and convenience stores often open until late and usually open over the weekend.

Banks are normally open from 9.30am to 4pm Monday to Thursday, and until 5pm Friday. The exception is in small towns where they may be open only one or two days a week.

Post offices are generally open from 9am to 5pm weekdays, but you can also buy stamps from newsagencies.

Restaurants typically open at noon for lunch and between 6pm and 7pm for dinner; most dinner bookings are made for 7pm or 7.30pm. Restaurants are typically open until at least 9pm but tend to serve food until later on Friday and Saturday. That said, the main restaurant strips in large cities keep longer hours throughout the week. Cafés tend to be all-day affairs that either close around 5pm or continue their business into the night (often to around 8pm). Pubs usually serve food from noon to 2pm and from 6pm to 8pm. Pubs and bars often open for drinking at lunchtime and continue well into the night, particularly from Thursday to Saturday.

Keep in mind that nearly everything is closed on Christmas Day.

CHILDREN
Practicalities

Most Australians have a relaxed attitude about breast-feeding or nappy changing in public; it's common to change the baby's nappy in the open boot of the car. Hobart and most major towns have centrally located public rooms where mothers (and sometimes fathers) can go to nurse their baby or change its nappy; check with the local visitors centre or city council for details.

Many motels and better-equipped caravan parks will be able to supply cots and baby baths and offer playgrounds, sandpits, minigolf, games rooms or swimming pools (lots of grass to run around on, at the very least). Top-end and some midrange hotels are well versed in the needs of guests with children; some may also have in-house children's videos and child-minding services. B&Bs, on the other hand, often market themselves as blissfully child-free – it's a good idea to ask if this is the policy.

It can be difficult to dine with kids in some better restaurants and booking in for the earliest sitting is one way to tackle this. While some cafés lack a specialised children's menu, many will provide small serves from the main menu if you ask. Some also supply highchairs.

Child concessions (and family rates) often apply for such things as accommodation, tours, admission fees, and air and bus transport, with discounts as high as 50% of the adult rate. However, the definition of 'child' can vary: from under 12 to under 18 years. Accommodation concessions generally apply to children under 12 years sharing the same room as adults. On the major airlines, infants travel free provided they don't occupy a seat – child fares usually apply between the ages of two and 11 years.

Items such as infant formula and disposable nappies are widely available in urban centres. Major car-hire companies will supply and fit booster seats for you for a minimal rate, sometimes for free. Lonely Planet's *Travel with Children* contains plenty of useful information for travel with ankle biters.

Sights & Activities

Tasmania is a naturally active kind of place. Take a boat cruise up or down the river, assail the heights of the local mountain, rent a bike and explore the cycling paths, or pack the kids into the van and go surfing. The minute you head out of town, the child-friendly options increase, with an abundance of animal parks, beaches, caves, nature walks and mazes to explore. There's almost always a forest or national park trail in the immediate vicinity. There's also an array of active pursuits available (nature walks, cruises, kayaking), although such activities may well mean a bit more financial outlay from parents.

Nearly all tourist attractions offer significant discounts for children, with the very young often admitted free. If the weather is poor in Hobart and you're confined to indoor pursuits, rainy-day attractions to satisfy your child (or inner child) include the Tasmanian Museum & Art Gallery (p87), the Maritime Museum of Tasmania (p87), the Cadbury Chocolate Factory (p88) and the Discovery Centre at the Royal Tasmanian Botanical Gardens (p89).

Not all of Tasmania's historic buildings and museums will hold the interest of kids, but there are still plenty of historical, natural or science-based exhibits to get them thinking – these range from wildlife parks and aquariums to ghost tours.

CLIMATE

Because Tasmania is small and also an island, it enjoys a maritime climate, which means that it's rarely extremely hot or extremely cold (of course, this is relative – many Australians find it a lot colder than anywhere on the mainland, and storms can deposit wintry conditions any time of year, including at the height of summer).

Tasmania experiences four distinct seasons. Summer (December to February), with its generally warm days and mild nights, is the most pleasant time of year. In general, the east coast of Tassie is nearly always warmer and milder than other parts of the state, and it may surprise you to learn that Hobart is Australia's second-driest capital (after Adelaide).

Bear in mind though that Tasmania is in the path of the 'Roaring 40s', a notorious current of wind that encircles the globe and produces very changeable weather. It's not surprising, then, that the west and southwest can be blasted by strong winds and drenched by heavy rain.

See p17 for more information on the seasons.

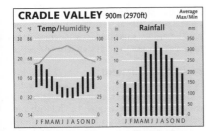

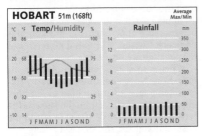

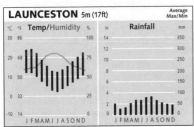

CUSTOMS REGULATIONS

For comprehensive information on customs regulations, contact the **Australian Customs Service** (☎ 1300 363 263, 02-6275 6666; www.customs .gov.au).

Overseas travellers entering Australia can bring most articles in free of duty, provided that they are for personal use and that you'll be taking them with you when you leave.

LIQUID REGULATIONS

Since 2007, all passengers flying to and from Australia on international flights are only permitted to carry small quantities of liquids, gels or aerosols in their cabin or carry-on luggage. Small containers of 100mL are permitted and must be sealed in a transparent plastic bag. Domestic travel is not affected by these regulations.

There's a duty-free quota per person (over 18) of 2.25L of alcohol, 250 cigarettes and dutiable goods up to the value of $900.

When it comes to prohibited goods, you should be particularly conscientious about drugs, which customs authorities are adept at sniffing out, and all food, plant material and animal products (see www.aqis.gov .au/whatcanti).

DANGERS & ANNOYANCES
Animal Hazards

You're unlikely to see many of Australia's more notorious creatures in the wilds of Tasmania, much less be attacked by one. For more information see p346.

INSECTS

For four to six warmer months of the year you'll have to cope with the mosquitoes (mozzies), which are most active around sunset; insect repellents go some way towards deterring these pests, and calamine lotion can soothe the bites, but it's best to cover up. Ticks, parasites that feed on human or animal blood, are found in moist bushy areas and can be avoided by covering up in light clothing; most people experience little or no symptoms of bites, but occasionally paralysis or allergic reaction to their toxins can occur. If you find a tick lodged somewhere on your body, gently remove it with a pair of fine-pointed tweezers by grasping as close to the skin as possible.

LEECHES

Leeches may be present in damp rainforest conditions. Trekkers often get them on their legs or in their boots. Salt or a lighted cigarette end will make them fall off. Do not pull them off, as the bite is then more likely to become infected. Clean and apply pressure if the point of attachment is bleeding. An insect repellent may keep them away and gaiters are a good idea when you're trekking.

SHARKS

Don't let paranoia keep you out of the beautiful oceans – attacks are rare, with only four deaths in the last 50 years in Tasmanian waters.

SNAKES

Tasmania's bushland is home to three species: tiger, white-lipped and lowland copperhead snakes (see www.parks.tas.gov.au/wildlife /reptile/snakes.html). Although all snakes in

INTERSTATE QUARANTINE

There are stringent rules in place to protect the 'disease-free' status of the agriculture of this island state, and fresh fruit, vegetables and plants cannot be brought into Tasmania. Tourists must discard all such items prior to their arrival (even if they're only travelling from mainland Australia). There are sniffer dogs at Tasmanian airports, and quarantine inspection posts at the Devonport ferry terminal; while quarantine control here often relies on honesty, officers are entitled to search your car for undeclared items.

Tasmania are venomous, they are not aggressive and, unless you have the bad fortune to stand on one, it's unlikely you'll be bitten. February is the month when snakes are at their most active.

To minimise your chances of being bitten, always wear boots, socks and long trousers (ideally gaiters) when walking through undergrowth where snakes may be present. Don't put your hands into holes and crevices, and be careful when collecting firewood. Most importantly, if you see a snake, leave it alone.

For information on treating snake bites, see p347.

SPIDERS & ANTS

There are only a couple of spiders to watch out for in Tasmania. Of least concern is the large, grey brown huntsman spider, which is quite common in the bush and often enters homes. Contrary to popular opinion, it can bite (resulting only in transient swelling and pain) but is generally shy and harmless. The white-tailed spider is a long, thin, black spider with (you guessed it) a white tip on its tail. It has a fierce bite that can lead to local inflammation. It is a ground scavenger rather than a web dweller, and can sometimes crawl into piles of stuff left on the floor. A spider found only in Tasmania is the Tasmanian cave spider, a relict species with its closest Gondwanan relatives in South America (see www.amonline.net.au/factsheets/cave_spider.htm).

Jack jumper ants have a brown body and orange pincers; they are quite aggressive and can sometimes 'jump' from the vegetation. They sting rather than bite. These critters are more common in Tasmania than in the other Australian states and their painful sting can cause a severe allergic reaction. Signs of an ant nest can include small pebbles at the entrance to the hole – try not to pitch your tent on one!

Bushfires & Blizzards

Bushfires are a regular occurrence in Australia and Tasmania is no exception. In hot, dry and windy weather, be extremely careful with any naked flame – cigarette butts thrown out of car windows have started many a fire. On a total fire ban day it's forbidden to use even a camping stove in the open. Locals will not be amused if they catch you breaking this particular law; they'll happily dob you in, and the penalties are severe.

When a total fire ban is in place (common from November onwards), bushwalkers should delay their trip until the weather improves. Get updates from the **Tasmania Fire Service** (www.fire.tas.gov.au). If you're out in the bush and you see smoke, even a long way away, take it seriously – bushfires move very quickly and change direction with the wind. Go to the nearest open space, downhill if possible. A forested ridge, on the other hand, is the most dangerous place to be.

At the other end of the elemental scale, blizzards can occur in Tasmania's mountains at any time of year. Bushwalkers need to be prepared for such freezing eventualities, particularly in remote areas. Take warm clothing such as thermals and jackets, plus windproof and waterproof garments. Carry a high-quality tent suitable for snow camping and enough food for two extra days, in case you get held up by bad weather. See p347 for information on hypothermia and how to minimise its risk.

Crime

Tasmania is a relatively safe place to visit but you should still take reasonable precautions. Don't leave hotel rooms or cars unlocked, and don't leave your valuables unattended or visible through a car window. Avoid walking around in the cities by yourself after dark.

Swimming

Surf beaches can be dangerous places if you aren't used to the conditions. Undertows (or 'rips') are the main problem. If you find yourself being carried out by a rip, the important thing to do is just keep afloat; don't panic or try to swim against the rip, which will exhaust you. In most cases the current stops within a couple of hundred metres from the shore and you can then swim parallel to the shore for a short way to get out of the rip and make your way back to land.

DISCOUNT CARDS

The **International Student Travel Confederation** (ISTC; www.istc.org) is an association of specialist student travel organisations. It's also the body behind the International Student Identity Card (ISIC), which is issued to full-time students aged 12 years and over, and gives the bearer discounts on accommodation, transport and admission to various attractions.

Senior travellers and travellers with disabilities who reside in Australia are eligible for concession cards; most states and territories issue their own version and these can be used Australia-wide (for more, see p329).

See Tasmania Card

The **See Tasmania Smartvisit Card** (☎ 1300 661 711; www.seetasmaniacard.com) might be of interest to short-term visitors. Purchase of the card allows free or discounted entry to some 60 attractions and activities around the state (including national parks, National Trust properties and big-ticket drawcards such as the Port Arthur Historic Site and the Tahune AirWalk), plus a book and maps to help you plan your travels. The card is not cheap, however ($159/89 per adult/child for three days, $229/155 for seven days, and $299/189 for 10 days, where children are aged four to 15), and it's worth noting that it can only be used on consecutive days. Before purchasing, do some research to determine if it's a worthwhile investment – you should be intending to do a lot of sightseeing in a relatively short time. Cards can be purchased online from many travel agents in Tasmania.

EMBASSIES & CONSULATES

The principal diplomatic missions to Australia are in Canberra. There are also representatives in other major cities, particularly from countries that have strong links with Australia, such as the USA, the UK and New Zealand.

Consular offices in Hobart include the following. For a complete listing, look in the Tasmanian **Yellow Pages** (www.yellowpages .com.au).

Denmark (☎ 62730677; 18 Bender Drv, Derwent Park)
France (☎ 6223 8239; 143 Hampden Rd)
Germany (☎ 6223 8239; 143 Hampden Rd)
Netherlands (☎ 6225 3951; 439A Sandy Bay Rd)

FESTIVALS & EVENTS

Tourism Tasmania (www.discovertasmania.com/events) lists everything going on in Tassie, so you can plan your trip around festivals and shows, sport, exhibitions, performances or markets. See also the Festivals & Events sections of the Hobart (p94) and Launceston (p207) chapters; other destination chapters will mention festivals and events on the ground.

Major statewide or region-specific festivals include the following.

March

Taste of the Huon (www.tasteofthehuon.com) Two-day festival in early March celebrating the food, wine, music and crafts of the Huon Valley, D'Entrecasteaux Channel area and Bruny Island.
Ten Days on the Island (www.tendaysontheisland .com) Tasmania's premier cultural festival is held in odd-numbered years and usually runs from late March until early April.
Three Peaks Race (www.threepeaks.org.au) Every Easter (March and April), over four days, competitors sail from Beauty Point north of Launceston to Hobart. Each yacht sends two runners to scale Tasmania's highest peaks: Mt Strzelecki on Flinders Island, Mt Freycinet and Hobart's Mt Wellington.

April

Anzac Day National public holiday (25 April) commemorating the landing of Anzac troops at Gallipoli in 1915. Memorial marches by returned soldiers are held all over the country.
Targa Tasmania (www.targa.org.au) Six-day rally of exotic cars that hoons around the entire state, appropriating 200km of roads as it goes.

September

Blooming Tasmania Beginning in spring and lasting over six months, this is a coordinated set of festivals, displays and open gardens around the state. A special brochure is produced every year detailing when each festival occurs and when gardens are open to the public (available online at www.discovertasmania.com – click on Activities & Attractions, then Outdoor Activities, and go to Gardens).

October

Royal Shows The royal agricultural and horticultural shows of Hobart, Burnie and Launceston are held during this month.

FOOD

The innovative food offered in top-quality Tasmanian eateries doesn't always cost a fortune. Best value are the modern cafés, where you can get a good meal in casual surroundings for under $20. A full cooked breakfast at a café costs around $14. Some inner-city pubs offer upmarket restaurant-style fare, but most pubs serve standard (often large-portion, meat-heavy) bistro meals, usually in the $15 to $25 range, in the dining room or lounge bar. Bar (or counter) meals, which are eaten in the public bar, usually cost between $10 and $15. Top restaurants have main meals (generally showcasing the state's fantastic produce) in the $24 to $36 price range.

For general opening hours, consider that breakfast is normally served between 6am and 11am, lunch starts around noon and lasts until 2pm or 3pm, and dinner usually starts after 6pm.

See the Food & Drink chapter (p40) for more information on Tassie food.

GAY & LESBIAN TRAVELLERS

It wasn't always so, but Tasmania is now considered by gay- and lesbian-rights groups to have greater equality in criminal law for homosexual and heterosexual people than most of the other Australian states.

The **Gay and Lesbian Community Centre** (GLC Centre; www.glctas.org), based in Hobart but with Tasmania-wide links, is one source of information on upcoming events. There is a **Gay Information Line** (☎ 6234 8179) with a host of contact numbers for support groups, plus details of coming events and gay-friendly bars and restaurants. There's also a fair bit of high-quality gay-owned accommodation in Tasmania: see www.gaystayaustralia.com.

HOLIDAYS
Public Holidays

The holidays listed are statewide unless indicated:

New Year's Day 1 January
Australia Day 26 January
Hobart Regatta Day 2nd Monday in February (southern Tasmania)
Launceston Cup Last Wednesday in February (Launceston only)
Eight Hour Day 2nd Monday in March
Easter March/April (Good Friday to Easter Tuesday inclusive)
Anzac Day 25 April
Queen's Birthday 2nd Monday in June
Burnie Show 1st Friday in October (Burnie only)
Launceston Show 2nd Thursday in October (Launceston only)
Hobart Show 3rd Thursday in October (southern Tasmania)
Recreation Day 1st Monday in November (northern Tasmania)
Devonport Show Last Friday in November (Devonport only)
Christmas Day 25 December
Boxing Day 26 December

School Holidays

The Christmas holiday season, from mid-December to late January, is part of the summer school vacation and is the time when accommodation often books out. There are three shorter school holiday periods during the year, but they vary by a week or two from year to year, falling from early to mid-April, late June to mid-July, and late September to early October. For a useful list of school holidays in all Australian states, see www.dest.gov.au/portfolio_department/calendar_dates.

INSURANCE

Don't underestimate the importance of a good travel insurance policy that covers theft, loss and medical problems. Most policies offer lower and higher medical expense options; the higher ones are chiefly for countries that have extremely high medical costs, such as the USA. There is a wide variety of policies available, so compare the small print.

If you plan on doing any outdoor activities in Tasmania, make sure the policy you choose fully covers you for scuba diving, motorcycling, skiing and even bushwalking (some policies specifically exclude designated 'dangerous activities').

You may prefer a policy that pays doctors or hospitals direct rather than you having to pay on the spot and claim later. If you have to claim later, make sure you keep all documentation. Check that the policy covers ambulances and emergency medical evacuations by air.

Worldwide travel insurance is available at www.lonelyplanet.com/travel_services. You can buy, extend and claim online any time, even if you're already on the road.

See also Before You Go (p344) in the Health chapter. For information on insurance matters relating to rental cars, see p339.

INTERNET ACCESS

Whether you use internet cafés or bring along your own laptop, it's easy to get connected in Tasmania. You'll find cafés in the main towns, and kiosks or terminals at many hostels and hotels. As part of a government-funded telecommunications scheme, online access centres have been set up in 66 of the state's towns. They are intended primarily for rural Tasmanians, but also provide net access for visitors. For a complete listing of these centres, which charge reasonable rates and are located primarily (but not exclusively) in libraries and schools, pick up the *Tasmanian Communities Online* brochure at many visitors centres, or visit the scheme's website at www.tco.asn.au.

LEGAL MATTERS

Most travellers will have no contact with the Tasmanian police or any other part of the legal system. Those that do are likely to experience it while driving. There is a significant police presence on the state's roads, with the power to stop your car and ask to see your licence (you're required to carry it), check your vehicle for roadworthiness, and also to insist that you take a breath test for alcohol (note that the legal limit in Australia is 0.05%). Needless to say, drink-driving offences are taken seriously here.

If you are arrested, it's your right to telephone a friend, relative or lawyer before any formal questioning begins. Legal aid is available only in serious cases and only to the truly needy (for links to Legal Aid offices see www .legalaid.tas.gov.au). However, many solicitors do not charge for an initial consultation.

MAPS

The selection of maps available is wide, but many are of average quality. One of the best road maps of the state (1:500,000) is produced by the **Royal Automobile Club of Tasmania** (RACT; ☎ 13 27 22; www.ract.com.au) and is on sale in the organisation's offices around the island. This sheet map includes detail of main city centres.

For more detail, including contours, the maps (1:250,000) published by the state government's Department of Primary Industries and Water (DPIW), more specifically its map publication arm **Tasmap** (www.tasmap.tas.gov.au), are recommended. The state is covered in four sheets, which are available from map retailers or online. DPIW also produces 1:25,000 topographic sheets appropriate for bushwalking, ski touring and other activities requiring large-scale maps. Many of the more popular sheets, including day walks and bushwalks in national parks, are usually available over the counter at shops specialising in bushwalk-

ing gear and outdoor equipment, and also at urban and national park visitors centres, **Service Tasmania** (Map p82; ☎ 1300 135 513; www.service.tas.gov.au; 134 Macquarie St, Hobart; ⏱ 8.15am-5.30pm Mon-Fri) and the **Tasmanian Map Centre** (Map p82; ☎ 6231 9043; www.map-centre.com.au; 100 Elizabeth St, Hobart; ⏱ 9.30am-5.30pm Mon-Fri, 10am-4pm Sat).

The best atlas is the *Tasmania Country Road Atlas* ($31), published by UBD. It contains clear, detailed maps of over 45 significant towns in the state. It's available from petrol stations, newsagencies, bookshops and visitors centres, at Service Tasmania or the Tasmanian Map Centre.

MONEY

Australia's currency is the Australian dollar, made up of 100 cents. There are 5c, 10c, 20c, 50c, $1 and $2 coins, and $5, $10, $20, $50 and $100 notes. Although the smallest coin in circulation is 5c, prices are often still marked in single cents and then rounded up to the nearest 5c when you come to pay.

See p17 to get an idea of expenses in Tasmania.

ATMs, Eftpos & Bank Accounts

In the smaller Tasmanian towns, banks are often open only two or three days a week. Local post offices act as agents for the Commonwealth Bank, although they are open only restricted weekday hours. Even the 24-hour ATMs, most of which accept cards from other banks and can be used to withdraw up to $1000 a day (cash amount varies depending on the bank), can be few and far between outside the state's largest centres. However, there's usually at least one pub, supermarket, general store, petrol station or newsagent in town that offers an Electronic Funds Transfer at Point Of Sale (Eftpos) service.

Credit Cards & Debit Cards

Australia is well and truly a card-carrying society – credit cards such as Visa and MasterCard are widely accepted for everything from a hostel bed or a restaurant meal to an adventure tour, and a credit card is pretty much essential (in lieu of a large deposit) if you want to hire a car. They can also be used to get cash advances over the counter at banks and from many ATMs, depending on the card, but be aware that these incur immediate interest. Charge cards such as Diners Club and

American Express (Amex) are not as widely accepted.

Apart from losing them, the obvious danger with credit cards is maxing out your limit and going home to a steaming pile of debt and interest charges. A safer option is a debit card with which you can draw money directly from your home bank account using ATMs, banks or Eftpos machines around the country. Any card connected to the international banking network – Cirrus, Maestro, Plus and Eurocard – should work, provided you know your PIN. Fees for using your card at a foreign bank or ATM vary depending on your home bank; ask before your leave. Companies such as Travelex offer debit cards (Travelex calls them Cash Passport cards) with set withdrawal fees and a balance you can top up from your personal bank account while on the road – nice one!

The most flexible option is to carry both a credit and a debit card.

Exchanging Money

Changing major forms of foreign currency or travellers cheques is usually no problem at banks throughout Australia or at licensed moneychangers such as Travelex or Amex in the major cities.

See the table on the inside front cover of this book for exchange rates at the time of publication.

Taxes & Refunds

The Goods and Services Tax (GST) is a flat 10% tax on all goods and services – accommodation, eating out, transport, books, furniture, clothing (but basic foods such as milk, bread, fruits and vegetables are exempt). By law, the tax is included in the quoted or shelf prices, so all prices in this book are GST-inclusive. International air and sea travel to/from Australia is GST-free, as is domestic air travel when purchased outside Australia by nonresidents.

If you purchase goods with a total minimum value of $300 from one store no more than 30 days before you leave Australia, you are entitled under the Tourist Refund Scheme (TRS) to a refund of any GST paid. The scheme only applies to goods you take with you as hand luggage or wear onto the plane or ship. For more details, contact the **Australian Customs Service** (☎ 1300 363 263, 02-6275 6666; www.customs.gov.au, click on Travellers).

Travellers Cheques

If your stay is short, then travellers cheques are safe and generally enjoy a better exchange rate than foreign cash in Australia. Also, if they are stolen (or you lose them), they can readily be replaced. There is, however, a fee for buying travellers cheques (usually 1% of the total amount) and there may be fees or commissions when you exchange them.

Amex, Travelex and other well-known international brands of travellers cheques are easily exchanged. You need to present your passport for identification when cashing them. Fees per transaction for changing foreign-currency travellers cheques vary from bank to bank.

Buying travellers cheques in Australian dollars is an option worth looking at. These can be exchanged immediately at banks without being converted from a foreign currency and aren't subject to commissions, fees and exchange-rate fluctuations.

POST

Australia's postal services are efficient and reasonably cheap. **Australia Post** (www.auspost.com .au) post offices are usually open from 9am to 5pm Monday to Friday. There are also many post office agencies lurking within general stores and newsagencies.

It costs 50c to send a standard letter or postcard within the country. International destinations are divided into two regions for letters: Asia-Pacific and Rest of the World; airmail letters up to 50g cost $1.30/1.95 respectively. The cost of a postcard (up to 20g) is $1.25 across the board.

Sending & Receiving Mail

All post offices will hold mail for visitors, and some city GPOs (main or general post offices) have busy poste restante sections. You need to provide some form of ID (such as a passport) to collect mail.

There are four international parcel zones and rates vary by distance and class of service. Airmail offers reliable delivery to over 200 countries in three to 10 working days. If it's not urgent, the cheapest way to send larger items back home is by sea mail (everywhere except New Zealand and Asia).

Express Post delivers a parcel or envelope interstate within Australia by the next business day; otherwise allow two days for urban deliveries, longer for country areas.

SOLO TRAVELLERS

Solo travellers are quite a common sight throughout Tasmania and there is certainly no stigma attached to lone visitors. Women travelling on their own should exercise caution when in less populated areas, and might find that guys get annoyingly attentive in some drinking establishments; see also Women Travellers (p330).

TELEPHONE

Many mainland visitors to Tasmania take their mobile (cell) phone along for the journey, figuring it will be useful for staying in contact with folks back home, phoning ahead to secure accommodation, or making all-important dinner reservations at Tassie's finest restaurants. If you're not on the **Telstra** (www.telstra.com .au) mobile network, coverage can be patchy. Other network coverage is all but nonexistent outside of Hobart, Launceston, Burnie and Devonport. If you plan to spend some time touring Tasmania, it might be worth purchasing a Telstra prepaid SIM card for your mobile phone – you'll still struggle to find a signal in the more remote parts of the state, but overall coverage will be a vast improvement over that of **Optus** (www.optus.com.au) or **Vodafone** (www .vodafone.com.au).

Information & Toll-Free Calls

Numbers starting with ☎ 190 are usually recorded information services, charged at anything from 35c to $5 or more per minute (more from mobiles and payphones).

Toll-free numbers beginning with ☎ 1800 can be called free of charge from anywhere in the country, though they may not be accessible from certain areas or from mobile phones. Calls to numbers beginning with ☎ 13 or ☎ 1300 are charged at the rate of a local call – the numbers can usually be dialled Australia-wide, but may be applicable only to a specific state or STD (Subscriber Trunk Dialling) district. Telephone numbers beginning with either ☎ 1800, ☎ 13 or ☎ 1300 cannot be dialled from outside Australia.

To make a reverse-charge (collect) call from any public or private phone, just dial ☎ 1800-REVERSE (1800 738 3773), or ☎ 12550.

International Calls

Most payphones allow ISD (International Subscriber Dialling) calls, the cost and international dialling code of which varies de-pending on the service provider. International calls from Australia are cheap and subject to specials that reduce the rates even more, so it's worth shopping around – look in the *Yellow Pages* for a list of providers.

The **Country Direct service** (☎ 1800 801 800) connects callers in Australia with operators in nearly 60 countries to make reverse-charge (collect) or credit-card calls.

When calling overseas, you need to dial the international access code from Australia (☎ 0011 or ☎ 0018), the country code and the area code (without the initial 0). So for a London number you'd dial ☎ 0011-44-171, then the number. Also, certain operators will have you dial a special code to get access to their service.

If calling Australia from overseas, the country code is ☎ 61 and you need to drop the 0 in the state/territory area codes.

Local Calls

Calls from private phones cost 15c to 25c while local calls from public phones cost 50c; both involve unlimited talk time. Calls to mobile phones attract higher rates and are timed. Blue phones or gold phones that you sometimes find in hotel lobbies or other businesses usually cost a minimum of 50c for a local call.

Long-Distance Calls & Area Codes

For long-distance calls, Australia uses four STD area codes. STD calls can be made from virtually any public phone and are cheaper during off-peak hours, generally between 7pm and 7am. Long-distance calls (to more than about 50km away) within these areas are charged at long-distance rates, even though they have the same area code.

Broadly, these are the main area codes:

State/Territory	Area Code
ACT	☎ 02
NSW	☎ 02
NT	☎ 08
Qld	☎ 07
SA	☎ 08
Tas	☎ 03
Vic	☎ 03
WA	☎ 08

When calling from one area of Tasmania to another, there's no need to dial 03 before the local number (and you don't need to add the 03 when calling Victoria either). Local numbers start with the digits 62 in Hobart and southern Tasmania, 63 in Launceston and the northeast, and 64 in the west and northwest.

Mobile (Cell) Phones

Local numbers with the prefix ☎ 04 belong to mobile phones. Australia's two mobile networks – digital GSM and digital CDMA – service more than 90% of the population but leave vast tracts of the country uncovered. Major towns in Tasmania should get good reception, but elsewhere it's haphazard or nonexistent (see p327).

Australia's digital network is compatible with GSM 900 and 1800 (used in Europe), but generally not with the systems used in the USA or Japan. For overseas visitors, GSM 900 and 1800 mobiles can be used in Australia if set up at home first – contact your service provider before you travel.

It's easy and cheap enough to get connected short-term, though, as the main service providers (Telstra, Optus and Vodafone) all have prepaid mobile systems. Just buy a starter kit, which may include a phone or, if you have your own phone, a SIM card (around $25) and a prepaid charge card. The calls tend to be a bit more expensive than with standard contracts, but there are no connection fees or line-rental charges and you can buy the recharge cards at convenience stores and newsagents. Don't forget to shop around between the three carriers as their products differ.

Phonecards

A wide range of phonecards is available. These can be bought at newsagents and post offices for a fixed dollar value (usually $10, $20 or $50) and can be used with any public or private phone by dialling a toll-free access number and then the PIN on the card. Once again, it's well worth shopping around, as call rates vary from company to company. Some public phones also accept credit cards.

TIME

Australia is divided into three time zones: Western Standard Time (GMT/UTC plus eight hours) applies in Western Australia; Central Standard Time (GMT/UTC plus 9½ hours) covers the Northern Territory and South Australia; and Eastern Standard Time (GMT/UTC plus 10 hours) covers Tasmania, Victoria, NSW and Queensland.

DAYLIGHT SAVING

Daylight Saving in Tasmania begins on the first Sunday in October and ends on the last Sunday in March. This start date is three weeks earlier than the Victoria, NSW, SA, WA and ACT commencement date, and this end date is a week earlier. Daylight Saving does not operate in Queensland or the NT.

During the Tasmanian summer things get slightly screwed up when Daylight Saving time (when clocks are put forward an hour; see boxed text on above) comes into play.

TOURIST INFORMATION

The main tourism authority for the state is **Tourism Tasmania** (☎ 6230 8235, 1300 733 258; www.discovertasmania.com; GPO Box 399, Hobart 7001), which has developed one of the better tourism profiles in Australia and runs a mighty slick website.

Alternatively, call a consultant at the **Tasmanian Travel Centre** (☎ 1300 780 867; www.holidays.discovertasmania.com; www.tastemptations.com.au), who can provide information on all things Tasmania, and can help you book accommodation, tours and transport.

For advice on independent budget travel, in person, **Tasmanian YHA Travel Centre** (Map p82; ☎ 6234 9617; www.yha.com.au; 9 Argyle St, Hobart) has info on air fares, travel passes, car rental, travel insurance, day tours and tour packages.

Local Tourist Offices

Tasmania's visitors centres are privately run and the key ones are located in Hobart, Launceston, Devonport and Burnie (see the relevant chapters for contact details). As well as supplying brochures, maps and other information, they will often book transport, tours and accommodation. They are generally open from around 8.30am or 9am to 5pm or 5.30pm weekdays and slightly shorter hours on weekends.

Other centres belonging to the Tasmanian Visitor Information Network are scattered in many smaller towns across the island. The standard of service provided varies enormously from place to place, and some centres are staffed by volunteers (resulting in irregular opening hours).

At visitors centres throughout the state you can pick up the invaluable free, bimonthly newspaper, *Tasmanian Travelways* (www

.travelways.com.au). It's packed with information, including comprehensive listings of accommodation, activities, public transport and vehicle hire, all with an indication of current costs throughout the state.

The visitors centres also stock a host of other free tourist literature, including *This Week in Tasmania* (an odd name given that it's published seasonally), the monthly newspaper *Treasure Island*, *Explore Tasmania*, and *Tasmania: The Visitors Guide*, published twice a year.

TOURS

A number of operators offer tours both to and within Tasmania. Many travel agents arrange package deals from the mainland that include transport to Tasmania (either by air or sea), car rental and accommodation. Contact Tourism Tasmania (opposite), **Qantas Holidays** (☎ 13 14 15; www.qantas.com.au) or **TasVacations** (☎ 1800 030 160; www.tasvacations.com) to get some ideas.

Once you're in Tasmania, there are operators who can guide you to the highlights (or off the beaten track), and many more who can offer a wilderness experience or activity-based tour (for these greener listings, see the GreenDex on p368). Most trips depart from Hobart, Launceston or Devonport. Some suggestions include:

Adventure Tours (☎ 1300 654 604, 08-8309 2277; www.adventuretours.com.au/tasmania-tours/) An Australia-wide company offering one- to seven-day tours in Tasmania. Participants can choose between hostel- or motel-style accommodation; prices for a one-/three-day tour start at $140/440.

Craclair Tours (☎ 6424 7833; www.craclair.com.au) Experienced walking tours, based in Devonport; offers guided walking tours (four- to 10-day trips) in national parks and wilderness areas, including the Overland Track at Lake St Clair. A three-day cabin-based Cradle Mountain trip costs $750.

Island Cycle Tours (☎ 1800 064 726, 6228 4255; www.islandcycletours.com) Offers a great range of guided cycling trips – day trips from Hobart (including a descent of Mt Wellington), budget-minded walking and cycling tours (from one to 10 days), 'indulgence' trips with more creature comforts (three to seven days) and new family adventure vacations. Prices are tailored.

TASafari (☎ 1300 882 415; www.tasafari.com.au) Offers three-, five- and nine-day, eco-certified 4WD tours that visit both the well-known and more remote parts of the state. There's bushwalking, bush camping and off-road driving – a three-day tour of the state's east is $470; five days in the west is $790.

Tasmanian Expeditions (☎ 1300 666 856, 6339 3999; www.tas-ex.com) Offers an excellent range of activity-based tours out of Hobart and Launceston, ranging in length from half a day ($100) to 16 days ($2690), with a choice of bushwalking, cabin-based walks, rafting, rock climbing, cycling and sea-kayaking (or a combination!).

Tassielink (☎ 1300 653 633, 6271 7333; www.tassielink.com.au) A program of coach tours (half- and full-day trips) to major attractions around Tasmania and Launceston. A half-day trip from Hobart to Huonville is $16; a full day to Freycinet is $85 ($73 concession).

Tiger Trails (☎ 6234 3931; www.tigertrails.green.net.au) Eco-tour company offering guided walks (one-day and multi-day) in pristine areas such as the Tarkine wilderness, Overland Track and Walls of Jerusalem, ranging from easy to challenging. They also host fundraiser walks.

Under Down Under (☎ 1800 064 726, 6362 2237; www.underdownunder.com.au) Offers pro-green nature-based, backpacker-friendly trips. There are tours from two to eight days, including a four-day Tassie Highlights tour ($525).

TRAVELLERS WITH DISABILITIES

In this guide particularly good or bad access is described in reviews. Disability awareness in Tasmania is pretty high. Many key attractions provide access for those with limited mobility and a good number of tour operators also have the appropriate facilities: call ahead and confirm this. There are also a number of local agencies that provide information and/or assistance to disabled travellers.

A downloadable PDF file, *The Wheelie Good Guide* on the website of the **ParaQuad Association of Tasmania** (☎ 6272 8816; www.paraquadtas.org.au), has information about accommodation, accessible toilets, mobility maps and attractions. Another source of reliable information is the **National Information Communication and Awareness Network** (Nican; ☎ 02-6241 1220, TTY 1800 806 769; www.nican.com.au), an Australia-wide database and directory providing information on access issues, accessible accommodation, sporting and recreational activities, transport and specialist tour operators (you have to give personal details to get to the information).

For urban travel, check out the *Hobart CBD Mobility Map* from the visitor information centre. If you're planning to get out and about, the **Parks & Wildlife Service** (PWS; ☎ 1300 135 513; www.parks.tas.gov.au) publishes a useful brochure, *Parks for all People* (PDF online), which outlines access for mobility-impaired visitors to Tasmania's national parks and reserves; also

DIRECTORY

see their pamphlet *National Parks, Forests & Waterways Tasmania Visitors' Guide.*

VISAS

All visitors to Australia need a visa (New Zealand nationals are exempt but receive a 'special category' visa on arrival). Visa application forms are available from Australian diplomatic missions overseas, travel agents or the website of the **Department of Immigration and Citizenship** (☎ 13 18 81; www.immi.gov.au). On average, applications are processed within seven to 10 days, though some can be processed in two days. There are several types of visa.

Electronic Travel Authority (ETA) (subclass 976)

This is designed for people who are outside Australia and want to visit for holidays, tourism, recreation or informal studies, for up to three months. It's free but a service charge applies ($20), and it is available to passport holders of 33 countries, including the UK, the USA and Canada, most European countries, Malaysia, Singapore, Japan and Korea. ETA applications are possible online at www.eta .immi.gov.au.

Tourist Visas (subclass 676)

This visa is for people who want to visit Australia for a holiday, to see family and/or friends, or to study for up to three months, especially if they would like to extend this stay. If you are from a country not covered by the ETA, you'll also need to apply for this visa. Standard visas (which cost $75) allow one (in some cases multiple) entry, stays of up to three months, and are valid for use within 12 months of issue. A long-stay tourist visa (also $75) can allow a visit of up to a year in certain circumstances.

Visa Extensions

Visitors are allowed a maximum stay of 12 months, including extensions. Visa extensions are made through the Department of Immigration and Citizenship and it's best to apply at least two or three weeks before your visa expires. The application fee is $215. It's nonrefundable, even if your application is rejected.

Working Holiday Maker (WHM) Visas (subclass 410)

You can supplement your holiday through short-term employment for up to 12 months if you are single, aged between 18 and 30, and from Belgium, Canada, Cyprus, Denmark, Estonia, Finland, France, Germany, Hong Kong, Ireland, Italy, Japan, Korea, Malta, the Netherlands, Norway, Sweden, Taiwan or the UK. You can apply online (www.immi.gov .au/visitors/working-holiday) for an application fee of $190. If you work in regional areas in Australia, you may be able to extend your visa for longer.

You can apply for this visa up to a year in advance, which is worthwhile as there's a limit on the number issued each year. Be sure to read about further conditions (which include having a return air ticket or sufficient funds for a return or onward fare).

WOMEN TRAVELLERS

Tasmania is generally a safe place for women travellers, although the usual sensible precautions apply. It's best to avoid walking alone late at night in major towns. The same applies to rural towns, where there are often a lot of unlit, semideserted streets between you and your temporary home. The new antismoking laws in Tassie have forced party-goers to light up outside pubs and restaurants in the evenings, and that can mean there's more action and shenanigans on the street. When the pubs close and there are drunks roaming around, it's probably not a great time to be out on your own.

Lone women should also be wary of staying in basic pub accommodation unless it looks safe and well managed. Stereotypically, the further you get from 'civilisation' (the bigger cities), the less enlightened your average Aussie male is probably going to be about women's issues. Having said that, many women travellers say that they have met the friendliest, most down-to-earth blokes in small-town pubs.

Lone female hitchers are tempting fate – hitching with a male companion is safer (and increasingly travellers are not hitching at all).

WORK

Casual work can usually be found in the high season (summer) at the major tourist centres and most jobs are in tourism, hospitality, labouring, gardening or farming. Seasonal fruit-picking is another prime possibility, though be warned that it's a tough way to earn a few dollars and pay is proportional to the quantity and quality of fruits picked (read: hard work!). In Tasmania the main harvest times are December to April, and the main areas are the Huon and Tamar Valleys. Grape-picking jobs are sometimes available in late autumn and early winter, as a number of wineries still hand-pick their crops. The best source for information on local work is on the website of **Australian Job Search** (www.jobsearch.gov.au). See also the information about the WHM visa, above.

Volunteer Work

Volunteering is an excellent way to meet people and visit some interesting areas of the country, with a number of worthy projects in Tasmania. The not-for-profit **Conservation Volunteers Australia** (☎ 1800 032 501, 03-5330 2600; www.conservationvolunteers.com.au) has offices in Hobart and Launceston and runs a variety of practical conservation projects (and information sessions) throughout the year. It organises volunteers (including overseas visitors) to get into the bush and get their hands

dirty: tree planting, walking-track construction and flora and fauna surveys are just a few examples. Most projects are either for a weekend or a week and all food, transport and accommodation is supplied in return for a small contribution to help cover the costs (about $30 per day).

Greening Australia (www.greeningaustralia.org.au) actively encourages volunteers to get involved with environmental projects. It has offices in Hobart and Burnie.

Willing Workers on Organic Farms (WWOOF; ☎ 03-5155 0218; www.wwoof.com.au) is a well-established program, with a number of host farms and businesses in Tasmania. The idea is that WWOOFers do a few hours' work each day on a farm or cottage business in return for bed and board, often in a family home. Some places have a minimum stay of a couple of days but many will take you for just a night. See the website: Tassie jobs at the time of writing included gardening, landscaping and blueberry-picking.

Transport

CONTENTS

GETTING THERE & AWAY

Tasmania is the land beneath 'the land down under'. It's a long way from just about everywhere except Antarctica, and getting here usually means a long-haul flight.

There are only a few direct international flights available to or from Hobart and Launceston, and these are from within the Australasian region (Asian capitals and New Zealand). Overseas visitors to the island state will usually need to fly to one of Australia's mainland cities and connect to a Tassie-bound domestic flight. Melbourne and Sydney airports have the most frequent direct air links to Hobart and Launceston.

Flights, tours and rail tickets can be booked online at lonelyplanet.com/travelservices.

ENTERING THE COUNTRY

Disembarking from your plane in Australia is generally easy enough, with only the usual customs declarations and the fight to be first to the luggage carousel to endure. Your flight number will be displayed on the screen above the carousel.

With increased security in mainland Australian airports, both in domestic and international terminals, Tasmania's customs procedures are generally less time-consuming. See p321 for more information on customs and quarantine.

> **THINGS CHANGE...**
>
> The information in this chapter is particularly vulnerable to change. Check directly with the airline or a travel agent to make sure you understand how a fare (and ticket you may buy) works and be aware of the security requirements for international travel. Shop carefully. The details given in this chapter should be regarded as pointers and are not a substitute for your own careful, up-to-date research.

Passport

There are no restrictions when it comes to citizens of foreign countries entering Australia. If you have a visa (see p330), you should be fine.

INTERNATIONAL AIR TRAVEL

There are many competing airlines and a wide variety of airfares if you're flying in from Asia, Europe or North America, but unless you book early, you'll still probably pay a lot for a flight. If you plan to fly during a particularly popular period (around Christmas is a notoriously difficult time to get into Sydney or Melbourne) or on a particularly popular route (such as Hong Kong, Bangkok or Singapore to Sydney or Melbourne), ensure that you make your arrangements well in advance.

Airlines

The east coast of Australia is the most common gateway for international travellers. Airlines that visit Australia follow (note that all phone numbers mentioned here are for dialling from within Australia):

Air Canada (airline code AC; ☎ 1300 655 757; www.aircanada.ca) Flies to most Australian capitals, including Hobart.

Air New Zealand (airline code NZ; ☎ 13 24 76; www.airnz.com.au) Flies to Melbourne, Sydney, Perth, Cairns, Canberra, the Gold Coast, Adelaide, Darwin, Hobart and Launceston.

British Airways (airline code BA; ☎ 1300 767 177; www.britishairways.com.au) Flies to Sydney.

Cathay Pacific (airline code CX; ☎ 13 17 47; www.cathaypacific.com) Flies to Melbourne, Sydney, Perth, Cairns, Canberra, the Gold Coast, Adelaide, Alice Springs, Darwin, Hobart and Launceston.

Emirates (airline code EK; ☎ 1300 303 777; www.emirates.com) Flies to Melbourne, Sydney, Brisbane and Perth.

Garuda Indonesia (airline code GA; ☎ 08 041 807 807; www.garuda-indonesia.com) Flies to Melbourne, Sydney, Darwin and Perth.

Japan Airlines (airline code JL; ☎ 1300 525 287; www.jal.com) Flies to Melbourne, Sydney, Brisbane and Cairns.

KLM (airline code KL; ☎ 02-9223 9835; www.klm.com) Flies to Melbourne and Sydney.

Malaysia Airlines (airline code MH; ☎ 603 7843 3000; www.malaysiaairlines.com.au) Flies to Sydney, Melbourne, Brisbane, Perth and Adelaide.

Royal Brunei Airlines (airline code BI; ☎ 1300 721 271; www.bruneiair.com) Flies to Brisbane, Sydney, Perth and Darwin.

Singapore Airlines (airline code SQ; ☎ 13 10 11; www.singaporeair.com.au) Flies to Melbourne, Sydney, Brisbane, Perth and Adelaide.

Thai Airways International (airline code TG; ☎ 1300 651 960; www.thaiairways.com.au) Flies to Melbourne, Sydney, Brisbane and Perth.

United Airlines (airline code UA; ☎ 13 17 77; www.unitedairlines.com.au) Flies to Melbourne and Sydney.

Tickets

Be sure you research the options carefully to make sure you get the best deal, online or otherwise. Round-the-world tickets can be a good option for getting to Australia.

Automated online ticket sales work well if you're doing a simple one-way or return trip on specified dates, but they're no substitute for a travel agent with the low-down on special deals, strategies for avoiding stopovers and other useful advice.

Paying by credit card offers some protection if you unwittingly end up dealing with a rogue fly-by-night agency in your search for the cheapest fare, as most card issuers provide refunds if you can prove you didn't get what you paid for. Alternatively, buy a ticket from a bonded agent, such as one covered by the **Air Travel Organiser's Licence** (ATOL; www.atol.org.uk) scheme in the UK. If you have doubts about the service provider, at the very least call the airline and confirm that your booking has been made. Most airlines will have an office in the country you're calling from; check their websites (usually to be found under 'Contact Us' or 'Customer Support').

For online bookings, start with the following websites:

Cheap Flights (www.cheapflights.com) Very informative site with specials, airline information and flight searches from the USA and other regions.

Cheapest Flights (www.cheapestflights.co.uk) Cheap worldwide flights from the UK; get in early for the bargains.

Expedia (www.expedia.msn.com) Microsoft's travel site; mainly US-related.

Flight Centre International (www.flightcentre.com) Respected operator handling direct flights, with sites for Australia, New Zealand, the UK, the USA and Canada.

Roundtheworldflights.com (www.roundtheworldflights.com) This excellent site allows you to build your own trips from the UK with up to six stops (it's a Global Village site).

STA (www.statravel.com) Prominent in international student travel but you don't have to be a student; site linked to worldwide STA sites.

Tiss.com (www.tiss.com) Truly international site for flight-only tickets; cheap fares and an easy-to-search database.

Travel Online (www.travelonline.co.nz) Good place to check worldwide flights from New Zealand.

Travel.com.au (www.travel.com.au) Good Australian site; look up fares and flights out of the country.

Travelocity (www.travelocity.com) US site that allows you to search fares (in US$) to/from practically anywhere.

Asia

Bangkok, Singapore and Hong Kong are usually the best places to shop around for discount tickets, however, flights between Hong Kong and Australia are notoriously heavily booked. Flights to/from Bangkok and Singapore are often part of the longer Europe-to-Australia route so they are also sometimes full. Plan your preferred itinerary well in advance.

Typical one-way fares to Sydney are A$500 leaving from Singapore, A$400 from Penang or Kuala Lumpur, and about A$650 from Bangkok. From Tokyo, fares start at A$650.

There are several good local agents in Asia:

STA Travel Japan (☎ 03-5391 2922; www.statravel.co.jp)

STA Travel Singapore (☎ 6737 7188; www.statravel.com.sg)

STA Travel Thailand (☎ 662-236 0262; www.statravel.co.th)

Canada

The air routes from Canada are similar to those from mainland USA, with most Toronto and Vancouver flights stopping in one US city, such as Los Angeles or Honolulu, before heading on to Australia. Air Canada flies from Vancouver to Sydney and from Toronto to Melbourne (both via Honolulu).

TRANSPORT

Canadian discount air ticket sellers' (consolidators') airfares tend to be about 10% higher than those sold in the USA. **Travel Cuts** (☎ 1 866 246 9762; www.travelcuts.com) is Canada's national student travel agency and has offices in all major cities.

Fares out of Vancouver to Sydney or Melbourne cost from C$1300/1900 in the low/high season via the US west coast. From Toronto, fares go from around C$1500/2300.

Continental Europe

From the major destinations in Europe, most flights travel via one of the major Asian cities such as Singapore, Bangkok, Hong Kong or Kuala Lumpur. Some flights are also routed through London before arriving in Australia. **eDreams** (www.edreams.com) is a fine website on which to compare multiple airfares from European capitals to Australia. In Germany, good travel agencies include the Berlin branch of **STA Travel** (☎ 069-743 032 92; www.statravel.de). Fares start at around €900/1000 in the low/high season. Other agencies:

Nouvelles Frontières (☎ 08 25 00 07 47; www.nouvelles-frontieres.fr) Fares from Paris in the low/high season cost from €550/800. Also has branches outside of Paris.

Holland International (www.hollandinternational.nl) Links to multiple travel sites. From Amsterdam, return fares start at around €650.

New Zealand

Air New Zealand and Qantas operate a network of flights linking Auckland, Wellington and Christchurch with most major Australian gateway cities, from where you can fly to Tasmania. Fares from New Zealand to Sydney/Melbourne cost around NZ$180/750 one-way/return, although prices can greatly vary depending on the time of year.

Trans-Tasman booking agents include:

Flight Centre (☎ 0800 243 544; www.flightcentre.co.nz) Has a large central office in Auckland and branches throughout the country.

STA Travel (☎ 0800 474 400; www.statravel.co.nz) Has offices in various cities.

UK & Ireland

There are two routes from the UK: the western route via the USA and Pacific, and the usually cheaper and more frequent eastern route via the Middle East and Asia. Some of the best deals around are with Emirates, Gulf Air, Malaysia Airlines and Thai Airways International. British Airways, Singapore Airlines and Qantas generally have higher fares but may offer a more direct route.

A popular agent in the UK is the ubiquitous **STA Travel** (☎ 0871 2300 040; www.statravel.co.uk).

Typical direct fares from London to Sydney are UK£650/900 one-way/return during the low season (March to June). In September and mid-December fares go up by as much as 30%, while the rest of the year they're somewhere in-between.

From Australia you can expect to pay around A$900/1800 one-way/return in the low season to London and other European capitals (with stops in Asia on the way) and A$1100/2050 in the high season.

USA

Airlines directly connecting Australia across the Pacific with Los Angeles or San Francisco include Qantas, Air New Zealand and United Airlines. There are also numerous airlines offering flights via Asia, with stopover possibilities including Tokyo, Kuala Lumpur, Bangkok, Hong Kong and Singapore, and via the Pacific, with stopover possibilities such as Nadi (Fiji), Rarotonga (Cook Islands), Tahiti (French Polynesia) and Auckland (NZ). In most cases, you'll need to purchase an additional fare to Hobart.

As in Canada, discount travel agents in the USA are known as consolidators. San Francisco is the ticket consolidator capital of America, although some good deals can be found in Los Angeles, New York and other big cities.

STA Travel (☎ 800 781 4040; www.statravel.com) has offices around the country, and can assist with tickets.

Student Universe (www.studentuniverse.com) specialises in cheap tickets for college students and faculty.

Typically you can purchase a return ticket to Melbourne or Sydney from the west coast for US$700/1700 in the low/high season, or from the east coast for US$950/1900. Note that taxes and fees will be extra (up to US$400).

Return low-/high-season fares from Australia to the US west coast cost around A$1640/1850, and to New York A$1500/1950.

DOMESTIC AIR TRAVEL

There are major airports located at Hobart and Launceston, as well as smaller operations at Burnie/Wynyard and Devonport. (Burnie/Wynyard airport is officially known as Burnie airport but is actually located 20km west of Burnie near the town of Wynyard. Due to the fact that some Tasmanians call the airport 'Burnie' and others call it 'Wynyard', we refer to it as 'Burnie/Wynyard' throughout this book.)

Flights are getting ever cheaper and it's straightforward to find a one-way flight for under A$100 from most Australian gateway cities. Airlines with services between Tasmania and the Australian mainland:

Jetstar (☎ 13 15 38; www.jetstar.com.au) Qantas' low-cost airline. Direct flights from Melbourne, Sydney, Brisbane and Adelaide to Hobart; also from Melbourne, Sydney and Brisbane to Launceston.

Qantas (☎ 13 13 13; www.qantas.com.au) Direct flights from Sydney and Melbourne to Hobart, and from Melbourne to Launceston. QantasLink (the regional subsidiary) offers flights from Melbourne to Burnie and Devonport.

Regional Express (REX; ☎ 13 17 13; www.regional express.com.au) Flies from Melbourne to Burnie/Wynyard and King Island.

Tiger Airways (☎ 03-9335 3033; www.tigerairways .com.au) Flies from Melbourne to Hobart and Launceston.

Virgin Blue (☎ 13 67 89; www.virginblue.com.au) Direct flights from Melbourne, Sydney, Brisbane and Adelaide to Hobart, and from Melbourne and Sydney to Launceston.

Qantas and Virgin Blue have connecting flights from most other mainland capitals.

PACKAGE DEALS

These include transport to Tasmania (either by air or sea), car rental and accommodation – and can often work out considerably cheaper than purchasing each component separately. As you would expect, the biggest discounts apply in the quieter periods of autumn, winter and spring, whereas in summer the deals rise in price. Most package deals have conditions attached to them, of which the most common is twin share (two people), and sometimes an itinerary is fixed at booking.

Contact **Tourism Tasmania** (p328), **Qantas Holidays** (☎ 13 14 15; www.qantas.com.au) or **TasVacations** (☎ 1800 030 160; www.tasvacations.com) for ideas.

Package deals are a particularly good idea if you're visiting King or Flinders Islands. See p309 and p314 for details.

DEPARTURE TAX

There is a $38 departure tax when leaving Australia. This is included in the price of airline tickets.

See p309 and p314 for information on airlines servicing King and Flinders Islands respectively.

Fares

Air fares to Tasmania are constantly changing and you can get some good deals, especially if you book well in advance or if you're planning a wintertime trip. Few people pay full fare on domestic travel, as the airlines offer a wide range of discounts that come and go. There are also regular special fares, so keep your eyes open and check the airlines' websites. Regular one-way and return domestic fares are similar on Qantas and Virgin Blue, while Tiger Airways and Jetstar offer some very good bargains, usually (but not always) cheaper than the two major airlines. Lowest one-way prices (at the time of writing) from Melbourne to Tasmania are in the $40 to $150 range; Sydney to Tassie costs $90 to $160, from Brisbane costs from $150 to $200, and from Adelaide costs from $130 to $155, although it is likely you'll pay towards the middle of these ranges.

Advance-purchase deals provide the cheapest airfares. Some advance-purchase fares offer up to 33% discount off one-way fares and up to 50% off return fares. You have to book one to four weeks ahead, and you often have to stay for at least one Saturday night. There are restrictions on changing flights and you can lose up to 100% of the ticket price if you cancel, although you can buy health-related cancellation insurance.

There are also special deals available only to foreign visitors (in possession of an outbound ticket). If booked in Australia these fares offer a 40% discount off a full-fare economy ticket. They can also be booked from overseas (which usually works out a bit cheaper).

SEA
Cruise Ship

Just about the only way to see the spectacular diversity of wildlife on remote, sub-Antarctic Macquarie Island, proclaimed Tasmania's second World Heritage area in 1997, up close is to take one of the sub-Antarctic islands cruises scheduled by New Zealand–based **Heritage Expeditions** (☎ 0800 262 8873; www.heritage-expeditions.com). At the time of writing the company offered a couple of wonderful options in the austral summer, such as the Footsteps of Mawson tour, a 26-day trip to Antarctica taking in various sub-Antarctic islands and incorporating two days on Macquarie Island (1500km from Tasmania). Prices per person for the this cruise range from around US$10,882 for triple share (shared facilities) to US$15,345 for a suite, plus US$400 for landing fees. Check the comprehensive website for more information (download brochures on all expeditions).

Ferry

There are two high-speed *Spirit of Tasmania* ferries operated by **TT-Line** (☎ 1800 634 906; www.spiritoftasmania.com.au) that ply Bass Strait nightly in each direction between Melbourne and Devonport on northern Tasmania's coast. The crossing takes between nine and 11 hours (departs at 9pm, both arriving at their destinations at approximately 7am the next morning). The Devonport terminal is on The Esplanade in East Devonport; the Melbourne terminal is at Station Pier in Port Melbourne. Each ferry can accommodate 1400 passengers and around 650 vehicles and has restaurants, bars and games facilities. The public areas of the ships have been designed to cater for wheelchair access, as have a handful of cabins.

Fares depend on whether you're travelling in the peak season (mid-December to late January), shoulder season (late January to early May, and September to mid-December) or off-peak season (May to the end of August), and there's a range of seating and cabin options. 'Ocean view recliner' seats are the cheapest and resemble airline seats. Cabins are available in twin or four-berth configurations, with or without porthole windows, or you can opt for a 'deluxe' cabin (with a queen-size bed and complimentary bottle of sparkling wine). All cabins have a private bathroom. Child,

---

QUARANTINE

There are stringent rules in place to protect the disease-free status of the agriculture of this Tassie, and plants, fruit and vegetables cannot be brought in. Tourists must discard all items prior to their arrival (even if they're only travelling from mainland Australia).

TRANSPORT

WARNING TO WEAK STOMACHS!

Bass Strait is known as one of the roughest shipping channels in the world, so landlubbers prone to seasickness should prepare themselves (just in case).

---

student, pensioner and senior discounts apply to all accommodation except for deluxe cabins. Prices do not include meals, which can be purchased on board from an à la carte restaurant or cafeteria.

One-way prices (per adult) are as follows. Booking online saves a further A$5 each way. Fares listed here (except for deluxe cabins) are the less flexible, nonrefundable 'ship saver' fares (conditions are similar to discount airlines):

Fare	Peak	Shoulder	Off-peak
Ocean-view recliner seat	$145	$123	$117
Inside 4-berth cabin	$185	$170	$134
Inside twin cabin	$221	$189	$148
Deluxe cabin	$418	$354	$326
Daytime sailings (seats only)	$168	$120	$114
Standard vehicles	$61	$61	$61
Campervans up to 5m length	$103	$103	$103
Motorcycles	$50	$50	$50
Bicycles	$8	$8	$8

GETTING AROUND

Driving around Tasmania is the easiest, most flexible way to see the state. If you do drive, don't make the mistake of drawing up exhaustive itineraries with carefully calculated driving times between each destination. Though this is sometimes necessary to catch a particular tour on a particular day or to check in at a prebooked B&B, it runs contrary to the real idea behind driving around Tasmania: that you can stop for a spontaneous photo or a leisurely browse, or divert down a side-road to explore the unfamiliar whenever you feel like it. Too many people make the mistake of thinking they can see all of Tasmania's top attractions in one week, madly dashing from the west coast to the east (via Cradle Mountain, Hobart and Port Arthur) – they usually end up going home in desperate need of a holiday.

While public transport is adequate between larger towns and popular tourist destinations, visiting remote sights might prove frustrating due to irregular or, in some cases, nonexistent services. There are, however, plenty of car-rental companies offering decent rates for early-model vehicles, an option you should seriously consider when planning your itinerary, particularly if your time is limited and the places you want to visit are far-flung.

AIR

As distances within Tasmania are far from huge, air travel within the state is not very common. Of more use to travellers are the air services for bushwalkers in the southwest, and links between major towns and King and Flinders Islands.

There are a few small regional airlines within the state:

Airlines of Tasmania (☎ 1800 144 460, 6248 5490; www.airtasmania.com.au) Flies daily between Launceston and Flinders Island (adult one-way/return $145/340). Also flies to Cape Barren Island from Launceston ($240 return).

Par Avion (☎ 6248 5390; www.paravion.com.au) Flies from Hobart to Melaleuca in the southwest wilderness (adult one-way $160). Good for scenic flights and bushwalker pick-ups/drop-offs; also offers a southwest off-season special ($180, May to October).

Tasair (☎ 1800 062 900, 6248 5088; www.tasair.com .au) Flies daily to King Island from Devonport and Burnie/ Wynyard (adult one-way $198, student discounts apply). Flies weekdays between Burnie/Wynyard and Hobart (one-way $198). Also offers charters and scenic flights, plus a bushwalkers' service to Cox Bight and Melaleuca (one-way $176).

BICYCLE

Cycling Tasmania is one of the best ways to get close to nature (and, it has to be said, to log trucks, rain and roadkill). If you're prepared for steep climbs and strong headwinds in certain sections, you should enjoy the experience immensely.

It's worth bringing your own bike, especially if you're coming via ferry as transport on one of the *Spirit of Tasmania* ferries costs $8 each way any time of year. If you wish to fly in, check with the airline for costs and the degree of dismantling and packing required. Also consider buying a bike in Hobart or Launceston and reselling it at the end.

Bike rental is available in the larger towns, and there are also a number of operators offering multiday cycling tours or experiences such as mountain-biking down Mt Wellington in Hobart. See p59 for more information.

While the same road rules that apply to cars also apply to bicycles, riders should also follow another rule – if in doubt, give way or get out of the way. When cycling on the state's many narrow, winding roads, always keep your eyes and ears open for traffic. Also watch out for wooden bridges with gaps between the slats that can trap bicycle wheels, and try not to cycle at night. Note that bicycle helmets are compulsory in Tasmania (and all other states and territories of Australia), as are white front lights and red rear lights if you are riding in the dark.

Full notes and lots of practical advice for cycling around the state can be found at www .biketas.org.au/giro.php.

BOAT

A car ferry runs at least eight times a day from Kettering to Bruny Island in Tasmania's southeast ($30 one way). To effectively explore this rather long (and beautiful) island, you'll need your own car or bicycle. See p141 for details.

At the time of writing there was a twice-daily service from Triabunna on the east coast to Maria Island, which is a national park, carrying only passengers and bicycles as vehicles aren't allowed on the island. The services may be limited during winter. See p171 for details.

There is also a small weekly passenger and car ferry from Bridport in Tasmania's north-east to Flinders Island (the ferry continues on to Port Welshpool in Victoria on demand). See p314 for more information.

BUS

Tasmania has a reasonable bus network connecting major towns and centres, but weekend services are infrequent, which can be inconvenient for travellers with limited time. There are more buses in summer than in winter, but smaller towns are still not serviced terribly frequently.

The main regional bus lines are **Redline Coaches** (☎ 1300 360 000, 6336 1446; www.redlinecoaches .com.au) and **Tassielink** (☎ 1300 300 520, 6230 8900; www.tassielink.com.au). They cover most of the state between them.

Buses run along most major highways year-round. Redline services the Midland Hwy between Hobart and Launceston,

the north coast between Launceston and Smithton, north from Launceston to George Town, and to the east coast. Tassielink runs from both Hobart and Launceston to the state's west (Cradle Mountain, Strahan, Queenstown, Lake St Clair) and to the east coast (St Helens, Bicheno, Swansea), from Hobart to Port Arthur, and south from Hobart down the Huon Valley. It also runs the 'Main Road Express', an express services connecting Bass Strait ferry arrivals/departures in Devonport to Launceston, Hobart and Burnie.

Over summer, Tassielink buses also run to popular bushwalking destinations. Special fares that enable you to be dropped off at the start of a walk and picked up at the end are offered. Buses take the link road from Devonport past Cradle Mountain to the Lyell Hwy, and services also run from Hobart past Mt Field and Maydena to Scotts Peak, and from Hobart past Dover to Cockle Creek in the south. See the website (click on 'Walking Track Links') or these destinations in the relevant chapters for more information.

Additionally, **Hobart Coaches** (☎ 13 22 01; www .hobartcoaches.com.au) runs regular services south from the capital as far as Woodbridge and Cygnet, and north to Richmond and New Norfolk. See the relevant chapters for details of these and other regional services.

There are smaller transport operators offering useful bus services on important tourist routes (eg between Bicheno and Coles Bay, or within the Cradle Mountain–Lake St Clair region); details of these are given in the relevant sections of this book.

Note that all bus fares and conditions quoted throughout this book are subject to change and should be used as a guide only.

Bus Passes
TASSIELINK

Tassielink offers an Explorer Pass valid on all scheduled services for unlimited kilometres. The pass can be bought from mainland Tasmanian travel centres, YHA and STA Travel offices, most other travel agents or directly from Tassielink. If you intend to buy an Explorer Pass, ask for Tassielink's timetables in advance or check the company's website and plan your itinerary carefully before making your purchase – this is the best way to ensure you'll be able to get where you want to go within the life of the pass.

Explorer Pass	Valid for	Cost
7-day pass	travel in 10 days	$189
10-day pass	travel in 15 days	$225
14-day pass	travel in 20 days	$260
21-day pass	travel in 30 days	$299

REDLINE COACHES

Redline offers its own form of bus pass, the Tassie Pass, with unlimited travel on its services. As the Redline bus network is not nearly as comprehensive as that of Tassielink, it's especially worth checking Redline's website and timetables to ascertain its worth to you before you purchase.

Tassie Pass	Cost
7-day pass	$135
10-day pass	$160
14-day pass	$185
21-day pass	$219

Costs

Fares are quite reasonable for bus travel within Tasmania. To give some idea of the fares and travel times, a one-way trip between Devonport and Launceston is around $20 and takes 1½ hours, Hobart to Launceston is $31 (2½ hours) and Hobart to Devonport is $52 (four hours).

CAR & MOTORCYCLE

Travelling by car is the best option in Tasmania, as it gives you the freedom to explore according to your own timetable. You can bring cars from the mainland to Tasmania on the ferry (p336), so renting may only be cheaper for shorter trips. Tasmania has many international, national and local car-rental agencies. There are also bus passes that allow you to travel for unlimited kilometres within a certain period (see opposite).

Motorcycles are another popular way of getting around, and the climate is OK for bikes for a large part of the year. You can bring your own motorbike across on the ferry from the mainland for a small fee, or hire one once you get here.

Automobile Associations

The **Royal Automobile Club of Tasmania** (RACT; ☎ 13 27 22; www.ract.com.au) provides an emergency breakdown service to members and has reciprocal arrangements with services in other Australian states and some from overseas. It also provides tourist literature, excellent maps and detailed guides to accommoda-

tion and camping grounds. The roadside assistance number is ☎ 13 11 11. There are branches in Hobart (corner of Patrick and Murray Sts) and Launceston (corner of York and George Sts).

Bring Your Own Vehicle

If you're departing mainland Australia from Melbourne, it's easy to bring your own vehicle across on the ferry. Before you book a ferry ticket, however, it's worth doing some calculations to determine whether it's the most economical option for your intended trip.

Driving Licence

You can generally use your own home-country's driving licence in Australia, as long as it's in English (if it's not, a certified translation must be carried) and has an identifying photograph. Alternatively, it's a simple matter to arrange an International Driving Permit (IDP), which should be supported by your home licence. Just go to your home country's automobile association and it can issue one on the spot. The permits are valid for 12 months. For more, see the website of the **Australian Automobile Association** (www.aaa.asn.au/touring/idp.htm).

Fuel

Fuel (super, diesel and unleaded) is available from service stations sporting the well-known international brand names. In small towns there's often just a pump outside the general store, while the larger towns and cities have conventional service stations and garages. Most are open from 8am to 6pm weekdays, but fewer are open on weekends, and fewer still are open late at night or 24 hours, something to keep in mind if you intend travelling long distances at night.

Fuel prices vary from place to place and from price war to price war, but basically fuel is heavily taxed and continues to hike up, much to the shock of Australian motorists. With petrol prices erratic but rising at the time of writing, the only reasonably steadfast fact is that once you get out into the small rural towns, unleaded petrol prices can rise about 10c a litre compared to larger cities and towns.

Insurance

In Australia, third-party personal injury insurance is always included in the vehicle registration cost. This ensures that every

TRANSPORT

registered vehicle carries at least minimum insurance. It's wise to extend that minimum to at least third-party property insurance as well – minor collisions with other vehicles can be amazingly expensive.

When it comes to hiring cars from a hire company, know exactly what your liability is in the event of an accident. Rather than risk paying out thousands of dollars if you do have an accident, you can take out your own comprehensive insurance on the car, or (the usual option) pay an additional daily amount to the rental company for an 'insurance excess reduction' policy. This brings the amount of excess you must pay in the event of an accident down from between $2000 and $5000 to a few hundred dollars.

Be aware that if you're travelling on dirt roads you will not be covered by insurance unless you have a 4WD – in other words, if you have an accident you'll be liable for all the costs involved. Also, most companies' insurance won't cover the cost of damage to glass (including the windscreen) or tyres. Always read the fine print.

Purchase

If you're planning a stay of several months that involves lots of driving, buying a secondhand car will be much cheaper than renting. But remember that reliability is all-important.

You'll probably get any car cheaper by buying privately through a local newspaper rather than through a car dealer. Buying through a dealer does have the advantage of some sort of guarantee, but this is not much use if you're buying a car in Sydney for a trip to Tasmania.

When you come to buy or sell a car, there are usually some local regulations to be complied with. You can get advice on how to make buying a car simpler and safer from www.justice .tas.gov.au/fair_trading/motor_vehicles. To avoid buying a lemon, you might consider forking out some extra money for a vehicle appraisal before purchase – the RACT offers this kind of inspection for a fee.

Rental

Tasmania has many international, national and local car-rental agencies; www.travelways .com.au lists many of the rental options.

Before you decide on a company, ask about any kilometre limitations and find out what the insurance covers. Ensure there are no hid-

den seasonal adjustments. However, it is quite normal for smaller rental companies to ask for a bond of $300 or more. Also remember that most companies do not cover accidents that occur on unsealed roads, and hike up the excess in the case of damage or an accident on such a road – which is a considerable disadvantage in a state where so many of the best destinations can only be reached via unsealed roads and where roadkill is so common.

Larger international firms have booking desks at airports and offices in major towns. They have standard rates from about $40 to $60 for high-season, multiday hire of a small car. By booking in advance and choosing smaller cars, rates can be lower still. Big-name companies include the following:

AutoRent-Hertz (☎ 1800 030 222, 6237 1111; www.autorent.com.au)

Avis (☎ 13 63 33, 6234 4222; www.avis.com.au)

Budget (☎ 13 27 27; www.budget.com.au)

Europcar (☎ 1800 030 118; www.europcar.com.au)

Thrifty (☎ 1800 030 730; www.tasvacations.com.au)

You can sometimes save money by choosing the smaller operators, but this must be weighed against the rental conditions and general condition of the vehicle – make sure you're familiar and confident with both before you sign. Small local firms rent older cars for as little as $35 a day, depending on the season and how long you hire the vehicle for. Prices then increase according to the model and age of the cars. The smaller companies don't normally have desks at arrival points but can usually arrange for your car to be picked up at airports and the ferry terminal in Devonport. Operators include the following:

Lo-Cost Auto Rent (www.locostautorent.com); Hobart (☎ 6231 0550); Launceston (☎ 6334 6202); Devonport (☎ 6427 0796)

Rent-a-Bug (☎ 6231 0300; www.rentabug.com.au) Office in Hobart, offering cheap Volkswagen Beetles, plus older-model vehicles and campervans.

Selective Car Rentals (☎ 6234 3311; www .selectivecarrentals.com.au) Office in Hobart.

CAMPERVANS

Tasmanian Travelways has a listing of campervan rental companies. Hiring three-berth campervans costs around $700 per week from May to mid-September, rising in stages to a hefty $1540 in the peak period from Christmas to mid-January. Other companies offer campervan rental:

> ### CAMPERVANNING IN TASMANIA
>
> Check your rear-view mirror on any far-flung Tasmanian road and you'll likely see a shiny white campervan packed with liberated travellers, surfboards and portable BBQs cruising along behind you. Campervanning around Tassie has really taken off – it's flexible and affordable, and you can leave the trampled tourist trails behind and crank up the AC/DC. Most towns have a campground or caravan park where you can park for around $20 a night, or seek out a remote beach/mountain/valley and dream in isolation. One warning: some rental companies aren't thrilled about their vehicles traversing unsealed roads (Bruny Island, Friendly Beaches, Mt William National Park etc). To avoid any acrimony, read the fine print and discuss your itinerary with them first.

Autorent-Hertz (☎ 1800 030 500; www.autorent .com.au)

Britz (☎ 1800 331 454; www.britz.com)

Cruisin' Tasmania (☎ 1300 664 485, 6248 4035; www.cruisin-tasmania.com.au).

Maui (☎ 1300 363 800; www.maui-rentals.com)

Tasmanian Campervan Hire (☎ 1800 807 119; www.tascamper.com) Specialises in two-berth vans.

MOTORCYCLES

Tasmanian Motorcycle Hire (☎ 6391 9139; www .tasmotorcyclehire.com.au; 17 Coachmans Rd, Evandale) has a range of touring motorbikes for rent from $110 per day (cheaper rates for longer rentals and half-day rentals also available); full pricing details are listed on the website. Evandale is south of Launceston, not far from the airport.

YHA CAR & HOSTEL PACKAGES

Available from the office of the **Tasmanian YHA office** (Map p82; ☎ 6234 9617; www.yha.com.au; 9 Argyle St, Hobart; ◷ 9am-5pm Mon-Fri) is the car rental and accommodation deal, whereby you purchase a Tasmania Adventure Freedom Pass and YHA hostel accommodation package for either seven, 10, 14 or 21 days. Twenty-one nights' dorm-style accommodation and car-hire pass costs $1042 (based on two persons). While these packages might appear to offer reasonable value, it's important to remember that YHA hostels are not widespread in Tasmania – there are no YHA hos-

tels on the west coast, for example, or south of Hobart, or along the Midland Hwy, or in the popular east-coast towns of Swansea or Bicheno. Our advice is to pay your accommodation as you go and not commit yourself to any one form of accommodation. There may not be a YHA hostel at your destination of choice, but there may well be an independent hostel, cheap pub room or budget cabin you can stay in.

Road Conditions & Hazards

Watch out for wildlife while you're driving around the island – the huge number of carcasses lining main roads is sad testimony to the fact that many drivers don't use enough caution. Many local animals are nocturnal and often cross roads around dusk, so try to avoid driving in rural areas when darkness falls and if it's unavoidable, remember to slow down. And be warned that hitting a wombat not only kills the unfortunate animal, but can also make a mess of your car.

Distances may appear short when looking at a map of Tasmania (especially in relation to distances on the mainland), but roads are often narrow and winding, with many sharp bends and, occasionally, one-lane bridges that aren't clearly signposted. This can make trip durations considerably longer than anticipated. There are also many unsealed roads leading to sites of interest throughout the state – bear this in mind when renting a car, as many insurance policies won't cover you for damage or accidents incurred while driving on such roads.

Cycling is popular on some roads (particularly on the east coast) and when encountering bicycles you should wait until you can pass safely. Log-trucks piled high and coming around sharp corners also demand caution. Finally, in cold weather be wary of 'black ice', an invisible layer of ice over the bitumen, especially on the shaded side of mountain passes. It's wise to drive a little more slowly and allow more time to react to these hazards.

Anyone considering travelling on 4WD tracks should read the free publication *Cruisin' Without Bruisin'*, available and at visitors centres around the state or online from the website of the **Parks & Wildlife Service** (www.parks.tas.gov.au). It details over 20 tracks (graded easy to hard) and explains how to

TRANSPORT

ROAD DISTANCES (km)

	Burnie	Deloraine	Devonport	Geeveston	Hobart	Launceston	New Norfolk	Oatlands	Port Arthur	Queenstown	St Helens	Scottsdale	Smithton	Sorell	Strahan	Swansea
Deloraine	100															
Devonport	50	50														
Geeveston	381	281	331													
Hobart	328	228	278	53												
Launceston	137	51	87	254	201											
New Norfolk	290	190	240	91	38	197										
Oatlands	246	146	196	136	83	118	79									
Port Arthur	386	286	336	148	95	258	133	140								
Queenstown	148	204	198	312	259	251	221	261	354							
St Helens	293	207	243	304	251	156	247	168	299	407						
Scottsdale	197	111	147	314	261	60	257	178	318	311	96					
Smithton	88	188	138	469	416	225	378	334	474	236	381	285				
Sorell	316	216	266	78	25	188	63	70	70	284	229	248	404			
Strahan	183	222	209	353	289	271	253	370	388	41	405	330	224	325		
Swansea	264	164	214	189	136	136	174	114	181	395	118	214	352	111	352	
Triabunna	314	214	264	139	86	186	124	131	131	345	168	264	402	61	249	50

These are the shortest distances by road; other routes may be considerably longer.
For distances by coach, check the companies' leaflets.

minimise your impact on the regions you drive through.

Road Rules

Driving in Tasmania holds few surprises, other than the odd animal caught in your headlights. Cars are driven on the left-hand side of the road (as they are in the rest of Australia). An important road rule is 'give way to the right' – if an intersection is unmarked (which is unusual), you must give way to vehicles entering the intersection from your right.

In towns and cities, the general speed limit is 50km/h, while on the open road the general limit is 100km/h, although on major highways such as the Midland Hwy it's 110km/h. Speed cameras operate in Tasmania and are usually carefully hidden.

Wearing a seat belt is compulsory – you'll be fined if you don't use them. Young children must be strapped into an approved safety seat. Talking on a hand-held mobile phone while driving is illegal.

The other main law applies to drinking and driving: a strict limit of 0.05% blood alcohol content applies. There are heavy penalties if you break this law – your licence will be cancelled and jail sentences are imposed on offenders with multiple convictions. Random breath tests are regularly conducted by police. All in all, the best policy is not to get behind the wheel if you've been drinking.

HITCHING

Travelling by thumb in Tassie is generally good, but wrap up in winter and keep a raincoat handy. Many of the state's minor roads are still unsurfaced and traffic on them can be very light, so although some of these roads lead to interesting places, you'll probably have to give them a miss if you're hitching.

That being said, hitching is never entirely safe in any country and we don't recommend it. Travellers who decide to hitch should understand that they're taking a small but potentially serious risk. People who do choose to hitch will be safer if they travel in pairs and let someone know where they are planning to go.

People looking for travelling companions for car journeys around the state often leave notices on boards in hostels and backpacker

accommodation. The website www.needaride
.com.au is a good resource.

LOCAL TRANSPORT

Metro (☎ 13 22 01; www.metrotas.com.au; ☻ information line 5am-11.30pm Mon-Thu, 5am-1.30am Fri, 5.30am-
1am Sat, 8am-10.30pm Sun) operates bus networks
in Hobart, Launceston and Burnie, offering
visitors inexpensive services enabling them
to reach some out-of-the-way attractions.
See online for schedules and price lists of the
Hobart services.

Taxis are available in all major towns and
can be a handy way of getting to places otherwise not easily reached; see regional chapters
for listings. Outside the major towns, local
transport is limited.

TRAIN

For economic reasons there are no longer
any passenger rail services in Tasmania, except for the West Coast Wilderness Railway
(p286) between Queenstown and Strahan (a
scenic 34km).

Health Dr David Millar

Australia and Tasmania are healthy places in which to travel. Diseases of insanitation such as cholera and typhoid are unheard of. Thanks to isolation and quarantine standards, even some animal diseases such as rabies and foot-and-mouth disease have yet to be recorded.

Few travellers to Australia will experience anything worse than an upset stomach or a bad hangover, and the standard of hospitals and health care is high if you do fall ill.

BEFORE YOU GO

Since most vaccines don't produce immunity until at least two weeks after they're given, visit a physician four to eight weeks before departure. Ask your doctor for an International Certificate of Vaccination (otherwise known as the 'Yellow Booklet'), which will list all the vaccinations you've received. This is mandatory for countries that require proof of yellow fever vaccination upon entry (sometimes required in Australia, see right), but it's a good idea to carry a record of all your vaccinations wherever you travel.

Bring medications in their original, clearly labelled, containers. A signed and dated letter from your physician describing your medical conditions and medications, including generic names, is also a good idea. If carrying syringes or needles, be sure to have a physician's letter documenting their medical necessity.

INSURANCE

Health insurance is essential for all travellers. While health care in Australia is of a high standard and is not overly expensive by international comparisons, costs can build up and repatriation is extremely expensive.

If your health insurance doesn't cover you for trips abroad, consider getting extra insurance; check lonelyplanet.com for details. Find out in advance if your insurance plan will make payments directly to providers or reimburse you later for overseas health expenditures. In Australia, as in many countries, doctors expect payment at the time of consultation. Make sure you get an itemised receipt detailing the service and keep contact details for the health provider. See opposite for details of health care in Australia.

RECOMMENDED VACCINATIONS

If you're really worried about health when travelling, there are a few vaccinations you could consider for Australia. The World Health Organization recommends that all travellers should be covered for diphtheria, tetanus, measles, mumps, rubella, chickenpox and polio, as well as hepatitis B, regardless of their destination. The travel-planning period is a great time to ensure that all routine vaccination cover is complete. The consequences of these diseases can be severe, and while Australia has high levels of childhood vaccination coverage, outbreaks of these diseases do occur.

REQUIRED VACCINATIONS

Proof of yellow fever vaccination is required only from travellers entering Australia within six days of having stayed overnight or longer in a yellow fever–infected country. For a full list of these countries visit the websites of the **World Health Organization** (www.who.int) or the **Centers for Disease Control and Prevention** (wwwn.cdc.gov).

INTERNET RESOURCES

There is a wealth of travel health advice online. The **World Health Organization** (www.who.int) publishes *International Travel and Health,* which is revised annually and is available online at no cost. Another website of general interest is **MD Travel Health** (www.mdtravelhealth.com), which provides travel health recommendations and is updated daily.

MEDICAL CHECKLIST

- acetaminophen/paracetamol or aspirin
- adhesive or paper tape
- antibacterial ointment (for cuts and abrasions)
- antibiotics
- antidiarrhoeal drugs (eg loperamide)
- antihistamines (for hay fever and allergic reactions)
- anti-inflammatory drugs (eg ibuprofen)
- bandages, gauze, gauze rolls
- DEET-containing insect repellent for the skin
- iodine tablets or water filter (for water purification)
- oral rehydration salts
- pocket knife
- permethrin-containing insect spray for clothing, tents and bed nets
- scissors
- safety pins
- steroid cream or cortisone (for poison ivy and other allergic rashes)
- sun block
- thermometer
- tweezers

FURTHER READING

Lonely Planet's *Travel with Children* contains advice on travel health for younger children. Also try reading *Traveller's Health* by Dr Richard Dawood (Oxford University Press) and *International Travel Health Guide* by Stuart R Rose, MD (Travel Medicine Inc).

IN TRANSIT

DEEP VEIN THROMBOSIS

Blood clots may form in the legs during plane flights, chiefly because of prolonged immobility. The longer the flight, the greater the risk. Though most blood clots are reabsorbed uneventfully, some may break off and travel through the blood vessels to the lungs, where they could cause life-threatening complications.

The chief symptom of deep vein thrombosis is swelling or pain of the foot, ankle or calf, usually – but not always – on just one side. When a blood clot travels to the lungs, it may cause chest pain and breathing difficulties. Travellers with any of these symptoms should immediately seek medical attention.

To prevent the development of deep vein thrombosis on long flights, you should walk about the cabin, perform isometric compressions of the leg muscles (ie flex the leg muscles while sitting), drink plenty of fluids and avoid alcohol and tobacco.

JET LAG & MOTION SICKNESS

Jet lag is common when crossing more than five time zones, resulting in insomnia, fatigue, malaise or nausea. To avoid jet lag try drinking plenty of (nonalcoholic) fluids and eating light meals. Upon arrival, expose yourself to natural sunlight and readjust your schedule (for meals, sleep etc) as soon as possible.

Antihistamines such as dimenhydrinate and meclizine are usually the first choice for treating motion sickness. Their main side effect is drowsiness. A herbal alternative is ginger, which works like a charm for some people.

IN TASMANIA

AVAILABILITY & COST OF HEALTH CARE

Australia, including Tasmania, has an excellent health-care system. It's a mixture of privately run medical clinics and hospitals alongside a government-funded system of public hospitals. The Medicare system covers Australian residents for some health-care costs. Visitors from countries with which Australia has a reciprocal health-care agreement are eligible for benefits specified under the Medicare program. Agreements are currently in place with New Zealand, the UK, the Netherlands, Sweden, Finland, Italy, Malta and Ireland – check the details before departing these countries. In general the agreements provide for any episode of ill-health that requires prompt medical attention. For more, see www.health.gov.au. However, you should carry insurance (see opposite).

There are excellent, specialised, public health facilities for women and children in Australia's major centres.

HEALTH

Pharmaceutical Supplies

Over-the-counter medications are widely available from privately owned chemists throughout Australia. These include painkillers, antihistamines for allergies and skin-care products.

You may find that medications readily available over the counter in some countries are only available in Australia by prescription. These include the oral contraceptive pill, most medications for asthma and all antibiotics. If you take medication on a regular basis, bring an adequate supply and ensure you have details of the generic name as brand names can differ between countries.

Self-Care

In Australia's remote locations, including those in Tasmania, it is possible there'll be a significant delay in emergency services reaching you in the event of serious accident or illness. An increased level of self-reliance and preparation is essential.

Consider taking a wilderness first-aid course, such as those offered at the **Wilderness Medicine Institute** (www.wmi.net.au); take a comprehensive first-aid kit that is appropriate for the activities planned; and ensure that you have adequate means of communication. Tasmania's often-limited mobile phone coverage can mean that additional radio communication is important for remote areas.

INFECTIOUS DISEASES

Giardiasis This is widespread in waterways. Drinking untreated water from streams and lakes is not recommended. Water filters and boiling or treating water with iodine are effective preventatives. Symptoms consist of intermittent bad smelling diarrhoea, abdominal bloating and wind. Effective treatment is available (tinidazole or metronidazole).

Hepatitis C This is still a growing problem among intravenous drug users. Blood transfusion services fully screen all blood before it is used.

HIV Rates of this disease have stabilised in Australia and levels are similar to other Western countries. Clean needles and syringes are widely available through all chemists.

Meningococcal disease Occurs worldwide and is a risk with prolonged, dormitory-style accommodation. A vaccine exists for meningococcal A, C, Y and W. No vaccine is presently available for the viral type of meningitis.

Ross River fever This virus is widespread in Australia, spread by mosquitoes living in marshy areas. In addition to fever it causes headache, joint and muscular pains and a rash, and resolves after five to seven days.

Sexually transmitted diseases These occur at rates similar to those in most other Western countries. The most common symptoms are pain while passing urine and a discharge. Infection can be present without symptoms so seek medical screening after any unprotected sex with a new partner. You'll find sexual health clinics in all of the major hospitals. Always use a condom with a new sexual partner. Condoms are readily available in chemists and through vending machines in many public places including toilets.

Tick typhus Cases of this illness have been reported throughout Australia, but are predominantly found in Queensland and New South Wales; however Flinders Island spotted fever occurs in Tasmania and Flinders Island in Bass Strait. A week or so after being bitten, a dark area forms around the bite, followed by a rash and possible fever, headache and inflamed lymph nodes. The disease is treatable with antibiotics (doxycycline) so see a doctor if you suspect you have been bitten.

TRAVELLERS' DIARRHOEA

If you develop diarrhoea, be sure to drink plenty of fluids – preferably an oral rehydration solution containing lots of salt and sugar. A few loose stools don't require treatment but if you start having more than four or five stools a day, you should start taking an antibiotic (usually a quinolone drug) and an antidiarrhoeal agent (such as loperamide). If diarrhoea is bloody, persists for more than 72 hours or is accompanied by fever, shaking, chills or severe abdominal pain you should seek medical attention. Also see Water (p348) for more information.

ENVIRONMENTAL HAZARDS
Animal Bites
INSECTS

Various insects can be a source of irritation and, in Australia, may be the source of specific diseases (eg dengue fever, Ross River fever). Protection from mosquitoes, sandflies, ticks and leeches can be achieved by a combination of the following strategies:

- wearing loose-fitting and long-sleeved clothing
- applying a 30%-DEET insect repellent to all exposed skin and repeating every three to four hours
- impregnating clothing with permethrin (an insecticide that kills insects but is safe for humans).

SHARKS

Despite extensive media coverage, the risk of shark attack in Australian waters is no greater than in other countries with a lot of coastline. Great white sharks are now few in number in the temperate southern waters. Check with surf lifesaving groups about local risks.

SNAKES

Australian snakes have a fearful reputation that is justified in terms of the potency of their venom, but unjustified in terms of the actual risk to travellers and locals. Snakes are usually quite timid in nature and in most instances will move away if disturbed. They only have small fangs, making it easy to prevent bites to the lower limbs (where 80% of bites occur) by wearing protective clothing (such as gaiters) around the ankles when bushwalking. The bite marks are very small and may even go unnoticed.

In all confirmed or suspected bites, preventing the spread of toxic venom can be achieved by applying pressure to the wound and immobilising the area with a splint or sling before seeking medical attention. Firmly wrap an elastic bandage (you can improvise with a T-shirt) around the entire limb, but not so tight as to cut off the circulation. Along with immobilisation, this is a life-saving first-aid measure.

For more on Tasmanian species see p51.

SPIDERS & ANTS

Australia has a number of poisonous spiders. Redback spiders, although rare in Tasmania and rarer still in winter months, are found throughout the country. Bites cause increasing pain at the site followed by profuse sweating and generalised symptoms (muscular weakness, sweating at the site of the bite, nausea). First aid includes application of ice or cold packs to the bite, then transfer to hospital. White-tailed spiders can also give a nasty bite. Clean the wound thoroughly and seek medical assistance.

Jack jumper (or bull) ants are more common in Tasmania than the other Australian states, and their painful sting can cause an allergic reaction, the most severe of which is anaphylaxis, including swelling and difficulty breathing. Travellers who know they are allergic should carry an EpiPen and seek urgent medical attention.

Hypothermia

Hypothermia is a significant risk, especially during the winter months in southern parts of Australia – and especially in Tasmania. Strong winds produce a high chill factor that can result in hypothermia even in moderately cool temperatures. Early signs include the inability to perform fine movements (such as doing up buttons), shivering and a bad case of the 'umbles' (fumbles, mumbles, grumbles and stumbles). The key elements of treatment include moving out of the cold, changing out of any wet clothing into dry clothes with wind- and water-proof layers, adding insulation and providing fuel (water and carbohydrate) to allow shivering, which builds the internal temperature. In severe hypothermia, shivering actually stops: this is a medical emergency requiring rapid evacuation in addition to the above measures.

Surf Beaches & Drowning

Australia has exceptional surf. Beaches vary enormously in their underwater conditions: the slope offshore can result in changeable and often powerful surf, rips and undertows. Check with local surf lifesaving organisations and be aware of your own expertise and limitations before entering the water. If a beach is patrolled by surf lifesavers, always swim between the red-and-yellow flags. If you are caught in a rip, don't try to swim against it. Instead, swim laterally along the beach to exit the rip, then head for shore.

Sunburn

Australia has one of the highest rates of skin cancer in the world. Tasmania's latitude makes it a risky destination, especially if you're spending lots of time outdoors. Monitor your exposure to direct sunlight closely, especially if you are fair or have moles and freckles. UV exposure is greatest between 10am and 4pm so avoid skin exposure during these times. Always use sun protection factor 30+ sunscreen; apply 30 minutes before going into the sun and reapply regularly to minimise damage.

> **TRAVEL HEALTH WEBSITES**
>
> It's usually a good idea to consult your government's travel health website before departure, if one is available.
> **Australia** (www.smarttraveller.gov.au)
> **Canada** (www.phac-aspc.gc.ca)
> **UK** (www.fco.gov.uk)
> **USA** (wwwn.cdc.gov/travel)

HEALTH

Water

Tap water in Tasmania is usually safe but there are some small towns (Swansea on the east coast, for example) where it is recommended that you boil tap water before drinking. It's worth asking for advice if you're unsure about the safety of tap water in the areas you're visiting.

Increasing numbers of waterways are being contaminated by bugs that cause diarrhoea, making water purification essential. The simplest way of purifying water is to boil it thoroughly.

Consider purchasing a water filter. It's very important when buying a filter to read the specifications, so that you know exactly what it removes from the water and what it doesn't. Simple filtering will not remove all dangerous organisms, so if you can't boil water it should be treated chemically. Chlorine tablets will kill many pathogens, but not some parasites such as giardia and amoebic cysts. Iodine is more effective in purifying water and is available in tablet form. Follow the directions carefully and remember that too much iodine can be harmful.

HEALTH

Glossary

arvo – afternoon
Aussie Rules – Australian Rules football, a game (vaguely) resembling rugby played by teams of 18

barbie – barbecue
barrack – cheer on team at sporting event, support ('Who do you barrack for?')
battler – struggler, someone who tries hard
beanie – woolly hat
beaut, beauty – great, fantastic
bloke – man
bludger – lazy person
body board – half–sized surfboard
bogan – loutish ruffian; term of social derision
boogie board – see *body board*
booze bus – police van used for random breath testing of drivers for alcohol
bottle shop – liquor shop, off-licence
brekky – breakfast
bush tucker – native foods
bush, the – country, anywhere away from the city
bushwalking – hiking
BYO – bring your own; a type of restaurant licence that allows customers to quaff bottles of wine (and sometimes beer) purchased elsewhere; a 'corkage' charge (say, around $5 per bottle) is added to the bill for this privilege

cask wine – wine packaged in a plastic bladder surrounded by a cardboard box (a great Australian invention)
catch ya later – goodbye, see you later
chook – chicken
cooee – to be 'within cooee' is to be within close range. A 'cooee' is a call from one person to another.
counter meal – pub meal
crack the shits – to express utmost irritation
crook – ill or substandard
cut lunch – sandwiches (to cut someone's lunch is to steal their girlfriend/boyfriend)

dag – dirty lump of wool at back end of a sheep; also an affectionate or mildly abusive term for a socially inept person
dinky-di – the real deal
dob in – to inform on someone
Dreaming – complex concept that forms the basis of Aboriginal spirituality, incorporating the creation of the world and the spiritual energies operating around us; 'Dreaming' is often the preferred term as it avoids the association with time
dunny – outdoor lavatory

earbash – to talk non-stop
Esky – large insulated box to keep your beer and sausages cold

fair dinkum – honest, genuine
fair go! – give us a break!
flake – shark meat, often the fish in fish and chips
flannie – flannelette shirt; often worn by *bogans*
flat out – very busy or fast
footy – football (in Tasmania, Aussie Rules is the code of choice)

galah – noisy parrot, thus noisy idiot
g'day – good day, traditional Australian greeting
good on ya! – well done!
grog – alcohol

hard yakka – hard work
having a lend – humorous deception
homestead – residence of a *station* owner or manager
hoon – idiot, hooligan

icy pole – frozen lollipop, ice lolly
iffy – dodgy, questionable

kick the bucket – to die
Kiwi – New Zealander
knackered – broken, tired
knock – to criticise, deride

larrikin – hooligan, mischievous youth
little ripper – extremely good thing; see also *ripper*
lollies – sweets, candy
loo – toilet

mainlander – someone from mainland Australia
mainland refugee – a *mainlander* who has relocated to Tasmania
map of Tassie – aside from its literal meaning, this is also a crude term for a woman's pubic hair (think about it – especially the island's shape...)
mate – general term of familiarity, whether you know the person or not
milk bar – small shop selling milk and other basic provisions
mobile phone – cell phone
Mod Oz – modern Australian cuisine influenced by a wide range of foreign cuisines, but with a definite local flavour
mozzies – mosquitoes

no-hoper – hopeless case
no worries! – no problems! That's OK!

ocker – uncultivated or boorish Australian
off-sider – assistant, partner, right-hand man
outback – remote part of the *bush*

paddock – fenced area of land, often full of sheep
perv – to gaze with lust
piss – beer
piss up – boozy party
piss weak – no good, gutless
pissed – drunk
pissed off – annoyed
plonk – cheap wine
pokies – poker machines
pom – English person

rapt – delighted, enraptured
ratbag – friendly term of abuse
ratshit – lousy
rip – strong ocean current or undertow
ripper – good; see also *little ripper*
root – to have sexual intercourse
rooted – tired, broken

sanger – sandwich
scrub – *bush*
sealed road – bitumen road
shark biscuit – inexperienced surfer
sheila – woman
she'll be right – no problems, no worries
shonky – unreliable

shoot through – to leave
shout – to buy a round of drinks ('Your shout!')
sickie – day off work ill (or malingering)
smoko – tea break
snag – sausage
sparrow's fart – dawn
squatter – pioneer farmer who occupied land as a tenant of the government
station – large farm
stolen generations – Aboriginal children forcibly removed from their families during the government's policy of assimilation
stroppy – bad-tempered
stubby – 375ml bottle of beer
sunbake – sunbathe (well, the sun's hot in Australia!)

taking the piss – see *having a lend*
thongs – flip-flops (definitely *not* a g-string!)
tinnie – aluminium boat or beer can
trucky – truck driver
tucker – food
two-pot screamer – person unable to hold their drink

unsealed road – dirt road
ute – utility; a pick-up truck

wag – to skip school or work
weatherboard – timber cladding on a house
whinge – to complain, moan

yobbo – uncouth, aggressive person
yonks – a long time

The Authors

CHARLES RAWLINGS-WAY   Coordinating Author, Hobart & Around, Tasman Peninsula & Port Arthur, The Southeast, Midlands & Lake Country

The son of a Devonshire flour miller and a Belfast belle, Charles was falsely convicted of stealing two potatoes and transported to Van Diemen's Land at the age of three. His suggestion of changing the island's name to Tasmania was only ever semi-serious, but it earned him a pardon from Governor Arthur. A free man on the open road, Charles funded his adventures with stints as an architect, croissant chef, deckhand, cinema cleaner and crucial cog at Lonely Planet's Melbourne HQ. An underrated rock guitarist and delighted new dad, this was Charles' second trip to Tasmania for Lonely Planet.

MEG WORBY   Coordinating Author, Bass Strait Islands

After six years at Lonely Planet in the languages, editorial and publishing teams, Meg swapped the desktop for a laptop, in order to write while travelling on maternity leave. On her first trip to Tasmania, she flew from the Torres Strait Islands to Hobart (over 4000km), just in time to see the Sydney-to-Hobart yachts arrive and the party start up in Salamanca Place. Since then, these have become a few of her favourite Tasmanian things: the magnificent Overland Track, roadside raspberries, Launceston's mysterious Cataract Gorge; the selection of knitted beanies in Ross; Mt Wellington reveries; Swansea's serene stone cottages; and King Island cheese. She looks forward to introducing her newest and smallest travel companion to them all.

GABI MOCATTA   East Coast, The Northeast, Launceston & Around, Devonport & The Northwest, The West, The Southwest

A bit of gypsy from an early age, Gabi has always lived and travelled in far-flung parts. Eight years ago she innocently alighted on Tasmania, a wonderful turn of events for anyone who loves the outdoors. Beautiful South Hobart is now home-base for Gabi – a place where you can be in the forest in an instant, or wander down for a coffee-and-catchup at one of the coolest cafes in town. Gabi beachcombed the east and west coasts for this edition, as well as enjoying the gourmet tastes of Launceston; getting wind-scoured in the wild Northwest; and being breath-taken in the even wilder southwest, a sea-kayaker's delight and one of the last true wildernesses on earth.

LONELY PLANET AUTHORS

Why is our travel information the best in the world? It's simple: our authors are passionate, dedicated travellers. They don't take freebies in exchange for positive coverage so you can be sure the advice you're given is impartial. They travel widely to all the popular spots, and off the beaten track. They don't research using just the internet or phone. They discover new places not included in any other guidebook. They personally visit thousands of hotels, restaurants, palaces, trails, galleries, temples and more. They speak with dozens of locals every day to make sure you get the kind of insider knowledge only a local could tell you. They take pride in getting all the details right, and in telling it how it is. Think you can do it? Find out how at **lonelyplanet.com**.

THE AUTHORS

CONTRIBUTING AUTHORS

Senator Bob Brown wrote the 'Simple Steps for Saving the Forests' boxed text in the Environment chapter. He was elected to the Tasmanian parliament in 1983 and first elected to the Senate in 1996. His books include *The Valley of the Giants* (The Wilderness Society, with Vica Bayley, 2005). Read more about Bob Brown at www.bobbrown.org.au.

Tim Flannery wrote the 'Australian Environmental Challenges' boxed text in the Environment chapter. Tim is a naturalist, explorer, writer and climate-change activist. He was named Australian of the Year in 2007, and is currently an adjunct professor at Macquarie University in NSW. He is the author of a number of award-winning books, including *The Future Eaters* and *Throwim Way Leg* (an account of his adventures as a biologist working in New Guinea) and the landmark ecological history of North America, *The Eternal Frontier*. His most recent book is *Chasing Kangaroos* (2007).

Behind the Scenes

THIS BOOK

This is the 5th edition of *Tasmania*. The 1st edition was researched and written by John and Monica Chapman back in 1996. Lyn McGaurr updated the 2nd edition, and Paul Smitz researched and wrote the 3rd edition. For the 4th edition, Carolyn Bain and Gina Tsarouhas covered the island. For this edition, Charles Rawlings-Way, Meg Worby and Gabi Mocatta covered countless miles in their quest to get the lowdown on all of Tassie's delights. Charles also researched the Journeys, Itineraries, Environment, Tasmania Outdoors and National Parks chapters, while Meg covered the Destination Tasmania, Getting Started, History, The Culture, Food & Drink, Directory and Transport chapters. In the Environment chapter, Tim Flannery wrote the boxed texts 'Australian Environmental Challenges' on p48 and the 'Watching Wildlife' on p53, and Senator Bob Brown wrote the boxed text 'Simple Steps for Saving the Forests' on p50. Lonely Planet founder Tony Wheeler wrote the 'Fire Walking' boxed text in The Northeast chapter. Dr David Millar contributed the Health chapter.

This guidebook was commissioned in Lonely Planet's Melbourne office, and produced by the following:

Commissioning Editor Emma Gilmour, Kerryn Burgess
Coordinating Editors Sasha Baskett, Averil Robertson, Gina Tsarouhas
Coordinating Cartographers Hunor Csutoros, Anthony Phelan
Coordinating Layout Designer Jacqui Saunders
Managing Editor Geoff Howard
Managing Cartographer David Connolly
Managing Layout Designer Celia Wood
Assisting Editors David Andrew, David Carroll, Daniel Corbett, Pete Cruttenden, Penelope Goodes, Anne Mulvaney, Rosie Nicholson, Charlotte Orr
Assisting Cartographers Corey Hutchison, Erin McManus, Jacqueline Nguyen, Mandy Sierp
Assisting Layout Designers Jim Hsu, Paul Iacono
Cover Designer Pepi Bluck
Cover Artwork Pablo Gastar
Colour Designer Indra Kilfoyle
Indexer Rosie Nicholson
Project Manager Sarah Sloane

Thanks to Trent Paton, Lisa Knights, Katie Lynch, Mark Germanchis, John Mazzocchi, Adam McCrow, Darren O'Connell

THANKS

CHARLES RAWLINGS-WAY

Thanks to the following folks for their input, generosity, friendship and distraction during the creation

---

THE LONELY PLANET STORY

Fresh from an epic journey across Europe, Asia and Australia in 1972, Tony and Maureen Wheeler sat at their kitchen table stapling together notes. The first Lonely Planet guidebook, *Across Asia on the Cheap,* was born.

Travellers snapped up the guides. Inspired by their success, the Wheelers began publishing books to Southeast Asia, India and beyond. Demand was prodigious, and the Wheelers expanded the business rapidly to keep up. Over the years, Lonely Planet extended its coverage to every country and into the virtual world via lonelyplanet.com and the Thorn Tree message board.

As Lonely Planet became a globally loved brand, Tony and Maureen received several offers for the company. But it wasn't until 2007 that they found a partner whom they trusted to remain true to the company's principles of travelling widely, treading lightly and giving sustainably. In October of that year, BBC Worldwide acquired a 75% share in the company, pledging to uphold Lonely Planet's commitment to independent travel, trustworthy advice and editorial independence.

Today, Lonely Planet has offices in Melbourne, London and Oakland, with over 500 staff members and 300 authors. Tony and Maureen are still actively involved with Lonely Planet. They're travelling more often than ever, and they're devoting their spare time to charitable projects. And the company is still driven by the philosophy of *Across Asia on the Cheap*: 'All you've got to do is decide to go and the hardest part is over. So go!'

of this book: Megan Worby; Gabi Mocatta; Mark, Cath and the irrepressible Oscar and Rufus Bresnehan; Fred, Lucy and the Ward collective: Lili, Abi, Holly and 'Noah's Ark' Ned; Dave, Susan and Byron Canty; Norm and Janelle Cummins for a sporting day at the cricket; David Button, Ed Parker, Tasmin and Hugh McNaughtan, and of course Paul 'Sunstroke' Roebuck. Special thanks to Emma Gilmour for allowing me to slake my Tasmanian addiction, and the in-house LP production staff.

More than ever, thank you my darling Meg for your eternal patience, bottomless wit and unparalleled glamour. Without you, our gorgeous daughter would look like me…

MEG WORBY

Grateful thanks to Emma for the gig, to Errol, Piers and Jane for the time in which to do it, and to the team in-house at Lonely Planet Footscray for their hard work. Thank you to co-author Gabi, it was great working with you. Muchas grassy-ass to Tasmin and Hugh McNaughtan: most excellent people with whom to share campsites, feasts, laughter, fictional journal entries and Lake St Clair scenery. Thanks to our crew in Hobart for such regular, warm welcomes. Heartfelt thanks, as ever, to Charles: for extreme coordination, seasoned travel advice, collaboration, wit and tups of cea – and for sharing a vocation. And thank you to dear little Ione, who was late so we could make the deadline!

GABI MOCATTA

Thanks to all those who helped me to scale a daunting mountain of research and writing, and come down, much relieved, the other side. To Emma Glimour at Lonely Planet, thank you for your patience with my Felix questions, and my slowness. Thanks also to coordinating authors Charles Rawlings-Way and Meg Worby, who quite astoundingly managed to make this book happen while bringing a baby into the world. To Annabelle Sweetman and Daniel McMahon, my dear friends and Launceston experts, who also watered my plants while I was away researching, thank you. To Helen and Boxer at Devonport, Max and Loraine at Allendale, and Margaret Galbraith at Swansea, it was such a pleasure to stay in your homes – I'm so grateful. Thanks to all the wonderful volunteers at the tourist information centres who made my job so much easier, and to all the great Tasmanian locals who gave me tips on what was hot, especially Libby Lutzmer who whipped me round Boat Harbour in an instant. Finally, to Jake, who was so wonderful to talk with, and share this with, all along the way – namaste.

OUR READERS

Many thanks to the travellers who used the last edition and wrote to us with helpful hints, useful advice and interesting anecdotes:

Peter Adams, Steven Alford, Doris Anderson, Erna Janssen Andeweg, Charles Barfield, Carmelo Bazzano, Klaus Bettenhausen, Billi Bierling, Margaret Boyd, Pip Cartmell, Joy Cassidy, Andrew Clissold, Judy Consden, Helen Crump, Alan Delew, Christine Denny, Aurora Dobson, Leah Dwyer, Sally Edsall, Hannah Ewers, Kay Fanslow, Erica Farish, Erik Fenna, Suzanne Ferriss, Des & Roni Fitzpatrick, Craig Fitzsimmons, Leila Fonseca, Ian Fox, Geraldine Fradgley, Michelle Godwin, Paul Grgurich, Lorraine Hamling, Scott Hannigan, James Hansen, Ian Harrison, Stefan Hilpert, Court Hobday, Claudia Hoehne, Michelle Homewood, Jessica Hope, Thomas Hühn, Lauren Jaeschke, Simon James, Melanie Johnson, Sarah Johnson, Mel Johnston, Gilles Karolyi, Tobias Kaupp, Andre Kreitlein, Jason Laverack, Jane Lawrence, Veronica Lever-Shaw, Daphna Levin-Kahn, Foh Lim Lim, Manuela Maly, Nicole Mattson, John May, Lewis Mckillop, Gabrielle Methou, Sharon Miller, Jonathon Mills, Frank Molloy, Marie Murray-Arthur, Michael Nankervis, Robert Nicholls, Rob Olston, Alan Oxenham, Tracy Page, Anna Palthe, Beris Penrose, Roberta Penrose, Alana Read, Angelika Schwerin, Ann Ten Seldam, Valerie Shallvey, Michael Skully, Millie Slaytor, David Spielvogel, Sten Starner, Tana Stickler, Rachel Stivicic, Gemma Swindle, Anne van Put, Gill Der van Watt, Pip Vice, Madalena Wagenaar, Jeanette Wall, Andrea Webb, Michiko Weinmann, Gabriela Weiss, Catherine Wescott, Liz White, Angelika Wick, Wendy Wilkikns, Caroline Wilkinson, Adam Williams, Sarah Witt, Ursula Ziegler.

SEND US YOUR FEEDBACK

We love to hear from travellers – your comments keep us on our toes and help make our books better. Our well-travelled team reads every word on what you loved or loathed about this book. Although we cannot reply individually to postal submissions, we always guarantee that your feedback goes straight to the appropriate authors, in time for the next edition. Each person who sends us information is thanked in the next edition – and the most useful submissions are rewarded with a free book.

To send us your updates – and find out about Lonely Planet events, newsletters and travel news – visit our award-winning website: **www.lonelyplanet.com/contact**.

Note: we may edit, reproduce and incorporate your comments in Lonely Planet products such as guidebooks, websites and digital products, so let us know if you don't want your comments reproduced or your name acknowledged. For a copy of our privacy policy visit www.lonelyplanet.com/privacy.

ACKNOWLEDGMENTS
Many thanks to the following for the use of their content:

Globe on title page ©Mountain High Maps 1993 Digital Wisdom, Inc.

Internal photographs: Wibowo Rusli p71-2 (#2), p72 (#3). All other photographs by Lonely Planet Images: p75 (#3) John Banagan; p69, p76 (#2) Rob Blakers; p73 (#2) p76 (#1) Grant Dixon; p73 (#3) Krzysztof Dydynski; p74 (#1) John Hay; p70 (#1) Gareth McCormack; p73 (#4) Andrew Peacock; p72 Paul Sinclair; p74 (#2) Oliver Strewe.

All images are the copyright of the photographers unless otherwise indicated. Many of the images in this guide are available for licensing from Lonely Planet Images: www.lonelyplanetimages .com.

Index

INDEX

INDEX

GreenDex

GOING GREEN

It seems like everyone's going 'green' these days, but how can you know which businesses are actually ecofriendly and which are simply jumping on the eco/sustainable bandwagon?

The following attractions, tours, accommodation, eating and drinking choices have been selected by Lonely Planet authors because they demonstrate an active sustainable-tourism policy. Some are involved in conservation or environmental education, and many are owned and operated by local and indigenous operators, thereby maintaining and preserving local identity and culture.

Some of the listings below have also been certified by Ecotourism Australia (www.ecotour.org .au), which means they meet high standards of environmental sustainability, business ethics and cultural sensitivity.

We want to keep developing our sustainable-tourism content. If you think we've omitted someone who should be listed here, or if you disagree with our choices, email us at talk2us@lonelyplanet .com.au and set us straight for next time. For more information about sustainable tourism and Lonely Planet, see www.lonelyplanet.com/responsibletravel.

ACCOMMODATION

Bass Strait Islands
Healing Dreams Retreat 313
North-East River Campsite 313
Swan Island Retreat 315

Devonport & the Northwest
Beachside Retreat West Inlet 263
Carinya Farm Holiday Retreat 245

East Coast
Mount Paul on Freycinet 180

Hobart & Around
Henry Jones Art Hotel 97
Moorilla Estate Suites & Chalets 98
Platypus Playground 115
Tree Tops Cascades 99

Launceston & Around
Arthouse Backpacker Hostel 208
Cherry Top & Eagle Park 222
Plovers Ridge Host Farm 222

Midlands & Lake Country
Over the Back 163

Northeast, The
Platypus Park Country Retreat 199

Southeast, The
Far South Wilderness Lodge & Backpackers 150
Mickeys Bay Eco Retreat 140
Morella Island Retreats 140
Peppermint Ridge Retreat 142

Southwest, The
Giants' Table & Cottages 300

Tasman Peninsula & Port Arthur
Potters Croft 123

EATING & DRINKING

Bass Strait Islands
Boathouse 309
Bold Head Brasserie 309
Boomerang by the Sea 309
Flinders Island Bakery 314
Furneaux Tavern 314

Devonport & the Northwest
Groovy Penguin Café 251
Rosehip Cafe 236
Ulverstone Deli Central 250

East Coast
Banc 174
Purple Possum Wholefoods 186

Hobart & around
Amulet 103
Nourish 101
Sirens 101
Tricycle Café Bar 101

Launceston & Around
Café Rossilli 211
Fresh 211
Tant pour Tant 211
Trevallyn Deli Café 212

Midlands & Lake Country
Jackson's Emporium 163

Northeast, The
Holy Cow! Café 193
Village Store & More 194

Southeast, The
Dover Hotel 151

Southwest, The
Giants' Table & Cottages 300

Tasman Peninsula & Port Arthur
Eucalypt 130

SIGHTS & ACTIVITIES

Bass Strait Islands
Calcified Forest 307
Furneaux Museum 310
Wybalenna Historic Site 310

Devonport & the Northwest
41° South Aquaculture 240
Allendale Gardens & Rainforest 266
Artwork in Silk 239
Creative Paper 253
Deloraine Folk Museum & YARNS: Artwork in Silk 239
Flowerdale Lobster Haven 257
Greening Australia 331
Highland Trails Horseriding 245
Penguin watching at West Beach 233

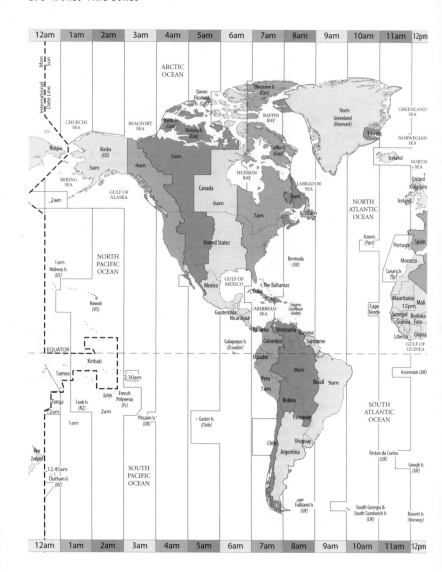